74e PARIS-

(DIMA

L'ÉQUIPE

TROPHÉE BNP

Epreuve comptant pour la COUPE du MONDE de l'A.I.O.C.C.

LES ZONES DE MAUVAIS PAVÉS

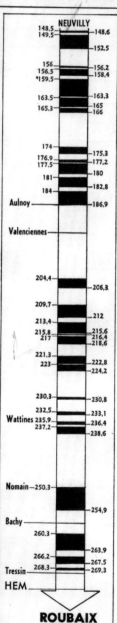

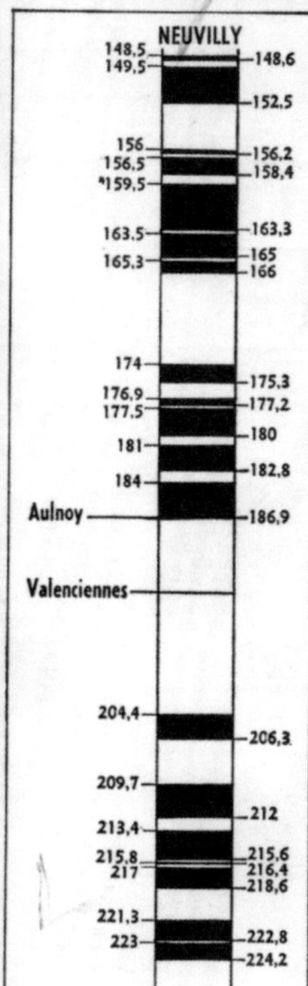

L'OFFICIEL DE LA COURSE

- **PARIS** (Journal « L'ÉQUIPE », 10, rue du Faubourg-Montmartre, Paris-9e).
  - **Vendredi 9 avril à 18 h 30 :** Réunion des Commissaires de course (salle de conférence du Tour de France, 1er étage, sous la voûte).
  - **Samedi 10 avril, de 10 h à 12 h et de 14 h à 18 h :**
    — Remise des pièces officielles aux coureurs et suiveurs accrédités.
    — A 17 heures : Réunion des Directeurs sportifs. Tirage au sort de l'ordre de marche en course des voitures techniques d'équipes.
- **CHANTILLY** (36 km de Paris, R.N. 16).
  - **Dimanche 11 avril** (Place Omer-Vallon) :
    — De 8 h à 9 h : Contrôle de départ des coureurs. Remise des valises au véhicule bagages.
    — 9 h 05 : Appel des coureurs et rassemblement pour le départ.
    — 9 h 15 : Départ en groupe par la rue du Connétable, la place de l'Abbé-Charpentier, la rue de Senlis puis VINEUIL-SAINT-FIRMIN (distance : 2,500 km).
- **VINEUIL-SAINT-FIRMIN**
  - 9 h 20 : Départ réel **lancé** du 74e PARIS-ROUBAIX.
- **ROUBAIX** (arrivée)
  - Contrôle médical : Caravane Aspro (pelouse du stade-vélodrome).
  - Douches : Ecole de Plein Air.
  - Bagages : Cour de l'Ecole de Plein Air.
  - Permanence : Ecole de Plein Air.
  - Salle de Presse (télex) : Ecole de Plein Air (salle du réfectoire).
  - Téléphones : Bureau principal des P. et T. de Roubaix.

Service TV Presse LOCATEL

SUIVEURS, ATTENTION !..

- **LIAISONS RADIO.** — Les Organisateurs rappellent aux Directeurs sportifs et aux journalistes qu'ils ne seront autorisés à prendre le départ de l'épreuve que si leurs véhicules sont équipés d'un récepteur radio spécial en ordre de marche permettant de capter les informations transmises par la Direction de la course.
- **VÉHICULES PRESSE.** — Ils devront, à partir de **Neuvilly** (Km 148,5) :
  — ou précéder la course sans jamais se laisser rejoindre par les motocyclistes de l'Escorte de la Garde Républicaine porteurs d'un drapeau rouge,
  — ou suivre l'épreuve derrière la voiture « Commissaire de course » portant un drapeau jaune.
  En vue d'éviter tout incident susceptible de gêner le déroulement de « PARIS-ROUBAIX », durant le passage difficile entre Neuvilly et Saint-Python, les organisateurs de l'épreuve ont décidé d'appliquer la règle suivante :
  1° **Seules les voitures de Presse se présentant 15 minutes avant l'heure « H » de la course à Neuvilly seront autorisées à emprunter l'itinéraire normal et sans s'y arrêter, jusqu'à Saint-Python, de manière à permettre aux journalistes les occupant de s'imprégner du « décor » de l'itinéraire.**
  2° **Les véhicules Presse qui se présenteront en dehors du créneau horaire prévu utiliseront l'itinéraire de dérivation suivant :**
  — N. 355 - NEUVILLY - SOLESMES - SAINT-PYTHON (au total : 5 km).
  La direction de la course ne manquera pas de rappeler cette consigne impérative aux suiveurs de l'échelon Presse après le ravitaillement à Saint-Quentin.
  Les motos Presse (cameramen, photographes) pourront utiliser l'itinéraire normal.
- **MOTOS ÉMETTRICES.** — Elles ne pourront évoluer dans le sillage des coureurs de tête qu'aux heures d'émission et si le déroulement de la course les y autorise.
- **ATTENTION ! PASSAGE A NIVEAU :**
  — ARTRES (Km 181) : autorail Aulnoye-Valenciennes ;
  — WALLERS (Km 203) : train Valenciennes-Louvain.

PARIS - ROUBAIX
Départ de CHANTILLY

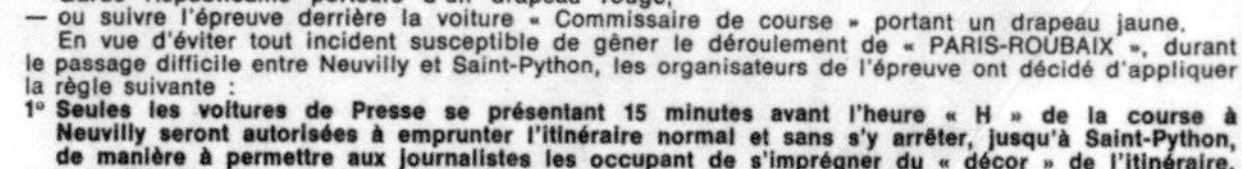

SUNDAY IN HELL

With all best wishes
William

WILLIAM FOTHERINGHAM

SUNDAY IN HELL

Behind the Lens of the Greatest Cycling Film of All Time

YELLOW JERSEY PRESS
LONDON

1 3 5 7 9 10 8 6 4 2

Yellow Jersey Press, an imprint of Vintage
20 Vauxhall Bridge Road
London SW1V 2SA

Yellow Jersey Press is part of the Penguin Random House
group of companies whose addresses can be found at
global.penguinrandomhouse.com

Penguin
Random House
UK

First published by Yellow Jersey Press in 2018

www.vintage-books.co.uk

A CIP catalogue record for this book is available from the British Library

ISBN 9780224092029

Typeset in 11/15 pt Fairfield LH
by Integra Software Services Pvt. Ltd, Pondicherry

Printed and bound by Clays Ltd, St Ives plc

To the memory of Albert Bouvet, without whom the Paris–Roubaix we know and love today would not exist in its current form.

A NOTE ON THE TIME CODES AND VERSION OF FILM

Throughout this book you will find in the margins time codes which relate to key moments in *A Sunday in Hell*. There are at least three versions extant of the film that I know of, on DVD and other media. These time codes relate specifically to the Danish Film Institute DVD issued in the box set *Jørgen Leth 2: Sports Films*.

CONTENTS

PRELUDE: THE LOVE AFFAIR

We start with the sound of a chain, the tick-tick-tick of 0:12
the links running over the bar that has been thrust into the gap between the drop-outs of the silvery frame as a mechanic lovingly brushes the transmission with diesel. After fifty seconds, the camera pans upwards to the man's face. We don't know to whom the bike belongs or, initially, what make it is. We never learn the identity of the mechanic; we are aware only that he is intent on his work. We can eventually surmise, from his green jersey, that he belongs to the Sanson team . . . but we can only do this in hindsight; as we watch initially, the colour means no more than the images. A minute in, the mournful sound of a cello starts up.

As we wait to find out what is going on, we are allowed to feast our eyes for a full three minutes on the finest products from Campagnolo's Italian stable: a three-quarters rear shot of the finely sculpted Record chainset, the black anodised pedal with its perfectly arranged leather toestrap, the bars waiting to have tape wound onto them. The cameramen, Henrik Herbert, has captured the mechanic's total involvement so lovingly, so lingeringly, that it feels almost fetishistic. Intent though he is, the mechanic is still brisk as he rotates the cranks, checks the tyres, taps the brake blocks into place with a hammer, puts a wheel into the rear dropouts and finally runs through each gear. Click. Click. Click. Tap tap. Brush brush. Whirr whirr.

It takes nearly two minutes for the credits to come up, and another minute and a half before we get any sense of what might be going on, as David Saunders intones the opening words on the English soundtrack. Nearly four minutes go past before the bike race, Paris–Roubaix, even merits a mention. All this time there is sound and image – and wonder. Even if we know – as we most probably do on first viewing – that this film is about the 'Hell of the North', we are made to wait before we enter it.

Something is brewing. Something is building.

'It's the afternoon of Saturday the tenth of April. Roger De Vlaeminck arrives at the Brooklyn team's hotel in Lamorlaye, north of Paris . . .'

In 2010, I was asked to act as the compere when a Bristol film festival ran a screening of the film *A Sunday in Hell*,* the Danish director Jørgen Leth's full-length documentary account of the 1976 Paris–Roubaix. We watched the film on the big screen – a rare enough event in itself – after which I hosted an audience question-and-answer session with Leth, who had travelled from Denmark just for us.

We all knew the race: Paris–Roubaix is not cycling's most celebrated one-day Classic for nothing. Its reliance on archaic cobbled lanes nicknamed 'the Hell of the North' makes it the stand-out event in a sport that hinges primarily on the interaction of man, bike and landscape, and where the fundamental premise is extreme: asking man and bike to do things they are not intended to do. 'Paris–Roubaix is cycling's Cape Horn,' said the double winner Marc Madiot – in other words, its ultimate challenge – adding that, 'in an era of cycling by computer it sublimates the artists who use pen on paper. It's as beautiful as a parchment manuscript.' This race is anachronistic, but glorious.

* Details matter in Leth's film, and those details include the title. In its original Danish version, the film is called *En forårsdag i helvede* – 'A Spring Day in Hell'. That was translated as *A Sunday in Hell* when the film acquired an English soundtrack after production. The director's preference is for the latter title.

I'd become completely smitten the fifth time I reported the event, on 10 April 1994, when a blizzard struck the field as they left the start. That marked the point when you paused for breath and realised just how insane this entire exercise was. And, therefore, just how special. Every one-day Classic makes massive demands on the participants for the same basic reason: they are the most coveted single-day races in cycling, the action condensed over the hardest courses. Wet editions of Paris–Roubaix are rarities because truly sodden springs are relatively infrequent, and the cobbles drain fast when the weather dries up; in spring 1994 the press corps had been scanning weather reports and speculating for weeks about how bad this one might be – or good, depending which side of the computer keyboard you were on.

The 1994 edition of Paris–Roubaix was the toughest race for many years, the cobbles so slippery that at one point there was not a single motorcycle left upright to carry a television camera, and conditions so tough that sixty kilometres from home there was only one rider left in front of the field: a chippy little former Soviet called Andrei Tchmil, who sported a banana-shaped grin on good days and a fixed Stalinesque set to his jaw on the bad ones. This was a Stalin-mask day. There were no other cyclists in sight at times. The motos and the drivers had been defeated and all of Tchmil's pedal-powered rivals had either fallen off, punctured, or simply been unable to handle the cold, wet, mud and stress. There was just Tchmil and the gloop.

Leth's film was shot eighteen years before Tchmil's glorious ride through the snowstorm, but it has all the elements that still make up the madness that gives me and hundreds of thousands of others around the world that collective tingle down our spines every second Sunday in April – the chaos, the crashes, the passion, the suffering, the humanity. But the director has added an epic dimension that sums up what really appeals to us: this race is so much larger than life. There are close-ups of muscles as they are battered by the cobbles like jellies balanced on a pneumatic drill, surreal music, scenic vistas from soaring viewpoints, intimate human details, and a smattering of humour.

There is more to it than his personal vision, however. This film is a snapshot of a moment in cycling history, a time capsule of a sport about to emerge from the homespun post-war era and become a bigger, more sophisticated, more anonymous entity.

There is a poignant touch in that the winner of the 1976 race, Marc Demeyer, died tragically young – the English version of the film is dedicated to him – and most of the men who contested that year's race with him were household names. Eddy Merckx looms large, as he always did. His successor as a five-time Tour de France winner Bernard Hinault makes a cameo appearance, in complete anonymity. France's most popular cyclist ever, Raymond Poulidor, has a walk-on role. The film's other stars – Roger De Vlaeminck, Francesco Moser, Freddy Maertens, Walter Godefroot, Hennie Kuiper, Joop Zoetemelk, Bernard Thevenet – make up a hit-list of cycling greats of the late 1970s and early 1980s. 1976 was a key generational turning point: Merckx was past his best; Poulidor was about to retire, closing a protracted coda to the 1960s when he and Jacques Anquetil had ruled the roost. It was one hell of a generation captured on celluloid in a single slice of time.

The film is also peppered with lesser-known personalities who were still on the circuit in 1994 – tending to be older and fatter – which makes the sense of continuity still greater; men such as the voice of the Tour de France for forty years, Daniel Mangeas, who is the voice at the start of Leth's *Sunday*; the television commentators, some of the lesser riders. Among the bit-part players who can be spotted are two men who drove me and the photographer Graham Watson along the route of the race one memorable winter afternoon in the early 1990s. Albert Bouvet pops up now and again waving a baton, showing exactly the same body language as when he worked on the Tour de France and other races in the nineties. His sidekick Jean-François Pescheux was actually riding the 1976 race, and can be spotted in the background.

A Sunday in Hell is also a paean to a kind of race that had disappeared during the 1980s: the one-day Classic contested by stars of the Tour de France. By the time I first visited Paris–Roubaix, in 1989 – just thirteen years after Leth captured it – the sport's most high-profile champions no longer turned up at the race. Cycling was increasingly specialised, as the Tour de France became the focus of an increasingly skewed season. A star targeting the Tour didn't want to be in form in April, and if racing he didn't want to risk a broken leg on the cobbles. Only Laurent Fignon and Greg LeMond kept the faith. As a result, for a spell, the one-day Classics became increasingly peripheral and devalued as far as mainstream media were concerned.* The Tour de France became the only focus.

* Although the Tour specialists still tend to eschew the cobbled Classics, the cobbled Classics themselves have regained much of their old aura. This is partly down to astute marketing by Flanders Classics, who own most of the major Flemish races and have created a new narrative for bike racing through spring. Plus, as the Tour has become increasingly specialised, the bike riders have realised that they can't all do well in France in July; hence, it's all far more competitive. Other Classics are still more marginal though, but that is a different story for a different book.

Leth's film is a lasting reminder of the eternal values of a one-day annual event on a unique course: a Classic.

As well as the essential madness of the spectacle itself, this timelessness draws fans and media to major bike races. Each year's Tour de France, Milan–San Remo or Giro d'Italia, Tour of Flanders or Paris–Roubaix is a single moment in a greater continuum. The essentials don't change. So the villages where Leth shot his masterpiece don't look that different over forty years later, and nor do the spectators, who still turn out in April – in greater numbers admittedly – at some of the same places their fathers, grandfathers and uncles have done, to crane their necks and shout at their heroes in exactly the same way.

Paris–Roubaix is timeless in its own unique fashion, and so is the film. The challenge of surviving those cobbled roads on a bike was essentially the same in the early twenty-first century – better tyres and factory-made wheels notwithstanding – as it had been when Leth made the film in the 1970s. The *pavés* themselves, although not always exactly the same ones, were as treacherous as they had been when I drove them with Bouvet and Pescheux and when Tchmil rode through the gloop left by the snow in 1994. The place names we passed were still the same – Orchies, Compiègne, Valenciennes, Templeuve, Gruson, Hem – and in a few cases the cobbled sections were virtually unchanged from when they had appeared in the film. There were individual spots that could be recognised down to the last metre: a disused railway bridge, a village church spire, a town square, a level crossing or two.

However, it was not preserved in aspic, far from it. Road races are picaresque events where individual characters appear and develop, live and die, suffer and thrive, all against an ever-changing backdrop. One-day Classics look like a bastion of stability in many ways, but the continuity is only in their essentials: they evolve as well.

I'd surmise that most of us at the showing had some idea of what we were seeing. But having Leth in front of us changed everything: we were made to look at what he had tried to do, how he had tried to do it, and how much of it he had actually achieved.

The director himself was – and still is – a larger-than-life figure, his vision of the race a poetic one. He didn't just set out to put together a film of a bike race because it seemed like a good idea or because the money was good. He had a vision and he had passion, immense passion, probably on a par with the riders who went to such lengths to get through the toughest one-day race their sport had to offer. Like me, like all of us in that hall, like those who make their annual pilgrimage to their chosen desolate corner of the depths of northern France, he clearly loved this race.

Asked to describe the cobbles, Leth once said: 'It's like the stones have just been thrown there, the roads are falling apart. It's fascinating from a film-maker's point of view. It gives you a certain tingle, a feverish feeling, when you come to these races every year. It's fantastic to imagine that the next day, the Sunday, whether it rains or shines, the race will come here full power and the riders are not blindly riding out on these fantastic obstacles, but with a lot of courage.'

Leth had gone to immense lengths to capture the essence of Prais–Roubaix, that much was clear. Portraying cycling is brutally reductive, as I had been painfully aware since day one of my career as a journalist. There are myriad sources of inspiration: the sport's sense of place, its colour and flavour, the deeper character of its participants, and their back stories, the ever-changing backdrops. Unfortunately, these tend to be reduced to footnotes because of the immediacy of reporting on what happens in a race amid the constraints of time and space.

We now see sport as a televisual entity, but television and radio are still more challenging when it comes to painting a complete picture of a bike race. The small screen is where we experience sport, so our view of almost every major sports event is mediated by the editors' choices of images and angles, and by the commentators' words. Unlike a stadium sport, if we read a report of a stage of the Tour de France – except on very rare occasions – we are looking at the reporter's interpretation of what he has been shown on television. What happens is mediated twice over; that makes for distance, uncertainty, grey areas.

A Sunday in Hell is an attempt to capture visually a one-day Classic in its entirety, to move outwards from the racing to the qualities that make every bike race unique: location, people, characters, history. That was a first. When the film was made, television stations across Europe showed only the final hour of many major races; we take it for granted today that we will know everything of note that has happened in a major cycle race and that, in the biggest races, we will be able to watch most of it on screen.

In the 1970s, Leth's objective of capturing every key moment in an entire bike race on screen was a radical one. Today, races are increasingly shown from start to finish with every minute live on television – the Tour de France, the Tour of Britain – and it is somehow appropriate that the trend began with Paris–Roubaix in 2016, forty years after the director tried to do something similar in spirit.

*

Cycling has spawned a vast, diverse culture: novels, photographs that could happily hang in any gallery, movies of all shape and size, poetry, drama, opera, some of the greatest sports writing; cartoons, caricatures and magazines as well as clothing and bikes and components which frequently have an artistic element to them – the delicate fretwork of a Magnum Bonum steel lug on a 1950s Hetchins frame for instance – and on occasion are made into works of art by the likes of Damien Hirst and Paul Smith.

The cultural diversity has various explanations: cycling functions on more levels than most other sports. It is not something that has been artificially created and which is restricted to the confines of a stadium. The social context is massively varied, so too the backdrops, not to mention the random factors when it takes place on the open road – punctures, crashes, weather, aggressive fans – and the infinite variety of tactics and politics forged by an individual sport contested by teams. The componentry involved has always brought with it an element of craftsmanship akin to the small custom Formula One car builders of the 1940s and 1950s; in some ways, that remains the same.

In relation to other sports, professional cycle road racing stands alone because of its variegated backdrops and cultural settings, but most of all due to its fundamental madness. You cannot describe the FA Cup or Wimbledon as bonkers. You can marvel at the skill on display on turf or lawn and love the twists and turns of a Cup run or a Men's Final, but any innate wackiness stems from the participants and fans, rather than the nature of the event itself. Cycling's eccentricity goes back to its roots, to the days when promoters wanted more and more extreme feats from the participants in their events: riding from Bordeaux to Paris, partly behind motorbikes; cycling around France in three weeks over every mountain that could be found; racing for six days straight on a track that might measure a mere 200 metres round; racing from the French capital to the Belgian border or the Riviera.

Leth's film remains the best depiction of a uniquely outlandish event in a uniquely extreme and demanding sport. Over forty years after it was made, it still appeals on so many levels: an introduction for the newcomer to cycling, a montage of bike porn for those who fetishised the equipment of the period, portraits of legendary figures, a depiction of one region's big day out, and so on.

'I still think it's one of the best sports films I've ever seen,' says Morten Piil, the consultant who originally commissioned the film, and who became a leading authority on Danish cinema. 'It's clean in a way; it's not trying to be psychological, or critical or sociological in a way that overstates things. It's lyrical, heroic, beautiful, but also matter-of-fact, and the composition of the film is superior. It takes its time. It's a kind of heroic poem.'

It is also the product of a unique cinematographic exercise in terms of documentary, and in sport. In Bristol that evening, Leth went through the resources he had devoted to his film: the planning, the hours of footage distilled into what we had just seen, the legwork he and his team had put in to find locations such as the café at a feed station that would be – briefly – at the centre of the cycling world as the early stragglers climbed off their bikes right outside. Clearly, the making of this film was a story in itself, with its own heroes, villains, untold tales, and mysteries.

Leth's project was a massively ambitious one, bordering on foolhardy: to capture on camera every major happening in a single event taking place over a course of more than 150 miles through open countryside, and to turn it into a coherent narrative that celebrated the race's heroes in epic style. The constraints that this implied, not to mention the possibility of outside events intervening – as they did on the day – made this a risky investment, the more so as Leth had not actually seen the race before he started shooting. It was the ultimate one-day shoot with no second takes. The question is simple: just how the hell did he do it?

Great art transcends time. *A Sunday in Hell* is great art, but that does not mean its subject matter is immutable or untouchable. Rather the opposite, which is where this book comes in. The film raises questions aplenty, starting with the story of how it was born and developed to maturity. There is its creator's story, and the unheard tales of the men who helped him make this *meisterwerk*. Was there anything that Leth missed out, by accident or design?

The film has its back story: the era in which, when we watch it, time stands still for almost two hours. Capture a moment in history, and you are bound to leave narrative threads hanging. So what has become of all those characters, the men exalted by Leth and assaulted by those cobbled lanes? What is left today of the race Leth depicted? Just as importantly, where *is* that café with the most hallucinogenic wallpaper and the most knowledgeable cycling fans in the whole of France?

CHAPTER 1: FÉLIX SMELLS KRONER

Standing in the heart of Paris on a winter morning late in 1975, the two men from Denmark were impressed but also a little intimidated. Jørgen Leth and Christian Clausen were newly arrived from Copenhagen, fresh from many hours clank-clanking southwards through Germany, Holland and Belgium, which had been lightened by several bottles of burgundy to get them 'in the mood for France'.

The building, 10 Rue du Faubourg-Montmartre, stood just south of the Gare du Nord, not far from the Folies Bergère, a typical four-storey office block in a busy Parisian street. The man they had come to meet, Félix Lévitan of the newspaper *Le Parisien Libéré*, had the power to make or break their project, a radical one: to film a documentary about the Paris–Roubaix single-day Classic, one of the biggest of the bike races organised by Lévitan's newspaper and its partner title *l'Equipe*. Leth, the director of the putative project, knew there was no question of Lévitan making any concessions by talking English to his Danish visitors. In fact, there was very little chance of his making any concession of any kind.

'Elegant, arrogant, almost criminal,' is how Leth recalls Lévitan, the commercial mastermind behind the Tour de France and the other events run by the two Parisian newspapers. 'Everyone was afraid of him. All the journalists were terrified of him – he could throw them off a race at no notice. I remember the way he used to talk to them. I had a friend who was a journalist at *Le Parisien*, we went ahead of the race to have lunch one day, and Lévitan phoned the restaurant to ask where he was.' As for their meeting, before they even got the cameras rolling, it turned out to be, 'a big drama. A big drama.'

A dapper little man who exuded chilly aristocratic hauteur and foxy, Machiavellian cunning, Lévitan had come a long way from running errands on a cycling magazine in his youth. Born into a family of Jewish shoemakers, he had survived internment during the round-ups of the Second World War – the most brutal moment, he recalled, was watching from his cell window in the Cherche-Midi prison as the editor of the communist paper *l'Humanité*, Gabriel Péri, was executed.

He had been made head of sport at *Le Parisien* when the capital's press was restructured after the liberation in 1945; and had joined forces with *l'Equipe's* editor Jacques Goddet when *Le Parisien*'s publisher Emilien Amaury had taken over *l'Equipe*. The two papers' list of events was a long way from the sprawling, multinational quasi-monopoly now enjoyed by their linear successor Amaury Sport Organisation, but the roster included one-day Classics such as Bordeaux–Paris and Paris–Tours as well as Roubaix, the Grand Prix des Nations time trial, the Critérium National and the under-25 Tour de l'Avenir.

There was a theatrical tenor to proceedings. Lévitan's office had a close-fitting, soundproof door. 'Spectacular', recalls Leth; 'they just whisked us in there.' It was all part of the aura that Lévitan liked to project; the hard commercial man compared to his co-organiser, Jacques Goddet, who seemed more approachable and cerebral. Lévitan would go as far as intervening in his own races to ensure the interests of his sponsors prevailed; on one occasion when he overruled his own judges' ruling on a sprint result it drew an angry protest from the British cyclist Barry Hoban, who questioned his right to make the call. Lévitan answered firmly: *'Moi, mon cher Barry, j'ai tout le droit.'* He could do whatever he wanted.

Leth and Lévitan had history; the film-maker describes their relationship as 'strange' and 'difficult'. Five years earlier, Leth had turned up at the Tour for the first time, a rising star of Danish film-making with seven years of radical cinematography behind him. He and his collaborator Henning Camre wanted to make studies for a proposed feature film on the Tour, funded by the Danish Film Institute. In those days, official visitors to the Tour who did not speak French (or who happened to be female) received a somewhat chilly welcome until they had been accepted into the family as long-standing members of the caravan. 'The relationship with Lévitan wasn't easy,' recalled Leth. 'We had the backing of Nordfilm in Denmark; they had written to him to get us access, but we had difficulty getting the accreditation we had previously secured in writing.' The film never saw the light of day – so Camre recalls – due to the potential cost.

Lévitan would not give the Danes permission to film the 1970 Tour. The picture rights to the race had not yet acquired the massive commercial significance they hold today, but Lévitan would not deliver anything relating to his races to any party unless he felt the price was right. In the 1970s, the Tour was, commercially at least, on shaky ground, and he was innovating constantly in repeated attempts to square the financial circle. 'Lévitan said to us, "Don't film anything,"' said Leth. 'So we had only a still camera and a Super 8 camera' – a classic cine camera made by Kodak and using 8mm film – 'which I wanted to get some footage on, for study.'

The Tour's commercial head and the experimental film-maker had lived contrasting lives. Born in Aarhus, Denmark's second city, in 1937, Leth had studied literature and anthropology there and in Copenhagen, and had started working life as a journalist for the magazines *Aktuell* and *Politiken*. He took a particular interest in jazz, sport, film and theatre. He started writing poems and making films almost simultaneously; they overlapped – and still do nearly sixty years on – with inspiration flowing from one to the other and vice versa in the spirit of the sixties. He was inspired by the anthropologist Malinowski, by Andy Warhol, by Jean-Luc Godard; inevitably for a Danish cineaste, by Carl Dreyer (*The Passion of Joan of Arc* remains one of his favourite films). His films at this stage were largely experimental; his curiosity for life was insatiable.

Some of the footage from the 1970 Tour eventually made it into Leth's 1973 experimental film, *Eddy Merckx in the Vicinity of a Cup of Coffee*: the stage finish in Rouen won by Walter Godefroot, the peloton topping Mont Ventoux, and a sequence at a stage start that focuses closely on the Cannibal. But Lévitan was not happy. 'At some point he saw me with that camera and said, "I've told you Mr Leth, no filming. If I see that again, you are out [of the race]." He threw people out all the time.'

Leth was inspired by cyclists and their sport, but in a far more abstract, mystical way than the cold-bloodedly commercial Lévitan. 'I had always been in love with cycling,' he recalled. He had begun riding on a 'big black bike'; his father had put a stick behind the saddle so that he could be safely steered along. He had raced for the local cycling club as a junior, without conspicuous success ('I didn't want to fall off the bike; I didn't want to repair it'). As a boy, he had seen the greats of track cycling on the velodrome at Aarhus, which was run by his uncle, Erik Linde, 'an excellent sprint champion', says Leth, who raced on the track himself.

Track sprinting is now largely reduced to the formalities of the Olympic Games, but in the 1940s and 1950s, at its zenith, it married the claustrophobic atmosphere and larger-than-life stars of the boxing ring with the spectacle and intrigue of WWF wrestling. From within the track centre – a special place for a youngster to be invited into – the teenaged Leth watched sprinters such as Jef Scherens, Reg Harris, Arie Van Vliet, Jan Derksen, and Toto Gérardin. It was, he said, 'a romantic era, when even the velodrome in the little town [of Aarhus] was full. Those fantastic matches stayed in my memory, and later became material for my Sports Poems.' Track racing opened his teenage eyes to the international world: exotic, eccentric foreign stars, flags fluttering for the Grand Prix. His curiosity was sparked.

He can still reel off those names, sixty years on: 'I still have the autographs of fifty of the greatest sprinters in my notebook.' He recalls Jef Scherens's 'double jump' – his ability to produce a second acceleration which would devastate his rivals – and Reg Harris sitting on the trackside ostentatiously smoking a pipe as his great rival Arie Van Vliet scurried around in a panic about his and Harris's seeding. Harris, four times a world sprint champion, and the most popular cyclist in Britain for many years – indeed one of the most popular British sportsmen of the fifties – attracted Leth because of his back story as a Second World War hero. 'You educate yourself from the stories these heroes tell you. Harris coming out of the burning tank – the only one who survived – I want to know more about that.'

Road racing came next, through Leth's friendship – which endures to this day – with Ole Ritter, the top Danish cyclist of the 1960s and 1970s, a double medallist at the world road-race championships, a multiple-stage winner in the Giro d'Italia, and holder of the prestigious world Hour record. The pair first met in 1961. 'Jørgen was a journalist and I was an amateur racer,' recalls Ritter. 'I was strong, and I rode in a special way, always trying to make solo breaks, maybe with fifty to sixty kilometres to the finish.' That quixotic approach struck a chord with Leth.

'The next year I got two silver medals at the world championship and we were always friends after that; we always wanted to make a film together.' The friendship was to influence all Leth's cycling work. One project was to film Ritter naked, painted blue, against a backdrop of white houses. 'He had the idea that all people were blue,' explains Ritter. The film was never made.

One early cycling hero was Fausto Coppi, whose story is, as his friend Raphael Geminiani told me,* a life worthy of a novel in itself, one of the narratives so beloved of Leth, who wrote a poem dedicated to the *Campionissimo* in his collection *Sportdigte*, in 1967.

Fausto Coppi

Fausto coppi.
was a fantastic human being
most at ease when alone

Invincible
in the mountains, he
was a fantastic human being

Took leave of this world prematurely
fausto coppi
fausto coppi

* *Fallen Angel: The Passion of Fausto Coppi*, Yellow Jersey, 2007

Another was the equally ill-fated Luis Ocaña, whose duel with Eddy Merckx in the 1971 Tour remains the stuff of legend, ending as it did with his dramatic crash and abandon while wearing the yellow jersey: 'For me it was the biggest Tour de France of all; the drama, the feeling of fate, the defeat, the lack of luck. Ocaña was a personality – [he showed] pride I'd never seen before, the way he was challenging Merckx was incredible, unprecedented. That stage at Orcières Merlette, the accident on the col de Menté. I'll never forget those images – him lying there, fantastic but terrible . . . hit by Agostinho and Zoetemelk. Then [the next day] Merckx refusing to take the yellow jersey – beautiful.'

At the back end of the 1960s and into the early 1970s, there was a romantic, exotic side to professional cycling. That was felt by only a few within the circumscribed group of European nations that made up its heartland – writers like Antoine Blondin – but it was part of what drew the small number who came from outside to discover a sport that was new to them. That sense of adventure and romance – cycling as road trip – underpinned a friendship which had begun in 1970 during Leth's first visit to the Tour when he met another newcomer, the cinematographer Dan Holmberg.

Holmberg, who would become Leth's closest collaborator, was shooting the event for Swedish television. He recalled: 'We had a brand-new rented Peugeot. It was light blue and had a sunroof that you could shoot from. I loved it, of course. It was an adventure. There was another Peugeot in the race. A much older one and it was black and had Danish number [plates]. The two Danes in the car were Jørgen and [another future collaborator] Henning Camre. Jørgen told me that they were researching for a possible film on bike-racing.

As the "expert on bike-racing-cinematography" I probably had a lot to say on the subject. After all I was an old hand at this . . . a few days of shooting in Italy and a few days in France. Ho ho.'

When the Tour reached Paris on the final Saturday, Leth and Holmberg went out to celebrate with 'a big bunch of journalists', over *choucroute* and wine, after which he lent Leth some money to enable his new-found friend to pursue the evening in the company of another new-found friend. 'The next morning I woke up when the maid was placing a very elegant tray on top of my bed with *café-au-lait* . . . orange juice freshly pressed . . . bacon and eggs . . . warm croissants and so on. It was a very nice hotel close to the Champs Elysées by name of Bellman. I fell asleep again of course and woke up this time with my right leg hurting from the hot *café-au-lait* and my left leg deep-frozen in orange juice and ice. Later that day Jørgen and I met again at the finish line [this would have been in the Piste du Bois de Vincennes in western Paris]. Jørgen paid back his short-term loan and from now on we were friends.'

Five years later, with two low-budget cycling documentaries to his name – *The Impossible Hour* and *Stars and Watercarriers* – Leth was in Paris again. The idea of a film about a single-day Classic came about after a conversation with a young producer, Steen Herdel, although each now claims the other man raised the idea first. Leth says that Herdel suggested he make another cycling film; the director recalled that his initial reaction was ' . . . It will need to be totally different from the first [cycling films], but if you really insist I will have to have a think, decide upon a one-day race and do it in a totally different way from the first one.'

Herdel's recollection is subtly different. 'Jørgen came into my office and said, "Have you seen this magazine, with this crazy bike race in northern France in it? I'm going to make a film about it – what do you think?" I said, "You should do it."' It was a shot in the dark in one sense. Leth had not actually seen cycling's greatest one-day Classic at this point. He had read about the race in the newspaper *l'Equipe* and magazines such as *Miroir du Cyclisme* (then as now, he was a voracious consumer of newsprint – 'it's fuel to me' – who still has to have his copy of the French newspaper when he is at the race today). He had discussed it with Ritter, his most important contact within the sport. 'I was always talking to him about it; I said it was a fantastic race and he should make a film on it,' recalls Ritter.

Leth knew enough to have made up his mind, but he was still taking a punt on an event he had never seen. 'I said, "I want to film the hardest race of all, I want all the cameras I need." I'd had a big success with *Stars and Watercarriers* so it was a good basis to come back for another cycling film. I wrote a proposal the same day for the Danish Film Institute.'

'Jørgen wrote six to eight lines to the guy at the DFI,' recalled Herdel. 'He knew Jørgen, he knew me, so it was very easy. Today, you wouldn't be allowed to make a film like that. People in offices educated at university wouldn't have the brain cells to see it.'

The earliest extant version of the proposal is a single page of typescript, dated Frederiksberg, 6 October 1975. Leth has written a prose poem, in elaborate, exalted language: lyrical, rhythmic, rhetorical.* It is less a business proposition than a paean to cycling's greatest one-day race. When he gets to the

* It forms Appendix 1 of this book.

cobbles, his cadence becomes reminiscent of a Nordic saga: 'Here the field is stretched, here the merciless weeding out takes place, here is the great manslaughter.' He talks of 'moments stretched out of time in a long frieze of incredible, emotionally captivating scenes'; of 'actors' heroic in stature; the 500 words is peppered with terms such as 'epic', 'ritual', 'mythology'. He concludes: 'I do not want to make an ordinary documentary about a subject from humdrum real life, but instead I hope to bring forth a scintillating, novel and epic film.'

It is an immense leap of imagination and faith to write so eloquently and in such exalted tones about something you have never actually seen. Only a poet could have done it.

The idea fell on receptive ears: the consultant at the Danish Film Institute, Morten Piil, was a cycling fan who did not know much about Paris–Roubaix, but who had reviewed *Stars and Watercarriers*, and had clearly loved it. 'We had an answer the same day,' said Leth. 'Today you'd have to wait for months. That was incredible.' Here, Leth got lucky. The system of allotting grants to films at the Institute gave immense power to consultants such as Piil, who had considerable input and close interaction with directors rather than merely looking at a script: 'What they wanted was the law,' says Piil. Thus, he could act rapidly. 'It wasn't difficult to decide and it wasn't difficult to get acceptance from the Board of Directors. It was one of the easiest decisions I ever made.'

'It wasn't a question of what [Jørgen] wrote as much as what he told me. Personal contact was very important,' says Piil. 'The decision was based on a long conversation I had with Jørgen, my knowledge of his writing, his whole attitude to professional cycling. He described so many details. This was to be the first film about cycle racing to follow an event in its totality. I found this idea very seductive. He had other projects that he'd sketched for me, but this was the best. One key point was that you couldn't see a whole race on film at that time, but he wanted to show it all.'

Within four days, Piil had released 10,000 kroner (about £800 at the time, or close to £5,000 today) for 'research expenses' to enable Leth and his producer to travel to Paris to negotiate with Lévitan, who had – so Piil's justification for the bill reads – 'already expressed his interest in writing', although that sounds like a stretch given the timescale involved.

Fixing an appointment with the Tour's head with a view to making a deal was the easy part. In the sealed meeting room in the office building in the Faubourg-Montmartre, the Frenchman's opening gambit was that Leth's project was not feasible.

'He wanted to scare us,' says Leth. 'He said, "Sit down. I've studied your letter. I can tell you that this is a very difficult project. Paris–Roubaix is an impossible race to film, very dangerous."' Leth stood his ground: 'I said, "That's why I want to make [this film]. I like all the drama and that's what we want to capture." Then I made a big tactical error. I played all my cards immediately. I said, "This is supported by the Danish Ministry of Culture. It is going to be in cinemas. It's going to be a big film."'

Lévitan could sense that his opponent had made his initial play, and he could see there was money, somewhere. It wasn't the first film rights deal he had struck with foreigners unfamiliar with cycling's finer points: the Hollywood rights to the Tour had been granted a couple of years before. He was only going to concede a limited amount of ground, and he was going to do it gradually.

'OK, that sounds OK. I will see if we can make a deal, but I warn you, it's the most dangerous race and you can only have a certain amount of access. There is a limit to [the number of] motorbikes in the race because priority goes to Eurovision and we can't mess with those guys – you can maybe have three [camera] motorcycles, maximum.' Three is actually a substantial number, given that in the biggest races, fewer than a dozen motorbikes are now permitted to circulate around a peloton to shoot stills and television images. In fact, getting three dedicated camera motorbikes to shoot any major Classic or Grand Tour solely for a film would be impossible in the twenty-first century.

With his artistic plan in place in his head – and sensing that getting those motorbikes in the race would permit him to get the moving images he needed – Leth was at least equal to this move. 'I said, "We will have a lot of cameras located in other places," and Lévitan answered, "OK, so what are you going to pay me?"'

At the table of a chic restaurant in the main square in Copenhagen, the director breaks into a chuckle and laughs loud and long: thirty-nine years ago in his memory, in the soundproofed room in Faubourg-Montmartre his French opponent is about to push a metaphorical chess queen across the board to declare 'checkmate'.

'I said, "I don't know, we have not calculated that."'

Knowing he was home and dry, Lévitan went for the jugular: 'You haven't? Then I don't understand why it should be difficult [to work out]. I see some structure here. You are making a feature film, you are supported by the state. What do I have to offer you? Take actors, I have actors. The story, I have it. The setting, I've got that. These things must have some cost in your budget. What is a feature film budget?'

As a business negotiation, it is all worthy of a place in any textbook: the opponent's defences are probed, he is given a glimpse of what he wants before the chess pieces are moved in for the kill; when the king has been pinned into that last square on the chessboard, Lévitan leaves his interlocutor hanging in the wind, as Leth recalls. 'And he said, "OK, so this is what you have to think about, and I must ask you to leave now because I have a phone call to take from a mayor [of a stage town]. You can go down and have lunch at the restaurant downstairs and come back in one hour with an answer, with a number." We were shellshocked by his directness.'

They should not have been surprised. The commercial history of the Tour de France in the postwar years had been written by Lévitan. Through the 1960s and 1970s, Lévitan expanded the Tour's publicity caravan, pressed hard to persuade Goddet to abandon the race's format of national teams in favour of commercially sponsored squads, and brought in sponsor after sponsor, most often on a small scale, often giving prizes in kind, frequently tied in to advertising in the two sponsoring newspapers. He had also brought the Tour to the Champs Elysées earlier in 1975; that remains his most enduring legacy.

Leth's approach to sport was far more mystical, more romantic. He had always been outside the mainstream, thanks to the emphasis he placed on heroism and myth. Leth felt he could see qualities in cycling that some others failed to discern. 'I thought it was a fantastic sport, with great stories, and I felt it deserved better than lousy sports journalism,' he said in a 2003 interview. 'It deserved to be sung about in big, epic films, and there were other ways of talking about it.'

Leth viewed himself as a storyteller who could see the world with the non-judgemental eyes of an anthropologist coming across new tribes, and he viewed cycling in the same way he saw other aspects of human life: sexuality, ballet, poetry, table tennis. All had narrative potential, all could be seen in new ways, through fresh, wide-open eyes.

Cycling attracted him because it 'is so full of fate, drama, characters who are bigger than life. I'm fascinated by the greatness of the riders, their facility, [their] charisma. It's enormous. It's simple. You admire them. You can rationalise why you like them – you like to look at them. I'm drawn to the tragic figures like Luis Ocaña, Fausto Coppi – I'm fascinated by the greatness of their acts, the non-rationality, courage. I like blind courage. That is something that is historic, an eternal quality. They ride irrationally. I like the madness. It's a quality in art and sport.'

As for Paris–Roubaix, the Hell of the North exemplified all the qualities he saw in cycling, but condensed into a single day – although, as we know, he had yet to see the race at this stage. Speaking much later, he explained: 'Paris–Roubaix and the Tour of Flanders are classics – people come to them because they see drama every year. [A classic] is a drama based on the sacrifices the riders must make, the accidents that can happen, the courage it takes. [A classic] makes big demands on the riders' psyche – [you need] very special people to do them right. It's fascinating from a film-maker's point of view.'

In 1976, the year that Leth was to shoot his film, the British writer Geoffrey Nicholson described what drew him to cycling in similar terms, hailing the 'strong narrative quality' of any road race, in the introduction to his book *The Great Bike Race*. Any such event, he explained, 'was a rounded, self-contained story with complex relationships, sudden shifts of action, identifiable heroes, a beginning, a middle and an end. When it was simply a stage in a longer race, then it became another chapter in a picaresque novel which each day introduced new characters in a different setting.' This chimes with Leth, who said, 'The riders create the races with the way they race. They create stories.' He would describe *A Sunday in Hell* as being 'like a novel, full of small details, an epic piece with a lot of details'. The Giro d'Italia, he said in *Stars and Watercarriers*, was 'a soap opera'.

Both Leth and Nicholson are in a strong tradition: the creation of strong narratives lies at road racing's core, because – as the Tour de France's founder Henri Desgrange realised in a moment of inspiration that has coloured the sport for 100 years – storylines are what draw in the public. In Desgrange's day – and Lévitan's – the plots emerged in newspapers, whose journalists created heroes with nicknames, personalities, and subplots to fill their pages with soap opera. Now, the tales are told through television and the internet, with print playing a subtly different role.

The meeting between the three men, Lévitan, Leth and Clausen, was significant in other contexts. *A Sunday in Hell* cannot be seen purely as a film about cycling which happens to have been made by a Danish director. It has specific significance as a Danish film; it was part of an early wave of films funded by the fledgling Danish Film Institute. The late 1960s and early 1970s marked something of a turning point in Danish cinema, with the founding of the National Film School of Denmark in 1968 and the Institute in 1972.

That investment in a national film culture had come about following what was perceived as a crisis in this area as television gained popularity, along with imports from America. 'By the early 1970s, it was clear that the survival of Danish film depended on the possibility of significant state support,' wrote Mette Hjort and Ib Bondebjerg in their introduction to the anthology *The Danish Directors*. That state support came with the founding of the film institute, specifically to fund home-grown films; now, according to John Sundholm's *Historical Directory of Scandinavian Cinema*, 'nearly all film production in Denmark is subsidised by the state'. Such a risky proposition as *A Sunday in Hell* could only have been made with state subsidy. It was a radical departure, given that 'funds were traditionally and exclusively reserved for fiction films shown in cinemas', according to the writer Henrik Jul Jensen.

Leth was one of a number of film-makers to benefit from a system specifically devised to promote Danish film-making that would reap immense benefits in the long term. Ironically enough, Leth had been turned down by the Danish national film school in 1968 on the grounds that he already had sufficient film-making experience. In terms of the DFI, however, he was one of the film-makers who got in there early, one of a select group whose work would lay the foundations of an international breakthrough in the 1990s headlined by the likes of Leth's erstwhile pupil Lars von Trier, which resulted in 'a return of the golden age of Danish cinema'.

Clearance to make the film also came at a significant moment for professional cycling, which in the 1970s was a small, parochial world: local sponsors, local riders, traditional races on small budgets. Americans, Australians, South Americans and Eastern Europeans were rare birds, so too sponsors from outside the heartland. That was changing, gradually. The arrival of Leth at Lévitan's soundproofed door marked another milestone in the gradual opening up of cycling to a wider world, initially not something that its organisers embraced with any ease. In a similar vein, 1976 saw the writing of one of the books that opened up the race to an English-speaking audience, Nicholson's *The Great Bike Race*; it appeared in 1977, the same year as Leth's film, followed two years later by Robin Magowan's ground-breaking book on the 1978 Tour de France, *The 75th Anniversary Race*.

Leth and Clausen had their lunch and between them thrashed out a figure, 'nothing compared to nowadays', recalls the director. The rest of the meeting was seamless: 'We came up, Lévitan said immediately, "Do you have a number for me?" and we said our number, 100,000 francs or whatever; he said, "OK but I feel it's . . ." and he mentioned a number a bit above, like 120,000; then we returned to something he had said before: "You must know I'm not making films, I'm just making cycle races, and you want my stock – you know better than me what it would cost." We said to him that he had had no idea of what his race was worth to us an hour earlier but, "Now you have a very precise idea of what you want, how come?" He pointed to his nose and said, "I can smell it."'

Nearly four decades on, the café in Copenhagen fills again with Leth's laughter. Just like his Danish visitors, Lévitan had been winging it all along.

CHAPTER 2: THE ANTHROPOLOGIST

'I am a storyteller. The race is the story, it's there for us to see, to use it, to interpret it well.'

Jørgen Leth

In Jørgen Leth's experimental film *Eddy Merckx in the Vicinity of a Cup of Coffee* the typewriter is as important as the bikes. The tap-tap-tapping flow of the keys provides the link between the two elements: dreamy sequences of footage from the Tour that Leth had shot in 1970 (without Félix Lévitan's wholehearted approval); hypnotic, straight-up in-your-face takes of the poet reading his oeuvre to a single camera. In between, a typewriter clack-clacking away.

The typewriter connects Leth's poetry and the Tour, which he describes at the start of *Eddy Merckx* . . . as 'my favourite novel, which continues year after year'. The sound has a sense of urgency that contrasts with the steady rhythm of Leth's voice and the soft-focus images of the bike race; its immediacy speaks of news being made, headlines being written. It would have been a familiar backdrop each day, 'year after year' at the Tour, as the journalists from around Europe wrote the daily episodes of that 'novel', each in his individual way, every evening after the day's stage. And it is also a connection to Leth's own beginnings as a print journalist. Of course, Leth doesn't mention any of this explicitly. It is for the viewer to make these connections: what Leth does is provide us with the opportunity to set our minds running.

The progression from *Eddy Merckx in the Vicinity of a Cup of Coffee* to *A Sunday in Hell* is clear: the earlier film has similar extended takes run unedited to illustrate the passage of the race in real-time, plus the impressionistic use of footage – in this case, from the Mont Ventoux finish – coupled with a disorienting musical soundtrack. There's also an element of mischief which we will see in *Sunday*, in the depiction of the finish outside the cathedral in Rouen three times, each time focussing on a new detail of Walter Godefroot's victory. The resonances are obvious: Merckx and De Vlaeminck are depicted 'ripping the cobbles apart on the notorious cobbles of the North' where, the laconic commentary tells us, 'fatal gaps open up . . . illusions are shattered'. The Hell of the North is depicted in a long, single shot on a corner, showing the entire race coming past. And then, we are back to the typing noise and the poetry.

Leth had no formal training in film-making; his first short film, *Stop for Bud* (1963) was made with other members of a 'congenial artists' collective'. Leth and his two collaborators lacked resources but got on with making their film with the same immediacy and lack of inhibition that Leth had brought to his poetry. It was very much in the counter-culture spirit of the sixties. 'I wanted to start a new film language, to turn everything upside down,' he said. As Leth saw it, the lack of available technology due to an absence of budget was less a restriction, more a chance to simplify things: hence, *Stop for Bud* has no synchronised sound. It's not sophisticated but it doesn't need to be. (It's also based on a linguistic joke, the road signs that are to be found in Denmark saying

Stopforbud – no stopping – one of which is shown in the film's opening.)

Leth's work was part of the broader way in which artists explored new frontiers in the 1960s, but there was a specific Scandinavian and Danish element to it. *A Cultural History of the Avant-Garde in the Nordic Countries 1950–75* refers to Leth as 'engaged in expanding and refining the traditional practices of art'. The essayist continues, 'The key terms in this endeavour were hybridisation and blending, especially of traditional art forms such as painting, poetry and opera with modern media, including radio and television.' The combination of poetry and image that marks Leth's career – and which we see in *Eddy Merckx in the Vicinity of a Cup of Coffee* – is a perfect example of this kind of mix, where the boundaries between different art forms are elided and broken down.

By the time Leth moved on to his first full cycling feature, *Stars and Watercarriers* in 1973, he had a dozen more films under his belt, most notably *The Perfect Human*, a surreal and hugely acclaimed thirteen-minute work from 1967. All his films had certain things in common: they were short in length, and they were largely experimental. *Ophelia's Flowers* (1968) is a seven-minute short shot with a single camera and one actress, focusing on a tiny part of Ophelia's descent into madness from Hamlet; *The Deer Garden: The Romantic Forest* (1970) a leisurely, pastoral look at a deer forest near Copenhagen, initially shot with four cameras to be shown on four different projectors at the same time; *Chinese Ping-Pong* (1972) is fourteen minutes of table tennis, shot on zero budget, often in slow motion and set to a piano soundtrack (played by Leth himself using the piano at the Danish Film School) mixed with the players' shoes squeaking on the gym floor.

The material was diverse, but there is a pattern of a kind: a transition from briefer studies of individuals to more extended investigations of more complex subjects, and from purely abstract topics towards more concrete subjects. It was in cycling, however, that Leth would find his first true inspiration for full-length films. *Stars and Watercarriers* tells the story of the 1973 Giro d'Italia; it came about at the initiative of Ole Ritter, by the early 1970s a regular stage winner at the Giro and a fixture in Italian cycling, who arranged for his Bianchi team to assist Leth with hotel accommodation and other support.

With a minimal budget from the Danish Film Institute, Leth travelled to Italy with a rudimentary team. Dan Holmberg wielded the single camera. It was a last-minute affair. In March 1973, Holmberg – who had not heard from Leth since the 1970 Tour de France – was in San Luis Obispo, California; he checked in by phone to Swedish television where the secretary told him to call 'a man speaking Danish, very important. Amazingly the lines worked and Jørgen answered the phone and I said yes and thanks to the offer to shoot *Stars and Watercarriers* in May–June the same year. I said thank you to the AT&T operator and she reminded me that I get my dime back when I hang up.'

There was a motorbike driver to convey Holmberg (that motorbike driver, Sergio Penazzo, was to become a legend in Italian cycling photography later in the decade; Penazzo would apparently jump off the motorbike during shooting *Stars and Watercarriers* to take still images). A friend of Leth's, a fellow poet and cycling fanatic named Eberts Habert, was in charge of sound; he was given a crash course in the subject before he headed for the start in Belgium. So tight was the budget that Ritter lent Leth his own car to use during the race – the Peugeot 407 that features in the final moments, where the cyclist packs his bike resignedly into the boot and heads off to his next race.

Stars and Watercarriers sets out to explain stage racing in its nuance and complexity to a non-expert public, by telling the story of one particular Giro. In this, it was pretty much identical in its aims and method to Geoffrey Nicholson's 1977 sports-literature masterpiece *The Great Bike Race*. However, the two men differ in their approach. What Leth wanted to do was 'to make a film which went beyond the result . . . beyond the daily reporting of the result . . . I was interested in emphasising the mythological content of bike racing and to show bicycle sport as an epic. I wanted to give the audience a deeper understanding of the sport.' In telling the story of the 1976 Tour de France, Nicholson is far more matter-of-fact, mildly ironic, slightly down-beat. His interest is more in the narrative per se.

Leth's film, on the other hand, adopts an exalted, mythical approach to the race and its central characters – sub-headings such as 'A Road of Pain', and extended sequences showing Merckx and his main opponent, the mercurial Spanish climber José Manuel Fuente. The race was, he felt, ' . . . the material of novels, great storytelling'. He acknowledged that he was 'projecting certain qualities onto the sport – but I think they are there.' He saw what he describes as 'mythological values' in that Giro: 'the glories, the falls and the tragedies and the triumphs.' The objective, he said, was 'to get inside, rather than being critical in the journalistic sense of the word. I wanted to sing about the riders.'

Stars and Watercarriers places the battle for supremacy between Merckx and Fuente* centre stage, but also examines

* Nicknamed *El Tarangu* – Asturian for a man of great strength – Fuente won the Vuelta a España twice, and pressed Eddy Merckx hard in the 1972 Giro d'Italia, hence the 1973 rivalry. He retired at only twenty-nine due to liver disease, and died at fifty of the condition.

the intra-Italian rivalries between the likes of Felice Gimondi and Giovanni Battaglin, as well as Ritter's personal odyssey through the three weeks. It delves into the internal life of a team – naturally Ritter's Bianchi – and there are cameo roles for the world champion Marino Basso and the 'water-carriers', one of whom is followed riding up to the bunch with three vast glass bottles precariously balanced in a jersey pocket.

The low budget is betrayed by features that give the film some of its charm: the use of the cardboard gradient profiles issued by the race organisers as a framing device; black-and-white photographs culled from a magazine. Having a single camera is less of a limitation than might be imagined, given the wealth of filming opportunities offered in a three-week race. The sonorous voiceover in Danish is narrated by Leth himself, and even with English subtitles it has a poetic quality that is familiar if you have listened to *Eddy Merckx* . . . It also starts with a classic Leth sequence: uncut footage from one camera of the race passing through a town in real-time, a cavalcade lasting close to two minutes from the first motorbike outriders to the service cars. It is the perfect illustration of the scale of the event, even as we are told something of its dimensions.

It was Ritter's idea, Leth said, to ask the riders to interview each other while riding along in the peloton at a quiet moment in the race (the perils of a microphone attached to a motorbike by a sound cable amid a horde of moving bikes can only be imagined). 'I would never have dared to ask them. I couldn't believe it was possible to do it but he insisted it could be done. He was a popular figure in the bunch and he could make it possible.' Amid the hilarity is a moment where a rider asks Merckx to allow him to win something, anything – to the Cannibal's obvious annoyance. This jars: Merckx clearly doesn't get the joke. 'It's a moment of truth – a rare glimpse of Merckx's personality,' says Leth. 'He was insulted – he didn't want to deal with the question.'

Getting on for half a century after he stepped into the world of cycling, Leth cuts a distinctive figure as we share a long breakfast in a café on a main square in Copenhagen. It is a breakfast that morphs, via many coffees and many digressions, into lunch. As a sports journalist, it is not often that you get the feeling that you are alongside someone who can be described as a genuine cultural institution, in a country where such people are valued and recognised. A well-known actor comes over to the table to say hello. People stop Leth in the street and chat as we walk to the Danish Film Institute to pick up a box-set or two. It's hard to imagine this happening to a British film-maker.

According to his close collaborator Henning Camre (he of the black Peugeot in the 1970 Tour), who began working with Leth in 1967, this is a relatively recent phenomenon, as Leth has moved from being a left-field artist of minority interest to being appreciated by a far larger, and largely younger, audience, many of whom were born long after he began making films. 'This is something new. Jørgen was always considered an elitist. When we made *Notes on Love* [1989], you could count the number of people who came to see it. There is a big young audience now, they know his films and are mesmerised. It's linked to his way of talking – now he is a public figure. It's very unusual, everyone seems to know him.'

Part of Leth's status can be traced to his much-loved television commentaries on the Tour de France, laced with a trace of tabloid notoriety following a scandal after publication of his autobiography *Det uperfekte menneske* ('The Imperfect Human') in 2005. 'The commentaries paved the way to his popularity,' says Morten Piil. 'They are done with his special way of doing things, that special attitude – the same attitude you see in *A Sunday in Hell*. I'd divide his films into the sport ones and the experimental – the films about sport communicated much better than the other films, which are more for a small minority. They are often very beautiful, but in sport when he makes films he makes a gift of drama.

'For him, bicycle racers are heroes; they have their own characteristics but he's not digging too deep,' continues Piil. 'He's unique in Denmark in having this romantic attitude, among directors, intellectuals and writers – or he was unique, because he's influenced the way people think. It's not so much his poems and his strange films as his personality. His own story is very seductive; he's a seductive person, and that's the case the more he's interviewed. He's good at putting his personality forward: he follows his own views, he's true to himself, he doesn't compromise. His way of being a bon-vivant is seductive too.'

Approaching his eightieth year, Leth still resembles the intense young man who stares into that single camera in *Eddy Merckx in the Vicinity of a Cup of Coffee*, and who can be spotted occasionally on the margins of a shot or two in *Stars and Watercarriers* and his third cycling film, *The Impossible Hour*, where he acts as French translator at one point. The face is marginally more craggy and lined, but the lion's mane of hair that frames it is still there, as wild as it ever was; the look remains as intense, the focus on every question as acute. Everything seems to interest him.

He is an exotic mix of constantly reinvented bohemianism, whose intellectual curiosity has not dulled. He exudes the sense of a man who loves to engage with an audience, not because he wants applause, but because he never quite knows what will emerge from that engagement. He comes across as a man whose involvement with his work is total, whether that work is recalling a film he made forty years ago, speaking to an audience about what he does, reading poetry to music, or commentating for Danish television. He is a man for whom there is no concept of a day job.

Ritter was also the key to *The Impossible Hour*, one of three documentaries produced by Leth in 1975, alongside a short, eponymous film on the writer Klaus Rifbjerg, and the experimental *Good and Evil*, described in Leth's filmography as 'a pseudo-documentary portrayal of life, no less . . . a series of sketches plucked out of different everyday contexts'. Leth's second cycling documentary depicts his fellow Dane's three unsuccessful attempts to regain the Hour record from Eddy Merckx; Ritter had pushed the distance to 48.653km in Mexico as a complete unknown in 1968, breaking new ground by being the first man to profit from the thin air at high altitude; Merckx set what would be the definitive distance, 49.431km, four years later.

In November 1974 and at the age of thirty-three, not for from the end of his career, Ritter went back for what he hoped would be a properly resourced attempt. Leth had given up an initial project to film the record due to lack of funds, before Ritter called him from Mexico 'about a week' before his first record attempt: his bike maker, Benotto, had come up with the money. Ritter had also press-ganged a French television crew, who had come to film him, into putting themselves at Leth's disposal as well. The crew included France's most popular commentator of the time, Jean-Michel Leulliot, and a cameraman of enigmatic genius, Paul Constantini. The credits for *The Impossible Hour* contain pseudonyms; the French crew could not be identified because they were already under contract to the company which had sent them to Mexico in the first place.

The film is a study in failure, showing how Ritter ended up with the second, third and fourth best distances in the world, while Merckx remained untouchable. Indeed, considering the intensity that envelops most Hour record attempts, there is a distinct lack of obvious disappointment or drama. Ritter was in optimal form, but what the film does not show was his version of events, a series of what he termed 'stupid mistakes' that prevented him from overtaking Merckx's distance, and which frustrated him so much that he ended up going to Acapulco for a holiday. The director had a different mission:

'I was trying to lift the event into the mythological space, and also [explore] the emotional part of men trying to pass their own limits. That's the essence of it.'

Once Lévitan had obtained his pound of Danish flesh, Leth and his collaborators had to move urgently, with just four months to pull their entire project together. A further 40,000 kroner were released by Piil on 9 February to cover pre-race research; the grant, by then, had been finalised at 1,053,000kr (£84,000 at 1976 rates), with up to 66 per cent going on pre-production costs. The final contract with *La Société d'Exploitation du Tour de France*, the umbrella company that owned *l'Equipe's* races, is a mere three pages and is dated 26 February 1976, less than six weeks before the race was to take place. The final fee for the rights was 90,000 francs, about £10,000 at the time, or close to one-eighth of the film's budget. Prior to that, the two parties had negotiated by letter; in one, dated 29 January, Lévitan accepts a role as 'French expert', although it is not clear what that actually involves, or whether it merited any remuneration.

The contract stipulates that Leth can have two motorcycles shooting 'in the race', and two more to supply them with film; two cars in the convoy; and one helicopter; the contract, once signed, is to be accompanied by a letter certifying *bona fides* from the Danish embassy in Paris. There were attempts to pull in sponsorship – from the Danish Sports Federation, from a supermarket chain, from various banks – and there were worries about the use on French soil of cameramen from a country other than France due to the strict labour laws and the militancy of arts unions. A letter from the Danish embassy in Paris mentions – in jest – the possibility that the non-French camera crews might have to be 'smuggled in'.

Four months was a short time frame compared to most projects involving small or large screen, but it was ample compared to the rushed, impromptu way in which Leth had had to pull together *Stars and Watercarriers* and *The Impossible Hour*. The priority was to look at the route, and the best opportunity was when it was examined by Lévitan and Goddet's right-hand man Albert Bouvet, who made an annual trip to see which sections had eluded the tarmacking machines of the local authorities and to assess the condition of what was left.

That trip took place in December or January, and it marked Leth's first physical encounter with the world of Paris–Roubaix. Like many before and since, he fell in love with the *pavé*. 'We stopped now and then, and Albert told us crazy stories,' he told me. 'I loved the madness of it all. He said the race had to be monstrous or it was no good. I loved that. I still believe the harder the better. I hate it when they cut races short because of rain or snow. I thought it was wonderful. You can't get away from the little injustices of it. There are accidents, bad luck, big dramas, life and death. I was fascinated walking on the cobbles. I fell in love with [the race] immediately. I felt that it was going to be a fantastic film.'

From there Leth and Holmberg had to decide where to put their fixed position cameras. 'We had to choose places which were important, strategic. We decided on this trip – we looked at localities and locations but they were not definite because the route changed a little bit from year to year. From there we began calculating. We knew we could have three motorbikes with cameras in the race, and a fourth to feed the cameramen their film during the race. We began to hire people.' The producer Christian Clausen sent a 'situation report' to the Danish Film Institute on 19 January 1976. The core members of the camera crew were in place: Constantini, Holmberg, cameramen Peter Roos and Dirk Brüel, and Ron Goodman, a Canadian specialist in the use of a radical helicopter-mounted camera, the Wesscam.

The compact nature of the Hour Record – one man, one principal location, one hour – made *The Impossible Hour* a feasible project for a small crew. The low budget for *Stars and Watercarriers* meant Leth's only option was to use a small, hand-picked team; it was an ambitious project, but three weeks on the road in Italy gave them opportunities aplenty to amass the footage they needed. *Sunday in Hell* was different. Leth would use broadly similar techniques that can be traced as far back as *Stop for Bud* and *Eddy Merckx in the Vicinity of a Cup of Coffee* but on a more extensive and lavish scale. The wider themes of myth and epic that are touched upon in *Stars and Watercarriers* would be explored again, blended with what marks out *The Impossible Hour*: the intense focus upon how human beings cope with an athletic challenge, ending in failure.

Leth's view of Paris–Roubaix itself dictated his approach to the film. 'It's a race that has a very special, epic quality and that's the story I wanted to tell. First of all, I think it is a story, a great story, an epic story, more than a circus. It's not a circus, it has many disturbing elements, a lot of things to keep hold of. A circus is more disorganised. [Paris–Roubaix] has a dramatic narrative in itself, which a circus does not. It starts there and it ends there, and in between a lot of things are happening, and in the end it is rising suspense. That was the idea that carried my film. That this is a story. I just need to instrument it, orchestrate it and tell it well enough.'

In other words, it wasn't merely a matter of sending a load of cyclists down some bad roads and seeing how many fell off. Leth viewed the race as a 'novel', with multiple strands to interest the 'reader'; these had to be identified and then he had to assemble material in order to produce the narrative. 'The bicycle race is more than just the riders going from one place to another. There is everything that is happening in between, all kinds of aspects. Like a novel, it has a lot of small pieces, a lot of characters, even the lesser ones, like the people in the café, the guys in the media and so on. It's not a small-scale task.'

Given the financial restrictions he had experienced in his previous three cycling films, he viewed this as his one opportunity to produce the cycling documentary of his dreams. Paradoxically, however, Leth actually didn't want the entire shoot to be plain sailing, with everything proceeding seamlessly, under total control. He had made a point of working 'with obstructions' since the very start of his career, from the point where he and his friends had shot Bud Powell with limited kit and without the benefit of synchronised sound. (Later, in 2003, he and his former pupil Lars von Trier would put together an entire project based on the notion that the artist should work under defined, strict limitations rather than having a free rein.)

'All the films Jørgen and I worked on together, we set the rules and the limitations,' Henning Camre told me. 'You can't just do whatever [you like]. For *Life in Denmark* [1972] it was all shot in a studio against a black background, all fixed shots. There are only five or six exterior shots – the sea, a village, to remind you of where we are. When you work that way, it adds to it. If you think everything is possible and you want to do everything you end up in a mess. Jørgen would never get involved in a film where everything is possible.' One parallel is in soap opera, where the timescale for honing and rehearsing each weekly episode comes down to a few days; that obvious 'limitation' is usually a spur to creativity.

The 'limitations' for *A Sunday in Hell* were inherent in the race itself, in its timescale and location, and in how Leth wanted to tell its story, rather than related to his budget. 'I wanted this race to be totally different from *Stars and Watercarriers*. I was determined to have a chronological account of the race.' That meant depicting – in some way – everything of note that happened between the evening before the start at Chantilly and the finish, while delving into the minutiae around the event.

Leth would face another 'obstruction'. In an era before mobile phones, with his teams of cameramen, drivers and soundmen spread across 150 miles of northern France, on the day of the race he would have no contact with any of the personnel who would be doing the hard artistic graft. The race organisers would not allow him and his team to communicate via radio, because of the understandable risk that if a separate short-wave network was established around the race, there was a chance it would interfere with the race's own internal broadcast system and jeopardise the running of the event. Such a lack of communication would be unthinkable today.

In total contrast to a modern-day television director monitoring several screens displaying a plethora of live footage, and thus in a position to instruct each team member how to work – focus here, zoom in on that, keep watch for this – Leth had absolutely no hope of affecting how any of his team functioned on the day: where they went, how they shot, what they shot. Everything would have to be delegated to the individuals. There would be no chance to put contingency plans in place, to redirect personnel if something went wrong, or rather *when* it did. No matter how much he and Holmberg put into their planning, he would have absolutely no control over what any of the fifty personnel did with their cameras and microphones when confronted with a bike race and all that went around it.

In fact, Leth would actively embrace this limitation and turn it into an artistic virtue. In the 2002 special issue of *FILM* magazine compiled by the Danish Film Institute, he explained how he liked to work, under the heading 'Working Credo':

> Film is a series of images put together. Not a sequence, not a story, but a series of images, nothing more. The order of the images is less important than the single image. The final consequence of that assertion is that the images may be put together blindfolded. That their order may be determined by a means of rules that make allowance for a strong element of chance. . . I allow chance some leeway in my films, during shootings, but often during editing, too. In various ways, I invite chance to join in the game . . . When everything is in place, when the rules are fixed, then the attitude is: let's see what happens.

This should not be seen in isolation. In *The Big Screen*, David Thomson's overview of cinema history, he writes that Leth's hero Andy Warhol 'had felt the appeal of letting time and some very humdrum activity unfold in front of a camera . . . Warhol the painter and conceptual artist fell on the camera with drained glee because it made "art" so much easier. You turned the thing on and it happened; if something occurred in front of the camera, that was a bonus.' The Merckx interview in *Stars and Watercarriers* described earlier is a classic example: the camera and microphone were put in place, but Leth had no notion when he set up this part of the shoot that he might gain the insight into Merckx's character that emerged. It was pure good fortune that it worked out as it did.

A *Sunday in Hell* would be founded on this principle. As cycling fans we take for granted the fact that Paris–Roubaix is a one-day race. But single-day shoots are not the norm in the film world. There would be no second takes. 'Either you get it or you don't,' said Camre. 'This is what makes this film unique, so different from what we normally do. There was nothing in between. We ought to work like that all the time – why do we have to think, "This must be perfect"? I have seen people shooting hundreds of hours of footage, losing their way because they don't make a clear decision. It is not always better to do things again and again.'

'That was part of my game,' Leth explained to me. 'I liked to be deprived of control. You don't know what you will get – you only know the location, the place itself but you can't guess how many gifts you will get in such a situation. Chance often smiles on you if you risk your arm. Chance can help you in crazy situations and help you do something you don't expect. You have to have a contract with chance.'

CHAPTER 3: HEROES PART 1

'Roger De Vlaeminck gets ready . . . Paris–Roubaix is a special challenge for him. Like Merckx, De Vlaeminck has won the race three times. It's his ambition to set the record of four wins in the finest and most difficult Classic in professional racing. He knows that his arch-rival Merckx might be the one to do it tomorrow – four victories.'

As he gets out of his team car in his red top and strolls around 3:05
the back to look at the bike he will ride on Sunday, Roger De Vlaeminck has the watchful look of a street fighter waiting for the flick-knife to be pulled, or a boxer who has just entered the ring. Forty years on, he still has that aura of a man looking to respond to the first move, even as he enters his seventies. He is always, you feel, looking for an edge.

Of the four stars Leth chose to follow through their respective Sundays in Hell, De Vlaeminck is the one that the director appreciates the most. 'He's not an admirable person as such. He is like an artist who's gone crazy. [For] all his social limitations he's a fantastic character – the pride, the way he masters his riding on the cobbles. I can never tire of admiring the smoothness of his riding on the *pavé*, his view that penetrates everything – more than vision, it's focus, when you lose [the sense of] your body to find something. I can never tire of his clarity in avoiding the potholes. It's wonderful, it's masterly and it's done in such a smooth, musical way.

He X-rays the road in front of him. He X-rays ten metres in front, constantly.'

For Leth, De Vlaeminck slotted neatly into a certain template. The director had always been fascinated with 'great figures, wonderful, brilliant performers', experts at their art, beginning with the jazzmen and track sprinters he encountered early in his career; he still thinks that way today. Leth's views on sport went counter to the egalitarian current of 1960s thinking, which he has described as 'disturbing and sterile': his 1967 book of sports poetry, *Sportdigte*, was, he recalled, 'not highly regarded by intellectuals. It was a breakthrough to write about sport in a serious way.' The poems were elitist, celebrating greatness; as he put it, 'They cultivated the sportsman as a hero, as a model, as someone who's capable of moving us.' Leth described his breakthrough documentary, *The Perfect Human*, made in the period when he wrote his sports poems, as 'a kind of polemic against imperfection [and] the cultivation of mediocrity'.

Leth's hero with the X-ray eyes and the Teddy boy's walk was born in Eeklo, in the polder region of Flanders where the wind blows across the flat marshes, broken only by lines of pollard willows. His parents were travelling clothiers; hence his nickname, 'the Gypsy'. Like his big rival Merckx, he was initially a soccer player, until the day when the club president asked him who he was when he got off the first team's bus. His pride piqued, he decided to follow the example of his elder brother Erik, who lent him his bike to ride his first race.

Like his brother, his early speciality was cyclo-cross; he turned professional in 1969 after taking silver at the world championships. 'I remember doing a press conference in Genoa once with him,' recalled Ole Ritter. 'It was on the fifth floor of a hotel, and he got his bike and rode down the stairs to the garden.' It is said that he practised riding with his tyres between tramlines to hone his bike handling. If the story is not true, it should be. His team manager Franco Cribiori said that after Paris–Roubaix, the team would go through all the riders' wheels: only De Vlaeminck's would be good enough to be used again. 'They were as good as new.'

By the time he turned up at the Hostellerie du Lys in Lamorlaye, just south of Chantilly, to be looked over by the medical staff ('Let's see if you slept well last night,' says Brooklyn's Dr Modesti as he palpates his liver), he had spent several years as Merckx's biggest rival, his 'personal gadfly in the Classics', as Geoffrey Nicholson wrote. *In the Classics* is the crucial qualifier. De Vlaeminck's first Tour de France in 1969 ended after ten stages, and so did any illusions that he might take on the Cannibal over three weeks. After that he turned to one-day races, building a *palmarès* in these that rivalled the two greats: Rik Van Looy and Merckx.

As he did so, he came to be seen in Belgium – inevitably – as the anti-Merckx, 'the last bastion of independence and humour, a non-conformist amid the homogeneity of a nation conquered [by Merckx]', as Olivier Dazat wrote in *Seigneurs et Forcats du Vélo*. A year after *A Sunday in Hell*, he won his fourth Paris–Roubaix to become the event's record holder, a status he now holds jointly – and not remotely to his satisfaction – with Tom Boonen.

Merckx had asked De Vlaeminck to join his Faema team when he turned professional; the younger man declined, knowing that he would have to bury his talent in Merckx's service. Instead, he raced for the Flandria squad, led by his friend and training partner Walter Godefroot. The episode that brought the rivalry with Merckx centre stage came in the 1970 Liège–Bastogne–Liège when Erik obstructed Eddy as Roger began his finish effort; losing in this way was not something that Merckx would take lightly. Although De Vlaeminck admitted that he would always look at a result to see where Merckx had come, and that his favourite results were those where the Cannibal finished second, he and Merckx had overcome their differences by 1976. Now, De Vlaeminck believes the greatest win of his career was the 1975 edition of Roubaix, when Merckx came second while wearing the rainbow jersey of world champion – the one great single-day race that the Gypsy never conquered.

Ironically, De Vlaeminck now says that Roubaix was not his favourite race, although it was probably the event that suited him best because he was 'the best cyclo-cross rider among the road racers'. The fact that it was in France, a country he did not like in the slightest – 'I would never go on holiday there' – did not recommend it to him. He felt the Tour of Lombardy was the finest Classic of them all, but Roubaix was still *his* race, according to his former team manager Franco Cribiori, who recalls how in 1973, his leader insisted on riding in spite of having been brought down by a television motorbike on a descent a few days earlier in Ghent–Wevelgem, requiring over thirty stitches in a cut to his arm.

De Vlaeminck's first win in Roubaix came in 1972 – a wet, cold edition which he took in a 23km solo escape. That came shortly after his transfer to the Italian squad Dreher, sponsored by a beer company; the following year, the team became Brooklyn when a chewing gum manufacturer picked up the reins and, with Cribiori at the helm, wins in the Hell of the North followed in 1974 and 1975.

*

Like so much in *A Sunday in Hell*, the opening sequences have their forerunner in *Stars and Watercarriers*, which has a section dealing with Ole Ritter's build-up to the time trial at Forte dei Marmi, where Leth cuts between footage of the mechanic's painstaking preparation of his friend's Bianchi bike and shots of Ritter carefully eating his lunch, cutting his orange just so. In both films athletes go through their rituals as they prepare for a massive, personal challenge; we are reminded as Roger De Vlaeminck shaves his legs that 4.40 this is, 'one of the most important steps in preparing each individual rider'; we are told as the soigneur slaps his calves that 'the muscles must be softened for the torture ahead'. Eddy Merckx *personally* supervises the preparation of his machine, and so on.

Leth guides us teasingly, gradually, to Paris–Roubaix, unlike the beginning of *Stars and Watercarriers*, which takes us straight to the heart of the Giro d'Italia and tells us immediately where we are (confusingly, that year's race started in Belgium). Here, the director has become more ambitious, thanks in part to the resources at his disposal – he can source footage from several

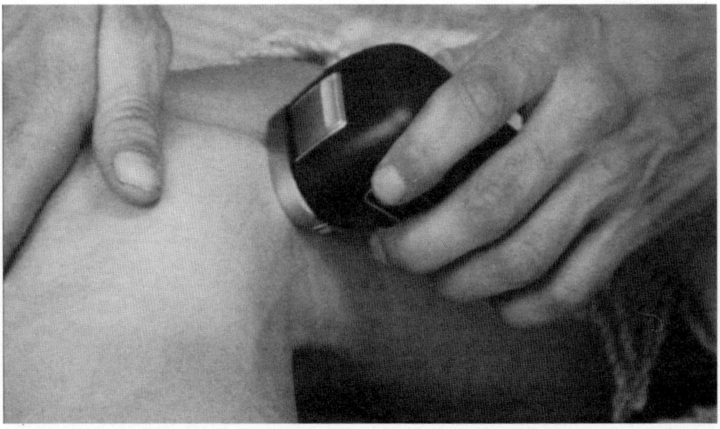

different places simultaneously – and he shows greater confidence. In the earlier film there is an obvious need to explain and guide the viewer – hence the beginning *in medias res*, straight to the Giro; in *Sunday*, we can wait.

'I wanted to create some suspense, waiting to lay out the story,' Leth told me. 'This is a conscious method . . . to present some concrete details, and create some expectation. What is going on? What are they doing? There are so many weird and wonderful rituals in this sport – I want to find out how it unfolds. This is a story that wants to be told.'

'The film isn't rushing into things,' says the consultant and long-standing film critic Morten Piil. 'This is a place here . . . This is a place there. The more we learn about how the race is going to unfold, the more interesting it is when it starts.'

Leth has chosen four heroes: Franceso Moser, Freddy Maertens, De Vlaeminck and Merckx; their preparations for the great race form our introduction to the Hell of the North. Initially, he sent a camera crew to follow a fifth rider, Walter Godefroot of Ijsboerke – the stage winner at Rouen depicted in *Eddy Merckx in the Vicinity of a Cup of Coffee* – but the footage did not make it past the cutting-room floor. Godefroot recalls now that he had no idea what the Danes who turned up at his hotel room actually wanted; they spoke no Flemish. 'They wanted to shoot me brushing my teeth; I had no problem with it, but I didn't know it was for a film of that kind. I saw the film afterwards; I wasn't in there, presumably because I didn't win.'

The director's choice of the quintet tallies exactly with the view at the time of how this edition of Paris–Roubaix was going to pan out. As the banner headline in *l'Equipe's* edition of Saturday 10 April put it: 'Moser Served up to the Voracity of the Belgians'. However, there is more to Leth's choice of protagonists than a quick skim along the top of the newspaper.

Speaking of his 1978 documentary about the Danish Royal Ballet star Peter Martins, Leth described what he saw in great performers: '. . . charisma, the ability to facilitate or transmit certain experiences. These experiences are transcendental: a great performance is something that enriches our lives. My aim is to penetrate and reveal what it is exactly that the performers do, the mechanisms underwriting their accomplishments. I maintain admiration and respect as my starting point.'

Sport, Leth felt, was worthy of a place in the human pantheon. 'A great sports performance is like theatre where we can see the qualities of our lives explosively displayed in purified form . . . Outstanding sports accomplishments resemble Greek theatre where all kinds of characters and traits were put on display – heroes, villains, virtues and vice. We owe it to the great performers to respect them for this aspect of what they do.'

Leth is a man who admires larger-than-life figures. His 2015 book *Mine Helte* – 'My Heroes' – contains an eclectic set of pen portraits of the people who have made the biggest impression on him throughout his life. *Mine Helte*, he told me, was 'another way of writing your memoirs, about people I met, people who had an influence'. From the Yugoslav performance artist Marina Abramović, he scrolls through a range of sportsmen, ballet dancers, jazz artists, dictators, anthropologists, strongmen, politicians. Andy Warhol rubs shoulders with Roberto d'Aubuisson – interviewed by Leth for his documentary *Haiti Express* – and Papa Doc, George Balanchine and Chet Baker. The anthropologist Bronislaw Malinowski is there, so too Dennis Hopper, Dustin Hoffman and Leth's fellow director Lars von Trier. The criteria for their inclusion are universal: in Leth's view they are larger-than-life as human beings, people of impact.

Leth selected cycling's two greatest tragic heroes – Fausto Coppi and Luis Ocaña – plus the track sprinters who provided the colourful backdrop to his early years as a teenager in the velodrome at Aarhus: Reg Harris, Arie Van Vliet and Jef Scherens. 'I've been very selective writing about sportsmen. I didn't want to write a normal cycling story. I selected them [for the book] so carefully. I want to remember them in that context of general experience in life. You admire them and you learn from them. I include only the most important ones, the ones who fired my imagination.'

He was not the first to depict cycle racing as mythological epic. When he founded the Tour de France, Henri Desgrange was looking to create heroes and mythology for the twentieth century, although, prosaically, this was in order to sell newspapers rather than for any higher purpose. Benjo Maso's history of the sport is not lightly entitled *The Sweat of the Gods*. Roland Barthes's view that cycling is modern-day mythology was current in the 1950s but is widely quoted to this day. Leth's cycling films fit into this bigger picture.

'I'm drawn to the more tragic figures like Ocaña and Coppi,' Leth explained to me. 'I'm fascinated by the greatness of their acts, the non-rationality. I like blind courage. That's something that is historical, an eternal quality. They create the races with the way they ride; they ride irrationally – Coppi didn't ride rationally, and that makes him great for me. The same for Ocaña. Merckx is more rational, [but] I like the madness.' But Leth's documentaries about special human beings all have this in common: 'It's not enough simply to admire a given achievement. My aim is to ask how and why.'

In *A Sunday in Hell*, the goal is not merely to say that to race across the cobbles is a magnificent, mythical feat – we have to be taken inside that event and made to understand that the men who do it are outstanding individuals. 'My main motivation was to make it deeper,' Leth explained to me. 'I'd always been unhappy with people diminishing the character of sports heroes. They are not heroes for nothing. They are heroes because of their character and personality. I wanted to find out how they did it, how they created their masterstrokes. I want to convey my experiences to other people.'

We may wonder what is going through De Vlaeminck's mind as he shaves his legs and lies there on the massage table, the answer is – he says now – not a lot. Forty years on, it's hard for him to cast his mind back to that distant era. He wasn't thinking strategy; his way was to ride as hard as he could for as long as he could. (Eddy Merckx and Walter Godefroot took the same approach.) He isn't stressed, because the pressure was less in those days. This was a race with many favourites, not just a few; it was an era when champions such as Merckx, De Vlaeminck and Maertens won every week, averaging fifty victories a year. (De Vlaeminck contrasts this with the present day; he knows a good rider now, he says, who has won twice in ten years.) With the wins ticking over, the press and fans stayed off a rider's back. As for the pressure he put on himself, it was the same for a *kermis* – a local race in Belgium – a cyclo-cross or a Classic.

De Vlaeminck being De Vlaeminck, he's still looking for that edge by manipulating the *actualité* a little. 'He was always very nervous before Roubaix, because it was a race that touched him emotionally, he set a lot of store by it; it was his race,' recalls Cribiori, with whom De Vlaeminck won the race four times. 'They were good nerves.' De Vlaeminck himself won't admit to stress, or go into what he was thinking. 'I am just thinking about winning Paris–Roubaix. That's all,' he says now. However, he would sleep the night before a Classic with his bike in his hotel room, just to make sure that no one could tamper with it. That is not a man with a casual attitude. He took great pride in his profession, so much so that he had his own track mitts custom made in Italy with his name on – egotistical, yes, but many were given away to his fans.

The intimacy of the footage is foreshadowed in *Stars and Watercarriers* in the sequences of Ole Ritter contemplating defeat in his single bed in his spartan hotel room and pondering the challenge of the time trial from his lonely lunch table. Leth recalls the Gypsy cooperating fully as, variously, he was captured shaving his legs with that buzzy razor – the look of intense concentration as he does so is brief but speaks volumes – complaining in perfect Italian of his sore back as he is massaged and discussing with the doctor whether he has had any nocturnal adventures that might have impinged on his rest ('*Possibile, ma non sicuro*,' – maybe, but I'm not sure – he says ambiguously.)

6:27 *'Eddy Merckx personally supervises the preparation of his machine. He has the reputation of being a super perfectionist, a maniac about mechanical details. Something always needs to be adjusted, especially the height of the saddle.'*

The Cannibal, shot by the Danish cameraman Dirk Brüel, is a contrast to his big rival De Vlaeminck as he arrives at his hotel: early 1970s cool personified in his well-fitting jacket, dark sunglasses, and impeccably coiffed Teddy-boy quiff above what one writer termed 'the graven features of a statue'. The resemblance to the cat-like young Elvis Presley is disconcerting, although with his sunglasses removed to help him examine the bike being shown to him by the mechanic Julien de Vries – later to wield a spanner for Greg LeMond and Lance Armstrong – the Cannibal takes on a slightly less confident mien.

Merckx had an external veneer of stylish cool and dominance, hiding a sensitive and more insecure interior: 'a worrier', his confidant Jean Van Buggenhout said. In the film, his personal obsession with adjusting his bike makes as much of an impression as the way he tries to compete. He travelled to a race with seven or eight machines, all of them of subtly different design; his Molteni team car was piled high with spare parts – different stems fitted to different bars – and he was not above calling on his support crew to change stem and bars on his race bike *during* a stage of a major Tour. The *directeur sportif* Bob Lelangue and de Vries could manage it between them in two minutes.

De Vlaeminck's focus is on himself; Merckx's attention is on his bike: watching his mechanic measuring and re-measuring his saddle height. The manoeuvre is carried out using what is clearly a specially made tool to check that the saddle is completely level. It's almost counter-productive, given the confusion among the mechanics Giacomo and Julien about who has done what. In contrast, his teammate Jos Bruyère puts his leg over his bike and says nothing. This obsession dated back to Merckx's crash on the velodrome at Blois in late 1969, which left him with long-term sciatica in his left leg due to compression of the vertebrae in his lower back. He has felt the consequences throughout the rest of his life, and the constant issues in his racing years were what led him to change his position almost on a daily basis. '*Something always needs to be adjusted, especially the height of the saddle,*' intones Saunders. Or checked: the relative height of the brake levers in this case.

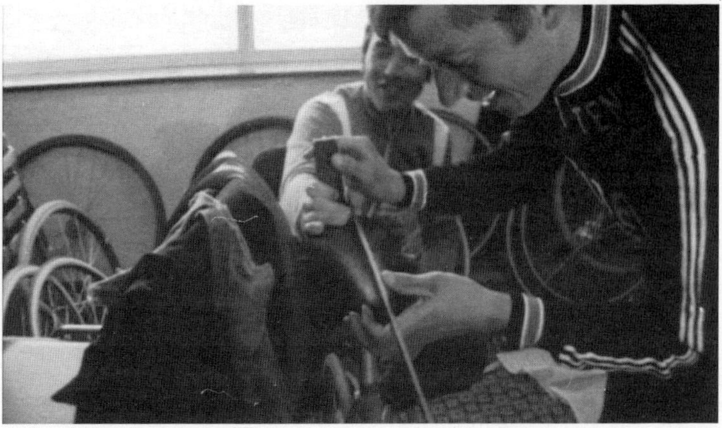

Like De Vlaeminck, Merckx was happy to cooperate with Leth's crew. 'He maybe seems more reserved,' Leth told me. 'But he was doing this stuff with the bike, we didn't interfere. That's the whole idea. It is – for me – an important idea for documentary film-making. And that played well with the riders.'

In *Eddy Merckx in the Vicinity of a Cup of Coffee*, Leth described the Cannibal as 'a phenomenal athlete, strong on every type of road in all kinds of weather and almost intolerably ambitious. He doesn't just want to win. He wants to win gloriously.' At the time, it was a reasonable summary, but six years later much had changed. In 1970, Merckx was at the height of his powers; he started 138 races and won fifty-two of those. He had hit the zenith of the most incredible career cycling has ever seen, a picture of utter dominance on every terrain.

The son of a grocer in the Brussels suburbs, Merckx was a hyperactive child who inherited his father's love of cycling; his entire career was impelled by conflicting needs: to satisfy his perfectionistic dad while placating his overprotective mother. He was also that rare thing, a cycling champion who sprang from the lower middle-class rather than the impoverished peasantry or industrial working class.

When he climbed out of his orange Volvo near Chantilly, the Cannibal retained the aura of his heyday but he was on the edge of the abyss. On 19 March 1976, he had taken the last Classic win of his career ahead of a new professional, Jean-Luc Vandenbroucke. Finally, his body was giving way in the face of the intense punishment it had sustained for ten years. Mentally too, those around him noted that he didn't have his old insatiability. Moreover, the question of Merckx's succession was becoming increasingly important and new rivals had come along to threaten both him and his old sparring partner De Vlaeminck.

8:43

> *'In Chantilly, the Flandria people are very optimistic . . . They are counting on the Belgian duo of Freddy Maertens and Marc Demeyer. Maertens is twenty-four years old, the new superstar of Belgian racing.'*

Whether or not it was an act put on for Leth's cameras, it is no surprise when the hangers-on around the Flandria team join Maertens and Demeyer for bit of a sing-song in the bar of the Hôtel du Château in Chantilly the afternoon before Paris–Roubaix. This is a classic example of Leth's 'contract with chance'. The shot was not set up. It just so happened that the team who were asked to follow Maertens (the cameraman was Jan Weincke) ended up in the same room as the eventual race winner and his team leader.

The relaxed atmosphere – polo-neck jumpers and louche sunglasses to the fore, not a tracksuit in sight – contrast with Merckx's perfectionism and De Vlaeminck's intent inward focus, but it is understandable. After years of struggle against the Cannibal, the spring of 1976 was Flandria's collective moment; Maertens, as Saunders drily notes, had been, '*the predominant rider this season . . .*' The character in the white polo neck is Walter Verlee, who was assistant *directeur sportif*, and who went on to work at the Dutch TVM squad into the 1990s. The gentleman with the glasses who sings of white wine and women was – so Freddy recalls – known as 'Harlequin'; he came from Brussels, 'had a lot of money', and was a big man for betting on the horses.

Harlequin was a close friend of the manager Lomme Driessens, who appears last, and briefly. He was a larger-than-life figure, as Leth suggests. 'He was a massive motivator, the best for that,' recalls Walter Godefroot, who rode under his direction early in his career. 'A good director,' Maertens says, 'who would always make sure the hotel rooms were close to the restaurant and was correct with money.'

He would wax lyrical about his time spent as Fausto Coppi's *soigneur* but was a ruthless operator well versed in the tricks of the trade; a rival rider of the time recalls how he was run off the road by Driessens. His relationship with Maertens is ambiguous: the rider maintains it was good, history suggests that Driessens was exploitative. The story goes that after Maertens's world championship victory later in 1976, Driessens arranged for a champagne reception in Epernay for the rider. The company, Lanson, gave the rider 1,000 bottles of champagne. These were appropriated by the *directeur sportif*, on the grounds that they might be prejudicial to Maertens's health, as 'Freddy was too fond of champagne'; he would 'pass them on later'. However, the rider never saw them.

Flandria was a long-established squad backed by the bike company of that name, which spoke of regional dominance in the most bike-mad hotspot in the world. Its history dated back to the nineteenth century, to a blacksmith's forge in the little town of Zedelgem; the company was selling a quarter of a million bikes by the 1950s, although a family falling-out had led to a schism that is worth a novel in its own right. The marque began backing a team in 1959, and it grew into Belgium's greatest ever squad, sponsoring the nonpareil Rik Van Looy in the twilight of his career and managed by an older Flandrian legend, the evocatively named 'Brick' Schotte. Its red jersey remains one of the sport's most feted team strips.

Whereas Merckx and De Vlaeminck spent the bulk of their respective careers racing for Italian teams, Flandria – where the Gypsy started out – had a solid Flemish identity with the bulk of Belgium's stars going through their books, men like Walter Godefroot, Eric Leman and Jean-Pierre Monseré. By 1976, the team had reached its definitive form with Maertens, Demeyer and the third 'musketeer', Michel Pollentier. They were a contrasting trio: Maertens, blond, lanky and a super stylist; Demeyer, a burly bulldog; Pollentier, a balding all-rounder who could climb with the best but with the poise of a rat clutched in the jaws of a terrier. Maertens's fondest cycling memories are of their time together, before they split up at the end of 1978 when Pollentier transferred to the Splendor team.

Even though they worked well together on the road under Demeyer's guidance, Flandria did not have an unrelenting focus on a single leader backed by a group of strong *domestiques*. That was the hallmark of Merckx and De Vlaeminck's teams; the Italian tradition, dating back to the postwar innovations of Fausto Coppi, was more organised, more cohesive. That tradition was upheld by the men of the fifties and sixties who ran these *squadre*: Cribiori, Giancarlo Ferretti, Waldemaro Bartolozzi. Like its French equivalent, Peugeot – also owned by a storied bike company, again with a legendary jersey – Flandria was a group of randomly selected riders thrown together in the hope that they would blend into a unit.

Maertens was literally the blue-eyed boy, with piercing azure eyes, a pointy chin, and a lovable mop of blond hair; a gentle character, recalled his former teammate Sean Kelly, in contrast to the bruiser Demeyer. His was a shop-owning family like Merckx's, from the northern town of Nieuwpoort; his father was a tyrannical character, who sawed his son's bike in half when he saw him dating a girl. Having delivered newspapers on his bike as a lad, he stayed on at school to study economics – ironically, given the chaos that marked his financial affairs in later life – and showed instant promise on turning professional with Flandria; he had been on the point of signing for the Italian team SCIC-Colnago, but the bike company offered a dealership to his father and the rest was history.

Maertens reached cycling maturity in 1975, when he won three major Classics – Ghent–Wevelgem, Paris–Tours and Paris–Brussels – but there was a caveat: he was seen as a sprinter who could turn his hand to a one-day race, rather than an all-rounder in the Merckx mode. His run of victories in the month before the 1976 Paris–Roubaix made him the overwhelming favourite: six out of ten stages in Paris–Nice; the Dutch Classic Amstel Gold – held that year at the end of March – and Ghent–Wevelgem again.

He was the obvious man to watch, but, he now says, there was no great stress. 'I never really felt under pressure; if you feel under pressure, that's because you haven't prepared right.

I knew I was ready; we had looked over the course on the Tuesday and Thursday, to see what had changed from the last year.'

Ghent–Wevelgem was a sprint victory from an elite group of ten men including Merckx, Moser and De Vlaeminck, plus solid Classics specialists such as André Dierickx and Frans Verbeeck. Most of the other 172 starters were over six minutes back. That came just five days before Harlequin broke into song in the hotel bar in Chantilly. He and the others had good reason to be optimistic.

> *'In Italy, Francesco Moser is hailed as the new great hope.* 11:03
> *At last a new* campionissimo *who might live up to the*
> *glorious past, reminiscent of the great Fausto Coppi . . .'*

Leth's fourth hero is different again. The young Francesco Moser sits watchfully, almost suspiciously, in the back seat of the team meeting hosted by his *direttore sportivo* Waldemaro Bartolozzi, captured by the cameraman Henrik Herbert. Bartolozzi must be making his script up for the cameras, as his tactical analysis – 'a difficult race, thanks to the *pavé*' – is hardly incisive. Perhaps Moser is embarrassed. Perhaps he doesn't like the camera. Somewhere among the *gregari* – anonymous teammates – is one of two Englishmen on the start list, the late Phil Edwards, a strong rider from Bristol.

There is a sullen, sultry style about Moser, 'a whiff of after-shave from the ski slopes', as Nicholson wrote. 'He's quieter than De Vlaeminck, much more intense,' says Ritter. That hides the power that we see later on in the film, and that would take Moser to a sound beating of Merckx's Hour record (the one that had eluded Ritter). If De Vlaeminck erased the cobbles with his supple pedalling and bike handling, Moser obliterated them with brute force, grinding them beneath his tyres like pebbles. The young Italian from a cycling family in Trentino interested Leth nearly as much as De Vlaeminck – he felt he shared the Gypsy's X-ray vision – although the director never truly gets close to the saturnine, aloof character later known as 'the Sheriff'.

While De Vlaeminck and Maertens were at the height of their powers and Merckx's star was waning, 'Cecco' was rising fast. In his fourth year as a professional, aged twenty-four, he had won stages in the Tour de France, taken the Paris–Tours and Tour of Lombardy Classics, and had finished second in his first attempt at Paris–Roubaix in 1974. 'I was just curious that year. I had a look at a few sections the day before. I fell in the finale when I was in front on my own; I braked too hard and flew through the air. But I wanted to do it again. The cobbles didn't scare me. You can fall off, for sure, but you have to have no fear, not be scared of the other riders, crashes, punctures.'

At this early stage in his career, before he became conscious of the economic interest in turning himself into an almost exclusively Italian star, focused on a rather sterile rivalry with the younger Giuseppe Saronni, Moser was a rare creature: an Italian who had no hesitation about testing himself far from his homeland, in the tradition going back to the 1940s and 1950s 'Tuscan of Flanders', Fiorenzo Magni, and to the *campionissimo* Fausto Coppi. In later years, he turned Roubaix into a speciality; here, he is still feeling his way.

For observers of the 1976 campaign of spring Classics, there was also a subplot here in the three-way rivalry between De Vlaeminck, Merckx and Maertens. Maertens had fallen out with Merckx in his first season as a professional, when he refused to work for the older man at the 1973 world road-race championships. The feud lasted close to thirty-five years. De Vlaeminck and Merckx were at daggers drawn; Maertens and De Vlaeminck are still at loggerheads today. Godefroot played a joker's role: drawn to De Vlaeminck, correct with Merckx, not close to Maertens.

As the long era dominated by Merckx approached its end, Flandria's 'Three Musketeers' were the flag-bearers of what was expected to be the generation that would pick up the torch from Merckx, De Vlaeminck and Godefroot. However, the succession proved far from simple. In the shadow of the Cannibal, winning was not enough: victories had to be prolific and they had to be utterly crushing.

The intra-Flandrian rivalry meant that at times it was more important for one of the trio to stymie a victory for the others than it was to win in his own right. This had clearly been the case at the previous weekend's Tour of Flanders, where De Vlaeminck and Maertens had marked each other out of the race; the outsider Walter Planckaert had won, with Demeyer second. So, for Maertens and Demeyer, Paris–Roubaix was a chance for revenge; Merckx was contemplating the end of his glory days; De Vlaeminck knew he had yet another chance to work that chip on his shoulder; Moser had the legacy of his great cycling ancestors behind him.

For Leth, the back stories are secondary; what matters to the director is the minutiae. 'Everything is in the detail,' he repeats, forty-one years later, as if it were yesterday. 'Everything goes back to that. Look at the start of *Sunday* – how they work with their teammates, the team doctor, the mechanic. It's like in *Stars and Watercarriers*, Ole Ritter cutting up the fruit before the time trial. The key to the film is that. The key to it is taking care of those details. I want to know how and why, but I'm not rushing to it.'

In the twenty-first century, we are used to the idea that we must hear words from sportsmen, however meaningless. Leth doesn't do this: he is not a participant; it is for us to interpret their emotions in the next ninety minutes. The camera is present, but whereas today's television coverage would require interviews with the stars, Leth 'avoids banal questions from reporters', as he puts it. 'I'm an anthropologist in film-making. I want to look at things, study the details, and see when they open up. And that's also the reason why I don't want the actors to tell [us] what this is all about. No editorial dialogue.

'You can rationalise why you like [cyclists] – you like to look at them,' says Leth. 'It's the same with actors. Some actors I like, some I don't. I'm not interested in Demeyer at all – *at all*. And I'm not interested in Maertens either. I'm interested in Merckx but I'm more interested in De Vlaeminck because he seems more complicated. I like blind courage. And of course they tell stories. I don't know exactly what story De Vlaeminck is telling but he's definitely a guy who arouses my curiosity.'
11:13 And ours as we watch footage of the Gypsy pedalling pensively in training. ('*Roger De Vlaeminck gets ready; psychology plays a big part . . .*')

It is not until we are twelve minutes into this film that something immediate and jarring happens, an abrupt switch to vintage-looking black-and-white amid the timpani rolls that, finally, make it explicit to us what this is all about. (Artfully, some of the footage is actually from the race the year before, switched to monochrome for effect.) '*This hell consists of some primitive narrow country roads with centuries-old cobblestones –* les pavés du Nord *– roads no longer used for civilised traffic,* *but for driving cattle and for a bicycle race . . . Year after year . . . A setting for an incredible Dante's* Inferno *with tortures and even martyrdom.'*

This is where our heroes are headed.

CHAPTER 4: SUNDAY 11 APRIL

'Sunday 11 April. It's seven-thirty in the morning. From here the seventy-fourth Paris–Roubaix will start in a few hours.'

13:16 Henning Camre chose his spot carefully, to get the perfect view across Place Omer Vallon in the centre of Chantilly. A veteran collaborator of Leth's who was taking a two-day break from his post as director of the Danish Film School, Camre arrived before dawn, several hours before Paris–Roubaix was due to roll out of the marketplace. He took up station on the roof of a building in Rue de l'Hôpital looking across the square to obtain a bird's-eye view down towards

the start banner bearing the names of the organising newspapers, which was strung between two posts at the foot of Rue du Connetable.

It was bitterly cold before the sun began to rise just after 7 a.m.; the riders were due to roll out at 9.15. 'I was there a long time,' recalls Camre. 'We didn't know when the light would be right, how early the cyclists would begin to arrive. We put up the tripod and then you wonder for a minute or two if you are going to fall off.' The images of the square, deserted apart from the occasional pedestrian and car, meld into the chaos of the race start. This is the ephemeral, peripatetic world of bike racing, as seen at the end of *Stars and Watercarriers*: the event comes to town, it sets up camp, it breaks camp, it moves on elsewhere.

Camre's background was different to the other cameramen. He had never worked in reportage ('It doesn't interest me'); his background was in still photography. 'We almost grew up together; I trusted him totally,' Leth told me. The pair had worked together on the 1970 Tour de France and Leth's experimental films such as *Ophelia's Flowers*, *Chinese Pingpong*, *Good and Evil*, and most notably *The Perfect Human*. Camre already had a Bodil award for cinematography to his name, but Leth knew he had to be directed in a certain way. 'He was seen by some as too old and conservative, too slow, but he used the role he was given to the utmost; he wasn't too slow, it was a matter of defining his role. The square was something we knew he could do. We didn't want him fighting with other people so he didn't work in the team hotels; we wanted him for "golden shots".'

Camre's images of the start show a far smaller and much more homespun race than was the case even ten or a dozen years later. What we see is more akin to a race of the 1950s rather than, say, the 1980s. As with footage of Tours de France of that era, the tiny infrastructure around the race is striking: the small number of barriers, the relative absence of branding, the tiny space a far smaller race cavalcade requires to park up. 'Artisanal', is the epithet used by those who remember this period. Within ten years, any decent regional amateur event would be more impressive. 'The difference in the sport's standing, the budgets of everything around it – teams, organisation, media – is astounding,' says Roger Legeay, who was number 164 on the start list. 'Look at the size of the sign-on table. See how few gendarmes there are.' He is echoed by Jean-François Pescheux (*dossard* 182). 'The start is barely even barriered; you have one guy, Albert Bouvet, directing the vehicles. It's another world.'

This second section of the film – from Camre's image of the deserted square until the moment when the actual racing begins after the start proper – picks up on the rituals of the evening before and intersperses them with the themes, places and personages that will crop up again and again during our day in Hell. De Vlaeminck and his team eat breakfast; the same mechanic who cleaned the Sanson team's Benotto bikes puts them onto the roof of the team's Transit van – with a distinct lack of urgency – before driving to the start in the van laden with wheels, frames and team staff, in comedic style. It's pure Keystone Cops-style slapstick, as is the moment when one of Merckx's Molteni teammates begins to slalom his bike past the fountains of Chantilly's chateau en route to the start, but there is also beauty – Bernard Thévenet pedalling his Peugeot through the morning mist. Merckx, of course, has to adjust his handlebar height en route to the start under the concerned gaze of Julien de Vries ('*Rrr . . . rrr . . . rrr . . . stop*,' he mutters, before double checking the straightness of his stem). By now it is obvious that this is as integral a part of his pre-race routine as eating a raw steak and signing cursory autographs is for De Vlaeminck.

The peripherals of the sport may have changed, but the basic principles haven't. Even the twenty-first-century Tour de France still features bizarre *animation* along the lines of those fox-hunters blowing their horns, while the process of signing on and assembling the cavalcade remains key, '*a presentation ritual which gives the fans a chance to see their heroes*'. The chaos of colour, cars, cameras, crowds and cycles will always be the same and – in some cases – is still voiced by Daniel Mangeas, the speaker who appears at the start of *Sunday*, notebook in hand, hair longer, fresher faced and less grey than of recent date, but still with the same declamatory delivery of rider stats and uplifting information, equal weight given to fifth place in stage three of the Tour de l'Indre et Loire for an obscure *domestique* or second in Milan–San Remo for Raymond Poulidor (who nearly hits his head on the tiny caravan where the riders sign on). Mangeas retired from his post at the Tour de France in 2014 (he was still working at the odd race in 2017); on the morning of 11 April 1976 he was twenty-seven years and one day old, and less than two years into his career as speaker.

19:01 A more anonymous face in the crowd is Bernard Hinault (*dossard* 84, Gitane-Campagnolo), who is seen from behind as he signs on in front of Mangeas and does not merit a name check. (Ironically enough, just after Hinault passes the speaker, Saunders laments the lack of any French contenders
19:08 for the race – '*The French have long ago given up any illusions . . . The last French victory was twenty years ago.*') 'The Badger' was to win this event five years later. Pescheux too can be spotted, as can his future boss at the Société du Tour de France, Jean-Marie Leblanc. In his capacity as journalist for *La Voix du Nord*, he is politely given the brush-off by Merckx as the Cannibal rides in to sign on. Poulidor receives identical applause forty years on when he turns up at a Tour de France stage start; here is a sense of timelessness, of the race changing but elements of location, ritual and personnel remaining the same.

Leth had prepared his battle plan for the day with more precision than any of the cyclists he was filming. Some, like Godefroot and Merckx, didn't bother looking at the route; Flandria had gone over it twice during the week before 'to look for new sections', as Maertens put it. But Leth and Holmberg went through potential locations, 'metre by metre'. The director had travelled to France one month before the race, when the itinerary had been finalised by Albert Bouvet. 'There were four phases – the meeting in Copenhagen, the meeting in Paris, the research with Bouvet and Christian Clausen, and the research period before the race which was more technical and detailed,' said Leth.

Unlike a mountain stage in a major Tour where there will be a couple of key climbs, in Paris–Roubaix the decisive moment can come almost anywhere between the first section of cobbles and the last, be it a crash or puncture that eliminates a major player, a critical attack, or a key diversionary move. This race is completely unpredictable. In 2016, for example, the eventual winner, Matt Hayman, made his initial attack well before the race even reached the cobbles. That is what makes Paris–Roubaix so unique, but in turn that makes it hard to plan for. The plot develops on the road, but its structure only becomes clear once the final outcome is known. Given that Leth's intention was to miss nothing, to report on everything, that meant his people had to be everywhere – but how?

Holmberg, Leth and the producers, Sten Herdel and Christian Clausen, had arrived in Chantilly on 30 March. They had visited the one-day Classic Het Volk to get experience of how such a race functioned; earlier that week, they also made sure to visit the Tour of Flanders and Ghent–Wevelgem with an assistant and a sound engineer. Holmberg's notes record that they started the research for Paris–Roubaix, 'driving the actual race route', on Wednesday 31 March, eleven days from race day. 'This we do again and again the rest of the week. I often drive it on my own. It is now the planning of the shooting takes place. I remember a big map and a big piece of paper where all camera positions were marked.

'We were looking for the exact spots where the race would develop, where the action would develop,' said Leth. 'Me and Dan would evaluate how the cameras should frame the race at the spot. We chose a number of points where to put the cameras [and] we had to calculate out of that. We based that on a feeling of landscape [and] the cobblestones.' They decided to target one sector in particular, the first stretch of cobbles at Neuvilly – close to today's first section at Troisvilles* – with several static cameras, 'one by a big hole, one on the other side of the track'.

The pair's reconnaissances can still be traced in their respective notebooks, held in the Danish Film Institute Archive. Holmberg's kilometre-by-kilometre breakdown of locations lasts eight pages in considerable detail (for example position 2, early in the cobbles: 'On the N39 road between Inchy and Le Cateau small road out from white house with light blue fence opposite sign "Troisvilles 1.9km"), and is followed by itineraries and time-tables for the individual cameramen, with intricate instructions for the short cuts they are to follow.

The preparations gained in pace during the following week. Holmberg records discussions over the number of cars they were permitted in the race to 'service' the motorbikes, whose cameramen would be able to change film and camera batteries with their help. There were attempts to obtain special clothing for the motorcycle cameramen, but this did not materialise. They arranged 'guards' to keep the crowds away from the cameras in the Roubaix stadium (fruitlessly. as it turned out), and looked into fuelling possibilities for the helicopter that would convey the specialist, Ron Goodman; they found a wide-angle lens for the cameraman in the Brooklyn team car, Peter Roos.

Roos was one of the cameramen who would be held in specific locations for the day – the velodrome, a café en

* See Chapter 5: Mephisto's penknife.

route – and in vehicles behind the race – the Brooklyn team car and the broom wagon. Each of these editorial decisions was a shot in the dark, 'a gamble', as Leth puts it: there was no guarantee that any of the cameramen in the cars in particular would produce anything noteworthy and for every cameraman committed to a specific area for the entire day that meant that one less would be available to cover the action on the road.

Each fixed-position camera had a single operator, with no soundman, because synchronised sound was required only in a few locations where the cameramen would remain for the entire day. The cameras and operators could be transported from place to place on motorbikes with drivers hired just over the border in Belgium. 'We had to make certain hard decisions – we needed people on the road, there, there and there,' said Leth. 'We chose a lot of fixed points where we placed cameramen and they were to do certain shots. Then we calculated that some cameramen could do one point early and maybe one point later in the race if they moved around on other roads and hopefully even three points, but that was very optimistic because the traffic is chaotic on that day with all the small roads, and they could not move on the race route itself. This was all planned really precisely, and the kinds of transport that were needed for that. We had to not be too optimistic.'

There was another issue that stemmed from doing a single shoot in a single day, with twenty-seven cameras, a multitude of camera shots and a multiplicity of locations: how to tell what shots had been taken where and when? 'The real coup that we did was to acknowledge the problem of chronology, of being able to time the cameras covering this and that,' said Leth. 'That is not something that you can do without having prepared for it. So what we did – it was a smart guy among the producers who thought this up – was we got a deal with Longines watches, and every cameraman had to start every shot by shooting his watch.

'On the watch strap we could see a letter indicating his role and from that letter we knew where he was supposed to be at that time. Those letters corresponded to a battle plan, like a military plan, where you have those letters on a map – we would know that someone was to be here at this time, and we would hope that he would be able to move to somewhere else – sometimes in very optimistic hope that he could make it.' Each has his number, his locations, his times and his diversions – often complex; often, as Leth admits, hopeful rather than realistic.

It's all there in Holmberg's A5 notebook: Henning Camre, for example, is listed as 'Foto G'. His suggested itinerary begins with 'Chantilly, Main Street, Big Picture, km 0, 9:30' – the shot described at the start of the chapter. It continues with a location at 40km in Compiègne, 10:30, after which it's into the first *pavé* at Neuvilly, km 150 13:15. This is the first of twenty key locations listed in Holmberg's breakdown of the route, and specifies 'Up the first hill with the village in the background' – the classic shot as the race tackles the infamous Côte de Neuvilly. And so on to the finish in Roubaix.

Two days before the race, all the cameramen were taken around the locations in a bus (with a luggage compartment 'stocked with supplies of Kronenbourg' according to one of those present). It was Holmberg's job to brief them. 'We stop at each position where I explain what they should shoot,' he explains. 'And what not to shoot . . . because another cameraman has that job. This works . . . but I get concerned about many of the French cameramen. Some of them did not listen really. Maybe because of not understanding English . . . but more likely . . . they maybe did not care.'

There was something else that had to be covered in the briefing: continuity. Holmberg explains: 'When you see the movie screen [in *A Sunday in Hell*], Paris is to your right and Roubaix to your left. The peloton have their noses pointing to the left. You have to decide that. If you stand on the other side of the road and shoot they would travel in the opposite direction. John Wayne needed to travel in one specific direction to find the Indians without confusing the audience. He had the script girl helping him. When I shot *Stars and Watercarriers* I did not know about this or I did not think it was important. The result was that the editor had problems with the continuity.'

For *A Sunday in Hell*, Leth and Holmberg decided that, on screen, the race would be travelling from the right to the left. One reason for this, Holmberg says, is that because the riders tend to stick to the right-hand side of the road, the cars in the convoy – and, critically, the motorbikes that are filming the riders – tend to pass them on their left. As a result the motorbikes spend most of their time on the riders' left, and so most images are taken with the riders travelling from right-of-screen to left. 'It was an important thing to decide before the race started. Part of the plan. Very important to tell the camerapeople what side of the road to shoot from. What direction the riders were travelling . . . to avoid a mess in the editing table.' Hence, throughout his notebook, the Swedish words *höger-vänster* crop up again and again in the instructions for each position: right to left. Often another word is there: *viktig* – important.

Pre-race stress was not restricted to the riders. Leth, Sten Herdel says, was 'very nervous' the day before, he worried that his crews might run out of film, and dispatched the producer to Paris to buy an extra twenty rolls. 'We never used them, but it wasn't surprising he was concerned; there were fifty people on the road, a million kroner at stake. That feeds down to the production crews and there are different ways to show it. The guy in charge of hotels was overwhelmed, so I called a production manager I knew, he got in a car and drove like hell for ten hours and did the job.'

One cameraman came close to walking out a few hours before the start when he realised there were no footrests on his motorbike; it became clear that race day would be dusty, leading to another question: could the helicopter fly through the dust? As they prepared to leave their base at Senlis, it became apparent that no car was available for the DFI consultant Morten Piil, according to the journalist Henrik Jul Jensen; a vehicle was hastily borrowed from a French film crew. 'It was a nervous-breakdown job,' recalls Herdel, who had to deal with the details. 'We knew it could all go wrong, but we were a good team. I didn't sleep for days, but I love crazy things like this. It's better than sitting in a bank counting money.'

21:40 *'It's twenty minutes past nine. The seventy-fourth Paris–Roubaix is slowly getting under way . . . The riders are expected in Roubaix in a little more than seven hours. But how many will arrive?'*

It takes well over a minute of impressionistic, fractured images to show the caravan rolling out of the start area, from when an official comes past leaning out of the sunroof of a white Peugeot – nowadays it would be Christian Prudhomme in a Skoda – through to the broom wagon, with the world

champion Hennie Kuiper among the back markers sprinting to catch the back of the peloton. Leth shows all of it, the camera panning in and out of the crowd to capture the blur of jerseys and pedalling legs, set to a collage of sound – the put-putting of the motorbikes, the shouts and applause of the crowd – in the sudden hurry that marks any bike race heading out of any town.

The mood changes abruptly, and the theme of empty space being briefly filled by the bike race and its entourage returns with a brief visit to the velodrome (*'At the Municipal Velodrome in Roubaix, preparations are already being made to receive the race, still over seven hours away . . .'*) where the logo of race sponsor Banque Nationale de Paris is being traced on the tarmac, even as the riders pull out of Chantilly.

On the road, the 'contract with chance' went Leth's way almost immediately, when the riders and race convoy managed – eventually – to make it through the demonstration by striking print workers at the location at Vineuil-Saint-Firmin where the race was due to be flagged off. Thousands of copies of *Le Parisien Libéré*, looted from delivery vans, were spread on the 24:49

road to stop the race passing through. That caused the start to be delayed by an hour and eleven minutes, which was substantial for a race going out on live television. Once the cavalcade had finally got through, the start was moved up the road to Senlis.

For most of the cyclists who rode that year's race, the delay caused by the strike was the most memorable feature of the day. In the car containing the DFI consultant Morten Piil, there was consternation; the race might be called off, sending their entire project up in smoke. 'I was worried of course,' recalls Piil. 'It wouldn't have had consequences for me but politicians might have asked questions of the Institute.' The newly formed film body – it had been going for just four years – had already been marked by the lengthy scandal over the putative film *The Many Faces of Jesus Christ* by Jens Jørgen Thorsen – who had collaborated with Leth on his first film *Stop for Bud* – which was deemed blasphemous. That had led to questions over the same consultant system which had enabled Leth to get *A Sunday in Hell* under way so quickly.

The strike stemmed from a controversy of more recent date. The dispute dated back to February 1975, when Emilien Amaury, the owner of *Le Parisien Libéré, l'Equipe* and *Marie-Claire* (and head of the family which still owns Amaury Sport Organisation, the parent company of Paris–Roubaix and the Tour de France) decided to close his print works in Rue d'Enghien in Paris with the loss of 300 jobs; the CGT (Confederation Général du Travail) union fought back, sparking a confrontation which lasted for two and a half years. The print works was occupied for nineteen months and as Amaury tried to open new plants in France and Belgium, the union blocked delivery lorries and destroyed copies of the paper. The strikers occupied Notre Dame, blocked high-profile television programmes, occupied the Ministry of Work and targeted the bike races run by his newspapers. The first finish of the Tour de France on the Champs Elysées in July 1975 took place against a backdrop of demonstrations, and three months after Leth's Sunday, during the Nancy stage of the 1976 Tour, the print workers dumped newspapers on the road to obstruct the race, with the riders running the gauntlet of a corridor of protesters in exactly the same way that they do in *A Sunday in Hell*.*

It was by no means a given that the race would get through, considering the intensity of this particular dispute, the French police's penchant for using their batons, and the fact that this was only eight years after the massive riots that had paralysed Paris in 1968. Half a dozen years later, at the 1982 Tour de France, the team-time-trial stage through northern France would be cancelled due to a strike by steelmen; at the 1984 Paris–Nice, there would be a now-legendary punch-up between Bernard Hinault and a group of striking shipyard workers. Leth was fortunate but he could have been even more lucky: in 1990, when *agriculteurs* blocked the Tour de France outside Nantes, the then-director Jean-Marie Leblanc enlisted a local youth on a moped to guide the peloton on a diversion around the strike through some obscure local lanes. That would have truly been the jackpot.

'*This is where the race is to be let loose, with the chateau of Chantilly providing the backdrop*,' says Saunders, against the sound of distant chanting. The commentary doesn't mention

* The *manifestation* merits a few minutes in Leth's film but is also captured in a documentary of its own, *Libérez le Parisien*, which includes home footage shot by the strikers.

another significant factor: not only was this the race start, it was where Amaury owned a villa for weekends away from work. As is so often the case when demonstrations hit bike races, the demo is a relatively good-humoured affair, because – again, this is often the case – the strikers enjoy the close proximity to celebrity sportsmen that cycling offers, and that helps to diffuse any tension. The riders don't seem to mind the interruption either – take the Ijsboerke rider who puts his

hands over his ears, with a big grin all over his face. Clearly meeting a double Tour de France winner has made the day of the gnome-faced man in the green-striped bobble hat who slaps Bernard Thévenet on the shoulder; the riot police with rubber bullet guns and truncheons ready for action appear to be in a different mood. The demonstration also provided what 26:00
Leth views as the finest example of chance intervening in his favour. It was pure fluke that when Merckx decided to take advantage of the enforced break to – inevitably – adjust his saddle height, two of the director's cameras were on hand to capture the moment. 'The camera is following [him] because I have one camera that I have told just to go after Merckx. So he follows him back and fortunately he goes to the Brooklyn car where I have a camera, the only car where I have a camera inside. So you have two cameras covering that small episode. It's a crazy chance.'

This is one of the most insightful minutes of footage in all the coverage of Merckx's career. You can hear Bob Lelangue or Julien de Vries describe the Cannibal's obsession with his position on his bike, but to see this happen in real-time – the long look up the road to assess how long he might have for this brief operation, the good-humoured exchange with the Brooklyn manager Franco Cribiori as he blags the spanner – puts real flesh on the bones. It also enables Leth to put detail on the framework of his 'novel', as he explains. 'The whole story [of this race on this day] developed because we had the material.'

The footage of Merckx shot from within Cribiori's car was the work of a Dane, Peter Roos – 'a really good, innovative cameraman', said Leth – who had also shadowed De Vlaeminck the previous afternoon. Getting Roos in the car was, believed Leth, 'the best money we spent', and it was the result of direct negotiation with Brooklyn. Cribiori recalls little now about having Roos at his side. Not a great deal was said between the two of them during the day, he says, but that, he feels, means that Roos was clearly doing his job of just sitting there unobtrusively and getting on with his job while he dealt with his. Due to the confined space in the front seat, Roos had to operate a small camera – sixty-metre rolls of film as opposed to the usual 120 – and critically he also had a small tape recorder ('a mini Nagra', says Leth), although that meant he had to juggle the task of capturing both sound and image.

Like the footage of De Vlaeminck's preparation at the start – the scrawled autograph, the almost pained expression as he stands by the team car, his appearance of being completely in his own zone apart from the world – the Merckx episode keeps us close to this particular protagonist. But we are introduced to other characters and places that will crop up in the next few hours.

28:43 Roos struck pure gold in the character of the flat-capped, double-chinned *commissaire* who is sitting in the back seat of the team car behind Cribiori (and who can be spotted earlier lurking by the Brooklyn car at the start making sure he does not get left behind). *'A race* commissaire *from the French Cycling Union. He sees to it that everything proceeds correctly.'* He is not named by Leth, but, Pescheux says, remains easily recognisable to anyone racing at the time. The *commissaire* ('Such a fool,' says Leth. 'Peter didn't know he was going to get him') crops up from time to time in the rest of the film to provide an ironic counterpoint to the serious episodes in the Merckx–De Vlaeminck–Maertens epic. For those who can translate his French, he is the equivalent of the mechanicals in *A Midsummer Night's Dream* or the local watch in *Much Ado About Nothing*.

The *commissaire*'s opening gambit is a sententious monologue on the strike's implications for the riders, for which Leth doesn't offer a translation. It's delivered in the pontificating style of a man used to being listened to and is worth quoting in full: 'I say it's not funny for the riders, they've been up a fair while already, and standing about like that in their race kit . . . I've always said you shouldn't mix politics and sport. I said it last year and I'll say it again this year.' Harrumph harrumph.

The moments of comedy alongside the serious stuff on the cobbles are the most unexpected pleasure of *A Sunday in Hell*. The *commissaire* will have his moments but the finest farce stems from the regulars in the Café de la Place on Avenue Desandrouins in Valenciennes, close to where we see the banner being erected to denote the *zone de ravitaillement*, again in an early-morning hush that recalls the scene captured in Chantilly by Henning Camre. The street is essentially the same today. The lamp-post to the right from which the banner is hung can still be made out, adjacent to the lean-to garage with the curious stepped roof.

The Café de la Place is not quite the match of my abso- 29:50
lute favourite, a ropey room in Troisvilles with the welcome of a flyblown dive in a Sergio Leone western, where I would stop during 1990s trips to watch the race to fill in the hours before the peloton arrived at the first section of cobbles. That café used to serve the worst coffee in Europe (it was impossible to conceive of worse) below an elaborate mural showing racing pigeons. The birds themselves – this room was the base for the local pigeon-fanciers' club – cooed in

rows of boxes adjacent to the most spartan outdoor latrines west of the Urals.*

However, the Café de la Place has everything that an establishment in rural France ought to have, topped by the psychedelic wallpaper that would have been the *dernier cri* when the *patron* and *madame* slapped it on in a mid-1960s fit of optimism. The hallucinogenic horror is plastered with posters of bike riders and soccer teams on the wall, and heaves with customers who know more about the bike racing than the journalists waiting at the finish. Top customer is the legendary bloke in the chequered shirt with decidedly trenchant opinions fuelled by his morning *pastis*. As with the commissaire, Leth leaves his views untranslated, but it's a lacuna that is worth filling.

* With respect to the café in Troisvilles, a visit in late 2017 showed a marked improvement to the coffee, if not the latrines.

'The French don't seem to be very lucky . . .' 30:38

'Yes, that's right, [the last winner was] Louison Bobet in 1956. 1956.'

'Who do you particularly see as the favourite?'

'Merckx?"

'No.'

'Maertens?'

'Voilà! Exactement. *Maertens. I think so . . .'*

'Moser?

'Non, *the Italians are not used to the* pavé, *they are more used to the sun than the* pavé. *Eh? Eh?'*

That contract with chance works in the most mysterious ways.

CHAPTER 5: MEPHISTO'S PENKNIFE

'I hope the organisers are happy – is that really a bike race? You're having me on. It's a cyclo cross! You're taking the piss. It's show-jumping. Why go to so much trouble to get cyclists through these damn roads where the farmers won't even dare send their tractors?'

Bernard Hinault, 1980

Albert Bouvet makes his first appearance some twenty minutes into *A Sunday in Hell* blowing a whistle to put the cars and motorbikes in the right place at the start in Chantilly. Bouvet, who had guided Leth through the cobbles a few months earlier, is the short, harassed-looking chap with leather trousers and jacket, motorbike boots and a beer gut at the development phase asking politely '*Reculez, s'il vous plaît*' – go back, please!

The 1956 Paris–Tours winner, nicknamed 'the Bulldog of Fougères', Bouvet is described in the 1976 Paris–Roubaix programme as one of two *chefs des services techniques et sportives*, together with Jacques Lohmuller. While *directeurs* Jacques Goddet and Félix Lévitan took an overview of their respective newspapers' events – finances, stage towns, sponsors – it was Bouvet and Lohmuller who were tasked with ensuring the smooth running of the races on the day: making sure the cars went to the right places in Chantilly, that press motorbikes didn't stray too close to the action, and that team cars didn't get caught between break and bunch. Bouvet has an anonymous walk-on role at various points in Leth's film, but few who met him would ever forget him: his bow-legged way of standing, that look of perturbed disgust at a world which won't do what he wants, his affectionately gravelly voice.

Bouvet, who died in May 2017, played a role in the history of Paris–Roubaix that was argubly more important than any of the riders who have won it. There might now be no Paris–Roubaix at all had it not been for his intervention in 1967 and the drive – some would call it obsession – that impelled him to seek out new ways of routing the race until his retirement in the 1990s. Paris–Roubaix would probably have been still going in 1976, but it would probably not have been the same race that Leth filmed and it might not have had the same legendary status.

In early 2016, aged eighty-six, Bouvet was a diminished presence in an old folks' home outside Paris. What mattered, however, was that his memory was clear. The story of the modern Paris–Roubaix, the race we know and love today, the race that Leth shot in 1976, began on 10 April 1967, when Jacques Goddet summoned Bouvet into his office – the Tour de France founder Henri Desgrange's old *bureau*, no less – on the first floor of *l'Equipe's* headquarters in the Rue du Faubourg-Montmartre, the same building where eight years later Leth would conduct his negotiations with Félix Lévitan before launching his project.

'Paris–Roubaix, *c'est foutu*!' were Goddet's opening words: the race, held the previous day, was 'dead in the water . . . all those *pavés* have gone: look at Pas Roland at Mons-en-Pévèle, the Montée du Cimetière . . . cobbled last year; now it's tarmac.' The Pas Roland was a one-kilometre climb resembling a Flemish berg, climbing to a cemetery before a corresponding one-kilometre descent. 'Take a pen and paper, take a car, take a driver, go and find what's left,' continued Goddet. 'If you don't, in years to come, Paris–Roubaix will become *une course banale*, with nothing to test the riders. It will be just another race, where nothing at all will happen. So this is urgent.'

The conversation lasted ten minutes – 'Goddet was always succinct,' recalled Bouvet – and then the young ex-professional was on his own. 'I had an idea; I called an old friend, Jean Stablinski' – world road-race champion in 1963 and once a mainstay of the Ford-France team alongside Jacques Anquetil – 'who had a cycle shop in Valenciennes. I told him my mission, and what was at stake: we needed to find new cobbled sections, because if we didn't, in a couple of years Paris–Roubaix would not exist.'

Like Bouvet and Goddet, Stablinski had seen the extent of the road works which had been carried out on the roads of northern France during the 1950s and 1960s; he also knew the area intimately from hunting trips into the nearby countryside as well as from his training rides. Together with another local professional, Edouard Delberghe, 'Stab' showed Bouvet several cobbled sections to the south-east of Valenciennes: the hill at Neuvilly, which figures prominently in *A Sunday in Hell*, others which formed part of the route into the twenty-first century: Quérénaing, Hornaing, Aulnoy-lez-Valenciennes, and still more which now figure in the early part of the route around the villages of Viesly and Quiévy.

The key discovery came at the end of the first afternoon, just north-east of Valenciennes. 'Stablinski took me to the Forêt de Raismes and showed me the Trouée d'Arenberg, archaic *pavé*, thirty centimetres high, through an area where the soil was very unstable due to the coal mines underneath,' said Bouvet. 'It was officially known as le Drève des Boules d'Hérin, and it belonged to the Office des Eaux et des Forêts.' *Drève* is a term used locally for a lane; this was the one down which Stablinski used to ride on his way to work in the mine below where the lane ran. It ran in a dead straight line through the wood where he picked mushrooms and went hunting and fishing, under the bridge that used to take waste from the mine to the nearby dump. This single sector of cobbles though a dank forest north of Valenciennes is the most popular and notorious element in Paris–Roubaix and arguably the one that has guaranteed its survival to the present day.

'The riders had no choice; they either rode down this appalling *pavé* with spaces between them where they might get their wheels stuck, or they used the ditch. There was no pavement.' This last sentence was crucial, as Bouvet explained. 'The editions of Paris–Roubaix I rode, which lasted up to the 1960s, used the cobbles on major roads. Three-quarters of the peloton could avoid them by taking to the pavements. In the little lanes that I looked at with Jean Stablinski, the ones only used by tractors or horses and carts, it was the cobbles or the ditch: *pavé ou fossé*. We spent two days looking at the new sections, then came back to what was almost an identical finale: in La Grande Lille' – the city of Lille and its environs – 'there was only one cobbled road left.'

The start had already been moved north of Paris, to Chantilly, a couple of years earlier as Bouvet's predecessor Jean Garnault began an initial search for surviving sectors of cobbles. Now, the route was shifted eastwards, permanently as it turned out. The Classic had usually been run up the main route north from Paris to Lille through Amiens, Arras and Beauvais. Now, the course went more to the east, to include Stablinski's personal stomping ground around Valenciennes. That meant the first cobbles were encountered close to the little town of Solesmes.

Bouvet and Stablinski's proposal was not greeted with acclaim when it was presented to Goddet. 'I said the new route was hard to envisage; I brought in some photos. They showed a sea of mud covering the new sections of cobbles.' Goddet said: 'I asked you to find cobbles not a paddy field.' Bouvet: 'The cobbles are there, under the mud.'

A week before the race, at the final route meeting, Bouvet was worried, as the weather had been bad. 'Goddet said, "Keep me informed about whether the riders will be able to get through." I replied, "Well, maybe one of them will."' On the day, Eddy Merckx won; Bouvet fell off his motorbike four times – the thick mud had filled the tread on the tyres, making them slick – to the amusement of the riders. Forty-four of them finished, and the consensus was that the race was perfectly feasible. Bouvet went into the showers, where 'the riders were cleaning themselves up as best they could; they told me, "We can do it again, but not tomorrow." They gave me a nickname: "the Mephisto of the Cobbles".'

Mephisto: short for Mephistopheles, the devil's representative from the legend of Faust.

'These old cobbled roads are hardly ever used except by farmers on their way to the fields . . .'

In early December 1993, I took a trip to northern France with the photographer Graham Watson, to accompany Bouvet and Jean-François Pescheux, his colleague at the Société du Tour de France – as it was then, before its rebranding as Amaury Sport Organisation – as they took their annual trip to inspect those cobbled lanes, twenty-six years after Bouvet's first reconnaissance. The sky lowered over the bleak sugar beet fields – there was not a ray of sunshine all day – and their big Fiat Saloon splashed through the vast puddles on the sunken lanes, skidded on muddy corners, and lurched alarmingly over the potholes. During the day, the vehicle was rapidly transformed from a white car with brown pock-marks to an earth-brown *voiture* bearing not a hint of any other colour.

We drove down one mud-filled track after another, with our hosts grunting approvingly when the cobbles were of the required standard: not tarmacked over; still in reasonable shape without so many potholes as to make them too dangerous; bumpy enough to trouble all but the most courageous cyclist and to challenge the most robust of bikes. The sides were crucial: there was often subsidence because this was where vast modern tractors pressed the cobbles into the dirt below, but to run the race, it had to be possible for cars to get through without destroying their sumps on the *pavés* in the middle.

The references to races past were a continuous soundtrack; someone punctured here, someone fell there, someone else broke this bone or that bike part, a car got stuck in that pothole, that was the bend where a motorbike driver slid under a team support car. It all felt very timeless.

We stopped for a glass of champagne at the house of Edouard Delberghe, who lived close to the route, but that fizz was overshadowed by a salutary and depressing moment when we drove up a cobbled lane and were forced to stop and re-enter the twentieth century: the track had been blocked off with red plastic barriers. One of the race's key *pavé* sections had been turned into a construction site for one of the high-speed train lines that thread this part of France like blood vessels on a cyclist's calf. Watson's photograph of Bouvet looking at the mess captured him with the traumatised mien of a man who has nipped down to his favourite pub for a pint only to find it has closed overnight.

The pressures on the cobbles that are so vital to the race began mounting as the infrastructure of northern France was gradually improved after the Second World War. Amusingly enough, at one time, the race route was continually adjusted to *avoid* the worst stretches of *pavé*; soon after the war, the race still included sixty kilometres of cobbles largely on main roads, some through towns such as Amiens, far to the west of the current route. The final forty kilometres into Roubaix were entirely on cobbles.

By 1965, however, the total had been pared back to just twenty-two kilometres, with the toll mounting every time a local election was held, or if the local mayor happened to live on a cobbled lane. As well as the Pas Roland, Pescheux recalls sectors in places long forgotten: the Forêt d'Halempin, La Vache Bleue, Bachy.

Bouvet would meet mayors who were delighted that he was thinking of bringing his race through their small villages; they believed it might mean that their roads would be 'improved', and were somewhat less than impressed when they realised that his mission was to preserve the tracks that damaged their cars and tractors. 'You want us to keep the *pavé*,' the mayor of Camphin-en-Pévèle, an artichoke grower, told him: 'That's all very well, but we have to drive down them three hundred and sixty-five days a year.'

On one occasion in the 1970s, the journalist Jean-Marie Leblanc – later the race director – suggested to the official responsible for infrastructure in La Grande Lille, Pierre Mauroy, that perhaps the city could play a role in preserving the cobblestones: 'Forget it,' snapped Mauroy. 'They are lousy for the image of the *département du Nord*.'

The fight back began in earnest the following year with the formation of a body dedicated to saving the *pavés*: 'Les Amis de Paris Roubaix'. Bouvet was a founder member, along with local dignitary Jean-Claude Vallaeys; their campaign was backed by Leblanc and raised awareness along the route. 'It all turned in the 1990s,' Pescheux told me in 2016. 'The local villagers became aware that the race would promote their areas; the agricultural colleges realised they could repair the *pavé* roads as part of their studies. The *conseils régionaux* got behind us; now when they want to do something on a cobbled sector, they talk to us.'

Keeping the cobbles intact is far from a done deal; as late as 2015 there was intense debate around the cobbles in the Briastre area south-east of Valenciennes: the *pavé* tracks were being broken down by agricultural traffic, and it was not entirely clear who should be paying to look after them – the farmers themselves, as they were the ones doing the damage, and they were the main users, or the local *mairie*. The outcome at least was that the cobbled tracks were worth saving and the various parties should work together to this end; it was more positive than the more obvious solution of slapping on a ton or two of tarmac.

The impact of progress on the roads that Leth was preparing to shoot in 1976 is starkly illustrated. The diagram of the renewed race route in 1968 shows a solid black block of fifteen kilometres of unbroken *pavé* between the villages of Templeuve and Bachy through Nomain, just to the north of Orchies; the 1976 race programme includes the same roads, but in the intervening eight years that chunk has been cut down to a five-kilometre stretch. This is where the mayor ran a poster campaign one spring, around the time of the race, pushing for his roads to be properly surfaced: it showed a photo of cobblestones in a muddy pool, with the caption 'They don't deserve this.' When I drove between Nomain and Bachy in 2017, not one cobbled lane was immediately visible, although the remains of some – with cobbles protruding through the tarmac – could be seen.

Bouvet's role in saving the cobbles was recognised early on. In 1982 Henri Quiquéré wrote in *Miroir du Cyclisme*,

> The years pass and the *pavés* go. Since 1956 when the *Autoroute du Nord* was driven through the region the process has been speeding up. Some disappear under a thick coat of tarmac but most are ripped up by northern hands in the same way that *Midi* hands pull up vines. And they do it anonymously, during the week . . . Like little birds in winter, the bad *pavés* hide away to die.

The only friend of the *pavés*, the only one to bend over to enable the legend to live on, is Albert Bouvet. The title of Conservator of the Cobbles was handed down to him when he took over at the race organisers'. Each year as April approaches he comes to visit them, assesses the extent of the massacres in the name of progress. He caresses them, admires them, counts them and sets out across the fields to search for their brothers who have been forgotten by the road menders, the ones which will replace those who have fallen in some forgotten field . . . He is still managing it, but for how much longer? The day is not far away when there will not be enough left to make a lane. Perhaps the last ones will be put together to create his statue.

The very existence of the event that Leth was shooting in 1976 was threatened by the march of progress. He probably did not know it but the event that he was shooting could well have had a very limited life span.

The 1976 route as depicted in Leth's film included fourteen principal sections of cobbles, some of which subdivided into several segments. The fundamentals of the route remain similar today, but the details once the race gets to the serious stuff just to the south of Valenciennes have changed to the extent that the course we watch in *A Sunday in Hell* is barely recognisable in the twenty-first century. The start was moved north from Chantilly to Compiègne in 1977, to give Bouvet and his organising team more opportunity to send the route back and forth across the countryside in search of those elusive cobbles; today the start remains in Compiègne, and it still replicates the 1976 route north from the town through Noyon, Ham and Saint Quentin.

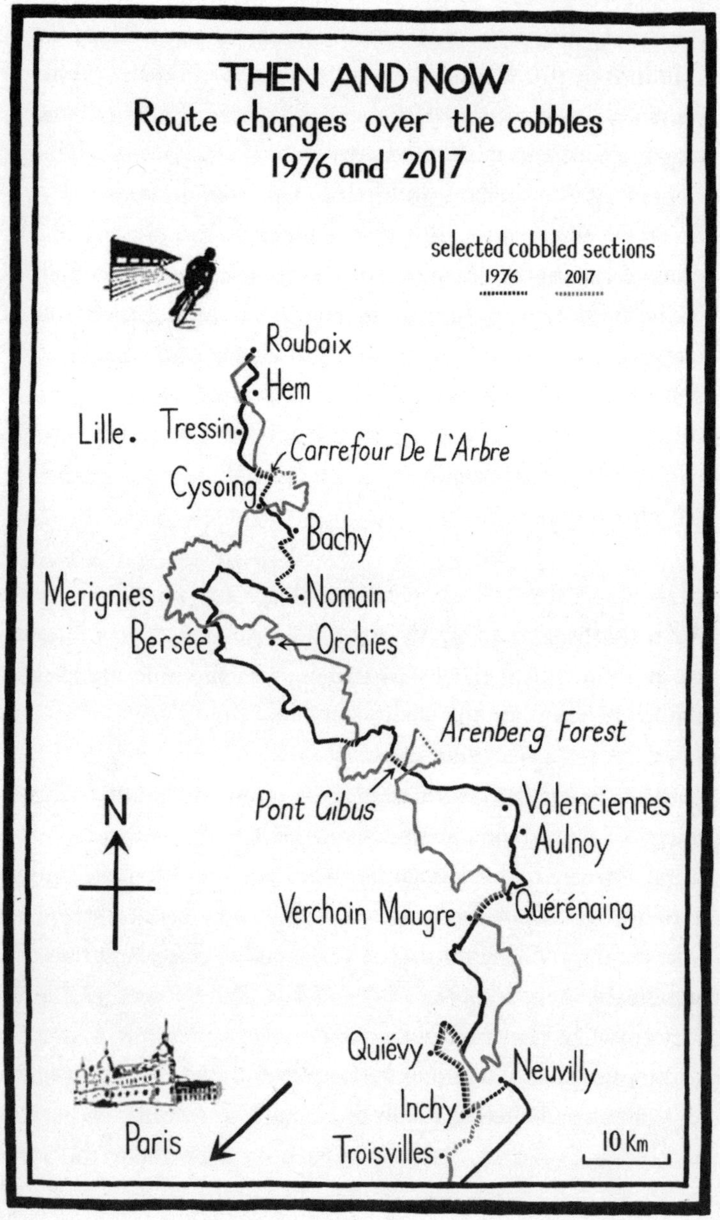
THEN AND NOW
Route changes over the cobbles
1976 and 2017
selected cobbled sections
1976
2017
Roubaix
Hem
Lille
Tressin
Carrefour De L'Arbre
Cysoing
Bachy
Merignies
Nomain
Bersée
Orchies
Arenberg Forest
Pont Gibus
Valenciennes
Aulnoy
N
Verchain Maugre
Quérénaing
Quiévy
Neuvilly
Inchy
Paris
Troisvilles
10 Km

The 1976 route travelled straight up the main road from the village of Bohain-en-Vermandois north-east to Le Cateau-Cambrésis, turning north-westerly to Neuvilly, notorious for years as the location of the first cobbles. The current route turns left off the main road at the village of Busigny, between Bohain-en-Vermandois and Le Cateau, heading for Troisvilles to cross what is usually the first sector in the race; after emerging from the village to turn left down Rue Jean Stablinski, formerly known as Rue de la Sucrerie, passing a plaque put up in honour of the man who guided Bouvet around these cobbles. This sector – number 29 in the 2017 route* – crosses the main D643 Cambrai to Charleville road onto another cobbled lane which in turn comes out at a crossroads of four cobbled tracks. Here the route turns left onto Rue de Neuvilly to descend into the village of Inchy; the road coming from the right is the 'hill' coming up from Neuvilly.

In the film, the race is shown sweeping across the empty town square in Neuvilly, *'immediately before the rough stuff'*, before heading up the distinctive hill: *'the first stretch of* pavé *is only two miles long, but terribly difficult. The surface is completely deformed and here . . . there is a steep hill as well.'* The 'hill' is gravelled at its foot where the turn is made off the main road into the village, and is surprisingly long – a good mile and a half to the crossroads. At the foot, the cobbles are wide and clean; higher up the track becomes narrower and the cobbles less well kept.

Only a few sections of cobbles which figured in the 1976 route were still included in their entirety in the 2017 course, two of which immediately follow the Inchy crossroads: number 28

* The sections of cobbles are traditionally listed in descending order, with number 1 the final brief stretch outside the velodrome in Roubaix.

'Viesly to Quiévy' beginning at Rue de la Chapelle, slightly descending, mainly straight, lasting 1.8km. number 27 'Quiévy to Saint Python' follows almost immediately out of the village via Rue de Valenciennes to the D113B minor road to the farm of Fontaine au Tertre. The 1976 race also used the cobbles known as 'Saint Python', which runs from the D134 road to the village of that name down route de Cambrai over 1.5km; this section was included in the route up to 2016, but was abandoned in 2017 in favour of two new sectors near the village of Briastre.

Close to Saint Python, the 1976 and 2017 routes diverge. The modern route goes eastwards to the cobbled sectors at Vertain and Capelle-Ruesnes, while the 1976 route went north-west to Saulzoir before tacking north-east, to tackle the sector between Verchain-Maugre and Quérénaing, which was also included in the 2017 route as number 23. It's a long-standing inclusion, and saw the winning move go clear in 1993. The current course then turns left into the Quérénaing-Maing sector, whereas the 1976 version headed north-east to Artres and Aulnoy-lez-Valenciennes, for one final stretch of cobbles before the seventeen-kilometre respite on tarmacked roads through Valenciennes, the location of the second feed zone.

Afterwards, the 1976 route headed due west to the village of Wallers, where it again bisects the current course, which has diverted to the west of Valenciennes through Douchy and Denain. In Wallers, the 1976 race went straight through the village and on to the sector now known as Pont Gibus, whereas the current course circles to the east, heading for Arenberg. There it turns left into the forest, then heads back towards Wallers to enter the Pont Gibus sector, which is instantly recognisable in the film – and on today's television pictures – because of the brickwork of a bridge from a disused railway, now painted in honour of the 1992 and 1993 winner Gilbert

Duclos-Lassalle, nicknamed 'Gibus', hence the name; in 2017 these *pavés* were number 18.

At the end of the 1.6km of the Pont Gibus cobbles, the current course turns left towards Hornaing while the 1976 route turns right towards Hasnon; the routes cross again in the village of Wandignies-Hamage as the current course heads north towards Beuvry-la-Forêt. Both routes then turn north-west to run roughly parallel but a few kilometres apart. The 1976 course misses out the town of Orchies – site of the evocatively named Rue des Abattoirs cobbled section in today's course – although the two routes coincide briefly in part of the Auchy-les-Orchies to Bersée cobbles (number 12 in 2017), rated among the toughest today; the 1976 *parcours* joins the current route from the left, before both head down Rue du Nouveau Monde into Bersée.

Here, they diverge again, with the 1976 route now staying to the east of the current course. In Leth's year, the race headed towards Templeuve – skirting the village to the south where the 2017 route is a little to the north – after which there was a twelve-kilometre respite without cobbles en route to the village of Nomain. Here the 1976 race turned north through a 4.6-kilometre zone of cobbles towards the village of Bachy; this has since been tarmacked over. The two routes cross again between Cysoing and Bourghelles, the 1976 course heading briefly west, today's travelling east to the cobbles of Wannehain and Camphin-en-Pévèle.

The final sector of cobbles which is replicated from the 1976 route is between Carrefour de l'Arbre and the village of Gruson. Today, the stretch of cobbles from Camphin-en-Pévèle to the Carrefour is seen as the most important, being the last truly hard stretch of cobbles before the finish. It's where the race is frequently decided, from Moser in 1980, Marc Madiot in 1985 and 1991 to Fabian Cancellara's win in 2006, or Johan

Vansummeren in 2011. However, in 1976, the race approached the Carrefour from a different direction, from the village of Bourghelles.

Both routes cover the relatively easy stretch of cobbles slightly downhill into Gruson – number 3 in 2017. Ten years after *A Sunday in Hell* was filmed, this was the site of another intriguing work of art, when the Algerian artist Mohamed Ben Bella painted twelve kilometres of the route in red, white and blue, using a sand mix to ensure the riders didn't slip. The artwork was visible for three editions of the race. After Gruson, the 1976 and 2017 routes again diverge, going in parallel northwards towards the village of Hem, just outside Roubaix, after which they are identical into the finish.

One question which is often asked about Leth's film concerns the absence of Bouvet's greatest discovery, the Arenberg 'trench', the section of cobbles which has become synonymous with the race. Bouvet was unable to include it in the route from 1974 to 1983 for reasons linked to safety, insurance and bureaucratic worries. 'We used the *tranchée* for six years, but it is private land; there were crashes – I remember a bad one involving Joop Zoetemelk where he got up as black as a coalminer – and there were worries about who was responsible. We couldn't pay them to let us through as then they would have been liable for any accidents. So they blocked it. Eventually we took out private insurance for it, Stablinski and I had dinner with the local *préfet*, and we agreed to make an annual donation to the ministry's charity. We weren't paying officially, but they were cooperating.'

The constant changes in the route demonstrate the constant battle to maintain the race's unique character. Bouvet and Pescheux had no option but to be creative; their successor Thierry Gouvenou faces precisely the same pressure, although he has greater public and institutional support.

The issue today remains the same as forty years ago: barely any cobbles remain in the area immediately south of Roubaix other than those currently being used for the race – which is why the final kilometres have changed little in recent years – whereas south of Valenciennes, where the cobbles are first encountered each year, there are apparently more than enough *pavé* tracks to run the race. The burning question is how long the sections at the end of the race can be kept from the tarmac machines.

Paris–Roubaix is now essentially kept in place as a historical relic. No other race has a preservation society and a movement to conserve its fabric. With this in mind, the recent trend for the Tour de France to use long stretches of the cobbles – in 2014, 2015 and 2018 – can do nothing but good, as this will underline their economic value in bringing tourist trade to the area. The chances of it losing its name seem slight – it's not going to become *Le Nord* or *Le Classique des Pavés* – but the fact there are so few cobbles that figure in both the 1976 and the 2017 routes speaks volumes. The transformation in the final 160 kilometres north of the first cobbled sections is testimony to the constant pressures on the *pavé* and the consequent need to keep readjusting the route.

Here is the irony: a race that is presented to the public as uniquely archaic, as the event which keeps cycling in touch with its nineteenth-century roots, has had to be reinvented annually. Leth's moment in time depicts an event that feels immutable, in surroundings that always feel familiar. In fact, the race organisers have had no option but to adapt time after time as the environment around it mutates. It is like the legendary penknife, which had had one new handle after another and a constant succession of replacement blades but which was widely held to be the same.

CHAPTER 6: SOUND AND SMALL FRY

'The time is ten-thirty. The race eventually started but with more than an hour's delay, and within a few miles three men have broken away and gained a slight advantage . . . Three French riders who do not have a chance, which is perhaps why they are trying to distinguish themselves at this early stage when the favourites are still idling and nobody is interested in increasing the pace.'

Like bats out of hell, the peloton sped away from the *départ réel*, having eluded the group of demonstrators, the man in the bobble hat, the gendarmes, the rubber-bullet guns, and the truncheons. 'We were all desperately impatient,' recalled Jean-François Pescheux. 'The start was completely messed up because of the demonstrations. There were wheels punctured, cars held up. That made everyone panic a bit. It was a very fast start, because everyone had been hanging around for so long at the demonstration.' Lévitan and Goddet's cars had their wheels punctured, as the *l'Equipe* boss lamented in an apocalyptic editorial the following day.

Jørgen Leth had rolled out of the start in a more relaxed frame of mind. He had taken station in a car driven by a couple of friends who were not part of the crew, one a photographer, one a writer. There are moments in the film itself, he says, when you can see the car in the background – it has no decals on it so only he can identify it. 'I know which one it is.

'There were a hundred people spread across the landscape – I knew they were there. I was excited and I could not do anything. I was sitting in the car behind the peloton. I couldn't move around the peloton because I didn't have the [necessary] accreditation but I didn't want to. That was part of my game. I liked to be deprived of control. I like the idea that, "OK, from this moment on I have no control, I'll see what happens." This is one of my favourite lines in all my work as an artist, as a film-maker: see what happens. I don't know, I have no control, I'll see what happens.

'I went through the landscape in the car, along the itinerary at [the back of the race]. I could see it, and think, "I'm sure they made this image," but I didn't know, because by the time I passed the cameramen were already gone. I could not get reports. When the race started I had no more contact with my crew. I couldn't see where they were. I didn't want to impose myself, and practically it would also have been impossible. I had no possibility to communicate with my crew – that's a very unique situation. I never heard about that in any other film.

'I had no idea what they were doing, I could only count on them to be following the orders of Dan Holmberg, and be there when they were supposed to be there, which was exciting. In this race so many things happen – unexpected things, first of all the strikes, the demonstrations, it was incredible to have such things and for the race to survive it. I was happy that this proves my golden rule – see what happens. It's a wonderful way to work.'

Camre, meanwhile, had packed up his kit in the Place Omer Vallon in Chantilly, and had jumped onto the back of his allotted motorcycle to head for his first location. He had looked at the licence of his motorbike driver: the writing read 'Job: motorcyclist'. At least he knew he was in the hands of a professional. He and his Belgian driver were sitting astride a massive Honda Goldwing, with huge saddlebags on either side into which he could put extra cassettes of film. The driver's nickname derived from those bags: Harry La Valise, 'the suitcase'. 'He was absolutely fearless. He'd stand up while he was driving, keep one hand on the handlebar, and with the other one he'd be waving at the crowds and the cars to get them to move out of the way.'

Camre also had a tripod, which was tied on to the back of the motorbike in a way that he recalls being 'very orderly' at the start of the day; it was closely tucked in to avoid contact with the convoy cars as the bike rubbed shoulders with them. As the race progressed and the stress of moving from location to location grew greater and greater, the fixing of the tripod became increasingly rushed until eventually he was sitting on the pillion clinging desperately on to it as it was buffeted by the wind.

The 'racing' phase of *A Sunday in Hell* opens with a classic 31:47 full-frontal shot, telephoto work by Jan Weincke, who was delegated to find avenues and shoot lingering images of the race and its convoy of motorbikes approaching. It is reminiscent of both Joel Santoni's beginning to *La course en tête* or the start of Leth's own *Stars and Watercarriers*. The race passes in slow motion; the gap between the break as it forms and the bunch behind is shown in physical rather than temporal distance – it is only 150 metres or so – in a brief sequence. There is real-time sound of the crackly race radio – probably from Peter Roos's microphone in the Brooklyn team car – transmitting the news of the formation of the three-man escape ('*La jonction est faite, Talbourdet et Boulas ont rejoint Martinez . . . les trois hommes ont quinze secondes d'avance sur la tête du peloton*'),* which morphs into the chorale. That unsettling, echoing sound will accompany us intermittently as far as the velodrome itself.

As with the preamble from the day before, Leth feeds us information slowly, almost unwillingly; it will be eight minutes before we find out more about the escapees beyond Saunders's laconic '*. . . three French riders . . .*' A full quarter of an hour – 120km in distance on the day – will elapse on screen until the favourites begin to stretch their legs as the Hell of the North draws near. Leth uses this interval as a gentle prelude to the chaos and intensity that is to come, mingling pastoral views of the race with brief spells of action. It is a micro-portrait of life in the peloton when times are quiet: the aftermath of a 33:10 minor crash captured from within the Brooklyn team car ('*nothing serious but considerable chaos*'), riders handing in

* 'They have joined forces, Talbourdet and Boulas have caught Martinez . . . the three men have fifteen seconds' advantage on the front of the peloton.'

clothing to their team cars, an explanation of just who these motorbikes are conveying, the race doctor at work – the kind of didactic material that occurs frequently in *Stars and Watercarriers* but is relatively rare here.

35:27 A close look at the sequence showing the gap between break and bunch in extended, if not real-time as they speed down a little hill somewhere in the depths of northern France shows how one of Leth's cameramen disobeyed the director's instructions to keep a single shot running for the entire passage of the race convoy. Between the moment when the motorcycles pass and the point when the peloton speeds past, a clear difference can be spotted in the position of the camera, if only a small one, because the backdrop remains largely the same.

This prelude is the 'no-hopers' chance for their fifteen minutes of fame. They were precisely the sort of riders you would expect to see in an early suicide move. Jacques Boulas and Mariano Martinez belonged to the two smaller of the five French teams in the race, Jobo-Wolber and Lejeune-BP respectively – the latter managed by Henri Anglade, a major figure in French cycling in the 1960s. Georges Talbourdet rode for the rather larger Gan-Mercier, which was led by Raymond Poulidor and Barry Hoban – the former the most high-profile French star of the 1970s (and in fact the most consistent home performer in the classic at the time), the latter an outside chance for victory after his third place in the 1972 edition.

The fifteen teams that started the 1976 Paris–Roubaix reflected a sport that was far smaller in scale and limited in its commercial appeal than that of today. Belgium, France and Italy dominated. The bulk of the peloton was Belgian (in other words largely Flemish, from only the Dutch-speaking northern half of the country) and French. Of the fifteen teams, seven had bike companies as their lead sponsors, of which Lejeune was definitely ranked among the minnows compared to Raleigh, Flandria and Peugeot. Jobo's riders were paid the SMIC, the French minimum wage. These were not affluent times in French cycling; two major *extra sportif* team sponsors in Bic and Sonolor had pulled out at the end of 1974 with no substitutes in sight. Hence the preponderance of small sponsors from within the still-vibrant French cycle industry: bike makers La France, Mercier and Lejeune, tyre manufacturers Wolber and Hutchinson, all now defunct except the latter.

'The biggest difference with today was the standing of the teams and the riders,' says Roger Legeay. 'Then, you could earn a good living at teams like Peugeot or [later] Renault, and if you got in there, there was a programme of major races. There was a big difference between the teams like Molteni, at the top, and Jobo, at the bottom. You could call Lejeune or Jobo a second- or third-division team, but the ProConti teams of today, in the second division, have a far better structure relative to the best teams today, and are truly worth their place in the biggest races.'

By the end of his career in 1985, Legeay would be riding for a Peugeot team whose budget had expanded to several million francs as salaries and team numbers grew massively through the 1980s. In 1976, however, the wages reflected the fact that this was still the 'artisanal' cycling of old. 'You could make a good living, but you had to make yourself known as a good rider. At Lejeune I earned sixteen hundred francs per month, or two hundred to three hundred francs above the SMIC.' The co-leader of Talbourdet's Gan-Mercier, Joop Zoetemelk (start number 132) earned around £80,000 for his year's contract; Lejeune's leader Roy Schuiten of Holland made around £20,000. For a superior *domestique* capable of winning major one-day races, the rate was just over £4,200. That was the pay packet Marc Demeyer was set to bring home in 1976, although his leader Freddy Maertens insisted later in the year that it should be doubled by Flandria.

For lesser riders, the wages were on a par with manual workers, but they would be topped up by appearances at the extensive calendar of small-scale track meets and criteriums that took place across France through June, July and especially August, after the Tour. That explains the importance of the early escape by the 'no-hopers' in this Paris–Roubaix. In the twenty-first century the riders in an early suicide move will be looking to get their sponsors' logos onto live television; in the 1970s, the escapees' hope was that they would raise their profiles with a long-distance escape, perhaps culminating in a little television exposure if they hung on until live coverage started in the final hour. That in turn would boost their fees from the organisers and agents who doled out the criterium contracts.

Their escape merits a photograph and a single paragraph in *l'Equipe's* resumé of the race: 'Mariano Martinez detached himself from the peloton at km 4, followed by Talbourdet and Boulas. At Saint Quentin, where a second demonstration blocked the race's following cars for a quarter of an hour, the three men passed through with 3min 30sec lead on the bunch.' But that paragraph equated to a pay rise: there was money to be earned for a man known as an *animateur*, *un offensif*, who was willing to liven up an event with aggressive riding, and that Monday morning's edition of *L'Equipe* would have been closely scanned by the men who mattered.

Of the three journeymen, it was Martinez, *'the smaller man with the glasses'*, who had the most notable career. Born in the

Spanish town of Burgos he won the French junior title in 1965 and in twelve years as a professional he took two mountain-stage wins in the Tour de France and the King of the Mountains jersey in 1978. He had already managed a bronze medal in the world road-race championship behind Merckx and Raymond Poulidor in 1974. Talbourdet and Boulas were not in his class. Boulas had finished as *lanterne rouge* in the previous year's Tour de France, was in the last year of a three-year career of almost total obscurity and would die in 1990 at forty-one. Talbourdet enjoyed a middle-ranking career that lasted six years. His greatest claim to fame is as a regular training partner of the young Bernard Hinault, a neighbour on the Breton coast near Saint Brieuc. He and another senior professional, Maurice Le Guilloux, came up with a nickname for their young companion, *blaireau*, which would become one of the sport's most legendary monickers: 'the Badger'.

Along with the *échappée matinale* of Boulas, Martinez and 36:38
Talbourdet, we also meet, albeit briefly, one of the most distinctive, radical features of *A Sunday in Hell*: the choral chant that will recur intermittently as far as the velodrome, picking up on the cello theme that introduced us to De Vlaeminck half an hour earlier. Like the rest of the incidental music for the film, this was the brainchild of Gunner Møller Pedersen. Pedersen was a little younger than Leth – born in 1943 to the director's 1937 – and was also born in Aarhus, where, the composer recalls, they had been 'part of the same avant-garde scene, although we didn't know each other; I knew about him, he knew about me.' He had begun to work with Leth not long before, composing the soundtrack for *Stars and Watercarriers,* which he saw as essentially, 'music for Jørgen's voice, rather than the pictures'.

Pedersen has enjoyed a lengthy career which is by far the most eclectic of any of Leth's collaborators. The label Naxos refers to him as 'one of Europe's leading composers of electronic music', but that is merely a starting point. His work includes ballet, opera, symphony, brass band and vocal work. Intriguingly, given the mythic nature of the work Leth was trying to create, twenty-three years later he collaborated on a reworking of Homer's *Iliad*, providing electronic incidental music for a rereading of one of the world's greatest epics. His most recent credits include elvish songs for Peter Jackson's *The Lord of the Rings*, while his most lengthy artistic collaboration was with another Aarhus native, the film-maker Nils Malmros, which began in 1973 with Mamros's breakthrough film *Lars Ole, 5c* and continued until 2009, encompassing seven films.

Like Leth, Pedersen had been among the pioneers of experimental art in Denmark during the 1960s; for example, his involvement with the group Show Bix, 'created some of the most artistic oddities of the decade', according to one review of Scandinavian avant-garde art in the mid-twentieth century. That included a 'gymnastic opera' entitled *Something*, and a piece of performance art called *Surrounding*, a multi-media experience involving images, light, sound, text and movement, which resulted in what one critic described as 'a bombardment of images'. He had studied in London and met Tristram Cary, described in his obituary in 2008 as 'the father of British electronic music', and who was among the team that designed the synthesisers used by the likes of Pink Floyd, Brian Eno and Jean-Michel Jarre.

In the early 1970s Pedersen worked on sound installations, most notably *A Sound Year*, consisting of twelve different pieces of music – one for each month – for the Glyptoteket

Conservatory in Copenhagen – on which he worked until 1982. The piece was played daily in the garden until 1999. In the 1980s and 1990s he experimented with works that combined sculpture and sound. One example was the *Dodekalites*, consisting of twelve vast human-like sculptures reminiscent of Easter Island statues in a field, to a background of his electronic music, although that project went sour after a dispute with the sculptor, to his immense distress. Another work, *Lamentation of Mururoa* was a composition for sopranos and choir expressing protest against French atomic testing in the Pacific.

This is a long and esoteric distance from an 'artisanal' sport which, in the 1970s at least, was low-budget and was still the province of manual workers and farm labourers, with the occasional interloper from the lower middle classes. 'He told me very emphatically that he had no interest in cycling,' says Leth. However, *Stars and Watercarriers* had changed that. 'I didn't like bicycle racing until I discovered it wasn't just about sport,' says Pedersen. 'It was a poem about human relationships, about what [cycling] does to your body and mind, the process of fatigue, of trying to overcome yourself and all this. That got me fascinated.' That led him to create the distinctive 'Bolero' which, in *Stars and Watercarrriers*, accompanies Merckx and Fuente through the mountains; an insistent tune with an unchanging rhythm, breaking eventually into brass which is his attempt to mirror the lengthy effort of a long mountain climb. 'Jørgen's voice was quite precise about what was happening; I made the music for his voice; when it changed, I changed. I came to like the whole process, even cycling.'

The composer's distance from the subject matter and the eclectic nature of his output go to the heart of what Leth achieved with *A Sunday in Hell*. Leth's background within experimental performance during the 1960s had meant he came into cycling with no preconceptions about how it should be covered. That in turn made it almost inevitable that he would depict the sport in a new way, assisted by an eclectic range of equally open-minded collaborators: Holmberg, Camre, Pedersen. In this melting pot he was also able to include more conventional cycling personalities, such as Ritter, and specialist cameramen – Goodman, Loiseleux and Constantini. This blend is what makes *A Sunday in Hell* so unique. 'We couldn't have made this film at any other time,' believes Pedersen, who says it is underpinned by an 'everything-is-possible attitude' that stems from the 1960s.

'I know it's extremely strange . . . but it's an original idea,' is Leth's view of the chorale. 'I'm very interested in how to do the music for different films. I always do it in an unconventional way. It's a matter of professionalism and personal pride. [Pedersen] saw the material and said, "This is screaming for having a choir – it has to have a choir because it's such an impressionistic image, so many riders in the landscape, and so on. We have to have a choir." I said, "Do you really think so?" I was surprised. But I decided to follow his instincts; you have to go with the man who has the inspiration. I didn't regret it. I just counted on him coming up with something interesting like he did in the other films.'

The tone for Leth's approach to sound in his films had been set with *Stop for Bud*, where he made a virtue out of the lack of synchronised sound. He did not see sound and image as necessarily being integrated. 'From the beginning, image is one thing, and sound is another thing,' he said in a 2010 interview. 'I think they are two equally important elements. It's not that obvious that sound is just illustrating image, it could also be something that's contradicting the image.' Asked how he had worked with Pedersen, he said: 'I kind of delegate the imagination to him. I think it's because I come from a different background to most film-makers. I'm used to having a lot of confidence in my collaborators – I like the inspiration from the others to influence my work. I know [the music in *A Sunday in Hell*] is extremely strange . . . but it's an original idea.'

'I thought, "Oh no, not another cycle film,"' says Pedersen. 'I came home with eight hours of film and didn't have a clue what to do about it musically. First, I decided we had to have a solo instrument for the hero' – De Vlaeminck's theme on the cello, played by Gerhart Hamann, which also plays the opening solo, entitled *l'Enfer du Nord* – 'and there was a timpani improvisation for the chaos. If you need something to be very loud and very cheap, you don't choose a violin.'

It is the chorale that is most striking, however, although its birth was not an easy process. 'I just sat and became more and more desperate, thinking, "What am I going to do with this?" I finally got the idea when it was now or never. When I saw the peloton, when it comes along, there is a helicopter shot of the whole thing, where the chorale starts. And I thought, "What a waste, all these men just sitting there trying to be the first to Roubaix. If they sang it would be wonderful." I thought, "Why don't you let them sing?" And that's what I did. They can't sing "ah ah ah" all the time. What they are singing is what they are doing . . . going from Paris' – he pronounces it *Pahree* – 'to Roubaix' – pronounced on a much lower note – 'that's what they are singing and nothing else. Until we come to the *pavé* . . .'

At which point, I do a double take: 'Are you going to tell me that they start singing *pavé* when they get to the *pavé*?'

'You didn't notice that? [He sings the words] *"l'Enfer, l'Enfer. . ."* and then *"Paris–Roubaix"* at the end, triumphant . . . The basic point is they have to have something to sing and they are singing what they are doing. That's what they are thinking about.'

Pedersen made his liturgical chorale with eight singers from the opera choir of the Royal Danish Theatre, recorded twice and overdubbed for greater effect. 'We doubled the sound by getting them to do it twice over.' The connection came through his sister, an opera singer. 'We knew some of her friends, we got a group together. They were not paid very well. But it has always been a Danish speciality to do sound cheaply, because film budgets are usually spent on pictures. You need to do it fast as well because of being careful with the money.'

While the words reflect the complete inner focus that is the hallmark of a sportsman in 'the zone', the sound recalls religious music that would once have been composed to make medieval peasant churchgoers lift up their eyes to the heavens. 'Afterwards came the question of whether the chorale was genius or whether it was completely idiotic. It divided people – if you are really a sports fan you think it's too much, or perhaps it should be something you don't have to take so seriously. Every time I meet people they argue about whether it should be there or not. But I got into the brain of the racers.'

In a bike-racing context the chorale exalts the riders' effort and sacrifice, dovetailing perfectly into Leth's project to create mythical cycling heroes. The sound is radical, but the effect is utterly fitting given the history and tradition of the race, once known as *La Pasquale*, because of its traditional Easter Sunday date. There is a religious tone to much of what Leth depicts on screen – the pre-race rituals (De Vlaeminck's leg-shaving, the team meeting, the massage), Merckx's fetishistic belief in the need for perfection, the sense of sacrifice and suffering, and the fact that this entire event has a celebratory aura. Cycling fans attend Paris–Roubaix as their forefathers worshipped at mass; more broadly, cyclists are frequently compared to penitents on the road of the cross.

Pedersen's chorale takes centre stage, but it is only one sonic element. Leth makes extensive, and more conventional, use of the sounds that occur in and around any major bike race. There are too many examples to list, but he begins doing this in the first minute with that delicate tick-ticking of the chain moving over the bar in the frame. The spoken word features as a sound effect without translation – the clips from race radio, the conversations in the Café de la Place, Merckx discussing his stem height with Julien de Vries, Mangeas introducing the cyclists at the start, and finally the commentator talking in the finish in the velodrome.

At times, the sound replicates exactly what is being said, where Leth has a soundman on hand to synch the two. At other times, it is what Pedersen describes as 'collages from voices, put together afterwards. We' – he and sound head Ole Orsted, for a while his brother-in-law later in their lives – 'were looking to [simulate] how it would sound in the heads of the cyclists. It's not synch sound but it actually sounds more real – the timpani, some voices, some prepared sounds which are like the *pavé*.' Hence the mixes of crowd shouts, commentators' voiceovers, airhorns, and the screeching brakes at one key crash when Freddy Maertens is almost squashed by a team car. And there are specially created sounds dubbed in during production: the birdsong during the early pastoral moments before the race reaches 'Hell', and the ticking sound as Jacques Boulas regains the break after having a wheel change.

Even in synch, the actual content of what is being said is often left hanging, although some translation is provided in the DFI DVD amid its English subtitles. Where I have provided a translation on some occasions in this book, it is to broaden the experience of watching the film, not because I feel its absence detracts in the slightest from the film as a whole. The sounds and their context matter as part of the entire bike-racing experience – there is always a sense of urgency in race radio at any event as the escape leaves the pack or as the finale intensifies; we can feel the passion in the trenchant opinions in the café, and the slightly forced humour in De Vlaeminck's casual chat with his masseur. The words may actually be banal or bathetic but that is irrelevant; it is the sound as part of the experience that is important in the film. 'The idea was to isolate some sounds – a sort of super naturalism – you take out a sound and clean it from the surrounding chaos,' said Leth. 'I use it in *Stars and Watercarriers* and I use it extensively in *A Sunday in Hell*.'

One further note. According to Pedersen, the restored DVD of *A Sunday in Hell* runs at twenty-five frames per second, while a traditional cine camera runs at twenty-four. This has not been adjusted on the restored DVD, thus the sound is slightly faster in tempo than intended. 'It's a bit quicker, a bit higher, a bit more strange. It's out of pitch, a little too fast and in mono . . . What else can they do to ruin it?'

As well as providing race ambience, the other effect of using Italian, Flemish and French without subtitles on occasion is to make the entire experience more exotic and to dislocate the viewer – what Russian formalists would call *ostranenie*, or defamiliarisation, where difference is emphasised to enhance our perception of what we are being shown. If the viewer does not know the meaning of what is being said, we will be forced to use our imaginations to interpret the intonation, the context, and whatever words we can make out. That results in a powerful sense of mystery, of the exotic. It is exactly like picking up a French or Italian cycling magazine as an adolescent, admiring the pictures and trying to make out what is meant by the words. To extend the religious analogy, if the chorale serves to uplift the spirit of the viewer, the snippets of verbal sound are like listening to the words of the liturgy being delivered in Latin in a Catholic church. We do not need to understand the precise meaning, what matters is the part the sounds play in the broader ritual and the emotions they induce.

For English-speaking fans, another key feature of *A Sunday in Hell*'s soundtrack is the elegantly understated, clipped commentary of the late David Saunders, which stands in distinctly British contrast to the voluble French speaker and the Italian and Belgian television commentators who form part of the sonic background. Saunders's 'Queen's English' accent and lapidary, unemotional delivery is reminiscent of celebrated English-language documentaries such as the British Transport Films of the 1950s.

Saunders worked from a translation of Leth's original commentory by Ken Tindall, a twenty-four-page script which Saunders amended, corrected and reworked in considerable detail; given so many of the words are his, this film is the commentator's testament as well as that of the winner Marc Demeyer, who died in 1981. His time in the sport went as far back as Tom Simpson's 1965 victory in the road-race world championship, and in the 1970s it was Saunders who talked ITV into taking highlights of the one-day Classics and the Tour de France on their *World of Sport* weekend roundup. By the time he died in 1978, he was the voice of cycling on British television.

A former guardsman – hence, perhaps, the clipped tones – Saunders had worked in marketing for the drinks company Corona, badgered them into sponsoring a four-day stage race in England's south-west, and had moved seamlessly from there into television commentary. Friends with the ITV sports establishment – Dickie Davies, Ron Pickering – he also had the ear of high-ups in the company: 'Very good at being in the right place at the right time, a man with a lot of panache,' his former driver Phil Liggett recalls. 'He had to really sell them the sport. He sold them it all on Merckx and the way he raced.'

Together with the legendary writer Geoffrey Nicholson, Liggett and Saunders 'laughed their way around France. We swanned around the Tour drinking the best wine and brandy,' staying in hotels so plush that fellow hacks dubbed the trio 'the kings of England', laying out a tablecloth on their car bonnet to hold picnics by the roadside before the peloton came past on the day's stage.

Somehow, Saunders managed to do all this on a retainer from ITV and the *Daily Telegraph*, while paying Liggett to be his gopher out of the proceeds; small wonder that he left little behind him other than great affection among his peers after his untimely death in a car accident on London's South Bank in March 1978. After his death, it was the young driver who took over his former mentor's various gigs, beginning a television career that has taken Liggett to the status of voice of cycling worldwide.

At eleven o'clock we revisit the Roubaix velodrome where '*the Eurovision production chiefs are worried about the delay,*' although they soon resolve their fears. There is also sumptuous scenery: a sweeping foreshortened sequence of the peloton entering the village of Verberie, the helicopter shot of the bridge over the river Aisne in Choisy-au-Bac using a relatively new technological miracle called the Wesscam, the image of the square in today's start town of Compiègne. There are punctures in break and bunch, a second demonstration by workers from the chemical company Rhône-Poulenc (*l'Equipe* records that this one merely slowed down the riders, and delayed the following cars for fifteen minutes) is dealt with briefly, and we return to the break: Boulas, Talbourdet, Martinez. 40:43

'The trio's advantage has begun to diminish. It isn't far to l'Enfer du Nord *and the field starts to accelerate . . . Through Le Cateau, only four miles to the first cobbles and the field have gathered speed.'*

The run-in through villages such as Fresnoy-le-Grand, Bohain-en-Vermandois and Le Cateau-Cambrésis remains essentially the same in today's race; we see little of it from Leth. But compared to the earlier tranquil, structured moments, there is a very obvious difference in the mood of the peloton – more closely packed, far more urgent, moving faster.

46:40 'You can't win at Roubaix without being in front here,' Moser said. 'If you are behind, something will happen and you can't put it right. The speed goes up bit by bit as you approach [the first section]. You have no choice: you absolutely have to be in front. It's a fight where you have to return blow for blow.'

'It's like a sprint finish that starts fifteen kilometres out,' is how another winner, Andrei Tchmil, described that battle. 'No one brakes because everyone wants to be in front.'

Approaching 48min we see a different angle; the large, empty-looking cobbled square with a gaggle of fans to the left . . .

'Neuvilly, immediately before the rough stuff. The time is ten minutes to two. A single rider in the lead – it's Talbourdet, one of the three breakaways . . . The other two, Martinez and Boulas, but there, also, is the field. It's important to be among the first in on the pavé *as the twisting cobbled roads cause an immediate spreading of the field.'*

Finally, we are at the cobbles.

CHAPTER 7: HEROES PART 2

'This is where Hell begins. The first stretch of pavé *is only two miles long but terribly difficult. The surface is completely deformed, and here past Neuvilly there is a steep hill as well. Who's the first man in? Talbourdet. He doesn't seem to have considered resigning yet.'*

Dan Holmberg knew they would be hitting the pothole some 48:30
time soon, but he knew he wouldn't see it coming: he was facing backwards on his motorcycle. On the plus side, he had an unmatched view of the frontrunners as they streamed into the first section of cobbles at Neuvilly like a herd of wild horses in a panic. He and Leth had targeted this opening stretch up the legendary hill towards the village of Inchy as a key location in the race. All he had to do was wait for Merckx, De Vlaeminck and company to turn up.

'I had done the research and I did know it was sort of dangerous,' he recalled. 'There was a considerable bump in the road at one spot.' The motorcycle pillion seat was too small to accommodate him and his driver safely. He had attempted to persuade the driver to weld a safety bracket onto the back of the bike, and put on two extra pins to take the weight of his feet, but that was never going to be done.

'It happened as we thought; the race really started here. They were racing . . . going fast. My motorcycle and my camera right in front. Sitting backwards I get the whole scene. A wonderful shot. Dust flying and Roger De Vlaeminck trying to wave me out of the way. This is not possible . . . my guy is going as fast as he can. Then comes the "bump", I am up in the air . . . but luckily land back on the seat. But barely.

'Take a look. It happens right after Roger De Vlaeminck tries to wave me away. The camera goes up to the sky. That is me flying.' Looking back at the day as a whole, there were other shots that Holmberg loved, but, 'mostly I'm happy I did not fall off the motorcycle in the bump and [get] killed by Roger De Vlaeminck's team car. It still scares the living shit out of me when I see it.'

'And then it happens. The front of the field catches up with [Talbourdet] and streams past, Roger De Vlaeminck followed by Walter Planckaert . . . De Vlaeminck is now in the clear and forcing the pace. There is panic in the field and signs of disintegration.'

De Vlaeminck's attack occurs immediately the race hits the 49:33
Neuvilly 'hill'. Talbourdet, the last survivor of the three escapees from the morning, is rapidly overhauled as the church spire and the cottages fade into the distance behind them. Asked about this move forty years later, the four-time winner is keen to emphasise the difference between his era and modern cycling. 'Every year it was the same: I would always go from Neuvilly, from the beginning of the cobbles. Now, the riders wait, wait, wait . . . I didn't want to leave it until the last forty kilometres. The idea was to test everyone, see if they were good.' *'To provoke a state of alarm and split the field'*, as the commentary has it.

The Gypsy adds that he was able to adopt this strategy only because of the distances that he covered in training in the run-in to the race, which gave him the confidence to begin making intense efforts 160km from the finish. 'The week before, it was the Tour of Flanders – 260km, and I would do 50km behind a motorbike immediately after, to make the day over 300km. During the week, I had Ghent–Wevelgem, which was 265km, four times up the Kemmelberg; a friend would wait on the finish line with the Derny, I'd do another 120km. So that would be almost 400km.' As Monty Python's Yorkshireman would say, you tell the kids of today that and they wouldn't believe it.

De Vlaeminck is known for making unfavourable comparisons between the two eras, and he has no hesitation in making his point. 'If you train only two hundred kilometres, you can't make more than a couple of attacks in Paris–Roubaix, because it's so long; that's why you see the riders of today wait in the wheels until close to the end of the race. If you are doing a 260km race, you have to do more than that in training. If you cover such a big distance in training, you don't worry if you have to attack fourteen or fifteen times. I didn't do that every week; I'd do it for special races like Roubaix or the Tour of Lombardy.'

The contrast in speed on the Neuvilly 'hill' between De Vlaeminck and the other favourites and the struggling Talbourdet is telling, but so is another detail: the amount of motorbike 'traffic' around the front of the peloton – still photographers, television cameras, radio reporters, *commissaires*, not to mention Holmberg and his driver. The riders receive a considerable amount of slipstream assistance, while – in the case of De Vlaeminck, at least – simultaneously being annoyed that the motos are in the way, throwing up clouds of dust.

Having acted as 'regulator' of the traffic around the front of the bunch at Paris–Roubaix for many years, Jean-François Pescheux does not feel this could happen now: 'You see the motorbikes constantly getting in the way of the riders in the film. [Now] the regulating of the motorbikes in and around the race makes for a more fluid race – there are more restrictions on the motorbikes today, but it means that the riders have the cobbled zones to themselves, which obviously wasn't the case in 1976.

'It's something that we worked hard to improve each year; we'd bring in new rules all the time, no motorbikes on the cobbled zones, no motorbikes in among the riders. We organised a pool system, with one [still] photographer's motorbike in front and one behind, one television motorbike in front and one behind, and all the other photographers working statically.' In the twenty-first century, those images of De Vlaeminck surrounded by motorbikes would not be seen, with access so limited – those still photographers that are allowed to use a motorbike have to shoot from the roadside, with their motorbike used to overtake the race to get them back to the next position.

Luke Evans, the only British motorbike driver to have made a career driving in European races, drove the still photographer Graham Watson in Paris–Roubaix for the first time in 1991, when conditions were still similar to those of the 1970s, with few restrictions on where the motorbikes could go in the race. 'The roads are so narrow that, for a photographer, you can't go alongside the riders, or you get a really tight pic, so you're working from three-quarters in front. The race explodes to such an extent that as early as just after Troisvilles you can be overtaking individual riders and small groups – there is no peloton, just groups of fifteen to twenty, and they are [lined out] on the crown of the cobbles or on the edge and are going just that bit slower than in a normal race so it's easier to pass them than in a usual race.

'It was a free-for-all back then. I've got a picture of me and Graham Watson alongside [race winner] Marc Madiot on the Carrefour de l'Arbre cobbles in 1991, which shows just how close you could get in there – that was the key attack and we snuck in. We just used to use normal big road motorbikes, although now you get guys on smaller bikes, sometimes with knobbly tyres, but that's a bit excessive. It's either dusty or muddy – in the wet, it's only dangerous if there is mud on the cobbles. The dust adds an extra element of danger because it can be so hard to see. I've nearly ridden into the back of a team car because I couldn't see where I was going. It doesn't matter what you put on, a bandana or whatever, you still can't breathe.'

Paul Constantini, who worked for over a quarter of a century as a motorbike cameraman, hails the complicity that could be created between the driver and passenger (something Watson has described as well). The Frenchman's regular driver was called Michel Sergeant, with whom he completed the Tour de France eighteen times. 'You work together. There is a kind of synchronicity. Without him on the motorbike it just wasn't the same.' He describes one occasion when Sergeant heard a rider change gear on the Col d'Izoard, and alerted him just as a key battle broke out between Lucien Van Impe and Eddy Merckx. 'He had a real feeling for what was happening in the peloton. He heard everything.'

Without this kind of partnership, communication between motorbike driver and cameraman could be a haphazard process, recalls Holmberg. 'You do it by some kind of instinct, but I can't remember it being a big problem. The drivers know the rules of the race. Sometimes it is better for the driver to lead and the cameraman to follow, sometimes the other way around. You work with the wind and your instinct. You let the driver know when you are shooting, so that he can help you by driving smoothly. You say in some hybrid EU language, "Stick with Fuente." When you are done, "OK . . . Let's drive ahead." All in a crazy mixture of English, French, Italian and Spanish.'

Leth's opening sequence on the cobbles between Neuvilly and Viesly blends footage from at least two motorbike cameras, the static cameras that had been set up by the roadside, with a lengthy shot of the leaders from the helicopter. That shows the peloton strung out in one single line on a sinuous stretch of cobbles, amid clouds of dust blowing gently across the fields like gun smoke in a battle. That image can (if you have the time and energy) be compared to footage from today's race and the location narrowed down to the twisting cobbled section

between Viesly and Quiévy, one of the few from the 1976 race that is still used today.

The dramatic shift in intensity when the set-pieces are reached is an integral part of Classic racing – the first cobbled sections en route to Roubaix; the succession of little hills known as the *capi* in Milan–San Remo – and Leth captures this with the timpani roll, the abrupt emergence of the solo cello as De Vlaeminck makes his move and is caught by Walter Planckaert and Ludo Dierickx, the switches between the extended sequence showing the motorbikes jostling in front of the Gypsy, and slow motion of the peloton, biceps vibrating in agonising close-up in a chaos of crowd noise, car horns. The dusty panorama places it all in context.

De Vlaeminck is riding in the classic manner: getting to the front and staying there. 'In Paris–Roubaix, the break can go anywhere,' the 1994 winner Andrei Tchmil told me. 'On the tarmac, on the *pavé*, after a crash. You can't expect anything so it's better to be in front all the time. Then you have to understand the moment, sense that the riders who have gone are the right ones. It's just down to intuition.'

'The strongest men stay out of trouble because they always stay at the front,' another specialist said. 'When riders are tired, they ride on the edge of the cobblestones and get punctures.' The strong men often favour the crown of the road – as Walter Godefroot did – with the entire width to play with, albeit with the risk that if the cobbles fall away steeply all of a sudden, the front wheel can be lost. In the wet, the crown of the road is a dangerous place to ride. 'When you are strong, you can lay off the wheel in front' – leave a small gap – 'and see where you are going. When you are tired, if you don't ride on the wheels you get dropped, so you ride blind and you can't see what's coming up. You just have to pray.'

Moser's tactic for Paris–Roubaix was the opposite to the one favoured by De Vlaeminck: 'Wait, and make as few mistakes as possible. You have to use the terrain, or you forget where you are. The difference in this race is a mental one. It's a waiting game, to the very end. The problem is that when you feel strong, you tend to be tempted to press just a little bit harder on the pedals. The risk then is that you end up devoid of strength in the end. Sometimes, if you are slightly below the best physically, you use your strength differently, you save what you've got, and you can win.'

The riders faced a common issue in the 1976 race, which is far less of a factor now: the difficulty of getting spare wheels and bikes when – not if – they punctured or crashed. 'The bikes are practically the same as in 1976 but what's different is that in almost every one of the cobbled zones, pretty much every team has organised for people to be there with spare wheels and bikes,' says Jean-François Pescheux.

'So in 1976 if a rider punctured, he either got a wheel from his team car or from a teammate or that was it. Today, there are so many people in the cobbled sectors that puncturing is barely a handicap.'

Peter Sagan would have every right to disagree after his disastrous brace of punctures in the 2017 race, but the general point stands. In the twenty-first century, teams have far greater resources than in the past. In the 1970s, even the richest teams such as Brooklyn or Molteni would turn up at Paris–Roubaix with only two team cars. One would travel behind the race, the other would go ahead to the feed zones at Saint Quentin and Valenciennes. There is no sign in Leth's film of any team personnel in any of the cobbled zones: the teams did not have staff or vehicles to spare. Nowadays, on the other hand, team-branded vans and cars line up at the end of almost every stretch of cobbles and riders can be seen taking bottles from helpers as they emerge.

That has a considerable impact on the twenty-first-century race compared to that of forty years ago. Because the wait for a new wheel would usually be far longer without static service points, those who did puncture or crash, as Maertens, Poulidor and Kuiper do early on in the 1976 race, faced a far harder chase, and potentially a far longer one, to get back to the front afterwards. That had a knock-on effect: later in the race, they would be more tired and more likely to puncture or crash again, even assuming they still had the legs to stay with the frontrunners.

The twenty-first-century race remains a lottery, but less so. Crashes still play their part, even in relatively dry conditions, as Team Sky riders such as Geraint Thomas and Luke Rowe, and Fabian Cancellara would attest after the 2015 and 2016 races. But due in part to considerable improvements in tyre technologies, puncturing is less common and the price a rider pays for a puncture can be lower. This in turn explains why in some modern editions of Paris–Roubaix more of the favourites stay together for longer. It also explains why over a hundred riders now make it to the Roubaix velodrome every year, whereas through the 1970s between thirty-five and fifty was the norm. If the organisers felt like turning the clock back and banning service from the roadside – limiting wheel and bike changes to teammates and vehicles accredited within the convoy – they would have an entirely different and far crueller contest. Purists might argue it would be more genuine as well.

Beside Leth's chosen quartet of De Vlaeminck, Merckx, Maertens and Moser, the director cites other heroes in *A Sunday in Hell*: the cameramen whose names appear on the credits at the end of the film. Inevitably, as Leth's director of photography and his most trusted collaborator, Holmberg was one of the three men selected by Leth for the most important role on 11 April: the motorbike camera. Leth had permission for two other cameramen to travel 'in the race' and their fortunes would provide an intriguing subplot.

In Mexico City during Ole Ritter's Hour record attempt a few years earlier, Leth had met a French cameraman called Paul Constantini, who was one of the television crew who were commandeered by Ritter to shoot *The Impossible Hour*. His name does not appear on the credits for Leth's film, as theirs was an unofficial arrangement.

'He was a curious person, a great cameraman, but a curious person,' said Leth. 'He was a star with French television, very smart, he had fantastic technical ideas for shooting a cycle race. I counted on him [but] I couldn't control him.' 'A small, lean guy,' recalls Holmberg. 'Probably not much of a cinematographer but he knew bike races and he had his own way of shooting them. He was good at riding a motorcycle in the horrible chaos that a bike race can be.'

Constantini had worked for French television since 1962, shooting colour pictures for post-race reports and working on the monthly documentary series *Les Coulisses de l'Exploit*, which ran from 1961 to 1972. 'A very good cameraman,' recalls the commentator Daniel Pautrat, 'a Corsican and proud of it.' 'Talented, enterprising, and also *debrouillard* – capable of looking after himself,' says the former television producer Régis Fourissier. Now eighty-two, Constantini is a colourful character, massively passionate about his work, who told me – down a telephone from France – a glorious tale of a lorry crash in Cuba in the 1970s, after which his death was prematurely made public, all of which, somehow, led to an improbable meeting with Fidel Castro.

The third cameraman was another Frenchman, Jacques Loiseleux, 'a wonderful talent', recalled Leth. A handsome man with an unruly head of hair and a lively face, Loiseleux had worked with Joel Santoni on *La Course en Tête*, the French director's tribute to Merckx, shot over the course of 1973 and 1974, and including footage of races such as the Giro d'Italia and world road championships. He was to become a major figure in French cinema, who sparked warm tributes when he died in 2014. His career encompassed over fifty films for television and big screen as photographic director, including work with Jean-Luc Godard, Maurice Pialat and Yves Boisset, and a book on cinematography, *La Lumière en Cinema*.

Loiseleux had a personal trick: changing position on the motorbike while being driven at speed, something distinctive enough that it merited mention in the eulogies after his death. 'He was the only one I have seen who could do that,' says Holmberg. 'the camera guys, stills and movie, sit looking forwards like the driver. Sitting backwards had its advantages but could get really scary if you got caught looking that way and you and the race began going downhill. I liked to sit backwards going up the mountains. It gave you easier framing. The plan was always to stop so that I could turn around on the bike, to go down the mountain.

'A few times we couldn't stop,' continues Holmberg, 'so I had to sit backwards going down a mountain at a hundred kilometres per hour among the cards and cyclists. No fun, and very dangerous. Loiseleux could do this changing position at speed. A huge advantage. How he did it I could not understand. He was that quick. When he showed up at Chantilly and got his motorcycle [and driver] he tried it out, of course. I looked at him and he did it. Twice . . . The show-off . . .'

The task of managing these disparate characters fell to Holmberg. 'Dan was supposed to direct all the others, tell them what to shoot, what not to shoot, and how to shoot,' said Leth. 'That was his job. [But] Constantini was a rebel; he didn't want to be directed by a Swedish cameraman. [He saw Paris–Roubaix as] his race. He didn't want to adjust to a new formula. That cost us something because he had a special trick and he had not really told us what he was doing.'

There was another issue, however, and it came close to scuppering Leth's project. Loiseleux had an accident on the morning of the race, for reasons that remain unclear today. 'It was a whole intrigue, a very dramatic story . . .. [Loiseleux] wasn't hurt but the camera was smashed so he was out. You can see it's a novel in itself. He didn't shoot a single metre.' With Loiseleux out of action, Leth was down to just two 'in

Top: Jørgen Leth gets in the saddle with Ole Ritter, who has inspired him for more than half a century

Bottom: Leth contemplates the day ahead on the start line of the 1976 Paris – Roubaix

The winning move in the final phase of the 1976 race: Francesco Moser leads Hennie Kuiper, Roger de Vlaeminck and Marc Demeyer

Then and now

Top: the Neuvilly "hill" where De Vlaeminck made his initial attack and found photographers' motorbikes in his way

Bottom: the Roubaix showers where "the Gypsy" contemplated a bitter defeat

Top and middle: Cinematographer Dan Holmberg prepares for his day out in the Hell of the North

Bottom: The late Alber Bouvet contemplates his beloved cobbles during a route recce in winter 1993

The late David Saunders, the "voice" of the film for English speaking fans

Remembering Marc; clockwise from top:

The finish sprint in Roubaix, with Moser, left, Demeyer, centre, De Vlaeminck right; celebrating victory; Demeyer's grave in Outrijve, West Flanders; the 1976 winner's plaque in the Roubaix showers; congratulated by Lomme Driessens

Top: Chemin de Bourghelles
Bottom: The former Café de la Place on venue Desandrouins, Valenciennes.

Top: Freddy Maertens, West Flanders, September 2017

Below: The author and Jørgen Leth, Copenhagen, September 2017.

race' cameramen, although he was not aware of it. 'It was an immense loss, but I didn't know about it until the evening. I thought he was there.' That would have a crucial impact later in the day.

Constantini's distinctive camerawork meant that his contribution to the film was a major one. 'He was shooting in his own way, half-reels of 16mm film with a small camera, a Bell and Howell,' said Leth. The reduced size of the camera meant that Constantini could move around the bike more easily, making his work more versatile. 'He is an artist. I loved what he was doing. The best footage in the film is his – everything that is centred on the bike, the faces, the hands, close-ups from the race on Merckx, Godefroot. He was a virtuoso – very selective with what he was shooting. He was very good at it [but] he didn't tell me or the other guys he was going to do it.'

'The camera that Constantini used was one of the old news cameras,' said Holmberg. 'You wound them up and then you could shoot approx thirty seconds before you had to wind up the spring in the camera again. Very old style. One problem with them was that you used thirsty metre rolls of film that should be loaded in subdued light, but when Constantini did it in full sunshine on the motorcycle a lot of the film [was made] useless by too much light exposing the film.

'The Constantini system was not a very good one,' continues Holmberg. 'He was the only one shooting like that. All other cameramen used modern [at that time] cameras with magazines that took 120-metre [400 feet] film rolls that lasted just over eleven minutes. And of course no winding up the camera – they ran on twelve-volt batteries. Then you can shoot one take as long as you like before the film runs out and you need to change magazine. I used Arriflex BL, a camera made in

Germany. Some used Eclair, made in France. They were the leading camera brands at that time.'

The criticism might be a little unfair: the particular way Constantini worked probably did not matter when it came to shooting 'colour' images for pared-down television features. Pautrat mentions a beautiful Constantini image of swans; the cameraman himself feels one of his best bits of work was an ice cream, placed on the ground, which he then lay down to shoot in the foreground as the peloton went past. In either case, the eventual cut would be a few seconds for an introduction to the reporter's work. The French cameraman had vision, but for the extended footage Leth required, and the need to try to capture every event in the race, his approach clearly had its limits.

Leth is far more forgiving than his cinematographer, but feels the big problem was that Constantini was focused on his own work rather than where it fitted into that of the group as a whole. Again, in a cameraman shooting atmospheric pictures largely on his own initiative – his brief was to set off each day and dream up what he could for the evening's feature piece – that was not surprising. In such a massive enterprise – and as one of only two motorbike cameramen active on the day – his individualism had two sides to it. Leth continues: 'When we saw the material several days after the race – [we are working with] film so it's not like today, I only see it on the editing table – I thought it was fantastic but I was surprised because I didn't know what he had in mind, I didn't know his technique.

'I was very happy when I saw what he'd done, but very angry – because he didn't communicate his tricks so we could have orchestrated something more, and because he was shooting so selectively. So on the one hand he's tremendously valuable for the film, but he shot too little, it was too exclusive. There was so little of it – when he was putting the rolls in there was a lot of light at the beginning and the end so there is only a little amount in the middle. He concentrated on the most important parts of the race. Holmberg was furious at him, but I loved his material. I couldn't have done the film without his shots. I couldn't have done it without him. He shot very little but it was all gold.'

The report in *l'Equipe* the next morning offered a brief summary of events in those first few stretches of cobbles: 'A first selection happens, with a hundred riders at the front including all the favourites, apart from [Hennie] Kuiper who is held up by a puncture and makes his way back to the front on his own at km 152. On the cobbles of Saint Python (km 155), there is a new selection. Maertens and Merckx, held up by various incidents, chase back to the front group.' For both men, the day was to be a nightmare: Maertens remains bitter to this day about the way his team rode, with the honourable exception of Michel Pollentier and Marc Demeyer, while Merckx is listed in one book as having had ten punctures. That seems like an exaggeration, but his race was riddled with incidents, which we do not see in the film.

Leth also omits the puncture to Kuiper – in the rider's view it was one that made little difference – but the picture he paints is the accurate one of an early phase in which the riders who will later be also-rans – Merckx, Maertens, Ritter, the biggest French star of the time Raymond Poulidor – are off the pace, using up valuable energy as they fight their way back to the front time after time; later, the cumulative effort will take its toll when they fade or fall. Poulidor's chase back to the front lasted many kilometres, as did that of Maertens. As

Moser says, much of Paris–Roubaix can resemble an individual time trial; the issue is whether that time trial is being ridden assertively to press the pace in front or desperately to regain contact from the rear.

A brief interlude with the broom wagon gives way to the chorale, combined with the timpani for epic effect, acting as soundtrack to one of the most distinctive sequences, shot in the Neuvilly cobbles and using, according to Leth, 'A very big slow-motion camera with an enormous lens, which cannot be hand-held, a static camera – you have that image where the whole peloton is coming towards you.'

The sight of the riders' biceps vibrating in slow motion – as one told me, riding the cobbles feels 'like sitting on a piledriver' – is unforgettable, so too the ghostly vision of team cars emerging from the miasma of dust, mechanics sitting on the car roofs like vultures waiting for prey. Walk on that section of cobbles now, and you see how fine the soil is between and over the cobbles; the dust, Freddy Maertens says, would still be in his eyes three days after a dry Roubaix, no matter how many eyedrops he used.

Leth is often asked whether he regrets that his Sunday in Hell was a dry one rather than the soaking-wet conditions that aficionados crave. The answer lies partly in that series of images.

'I face that question every year when I commentate Paris–Roubaix. We ask ourselves: do we want bad weather? From my experience with this film, I do not. I think strangely enough the race is more wild in the dry. That sounds crazy because of course I know when it's wet it's crazy and surreal – there [would] have been more bad chance in the film if we had filmed when it was totally wet. Of course, for instance, we would not have had the demonstration – they would not have been on the streets if it had rained. What surprised me was that Paris–Roubaix in dry weather has a totally different quality with the dust, the haze that hangs over the race. It adds something fantastic. That definitely outdoes the possibilities with a wet race. The race was tougher, cleaner, more visible.'

CHAPTER 8: PARIS–VALENCIENNES

'At the rear, the weak and the unfortunate are being left behind. This is where the broom wagon has something to do, when they start giving up.'

Once the 1976 Paris–Roubaix had sped through Neuvilly and onto the cobbles, the cameramen positioned behind the race in the broom wagon and in the Brooklyn team car truly came into their own. Among the footage of the backmarkers, most distinctive perhaps is the sight of Jacques Boulas, wheeling wearily along a dusty roadside after his morning in the limelight – which will earn him that paragraph in *l'Equipe* the following day – only for someone in the convoy to casually lift the *casquette* off his head as they drive past.

53:32 That almost feels like the ultimate indignity. According to one of the riders who was present at the race, the culprit was definitely a *commissaire*, bizarre as it may sound. 'The race officials were all amateurs brought in from the French regions and they would take home every souvenir they could lay their hands on.'

54:02 The true depths of despair, however, are reserved for those who climb wearily into the *voiture balai*, rattling and banging along the cobbled roads like an empty freight train going over a set of points – an outstanding use of sound that does much to illustrate the horror of the cobbles. We go inside 'the broom' only this once in the film, we see one man, but there is enough in the vignette shot by cameraman Henrik Herbert (he of the lingering sequence with the Sanson mechanic). *Dossard* 25 – the commissaire in the broom wagon brusquely asks him for the information as he clambers through the door – is Frans Van Looy, who came from Merksem, a town close to Antwerp, and who had finished sixteenth in Paris–Roubaix the year before.

That helps explain his disgust: of Merckx's eleven team-mates, he was one of the pure Classics specialists, good enough to finish in the top twenty, so he could have been expected to go on and help Merckx all the way to the finish. Van Looy was a successful professional, winner of various middle-ranking races, who went on to be a *directeur sportif* at the Histor-Sigma team, then alongside Walter Godefroot at the Telekom/T-Mobile squad.

Given how desperately Merckx leads the chase behind the winning break later on, having Van Looy beside him in this phase might have made a difference. Van Looy is justifiably

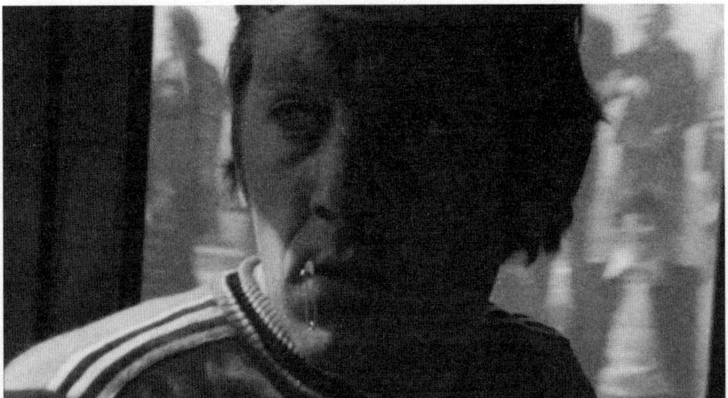

irritated when the van door refuses to close behind him. He tells of his long wait for the team car to get him a wheel – en route to Roubaix in the twenty-first century he would have picked up a spare from a helper at the end of the cobbled section. He is desperate to make it known to the official in the broom wagon that he has not quit because he is not good enough – he was with the front group of twenty, Merckx is probably on his own now . . .

The noise as the van rattles over the cobbles is mind-bending; the close-up of the safety pins dangling in the rider's mouth the kind of intimate image that Leth had been hoping for. 'There you see the whole principle of the shoot – [that rider's] story alone is worth one man's work for an entire day. It's a very telling detail. But that is the thinking behind it.'

In a small way, Van Looy became known for that fifteen-second sequence in the broom wagon, says the Danish cyclist Brian Holm, who rode for him at Histor and T-Mobile. 'Of course we reminded him about it – there aren't many cyclists who haven't been in that situation when it feels like you've fucked up the whole thing and you are really unhappy about it. It's those small details that make this film so real for any cyclist.'

> *'In fine weather, the crossroads are a good picnic spot for the nearby villagers. People wait to get a glimpse of this great race. They wait for a few fleeting moments of action, drama, torture and even heroism.'*

56:54 Leth includes two extended roadside sequences in the cobbles, one on either side of the second feed at Valenciennes. The first and relatively leisurely one on a right-angled bend in the middle of the section of cobbles between Quiévy and Saint Python may well be the work of the cameraman Dirk Brüel, who had worked with Leth a couple of years before on *Klaus Rifbjerg*, a twenty-two-minute film about the Danish writer.

Two middle-aged ladies deal cards onto a picnic blanket; a young fan glues his ear to his transistor radio (which informs us, cracklingly, that the race is taking place in a 'fog' of dust, and that Raymond Poulidor is among the early puncture victims). Old men in berets, middle-aged fans with binoculars, a young lad in a Poulidor cap; everyone is in their Sunday best, adding to the sense of Easter ritual. A Citroën Estate car appears flogging *casquettes* and *cadeaux*, with a vast loudspeaker on the roof reminiscent of the one Jake and Elwood steal and mount on their car in *The Blues Brothers*. It is timeless stuff, and time is milked to the full.

Ironically enough, the cameraman did not follow Leth's instructions to keep the camera in one place; he moves it around, focusing on the cobbles and grit as the first two groups come through in real-time; the camera is then moved around the corner for the shots of Maertens and the main field including Poulidor. 'Brüel shot wonderful bravura close-ups, but he missed the time measure,' said Leth. 'That was OK in that case. The main field split in pieces . . . Maertens hunting alone.'

The '*hapless*' Maertens had punctured, and his car was stuck behind the peloton; he took a wheel from his teammate Pol Verschuere. His quest to re-join the front of the race is the theme for the next few minutes, which includes another real-time sequence on an uphill stretch of cobbles, shot with a massive zoom lens used by the cameraman Jan Weincke, who was driven to and from locations by the producer Steen Herdel – the lens being too large to convey on a motorbike. Holmberg scouted stretches of straight road for Weincke (cameraman O in the list), and gave detailed instructions as to where he was to stand.

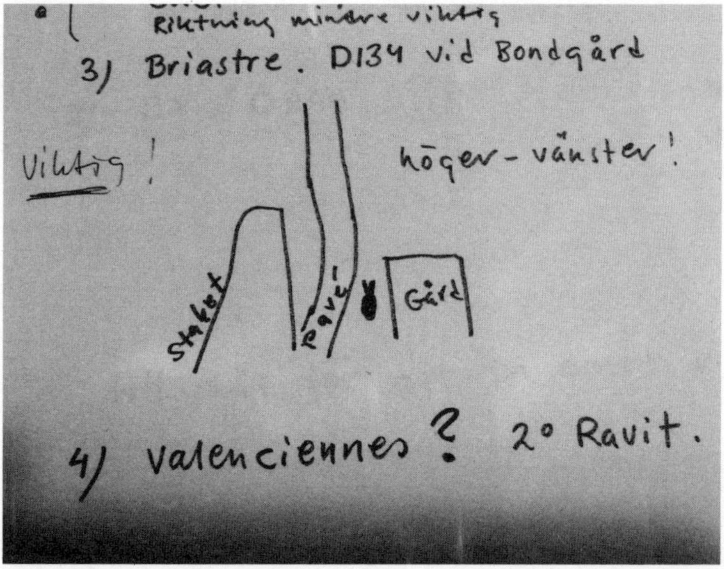

1:0:59 'I think it was a 600mm lens and I think he also had a 300mm with him,' says Holmberg. 'This was very important for the film. It worked at least at one spot. The caravan sort of dancing in the mist of dust towards the camera. The same way John Wayne and his pals sometimes ride towards you in the movies of our youth.' The shot is most probably taken at Weincke's third location, 162.5km into the race near the village of Briastre, where Holmberg's diagram shows the cobbles curving to the right at the point where Weincke is to stand on the outside of the bend looking up the straight stretch of pave. 'Important!' says the note. 'Right to left.'

Here Maertens's wingman Marc Demeyer is prominent; his brief was to mark the favourites if the Flandria leader had any issues. The problem was that most of the team's *domestiques* were stuck in the third group, behind Maertens: forty-one years later, he picks them out for me: Herman Van Springel, Albert Van Vlierberghe, Tino Tabak. Here, Leth's old friend Ole Ritter features for the only time before the finish. Now, the veteran Dane says he was especially motivated for that particular race, because he knew his friend was filming it. 'I wasn't someone who could win Roubaix, but that year I was good. I really wanted to be in the front that year. I saw the camera crews along the route, and knew what was going on.'

There is an interlude among the red Peugeots driven by the 1:03:30
race officials, a crash in which Hervé Inaudi is dragged unceremoniously off the road, and a rooftop wheel change from the Brooklyn car. That takes us to one of the most anachronistic – and frankly insane – visions in *A Sunday in Hell*: mechanics perching perilously on the roofs of the team cars, clinging for grim death to the roof racks. It looks crazy, and clearly was. However, the point, Walter Godefroot explains, was that the wheel changes had to be done as quickly as possible. So far, so obvious.

It seems self-evident that the need to swap the wheel rapidly was due to the fact that the rider had to get moving as soon as possible. However, that is only part of the story. What actually mattered more was to keep the car positioned high up the convoy of team vehicles so that the leader could receive a wheel or a bike rapidly if needed. 'On those roads, when the team car stopped to do a proper change for a rider, it would drop back to twentieth in the convoy – and as you came back up the line sometimes there would be rivals who would play it clever and block you – so you wouldn't want to stop,' said Godefroot, who worked as a *directeur sportif* for twenty-five years after quitting racing in 1979.

'You would want to pause for only a second or two. So the rider would undo the wheel himself, the mechanic would hold a good one down from the car, they would swap them, and the car would move on. Sometimes the mechanic would just throw the wheel down.'

A loose wheel going astray on the road would cause utter mayhem, which is why the organisers attempted to regulate this chaotic process. Race rule number 7, to be found in the official programme, stipulates that wheel changes must be made behind the bunch and 'when either the *directeur sportif* or the mechanic have a foot on the ground'. No bunging wheels off the roof; what then, to make of the fact that the Brooklyn mechanic does the swap without alighting, even though our mechanical friend the plump *commissaire* is sitting in the back seat below him to watch for precisely this kind of thing?

There was another reason for risking the mechanics' life and limb in this way; with punctures being more common than today, and no chance to change the wheels at static team-service points, all spare wheels had to come from the car, and there was a limit to how many (either flat or still inflated) could be contained within the back seat area. With the mechanic on the roof, there was no need to stop and switch wheels from the rack to the interior (we see the Brooklyn mechanic putting the wheel into the rack as the sequence ends). The practice was outlawed in the 1980s when health and safety finally – and not unreasonably – caught up.

As we approach Valenciennes, Cribiori comes up behind the main group – passing Merckx a few metres off the back wearing number 22 – to tell De Vlaeminck that his big rival is at *quaranta secondi*, forty seconds. Earlier, we are specifically told that the teams' service cars are still stuck behind the main bunch because the officials in the red Peugeots won't let them past. On occasion, Brooklyn got round this, recalls Cribiori, with a cunning plan that they had worked out among themselves: the *direttore sportivo* would get their team car in front of the race twenty kilometres before they reached Neuvilly. The car would overtake the field, and would then park up and wait at the end of one of the first sections of cobbles.

When De Vlaeminck's group came past – given his tactic of riding *la course en tête*, he would usually be among the leading string of riders – Cribiori would drop in behind his leader, thus avoiding what the *directeurs sportifs* dreaded: getting caught behind all the also-rans who began struggling behind the race when it hit the early cobbled sections. 'We would be the only car there; the race would be in ten groups by then, so otherwise he would have to wait two or three minutes for me.' Back there, it was utter chaos due to the constant splits and regroupings. As Maertens and Frans Van Looy found to their cost on that particular Sunday, it could be virtually impossible for riders to get rapid service if they punctured with only a single team car in the convoy behind the peloton.

Cribiori's strategy was a risky one. De Vlaeminck and his teammates would have to fend for themselves if they punctured during the hectic run-in to the cobbles, and once on the cobbles, any team member who got dropped and ended up behind the team car would have to find a wheel for himself if he punctured, most probably ending his race. However, the tactic would guarantee cover for the leader at a risky phase of the race, and would ensure that he could receive information from the car from the moment the true action began.

'Something happens just before Valenciennes. Two Brooklyn riders have broken away, the Belgian Johan De Muynck and the Italian Marcello Osler. This is a tactical manoeuvre. Neither is among the real contestants in this race. They've been sent by De Vlaeminck with the intention of forcing his rivals to greater activity. He's on the offensive, even with this ploy . . .'

1:05:52 De Muynck was the first to attack, some ten kilometres after Saint Python – in the cobbled sections around Verchain-Maugré and Quérénaing, both names familiar to followers of today's race – and he remained alone for ten kilometres, before being caught by his teammate Osler as the race approached Valenciennes, which was in the middle of an eighteen-kilometre tarmacked respite from the battering.

The image of the pair going over a level crossing is taken at the end of the cobbled section between Quérénaing and Artres (km 181), the last *pavé* before the break through Valenciennes. The road downhill to the level crossing, Rue du Tapage, is still cobbled and still has its strip of tarmac down the right. The location is listed in Holmberg's notebook as number 6; it is in Henning Camre's list of seven potential shots for the day, along with a complex description of how to get to the next one, 'a green house in Rue de Sablières in the village of Coutiches'.

According to Cribiori, the double attack was not a pre-planned move; the notion was simply for Brooklyn to get as many riders as they could as far towards the front of the race as they could, to ensure that De Vlaeminck would have riders to help him out if he punctured or crashed, rather than waiting for his team car to catch up. The thinking – similar to the tactic of getting the team car ahead – was that they would end up in front once the race hit the cobbled sections after the tarmacked interlude through Valenciennes, and De Vlaeminck would bring the selection of favourites up behind them when it formed. Plus, it did no harm to keep the pressure on Maertens – who had finally received some help in the chase from the third Flandria 'musketeer', Michel Pollentier – and Merckx, the Gypsy's key rivals.

Of the Brooklyn pair, De Muynck had the most interesting career. In this race he is a mere *domestique*; playing the same role, he unexpectedly found himself in the leader's jersey later that spring at the Tour de Romandie, giving him ambitions above his station of *domestique* when he arrived at that year's Giro d'Italia. There, he took a stage and led the race overall until his own team leader De Vlaeminck joined forces with – believe it or not – his erstwhile-rival Merckx to put the upstart in his place. He has not spoken to De Vlaeminck since. He finished second that year after a crash but would go on to win the 1978 Giro riding for the Bianchi team. Osler, on the other hand, never won another race to match his 1975 Giro stage victory, and rode out his career alongside Moser at Sanson until 1980.

The footage immediately afterwards of De Muynck and Osler together on the cobbles was probably taken after Valenciennes and used out of sequence. Approaching the tower blocks in the centre, the action switches to the back of the race, where a regrouping has taken place as it so often does in Paris–Roubaix during this interlude through the town – or in the twenty-first century, its south-western satellites – after the initial cobbled sections. *'Kuiper, Poulidor and Ritter have caught up. It was their last chance to be included in the finale, which begins after the feeding station in the town.'* We move to footage of the back of the bunch from one of the motorbike cameramen: riders scrambling to stay on the wheels, the urgent revving of a line of motorbikes behind the field, the sprint for the corners. This is only a respite of sorts.

> *'The second feeding zone is right outside the Café de la Place . . . it's also where many of the riders dismount. The hopelessly outdistanced, the weary support men who may feel they have done their duty . . . some even that it was well performed. They know that here the team personnel are ready to take care of them and there is transport to Roubaix.'*

All French cafés have certain things in common: the early-morning beer and *pastis* drinkers, the *patron* who has seen it all and either wiped it off the vinyl floor or chucked it out the door, the chalkboards displaying a manky *plat du jour*, toilets heaving with alien lifeforms. The location is crucial to the identity of the café in general and to the one in *A Sunday in Hell* in particular: the Café de la Place on Avenue Desandrouins in Valenciennes is not a town-centre establishment but feels more like one of its rural counterparts.

The café is technically in Valenciennes but it is not a totally urban environment. The Place is Place Taffin (named after Pierre Taffin, founder of the coal mines that run under the Arenberg Forest). It sounds far grander than it actually is, being no more than a wide street backing onto the Avenue, the main road out of the north-western side of town. Place Taffin is on the far side of the river Scheldt in the suburb of Saint-Vaast-le-Haut, which was presumably a community of its own in pre-industrial days. The critical point about the Place, as far as the 1976 Paris–Roubaix was concerned, would have been the parking space it provided for team cars as they waited for the peloton to arrive at the feed zone.

Leth is fond of the footage of the café, describing it as 'an LSD vision. We chose the locations deliberately. I knew this Café de la Place was the meeting place so I don't regret it, even though the wallpaper is crazy. The conversations in that café are so French, you have everything. You don't know what you will get – you only know the location, the place itself, but you can't guess how many gifts you will get in such a situation. Chance often smiles on you if you take chances.' The location, on the corner of the Place and the Avenue, is marked in a rough sketch in his notebook.

The director's decision to base a full crew here was inspired, and was prompted by Albert Bouvet, who explained to him that the race's second feed zone – the first was eighty-eight kilometres earlier, in the town of Saint Quentin – was where the bulk of the also-rans tended to abandon the race. As Jean-François Pescheux explained, Paris–Roubaix was a misnomer for many. The race actually boiled down to Paris–Valenciennes: 'For a lot of us that's all it was. If you were poorly placed at that [second] feed, if you'd punctured or just were behind for some reason – say you'd given a teammate a wheel – you knew

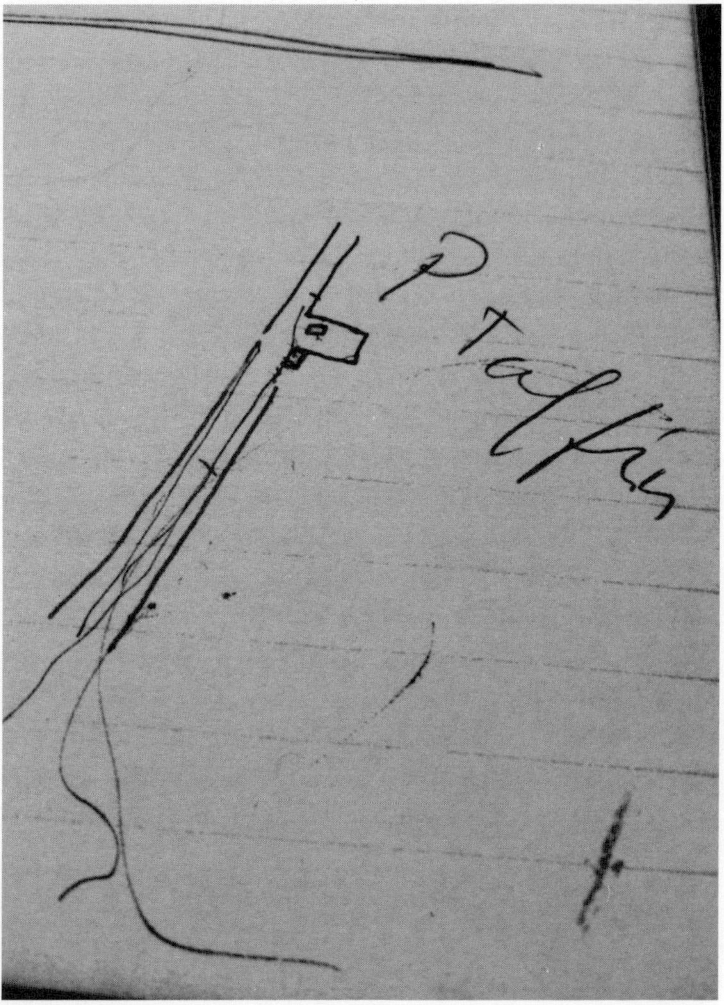

there were no more cars behind you, nothing at all in support. You couldn't take the risk of going any further because after the *ravito* at Valenciennes it would be almost the finish before you saw another car because that was the second feed. There would be no one behind you. You'd just have to find someone in the countryside to help you out.'

Even in the twenty-first century, riders still get lost amid the chaos of Paris–Roubaix. From the 2017 race, a video of the Italian Andrea Guardini trying to find his way to the finish along a motorway went viral. Guardini had got to the second feed and had been told by his team to ride across country to the finish, which is far easier said than done in these parts. He found his way onto the *autoroute*, where he was picked up by the police. In that respect, his experience was not dissimilar to that described by Pescheux over forty years earlier: 'When you punctured, if you missed out on a wheel you had to fend for yourself – hitch a lift off a spectator or just ride on the rim as far as the feed where the cars were. At that level you can see how basic it was. It's gone from an artisanal level to being a massive industry.'

It is not all epic heroics and bravura intensity. Like the earlier, intimate images of the broom wagon and the fans by the roadside, the feed station provides a small-scale, more human counterpoint. The *soigneurs* crane out into the road brandishing feed bags, riders dismount and are directed towards the team cars parked conveniently on Place Taffin. The Jobo team manager, resplendent in his orange tracksuit, has a mighty hissy fit over the strikers who have punctured the tyres of his support car.

We might assume he is a *soigneur*, but in fact he is Guy 1:08:20
Faubert, one of the senior members of the team (the *directeur sportif* who gives Jacques Boulas a wheel earl er is Christian Lapébie, son of 1929 Tour winner Roger). Leth merely uses his grumbles as part of the soundtrack; Faubert is telling the world he had 'four riders in the front group with Merckx and all the big riders, they have nothing [to eat] since the depart, barely a crumb for the whole of Paris–Roubaix. Nothing in their bellies and up the front with Merckx . . . *Incroyable,*

incroyable.' The point being that the earlier puncture to the team car had meant that it did not have time to get to the feed at Saint Quentin but instead has had no option but to come straight here.

'Some of them gave up long before Valenciennes.'

Leth's mission was not merely to create a work of art that would celebrate the heroic goings on in one particular Paris–Roubaix and turn them into modern-day myth. He also wanted to explain how the myth was created by showing the smallest details around it. 'My aim', he said of his cycling (and other) documentaries, 'was to ask how and why. It's not enough in my mind simply to admire a given achievement . . . the film is driven by my own curiosity. That is, there is something I myself want to know.' He has also said, 'I'm not motivated by moralising intentions. I simply want to explain something.' In other words, there is no message: it is all about the event and its depiction.

This curiosity is his trademark, his personal calling card: 'Show it to me and I want to explain it,' he said to me in September 2017. 'I don't do opinions. I study life with intense curiosity.' 'He is always curious,' said Camre. 'It's a very important asset.' That wide-eyed lust for learning about human beings harks back to Leth's background in anthropology – which he studied as a student – and his particular interest in the work of the anthropologist Bronislaw Malinowski, who he calls his 'hero' in the film *Notes on Love*. Leth also refers to Malinowski's book *The Sexual Life of Savages in North-Western Melanesia* [1929] as his 'bible'.

Discussing how he made *A Sunday in Hell*, Leth specifically told me, 'You do it like a little piece of anthropology.' He is adamant, however, that in his films he is not attempting to emulate the anthropologist's scientific studies of humanity (his interest in Malinowski, he said, is 'frivolous'); rather, to learn from his methods. 'What moves me is [Malinowski's] almost naïve relation to what he describes,' he explained. 'His straightforwardness and [his] way of describing things make him the romantic incarnation of the anthropologist sitting in a tent and looking at the natives. I've wanted to be someone who looks upon life with a sense of wonder, someone who asks the most awkward questions.'

To figure out what that translates to in terms of depicting men on bikes and all the stuff that goes on around them in *A Sunday in Hell*, it's best to turn the question around, and ask what the film would be like without that sense of wonder. Imagine it without Leth's ability to find every detail around the race interesting, be it the television producers wondering what time the finish will be at the Roubaix velodrome, the drinkers in the café in Valenciennes expounding their views of cycling over a brown beer or three, or Eddy Merckx tweaking his saddle height for the umpteenth time. None of this is treated as banal or everyday. Every detail becomes special because it relates to the central event, the act of human endeavour which Leth considers to be out of the ordinary.

The details count, but delving down to the smallest fragments of action calls for an artist with the ability to be the equivalent of the 'anthropologist sitting in a tent and looking at the natives'. It takes time and resources. 'You have to do it properly,' underlined Leth. The footage of the bar in Valenciennes is the example he gives of how this approach works at its best. 'You have to be there in the café for a long time, to get acquainted with these people – it's not like rushing in and going out again. That's not how you do it. You can't do it by sleight of hand.'

In the café, the feed zone, and in the broom wagon, there is the same intimacy as on the Brooklyn team's massage table or at the Sanson mechanic's work station. Aligning perfectly with Pescheux's recollections, Eduardo Gualazzini of Brooklyn (*dossard* number 6) and Serge Parsani of Bianchi (number 150 – and later a noted *directeur sportif*) have had to take a lift to the feed zone with a carful of cycling fans, who clearly believe that all their Christmases have come at once. Gualazzini is more concerned about where his wheels have got to as a girl in a Mondrian-design collar kisses him and filches his *casquette*. 'See you next year,' she says to the Ijsboerke rider with the pot belly and the Ray-Bans. Number 67, the solid near-veteran *flamand* Wilfried David, is not so sure he'll be back.*

1:09:54 Back in the café, the fans are expounding on their knowledge again, principally a craggy individual in a navy jersey, who is at least a little more sober than the Bobet fan we met earlier. He has come here every year for seven or eight years, he tells us between drags on his Gauloise. He fancies Moser for the win, but didn't see him because he was *distrait*, looking for Merckx.

'How does it compare to last year?'

'I have the feeling the race is a lot quicker.'

The *casquettes* lined up on the fans' heads speak for themselves – Miko, De Gribaldy, La France – although the random tam o'shanter remains unexplained. The Brooklyn rider who 'gave' the young lady his hat 'didn't abandon, he punctured', she insists to the interviewer. Her naïveté delighted Leth – and clearly made an impression as he

* David was killed in a car crash, together with his wife, in 2015.

went through the sound soon afterwards, as he recorded in his notebook the fact that she had described the rider who gave her the hat as '*un monsieur nommé Brooklyn*' – a rider called Brooklyn.

'I like the small scene with the girl who is explaining but she has everything wrong,' the director said. 'I love that scene, it has so much sweetness, so much enthusiasm. It's very pure in a way. It has so much innocence. Because I have several cameras in the location I can tell the truth of the story – the rider didn't give it to her, she took it from him ('Did he give it to you?' she is asked; 'Yes, he gave it to me,' she insists). His name wasn't Brooklyn, he was just a rider from Brooklyn. He didn't abandon, as she has it. I love all these small things.'

'What do you like about the race?' she is asked.

She is prompted from behind: 'The men.'

She giggles. And the fans starting singing over their beers.

The Café de la Place's former identity was clear as late as 2014, when another *Sunday in Hell* fan, Sir Bradley Wiggins, couldn't resist the temptation to go onto Google Streetview and locate it for me (for which I would like to thank him).

Most recently, it has been converted into a very basic sandwich-and-fried-chicken shop entitled Blé Delice. The walls are now painted plain white.

CHAPTER 9: FISHING FOR REALITY

> 'When we go out, we set a trap for reality . . . Things happen when they happen. We are just as clever and just as stupid as fishermen. We can go out when we like in any defined direction and sometimes we stumble over a magic moment. That is what we are searching for, but we must not be too eager or too sure of it.'
>
> *Jørgen Leth*

After the respite through Valenciennes, the 1976 Paris–Roubaix entered a fourth phase, where the intensity ratcheted up another notch. The race was not won in the sectors that followed, but here, as the final selection formed, it was lost: for Merckx, Maertens and Godefroot, as well as that perennial outside-chance-but-eventual-also-ran Raymond Poulidor and a more genuine hopeful in Walter Planckaert.

The cobbled sectors that preceded the old mining town had witnessed an initial sifting process. That in turn resulted in an elite selection of some forty riders who grabbed their *musettes* at the feed, then headed resolutely down Avenue Desandrouins to the bleak countryside around the villages of Wallers, Hornaing and Hasnon, '*where the paving stones of Hell start again*'.

Osler and De Muynck remained in the lead. Behind them in the lead peloton, Maertens, Merckx, Poulidor and Hennie Kuiper among others had expended valuable energy fighting their way back to the front group after punctures; Demeyer and Pollentier had had to help their leader, Maertens, along the way. Godefroot and Moser had ridden the perfect race – present and avoiding incident, yet saving their strength – while De Vlaeminck had raced quixotically, aware he was on a good day and unwilling to save his strength.

1:11.55 The cobbles of *l'Enfer du Nord* were encountered again on the section between the villages of Wallers and Hasnon. This is one of a handful of mid-race sections that feature in both the film and the present race (it was numbered 18 in 2017), and is one of the few where the *pavés* have been restored in recent years, solely for the race, at a cost of €1m. It also featured in the 2014 Tour de France, albeit in the opposite direction to that taken by Paris–Roubaix. It is easy to identify due to the footings of a disused railway bridge, featuring prominently in Leth's footage, which has recently been named Pont Gibus after the double French winner Gilbert Duclos-Lassalle. An embankment carried a railway long since closed, with a clear gap where the bridge used to carry the rails over the cobbled road; both sides of what used to be the bridge are now daubed with paint in honour of Duclos. Holmberg lists this as camera locations 8 and 9, with the wall of the old bridge listed as a possible position, in 'terrifying' *pavé*.

From Ron Goodman's perch in the Wesscam helicopter, and a camera perched on the level crossing that comes just before the former bridge, Leth provides two perspectives as Merckx can be seen leading the chase behind De Muynck and Ossler, who are caught not long after the end of this cobbled section. *'Merckx, as usual, has assumed the role all the others are keen to see him in . . . The lead position. Once in front he heads the pursuit like a locomotive . . . It falls into place for De Vlaeminck. Merckx has to ride hard behind the breakaway which De Vlaeminck has organised . . .'*

Reflecting the change of tempo after the second feed, Leth and his editor Lars Brydesen increase the pace and intensity from now until the end of the race, initially switching between images of Merckx attempting to *'break the others with his tremendous power'*, crashes – a Jobo rider wipes the blood off his head before we focus briefly and sickeningly on the massive open gash in his forehead – and punctures. There is drama everywhere. The interludes between sustained action become fewer; there are only two more of the extended takes that Leth so favours. Raymond Poulidor's cameo lasts fifteen seconds as 1:13:35
the 'Eternal Second' desperately waits for a wheel change. Few remember now that 'PouPou' was a regular at Paris–Roubaix, riding every year from 1960 to 1977 – his eighteen starts is a record. He finished eight times in the top twelve, with a highest placing of fifth, notching up at least a dozen punctures along the way, plus various broken bike parts, one disqualification for 'an irregular bike change' and several crashes. He told a *Vélo* magazine special on the race that he believed 1976 was 'the only time I had a chance of winning' but three punctures and a crash put paid to that. Hence his obvious anger. 'I've rarely been this cross. Instead of having to work to get back to the group, I would have been attacking. I was capable of it.' The explanation afterwards from his team was that they had not inflated their tyres to the correct pressure for the dry conditions; the low pressure used for wet roads meant that the tyres 'bottomed' out when ridden at speed over the cobbles.

In Leth's film we witness one moment in Poulidor's day. In fact, it is the tip of an iceberg of misfortune; but that gap between what we see and what actually happens is typical of a race where the confusion means so much remains hidden. In *l'Equipe*, the following morning, Jacques Goddet – presumably with an eye on the home market for his races and papers – went into PouPou's race in painful, exalted detail. His first puncture happened before the cobbles, his 'first return to the group, without a great deal of assistance, necessitated a pursuit of over forty kilometres, because the race was already in pieces. Managing to overtake around a hundred men spread across the countryside in the middle of a crazy mass of cars and motorbikes and regaining his place with the leaders was an exploit in itself.

'Suffering three more punctures, the third coming when the victim had just managed to get back to the front after the second, felt like a form of penance. The fourth incident [Goddet believes this was a puncture; later reports have it as a crash] looked like persecution. PouPou threw his wheel across the road, but repaired it again and set off again . . .'

This is the third of Poulidor's punctures, hence his anger, but the greater message of man afflicted by misfortune is what matters more. At twenty minutes to four – the repeated 1:14:20
returns to the timeline add to the building suspense, like the constant depiction of clocks in *High Noon* – we cut briefly back to the velodrome. The contrast is made between the relative calm at our destination and the intensity of the action on the road. Gendarmes prowl, track racers compete in the traditional warm-up events (Leth tipping his hat to his origins at the Aarhus velodrome?), a hawker flogs *casquettes*, the commentators limber up their vocal cords, and the fans listen intently to their radios.

> *'A few things have been happening in Hell. The Brooklyn breakaways have been overtaken and straight after a lone rider took off. It's Frenchman [Guy] Sibille who bravely takes his life in his hands. But he doesn't get very far.'*

Demeyer, with his mind on his team duties for his *kopman* Maertens, chases down Sibille together with Godefroot. Then come '*more mishaps*', including a significant faller in the previous weekend's Tour of Flanders winner Walter Planckaert. At this 1:16:38
crash close to the village of Marchiennes, sixty-one kilometres from the finish, the cameraman is Peter Roos, who, according to Herdel, had moved out onto the roof of the Brooklyn car to wield his little camera. The other team cars take to the bike path to avoid the fallers, who include the French champion Régis Ovion of Peugeot, and number 122, Régis Délépine from Gan-Mercier.

It is De Vlaeminck who begins the final sorting-out process 1:17:42
in the sections of cobbles around the village of Wattines

between forty-nine and forty kilometres to go. It is a classic surge of lung-bursting speed in his unique style, with his arms flat, hands on the brake levers. Moser's response is more brutal, but equally familiar: torso horizontal, fists in the drops of the handlebars, arms in line with the flat part of the bars, head inclined to the right. Behind the flat-out Maertens, the world of one-day Classic racing is summed up in a single image: the line of favourites struggling desperately to stay within reach of the wheel ahead. *L'Equipe* records that this phase eliminates second-string contenders such as the mercurial German Dietrich Thurau, Maertens's sidekick Pollentier, and the multiple Tour of Flanders winner Eric Leman.

It all takes place to a bubbling electronic soundtrack from Gunner Møller Pedersen, overlaid with his dramatic timpani. It is 'a fast-moving sound', the composer says. 'I had a very old, primitive rhythm box; I could turn the speed up and if I connected some of the programmes, turned it up very loud and put it through a wah-wah pedal – even played it backwards – you get the sound of things going very fast, flying across you, flying by.'

1:19:08 Suddenly, unexpectedly, the unthinkable happens. There are thirty-six kilometres to go, we are on a left-hand curve in the village of Templeuve, during a twelve-kilometre respite between the cobbled sections at Molpas and Nomain, where the final wave of *pavé* sectors begins.

'Now there is a new faller. It's Maertens.'

The crash that eliminates the favourite is – arguably – the key moment of the entire race, as it dictates the way the rest of the afternoon pans out, and helps to explain the identity of the eventual winner.

As with earlier moments, the way it is covered vindicates Leth and Holmberg's *modus operandi*, positioning cameramen everywhere they could and relying on the 'contract with chance'. Leth explains: 'We have the image from the top of the Brooklyn car where the camera is sitting – we have it when it happens, then the car continues; it has nothing to do with Maertens. Then the other camera, Constantini, who is there, he stops, he gets off the bike and tells the whole story: Maertens who can't get back up and can't continue.'

There is a screech of brakes as the Ijsboerke car (driven by one of the more unpredictable drivers among the *directeurs sportifs*, Willy Jossard) almost collides with Freddy, who lies on the floor in agony before being gently removed from the road in an attitude redolent of the crucified Christ being taken off the cross. Briefly, 'Harlequin' – he of the songs in the Flandria team hotel bar an hour or so ago in the film – appears in the picture, having jumped out of the Flandria car along with the mechanic to assist their *kopman*, to no avail; Van Springel and Pollentier also try to help.

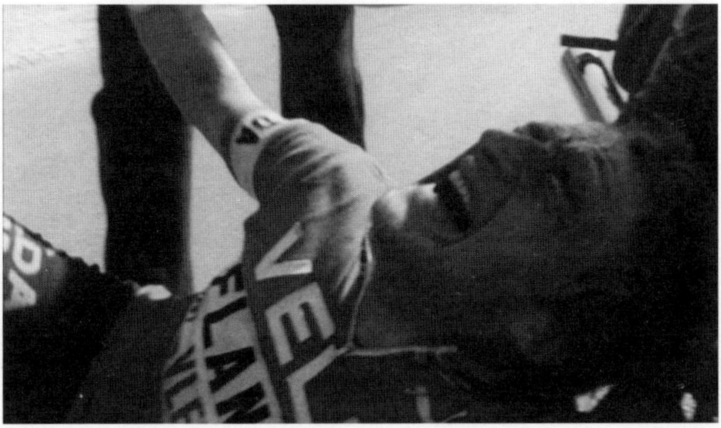

'A French television motorbike fell on me; it was at the front, taking pictures,' recalls Maertens. 'It's one of those things – the driver came and found me afterwards to apologise. But it had gone over my feet and my leg. What can you say? That's Paris–Roubaix.'

> *'The young Belgian star has no hope now of success.*
> *The race is over for the man considered the top favourite.*
> *Maertens sadly ends the race as a passenger in the*
> *doctor's car.'*

With Maertens disconsolately out of the race, the focus switches suddenly to Godefroot, a regular Classic winner who is often overlooked in comparison to the towering figure of Merckx, the glowering De Vlaeminck and the tragi-comic Maertens. At thirty-two, Godefroot was a near-veteran, old enough to recall the days before Albert Bouvet's restructured 1968 route; he had won Paris–Roubaix in 1969, and had found early in his career that the cobbles suited him.

'I was better on the *pavé* than on the tarmac. On the *pavé*, you get a kick through your legs that drives you along; when you get back on the tarmac your legs feel blocked, you search for the perfect *coup de pédale*. Then you get back onto the cobbles and get the kick again. That was why I liked Paris–Roubaix. I never wore gloves, never put extra padding on the bars, never wore a crash hat. I didn't need them. There were no tactics; when you are good, you ride in the middle of the cobbles. But I punctured a lot.'

1:20:13 Godefroot is captured in a sequence shot by Paul Constantini, one of the mysterious cameraman's finest pieces of work. As well as his use of a smaller, lighter, more manoeuvrable camera, the French cameraman could do something else. Leth explains:

'[He] had another trick up his sleeve, unknown to us, which he could have shared – he was shooting with delay, thirty or thirty-one frames not twenty-four frames per second, slightly slow-motion. It gave him the [chance to] make a very fluid quality in the images. The idea of slowing down the shooting was great. He was an artist, no doubt about it.

'Constantini gave me images that I couldn't have gotten in any other way than by his extremely personal and I'd say daring way. He was an acrobat. What he shot from the motorbike was extraordinary. For example: Godefroot's watch dancing on his arm, the vibrations on arms and legs, the chain moving in slow motion. In these images you get a sense of how vibrations travel though the limbs and body.'

Slow motion remains a predilection of Constantini's: as he discusses his work today, he mentions a shot in which he has slowed a tennis player's action to 400 frames per second: 'as you see the tennis ball arrive on the racket, you can see the ball flatten out and the racket strings deforming as it strikes . . .' It is classic technique known as 'overcranking'.

For the Godefroot sequence, the camera is not particularly steady, and it has a couple of streaks of dirt on the lens, but Constantini gets close in. The 'Bulldog of Flanders's' hair flows in the wind, his eyes lack protective glasses, the muscles of his arms work in counter-motion to his legs, his hands are bare (he never wore gloves except if it was snowing) and most distinctive of all, that watch bounces up and down as his body and bike are battered by the cobbles.

More than forty years on, Godefroot still remembers the watch; the makers' name, Rodania, is visible on the strap. He had a sponsorship deal with the company (which also sponsored the lead car in many Belgian races, with its own ear-wormy jingle) and the same watch can be seen on his wrist in photographs from later in his career. Godefroot says now, 'I was never, ever without my watch.' He recalls a Seiko earlier in his career, bought at the Tokyo Olympics.

He has good reason to hark back to his timepieces. Before the invention of the cycle computer, he says, the watch was a vital source of accurate information amid the confusion that turned most bike races into a game of blind man's buff on two wheels.

'You had no way of calculating the distance, so you worked it out through time. You didn't know exactly where you were, so you would figure out, perhaps, that you had done two or three hours, at forty kilometres per hour, and the first feed might be, perhaps, at 120 kilometres. You would learn to feel if you were going quick or slow and work from there.' This would probably be done from a simple, long-forgotten expedient: whether the downtube gear lever had been predominantly forward, on a high gear, or pushed back, on a lower ratio for a slower speed.

'You had a piece of paper in plastic with the distance of the cobbled sections written on it; you knew the route, you worked

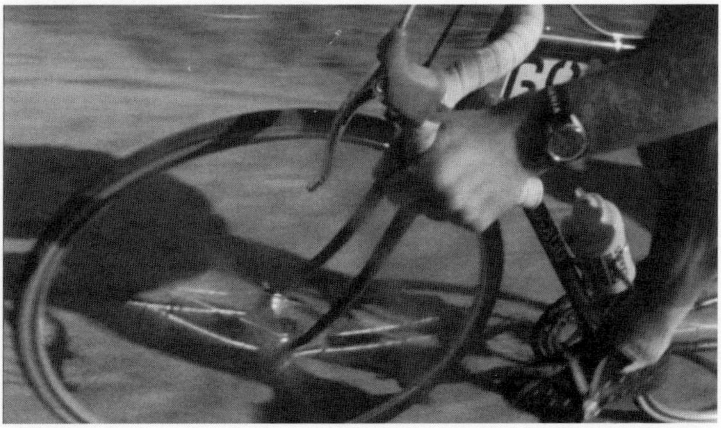

from your watch using the speed, and the team cars came up to talk to you all the time, because there were many fewer cars in the convoy, so it was all less complex. A lot of it came down to the reflexes that came with experience, but all the Classics are like that.'

'Now it is his turn to force the pace so it hurts.' It is Godefroot who sparks the winning break in the cobbles between the villages of Nomain and Bachy – almost five kilometres of *pavé* which have now been tarmacked over – with his effort drawing De Vlaeminck and Hennie Kuiper in his wake. Ron Goodman in the Wesscam helicopter captures the human moment: De Vlaeminck looks back, sees no sign of Merckx or Maertens (we know he has crashed; does the Gypsy?), and makes the instantaneous decision to press on.

The quartet is joined by Moser, whose immense power – and 1:21:25
courage in the way he drives his bike across the *pavé* – is captured as he speeds between Raymond Poulidor and Jean-Pierre Danguillaume. The fact Poulidor is there at all after his earlier issues speaks volumes for his form, the day before his fortieth birthday. The French pair flounder as they attempt

briefly to hold Moser's wheel. *'His distinctive style, his still, aerodynamic position on the bicycle is an imposing sight of almost effortless rotary action.'* It's something most competitive cyclists can relate to: force so superior as the rival goes past that you can only look on and wonder.

What we don't know is that Danguillaume is struggling with a broken back wheel, which he did not want to change. Afterwards, he complained that he had spent fifteen kilometres just fifty metres behind the leaders – a slight exaggeration as Leth's pictures would later show – and that he would have made contact with Moser, Demeyer, De Vlaeminck, Godefroot and Kuiper without the bent back wheel touching his brake blocks and slowing him down. He had faced the classic dilemma: chase with defective equipment, or stop and lose everything.

There is one more twist as the winning break forms. Godefroot is philosophical now about the number of times he punctured in Paris–Roubaix. He is resigned to the capricious way in which fate points the finger in this race. 'I always punctured at bad moments. The year I won I punctured. I was in a small peloton of about fifteen, I think, I slipped to the back, survived to the end of the section, then the team car came at once and I got the change. I got back to the group, and Erik De Vlaeminck asked why I was riding at the back. No one saw that I had the puncture. Other times, you wait several minutes.'

This time, he is out of luck. When Godefroot's front tyre goes down on a right-hand bend, the Ijsboerke car is stuck behind the chasing group containing Merckx and company. As far as winning is concerned, his race is over. *'A real disaster for him and so another man's chance has gone.'*

Back in the Brooklyn team car, there is confusion, briefly, 1:22:45
as Cribiori and the *commissaire* try to work out who is in the front group, partly by a process of elimination ('Moser is not there,' they agree, referring to the chase group in front of them which contains Merckx and Willy Teirlinck among others; they can't see Moser in front of them, hence he must be in the break). It's a situation that has occurred in countless team cars in countless races at all levels; that moment when the race radio simply won't say precisely who is where.

However, the final selection has formed: *'The Italian Moser, the rival Belgians De Vlaeminck and Demeyer, the Dutchman Kuiper in the world champion's rainbow jersey, these are the four who have gained for themselves a vital position.'*

In 2003, Leth collaborated with his fellow countryman, fellow director and former pupil Lars von Trier on a film entitled *The Five Obstructions*. It was an astonishing, experimental project, which rightly made headlines: von Trier commissioned the old master to remake his 1967 film, *The Perfect Human*. The twist was that Leth had to work within impediments dictated by von Trier – the 'Obstructions' – for example shooting in the 'most miserable place' that Leth could imagine.

Among the 'Obstructions' was one which had deep resonance for Leth and lovers of his work. It was a truly mischievous stroke by von Trier: Leth would be permitted to hold no single shot for longer than twelve frames. The director's love of the long, uninterrupted image can be seen throughout his work: the single shot that makes up most of *Ophelia's Flowers*, the *pavé* in *Eddy Merckx in the Vicinity of a Cup of Coffee*, the lengthy frontal sequences as Peter Martins dances.

'It was torture but it was fun,' recalls Leth of the 2003 challenge. 'I mastered it. He knew my softest point. It was playful for both of us. It was a flattering move, to take me down from my pedestal.'

The long take is something that Leth traces back to inspirations such as Jean-Luc Godard, Andy Warhol and Carl Dreyer. The value of the technique is seen in David Thomson's* description in his book *The Big Screen*, of a scene in Godard's film *Vivre Sa Vie*. The character played by the lead actress Anna Karina is writing an application to join the staff of a brothel. ' . . . It takes time,' wrote Thomson. 'As one watched this scene for the first time in 1962 it was impossible not to think, "Ah a letter-writing scene. He'll show the start of the action and then he'll cut to the finished letter . . . a couple of shots and editing them together. That is how movie works." But then you watched and the action of writing stretched out in time. It became the scene . . . Godard was saying, just look at the now of it, look at her presence, her being.'

Thomson describes Godard as 'in love with the primacy of seeing, of an age before [camera] angles when we were amazed.' This closely resembles Leth's ability to see a scene with new eyes, wide open in wonder, which underpins so much of *A Sunday in Hell*. 'The part of a film I enjoy the most is when one can feel time flow through a single scene,' wrote Leth. 'There should always be room for time. A film should breathe naturally.' And it goes back to the anthropologist's desire to watch things happen without comment or

* British-born, US-based, Thomson is a veteran film critic, who has been described as 'the greatest living writer on the movies' with more than twenty books to his credit.

criticism; as Leth said in a 2003 interview: 'I'm an observer, not a participant'.

The director's love of the unbroken frame was key to his and Holmberg's vision for the day's filming. Their initial plan was for every camera at every roadside location to make sure to film the entire passage of the race. 'We were very particular. We wanted always the camera to stay, watch the action pass, and count down the seconds between different groups or riders as they came through,' said Leth. 'Real-time is so important. The idea is not to cut it up into bits and pieces as the modern style of filming action requires. I really like long shots. That's what this kind of story-telling deserves and needs. That was a very big point, but it was only done once.'

The only cameraman who managed to fulfil Leth and Holmberg's vision was Henning Camre, who was a fan of the restricted approach that experimental film-making imposed. 'I had a different point of departure – still photography, architecture. There, there is no compromise, it matters where you direct the camera.'

The instructions that he and Holmberg gave the cameramen were specific: they should keep the camera running as long as possible. 'Many cameramen get confused, they think, "OK the riders have passed now we have to take a different shot."'

Camre's extended moment comes after the escape forms, 1:25:48
as the quartet cements its lead through the cobbles, with the crowds craning forward to watch them pass; a couple of the braver spectators have climbed the electricity pylons for a better view. The motorbike comes first; then the four spectral figures in the dust – Moser to the left, De Vlaeminck to the right, in the centre Demeyer concealing Kuiper. *'The four breakaways, how big an advantage do they have?'* The team cars pass, and Saunders counts down the time: *'Ten seconds, fifteen, twenty,*

twenty-five . . .' as the dust cloud slowly subsides, and the bubbling electronic soundtrack resurfaces.

There is time for one or two spectators to cross the road before the next motorbike arrives (just as in Godard's *Vivre Sa Vie*, we have the extended opening take of Karina shot from behind, with cars and people crossing the line of vision). Then comes '*a single rider*' Jean-Pierre Danguillaume and the Peugeot team car, about forty-five seconds behind; again, the dust clears before Merckx, Jan Raas, Godefroot and Teirlinck and the rest of the chasers pass, roughly a minute in arrears.

It is, says Camre, 'the shot that is the most important . . . It's used full length in the film, exactly the way it was done – we wanted more of that kind.'

'That's the only scene in the film that exemplifies my plan: to measure time with one unbroken frame,' Leth told me. 'He's doing exactly what I asked him to do – he's not being confused by the riders passing, he keeps the frame [on the cobbles] shooting even after the riders pass, and that way you get the real time between the lead group and the chasing group. Choose your frame and stay with it. Simple, but seemingly not so easy to maintain.'

And not so easy or simple to create. Camre was being driven down the course between his appointed locations when he decided to innovate. 'There are lots of things you mustn't do and one of them is you mustn't drive against the race, but I made my driver do it,' recalled Camre. 'I realised this could be an interesting shot, which is why I persuaded my driver to do it. I thought, "This is where I have to be." That shot was not planned. It was an opportunity that I saw. I knew they would have to pass there, and there would probably be a split in the group.'

'Most of [the cameramen], the Danes as well as the French, were impatient,' said Leth. 'They think, "I have made one great frame; while we wait for the [next] riders to come I can make it a little bit different." It still came out well in the end but there were lots of situations where it was not done as we had decided.'

'We didn't have a lot of time to instruct people,' recalled Camre. 'We were probably a bit naïve about how easy it would be. We needed a hell of a lot of cameramen, most of them came from Belgium and France and it was hard to get them to understand what Jørgen actually wanted.'

1:27:21 Shortly afterwards, the same phalanx of motorbikes and team cars that was shot by Camre concertina into each other after a motorbike fails to make it around a right-hander. *'On these misshapen roads, in these dust clouds, a lot can happen.'* Indeed. This is also Albert Bouvet's moment in the limelight. Leth doesn't name him: in the context of the film he is merely one element in a sequence shot in real-time that depicts the build-up, colour and chaos as the race passes. But it is Bouvet who jumps off his motorbike and waves his lollipop baton frenetically to get the whole caravan moving again before Jean-Pierre Danguillaume, Eddy Merckx, Walter Godefroot and all the others pile into their rear bumpers.

The chaotic scene ends as the official leaps back onto his motorbike, just about making it with a bit of a scramble; the bike is poorly parked on the exit from the bend and Danguillaume comes close to colliding with it, to Bouvet's obvious consternation. Merckx and his group come next as

Gunner Møller Pedersen's tuba barps mournfully in the background. A process of elimination suggests this is somewhere between Bourghelles and Carrefour de l'Arbre, in the final long stretch of cobbles before the run-in to the finish.

Now a vital part of the modern Paris–Roubaix, 'the Junction of the Tree' is an isolated spot in flat fields between the A27 motorway to the north, the Belgian border to the east and the Lille–Brussels TGV line to the south. The vast agglomeration of Lille looms to the north-east. The crossroads, *le carrefour*, is named after a red-brick restaurant, which takes its name from a clump of about twenty poplar trees to one side of the restaurant; when viewed from a distance, they give the impression of being one single vast tree. The restaurant, renamed l'Arbre Gastronomique, is well appointed now but in the 1960s, Albert Bouvet recalled, it had no electricity and was thus without a fridge, so the *patronne* would go down to the cellar to collect a cold beer when he passed on reconnaissance missions.

Compared to the current route, in 1976 the riders faced a different approach. In the twenty-first century, the race reaches l'Arbre via the slightly rising section of cobbles leading out of Camphin-en-Pévèle – the strategically critical five-star rated sector known as Carrefour de l'Arbre which has been in the route since 1980. In 1976, the race used the Chemin de Bourghelles, which arrives at the junction between the clump of poplars and the restaurant to the right of the track from Camphin-en-Pévèle. It is advertised as a mountain-bike route and is still cobbled – if not in a particularly good state – but has been cut in two by a railway line. After crossing the main D90 road, the 1976 race re-joins the current course on the cobbles of Gruson, where there are patches of blue slate setts among the granite.

The location is only part of the story. This is a glorious vignette, a tiny moment that sums up the confusion and organised chaos that accompanies any bike race, a classic example of Leth's 'contract with chance'. As he would put it: 'In our work we are armed with our instinct, our eyes and ears. We concentrate on empty space as well as occupied space. We observe silence and noise. We trust in chance's limitless gifts and yet the place in which we find ourselves isn't necessarily a product of chance. The moment suddenly comes when we are no longer astonished by its appearance. We are ready to capture it. We don't know where it will lead us.'

In other words, his cameramen are on the spot, they do what feels right at the time, and – on occasion – they are rewarded.

As for the race behind the lead quartet . . . *'There are only twelve riders in the* [*chase*] *group with Merckx. The rest are scattered in the dust.'*

CHAPTER 10: THE "FINAL"

> *'Moser and De Vlaeminck are doing all the work in the lead group. They are the ones making sure the distance between them and their pursuers is constantly increasing. Neither Demeyer or Kuiper take the lead – they are just hanging on, or are they being crafty and saving their strength?'*

Alongside Leth's 'heroes' De Vlaeminck and Moser, and the Flandria man Demeyer, the leading quartet included one unexpected member: Hennie Kuiper. Leth had not included him in the 'heroes' that his cameramen were to shoot on the day before the race, but that was understandable. Kuiper had ridden strongly in Paris–Roubaix before, but never this well. That was a pattern: he had strength and tactical expertise but flew under the radar year after year, never quite enjoying the elevated profile of the biggest stars, but notching up a string of major victories from 1972 to 1988 that give him an extremely enviable *palmarès*. That includes Paris–Roubaix, the Tour of Lombardy, Milan–San Remo and the Tour of Flanders: four of the five Classics ranked as 'monuments' of the sport.

Kuiper would, however, have been well known to his colleagues in the break: De Vlaeminck and Moser had figured in the chasers when he won the world title the previous August in the Belgian town of Yvoir, taking full advantage of the fact that he had two Dutch teammates to mark the Gypsy, the

Sheriff and the inevitable Merckx, plus, *inter alia*, the Tour de France winner of that year, Bernard Thévenet. He had taken the rainbow jersey in one of the solo breaks that were his trademark – a similar move had given him the Olympic title in 1972 in Munich. This year, he felt he had to prove he was worthy of his new status.

Now sixty-eight, back then he was part of the 'new generation' that would succeed Merckx, De Vlaeminck and Godefroot; later, he would face a dilemma over whether to devote his attention to the Tour de France – where he finished second in 1977 – or the Classics, which would be his focus from 1981. His origins were somewhat different to his fellow Classic stars, however: from Eastern Holland, he had not grown up to a background where cobbled Classics were paramount. His first acquaintance with *pavé* had come when he was nineteen and made a convoluted journey – bike, train, then a long drive in a car with a fellow cyclist – across Holland and Belgium. It had rained and thundered, the *pavé* had been like a skating rink, and he had finished dead last. But he was hooked.

Riding for the small German team Rokado, he had also finished way behind in his first attempts at the Tour of Flanders and Paris–Roubaix, coming in half an hour down each time; riding to Roubaix for the second time, in 1974, he had figured in a break for 120 kilometres. He would tackle the Hell of the North fourteen times, and it would take him until 1983 to win it. 'I came from a part of Holland where there were no professional cyclists, no one to learn from. So I had to learn. My mindset was fantastic though; I never wanted to quit.' In 1976 he had moved up to the TI-Raleigh squad run by his fellow Dutchman Peter Post, and his career had turned a corner: 'I was the world champion; all the journalists, all the newspapers were looking at me, so I had to be serious, show the jersey, fight as best I could.'

1976 was one of his better years: he was close to the win in the opening Classic, Het Volk, then finished second in Paris–Nice, and he would come close to winning the Tour of Spain a few weeks after that Paris–Roubaix. He also gave TI-Raleigh its first Tour de France stage win that July, beginning a run of Tour successes that would last into the 1980s. The Dutch-run squad, backed by the legendary British bike maker, is remembered as one of cycling's greatest ever teams. Post's philosophy was a new one known as 'total cycling'; his teams did not rely on a single leader as those of Merckx, Moser and De Vlaeminck did, but brought together a number of all-rounders who would work for the best rider on any given day. That year, Raleigh included talents such as Kuiper and his fellow Dutchmen Gerrie Knetemann and Jan Raas, who can be seen fleetingly as the battle in Hell came to the boil in 1976.

A legend of track cycling – and the winner of an extremely fast Paris–Roubaix in 1964 – Post's strength was his personality, which enabled him to bring a group of ambitious individuals together and make them unite in a common cause. 'He was a good man, but not a psychologist,' recalls Kuiper. 'He wasn't the best at dealing with the riders, but he was a good organiser, and for me what mattered was that he had discipline. We were all young, and sometimes when you win something big, you start to think that you are a big champion, but with Post, every time you got on the start line you had to start from zero. He opened everyone's eyes.'

With Post behind him in the TI-Raleigh car, Kuiper had got through the early phases of his fourth Paris–Roubaix in good shape. He doesn't recall his earlier puncture, and he feels there must be a good reason for that: 'If I don't remember it, that's because it wasn't a hard chase to get back on, so I was going well.' Now, he remembers a dry, dusty race (the one he would win, in 1983, was one of the wettest and muddiest editions), run at high speed, with a surprisingly large group of riders staying together until relatively close to the finish. When Godefroot made his effort to pull away the final move, Kuiper was in the right place. 'It was a big acceleration. I was about tenth in line. The pace he set was so fast that I didn't need to look back. I knew I was in a break with a handful of riders. Then Godefroot punctured, and we were four in front.'

With Leth sitting in his car, powerless to affect events as they unfolded, the cameramen such as Constantini, Holmberg and Camre were able to work as they saw fit, with both the upsides and downsides implied by that, the hits and the misses. Another who did not fit into the conventional mould was the Canadian Ron Goodman, who had been hired to work the Wesscam* helicopter-mounted camera, then a piece of technology in its infancy. As the race reached its climax, and Leth's motorbike cameramen struggled to work at the

* Within cycling, the generic term for a helicopter mounted gyroscopically controlled camera is Wescam, but in fact this is only one of a number of such devices on the market; the current company L-3 WESCAM stems from the offshoot of Westinghouse which initially produced the camera, and markets them principally for military surveillance. The camera was first marketed as Wesscam – Westinghouse Steered Stabilized Camera Mount. Current similar models include Cineflex, Shooter and Goodman's own Spacecam. Recently, drones have increasingly been used for work which would previously have been the province of helicopter-mounted systems and this trend is set to continue.

front of the race, for various reasons, Goodman and his 'bubble' became more important.

The 'bubble' camera under the helicopter was a radical innovation and Goodman was one of only a couple of operators in the world. The 'bubble' was the fibreglass mounting for a helicopter-mounted, remotely operated, gyroscopically stabilised camera, which is now integral to television coverage of cycle races. In 1976, however, few had imagined what it could offer to a sport such as professional road cycling, where the backdrop varies constantly and the participants change direction incessantly.

'The whole system was pretty new at the time,' says Holmberg. 'There were older systems but they involved a camera operator sitting halfway outside the helicopter. I used to do it on the cheap: remove the door of the helicopter, tape yourself and the safety belt really well, then sort of hang out of the door opening with the camera on your shoulder.'

The critical quality of the Wesscam was its stability: kept in place by gyroscopes, the stillness of the camera meant that it could be used for lengthy single takes using cine-quality film. It could focus in tightly on a subject from the air, then zoom out in a single shot to put its subject in perspective. The contrast with what went before is relatively simple to see: before interviewing Hennie Kuiper, I had a quick look at the television footage of his world-championship victory in August 1975. There are helicopter images, but the focus barely changes, and the riders appear as tiny dots on a blurred screen.

Leth had a good idea of what the new technology might enable him to do in his film. 'What you gain compared to early helicopter shots is clarity, the possibility of zooming, as you see in the shots of the peloton in the landscape – first very

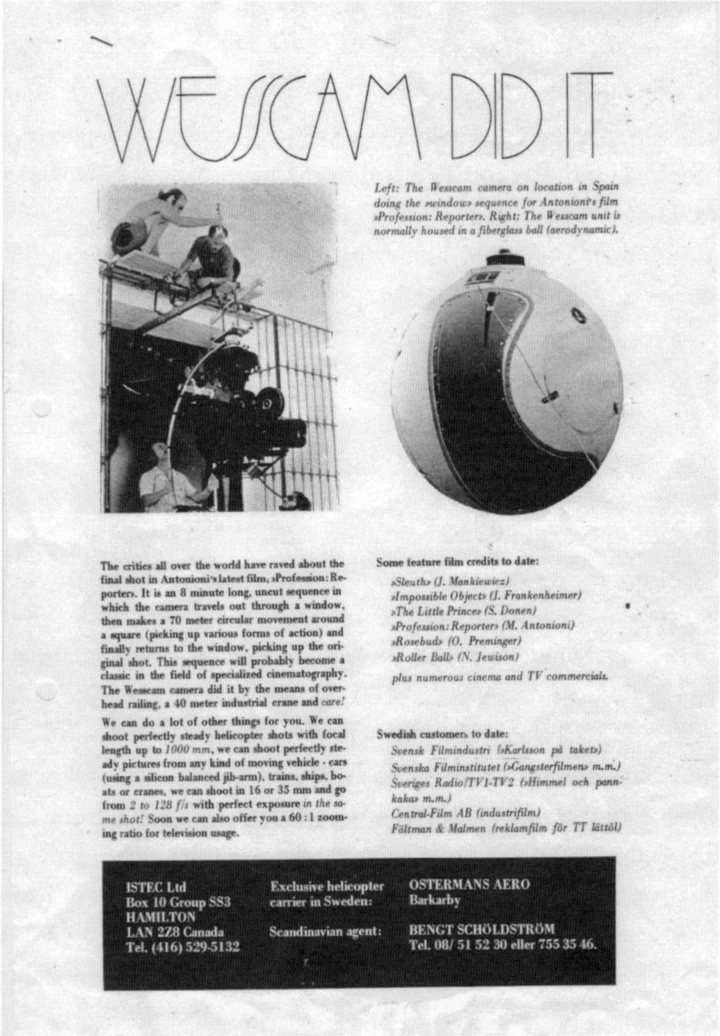

small, then going close in in one shot without cutting to another shot,' said Leth. 'That's wonderful, it's part of the poetic quality of the film. The helicopter shots were a very unique thing at the time for their quality.'

The camera's makers were also aware of the device's potential. 'Wesscam Did It' states the publicity flyer, with the picture of what looks suspiciously like a tennis ball alongside a shot of a group of technicians with a Heath Robinson-esque device perched on a beam. The rate card is in the DFI Archive: USD$1,150 per day for the HC32 camera with a crew of two; $1,850 for the HC33, half that for reconnaissance and travel days; daily expenses of $35 per day per person.

The gyroscope-stabilised camera mount for a helicopter had been dreamed up by a Canadian branch of the military technology firm Westinghouse (hence its name), to be used to observe what was happening on battlefields. Using 35mm film, it was adopted during the 1960s to a limited extent for films including the blockbuster *Tora! Tora! Tora!* Goodman had grown up close to the factory in Hamilton, Canada, where the Wesscam was made and during a lengthy stay in Europe eventually reworked the original system and began marketing the system in its own right.

The blurb on the flyer states, 'critics all over the world have raved about the final shot in [Michelangelo] Antonioni's latest film, *Profession: Reporters* [later renamed *The Passenger*]. It is an 8 minute long, uncut sequence in which the camera travels out through a window, then makes a 70 meter circular movement around a square (picking up various forms of action) and finally returns to the window. This sequence will probably become a classic . . .'

This 'seven-minute take that has seldom been equalled' – as Derek Malcolm put it in his 'Century of Film' series for the *Guardian* – was Goodman's work, and it certainly inspired Leth. Goodman recalls using between 30 and 40 feet of garage door tracking as a slider, with a trolley to carry the Wesscam up to the window, and a quick release so that it could be transferred seamlessly from the crane cable to the trolley. In their pitches to the DFI and putative sponsors, both Leth and the DFI consultant Morten Piil made much of the visual potential of the Wesscam, with good reason, and to their ultimate credit.

'The guy in charge of it was Robert Pilkington of the glass company; they had two of the cameras, but one had been destroyed falling off a rig,' recalls Goodman. 'Pilkington lost interest so I let Westinghouse know I wanted to work with them. Then I was let loose on the road in Europe for fourteen years; *A Sunday in Hell* was a short job among hundreds, and not one of the major ones.' For Goodman, who went on to shoot aerial sequences in numerous other films, most notably *The Empire Strikes Back*, *Return of the Jedi* and *Superman*, Leth's film was not a massively memorable job in the context of half a century of aerial photography, but for cycling it was revolutionary.

'I'm very proud of this,' says Leth. 'This was a new system – it's absolutely integral. The bubble-balanced camera – the camera suspended in a glass bubble under the helicopter – was an innovation at that time. It was a fantastic find, never been used before [at a bike race]. We read about it and had heard about it – we looked into it, from the production side, and later it was adopted by SFP.' The production company SFP (Société Française de Production) was hived off from the French national broadcaster ORTF and is now responsible for supplying live images from the Tour de France and other major races.

The helicopter was a minor bugbear for Leth and his producers from the start. There was negotiation with the Société du Tour de France over which chopper could be used – initially there was the chance of a place in one sponsored by

Stella Artois – before the Danes opted to rent Goodman's Alouette. 'It needed fuel, of course,' recalled Herdel. 'We couldn't get permission for it to refuel anywhere official, so we had to put barrels of fuel and a pump out in various places, just put it there and hope. Nothing happened.' The Wesscam didn't fit in the helicopter initially, according to Herdel, 'and we had to get approval from the authorities to use it with the doors off'.

Goodman was one of only two cameramen in Europe who could work the Wesscam at the time. Holmberg recalls that he 'drove a van up from Switzerland with the ball with the camera inside; the producer started to talk shooting with him, but got interrupted immediately: "I'm tired, take me to my room so I can take a shower, let me eat something, give me some money up front and then we talk."'

With the protective fibreglass housing around the workings, the contraption used in 1976 was massive in size, a sphere almost 1.5m across – a current device might be 45cm – and it weighed over 90 kilograms. 'It was bigger and generally more crude,' says Goodman. 'It was based on mechanical gyroscopes, now it would be fibre optics. One of the reasons that I redesigned it was that I couldn't get the subtle movements that I wanted.' This boiled down to the fact that the Wesscam had come from the military: on a battlefield aesthetics are not relevant; soldiers just want images of what is out there.

There were limitations for the cameraman with such an unwieldy device, which was controlled from a joystick within the helicopter, with the operator looking at the images on a small video screen. 'You could steer it 360 degrees, and pan continuously. You could look 90 degrees straight down and 30 to 40 degrees upwards from the horizontal. It was very sensitive, but the video was grainy black and white, and it wasn't easy to use because half of the image was what you were seeing, half wasn't.'

Actually mounting the camera on the helicopter was the major issue. Goodman possessed the only side-mounted bracket in the world at the time. His first job in Europe had been with the Swiss Army, and a group of their engineers custom-built him a bracket for an Alouette 3 helicopter, after which he persuaded them to pass it on to him. 'It gave tremendous flexibility. Before that, we were carrying the camera on a cable from the cargo hook – you couldn't just land for refuelling because you needed ground crew to take the camera off as you landed.'

Holmberg's itinerary for Goodman offers a guide to possible scenic shots as far as the village of Busigny, not far before the first stretch of cobbles at Neuvilly. Entry a) refers to the village of Choisy-au-Bac, forty-six kilometres into the race, and reads: 'Still picture against the river and bridge. Backlight!!! Then moving over the village. Start: right-left.'

His instructions were specific; clearly Holmberg has attempted to envisage how the route will appear from the air as he drives it. ('Through the woods . . .' he writes. 'What does it look like?') The fuelling station is at an airfield near the village of Roupy. Classic French treelined avenues, backlit shots, possible cross winds splitting the field, attractive villages; these are Goodman's initial targets before the race gets serious at the Neuvilly cobbles.

If the images sound familiar, that's because they reflect pretty much how a Wescam-mounted helicopter would cover a major bike race today. Leth points to the significance of the Wesscam in several areas: this was an early major project involving a lengthy single-day shoot where aerial work provided

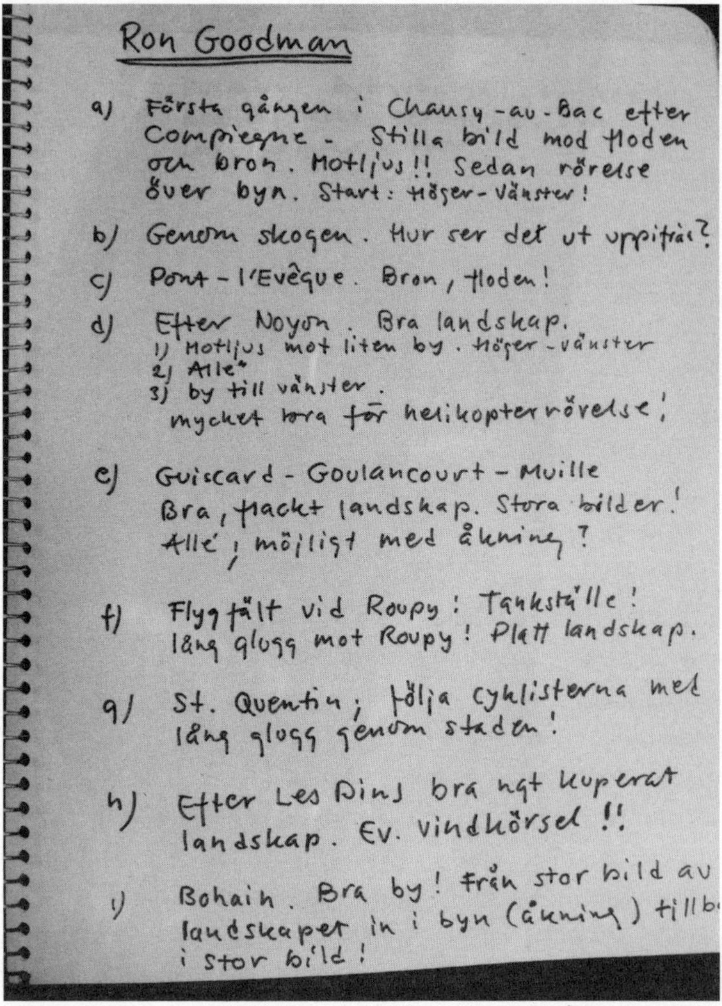
Ron Goodman

a) Första gången: Chaussy-au-Bac efter Compiègne - Stilla bild mod floden och bron. Motljus!! Sedan rörelse över byn. Start: höger-vänster!

b) Genom skogen. Hur ser det ut uppifrån?

c) Pont-l'Evêque. Bron, floden!

d) Efter Noyon. Bra landskap.
1) Motljus mot liten by. höger-vänster
2) Alle*
3) by till vänster.
mycket bra för helikopterrörelse!

e) Guiscard - Goulancourt - Muille
Bra, flackt landskap. Stora bilder!
Allé, möjligt med åkning?

f) Flygfält vid Roupy: Tankställe!
lång glugg mot Roupy! Platt landskap.

g) St. Quentin; följa cyklisterna med lång glugg genom staden!

h) Efter Les Dins bra ngt kuperat landskap. Ev. vindkörsel!!

i) Bohain. Bra by! Från stor bild av landskapet in i byn (åkning) tillb
i stor bild!

a key additional perspective, meaning that for the innovation itself 'so early in its development it was a big thing for them to succeed'. There was scepticism among directors, so Goodman recalls, and the device itself gained credibility for the way it worked so well in *A Sunday in Hell*.

Goodman's work first appears half an hour into the film, with images of the peloton from the side, as the helicopter tracks the bunch at the same speed. A few minutes later it provides a spectacular image of the peloton from above, snaking through curves, followed closely by the gloriously pastoral vision of the race crossing the river Aisne in Choisy-au-Bac. The device's potential is clearly seen at the second demonstration near Saint Quentin: the camera zooms out and back in to show the general situation as well as the human details of what Leth terms 'chaos'. Later, briefly, we have the sumptuous foreshortened vision of a different kind of 'chaos', the type envisaged by the race organisers and dreamed of by the fans as the race threads through clouds of dust in the cobbles between Neuvilly and Inchy.

The development of cycling over the last thirty years owes much to such helicopter shots. In the twenty-first century, the Tour de France and other major races – 'created by journalists, glorified by television', as the Tour's head Christian Prudhomme put it – are massively dependent on the type of dramatic visual images of the peloton amidst scenery that a helicopter-mounted camera can capture: great bridges, desolate mountainsides, high plateaux and bright yellow sunflower fields. Tourist authorities want the Tour and other major events to visit their regions so that their scenic splendours can be transmitted to the world in a giant marketing exercise. Crucially, for the economic well-being of the sport, they will pay for this.

The work of the Wescam, refined over the years, is integral when it comes to marketing cycling. The Tour de France route is now specifically planned to include scenic backdrops – the gorges of the Ardeche, the hairpins of Montvernier, the Mont-Saint-Michel – to appear on television screens. It has also been recognised that since the scenic side of television coverage began to gain importance, a whole new audience has emerged, one that does not have much interest in the actual racing, but which loves to see the scenic side of the Tour. People watch the Tour and other races and book holidays on the back of what they see.

This started in around 1990; in other words, Leth was a dozen years ahead of the rest of the cycling world in the way he used the Wesscam. The producer who brought the fresh scenic focus to the Tour and other races was Régis Fourissier, who worked at the Tour from 1990 to 1996. The Wescam entered the fray in the mid-1980s, he recalls.

'I remember discussing it with the producer who preceded me; I felt they showed only the race, they didn't show a great deal of interest in what was around the race – they would show the peloton, the riders, the break and so on. The Wescam was used more as an additional motorbike camera. They used tight shots because they wanted to show what was happening. I wanted to show the decor while showing the race at the same time – all the countryside, the chateaux, the churches. I wanted to move the camera in an astonishing way.

'There was one Wescam helicopter then, now they have two, but they didn't use the one they had in a good way. You can do fantastic scenic pictures, get thrilling images. I just felt that the Tour was missing out on something formidable – it seemed to me that we needed to show *la belle France* as well as the race. After we made that small change, the Tour's audience ratings went up, and so did the satisfaction levels.'

Without the Wescam and its ability to focus on a moving peloton in a scenic backdrop, in a sport where backdrops constantly change, day by day, hour by hour, none of this would have happened. Without this broader context, *A Sunday in Hell* would be merely a sumptuous vision. Put into the history of visual coverage of cycling – and that means primarily televisual – Leth's loving embrace of the Wesscam now looks like a key moment. 'Jean-Maurice Hooghe [the Tour's head of television] still respects that,' says Leth.

The Wesscam offers more than a way of placing cycling in a landscape: it also offers the opportunity to pick up images of the race from above as the action happens – a bird's-eye view that Leth exploits at the moment when the winning escape forms and Roger De Vlaeminck looks back to assess whether a chase is coming from behind.

1:29:08 The final phase opens with a helicopter sequence of the four leaders, Demeyer marking De Vlaeminck with Kuiper and Moser close behind as they emerge from the very last section of cobbles and cross the level crossing at Tressin. There are only ten kilometres remaining. The viewpoints alternate, with a long sequence from Roos on the Brooklyn car – with parts of the spare wheels showing at times – and the sound of air horns and race radio, the timpani and the bubbling rhythm box capturing the intensity of the final miles.

'Compared to the other Classics, the final phase [at Roubaix] is always far harder, because the riders are more tired,' the 1985 and 1991 winner Marc Madiot told me. But that has another effect: it is impossible to tell who has what left in the tank. 'You can never tell who is strong and who isn't,' the 1994 winner, Andrei Tchmil, told me. Here, though, it is clear who is strongest, because one sight is ubiquitous: De Vlaeminck at the front of the quartet.

'On the other hand,' says Saunders, *'Kuiper is always at the rear – is he tired or just waiting to get the jump on the others?*

That's his speciality and it's how, a little unexpectedly, he became the world champion last year.'

Kuiper's hallmark was his ability to find openings. 'I wasn't a sprinter, so I had to get away to win. Perhaps that was in my head, as I did win in a sprint a few times. But for sure I wasn't a field sprinter. Of the four of us in the final of that Roubaix, no one could drop any of the others, and after we came out of the final cobbled section I attacked four or five times. De Vlaeminck chased me down each time. It was difficult to get away; I would attack, De Vlaeminck would chase me, then we slowed down again. I created the opportunities, but Moser and Demeyer did not attack. Otherwise, I might have got away.'

Kuiper recalls that he wasn't 'tired'. 'It was an exciting day for me, in the break in Paris–Roubaix for the first time in my career. I wasn't empty. I had energy. I wasn't hanging. I could do my work. The problem was that Demeyer and Moser didn't work – they were watching De Vlaeminck.'

The Dutchman needed his fellow escapees to make repeated aggressive moves that would soften up De Vlaeminck so that he could counter-attack in the brief lull that would come immediately the group reformed. That never happened; Leth shows us one move by Moser, rapidly parried by De Vlaeminck. Kuiper placed in the top ten of over fifty one-day Classics, but the finale of this particular one was different: big names though they were, three of the four-man break were happy to wait for the sprint. 'The tactics here are so important,' Kuiper told me. 'In Paris–Roubaix, it's not usual for the big guys to sit on in a break; everyone will do their job.' He emphasises, however, that it is one thing to survive the final sort-out at a Classic; winning is a very different matter.

1:30:27 Leth shows one of Kuiper's moves, and De Vlaeminck's response, from several angles: first the focus on the world champion, then the close-up, then the helicopter shot of the actual attack, then De Vlaeminck's face shortly afterwards. As with Maertens's crash, and Merckx adjusting his handlebars as the race waits during the demonstration at the start, this is a single moment portrayed dispassionately from different viewpoints. 'This is what I love – this is the optimal result of planning a film in this way,' said Leth. 'You cover it from different angles and perspectives and then in certain points they meet. The moment can be described from different angles. It's wonderful when that happens.'

Kuiper sprints ahead, De Vlaeminck responds. And then we revert briefly to the confusion of the production studio and the commentators, to ratchet up the tension further, with the late Fred De Bruyne and Adriano De Zan – for many years key voices in respectively Flemish and Italian broadcasting – talking the race in, with De Zan speculating that the average speed may reach forty-two kilometres per hour, 'as the race approaches the outskirts of Roubaix'. Here, '*De Vlaeminck keeps the pressure on . . . he's hoping to drain the power from his three compatriots.*'

The Gypsy was also giving more than a few worries to his team manager Franco Cribiori in the Brooklyn team car behind the four-man break as he parried attack after attack from Moser and Kuiper. 'I could see that Demeyer wasn't working at all, or very little,' Cribiori told me. 'Kuiper wasn't doing a great deal and Moser wasn't very active either. I kept telling Roger not to work so much. I went up at least two or three times for sure and told him to rein it in. The problem in a small group like that is that if one guy pulls much harder than all the rest, they will be happy to let him do it.

'The only tactic is to do as little as the rest of them, then they will not figure out that you are the strongest, they will get worried because the break might not work, and they will pull. Maertens was out of the race, Merckx wasn't going to catch them. Roger didn't need to work so hard.' Kuiper recalls that De Vlaeminck, whom he greatly admires, was 'super nervous'. That suggests the Gypsy was bluffing when he tried to convince me that he felt very little when racing. The Dutchman adds, 'Sometimes his biggest competition was his nerves.'

Maertens says he was told after the race that as the escape formed, the cunning Driessens came up to Demeyer and told him not to collaborate in the break because his leader was 'only thirty seconds behind – but I was in the hospital!' In addition, at one point Driessens positioned his car so that Cribiori could not get past to tell Demeyer that the Flandria leader was out of the race. At some point, clearly, Cribiori did get past otherwise he would not have been able to tell De Vlaeminck to rein back his effort. However, by then it was too late. Driven by his obsession with Merckx, and his conviction that the race would be his, De Vlaeminck had damaged his chances.

In the finale, Leth indulges his affection for Merckx, who, 1:34:01
Saunders tells us, *'seems resigned to his fate.'* That is unlikely, given Merckx's character, but what is true is that *' . . . the race is over for him. He hasn't been able to dominate this one.'* The Cannibal's last flourish is a classic attack from behind up the blind side of the chase group that would grace any coaching manual. *'Only a Merckx would attack at this late hour . . .'* His attempted counter is captured side-on, and it paves the way for what the French like to term *un baroud d'honneur*, the final move from the defeated duellist, ensuring that the Cannibal

would at least contest the minor placings with two other defeated strongmen, Godefroot and Danguillaume.

'The rest of the way is ordinary asphalt road . . .' says Saunders; the final few kilometres into the celebrated velodrome remain the same; the approach up the dead straight tree-lined Avenue
1:34:50 Roger Salengro is easily recognisable today, as Kuiper in the lead quartet has *'time for a little relaxation before riding into the stadium'*, wobbling his thighs and stretching his shoulders. *'Which of the four is the best sprinter?'* asks Saunders of the quartet; it's a question that has been asked time and again as escapes have headed down for that much-loved right turn into the velodrome to the sound of the *speaker*.

'Normally it's De Vlaeminck . . . Just how fresh are Demeyer and Kuiper?

'The time is ten minutes past five.'

CHAPTER 11: THE LOST HERO

'The surprise winner . . . a tremendous triumph for this support rider who rode his own race when his star, Maertens, dropped out.'

Among the ornate nineteenth-century tombs and the bakers' dozen of First World War graves behind the church, the grey concrete slab in the little village churchyard of Outrijve is bright with flowers – pink, white and yellow – and is easy to find. It's a family grave: Parmentier and Van Huyse, and it bears a plaque with the black letters eroding like memories of the young man who won the Paris–Roubaix of Jørgen Leth's *A Sunday in Hell*: 'Our beloved son and brother Marc Demeyer, 19–4–50 to 20–1–1982'.

Demeyer's sudden death at the age of thirty-one is one of many premature demises that have marked cycling over the years. However, like the others it retains its full ability to shock, because sport is, above all, an affirmation of life – most often of youth, but far from exclusively – and pleasure. On 20 January 1982, Demeyer completed a 100-kilometre training ride in the morning, then went to visit his team manager, Albert de Kimpe; he was all set to ride that season for the Splendor squad. That evening, he was resting, filling out a crossword puzzle in his home in Merelbeke. He never reached the final clue. The diagnosis was a heart attack.

The local cycling clubs have left their plaques here: one from KSV Deerlijk, another from the local Vanweg Hand in Hand Wielercluh, and the oval photograph in the little marble block shows a fresh-faced, dark-haired youth, at odds with the haggard, tortured images of the cyclist in his racing heyday. And at odds with the way he sometimes raced. Demeyer was called 'the Man with the Whip' by his former teammate Sean Kelly in his autobiography *Hunger*, and described as ' . . . the captain of the [Flandria] team. He called the shots on the road and he could be a bully. He was built like a tank and could ride on the front all day if necessary and he expected everyone to be able to do the same.'

Demeyer is not forgotten, say the bouquets in the churchyard, as they do on Fausto Coppi's grave in Italy, and Tom Simpson's memorial on Mont Ventoux. The stone stands just twenty-two kilometres from the French town where Demeyer won the biggest race of his career – in other words, he was more of a local in the race than most of the French cyclists who rode it that year or have ridden it since. In 2012, thirty years after his death, the organisers of Paris–Roubaix made the trip here to leave flowers by the grave; he has his own cobblestone with his name carved into it on the final section of *pavé* in the streets of Roubaix. A few years earlier, the ASO had retrospectively awarded his family one of the cobblestone trophies which are now given to the race winners, but which had yet to materialise in 1976.

First a runner, then a cyclist alongside a job as a factory worker, Demeyer was famously uncompromising, nicknamed 'the Outrijve axeman' by some. In Kelly's first Paris–Nice, the young Irishman rode on the front on one stage until he felt he could do not more, then he swung off the front exhausted and struggled to hang on to the peloton, 'I thought I'd done a good job until Demeyer came up to me after the finish. He said that if I still had the strength to stay with the peloton, I could have done another kilometre on the front.'

Most agree: he was a hard, silent man, but, as both Freddy Maertens and Walter Godefroot put it, 'with a fine heart'. Jean-François Pescheux recalls, 'He was a hard man when going about his work, but a very, very nice character, very human.' Another contemporary, Roger Legeay, recalls Demeyer as '*hyper gentil*' and still marvels at the strength he possessed. 'Marc was nice, but he was a force of nature. He had this massive build, and when he accelerated you became aware of what a huge motor he had.' 'His heart was on his tongue, as we say in Flanders; he was a very correct character,' recalls Godefroot. 'There were no compliments, no false words. He was a bear, a beast, so strong. He rode on brute strength.'

He turned professional in the most rudimentary way, signing his first contract for Flandria on the bonnet of the team car before the Dwars door Vlaanderen semi-classic in the spring of 1972. He would win that race, at Waregem in West Flanders and would go on to take other major victories: Paris–Brussels, a stage in the Tour de France, two stages of the Giro d'Italia, the Scheldeprijs one-dayer. His was a typical Flandrian career: he was capable of getting close to the win in the biggest one-day Classics such as Milan–San Remo, Ghent–Wevelgem and the Tour of Flanders, of picking off smaller events and stages, and all the while working for the other members of the trio nicknamed the Three Musketeers: Maertens and Michel Pollentier.

'Markie' Demeyer epitomised Flandrian cycling: 'carved out of rock, seemingly built for the toughest tasks', said one writer, with his roots in deep countryside. His is an area of vegetable farms, featureless fields and one-horse villages where people still turn and look long and hard when a stranger comes into the single café. It's an area that could be Flanders or it could be northern France; since Schengen the borders have become blurred. This is an area that has changed hands over the years as armies have marched back and forth. Like so many Flandrian cyclists, he came from an impoverished rural background. In Outrijve – a satellite village of the small town of Avelgem – his father was a peasant farmer who supplemented his income by running a coal merchant's from their home in Oude Heestertstraat. His three brothers raced as well, if less successfully; one of the three, Wim, also died prematurely. And in Outrijve itself, the cycling roots ran deep: the village of just 1,200 inhabitants boasted the first winner of the Tour of Flanders in 1913, Paul Deman.

'He was a beast. He could ride, and ride, and ride, and ride,' recalls Pescheux. 'I remember his shoes. I don't know how big his feet were – 48 maybe? – and his hands, they were like this' – Pescheux puts both hands together. 'Big feet, 47 maybe, and great, great big hands,' says Maertens. He became one of the *patrons* of the peloton, as well as Maertens's personal bodyguard – when Maertens was struggling in the *autobus* on mountain stages at the Tour, it was Demeyer who would 'drive' the cumbersome group of stragglers. 'He was the one who arranged the whole thing in the *autobus*, for example when Martens had the green jersey in the Tour, and he would ride hard.' He was, says Pescheux, definitely one of the bigger personalities in the peloton, so his victory at Roubaix wasn't the victory of a lesser rider. 'He and Maertens were a real unit.'

'The time is ten minutes past five . . .' when the quartet enter the final turn into the velodrome, which has barely changed

since then. We see the sprint from several angles, including the eyes of the commentators De Zan and De Bruyne; the former's Italian talks us through the sprint, the latter's Flemish announces the victor to us; he punches the air in patriotic delight in synch with his countryman. *'De Vlaeminck makes the tactical error of riding a long sprint from the leading position. Moser attacks from above but doesn't box in Demeyer who slots in between them and rides a really explosive finale.'*

Pierre Chany's report in *l'Equipe* underlines how late 1:35:34
Demeyer left his effort, by stating repeatedly that the Belgian appeared to be beaten, first by De Vlaeminck – who accelerates progressively, moving slightly from side to side to discourage anyone from passing – and then by Moser, who attempts to use the height of the track to gain some impetus. 'Too intent on a fourth win that would have placed him at the top of the hierarchy above Merckx, Van Looy and Lapize, De Vlaeminck had under-estimated the strength of the wind, which was blowing against him as he came in front of the stands. He weakened at precisely the point where most had expected him to gain speed . . .'

Demeyer was well able to win a sprint from a small group as would be seen on numerous occasions during his career. It is a clear win, by a length from Moser; the textbook tactic of delaying the sprint into a headwind worked to perfection. Behind, Merckx, Godefroot, Raas and Danguillaume have escaped the chasers; watching the finish over forty years later, Godefroot is still happy at the turn of speed he shows through the final banking to win the sprint from fourth in the line, if resigned to the fact that it is only for fifth place.

Before Leth's cameras move back to capture Demeyer's 1:39:02
winning interview with the clearly delighted De Bruyne, and his celebrations on the tiny, amateurish podium with a

Banque Nationale de Paris banner haphazardly draped behind him, De Vlaeminck can briefly be seen pedalling past, looking at the Flandria rider. He has a face like thunder. For Demeyer, *'Victory,'* we are told, *'was especially sweet, snatched as it was from the hands of Maertens's arch-enemy, De Vlaeminck.'*

To this day, the Gypsy remains bitter about the result of the 1976 race. He appreciates the film because of the way it conjures up a past era, when one-day Classics had their true value, and would draw every one of the greats of cycling; he has seen it four times, but he doesn't like to watch it. In May 2016 he told me, 'I go crazy every time I see that film.' He finished second four times at Roubaix, once to Merckx, once to Hinault, but those defeats are easier to deal with because they were inflicted by two of the greatest names in cycling. 'If you are as good as I felt on that day, it's very, very painful. It's hard to explain.'

Cribiori had given De Vlaeminck his instructions before the quartet arrived at the velodrome. 'I told him not to go into the velodrome at the front of the group, he needed to go in in third or fourth place. It is a long track, it's not like a three hundred-metre indoor velodrome where you have to lead out the sprint. It's four hundred metres, it wears you out. You can't start the sprint first, you can't be in the wind for that long. He had already made the mistake of pulling the break too hard, and he made this mistake as well. These were not errors that he usually made. He wasn't that kind of rider.' Sometimes, as Walter Godefroot notes, you can just be too good in a race; 'Often, when you are certain you will win, you lose. It's like a boxer who thinks it's in the bag, and then the uppercut gets him on the chin.'

De Vlaeminck's confidence in his supreme ability had cost him a victory that should have been relatively straightforward. 'I was too good on that day,' he told me. 'I spent too many kilometres on the front. During the race, I was certain I would win. I was too confident. I wasn't clever enough. I should have saved my energy just a little bit. Look at Demeyer, he stays in the wheels for the last forty kilometres. I know that

[Flandria *directeur sportif*] Lomme Driessens told him that Maertens was chasing behind, so that he wouldn't have to work, but I have no problem with that. I just needed to be a bit more clever.'

'It was a race we should not have lost,' says Franco Cribiori forty years on. 'He was not the usual De Vlaeminck that day – he should have won easily. He was too enthusiastic. Perhaps he was too happy because he had dropped Maertens and Merckx, both of whom he was afraid of. He lost the race in two ways: he worked too much in the break and he led out the sprint.' 'He rode a good race, but not very intelligent,' sums up Maertens, still with a hint of smugness even forty years later. 'He began the sprint too early; Demeyer wasn't a bad sprinter once he got the big gear rolling.'

Roubaix marked revenge for the Flandria clan over their Brooklyn rival, as the following day's press reports made clear. 'Demeyer was not unhappy to have cut the grass from under De Vlaeminck's feet,' wrote Robert Silva in *l'Equipe*. 'In this sense at least, this suited Demeyer: "De Vlaeminck's little schemes cost Freddy the Tour of Flanders last Sunday, so I've avenged my friend's defeat by depriving De Vlaeminck of his fourth Roubaix win." A score had been settled. On this point, Maertens, Driessens and Demeyer were as one: Freddy had lost a battle the previous Sunday, and today, Marc was going to dedicate his war medal to him.'

Silva was referring to the Tour of Flanders, the race which – then as now – mattered above all others to Belgian riders and teams. There, Moser, De Vlaeminck, Maertens and Demeyer all featured in the decisive five-rider escape, with Maertens clearly the favourite to win, as he had the support of his principal *domestique*. Sensing this, De Vlaeminck had marked his Flemish rival so well that when the quintet split in the finale, with Moser, Demeyer and the eventual winner Walter Planckaert taking the lead, Maertens was unwilling to pull De Vlaeminck across the gap. De Vlaeminck's attitude was that, with a rider in support, it was up to Maertens to ensure his own victory and he would do nothing to help him.

Footage of the race shows Demeyer's obvious confusion: as the split occurs, he looks back to locate Maertens, and waves at his friend to encourage him to jump across the gap. But Maertens is more concerned about the possibility of setting up a win for De Vlaeminck, letting the other three pull away. Planckaert outsprinted the Flandria man, so neither of the rivals was happy about the outcome, nor were their home media; that in turn had ratcheted up the pressure a further notch on the road to Roubaix.

The banner headline across the front of *l'Equipe* from Monday 10 April is bizarrely defensive – 'Demeyer did not steal this success' – although in his preview the day before in *l'Equipe*, Pierre Chany had described Flandria's strength in depth in these terms: 'Roger De Vlaeminck appears to his rivals as the number-one [favourite], a title which would be contested by those who give the advantage to Maertens's team, because it marries quality and quantity better than others. Guillaume Driessens has the good fortune to direct Maertens, Pollentier, Demeyer and [Herman] Van Springel, four riders who would not disgrace the array of winners.'

Maertens watched the finish on television in his hotel; he had no issues with Demeyer's win, because his servitor had won, they were all going to get their bonus from Flandria, and 'we had said among ourselves that we had to stop De Vlaeminck winning. I was happy for Marc. The three of us, with Pollentier, we always played the game straight with each other.' On the other hand, he called the rest of the team together afterwards and told them they would get no money from him, because – other than the ever-faithful Pollentier – they had been less than helpful in the early sectors following his puncture, when he had wasted valuable energy chasing on his own.

Kuiper, on the other hand, believes that De Vlaeminck was both unlucky and injudicious. 'If Freddy Maertens had not crashed, then De Vlaeminck would have won Paris-Roubaix.' What he feels is that Maertens and Demeyer would have had to take on the task of driving the final break, which would have taken the pressure off the Gypsy. 'He had to catch me three or four times when I attacked,' says the Dutchman. 'Perhaps that was the reason he lost the race. For sure, he led the sprint out too early, but he lost it in 1981 with Hinault as well. That was De Vlaeminck, sometimes he got overheated, too nervous.'

De Vlaeminck, on the other hand, was only too happy to turn his fire on Flandria when asked to analyse his defeat on Flemish television. 'When Demeyer followed my attack, he knew already that Maertens was out of the race. That gave him the right to collaborate with us. He didn't do that. That's not very elegant. It's true, I'm very disappointed and revolted at the same time. I think I was the one who made the race happen, and I would like the guys who were with me to be able to say the same about themselves. More and more, you have the feeling that you are dealing with guys who have only one thought in their minds: putting one over you, profiting from the work you do so that they can reap the benefit and that's what happened today.'

In contrast to De Vlaeminck, Maertens and Godefroot are now sanguine about this defeat. 'I regret it, but I don't regret it,' says Maertens, who cannot resist seeing his career through the lens of his rivalry with the Gypsy and the Cannibal. 'OK,

I never won Roubaix but De Vlaeminck never won the world championship. We tried to win everything, but it wasn't possible. You can regret a lot of races, but I'm not Eddy Merckx.'

'When you make it to the final of Paris–Roubaix five times and you manage to win it once, you have to say you have been lucky, because you've been up there so often,' is how Godefroot rationalises this near-miss. 'The difference with De Vlaeminck? He was lucky. One year, I attacked with Moser; De Vlaeminck was behind us. The next day, we went training together and he told me how he saw it. I punctured; he said when he saw me standing on the roadside, he knew I had gone so he gave it a kick. Then Moser punctured, and he won.'

Where Demeyer differed from the likes of Maertens, De Vlaeminck and Merckx was in his view of himself and his role. Robert Silva's interview for *l'Equipe* after his Roubaix win underlines this. The journalist describes how, when Demeyer crossed the line in the velodrome, 'he had just one thought in his mind': it was not to celebrate the biggest victory of his career, but to look for his fallen leader, Maertens. His first act was to go and find Maertens, to gain news of the champion after his crash, and then to check that he had not offended his boss by racing for himself. 'He reassured himself, assuaged his fears that he might have committed treason. It was obvious that Demeyer would have been happier with a win for Maertens than for himself. It's incredible, but it's true.'

In the twenty-five editions of Paris–Roubaix that he had covered, Silva did not recall ever interviewing a winner like Demeyer. 'He repeated happily in French what he had just said in Flemish: "I ride 100 per cent for Freddy, that's all . . ." This forceful worker', wrote Silva, 'is entirely the opposite of a *patron* – a strong leader. He is a servant who is happy to have surrendered his independence. He says it: "I am not a team leader. I never will be."' Following Maertens's crash, he said, he had taken instructions from their *directeur sportif*, Lomme Driessens: 'Don't ride hard. Let De Vlaeminck make the race.'

No Roubaix is ever truly routine, but the 1976 race was not a legendary edition. That can be explained by various factors: the dry conditions, the crashes and punctures that put out Maertens and Godefroot, and Merckx's gradual decline, which meant he did not have his usual impact (Goddet described him as 'not having *un jour sans*, but certainly not having *un jour avec*'. Not a complete off day, but far from a good one.

Merckx was equally unforgiving on himself (one of his great qualities as a champion being his unwillingness to make excuses). Afterwards, he described a classic day out in Hell in which he had broken two wheels and had five bike changes, 'and to cap it all, I had so much trouble with my gears, to the point where I could not use the thirteen and fourteen sprockets'. That is quite a handicap, akin to a Formula One driver losing half his gearbox. 'When De Vlaeminck attacked with the others, I called my *directeur sportif* up to change my bike, but on those roads you have to wait so long for the car, and by the time we'd got it done, it was game over. That said, it's not an adequate excuse, because in that situation you have to be in front and I wasn't, obviously because I have yet to get back to my best.'

Although the 1976 race did not compare with some of the truly epic editions of the 1970s, these were rarities, often due to wet conditions. Leth, however, feels the race suited his purposes as a film-maker, just as he was favoured by the dry weather rather than the wet and mud most fans hope for: 'This race is a great race for heroic efforts, big courage, big events

[but] for my film it was more exciting that you didn't have a winner until the last moment – it kept it on a certain level of suspense until the very end. Of course, Merckx's efforts, his desperation in trying to catch the break, was an element I liked very much. He never gives up. I love that quality in him.'

In spite of all the plaudits that the film has attracted over the years, on the day itself, Leth in fact did not achieve what he had set out to do. For one thing, the cameramen did not produce the long static takes that he had asked for, but there was more. Leth did not have a motorcycle camera on hand to capture the final miles of the race. In his car as he drove in the race convoy, Leth did not know that his third cameraman, Jacques Loiseleux, had been unable to work due to a crash. Neither Constantini nor Holmberg can quite recall why they were not at the front of the race in the key moments; most probably it came down to decisions made by their individual motorbike drivers. In theory they had been given the right to drive 'in the race'; in practice, getting to the front would have depended upon individual commissaires being willing to let them through the convoy.

Leth was frustrated. 'I wanted to tell everything in the right order, the chronological order. I did not want to cheat with anything. I planned to be everywhere. With twenty-seven cameras I expected to be everywhere in all moments. Even that was not possible. I lost moments that I had to cover in different ways. There was a period of the race where I had no footage: that was the limitation. I had to solve that, because I was caught in my own formula.

'Of the twenty-seven cameras, I didn't have one covering that [final] phase of the race. I couldn't live with that. The moment when De Vlaeminck is trying to attack the group of favourites, Moser reacts, then Maertens a little later . . . these are crucial moments of the race. And also the phase where Moser impressively catches the leaders. These moments were not filmed by my people. So what do I do? I'm desperate. I need to have all these details of the race. I want to be faithful to these decisive moments. We decide to go to Paris to see French television, talk to them, see their archive for these moments and then buy it from them. That's why these images are different in texture – they are on video and the rest of the film is on Kodak film.' The change in the quality of the images can be seen one hour and seventeen minutes into the film, when the focus switches to the group of favourites as De Vlaeminck prepares to attack. The pictures from the roof of the Brooklyn car, and images from the back of the race – taken by either Constantini or Holmberg – are far more sharp.

When Leth arrived in Roubaix after the finish one of the first people he met was Félix Lévitan, who said, in characteristically acid style, 'I hope you are grateful that we completed the race.' The old fox was referring to the early assault by the strikers, which had threatened to put a stop to the entire event, to the consternation of all involved. 'I hope you appreciate that we went on with the race. I knew you were filming, so there was no way I could stop it.' The director laughs, fully aware of the mind games that the late Tour manager simply could not help playing. 'That was his tune, can you imagine . . . ?'

CHAPTER 12: THE SHOWERS AND THE SCULPTORS

'Eddy Merckx, inscrutable as ever . . . Roger De Vlaeminck, disappointed and furious . . . Marc Demeyer, the happy winner . . .'

The showers next to the Roubaix velodrome have a legendary status all of their own. They are simultaneously part of the legend and a bizarre throwback in their own right. Like the velodrome and the cobbles, they are subject to the vagaries of time. At the end of the editions of the race that I covered between 1989 and 1995, the post-race ritual for the journalist had not changed for generations: you went into the showers, notebook and tape recorder in hand, to interview whoever you could find.

All the riders went to the showers; there was nowhere else for them to go to wash off the muck and the blood and the sweat, and there was free access for the media amid the muddy footprints, ripped and dirtied kit on the floor, and the bruised bodies. Every rider had a story to tell – suffering, punctures, crashes and chases to regain a group – and while that story might have had nothing to do with the outcome of the race, it held immense personal significance. Each star drew a gaggle of press men, happily taking the risk of getting dirty water flicked onto a damp notebook so the biro wouldn't write.

There were always too many stories to fit in one magazine or newspaper, but it didn't matter. It was a rare – unique – moment of commonality between the men who rode the races and the men (cycling journalism was exclusively male back then) who wrote about them. The riders seemed to embrace the fact that we were there; for a journalist, it was the only race on the calendar where you would have completely unfettered access to the men who had made the event immediately afterwards. You emerged in the knowledge that, as a writer, you had been treading in the muddy foot-prints of press legends such as Pierre Chany, Gian Paolo Ormezzano and Jean Bobet.

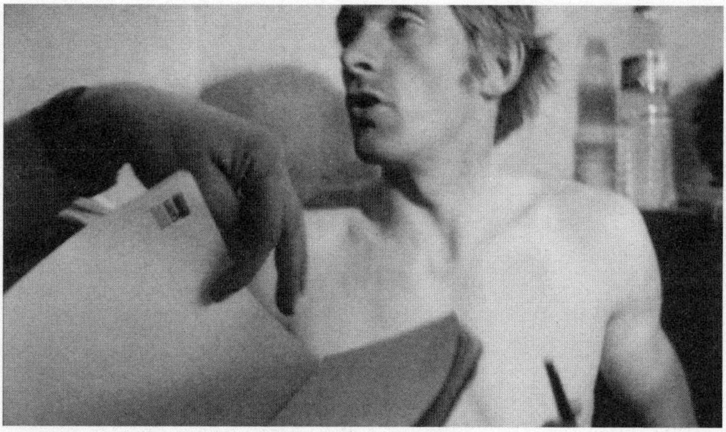

No more. Since the early 2000s the vast team buses that criss-cross Europe carrying the stars and watercarriers have parked up in a line outside the velodrome, air-conditioning motors humming; the riders can shower in peace inside and the press ants have no option but to select one bus, and cluster there in the hope that the one cyclist whose version of events they are interested in will deign to put in an appearance. In the list of crimes against pro-cycling culture that the buses have wrought, the death of the post-Roubaix shower ritual is probably the most heinous. As with the ritual of the Valenciennes abandon-fest, in his final sequence Leth was capturing an event that is now largely forgotten.

Only occasional die-hards buck the trend: the 2015 winner John Degenkolb, or the Frenchman Arnaud Demare who – riding for fdj.com, perhaps the most traditionalist team in the modern peloton – made a point of going there in 2017 to complete a day out in Hell which had given him sixth place. For him, it was a rite of passage akin to the fact of passing through Arenberg. One year recently, a team did go and use the showers, but it wasn't about tradition: they were backed by a shampoo maker, and they took their showers in the knowledge that the photos they released would do the rounds with the sponsor's products centre stage.

Forty years after Leth made his film, on a midwinter afternoon, the entire velodrome complex has a dilapidated, deserted air. The only sign of life stems from a pair of teenagers entwining amorously by one of the gates as I walk through. They are still entwined a good hour later when I exit in the opposite direction.

The shower building is anonymous, hidden between the old outdoor cement track where Paris–Roubaix still finishes and the sparkling, brand-new building which houses a 250-metre indoor velodrome named after Jean Stablinski, but almost always referred to as le Stab. There is a certain amount of official confusion about who has the key to the showers, who is permitted to show a visiting journalist around, and whether payment has to be made for the privilege. It falls to a pair of council employees, Touhan and Farid, to act as my guides, and, eventually, it is decided that no euros have to change hands.

Built in the 1930s, and thus contemporaneous to the velodrome, the two rooms are almost identical, the second slightly larger than the first, a large steam-streaked mirror on each wall. Against the left-hand wall is a row of shower heads, some rusty, some ending abruptly where the rose has been removed, each one stained with the hot water of many years; ten in the near room, sixteen in the further one. Between the shower heads and the entrance stand the changing cubicles, zig-zag walls of hard polished concrete – shoulder-high on a climber, sternum height on a lanky Classics man. The zigs and zags form a series of squares with alternate sides missing; the three-sided squares of concrete offer a modicum of privacy. There's a rusty coathook in each, a manky bench and, incongruously, a shiny cheap nameplate high up to the left, with the name of a previous winner (Degenkolb, when he showered here in April 2017, made a point of using 'his' cubicle – but the pictures he released on social media show him in glorious solitude).

Although the cyclists of the great race barely ever clean up here nowadays, the showers are still used occasionally, most often by the players of the third-division rugby club that practises here, hence the tell-tale plaques of stud-holed mud on the floor. The amateurs who ride the Paris–Roubaix races for lesser categories – junior and under-23 men – can be found here, so too some of the thousands of *cyclo-touristes* who bounce and clatter over the cobbles in the mass-participation events that use the race route. And there are visitors, people like me who just want to get a faint vibe of the Hell of the North; last week a Dutch group, Flemish, British, Americans.

The velodrome and the showers form part of a large multi-sport complex spread across several hectares: the outdoor velodrome, le Stab, the rugby pitches, athletics track, facilities for basketball, indoor football, yoga and archery. The BMX track is open long hours and is particularly popular. It's bounded by four roads: Avenue van der Meersch, Avenue du Parc le Sports, Rue Lannoy and Avenue Roger Salengro, off which the riders and the race cars have turned right and zig-zagged through the dog-leg into the velodrome April after April after April since 1942; the showers stand to the left of the dog-leg turn. The road through the dog-leg turn has what look like permanent white paint markings; one lane for the *coureurs* to turn right into the velodrome, a lane for the official *voitures* to park on the left.

The doors in the foot of the grandstand of the old open velodrome on Avenue du Parc des Sports are locked, but the wall above the way in has a delightful mural: '*Probita, Industria*'* it proclaims on either side of the town's coat of arms set above the locked blue metal doors. Higher up the walls are two socialist-realist mosaics of idealised athletes that wouldn't disgrace a stadium in the former Soviet Union. The elaborate, ceremonial entranceway to the athletics track and soccer pitches has a similar feel. Delapidated though it may be, the complex still oozes civic pride, harking back to the days when beneficent industrialists invested in the facilities of the towns where their workers lived and slaved.

The velodrome is only used now for the finish of Paris–Roubaix. Otherwise, it lies empty, apart from when cyclists turn up to ride the fabled bankings. The standing-room terraces built into the low hill on turns one and two recall

* 'Honesty, hard work.'

the days when thousands turned up for meetings such as the French national championship as late as 1971. It opened well into the heyday of open-air track racing, 1935, succeeding an earlier track that had been built in 1895 and which burned to the ground in 1924; this previous velodrome hosted the Paris–Roubaix finish until the outbreak of the Second World War.

The track is named after a local bar-owner, André Pétrieux – or possibly his son – whose hostelry stood on the corner of the Rue de Lannoy, and who founded the Velo Club Roubaix, the local cycling club – now known as VC Roubaix Lille Métropole – which has had charge of the track since its inception. The club's base is on site, in a battered-looking clubhouse named Au Pavé, where – if the vendors are at home and in the mood – you can buy official merchandise, and baby-sized cobbles at twenty euros apiece. Inside, a board above the bar lists the winners. There are supermarket trolleys full of cobbles for the *sportive* finishers: they are imported from nearby Belgium as French quarries no longer supply them.

Behind the attractive mosaic, the grandstand is crumbling. The frames in the windows are rotting. The building gets an annual coat of paint in late March, to ensure that it doesn't look too scruffy to host the greatest one-day Classic in cycling; the concrete track gets a look-over at the same time, to eliminate any cracks that may have been opened up by the winter. A few yards underneath the seating where guests watch the race finish the unused changing rooms are apparently a depressing scene. 'It's been left to rot for twenty-five years,' one municipal employee said in 2015. 'The exterior is done up before the race but no one cares about the interior; drug addicts and squatters force the doors and come in.'

Elsewhere in the complex is the base of Les Amis de Paris–Roubaix – the charity that watches over the *pavé* sectors, repairing them before they get so bad that local authorities have them tarmacked over. There have been moves to set up a permanent museum on the premises, along the lines of the Tour of Flanders museum in the town of Oudenaarde. There are rumours of a hotel being built, so that cycling fans can wake up, pull the curtains and see the velodrome bankings beneath them. It's the kind of economic boost that Roubaix needs, having gone through years of economic decline after the closure of the textile mills which made the city an economic powerhouse at the time the velodrome opened. Roubaix became legendary in a different way in the twenty-first century: 30 per cent unemployment, drug addiction and radical Islam; Trois-Ponts, the area close to the velodrome, became so known for urban deprivation that the local soccer club had to change its name. Ironically, few immediate locals now take up cycling, simply because it is too expensive for such a deprived area. There are hopes that the opening of le Stab will change that, but they have yet to be realised.

Leth's crews were still shooting – the shower footage, obviously – but after the adrenalin of the day came a sense of deflation and profound artistic doubts. The reports from the cameramen as they came up to him one by one were not promising, because to a man they were principally focused on what they had failed to achieve rather than what they had actually managed to get in the can. 'They told me they had missed this and this, they had missed that and that. I heard only terrible stories. I didn't hear any good stories. I only heard what they had missed. I was very depressed, as you often are after an exciting experience – you've built up to it and then there is the sense of let-down. So many people had told me they missed this and that. I began to think, "I wonder if there is a film in it." Those were my feelings.'

Most of the cameramen had not followed Leth and Holmberg's instructions and had not kept shooting for long enough. As a result, according to Camre, a good number of the twenty-six did not produce any footage that was used in the end. 'They were used to operating small cameras, shooting small clips to insert in TV reports. They didn't understand that Jørgen wanted to let the camera run as long as possible. Our method was to wait for something to happen and time was the key factor; it shouldn't be the cameramen who edited the film.'

Herdel, the producer, remembers mainly relief after the event; on the day, he was freaked out by the speed and the people. 'Today, I still think, "Oh my God, there was so much that could have gone wrong." We had guys on cars, hanging on with one hand while shooting, guys sitting backwards on motorbikes, overtaking cyclists and cars all the time. We were driving at 200 kilometres per hour in between the crowds, with kids in the road, people's hats blowing off. It was just so crazy.' He also recalls 'a huge party' in Roubaix; 'The city gave us a lot of champagne.'

Leth's feelings did not improve when he began the edit. In fact, he recalls, his depression was 'enhanced' in the first week of the process, when the task ahead of him seemed impossible. 'In the beginning, I felt sad and desperate. I thought the story wasn't there. I couldn't see any story in the film. I couldn't see where it led. I just saw chaos, a mass of chaos. It was so confusing to see the material from all these cameras, but where is the story?' 'Normally it's an amateur thing to shoot so much film,' says Herdel. 'But here it was necessary.' 'It's the opposite problem to now,' says Camre. 'Now, with digital, you can shoot for ever; here, there was a lot of material, but it was all in short shots.'

Leth and Holmberg had foreseen the issue of organising the mass of footage that would suddenly appear on the cutting table on the morning of 11 April 1976. They'd had to be inventive, hence the system of having the cameramen shoot the face of their Longines watches, along with the letters on the strap that could be checked back to Holmberg's plan. 'In principle we had every cameraman do three positions then go to Roubaix,' said Leth. 'So for every shot we have the exact time of the shot and the location of the shot – that gives you some indication of where it fits into the puzzle. Otherwise we'd be lost. We'd still be editing [the material] now.'

'One of the huge problems with shooting a film in one day with a hell of a lot of other cameramen you do not know is, of course, that you do not know what you [will] get,' says Dan Holmberg. '[You don't know] how good the others are . . . Can they frame . . . Can they move the camera . . . Can they hold the camera steady . . . Can they see . . . Can they make decisions . . . and so on.

'So shooting one race in one day with twenty-seven cameras is much harder than shooting a twenty-one-day race with one camera – mine! When I shoot myself, I know what I get. And I have to admit that I like my own way of framing and my own way of moving the camera best. This is not being snotty . . . I think it is perfectly normal. I am, after all, a professional.

'I can have an awful time seeing what others have shot. I think maybe like a good carpenter hates to see shoddy carpentry. In June of 1976 I was in Copenhagen and I spent time in Jørgen's home where the editing took place. I watched hours of raw material and I got more and more depressed. Far too much shoddy shooting . . . Far too many camerapeople not knowing or not caring what they were doing.

'I remember one French guy who was given a very good job. He was supposed to film people – the people watching the race; the people along the road. A very good project – a type of Cartier-Bresson job. . . . Sitting in the editing room in Copenhagen I saw the result of his work. A roll of film with people's feet. Nothing else! How is it possible? . . . I still cannot understand this.'

Another problem encountered by the crews, Holmberg recalls, was that after a camera had been put in its position on a tripod and everything looked in order, when the race came closer the audience crowded into the picture, looking for a good view. This happened, Herdel recalled, with the cameras at the velodrome for the finish; they were set up with a clear view, but when the race arrived, the cameraman was forced to use the long lens as a weapon to get the crowd to move.

'It didn't seem to be together in the beginning – there were so many things that we didn't capture or didn't get in a good way,' says Leth. 'But in the end there was more than enough to make a beautiful film. Except where I had to buy in the footage from French television.' The edit took four months, and it was done in Leth's home: 'I like to have it close to me.' Finally, Leth and his editor, Lars Brydesen, found some sense of narrative – perhaps the fact that this was the first and only time they would work together had contributed to the initial sense of disorientation.

'You have to have a very good editor to win this battle. He's a very good, respected editor and he did a wonderful job.' It was, Leth recalls, 'just old-fashioned editing. A big table, like two of these [in a café] put together, with three rolls [of film] on each side. And one or two soundtracks going through. Taking one roll after another. It was a very slow process.'

Part of the trouble stemmed from the sheer volume of material, and its multiplicity. 'When you have such a big lot of material it's a trap. You can get lost in the material. I think there was thirty hours of footage. Shot in one day. It's a trap if you just see it. You have to organise it – we did that from the letters and the times. I didn't want to get too involved in that. I didn't want to have to expose myself to getting tired of the material from working too sensitively with it. I asked Lars to organise it somehow, with the letters and the times so that we could see where we were, see some kind of rationale, understand where we were.

'You have to make a first cut, it could be double the length of the finished film – but even more than that. I was doing the editing process in my own home so it was difficult to get out of that. I wanted it in my home because I knew that this would be a different process. A lot depended on my knowledge of the riders, my enthusiasm for certain riders, for the reality of the race, my understanding of the race. I couldn't expect this expertise to lie with the editor. He knew nothing about cycling. Nothing. [But] you don't have to have an editor who is especially informed about your subject.'

What emerged was a different way of telling the story, compared to *Stars and Watercarriers*. '[There] I was commentating on every single development in the race through the various characters. The editor asked me questions all the time – "Why are they doing that? Why are they taking a bottle?" I had to explain everything. He said to me, "Jørgen, everything has to be told." That became the game – I would like to refer to *Stars and Watercarriers* as an educative moment for the Danish public where cycling was concerned because I explained everything. That was my first experience with that – then comes *A Sunday in Hell*.'

For *A Sunday in Hell*, Leth decided to be less didactic, to let the story tell itself. 'I had small images compared to *Stars and Watercarriers* – the story is told in images and I didn't want to over-tell it. There is another conflict here – in the history of documentary film-making . . . [in *Sunday*] I was breaking with a tendency at that time which consisted of a lot of explaining, [as] with English documentaries. The Danes began to look from a distance, explaining in images and sound rather than telling you what to think. I was breaking a tendency at that time – with *A Sunday in Hell* I went back a little way, doing much less explanation of simple facts.'

Eventually, the narrative emerged. 'Finally I had the feeling . . . it was like a sculptor making a sculpture out of a big stone. There is nothing in the beginning and it only takes shape after a lot of work. A sculptor will attack a stone and slowly something comes out of it. Slowly it fell into place.' The crucial turning point – 'when you begin to see a continuum of events, simply something like that' – came after he and Brydesen had put together the lengthy, multi-faceted sequence shot on the opening section of cobbles between Neuvilly and Viesly. 'I think there it fell together, the use of several cameras, that whole strategy . . . it was successful when we cooordinated that to tell the story of how the race got through the first *pavé*. That's where I could see that the film would work.'

When released in February 1977 under the Danish name *En forårsdag i helvede* ('A Spring Day in Hell'), Leth, Piil and the others were vindicated: the plaudits were unanimous. 'A film that puts pure adrenalin in the blood of the viewer . . . a film about human endurance, strategy and almost absurd self-flagellation', one with 'Shakespearean heroes', 'ordered with incredible mastery'. Others saw it as 'an extraordinary success . . . this ambitious project has been realised 100 per cent . . . Blow this film 100 ardent kisses,' or 'an honest, appalling and very very beautiful and poetic film . . . The truth can be beautiful, grime encouraging and the inhuman human.'

'As the poet in words and pictures that he is, Jørgen Leth blends words and pictures into a beautiful whole that not only

gives an ignoramus like the undersigned' – wrote Per Calum in *Jyllands-Posten* – 'an initiation into the mystique of bike racing but also gives me a glimpse into the mysterious beauty the poet saw before he began making the film . . . This is far better than TV reports. Maybe it's even better than attending a real bicycle race.' One said simply: 'Surely this is one of the best sports films ever.'

1:41:30 In those grim stone showers, in what seems like a mirror of the opening introductory sequences with Merckx, De Vlaeminck, Moser, Maertens and their teams, *A Sunday in Hell*'s valedictory images take us briefly back to some of the lead actors. They don't include Marc Demeyer ('I'm not interested in Demeyer at all,' Leth told me, repeating emphatically, '*at all*. And I'm not interested in Maertens either.'); instead, Leth focusses on his *helden*, his heroes. We are taken into the showers by Gunner Møller Pedersen's final piece of music, another chorale, this time with no words. It was, the composer told me, inspired by a scene in Alban Berg's 1925 opera of *Woyzeck*, in which there is a dormitory of soldiers sleeping after combat.

They are shot by Dan Holmberg as they cope with defeat, for what seems an eternity: De Vlaeminck, in close-up: mucky, disappointed, his hair slicked down over his shoulder with its distinctive lump from what is obviously a collarbone displacement from a crash in the past. Merckx, initially shot attempting to find a showerhead that will actually work – clearly the maintenance of the showers was not perfect even back then. This is 1976, the twilight of the great Merckx's career, the final season where he was truly competitive with the best, a day when he had various mechanical issues, but he acknowledged that it was his fading strength that prevented him from challenging De Vlaeminck.

'Even with twenty-seven cameramen, without that shot, I 1:43:19
could not have made the film,' Leth told me. 'The key thing was to have the same frame for so, so long. That was Dan Holmberg.' Holmberg recalls shooting Ritter, and the contrast with the scrum around Demeyer: 'The other scene that I remember being mine is after the race . . . Ole Ritter's face when he is tired and taking a shower. A beautiful scene and the other twenty cameraman are then filming the winner (I do not remember his name) in the shower. A mob scene – the poor winner having twenty cameras on him washing his hair.'

The final, almost painfully slow, moments of the film belong to Ritter, the man who brought Leth into cycling in the first place, and who enabled him to build the connections that mattered so much in Hell. The close-ups show the sheen of the water on his hair and his skin, the movement of his hands as he kneads his hair and tries to rinse the dust of the day out of his mouth. It could be any of the field, hero or lesser light, a man who has completed Paris–Roubaix or one who has made it from Paris to Valenciennes. The champion, ultimately, is just another man who has been to Hell and returned to lick his wounds, physical and mental.

'And that was Paris–Roubaix 1976 – a great race with a surprise winner, a year with a very special character . . . A race with fluctuating fortunes in the dust of the Enfer du Nord . . . In a week or so the same cast will be assembled – the same actors, riders, journalists, officials. The rivalry will continue. But few will have forgotten that Sunday in Hell.'

POSTSCRIPT: THE LOST MASTERPIECE AND THE POETIC VISION

The blonde woman leans alluringly across the Condor road-racing bike, her naked breasts hanging down over the top tube, her sultry look inviting. The Pan paperback of Ralph Hearn's novel *The Yellow Jersey* is definitely the product of a different, less enlightened era. Published in 1973, this is an amusing tale, if you can get your mind past the narrator's unreconstructed habit of referring to women by using the term 'it'. Whatever the reasoning behind this, as a device it rapidly wears thin.

The Yellow Jersey is, loosely, a novel in the mould of Angry Young Men classics such as Alan Sillitoe's *Saturday Night and Sunday Morning* and David Storey's *This Sporting Life*, with a plot that involves a washed-up ageing professional cyclist, Terry Davenport, who makes a comeback for one last Tour de France to support a young star. Somehow, he finds himself in the *maillot jaune* after the riders at the top of the standings are – cue a wry smile given recent cycling history – all thrown off the race for doping. There is an intricate love triangle, and an entertaining final twist to the tale.

Taking the novel to the large screen should have been Leth's next, and probably final cycling project. After *A Sunday in Hell* he felt he could achieve little more in the field of documentaries about the sport. The feature film, on the other hand, remains the one that got away; his involvement in it lasted more than ten years, but ended in frustration.

The film rights to *The Yellow Jersey* were sold in November 1973 to a producer called Gary Mehlman, who struck a deal with Columbia the following May and rapidly acquired permission to shoot the feature at the Tour. By the time Leth was planning *A Sunday in Hell* in 1975, Michael Cimino had come on board as director; he visited that year's Tour and lent some serious Hollywood weight to the project: his script credits included one of Clint Eastwood's *Dirty Harry* series, and he had teamed up with Eastwood and Jeff Bridges on *Thunderbolt and Lightfoot*.

The initial 125-page script was written by John Sherlock, whose credits included the soap opera *Peyton Place* and the television series *Logan's Run* (made in 1976 as a spin-off from the film of the same name). Proposed locations included the velodrome in Ghent and the Alpine ski resort of Les Menuires. The script did the rounds of various studios – Columbia, Universal, Lew Grade's ITC – for the next few years as Cimino's star waxed and waned with *The Deer Hunter* and *Heaven's Gate*. Carl Foreman, the scriptwriter legendary for *High Noon*, *The Bridge on the River Kwai* and *The Guns of Navarone*, was next to join the ship; on the strength of watching *A Sunday in Hell*, he and Mehlman contacted Leth to act as cycling consultant.

By 1983 the project had come back to Columbia and what looked like a dream team had taken it on: Foreman as director, alongside him as scriptwriter Colin Welland, a man of the moment after *Chariots of Fire*, and, most crucially of all in terms of selling the idea to studios to whom cycling was completely unknown, Dustin Hoffman – fresh from *Tootsie* and *Kramer vs. Kramer* – in the lead role as the washed-up professional cyclist Terry Davenport. At the end of 1983, Foreman was invited to Paris to scout locations that would be used for the following year's Tour de France, which would begin in the French capital. The current Tour's head of press Philippe Sudres, then in his first job at the Société du Tour de France, was given the job of meeting Foreman in the stretch limo that had been hired for him, and conveyed him around the start and finish of the prologue time trial and first stage.

Given his history with Lévitan in the run-up to *A Sunday in Hell*, the moment Leth recalls with the greatest pleasure from the saga came early on. He had been invited to the Tour de France in 1984 to help with guiding Welland, Cimino and Hoffman around the race. 'Lévitan was totally happy with [the deal] and I had a great moment when I met Hoffman in Bordeaux – he said at dinner, the first time we met, loudly, "All I know about cycling is from your film *A Sunday in Hell*. I've watched it many times in my bedroom," and Lévitan heard that. That changed my status in the race, from that moment I could get anything. That was nice.

'There was really not a climate for doing a film on the Tour de France in Hollywood,' recalled Leth. 'In Hollywood it has to go through many hands – Foreman had big difficulties convincing any studio to do the film – [it would happen] only if they had a great star doing it, finally they persuaded Dustin Hoffman and then it was a different song.' Amusingly, Sylvester Stallone had also been sounded out.

It was Hoffman who initially took the film on board, although there were strings attached: he wanted his own director and screenwriter. 'He wanted to do it. He came over for a few days to the Tour de France, watched a few stages and was absolutely happy with what he saw,' said Leth. 'I was with him in the Renault hotel with Guimard, Fignon, LeMond. Guimard wanted to sell him a bike – just have him on a Renault because it was great publicity – but finally it was Merckx who gave him a bike.'

After that, the project stuttered again, due partly to Foreman's death in June 1984. By the time Leth finally got shooting in 1986, the project was on its last legs. Hoffman had been so enthusiastic about cycling that he told a television station that visiting the Tour was the most moving experience of his life after the birth of his child, and he had trained on his Eddy Merckx bike in Central Park for a few months, but he eventually lost interest. Columbia had changed their minds that March, having invested 1.6 million dollars by then, and in extremis Mehlman had picked up a new deal with Cannon.

The right to shoot footage at the Tour was about to expire, meaning that Cannon faced the collapse of the entire project unless they got cameras on that year's Tour. 'In the summer of 1986 they called me,' Leth recalled, 'and asked me to come to France and direct the second unit – all the real stuff, the documentary parts of the film, the parts that can be done without the actors present, all the ambiance, with all the other riders present. Then they speculated that they could construct some scenes with actors later, maybe in France . . . that was normal practice.'

It was a massive project. The material in the Danish Film Institute includes a in-depth shooting schedule involving thirty-three people, eight cameras, and an intricate schedule around a lengthy list of proposed locations, and a mass of handwritten and typescript notes. The budget for that summer, according to the newspaper *Les Cahiers du Cinéma*, was half a million dollars. 'I was going to do all the stuff that they needed from the Tour; I got a big crew at my disposal, a helicopter for some shots and [motor]bikes and a special car built for shooting,' said Leth. 'They paid a lot of money so they had very good access to everything that they wanted – I shot all of this and I was very happy with it. It was all in Panavision. It was a very big production.' Alongside him was a largely French team headed by chief-operator Jean-Yves le Mener, who had worked with the French film director, Claude Lelouch.

'I was looking at this race from a very privileged position,' recalled Leth, 'from a car built for the purpose of shooting, called the 'insert car' but the riders called it *la voiture folle*, which means the crazy car, because we could go everywhere – we could go into the bunch and then move a little bit ahead . . . the camera was sitting on the back of the car and it was very movable.'

Leth ended that Tour with 200,000 feet of film – around thirty-five hours of footage – but in spite of the investment of the best part of a million dollars from Cannon, that was almost as far as it went. The Tour ended with controversy when a key figure, Avi Kleinberger, who acted as liaison between the crew and Cannon, was removed from the project, prompting angry correspondence from Leth and others. Not that Leth had given up. On 24 April 1987, he wrote to Mehlman care of his company Longstocking Productions on Sunset Boulevard. His letter proposed that he, Leth, become director, that the script should be simplified, and that a 'talented, athletic actor' be found for the lead role, rather than a big-name star. Leth's suggestion was Scott Glenn, later known for *The Silence of the Lambs* and *The Hunt for Red October* – 'tough and experienced like a pro from the Foreign Legion and he has a warmth beneath the rugged exterior'.

It was a vain hope. Shooting the rest of the film was constantly postponed and the project died a death in 1988 when Cannon went bankrupt. No one knows now where Leth's 200,000 foot of film is. 'I have only seen the stuff once – I tried several times to convince the original producers and owners of the copyright and so forth that they should do a documentary out of this material or start all over again on a more modest basis. I was really interested in helping them.'

What has been lost is, according to *Les Cahiers du Cinéma*, 'a massive quantity of the most beautiful images ever shot on the Tour, climaxing on the Champs Elysées filmed with twelve cameras including one perched on the Arc de Triomphe'. The magazine's piece on *The Yellow Jersey* from November 1986 is entitled 'Pictures in Search of a Film' and correctly states that the images will either 'take shape as a film or wander on until the end of time'.

The film was never made – and no truly successful Tour de France feature has ever emerged – partly because of cycling's minority status at the time in the US, where it remained a largely niche interest through the LeMond era. It was not until Lance Armstrong's comeback from cancer that the sport reached anything approaching the mainstream. There was another reason: the raw material available for a cycling scenario has never been able to match the stories thrown up by the real-life world of cycling.

That has been particularly the case since the Festina scandal of 1998 through to the Armstrong cataclysm. What degree of inventiveness would it take to dream up those scenarios? Could a master thriller writer (think Chandler, think Stieg Larsson) have bettered them? Even before cycling's years of doping doom, what kind of novelist could have dreamt up something as contorted as the Bernard Hinault–Greg LeMond Tour of

1986, as insane as the racing in Hinault's 1979 Tour win? Most often, fiction struggles to equal reality in this sport. *The Yellow Jersey* might have got round that problem thanks to the resources at its putative creators' disposal, and the unfettered access Leth enjoyed, but it remains the masterpiece that never was. The script is still in the Danish Film Institute archive if anyone is interested.

As for the other players on that Sunday in Hell, their paths diverged, crossed and kept running parallel. Demeyer's tragic early demise has already been detailed. Merckx was at the end of his tether in 1976, keeping on racing largely thanks to his superlative willpower as his physical powers gradually waned. After that spring his only major victory was a stage win in the Tour de Romandie, following which he tackled the Giro d'Italia with a saddle boil on his nether regions – a complaint that had affected him before. He refused to pull out because of the obligation he felt to his Italian sponsor Molteni, which in turn ruled him out of the Tour de France.

His victory list that year was thin, a mere fifteen races as opposed to the forty or fifty he had managed in his prime; for the first time in his career, he finished his season early. Unable to ride his bike by September, he spent six weeks treating his back. He returned in 1977 with a new sponsor, Fiat, but struggled in that year's Tour de France and his stage win in that year's Tour of Switzerland was to be his last major victory. He retired in the spring of 1978.

De Vlaeminck lasted longer. He finished first, second twice and third once in his next four attempts at Paris–Roubaix, but, like Merckx, he struggled to give up racing; his last appearance in Hell was in 1982, when he finished sixth. He kept going until the age of forty, and wound up riding cyclo-cross for a couple of winters. From 1988 to 2000 he was an irascible and not always successful *directeur sportif* – Hitachi, Tonton Tapis, Palmans. In 2004 he tried coaching, over-seeing Zimbabwean cyclo-cross racers.

In his sixties, he was dipping in and out of the sport, at times expressing views on professional cycling that were so uncompromising they invited satire. The early death of his elder brother Erik – after a long battle with drugs, alcohol and mental illness – was tough for him, so too the premature demise of his nephew, Erik's son Geert, who keeled over and died of a heart attack while racing. A key interest is the racing career of his son, born in 2001, and named Eddy as a sign of reconciliation with his old rival, who sponsored him in his final season racing cyclo-cross.

Others of that generation of Flandrians – probably the greatest generation ever from that tiny province – have also struggled to come to terms with life post-cycling. Freddy Maertens's crash and burn is now legendary, but as an example to be eschewed. The form that had made him the favourite for Paris–Roubaix in that spring of 1976 continued, with a flurry of wins in early May: the Henninger Turm at Frankfurt, the Championship of Zurich, and the Four Days of Dunkirk. He continued in that vein through June and July, taking the Belgian national championship, adding eight stages in the Tour de France – a record he still holds jointly with Merckx – and the points prize, then concluding with the world road-race title and the Grand Prix des Nations. It remains one of the greatest seasons any professional cyclist has put together.

In 1977, as Merckx's star waned, Maertens looked well worthy of his designation as the successor to the Cannibal, taking Paris–Nice and the Tour of Catalonia and landing thirteen stages and the overall title at the Vuelta, then the Giro d'Italia, where he took seven stages in the first nine days of racing before a spectacular crash in which he broke his wrist. He was never the same rider again, although he returned to take two stages and the points title at the Tour de France in 1978.

That was followed by a period in the wilderness and then an unexpected comeback in 1981, when he took five Tour stages and a second world championship, before his career again went over the cliff. There were four positive drugs tests in 1977, problems with failed investments and unpaid wages; by the mid-1980s Maertens was a shadow of himself; when we met at the end of 2017 he was unemployed, and had just got over heart surgery, although he seemed finally reconciled to everything that had beset him.

Flandria also fell on hard times. The team continued until 1980, shortly before the bankruptcy of the original bike company in 1981, with its lustre fading after Maertens's decline and a major drugs scandal involving Pollentier at the 1978 Tour de France. It was bought out by a company named Splendor, but Splendor-Flandria never flourished as a brand, and it closed in 1986. The current company bearing that name is based in Britain, having been launched in 2004 in the spirit of its predecessor.

Of the other Roubaix players, Walter Godefroot was close to the end of his career by the time he rode that 1976 Roubaix, but he continued to land major wins – Bordeaux–Paris later that spring, a final, nostalgic Tour of Flanders in 1978, when he was thirty-four years old. His career ended in 1979, after which he immediately became a *directeur sportif*; by the early 1990s he was working at the nascent Telekom squad, backed by Germany's national phone company. With their later incarnation, T-Mobile, he scaled the heights, winning the Tour de France in 1996 with Bjarne Riis and the 1997 Tour de France with Jan Ullrich, who turned into Lance Armstrong's main rival in the noughties. But Godefroot was undone when T-Mobile unravelled amid revelations of systematic doping – although there was no *prima facie* evidence he was involved in it – and when I first visited him in 2011, it was clear that he felt excluded by the cycling world which had been his focus for so long.

Moser would keep racing to Roubaix until 1987, winning the race in 1978, 1979 and 1980 – a hat-trick that has never been equalled – before turning his hand to the Hour record in 1984; with the help of new technology and, he admitted, the then-legal practice of blood doping, he would succeed in beating Merckx's 1972 distance where Leth's old friend Ole Ritter had found it impossible. He now divides his time between making bikes and pressing wine on his estate near his home town of Trento in northern Italy.

Hennie Kuiper enjoyed an equally long career, twice finishing second in the Tour de France before reinventing himself as a one-day rider, winning the Tour of Lombardy and the Tour of Flanders in 1981, and finally taking Paris–Roubaix in 1983 at the age of thirty-four and on his eleventh attempt. He retired in 1988 and became a *directeur sportif*, first with the Stuttgart squad, subsequently with the Motorola team.

Félix Lévitan ended his career in bitter circumstances. He remained at the helm of the Tour de France alongside Jacques Goddet into the 1980s, but fell foul of his own financial dealings. By the mid-1970s, he was aware of the need to open up the Tour and its races to the wider world, and he had his eyes on the USA – hence his support for Mehlman's Hollywood feature film detailed above, and his enthusiasm when Greg LeMond emerged in the early 1980s. Lévitan backed a short-lived project to run a Tour of America, which was killed off after making huge losses. In 1987, following a change of senior management at the Tour organisation after the death of Emilien Amaury, he was summarily sacked – at a meeting in that same office with the soundproof door where he had met Leth – amid allegations that he had used funds from the Tour de France to subsidise the American venture. Before his death in 2007 he was effectively estranged from the Tour organisation, and was not comfortable discussing the event.

His co-organiser Jacques Goddet, retired at roughly the same time as Lévitan, died in 2000 aged ninety-five and was widely mourned within cycling. Daniel Mangeas continued working for the Tour de France organisers and became the most celebrated voice in cycling long before his retirement in 2014. Albert Bouvet became a key figure at the Tour organisation under Goddet's successor Jean-Marie Leblanc, as did Jean-François Pescheux. Franco Cribiori continued working as a *directeur sportif* until 1989; the Brooklyn team folded at the end of 1977 but Cribiori wound up at another squad with a highly distinctive kit: Atala. He now works as a commentator for Italian television.

Leth moved on at pace following *A Sunday in Hell*, after which he made over twenty documentaries on topics as various as ballet (*Dancing Bournonville*, and *Peter Martins: A Dancer*, both 1979; *Step on Silence*, 1981), boxing (*Kalule*, 1979), the Basque ball game *Pelota* (1983), the Danish soccer legend *Michael Laudrup* (1993), sex (*The Erotic Man*, 2010), the USA (*66 Scenes from America*, 1982; revisited as *New Scenes from America*, 2002) and his adopted home of Haiti (*Haiti Express*, 1983).

His collaborators moved on too: Holmberg continued to work with Leth on most of his projects, but is now retired and lives in Honduras. Henning Camre went on to become principal of the Danish Film School, later heading up the British National Film and Television School before returning to the DFI and later becoming head of the think tank on European Film Policy. Herdel still runs his own production company; the editor Lars Brydesen amassed a range of further credits as producer and editor, while Dirk Brüel – who captured many of the images of Merckx – is still shooting after some ninety credits as director of photography in Danish film, winning Robert Awards for cinematography in 1991 for *Springflod* ('Spring River'), and 2000 for *The Magnetist's Fifth Winter*.

Morten Piil eventually resumed his career as a film critic and wrote three books on Danish cinema (*Danish Film Actors*, 2001; *Danish Film-Makers*, 2005; *Gyldendal's Danish Film Guide*, 2008), which jointly provide a comprehensive guide to Danish film. Paul Constantini continued working for French television until 1988; now eighty-two, he runs a company specialising in the production of helicopter images for car makers and motor events such as Paris–Dakar.

A Sunday in Hell has survived the passage of time remarkably well. In that sense, it too is a classic. 'I saw it the other year, I was surprised,' said Henning Camre. 'It's still OK. There aren't many films that you can look at after so many years. How many films are there that are forty years old that you still want to see? If you look at the way that sport is shown today, there are so many helicopters, cameras on bikes, whatever. There is much more sophisticated montage – here it was just shots from handheld cameras, we were much more limited. The drama still works. That's the essential thing, not the technique. You can have fantastic equipment and all that but it doesn't help if you haven't got the right idea. It's good to be reminded of that.'

Making the film was a courageous move for its director and financial backer: a film that could not be made today, a film that involved massive risks, a leap sideways for a largely experimental film-maker, but one who maintained a trend of doing what came to his heart.

The making of it did not work out entirely as Leth dreamed it might, but the director accepts that it has a key place in his career. 'It was like with my poetry in 1967, returning to my core interests. It was a kind of rebirth – finding that I knew something. It also meant a lot on the scale of the audience and the critics. After that, they were on my side. That helped my career, but I didn't want to stay with it. I couldn't go back, because I'd done what I needed to do. They [his cycling films] are the ultimate in that field. I fulfilled my ambition of telling big dramas about cycle races. In practical terms, it opened many ways to continue my career – I was more popular, and there were openings.'

A Sunday in Hell has fired up bike riders across the generations. In November 1977, a teenage cyclist defied a ban on night cycling imposed by his parents and rode for thirty miles through a dark, foggy East Anglia using flickering Eveready battery lights to watch a showing at an independent cinema in Norwich, getting home at midnight. 'It was my first experience of continental bike racing and it must have been the same for loads of us,' recalled Tim Harris. In the pre-satellite television age, bike racing barely ever appeared on screen. 'We never saw the guys racing,' says Harris, who went on to race across Europe as a professional and ended up running lodgings in Belgium where his successors live and race.

Another who drew inspiration from it was a young Danish cyclist named Brian Holm, who recalls saving up his pocket money and queuing outside a cinema on Strøget in Copenhagen when it came out. 'It made a big impression, and it still does forty years later. That's what you call a classic.' At the T-Mobile team in the 1990s, Holm's *directeurs sportifs* Walter Godefroot and Frans Van Looy – he of the broom-wagon sequence – would discuss the film, and when Holm became a manager at T-Mobile and later HTC, his riders would watch it before riding Paris–Roubaix. 'We had a video in the bus. There was a psychologist we worked with at one time who got the riders to watch a video with gladiators to motivate them; *A Sunday in Hell* was much more motivational.'

The film has maintained a place within modern-day cycling, making it far more than a mere archaeological record. It has an audience outside Netflix subscribers and hipster fans in arthouses, one which takes it back to its original roots. In the big-money world of twenty-first-century sport, there are those who feel it is critical for the athletes of today to retain a sense of history and heritage, to be aware of the wheel marks they are following. The film remains a snapshot of the past which conveys a sense of epic mission, as Leth intended; that which can make it appropriate to the task in hand when Merckx's successors are racing over the cobbles, even today.

'When I see it I feel like riding my bike, I think, "Fuck, let's go bike racing, let's get into the bike race,"' says Holm. 'When you see Moser on the cobbles, you think, "Fuck, I want to be the same." Hearing the gear clicking when the mechanic is cleaning the bike at the beginning gives me goose bumps. At the beginning, they all look like movie stars, no tracksuits, sideburns, leather jackets – but Merckx looks like a cross between Elvis Presley and James Hunt. As a movie, it's like a layer cake, it has so many levels – the broom wagon, the mechanics, how the race develops, although we all know the outcome, Marc Demeyer taking the biggest win of his life; and there is the whole retro thing. No helmets, no psychiatrists. Most of the riders I've worked with have got it – maybe 70 per cent – and most people who really love cycling love it.'

In 2010, Bradley Wiggins and his teammate Michael Barry watched the film in their hotel room on a portable computer before setting out across the cobbles during a stage of that year's Tour de France. The director loves the way his work has come full circle, with the stars of today drawing inspiration from his heroes of the past, thirty, forty and maybe fifty years after he and Clausen made their trip to Faubourg-Montmartre. 'What more can I ask? The film is still alive so long after it was made.'

Its maker has travelled far as well. June 2017 saw a series of events in Denmark to celebrate the eightieth birthday of a man who had become a fixture in its cultural life. Leth was still as involved with cycling as ever, returning from Haiti like a migrating bird each spring to commentate at Paris–Roubaix, remaining in for the summer to deliver his views on the Tour de France, that *'favourite novel, which continues year after year'*.

It is, when you think about it, an astonishing way for a 'cultural institution' – as the *Guardian*'s Xan Brooks described him in 2003 – to spend his summers, providing a link between the world of Warhol, von Trier, and Bud Powell and the sweatier, more basic milieu where men earn and lose livings by how fast they pedal and which side of a pile-up their own 'contract with chance' lands them.

Five years after he made *A Sunday in Hell*, Leth first visited Haiti, moving there in 1991, after which he gained the status of honorary Danish consul – an unpaid position where the responsibilities consisted of the occasional public function and the duty to assist any Danes who had issues on the island, hardly onerous, as he admitted in 2003 that the only fellow countrymen who visited tended to be his friends. Leth was drawn to the island, he said, by its sensuality, its voodoo culture and the people's generous spirit.

Leth has never left cycling or Paris–Roubaix behind, although he made no attempt to replicate *A Sunday in Hell*. The move into television commentary came after the demise of *The Yellow Jersey* project; that remained in his mind, and there were occasional suggestions that he should make another documentary: one on the Haitian cycling federation, one on the Tour de France from inside its organisation. There was a proposal to remake *Stars and Watercarriers* with a modern team (his preference was Movistar and Nairo Quintana) but his fear was 'I'd done it before – it might have been boring.' So *A Sunday in Hell* remained his ultimate cycling project, as he had felt at the time, and that seems only appropriate; 'I didn't want to repeat myself,' he told me, 'so the only way back was to take another road as a commentator.'

He made headlines in 2003 with *The Five Obstructions*, but that was followed by a spell in the wilderness following controversy over the content of his 2005 autobiography *The Imperfect Man*, which included an account of sexual relations with the seventeen-year-old daughter of his housekeeper in Haiti. 'It was a scandal, especially in the tabloids,' recalls the journalist Lars B. Jørgensen. 'It was a classic conflict between moralists and liberals. Eventually the tide turned; young people were not so interested in the sensational side and saw him as a guy who had just lived his life, a free thinker. He moved beyond cycle commentating to become something of a cult figure.'

Jørgensen was present when Leth – a pariah at the time, the writer recalls – commentated on a key stage of the 2008

Tour for a Danish newspaper's internet site. It was 'like watching Springsteen busk in the street', Jørgensen says. His rehabilitation came not long after. 'He was a victim of the moral majority and he suffered a lot personally,' says his fellow commentator Brian Nygaard. 'But often in the public domain if the media go hard after someone there is a reaction, public sympathy can change radically.'

In September 2017, Leth and I met again in Copenhagen. This time, lunch morphed into a long afternoon in another elegant café. (The director's liking for eating and sleeping in elegant locations is a recurring theme.) He had aged physically since we first spoke at length about his film two and a half years earlier, but was as sharp and intense as ever. His next film – provisionally titled '*I Walk*' was to be a 'kind of memoir or reflection on life in Haiti' which would reference his other films and those heroes who had dominated his work. Ritter would be among them: in his home, talking to a dog, and packing a bike into his car in a repetition of the closing scene from *Stars and Watercarriers*.

Leth is a born raconteur, who still tells stories of his early cycling heroes: Fausto Coppi, sprinters such as Reg Harris. One quality he admires in them is that they improved with age; Harris became British national champion at fifty-four. He clearly takes pleasure in the fact that a race named after him is run on the velodrome at Aarhus: the Jørgen Leth omnium. His views on cycling today are firmly nostalgic: against tabloid reporting of doping scandals, against night visits from doping control inspectors on privacy grounds, in favour of removing helmet radios, but his views of the fundamentals have not changed.

His commentaries on the Tour de France and Paris–Roubaix for Danish television are hugely popular, so too new departures such as poetry readings combined with music – selling out venues across Denmark including three nights at the national theatre in Copenhagen. There is the radio show named *Ask Jørgen*, in which he answers questions on every topic under the sun: what do you think about being called Jørgen? Why do you hate watermelons? How do you become a zombie? There is no sign of him slowing down. He will keep commentating on the Tour, he says, 'until I fall apart'. In the ultimate sign of joining the establishment, he's involved with the project to bring the Tour to Denmark in 2021, one which goes right up to the highest level – the prince and prime minister. Quite something for a child of the radical sixties.

As he is driven away by his producer, their car stops at a traffic light. A man on a bike begins talking to Leth, who winds down the window for a long chat. It's hard to conceive of any poet, television commentator or film-maker in the UK getting this treatment; let alone conceive of a British figure who combines such intellectual weight and popular appeal. 'He's a polymath; he appeals to people on so many levels,' says the film-maker Niels Christian Jung, who has known Leth since the early 1990s. 'He has a lack of intellectual fear or inhibition. He appeals to everyone because he's everything: he has his position as a documentary maker, his coolness about life, that sense of a classic old-school war correspondent who goes around the world making reports from strange places, talking to scary people like Aristide or Daubuisson. He's generous with people.'

'He's become a man that everyone wants to see and hear,' says Ole Ritter. 'Everyone wants to hear his voice. They like his voice.' Holm echoes him: 'Everyone in Denmark knows his voice.' Even for the English fan who does not understand Danish, the special nature of Leth's delivery is distinct, when you listen to him reading the voiceovers on *Stars and Watercarriers* or *Eddy Merckx in the Vicinity of a Cup of Coffee*. His speech has a mesmeric, rhythmic quality, like an incantation. 'Smooth, elegant, very clear, very articulate, a real sense of tempo, old but not old-fashioned,' says Jørgensen. 'He has no particular accent, so he sounds exotic but familiar.'

'When he commentates, it's like he's building up a movie script – with landscape, character, action – his way of working is very cinematographic,' says Nygaard. 'Either it comes from film-making or he always saw cycling like that. He has shaped the way an entire generation sees cycling. I see a lot of love for Jørgen in Denmark, with no boundaries in age group or background. It's not an elitist country, and the irony is that Jørgen is quite an elitist person in the sense that he makes films that are quite narrow in their audience, and poetry doesn't have a huge audience either. But he's unique for someone doing those kind of things in having such a big following.'

'In cycling in Denmark, everyone loves him,' said Holm, who acknowledges that the pair had their differences at one stage, but have patched up since then. 'He has been part of making cycling so big, and it goes both ways because cycling has made him big. He gives cycling poetry – it was a working-class thing, but he's given it a poetic quality. Some might say he's given it too much poetry – he talks more about history, wine, aesthetics and holidays than cycling tactics – but he's taken it to a new audience, to a new level.'

Leth's poetry, which sells in bookshops alongside Borges and Baudelaire, marked his beginnings and it remains the key factor for his musical collaborator Gunner Møller Pedersen. The composer sees in *A Sunday in Hell* a poet's vision of sport in its passion, and in the drive that meant a project that looked unfeasibly radical on paper actually made it to the screen. 'I've only ever seen it with Jørgen's voice. All those babbling sports reporters can get very annoying. He makes it all poetry. It's poetry with music when you listen to it. Without his poetry it would be just another shitty sports film.'

APPENDIX 1

Jorgen Leth's proposal for 'A Spring Day in Hell'.

I have long dreamed about making a film about the one-day classic Paris-Roubaix: the oldest, most distinguished and hardest of all the spring professional road races.

Paris-Roubaix is about 275km long. It has been run every year – with a few exceptions – since 1900, always in April, always as culmination of the traditional season of spring Classics on the medieval northern French and Flemish highways, the infamous *pavé du nord*, referred to with respect and horror as *l'Enfer du Nord* (*Helvedet Nordpå*).

I enclose for further information some articles on the topic.

I am attracted by the idea of making a full-length film about a bike race which will be settled on a single day – as opposed to the major multi-day stage races, for example the Giro d'Italia (*Stars and Watercarriers*) – because of the ability of a relatively large film team (at least 6–7 cameramen, as many assistants, helicopter etc.) to truly capture the decisive phases and the most dramatic situations in such a race; to dodge around the course and engage with the multiplicity of scenes akin to Dante's *Inferno*, a recurring ritual event, played out as soon as the field reaches the critical zone, the *pavé*, the small lanes of deformed cobblestones.

Here the field is stretched, here the merciless weeding out takes place, here is the great manslaughter. I envisage moments stretched out of time in a long frieze of incredible, emotionally captivating scenes and memorable images from the mythology of professional road cycling. As content for a film, I consider a race like Paris–Roubaix to be a fantastic gift: there is an immense degree of electrifying, epic material that is available here. And it takes shape in a coherent suspenseful narrative, an authentic fiction, a Living Theatre which takes shape in brilliant, moving real-life images. It has the generosity of the greatest competition as well as its value as ritual theatre.

I do not want to make an ordinary documentary about a subject from humdrum real life, but instead I hope to extract a scintillating, novel and epic film, a story simply about significant actors placed in the forefront of a ceremonial act, fascinating mythological figures with eye-catching, dramatically expressed human attributes, measured by a true test of each other's staying power as they venture into the legendary layers of cycling's Hell.

The jump from the single-camera method in *Stars and Watercarriers* to a kind of total 'image coverage' such as the one I have in mind is, in my view, very important. It underlines, among other things, that this variety of narrative has a highly elaborate and mercurial, ever-changing substance; there is only one history, and that is a highly concentrated and hugely exciting one.

APPENDIX 2

1976 Paris–Roubaix race results

Rank	Rider	Team	Time
1	DEMEYER Marc	Flandria-Velda	6:37:41
2	MOSER Francesco	Sanson	"
3	DE VLAEMINCK Roger	Brooklyn	"
4	KUIPER Hennie	TI-Raleigh-Campagnolo	"
5	GODEFROOT Walter	Ijsboerke-Colnago	+1:36
6	MERCKX Eddy	Molteni-Campagnolo	"
7	RAAS Jan	TI-Raleigh	"
8	DANGUILLAUME Jean-Pierre	Peugeot-Esso-Michelin	"
9	TEIRLINCK Willy	Gitane-Campagnolo	+1:45
10	VERBEECK Frans	Ijsboerke-Colnago	"
11	VAN KATWIJK Piet	TI-Raleigh	"
12	PINTENS Georges	Miko-De Gribaldy-Superia	"
13	POULIDOR Raymond	Gan-Mercier-Hutchinson	"
14	DE WITTE Ronald	Brooklyn	"
15	ZOETEMELK Joop	Gan-Mercier-Hutchinson	"
16	DE MUYNCK Johan	Brooklyn	"
17	SWERTS Roger	Molteni-Campagnolo	+2:10
18	PEETERS Willem	Ijsboerke-Colnago	+4:40
19	RITTER Ole	Sanson	"
20	PERIN Michel	Gan-Mercier-Hutchinson	+6:04
21	LEMAN Eric	Miko-De Gribaldy-Superia	+6:01
22	GEVERS André	Lejeune-BP	+6:35
23	THURAU Dietrich	TI-Raleigh	"

24	JACOBS Jos	Ijsboerke-Colnago	+9:01
25	BAERT Jean-Pierre	Miko-De Gribaldy-Superia	"
26	OVION Régis	Peugeot-Esso-Michelin	"
27	PEETERS Ludo	Ijsboerke-Colnago	"
28	BÉON Patrick	Peugeot-Esso-Michelin	+9:33
29	CORBEAU André	Jobo-Wolber-La France	"
30	SIBILLE Guy	Peugeot-Esso-Michelin	"
31	DILLEN René	Gitane-Campagnolo	+12:06
32	BRACKE Ferdinand	Lejeune-BP	+14:24
33	POLLENTIER Michel	Flandria-Velda	"
34	DELÉPINE Régis	Gan-Mercier-Hutchinson	+16:23
35	CAEL Eddy	Flandria-Velda	+21:47
36	MOLLET André	Maes Pils-Rokado	"
37	ABBELOOS Willy	Maes Pils-Rokado	"
38	OSMONT Bernard	Lejeune-BP	+35:25

GLOSSARY OF CHARACTERS

Bartolozzi, Waldemaro *Directeur sportif*, Sanson team.

Boulas, Jacques French rider for Jobo-Wolber, one of three riders involved in an early breakaway in 1976 Paris–Roubaix.

Bouvet, Albert Winner of Paris–Tours in 1956; Félix Lévitan and Jacques Goddet's right-hand man, instigator of the current Paris–Roubaix route; died 2017.

Brüel, Dirk Cameraman for *A Sunday in Hell*.

Camre, Henning Collaborator with Jørgen Leth on *A Sunday in Hell*; went on to head up Danish Film Institute and National Film and Television School in England.

Clausen, Christian Executive producer, *A Sunday in Hell*; together with Jørgen Leth pitched to buy rights to the race from Félix Lévitan .

Constantini, Paul Motorbike cameraman for *A Sunday in Hell*.

Cribiori, Franco *Directeur sportif*, Brooklyn team.

De Muynck, Johann Belgian rider for Brooklyn, involved in a mid-section breakaway in 1976 Paris–Roubaix; winner 1978 Giro d'Italia.

De Vlaeminck, Roger Classics star of the 1970s, holder of record four wins in Paris–Roubaix, one of four pre-determined heroes to be followed closely in *A Sunday in Hell*.

Demeyer, Marc Winner of 1976 Paris–Roubaix, teammate of Freddy Maertens at Flandria, died 1982.

de Vries, Julien Merckx's mechanic; later worked with Greg LeMond and Lance Armstrong.

Driessens, Lomme *Directeur sportif*, Flandria team; died 2006.

Goddet, Jacques Editor of *L'Equipe;* organiser of Tour de France, Paris–Roubaix and other races; died 2000.

Godefroot, Walter Belgian Classics star; winner of the stage featured in the Jørgen Leth film *Eddy Merckx in the Vicinity of a Cup of Coffee.*

Goodman, Ron Cameraman for *A Sunday in Hell*, specialist in helicopter photography.

Harlequin Friend of Driessens and his companion in the Flandria team car.

Herdel, Steen Producer, *A Sunday in Hell;* also one of the instigators of the project.

Herbert, Henrik Cameraman for *A Sunday in Hell,* shot the lingering opening sequence with the Sanson mechanic.

Holmberg, Dan Long-time collaborator with Jørgen Leth; cinematographer on many of his films, including *A Sunday in Hell* for which he also worked as a motorbike cameraman.

Kuiper, Hennie Dutch star of 1970s and 1980s, initially for TI-Raleigh; wears the rainbow jersey of 1975 world road race champion in *A Sunday in Hell.*

Leth, Jørgen Acclaimed Danish documentary film-maker, poet and director of *A Sunday in Hell.*

Lévitan, Félix Head of sport at *Le Parisien Libéré,* commercial gatekeeper and organiser of Tour de France and Paris – Roubaix.

Loiseleux, Jacques Motorbike cameraman for *A Sunday in Hell.*

Maertens, Freddy Belgian star of the 1970s and early 1980s, leader of Flandria, one of four heroes followed closely in *A Sunday in Hell.*

Martinez, Mariano French rider for Lejeune-BP, one of three riders involved in an early breakaway in 1976 Paris – Roubaix.

Merckx, Eddy Cycling's most prolific winner and feared star, one of four heroes followed closely in *A Sunday in Hell.*

Moser, Francesco Italian rider for Sanson, one of four heroes followed closely in *A Sunday in Hell*.

Orsted, Ole Danish soundtrack collaborator on *A Sunday in Hell*.

Osler, Marcello Italian rider for Brooklyn, involved in a mid-section breakaway in 1976 Paris–Roubaix.

Pedersen, Gunner Møller Danish composer who wrote the score for *A Sunday in Hell*.

Pescheux, Jean-François French rider for Jobo-Wolber, colleague of Albert Bouvet at the *Société du Tour de France* from the early 1980s.

Piil, Morten Consultant who originally commissioned the film on behalf of the Danish Film Instituate (DFI).

Pollentier, Michel Belgian rider for Flandria, teammate of Marc Demeyer and Freddy Maertens.

Poulidor, Raymond French rider for Mercier, nicknamed 'the Eternal Second'.

Ritter, Ole Danish rider for Sanson, Hour record-holder, team-mate of Francesco Moser and long-time friend of Jørgen Leth.

Roos, Peter Cameraman for *A Sunday in Hell,* responsible for footage from within the Brooklyn team car.

Saunders, David English narrator of *A Sunday in Hell*.

Stablinski, Jean Old friend of Albert Bouvet; responsible for creation of the current Paris–Roubaix route.

Talbourdet, Georges French rider for Mercier, one of three riders involved in an early breakaway in *A Sunday in Hell*.

Van Looy, Frans Belgian rider for Molteni, teammate of Eddy Merckx.

Verlee, Walter Assistant *directeur sportif*, Flandria.

Weincke, Jan Cameraman for *A Sunday in Hell*.

ACKNOWLEDGEMENTS

To Gunner Møller Pedersen, Henning Camre, Walter Godefroot, Freddy Maertens, Roger De Vlaeminck (ably translated by my Flemish colleague Joeri De Knop), Brian Holm, Steen Herdel, Ron Goodman, Hennie Kuiper, Jean-François Pescheux; many thanks for taking considerable time to be interviewed about a project and a race many years in the past. Many thanks are also due to Dan Holmberg for sharing his memories via a series of highly entertaining and illuminating emails from the other side of the world.

To Tim Harris, Phil Liggett, Philippe Sudres, Luke Evans, Franco Cribiori, Ole Ritter, Morten Piil, Régis Fourissier, Daniel Pautrat, Brian Nygaard, Paul Constantini; many thanks also for valuable insights on various occasions during the writing of this book.

For help, support and encouragement in Denmark, thanks are due to Nils-Christian Jung and Lars B. Jorgensen, with whom I shared a memorable 'Indiana Jones moment' at the Danish Film Institute Archive. At the DFI, Nikoline Riget was a massive source of assistance, while in the archive at the DFI Birgit Granhøj was immensely helpful with obtaining access to Jørgen Leth's papers.

I am indebted to Philippe Bouvet for supplying archive material from *l'Equipe*, and to Jean-François Pescheux for supplying archive material from ASO, most notably an original race programme from 1976, as well as an overview of the 1976 and current routes.

I first became aware of Jørgen Leth and his work in 1995 when, as features editor of the now-defunct *Cycle Sport* magazine, I was approached by the writer Adam Glasser who proposed a piece on the director and *A Sunday in Hell*. This book can to some extent be traced back to the article Adam wrote for us, which appeared in the April 1995 issue. I would like to thank Adam for making his original interview notes with Jørgen available to me.

Massive thanks are also due to my editor Tim Broughton at Yellow Jersey Press, designer Sophie Harris, Phil Brown in production, copy editor Justine Taylor, proof reader Alice Brett, Emmy Lopes for the terrific map, and to my former editor at Yellow Jersey Matt Phillips, who believed in this book when originally suggested several years back, also to my agent David Godwin.

To Caroline, Patrick and Miranda, many thanks for enduring hours of my watching *A Sunday in Hell* and at least one car journey to the sound of Gunner Møller Pedersen's chorale.

Last but far from least, this book would not have happened without the energetic support of Jørgen Leth, who made himself available for interview on several occasions and provided help by email and phone beyond the call of duty, while giving me ample distance to dissect and expand on his *meisterwerk*. It is quite humbling to be trusted in that way.

BIBLIOGRAPHY

The Big Screen: The Story of the Movies and What They Did to Us, David Thomson, Penguin, 2013.

Hunger: The Autobiography, Sean Kelly, Peloton Publishing, 2013.

A Century of Paris–Roubaix: 1886–1996, Pascal Sergeant, De Eecloonar.

Paris – Roubaix: A Journey through Hell, Philippe Bouvet et al., VeloPress, 2007.

'*A Roubaix, l'Envers de l'Enfer*', feature in *l'Equipe* magazine April 2015 by Alban Traquet.

Mine Helte, Jørgen Leth, Gyldendal, 2015.

The Danish Directors: Dialogues on a Contemporary National Cinema, Mette Hjort and Ib Bondebjerg, Intellect Books, 2001.

Small Nation, Global Cinema: The New Danish Cinema, Mette Hjort, University of Minnesota Press, 2005.

The figures for finishers in Paris–Roubaix over the years and the final result was taken from *Des Monuments et des hommes*, by Philippe Vandenbergh, Renaissance du live, 2017.

Figures for annual wages for various riders in 1976 quoted in Chapter 6 were taken from Geoffrey Nicholson's *The Great Bike Race*, Hodder & Sloughton, 1977.

The story about Freddy Maertens, Lomme Driessens and the Lanson champagne was kindly provided by Daniel Pautrat.

Xan Brooks's 2003 *Guardian* interview with Leth regarding his collaboration with Lars von Trier was also valuable.

Interview with Leth at the Sundance Film Festival 2003 from the box set of his work; audience and author interview with Jørgen Leth at the Cyclescreen festival in Bristol 2010 courtesy of Tommy Curtis.

Additional information about the Flandria bike company and its team was sourced from the excellent Flandria website www.flandriabikes.com.

Further information on Emilien Amaury and the strikes at his newspapers in 1975-6 can be found in Guy Vadepied's biography, *Emilien Amaury: La véritable histoire d'un patron de presse du Xxeme siècle*, Le Cherche Midi, 2009.

The quote about Leth's and Gunner Møller Pedersen's roles in the Danish avant-garde of the 1960s is taken from the essay 'Showtime! Notes on the Performance Practice of Per Højholt' by Karsten Wind Meyhoff in *A Cultural History of the Avant-Garde in the Nordic Countries 1950–1975*, Rodopi, 2016.

Vélo magazine special editions April 2001, April 2014; *Miroir du Cyclisme* special edition, April 1982; *Cycle Sport* April 1995.

Quotes from the writer Henrik Jul Jensen in Chapter 1 come from the sleeve notes to the DFI box set of Leth's films, Jørgen Leth 2. Sports Films; so too the story about Morten Piil and the car in Chapter 4.

Piece on the abortive feature film *The Yellow Jersey*, '*Images cherchent film*' by Frédéric Sabouraud in *Cahiers du Cinéma* 389, November 1986; letter Jørgen Leth to Gary Mehlman, 24 April 1987, both from the Danish Film Institute Archive.

LIST OF ILLUSTRATIONS

Demeyer congratulated by Lomme Driessens (Offside/Presse Sports)

The 1976 winner's plaque in the Roubaix showers (Author's own)

Demeyer's grave in Outrijve, West Flanders (Author's own)

Chemin de Bourghelles (Author's own)

The former Café de la Place on Avenue Desandrouins, Valenciennes (Author's own)

Freddy Maertens, West Flanders, September 2017 (Author's own)

The author and Jørgen Leth, Copenhagen, September 2017 (Author's own)

Jorgen Leth and Dan Holmberg's notebooks pages 144, 152 and 189 and film poster page 223 reproduced courtesy of Danish Film Institute

Every effort has been made to trace and contact copyright holders. The publishers will be pleased to correct any omissions or mistakes in future editions.

EST.1998

Yellow Jersey Press celebrates 20 years of quality sports writing

Yellow Jersey Press launched in 1998, with *Rough Ride*, Paul Kimmage's William Hill Sports Book of the Year. In those early days, the Yellow Jersey list sought to give a platform to brilliant stories, which happened to be framed within a sporting environment. Over the past two decades, its name has become synonymous with quality sports writing, covering all sports from the perspective of player, professional observer and passionate fan.

Sport is about more than simple entertainment. It represents a determination to challenge and compete. It binds individuals with a common goal, and often reflects our experiences in the wider world. Yellow Jersey understands this as much as its readers.

This edition was first published in the Yellow Jersey Press 20th Anniversary Year.

YELLOW JERSEY PRESS
LONDON

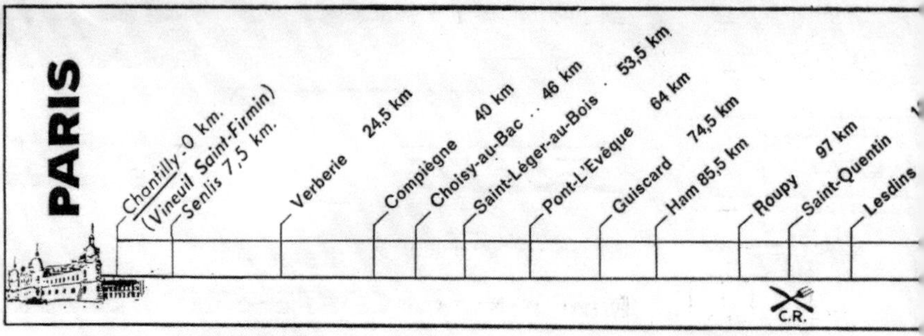

ITINÉRAIRE - HORAIRE

Km parcourus	Km à parcourir	Routes empruntées	LOCALITÉS	Horaire probable 40 km/h
			OISE (60)	
			Chantilly (Place O.-Vallon),	9 15
			départ fictif	9 20
0	279	N. 324	Vineuil-Saint-Firmin (2,5 km), **départ réel**	9 24
3	276		Courteuil	9 31
7,5	271,5		Senlis (N. 324 - N. 17)	9 33
8,5	270,5	N. 17	Carrefour N. 17 - N. 32	9 35
10	269	N. 32	Chamant	9 48
18,5	260,5		Villeneuve-sur-Verberie	9 57
24,5	254,5		Verberie	10 07
31,5	247,5		La Croix-Saint-Ouen	10 20
40	239		Compiègne (N. 32 - N. 31) ..	10 27
44,5	234,5	N. 31	Carrefour N. 31 - D. 130	10 29
46	233	D. 130	Choisy-au-Bac (D. 130 - D. 66)	
51	228		Carrefour D. 130 - D. 165	10 37
53,5	225,5	D. 165	Saint-Léger-au-Bois	10 41
55,5	223,5		Bailly	10 44
62,5	216,5		Sempigny	10 54
64	215		Pont-L'Evêque	10 56
64,5	214,5		Carrefour D. 165 - N. 32	10 57
65,5	213,5	N. 32	Noyon	10 58
74,5	204,5		Guiscard	11 12
80,5	198,5		Golancourt	11 21
			SOMME (80)	
82,5	196,5		Muille	11 24
84,5	194,5		Passage à niveau	11 27
85,5	193,5		Ham (N. 32 - N. 30)	11 29
			AISNE (02)	
97	182	N. 30	Roupy	11 46
104	175		Passage à niveau	11 57
105,5	173,5		Saint-Quentin **(1er ravitaillem.)**	11 59
106,5	172,5		Carrefour N. 30 - D. 8	12 00
113	166	D. 8	Lesdins	12 10
121,5	157,5		Fresnoy-le-Grand	12 22
127	152		Bohain-en-Vermandois	12 30
—	—		Carrefour D. 8 - D. 763 - D. 21	—
			NORD (59)	
133,5	145,5	D. 21	Busigny	12 40
143	136		Le Cateau (D. 21 - N. 355) ..	12 54
146	133	N. 355	Montay	12 58
148	131		Carrefour N. 355 - D. 98	13 01
148,5	130,5	D. 98	Neuvilly	13 02

Km parcourus	Km à parcourir	Routes empruntées	LOCALITÉS	Horaires probables 36km/h	38km/h	40km/h
149	130	D. 98	Carrefour D. 98 - V.O.	—	—	—
149,5	129,5	V.O.	Carrefour V.O. - V. 5	13 04	13 04	13 04
152,5	126,5	V. 5	Inchy (V. 5 - D. 134)	13 09	13 09	13 08
155,5	123,5	D. 134	Viesly (D. 134 - V.O.)	13 14	13 14	13 13
158,5	120,5	V.O.	Quiévy (entrée) (V.O. - D. 113 - D. 113 B)	13 19	13 18	13 17
160	119	D. 113B	Carrefour D. 113 B - D. 135	—	—	—
162,5	116,5	D. 134	Carrefour D. 134 - D. 113 ...	—	—	—
163	116	D. 113	Carrefour D. 113 - C. 309 ...	—	—	—
164,5	114,5	C. 309	Carrefour C. 309 - N. 342 ...	13 29	13 28	13 26
165,5	113,5	N. 342	Saint-Python (N. 342 - N. 355)	13 31	13 30	13 28
168,5	110,5	N. 355	Haussy	13 36	13 34	13 32
171,5	107,5		Montrécourt	13 41	13 39	13 37
172,5	106,5		Saulzoir (N. 355 - V.O.)	13 43	13 40	13 38
176,5	102,5	V.O.	Verchain-Maugré (V.O. - D. 40)	13 49	13 47	13 44
180	99		Carrefour V.O. - N. 358	13 55	13 52	13 49
180,5	98,5	N. 358	Quérenaing (N. 358 - D. 59) ..	13 56	13 53	13 50
181	98		Passage à niveau	13 58	13 55	13 53
182,5	96,5	D. 59	Artres	13 59	13 56	13 54
183	96		Carrefour D. 59 - D. 100	—	—	—
187	92	D. 100	Aulnoy-les-Valenciennes (D. 100 - D. 488)	14 07	13 03	14 00
187,5	91,5	D. 488	Carrefour D. 488 - N. 358 ..	14 08	14 04	14 01
189	90		Trith-Saint-Léger (D. 488 - D. 88)	—	—	—
193	86	D. 88	Valenciennes (D. 88 - N. 358 - N. 29 - D. 13) **2e ravitaille.**	14 17	14 13	14 09
198	81	D. 13	Carrefour D. 13 - D. 313	—	—	—
198,5	80,5		Près Bellaing	14 23	14 18	14 14
199,5	79,5		Passage à niveau	—	—	—
201,5	77,5		Wallers (D. 13 - D. 40)	14 28	14 23	14 18
202	77	D. 40	Carrefour D. 40 - V.O.	—	—	—
203	76	V.O.	Passage à niveau	—	—	—
204	75		Carrefour V.O. - N. 355	14 32	14 27	14 22
206,5	72,5	N. 355	Hasnon (N. 355 - V.O.)	14 37	14 31	14 26
208	71	V.O.	Carrefour V.O. - D. 99	—	—	—
211,5	67,5	D. 99	Carrefour D. 99 - D. 299	14 46	14 39	14 34

Km parcourus	Km à parcourir	Routes empruntées	LOCALITÉS	Horaires prob[...] 36km/h	38km/h
213	66	D. 299	Carrefour D. 299 - D. 81	—	—
214	65		Wandignies - Hamage	14 50	14 44
216,5	62,5		Carrefour D. 299 - D. 957	—	—
218	61	D. 957	Marchiennes	14 57	14 51
219,5	59,5		Carrefour D. 957 - V.O.	—	—
221,5	57,5	V.O.	Carrefour rue des Jardins - rue des Marais	—	—
223	56		Carrefour rue de Hem - rue Allard	—	—
223,5	55,5		Bouvignies (rue Allard - D. 30)	15 07	15 01
—	—	D. 30	Carrefour D. 30 - D. 230	—	—
225,5	53,5		« Le Fromet » (D. 30 - V.O. 4)	15 11	15 04
227	52	V.O. 4	Carrefour V.O. 4 - V.O. 3 ..	—	—
227,5	51,5	V.O. 3	Carrefour V.O. 3 - N. 50	15 14	15 07
228,5	50,5	N. 50	Coutiches (N. 50 - D. 30) ..	15 16	15 09
230	49	D. 30	Grupez (D. 30 - V.O.)	15 19	15 12
231	48		Carrefour D. 30 - D. 30 A ..	—	—
231,5	47,5	D. 30 A	Carrefour D. 30 A - V.O.	—	—
232,5	46,5		« La Broderie » (D. 30 A - V.O.)	15 23	15 16
233,5	45,5	V.O.	Carrefour V.O. - N. 354	15 25	15 18
	—	N. 354	Carrefour N. 354 - V.O.	—	—
235	44	V.O.	Carrefour rue de la Ricarderie - rue d'Argérie	—	—
		V.O.	Carrefour rue d'Argérie - rue du Nouveau-Monde	—	—
235,5	43,5		Carrefour rue du Nouveau-Monde - D. 127	—	—
236	43	D. 127	Wattines	15 29	15 22
	—		Carrefour D. 127 - V.O.	—	—
237	42	V.O.	Carrefour route de Bersée - rue de la Poissonnerie	—	—
239	40		« Le Molpas » (V.O. - V.O. C)	15 34	15 26
241	38	V.O. C	Carrefour V.O. C - N. 353 - D. 19	15 38	15 30
243	36	D. 19	Templeuve	15 41	15 33
243,5	35,5		Carrefour D. 19 - V.O.	—	—
244	35	V.O.	Carrefour V.O. - D. 128	—	—
246	33	D. 128	Huquinville (P.N.)	15 46	15 37
—	—		Carrefour D. 128 - D. 127	—	—
248,5	30,5		Ouvignies	15 50	15 41
250,5	28,5		Nomain	15 53	15 45
—	—		Carrefour D. 128 - V.O.	—	—
252	27	V.O.	Carrefour V.O. - V.O.	—	—
—	—		Rue Dérain - La Rue Haute ..	—	—
—	—		Le Quimberge	—	—
254,5	24,5		Carrefour D. 145 - D. 93	—	—
257	22	D. 93	« La Posterie » (D. 93 - D. 93 A)	16 04	15 55
258	21		Bachy (D. 93 - N. 355)	16 06	15 56
260,5	18,5	N. 355	Bourghelles (N. 355 - D. 93) .	16 10	16 00
262	17		Cysoing (N. 355 - D. 90)	16 12	16 02
262,5	16,5	D. 90	Carrefour D. 90 - V.O.	—	—
264,5	14,5	V.O.	Gruson (V.O. - D. 94)	16 17	16 06
267	12	D. 94	Anstaing (P.N.)	16 21	16 10
268,5	10,5		Le Petit Paris (D. 94 - N. 41 - V.O.)	16 23	16 12
270	9	V.O.	Tressin (P.N.)	16 26	16 15
272	7	V.O.	Forest - sur - Marque (V.O. - N. 352)	16 29	16 19
274	5	N. 352	Hem (N. 352 - D. 64)	16 32	16 22
274,5	4,5		Carrefour N. 352 - D. 6	—	—
275	4		Carrefour N. 352 - D. 264	16 34	16 23
278	1	D. 264	Roubaix (entrée Centre Sportif)	16 39	16 28
279	0		Roubaix (Vélodrome), la distance (300 m) plus un tour complet (500 m)	16 41	16 30

Oxford Handbook of

Clinical Pathology

Published and forthcoming Oxford Handbooks

Oxford Handbook for the Foundation Programme 4e
Oxford Handbook of Acute Medicine 3e
Oxford Handbook of Anaesthesia 4e
Oxford Handbook of Applied Dental Sciences
Oxford Handbook of Cardiology 2e
Oxford Handbook of Clinical and Healthcare Research
Oxford Handbook of Clinical and Laboratory Investigation 3e
Oxford Handbook of Clinical Dentistry 6e
Oxford Handbook of Clinical Diagnosis 3e
Oxford Handbook of Clinical Examination and Practical Skills 2e
Oxford Handbook of Clinical Haematology 4e
Oxford Handbook of Clinical Immunology and Allergy 3e
Oxford Handbook of Clinical Medicine – Mini Edition 9e
Oxford Handbook of Clinical Medicine 9e
Oxford Handbook of Clinical Pathology
Oxford Handbook of Clinical Pharmacy 2e
Oxford Handbook of Clinical Rehabilitation 2e
Oxford Handbook of Clinical Specialties 9e
Oxford Handbook of Clinical Surgery 4e
Oxford Handbook of Complementary Medicine
Oxford Handbook of Critical Care 3e
Oxford Handbook of Dental Patient Care
Oxford Handbook of Dialysis 4e
Oxford Handbook of Emergency Medicine 4e
Oxford Handbook of Endocrinology and Diabetes 3e
Oxford Handbook of ENT and Head and Neck Surgery 2e
Oxford Handbook of Epidemiology for Clinicians
Oxford Handbook of Expedition and Wilderness Medicine 2e
Oxford Handbook of Forensic Medicine
Oxford Handbook of Gastroenterology & Hepatology 2e
Oxford Handbook of General Practice 4e
Oxford Handbook of Genetics
Oxford Handbook of Genitourinary Medicine, HIV and AIDS 2e
Oxford Handbook of Geriatric Medicine 2e
Oxford Handbook of Infectious Diseases and Microbiology
Oxford Handbook of Key Clinical Evidence
Oxford Handbook of Medical Dermatology 2e
Oxford Handbook of Medical Imaging
Oxford Handbook of Medical Sciences 2e
Oxford Handbook of Medical Statistics
Oxford Handbook of Neonatology
Oxford Handbook of Nephrology and Hypertension 2e
Oxford Handbook of Neurology 2e
Oxford Handbook of Nutrition and Dietetics 2e
Oxford Handbook of Obstetrics and Gynaecology 3e
Oxford Handbook of Occupational Health 2e
Oxford Handbook of Oncology 3e
Oxford Handbook of Ophthalmology 3e
Oxford Handbook of Oral and Maxillofacial Surgery
Oxford Handbook of Orthopaedics and Trauma
Oxford Handbook of Paediatrics 2e
Oxford Handbook of Pain Management
Oxford Handbook of Palliative Care 2e
Oxford Handbook of Practical Drug Therapy 2e
Oxford Handbook of Pre-Hospital Care
Oxford Handbook of Psychiatry 3e
Oxford Handbook of Public Health Practice 3e
Oxford Handbook of Reproductive Medicine & Family Planning 2e
Oxford Handbook of Respiratory Medicine 3e
Oxford Handbook of Rheumatology 3e
Oxford Handbook of Sport and Exercise Medicine 2e
Handbook of Surgical Consent
Oxford Handbook of Tropical Medicine 4e
Oxford Handbook of Urology 3e

Oxford Handbook of Clinical Pathology

SECOND EDITION

Edited by

James Carton
Consultant Histopathologist
Imperial College Healthcare NHS Trust
London, UK

OXFORD
UNIVERSITY PRESS

OXFORD
UNIVERSITY PRESS

Great Clarendon Street, Oxford, OX2 6DP,
United Kingdom

Oxford University Press is a department of the University of Oxford.
It furthers the University's objective of excellence in research, scholarship,
and education by publishing worldwide. Oxford is a registered trade mark of
Oxford University Press in the UK and in certain other countries

First Edition published in 2012
Second Edition published in 2017

Impression: 1

Published in the United States of America by Oxford University Press
198 Madison Avenue, New York, NY 10016, United States of America

British Library Cataloguing in Publication Data
Data available

Library of Congress Control Number: 2017931114

ISBN 978–0–19–875958–4

Printed and bound in China by
C&C Offset Printing Co., Ltd.

To my parents, Paul and Shirley,
for all they have done for me,
and to Rob for making me so happy.

Preface to the second edition

The first edition of the *Oxford Handbook of Clinical Pathology* was very well received and I have been delighted to receive much positive feedback since its publication.

Pathology continues to advance at a tremendous pace, particularly in the field of tumour pathology, with new immunohistochemical and molecular diagnostic tools transforming the way in which tumours are diagnosed and classified. This new information has been a particular focus for the updates in this second edition. A dedicated head and neck pathology chapter has been written and colour photos have also been included.

An ever increasing burden in routine diagnostic work has meant that updating the book by myself became an impossibility, so I have been aided by a number of contributors, all of whom are experts in their particular subspecialty. I thank them all for their help, without which this new edition would not have been possible. I am also grateful to the team at Oxford University Press, especially Liz Reeve and Michael Hawkes.

James Carton
2016

Contents

Contributors

Dr Giuseppe Culora
Consultant Histopathologist, Guys' & St Thomas' NHS Trust, London, UK

Professor Adrienne Flanagan
Royal National Orthopaedic Hospital NHS Trust, Stanmore, UK

Professor Robert Goldin
Professor of Liver and GI Pathology, Imperial College Healthcare NHS Trust, London UK

Dr Monika Hofer
Consultant Neuropathologist, Oxford University Hospitals NHS Trust, Oxford, UK

Dr Luis Perez-Casanova-Gomez
Royal National Orthopaedic Hospital NHS Trust, Stanmore, UK

Dr Rathi Ramakrishnan
Consultant Histopathologist, Imperial College Healthcare NHS Trust, London, UK

Dr Manuel Rodriguez-Justo
Consultant Histopathologist, University College Hospitals NHS Trust, London, UK

Dr Candice Roufosse
Consultant Histopathologist, Imperial College Healthcare NHS Trust, London, UK

Symbols and abbreviations

&	and
~	approximately
%	per cent
=	equal to
×	multiply
±	plus/minus
>	greater than
<	less than
≥	greater than or equal to
≤	less than or equal to
Δ	delta
α	alpha
β	beta
ε	epsilon
γ	gamma
κ	kappa
♀	female
♂	male
↓	decreased
↑	increased
→	leading to
❗	warning
►	important
►►	don't dawdle
®	registered trademark
➲	cross-reference
ACTH	adrenocorticotropic hormone
ADH	atypical ductal hyperplasia
AFP	alpha-fetoprotein
AIDP	atypical intraductal proliferation; acute inflammatory demyelinating polyneuropathy
AIDS	acquired immune deficiency syndrome
AIH	autoimmune hepatitis
AIN	anal intraepithelial neoplasia
AITL	angioimmunoblastic T-cell lymphoma
AKI	acute kidney injury
ALCL	anaplastic large cell lymphoma
ALH	atypical lobular hyperplasia

ALL	acute lymphoblastic leukaemia
ALS	amyotrophic lateral sclerosis
ALT	atypical lipomatous tumour
ALVAL	aseptic lymphocytic vasculitis-associated lesion (score)
AMAN	acute motor axonal neuropathy
AML	acute myeloid leukaemia
AMSAN	acute motor sensory axonal neuropathy
ANCA	anti-neutrophil cytoplasmic antibody
APKD	adult polycystic kidney disease
APOE	apolipoprotein E
APP	amyloid precursor protein
APTT	activated partial thromboplastin time
ARDS	acute respiratory distress syndrome
ARF	acute renal failure
ASD	atrial septal defect
ASH	alcoholic steatohepatitis
ATLL	adult T-cell lymphoma
ATM	ataxia-telangiectasia mutated (gene)
AVSD	atrioventricular septal defect
BAL	bronchoalveolar lavage
B-ALL	acute B-lymphoblastic leukaemia
BL	Burkitt's lymphoma
BPH	benign prostatic hyperplasia
BSE	bovine spongiform encephalopathy
CADASIL	cerebral autosomal dominant arteriopathy with subcortical infarcts and leukoencephalopathy
CD	Crohn's disease
CF	cystic fibrosis
CFTR	cystic fibrosis transmembrane conductance regulator
CGIN	cervical glandular intraepithelial neoplasia
CHD	congenital heart disease
cHL	classical Hodgkin's lymphoma
CIN	cervical intraepithelial neoplasia
CIS	carcinoma *in situ*
CJD	Creutzfeldt–Jacob disease
CKD	chronic kidney disease
CLL	chronic lymphocytic leukaemia
cm	centimetre
CML	chronic myelogenous leukaemia
CMV	cytomegalovirus
CNS	central nervous system

COPD	chronic obstructive pulmonary disease
CPPD	calcium pyrophosphate crystal deposition
CSF	cerebrospinal fluid
CT	computed tomography
CVID	common variable immunodeficiency
DCIS	ductal carcinoma *in situ*
DDD	dense deposit disease
DFSP	dermatofibrosarcoma protuberans
DIC	disseminated intravascular coagulation
dL	decilitre
DLBCL	diffuse large B-cell lymphoma
DNA	deoxyribonucleic acid
DPLD	diffuse parenchymal lung disease
EATL	enteropathy-associated T-cell lymphoma
EBV	Epstein–Barr virus
ECG	electrocardiogram
e.g.	*exempli gratia* (for example)
ELISA	enzyme-linked immunosorbent assay
EMA	eosin-5-maleimide
EPA	eosinophilic granulomatosis with polyangiitis
ER	oestrogen receptor
ERCP	endoscopic retrograde cholangiopancreatography
ESR	erythrocyte sedimentation rate
ET	essential thrombocythaemia
ETEC	enterotoxigenic *Escherichia coli*
FAB	French–American–British (scheme)
FAP	familial adenomatous polyposis
FEV_1	forced expiratory volume in 1 second
FGF	fibroblast growth factor
FIGO	International Federation of Gynaecology and Obstetrics
FiO_2	fraction of inspired oxygen
FISH	fluorescence *in situ* hybridization
FMTC	familial medullary thyroid carcinoma
FNA	fine-needle aspiration
FOB	faecal occult blood
FS-DSFP	fibrosarcomatous dermatofibrosarcoma protuberans
FSGS	focal segmental glomerulosclerosis
FSH	follicle-stimulating hormone
ft	foot
FVC	forced vital capacity
g	gram

GBM	glioblastoma
GBS	Guillain–Barré syndrome
GCNIS	germ cell neoplasia *in situ*
GFR	glomerular filtration rate
GH	growth hormone
GI	gastrointestinal
GN	glomerulonephritis
GPA	granulomatosis with polyangiitis
G6PD	glucose-6-phosphate dehydrogenase
h	hour
HAV	hepatitis A virus
Hb	haemoglobin
HBcAg	hepatitis B core antigen
HbF	fetal haemoglobin
HbS	sickle haemoglobin
HBsAg	hepatitis B surface antigen
HBV	hepatitic B virus
HCC	hepatocellular carcinoma
HCG	human chorionic gonadotrophin
HCM	hypertrophic cardiomyopathy
HCT	haematocrit
HCV	hepatitis C virus
HDV	hepatitis D virus
HEV	hepatitis E virus
HHV	human herpesvirus
HIF	hypoxia inducible factor
HIV	human immunodeficiency virus
HLA	human leucocyte antigen
HMA	homovanilic acid
HNPCC	hereditary non-polyposis colorectal carcinoma
hpf	high-power field
HPV	human papillomavirus
HRS	Hodgkin/Reed Sternberg
HRT	hormone replacement therapy
HSV	herpes simplex virus
HUS	haemolytic uraemic syndrome
i.e.	*id est* (that is)
IFN	interferon
Ig	immunoglobulin
IgA	immunoglobulin A
IgAN	IgA nephropathy

IgE	immunoglobulin E
IgG	immunoglobulin G
IgM	immunoglobulin M
IL	interleukin
in	inch
IPF	idiopathic pulmonary fibrosis
IPMN	intraductal papillary neoplasm
IPSID	immunoproliferative small intestinal disease
ISUP	International Society of Urologic Pathologists
ITP	idiopathic thrombocytopenic purpura
JAK2	Janus kinase 2
kDa	kilodalton
kg	kilogram
kPa	kilopascal
L	litre
LCIS	lobular carcinoma *in situ*
LDH	lactate dehydrogenase
LDL	low-density lipoprotein
LEF1	lymphoid-enhancer-binding factor 1
LFT	liver function test
LH	luteinizing hormone
LLETZ	large loop excision of the transformation zone
LP	lymphocyte-predominant
LPL	lymphoplasmacytic lymphoma
LRPP4	low-density lipoprotein receptor-related protein 4
LUTS	lower urinary tract symptoms
LVF	left ventricular failure
m	metre
MALT	mucosa-associated lymphoid tissue
MASP	mannose-binding lectin-associated serine protease
MCD	minimal change disease
MCHC	mean corpuscular haemoglobin concentration
MCV	mean corpuscular volume
MDS	myelodysplastic syndrome
MDS-U	myelodysplastic syndrome, unclassified
MEN	multiple endocrine neoplasia
MFH	malignant fibrous histiocytoma
mg	milligram
MGUS	monoclonal gammopathy of undetermined significance
MHC	major histocompatibility complex
min	minute

mL	millilitre
mm	millimetre
mmHg	millimetre of mercury
mmol	millimole
MMSE	Mini-Mental State Examination
MoM	metal-on-metal (prosthesis)
MPA	microscopic polyangiitis
MPNST	malignant peripheral nerve sheath tumour
MRI	magnetic resonance imaging
MRSA	meticillin-resistant *Staphylococcus aureus*
nAChR	nicotinic acetylcholine receptor
NADH	nicotinamide adenine dinucleotide dehydrogenase
NAFLD	non-alcoholic fatty liver disease
NASH	non-alcoholic steatohepatitis
NF-κB	nuclear factor kappa B
NHS	National Health Service
NIFTP	non-invasive follicular thyroid neoplasm with papillary-like nuclear features
NK	natural killer
NLPHL	nodular lymphocyte-predominant Hodgkin's lymphoma
NOD2	nucleotide oligomerization binding domain 2
NOS	not otherwise specified
NSAID	non-steroidal anti-inflammatory drug
PaO_2	partial pressure of oxygen in arterial blood
$PaCO_2$	partial pressure of carbon dioxide in arterial blood
PAN	polyarteritis nodosa
PanIN	pancreatic intraepithelial neoplasia
PAS	periodic acid–Schiff
PBC	primary biliary cirrhosis/cholangitis
PCR	polymerase chain reaction
PCV	packed cell volume
PDA	patent ductus arteriosus
PET	positron emission tomography
PID	pelvic inflammatory disease
PIN	prostatic intraepithelial neoplasia
PMF	primary myelofibrosis
PR	progesterone receptor
PrP	prion protein
PSA	prostate-specific antigen
PSC	primary sclerosing cholangitis

PT	prothrombin time
PTCL	peripheral T-cell lymphoma
PTH	parathyroid hormone
PV	polycythaemia vera
RA	rheumatoid arthritis
RAEB	refractory anaemia with excess of blasts
RARS	refractory anaemia with ring sideroblasts
RBC	red blood cell
RCC	renal cell carcinoma
RCMD	refractory cytopenia with multilineage dysplasia
RCU	refractory cytopenia with unilineage dysplasia
REM	rapid eye movement
RhF	rheumatoid factor
RNA	ribonucleic acid
RVF	right ventricular failure
s	second
SLE	systemic lupus erythematosus
SLL	small lymphocytic leukaemia
SS	systemic sclerosis
STIC	serous tubal intraepithelial carcinoma
TB	tuberculosis
TGF	transforming growth factor
TIA	transient ischaemic attack
TIBC	total iron binding capacity
TIN	tubulointerstitial nephritis
t-MDS	therapy-related myelodysplastic syndrome
TNF	tumour necrosis factor
TNFR	tumour necrosis factor receptor
TSH	thyroid-stimulating hormone
TTP	thrombotic thrombocytopenic purpura
TURP	transurethral resection of the prostate
UC	ulcerative colitis
UIP	usual interstitial pneumonia
UK	United Kingdom
UTI	urinary tract infection
UV	ultraviolet
VAIN	vaginal intraepithelial neoplasia
VHL	von Hippel–Lindau
VIN	vulval intraepithelial neoplasia
VMA	vanillylmandelic acid

VSD	ventricular septal defect
VUR	vesicoureteric reflux
vWF	von Willebrand factor
VZV	varicella-zoster virus
WCC	white cell count
WHO	World Health Organization
y	year

Chapter 1

Basic pathology

Pathological terminology

Nomenclature of disease

- **Aetiology** refers to a disease's underlying cause. Diseases whose aetiology is unknown are described as **idiopathic**, **cryptogenic**, or **essential**.
- **Pathogenesis** refers to the mechanism by which the aetiological agent produces the manifestations of a disease.
- **Incidence** refers to the number of new cases of a disease diagnosed over a certain period of time.
- **Prevalence** refers to the total number of cases of a disease present in a population at a certain moment in time.
- **Prognosis** is a prediction of the likely course of a disease.
- **Morbidity** describes the extent to which a patient's overall health will be affected by a disease.
- **Mortality** reflects the likelihood of death from a particular disease.
- **Acute** and **chronic** refer to the time course of a pathological event. Acute illnesses are of rapid onset. Chronic conditions usually have a gradual onset and are more likely to have a prolonged course.
- A **syndrome** refers to a set of symptoms and clinical signs that, when occurring together, suggest a particular underlying cause(s).

Classification of disease

- **Genetic** diseases are inherited conditions in which a defective gene causes the disease, e.g. cystic fibrosis (CF).
- **Infective** diseases are the result of invasion of the body by pathogenic microbes, e.g. malaria.
- **Inflammatory** diseases are due to excess inflammatory cell activity in an organ, e.g. rheumatoid arthritis (RA).
- **Neoplastic** disease results from an uncontrolled proliferation of cells, e.g. breast carcinoma.
- **Vascular** diseases arise due to disorders of blood vessels, e.g. ischaemic heart disease.
- **Metabolic** disorders arise due to abnormalities within metabolic pathways, e.g. diabetes mellitus.
- **Degenerative** diseases occur as a consequence of damage and/or loss of specialized cells, e.g. loss of neurones from the cerebral cortex in Alzheimer's disease.
- **Iatrogenic** disease is the result of the effects of treatment, e.g. osteoporosis due to long-term glucocorticoid treatment.
- **Congenital** diseases are present at birth, whereas those occurring after birth are known as **acquired**.

Cellular adaptations

Atrophy

- A reduction in size of a tissue or organ.
- May occur through a reduction in cell number by deletion (apoptosis) or a reduction in cell size through shrinkage.
- Atrophy may occur as a normal physiological process, e.g. thymic atrophy during adolescence and post-menopausal ovarian atrophy.
- Examples of pathological atrophy include muscle atrophy following denervation and cerebral atrophy due to cerebrovascular disease.

Hypertrophy

- An increase in size of individual cells.
- Due to an increase in cell proteins and organelles.
- Seen in organs containing terminally differentiated cells that cannot multiply, e.g. cardiac and skeletal muscle.
- Examples of physiological hypertrophy include the myometrium of the uterus in pregnancy and muscles of a bodybuilder.
- Examples of pathological hypertrophy include left ventricular hypertrophy due to hypertension (➔ Hypertension, p. 33) or aortic stenosis (➔ Valvular heart disease, pp. 54–5).

Hyperplasia

- An increase in cell number.
- Examples of physiological hyperplasia include endometrium and breast lobules in response to cyclical oestrogen exposure.
- Examples of pathological hyperplasia include benign prostatic hyperplasia (BPH) (➔ Benign prostatic hyperplasia, p. 228) and parathyroid hyperplasia (➔ Parathyroid hyperplasia, p. 315).

Metaplasia

- A change in which one cell type is switched for another.
- Thought to be the result of progenitor cells differentiating into a new type of cell, rather than a direct morphogenesis of cells from one type to another.
- Seen almost exclusively in epithelial cells, often in response to chronic injury.
- Metaplasia is named according to the new type of cell type, e.g. a change from non-squamous to squamous epithelium is called squamous metaplasia.
- Common sites of squamous metaplasia include the endocervix (creating the transformation zone where cervical neoplasia occurs) and the bronchi of smokers.
- Common sites of glandular metaplasia include the lower oesophagus in some people with reflux disease, creating a visible Barrett's oesophagus (➔ Oesophagitis, pp. 108–9).
- Metaplasia is a marker of long-term epithelial damage which, in some cases, may develop into epithelial dysplasia and eventually carcinoma.

Cellular death

Necrosis

- A poorly controlled form of cell death in which membrane integrity is lost with leakage of cellular contents and an inflammatory response.
- **Coagulative necrosis** is the most common form, characterized by the loss of cell nuclei, but with general preservation of the underlying architecture. The dead tissue is macroscopically pale and firm.
- **Liquefactive necrosis** leads to complete loss of cellular structure and conversion into a soft, semi-solid mass. This is typically seen in the brain following cerebral infarction.
- **Caseous necrosis** is a type of necrosis in which the dead tissue macroscopically appears like cream cheese. It may be seen in many conditions but is most commonly associated with tuberculosis (TB).
- **Gangrene** is a term that refers to necrotic tissues modified by exposure to air, resulting in drying (dry gangrene) or infection (wet gangrene). Toes deprived of blood in critical leg ischaemia usually show dry gangrene (➲ Chronic lower limb ischaemia, p. 34).

Apoptosis

- A controlled form of cell death in which no cellular contents are released from the dying cell, and thus no inflammatory reaction.
- Apoptosis may occur physiologically (e.g. removal of cells during embryogenesis and cells with deoxyribonucleic acid (DNA) damage) or pathologically.
- Apoptosis may be induced in two main ways (Fig. 1.1): by the engagement of surface death receptors, e.g. Fas or tumour necrosis factor alpha (TNF-α), (extrinsic pathway) or through cellular injury (intrinsic pathway).
- The end result is the activation of protease enzymes called **caspases** which dismantle the cell cytoplasm and nucleus.
- Apoptotic cells shrink down and fragment into apoptotic bodies, each of which retains an intact cell membrane.
- Apoptotic bodies are targeted for their rapid removal by adjacent cells.
- Disordered apoptosis is thought to be central to a number of important disease processes, particularly carcinogenesis.

Necroptosis

- Programmed form of cell death which results in release of cellular contents with an inflammatory reaction, hence shows hybrid features of apoptosis and necrosis.
- Triggered by ligation of TNF receptor 1 (TNFR1) or viral proteins.
- Signalling driven by a protein complex of RIP1 and RIP3.
- Caspase activation does not occur.

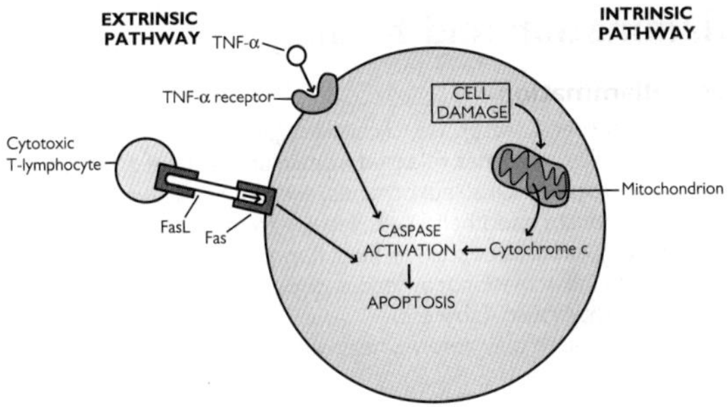

Fig. 1.1 Apoptosis may be triggered extrinsically by the ligation of 'death receptors' or intrinsically if cell damage causes the release of cytochrome c from mitochondria.

Reproduced with permission from *Clinical Pathology* (Oxford Core Texts), Carton, James, Daly, Richard, and Ramani, Pramila, Oxford University Press (2006), p. 9, Figure 1.3.

Inflammation and healing

Acute inflammation

- A rapid, non-specific response to cellular injury.
- Orchestrated by **cytokines** released from injured cells, e.g. histamine, serotonin, prostaglandins, leukotrienes, and platelet-activating factor.
- Cytokines activate endothelial cells, leading to the formation of an **acute inflammatory exudate** containing fluid, fibrin, and neutrophils.
- Severe acute inflammation may lead to a localized collection of pus within a necrotic cavity (**abscess**).
- Acute inflammation may resolve, heal with scarring, or progress to chronic inflammation.

Chronic inflammation

- Persistent form of inflammation in which there is simultaneous tissue damage and attempted repair.
- May arise from acute inflammation or occur from the outset.
- Characterized by the presence of chronic inflammatory cells, namely macrophages, lymphocytes, and plasma cells.
- More likely to heal with irreversible scarring than resolve.

Granulomatous inflammation

- A special type of chronic inflammation characterized by the presence of activated macrophages known as epithelioid histiocytes.
- Collections of epithelioid macrophages are known as **granulomas**.
- Granulomatous inflammation is associated with foreign bodies, persistent infections (e.g. mycobacteria), and diseases whose cause is unclear (e.g. sarcoidosis).

Healing

- Process of replacing dead and damaged tissue with healthy tissue.
- May occur through regeneration or repair.
- **Regeneration** (resolution) replaces damaged cells with the same type of cell and is the ideal outcome. This can only occur if the connective tissue framework of the tissue is not disrupted and if the tissue is capable of regeneration.
- **Repair** begins with the formation of granulation tissue which is then converted into a collagen-rich scar. Although the structural integrity is maintained, there is loss of function of the tissue that is scarred.

Innate immunity

Epithelial surfaces

- Epithelial surfaces form a physical barrier against infection.
- Low pH of skin and fatty acids in sebum inhibit microbial growth.
- The gut has gastric acid, pancreatic enzymes, mucosal immunoglobulin A (IgA), and normal colonic flora which act to prevent establishment of infection.
- The respiratory tract secretes mucus to trap organisms, and beating cilia transport them to the throat where they are swallowed.
- Continuous flushing of urine through the urinary tract prevents microbes from adhering to the urothelium.

Phagocytes

- Organisms breaching epithelial surfaces encounter tissue macrophages that recognize pathogens and attract neutrophils to the site.
- Macrophages and neutrophils are phagocytes that ingest microbes by phagocytosis into a phagosome.
- The phagosome is fused to cytoplasmic lysosomes that contain enzymes and reactive oxygen intermediates that kill the microbe.
- Phagocytes recognize organisms by pattern recognition receptors, e.g. mannose receptors, Toll-like receptors, and Nod-like receptors.

Acute phase proteins

- Cytokines produced by phagocytes stimulate the liver to rapidly synthesize and release acute phase proteins.
- **Mannose-binding lectin** recognizes microbial surface sugars and undergoes a conformational change, allowing it to bind a protein mannose-binding lectin-associated serine protease (MASP) and form a complex which activates complement.
- **C-reactive protein** binds to the phosphorylcholine portions of microbial lipopolysaccharide and targets them for phagocytosis by macrophages.

Complement

- A collection of circulating proteins that assist the immune system in killing microbes.
- May be activated by antibodies bound to a microbe (**classical pathway**), triggered automatically on microbes lacking a regulatory protein present on host cells (**alternative pathway**), or by mannose-binding protein (**lectin pathway**).
- A sequential cascade leads to the generation of C3 convertase, an enzyme that splits many molecules of C3 into C3b.
- Microbes coated in C3b are destroyed either by phagocytosis or the **membrane attack complex**, a polymer of the terminal complement components which forms holes in the cell membrane of the microbe.
- The complement system is tightly regulated to prevent uncontrolled activation. **Decay accelerating factor** disrupts binding to C3b to cell surfaces and **membrane co-factor** protein breaks down C3b.

Adaptive immunity

Antibody-mediated immunity

- Mediated by proteins called **antibodies** or **immunoglobulins** (Igs).
- Binding of antigen to the Fab antigen-binding region unmasks the binding sites on the Fc portion which mediates the functions of the antibody.
- Antibodies work in four main ways:
  - Neutralize the biological activity of a vital microbial molecule, e.g. a binding protein or toxin.
  - Target microbes for phagocytosis.
  - Activate complement.
  - Activate cytotoxic immune cells.
- Antibody production is initiated following binding of an antigen to its specific B-cell receptor on the surface of naïve B-lymphocytes in the presence of an additional signal from CD4+ helper T-lymphocytes (Fig. 1.2).

Cell-mediated immunity

- Predominantly mediated by T-lymphocytes (Fig. 1.3).
- CD4+ helper T-cells are activated by foreign peptides presented by class II major histocompatibility complex (MHC) molecules expressed by specialized antigen-presenting cells such as dendritic cells and macrophages.
- Activated CD4+ helper T-cells proliferate and secrete cytokines that mediate a variety of immune responses.
- Many subtypes of helper T-cells are recognized, depending on the cytokines they produce when activated, including Th1, Th2, Th3, and Th17.
- CD8+ cytotoxic T-cells are activated by foreign peptides presented by class I MHC expressed by all nucleated cells.
- Activated CD8+ cytotoxic T-cells destroy the presenting host cell either by stimulating apoptosis through the **Fas ligand** or by inserting a membrane pore called **perforin** through which the T-cell pours in proteolytic enzymes.

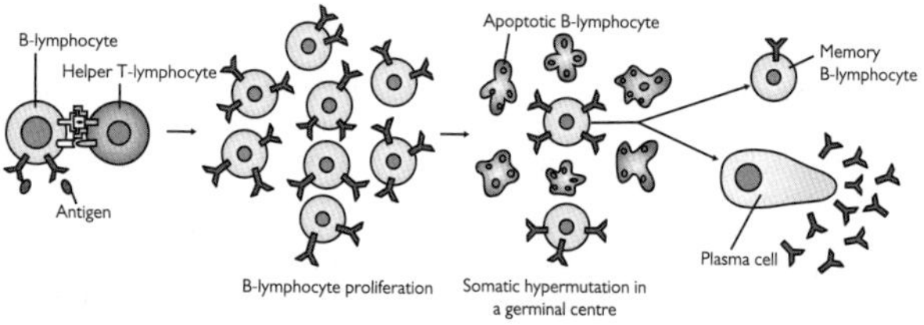

Fig. 1.2 Humoral immunity. Naïve B-lymphocytes that encounter their antigen and receive appropriate T-cell help enter a germinal centre where they proliferate and undergo somatic hypermutation of the immunoglobulin gene. Only B-lymphocytes with the best fitting immunoglobulin are selected to survive and differentiate into memory cells or plasma cells. The remainder are doomed to die by apoptosis in the germinal centre.

Reproduced with permission from *Clinical Pathology* (Oxford Core Texts), Carton, James, Daly, Richard, and Ramani, Pramila, Oxford University Press (2006), p. 41, Figure 4.5.

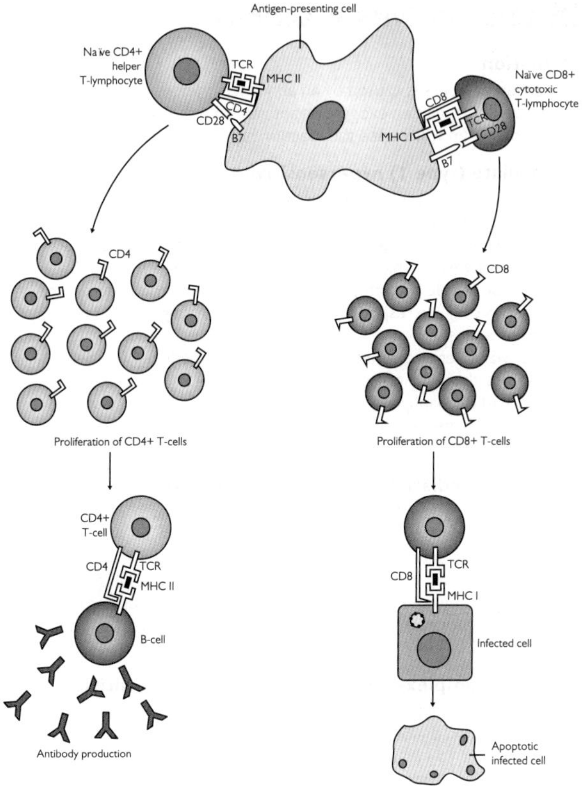

Fig. 1.3 Cellular immunity. T-lymphocytes activated by antigen-presenting cells proliferate and express genes appropriate to their actions. Activated CD4+ helper T-cells interact with other cells of the immune system such as B-lymphocytes, whilst activated CD8+ cytotoxic T-lymphocytes destroy infected host cells.

Reproduced with permission from *Clinical Pathology* (Oxford Core Texts), Carton, James, Daly, Richard, and Ramani, Pramila, Oxford University Press (2006), p. 43, Figure 4.6.

Hypersensitivity reactions

Definition

- A group of diseases caused by an abnormal immune-mediated reaction.
- May be directed at an exogenous antigen from the environment or a self-antigen (in which case the reaction is a form of autoimmunity).

Immediate (type 1) hypersensitivity

- Characterized by the production of immunoglobulin E (IgE) antibodies in response to an antigen.
- Cross-linkage of surface IgE receptors on mast cells releases mediators, such as histamine, which stimulate acute inflammation.
- Typical of people with **atopy**, a genetic disposition to produce large quantities of IgE in response to environmental antigens such as pollen and house dust mites.
- **Anaphylaxis** represents a systemic form of immediate hypersensitivity caused by the widespread release of histamine. In its most severe form, it can lead to **anaphylactic shock** (➔ Shock, p. 32).
- Immediate hypersensitivity diseases affect >20% of people and the incidence is rising.

Antibody-mediated (type 2) hypersensitivity

- Caused by immunoglobulin G (IgG) or immunoglobulin M (IgM) antibodies binding to a fixed antigen in a tissue.
- Binding of the antibody may activate complement and lead to cellular injury, e.g. bullous pemphigoid (➔ Bullous pemphigoid, p. 392), or cause a change in cellular function, e.g. thyroid-stimulating hormone (TSH) receptor-stimulating antibody in Graves' disease (➔ Graves' disease, p. 305).

Immune complex-mediated (type 3) hypersensitivity

- Caused by circulating IgG or IgM antibodies forming immune complexes with antigen in the blood and depositing in tissues where they activate complement.
- Sites of predilection for the deposition of immune complexes include small blood vessels, kidneys, and joints.
- Immune complex-mediated hypersensitivity reactions tend to be multisystem diseases in which vasculitis, arthritis, and glomerulonephritis feature, e.g. systemic lupus erythematosus (SLE) (➔ Systemic lupus erythematosus, p. 492–3).

T-cell-mediated (type 4) hypersensitivity

- Caused by activated T-lymphocytes that injure cells by direct cell killing or releasing cytokines that activate macrophages.
- Because T-cell responses take 1–2 days to occur, this type is also known as delayed-type hypersensitivity.
- Examples include contact dermatitis (➔ Eczema, p. 386), Hashimoto's thyroiditis (➔ Hashimoto's thyroiditis, p. 304), primary biliary cholangitis (PBC) (➔ Primary biliary cholangitis, p. 155), and TB (➔ Tuberculosis, p. 20).

Neoplasia

Definitions

- A **neoplasm** is an abnormal mass of tissue which shows uncoordinated growth and serves no useful purpose. The word is often used synonymously with the word **tumour** which simply means a swelling.
- **Benign** neoplasms usually have a slow rate of growth and remain confined to their site of origin. Benign neoplasms usually run an innocuous course but can be dangerous if they compress vital nearby structures or if the neoplasm secretes hormones uncontrollably.
- **Malignant** neoplasms have capacity to spread or metastasize to distant sites and produce secondary tumours called metastases which can grow independently from the primary tumour.
- **Cancer** is a broad term for any malignant neoplasm.

Nomenclature of neoplasms

Epithelial neoplasms

- Benign neoplasms of squamous epithelium are called **acanthomas** if they are flat or **papillomas** if they grow in branching fronds.
- Benign neoplasms of glandular epithelium are called **adenomas**.
- Epithelial malignancies are called **carcinomas**. Carcinomas showing squamous differentiation are called **squamous cell carcinomas**. Carcinomas showing glandular differentiation are called **adenocarcinomas**.
- Carcinomas are often preceded by a phase of epithelial **dysplasia**, in which the epithelium contains neoplastic cells but invasion beyond the confines of the epithelium has not yet occurred.

Connective tissue neoplasms

- Lipoma is a benign adipocytic tumour.
- Leiomyoma is a benign smooth muscle tumour.
- Rhabdomyoma is a benign skeletal muscle tumour.
- Angioma is a benign vascular tumour.
- Osteoma is a benign bony tumour.
- Liposarcoma is a malignant adipocytic tumour.
- Leiomyosarcoma is a malignant smooth muscle tumour.
- Rhabdomyosarcoma is a malignant skeletal muscle tumour.
- Angiosarcoma is a malignant vascular tumour.
- Osteosarcoma is a malignant bony tumour.

Other types of neoplasms

- Lymphomas, leukaemias, and myeloma are haematological malignancies derived from cells of blood or the bone marrow.
- Malignant melanoma is a malignant melanocytic neoplasm.
- Malignant mesothelioma is a malignant mesothelial tumour.
- Germ cell tumours usually arise in the testes or ovaries.
- Embryonal tumours are a group of malignant tumours seen predominantly in children and composed of very primitive cells, e.g. neuroblastoma (➲ Neuroblastoma, p. 322) and nephroblastoma (➲ Childhood renal tumours, p. 224).

Carcinogenesis

Definition

- The sequence of events leading to growth of a malignant neoplasm.

Aetiology

- Radiation or chemicals which damage DNA, e.g. sunlight in skin carcinomas and cigarette smoke in lung carcinomas.
- Chronic inflammatory diseases which stimulate persistent proliferation of cells, e.g. ulcerative colitis (UC) predisposes to colonic carcinoma.
- High levels of hormones cause proliferation of hormonally responsive tissues, e.g. oestrogens in breast and endometrial carcinomas.
- Certain oncogenic viruses produce proteins which promote uncontrolled cell division, e.g. human papillomavirus (HPV) in cervical carcinoma.

Pathogenesis

- DNA damage to genes whose protein products are involved in the control of cell division allows deregulated growth of cells.
- Genes controlling cell division are divided into **oncogenes** and **tumour suppressor genes**.

Oncogenes

- Mutated genes that promote cell division (Fig. 1.4).
- Mutations usually result in overexpression of the gene product or constitutive activation of the protein product.
- Examples of oncogenes commonly mutated in malignancies include *KIT*, *RAS*, and *MYC*.

Tumour suppressor genes

- Genes encoding proteins that normally inhibit cell growth.
- Loss of activity of both gene copies is usually required for a tumour-promoting effect.
- Examples of tumour suppressor genes commonly mutated in malignancies include *p53*, *CDKN2A*, and *Rb* (Fig. 1.5).

Metastasis

- Acquisition of metastatic potential is a pivotal event in the evolution of a neoplasm as this is one of the major reasons why malignant tumours eventually lead to death.
- Malignant neoplasms metastasize via three main routes: **haematogenous spread** to distant organs (e.g. lungs, liver, bone, brain), **lymphatic spread** to regional lymph nodes (e.g. axillary lymph nodes in breast carcinomas), and **transcoelomic spread** whereby malignant tumours growing near a body cavity, such as the pleura or peritoneum, can seed into these spaces and spread to other organs.
- Successful metastasis requires a number of hurdles to be overcome: loss of adhesion from neighbouring cells, eroding the extracellular matrix, penetrating the lumen of a vessel, surviving in the circulation whilst travelling to a distant site, exiting the vessel, and successfully implanting at the new site and multiplying.

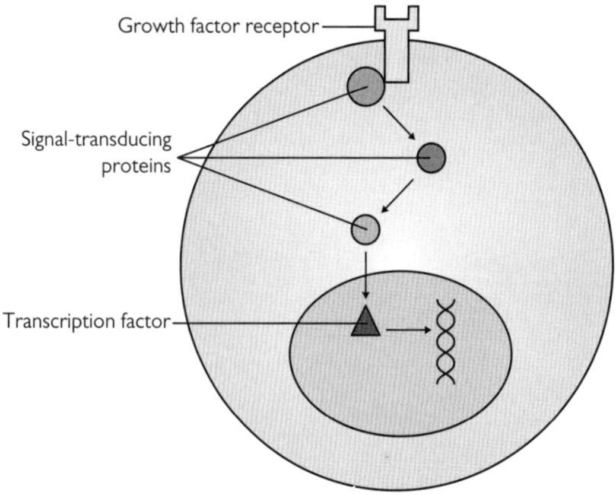

Fig. 1.4 Oncoproteins. Oncogenes code for proteins with key roles in growth-stimulating cell signalling pathways.

Reproduced with permission from *Clinical Pathology* (Oxford Core Texts), Carton, James, Daly, Richard, and Ramani, Pramila, Oxford University Press (2006), p. 56, Figure 5.5.

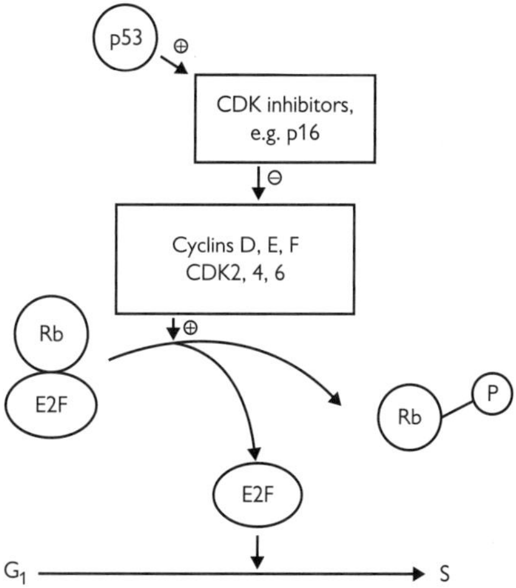

Fig. 1.5 Critical role of *p53* and *Rb* at the G_1 to S checkpoint.

Reproduced with permission from *Clinical Pathology* (Oxford Core Texts), Carton, James, Daly, Richard, and Ramani, Pramila, Oxford University Press (2006), p. 57, Figure 5.6.

Chapter 2

Infectious diseases

Microbes

Bacteria

- Single-celled organisms with their double-stranded DNA lying free in the cytoplasm surrounded by a cell membrane and cell wall.
- Most grow in air (aerobes) but can grow without it (facultative anaerobes). Some only grow in the absence of oxygen (strict anaerobes).
- Gram-positive bacteria have a thick cell wall composed of peptidoglycan and a second polymer, often teichoic acid.
- Gram-negative bacteria have a thinner peptidoglycan wall overlaid by an outer lipid membrane composed of lipopolysaccharide.
- Mycobacteria are a type of bacteria with a thick waxy cell wall which can be stained with the Ziehl–Neelsen stain.

Viruses

- Smallest and simplest microbes composed of genetic material in the form of DNA or ribonucleic acid (RNA) enclosed in a protein shell (capsid). Some viruses also have an outer lipid membrane acquired from the host cell in which they formed.
- Obligate intracellular organisms that can only replicate by infecting a host cell and hijacking its metabolic apparatus.
- Cause disease by destroying host cells (direct cytopathic effect) or due to the immune reaction against the infection.
- Some viruses are able to establish latent infection, e.g. herpes simplex.
- Some viruses are oncogenic and implicated in the transformation of the host cell and development of malignancy, e.g. HPV in cervical carcinoma (➔ Cervical carcinoma, pp. 250–1) and Epstein–Barr virus (EBV) in nasopharyngeal carcinoma (➔ Nasopharyngeal diseases, p. 98).

Fungi

- Contain DNA within a nucleus and have a cell membrane containing ergosterol and an outer cell wall composed of chitin.
- Yeasts are unicellular fungi that reproduce by budding, e.g. *Candida*.
- Moulds grow as branching filaments called hyphae that interlace to form a tangled mass known as a mycelium. Mycelia produce spores.
- Some fungi can exist in yeast and mould forms, e.g. *Histoplasma*.

Protozoa

- Single-celled organisms which may live inside host cells or in the extracellular environment.
- Intracellular protozoa derive nutrients from the host cell (e.g. *Plasmodium, Leishmania, Toxoplasma*).
- Extracellular protozoa feed by direct nutrient uptake and/or ingestion of shed epithelial cells (e.g. *Giardia, Trichomonas*).

Helminths

- Complex multicellular parasitic worms, ranging in size from microscopic organisms to giant organisms several metres in length.
- Many have complex life cycles involving more than one host.
- Divided into nematodes (roundworms), cestodes (tapeworms), and trematodes (flukes).

Antimicrobial agents

Antibacterial agents

Inhibitors of cell wall synthesis

- Interfere with peptidoglycan synthesis.
- β-lactams, e.g. penicillins and cephalosporins.
- Glycopeptides, e.g. vancomycin and teicoplanin.

Inhibitors of protein synthesis

- Bind to bacterial ribosomes and prevent the elongation of protein chains.
- Aminoglycosides, e.g. gentamycin.
- Tetracyclines, e.g. doxycycline.
- Macrolides, e.g. erythromycin, clarithromycin.

Inhibitors of nucleic acid synthesis

- Interfere with the synthesis of DNA precursors or DNA replication.
- Sulfonamides, e.g. sulfamethoxazole.
- Trimethoprim.
- Quinolones, e.g. ciprofloxacin.
- Rifamicins, e.g. rifampicin.
- Nitroimidazoles, e.g. metronidazole.

Antiviral agents

- Aciclovir is a guanosine analogue which is phosphorylated by viral thymidine kinase. Aciclovir triphosphate is incorporated into viral DNA and terminates chain replication.
- Ganciclovir is related to aciclovir but is more active against cytomegalovirus (CMV).
- Modern human immunodeficiency virus (HIV) therapy involves combinations of reverse transcriptase inhibitors and protease inhibitors.

Antifungal agents

- Azoles act by blocking the synthesis of ergosterol, e.g. fluconazole.
- Polyenes impair fungal cell membrane function, e.g. amphotericin and nystatin.

Human immunodeficiency virus (HIV)

Pathogen

- Single-stranded, positive-sense, enveloped RNA virus.
- Member of lentivirus genus, part of the retrovirus family.

Epidemiology

- Very common worldwide, most notably in sub-Saharan Africa.
- Declared pandemic by World Health Organization (WHO).

Transmission

- Major routes of transmission are unprotected sex, contaminated needles, breast milk, and transmission from mother to baby at birth.
- Transmission via transfused blood products now virtually eliminated by stringent donor screening.

Immunopathogenesis

- Infects CD4+ helper T-lymphocytes, macrophages, and dendritic cells.
- Widespread seeding of lymphoid tissue occurs following infection.
- HIV-specific CD8+ cytotoxic T-cells initially control the disease.
- Eventually, HIV escapes immune control through antigenic mutation.
- Viral load rapidly rises and CD4+ counts fall precipitously.

Presentation

- Acute seroconversion causes a flu-like illness with fever, lymphadenopathy, sore throat, myalgia, rash, and mouth ulcers.
- Latency phase then follows, which is usually asymptomatic.
- Final phase presents with opportunistic infections and/or neoplasms (Fig. 2.1).
- (➔ Bacterial pneumonia, p. 74), pulmonary TB (➔ Tuberculosis, p. 20), *Pneumocystis* pneumonia, oesophageal candidiasis (➔ Oesophagitis, p. 109), cryptosporidiosis and *Mycobacterium avium* in bowel (➔ Intestinal infections, p. 126), cryptococcal meningitis, and cerebral toxoplasmosis.
- Common neoplasms include cervical/anal warts and carcinoma, non-Hodgkin's B-cell lymphomas, and Kaposi's sarcoma.

Histopathology

- Lymph nodes show florid follicular hyperplasia with follicle lysis. Lymphomas are usually of diffuse large B-cell type (➔ Diffuse large B-cell lymphoma, pp. 366–7).
- Bone marrow appears dysplastic with jumbling of haematopoietic lineages and increased numbers of plasma cells.
- Skin may show eosinophilic folliculitis (infiltration of hair follicles by eosinophils). Cutaneous Kaposi's sarcoma shows an irregular proliferation of human herpesvirus (HHV)-8-positive spindle cells in the dermis which form slit-like vascular spaces.
- *Pneumocystis* pneumonia shows a lymphocytic alveolitis with silver-positive organisms in the alveolar spaces.

Prognosis

- With modern anti-HIV therapy, many patients can expect to have a near normal lifespan such that they die with HIV rather than from it.

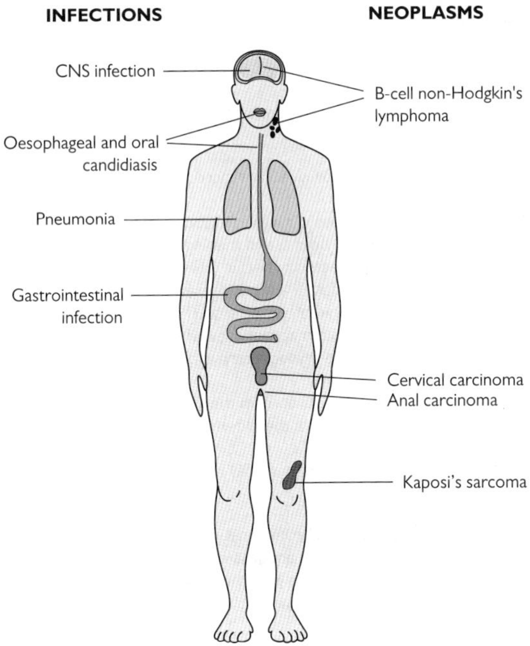

Fig. 2.1 Manifestations of advanced HIV infection.

Reproduced with permission from *Clinical Pathology* (Oxford Core Texts), Carton, James, Daly, Richard, and Ramani, Pramila, Oxford University Press (2006), p. 50, Figure 4.8.

Tuberculosis (TB)

Pathogen

- *Mycobacterium tuberculosis*, an acid-fast rod-shaped bacillus.

Epidemiology

- Most common infectious disease worldwide.
- Kills 2 million people per year.

Transmission

- Respiratory spread from an infectious patient with active pulmonary TB.

Immunopathogenesis

- Inhaled bacilli are engulfed by alveolar macrophages but can survive and multiply within them.
- Mycobacteria spread in macrophages in blood to oxygen-rich sites such as the lung apices, kidneys, bones, and meninges.
- After a few weeks, mycobacteria-specific CD4+ helper T-cells are activated following MHC class II antigen presentation by macrophages.
- Th1 subset helper T-cells secrete interferon (IFN)-γ, activating macrophages into epithelioid macrophages which aggregate into granulomas and wall off the mycobacteria in an anoxic and acidic environment.
- Most immunocompetent hosts contain the infection, leading to scarring.
- Active disease tends to occur in the elderly, malnourished, diabetic, immunosuppressed, or alcoholic.
- Active disease may be pulmonary (75%) or extrapulmonary (25%).

Presentation

- Pulmonary TB presents as a chronic pneumonia with persistent cough, fever, night sweats, weight loss, and loss of appetite.
- Extrapulmonary TB may present with meningitis, lymphadenopathy, genitourinary symptoms, and bone or joint pain.

Diagnosis

- Acid-fast bacilli may be seen in sputum, pleural fluid, or bronchoalveolar lavage (BAL) fluid.
- Culture is the definitive investigation but takes up to 12 weeks.
- Polymerase chain reaction (PCR) can be used for diagnosis and identification of drug-resistant strains.

Histopathology

- Necrotizing granulomatous inflammation.

Prognosis

- With antituberculous treatment, most people make a full recovery.
- Untreated, about half of people will eventually die of the infection.
- Prognosis is worse with coexisting HIV or organisms with multidrug resistance.

Infectious mononucleosis

Pathogen

- Epstein–Barr virus (EBV), a DNA herpesvirus.

Epidemiology

- Most patients are teenagers or young adults.
- No gender or racial predilection.

Transmission

- Saliva or droplet spread from an EBV-infected person.
- Incubation period of 4–5 weeks.

Pathogenesis

- EBV infects oropharyngeal epithelial cells via the C3d receptor and replicates within them.
- EBV also infects B-lymphocytes where the linear genome circularizes and persists as an episome.
- Viral persistence allows ongoing replication in oropharyngeal epithelial cells and the release of infectious particles into the saliva.

Presentation

- Sore throat, fever, malaise.
- Clinical examination may reveal lymphadenopathy, palatal petechiae, and splenomegaly.

Diagnosis

- Lymphocytosis.
- Peripheral blood film shows large atypical lymphocytes (these are not specific for EBV).
- 90% have heterophil antibodies (Paul–Bunnell; Monospot test).
- EBV-specific IgM antibodies imply current infection.

Histopathology

- Lymph nodes and tonsils show marked paracortical expansion by large lymphoid blasts which are a mixture of B- and T-cells.
- EBV-LMP1 antigen can be detected in some of the B-blasts immunohistochemically.

Prognosis

- In most cases, the illness is self-limiting.
- Rare complications include meningitis, encephalitis, cranial nerve lesions, Guillain–Barré syndrome, depression, and fatigue.

Malaria

Pathogen
- Plasmodia protozoa: *Plasmodium falciparum, P. vivax, P. ovale, P. malariae.*

Epidemiology
- Endemic in tropical Africa, Asia, and South America.
- ~10 million new infections each year.
- ~1 million deaths each year (mostly *P. falciparum*).

Transmission
- *Plasmodium* sporozoites are injected by the female *Anopheles* mosquito during a blood meal.

Pathogenesis
- Sporozoites infect hepatocytes and proliferate into merozoites.
- Merozoites infect and multiply in red cells, causing haemolytic anaemia.
- Sequestration of red cells heavily parasitized by *P. falciparum* causes acute renal failure (ARF) and cerebral malaria (Fig. 2.2).

Presentation
- Non-specific flu-like illness initially with headache, malaise, and myalgia.
- Fevers and chills then follow.
- Cerebral malaria presents with confusion, seizures, and coma.

Diagnosis
- Parasitized red cells may be seen on examination of blood films.

Prognosis
- Non-falciparum malaria has a very low mortality.
- Severe falciparum malaria can kill. Poor prognostic signs include high levels of parasitaemia, hypoglycaemia, disseminated intravascular coagulation (DIC), and renal impairment.

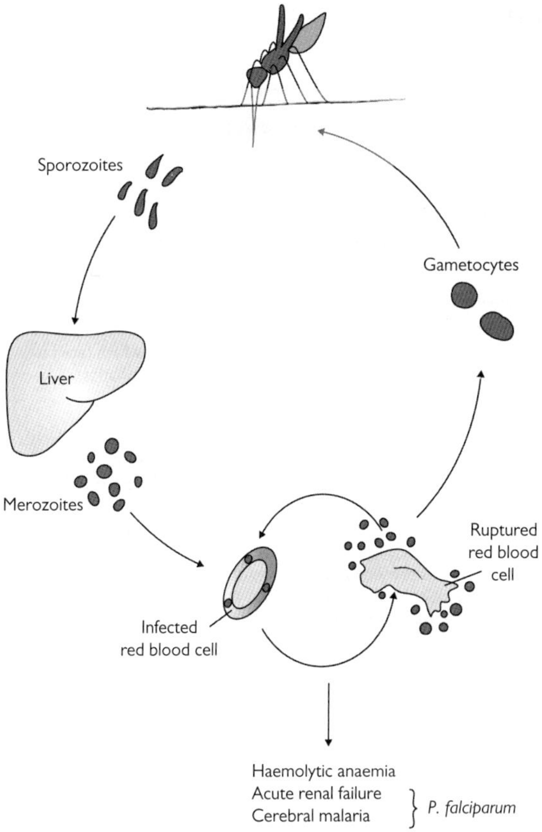

Fig. 2.2 Malaria life cycle. An infected mosquito injects sporozoites into blood which home to the liver and multiply in hepatocytes, forming merozoites. Merozoites released into blood infect red blood cells and multiply again, rupturing the red cells and infecting more red cells. Some merozoites mature into gametocytes which newly infect a mosquito, completing the life cycle.

Reproduced with permission from *Clinical Pathology* (Oxford Core Texts), Carton, James, Daly, Richard, and Ramani, Pramila, Oxford University Press (2006), p. 26, Figure 3.5.

Syphilis

Pathogen

- *Treponema pallidum*, a coiled spirochaete.

Epidemiology

- Worldwide distribution.
- Incidence increasing since the 1990s.

Transmission

- Almost always through sexual contact with an infected person.
- Can pass from mother to baby and cause congenital syphilis.

Pathogenesis

- Organisms enter the body via minor abrasions in epithelial surfaces.
- The organism produces a non-antigenic mucin coat which facilitates rapid spread throughout the body via blood and lymphatics.

Presentation

- Primary syphilis causes a firm, painless skin ulcer ('chancre') which appears about 3 weeks following exposure. The chancre occurs at the point of contact and is usually genital or perianal. There may be mild regional lymph node enlargement.
- Secondary syphilis presents 1–2 months after the chancre with rash, malaise, lymphadenopathy, and fever.
- Tertiary syphilis present years after exposure with so-called gummas in the skin, mucosa, bone, joints, lung, and testis. Gummas are inflammatory masses caused by a granulomatous reaction to the organism.
- Quaternary syphilis causes ascending aortic aneurysms, cranial nerve palsies, dementia, and tabes dorsalis.

Diagnosis

- In primary syphilis, the organisms may be visualized by microscopy of chancre fluid. Serology is often negative at this stage.
- In secondary syphilis, the organisms may be seen in the lesions and serology is usually positive.
- Organisms are usually not seen in later stages of syphilis, but serology usually remains positive.

Prognosis

- Antibiotic treatment during primary or secondary stages is usually curative and prevents risk of longer-term complications related to later-stage disease.

Lyme disease

Pathogen

- *Borrelia burgdorferi*, a spirochaete.

Epidemiology

- Found in temperate zones of Europe, North America, and Asia.

Transmission

- Arthropod-borne infection transmitted via ticks of the genus *Ixodes*.

Pathogenesis

- *Borrelia* organisms are injected into the skin via the tick bite where they establish infection and proliferate.
- Days to weeks later, *Borrelia* spreads via the bloodstream to distant sites, notably the joints, heart, and nervous system.
- *Borrelia* evades the immune system through antigenic variation of its surface proteins and inactivating complement components.

Presentation

- The earliest sign is an outwardly expanding erythematous rash at the site of the tick bite, known as **erythema migrans**. Many patients do not present with, or recall, the rash.
- Later signs include arthralgia, myalgia, neuropathies, changes in cognition, and palpitations.

► The presence of non-specific features across multiple body systems can make the diagnosis extremely challenging.

Diagnosis

- Western blot, enzyme-linked immunosorbent assay (ELISA), or PCR analysis on blood or cerebrospinal fluid (CSF).

Prognosis

- Most people diagnosed and treated recover fully with no complications.

Leishmaniasis

Pathogen

- *Leishmania* protozoa.

Epidemiology

- 1–2 million new cases each year worldwide.
- Seen in Africa, India, South America, the Middle East, and the Mediterranean.

Transmission

- Inoculation from the bite of an infected sandfly.

Pathogenesis

- The parasite is inoculated into the dermis and phagocytosed by dermal macrophages.
- The ability of each species to survive within macrophages and evade host immunity dictates the clinical outcome.

Presentation

- **Cutaneous leishmaniasis**, caused by *Leishmania tropica* and *L. mexicana*, usually present with a single nodule which ulcerates and heals with scarring.
- **Mucocutaneous leishmaniasis**, caused by *L. braziliensis*, presents with skin lesions resembling the cutaneous form which may spread to the mucosa of the nose, mouth, and pharynx.
- **Visceral leishmaniasis** (kala-azar), caused by *L. donovani*, presents with fever, anaemia, lymphadenopathy, and hepatosplenomegaly due to widespread dissemination of the organism via macrophages through the reticuloendothelial system.

Diagnosis

- Microscopy, culture, fluorescence *in situ* hybridization (FISH), or PCR.

Histopathology

- Skin biopsies show a heavy dermal inflammatory infiltrate composed of lymphocytes, plasma cells, and many parasitized macrophages.
- The organisms are round to oval, 2–4 micrometres in size, with an eccentric kinetoplast.

Prognosis

- Cutaneous disease usually resolves spontaneously over a period of months.
- Mucocutaneous disease should be treated early as outcome is less satisfactory once mucosal sites are involved.
- Visceral disease is fatal without treatment due to liver failure and bone marrow failure.

Chapter 3

Vascular pathology

Atherosclerosis

Definition

- An inflammatory disease of large and medium-sized systemic arteries, characterized by the formation of lipid-rich plaques in the vessel wall.

Epidemiology

- Almost universally present to some degree with ageing.

Aetiology

- Risk factors include age, male gender, diabetes mellitus, hypertension, smoking, and hyperlipidaemia.

► Men who smoke have a 70% increase in death rate from ischaemic heart disease, compared to non-smokers.

Pathogenesis

- Endothelial injury leads to an inflammatory and fibroproliferative reaction in the artery, culminating in atherosclerosis ('response to injury' hypothesis).
- Endothelium may be damaged by multiple factors, including smoking, hyperglycaemia, and oxidized low-density lipoprotein (LDL).
- Oxidized LDL is particularly potent at driving atherosclerosis through its proinflammatory and procoagulant effects.
- Stable plaques with few inflammatory cells and a thick fibrous cap narrow the lumen of the artery but are less likely to cause acute complications.
- Unstable plaques with more inflammatory cells have a thin fibrous cap vulnerable to erosion, cracking, or rupture. Exposure of the highly thrombogenic lipid core to the blood causes an acute ischaemic event in the organ that artery is supplying (Fig. 3.1).

Presentation

- Stable plaques cause symptoms of reversible ischaemia in the supplied organ, e.g. angina pectoris, chronic lower limb ischaemia.
- Unstable plaques cause acute ischaemic events, e.g. acute coronary syndromes, stroke, acute lower limb ischaemia.

Macroscopy

- Atherosclerotic plaques are yellow, lipid-rich lesions within the walls of large and medium-sized arteries.
- Superimposed thrombus has a dark brown appearance.
- Sites of predilection are the coronary arteries, abdominal aorta, iliac arteries, and carotid artery bifurcations.

Histopathology

- The intima is expanded by a plaque composed of a lipid-rich core with overlying fibrous tissue.
- If there has been superimposed thrombosis, then a fibrin-rich clot may also be present, occluding the artery.

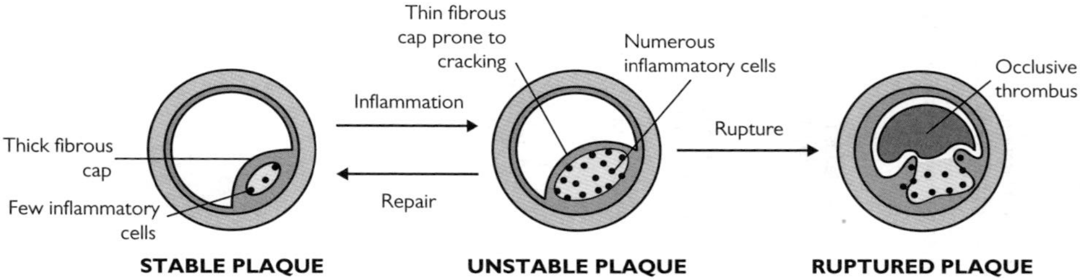

Fig. 3.1 Plaque stability. Stable plaques have few inflammatory cells with a thick fibrous cap. Increased inflammatory activity within an atherosclerotic plaque results in thinning of the fibrous cap, making it unstable and more liable to complications such as rupture.

Reproduced with permission from *Clinical Pathology* (Oxford Core Texts), Carton, James, Daly, Richard, and Ramani, Pramila, Oxford University Press (2006), p. 79, Figure 6.10.

Shock

Definition

- A generalized failure of tissue perfusion.

Aetiology

- Pump failure, e.g. acute myocardial infarction.
- Peripheral circulation failure, e.g. hypovolaemia, sepsis, anaphylaxis (➔ Hypersensitivity reactions, p. 10), tension pneumothorax (➔ Pneumothorax, p. 85), large pulmonary embolus (➔ Pulmonary thromboembolism, p. 69).

Pathogenesis

- Pump or peripheral circulation failure leads to cardiovascular collapse.
- Prolonged inadequate tissue perfusion risks the development of multiple organ failure.

Presentation

- Tachycardia due to increased sympathetic drive.
- Urine output declines (only apparent if the patient is catheterized).
- Hypotension.

❗ Note up to 15% of the circulating volume may be lost before any clinical signs become apparent.

Prognosis

►► Shock is a serious condition which leads to the development of multiple organ failure if not rapidly addressed.

Hypertension

Definition

- Persistently elevated systemic blood pressure.
- Stage 1 hypertension: clinic blood pressure is 140/90mmHg or higher and average home/ambulatory blood pressure 135/85mmHg or higher.
- Stage 2 hypertension: clinic blood pressure is 160/100mmHg or higher and average home/ambulatory blood pressure is 150/95mmHg or higher.
- Severe hypertension: clinic systolic blood pressure is 180mmHg or higher or clinic diastolic blood pressure is 110mmHg or higher.

Epidemiology

- Very common.
- Marked geographical and racial variability.
- Incidence thought to be as high as 25–30% in western countries.

Aetiology

- 95% of cases are idiopathic but appear to be related to both genetic and environmental factors. Genetic factors include sequence variations in the angiotensin and angiotensin receptor genes. Environmental factors include stress, obesity, smoking, physical inactivity, and heavy salt consumption.
- 5% of cases are due to chronic kidney disease (➔ Chronic kidney disease, pp. 182–3), phaeochromocytoma (➔ Phaeochromocytoma, p. 321), adrenal cortical adenoma (➔ Adrenal cortical adenoma, p. 319), coarctation of the aorta (➔ Congenital heart disease, pp. 42–3), pregnancy, and drugs, e.g. the oral contraceptive pill.

Pathogenesis

- Reduced renal sodium excretion may represent a final common pathway in the pathogenesis of hypertension.
- This leads to an increase in fluid volume, increased cardiac output, and increased peripheral resistance, causing an elevation in blood pressure.

Complications

- Accelerates atherosclerosis and its complications.
- Left ventricular failure (LVF).
- Aortic dissection.
- Chronic kidney disease.
- Intracerebral haemorrhage.
- Multi-infarct dementia.

Chronic lower limb ischaemia

Definition

- Persistent compromise of the arterial supply to the lower limbs.

Epidemiology

- Common.
- Affects 7% of men aged >50y.
- Male-to-female ratio is 2:1.

Aetiology

- Almost all cases are caused by atherosclerosis affecting the aorto-iliac, femoral, or popliteal and calf vessels, either singly or in combination.

Pathogenesis

- Single-level disease usually results in intermittent claudication.
- Two-level disease usually results in critical limb ischaemia.

Presentation

- Intermittent claudication is characterized by calf or thigh pain brought on by exercise and relieved by rest.
- Critical limb ischaemia is characterized by rest pain or tissue necrosis (gangrene or ulceration) or Doppler ankle pressure <50mmHg.

Prognosis

- One-third improves; one-third remains stable; one third deteriorates.
- 4% require an intervention and 1% result in amputation.

Acute lower limb ischaemia

Definition

- Abrupt sudden cessation of the arterial supply to the lower limb.

Epidemiology

- Incidence reported at 14 per 100000 people per year.

Aetiology

- 60% due to acute thrombosis in a vessel with pre-existing atherosclerosis.
- 30% due to thromboembolus from a distant site, usually the heart. Common cardiac associations are atrial fibrillation, acute myocardial infarction, or ventricular aneurysm. Common sites of impaction are the popliteal artery, common femoral artery, and aortic bifurcation.
- Rarer causes include aortic dissection, trauma, and iatrogenic injury.
- Iatrogenic injury is becoming more common with the growing use of endovascular procedures.

Pathogenesis

- Sudden occlusion of the arterial supply to the leg causes ischaemia.
- Without intervention, irreversible tissue damage occurs within 6h.
- Massive muscle necrosis leads to hyperkalaemia, acidosis, ARF, and cardiac arrest.

Presentation

- Sudden onset of pain and loss of sensation in the limb.
- On examination, the limb is pale and cold with reduced or absent pulses.

Prognosis

- Limb loss in 40% of cases.
- Death in 20% of cases.

Aortic dissection

Definition

- A tear in the aortic wall through which blood tracks.

Epidemiology

- Most cases occur in adults aged 50–70 years old.
- Male-to-female ratio is 2:1.

Aetiology

- Most cases are related to hypertension (➲ Hypertension, p. 33).
- Other associations include Marfan's syndrome and congenital bicuspid aortic valve (➲ Bicuspid aortic valves, p. 43).

Pathogenesis

- Precisely how hypertension leads to aortic dissection is controversial.
- Proposed that the initiating event is haemorrhage from a vasa vasorum into the media of the aorta. The intima is placed under stress and tears, allowing blood to track into the media and dissect along it.
- Dissections may propagate in the direction of the normal flow of aortic blood (anterograde) or against the normal flow of blood towards the aortic root (retrograde).
- Dissections may re-enter the aortic lumen at a distant site (creating a so-called 'double-barrelled' aorta) or rupture externally into the pericardial cavity, pleural cavity, or peritoneal cavity.
- ~75% involve the ascending aorta or aortic arch (type A).
- ~25% involve the descending aorta, without involvement of the ascending aorta or aortic arch (type B).

Presentation

- Acute severe 'tearing' chest pain which may closely mimic acute myocardial infarction.
- External rupture causes massive internal haemorrhage and shock.

Macroscopy

- A tear is usually visible in the intima of the aorta where the dissection starts and ends.
- If the dissection ruptures externally, large quantities of blood clot will be found around the site of rupture.

Histopathology

- Microscopy has limited value in explaining why dissection occurs.
- However, the presence of substantial degenerative changes in the aortic wall of patients aged <60y raises the possibility of an inherited aortopathy such as Marfan's.

Prognosis

- Untreated cases have a high mortality rate (50% within the first week).
- Treated cases have good initial survival but remain at risk of death from rupture of the dissection or development of a new dissection.

Abdominal aortic aneurysm

Definition

- A permanent dilation of the abdominal aorta >3cm in diameter.

Epidemiology

- Incidence is reported to be 5–10%.

Aetiology

- Almost all are caused by aortic atherosclerosis.

Pathogenesis

- Proteolytic enzymes weaken the media of the aorta, leading to aneurysmal change.
- Increased levels of matrix metalloproteinases have been found in aneurysmal aortas. These enzymes are known to degrade elastin.

Presentation

- Unruptured aneurysms are often asymptomatic but may cause abdominal or back pain. Most are discovered incidentally on abdominal examination or imaging.
- Ruptured abdominal aortic aneurysms present as a surgical emergency with abdominal pain and shock.

Macroscopy

- The aorta is dilated, usually below the level of the renal arteries.
- Extensive atherosclerosis is invariably present, often with secondary thrombosis and calcification.

Prognosis

- The natural history is that of gradual enlargement.
- Risk of rupture is exponentially related to the diameter.
- Mortality after rupture exceeds 80%.
- Elective surgical repair should be considered for aneurysms with a maximum diameter of 5.5cm or more.

Varicose veins

Definition

- Tortuous and dilated superficial leg veins associated with valvular incompetence.

Epidemiology

- Affect up to 20% of the population.
- Marked female predilection (female-to-male ratio 9:1).

Aetiology

- Most cases are primary and idiopathic.
- Secondary causes include pregnancy, large fibroids, and ovarian masses.

Pathogenesis

- Thought that valve cusps degenerate and develop holes within them.
- Incompetence of the valves increases strain on the valve downstream.
- Eventually, a column of valves become incompetent, leading to dilation of the vein.

Presentation

- Most patients present due to the unsightly nature of the veins.
- There may be associated discomfort, aching, itching, and swelling.
- Symptoms may be worse at the end of the day.

Complications

- Stasis (varicose) dermatitis.
- Varicose ulceration.
- Lipodermatosclerosis.
- Bleeding.
- Thrombosis (superficial thrombophlebitis).

Deep vein thrombosis

Definition

- Thrombosis within the deep leg veins.

Epidemiology

- ~1 in 1000 people each year.

Aetiology

- Related to stasis of blood and/or an increase in blood coagulability.
- Risk factors include immobility, pregnancy, recent surgery (particularly to the lower limb or pelvis), malignancy, long-haul flights, smoking, oral contraceptive pill, hormone replacement therapy (HRT), and thrombophilia.

► Multiple contributory factors will often operate within an individual.

Pathogenesis

- Sluggish blood flow and/or increased blood coagulability overcomes natural anticoagulant activity and causes thrombus to form in the deep leg veins.
- The thrombus may enlarge in size as it propagates along the lumen of the vein.

Presentation

- Warm, red, painful, swollen lower limb.
- Some cases may not produce symptoms or signs.

Complications

► Pulmonary thromboembolism (➲ Pulmonary thromboembolism, p. 69).

Chapter 4

Cardiac pathology

Congenital heart disease (CHD)

Ventricular septal defect (VSD)

- Most common type of CHD.
- An abnormal hole in the interventricular septum.
- May occur anywhere in the septum, but most occur in the upper part.
- A small VSD may have little functional significance and may close spontaneously as the child ages. There remains, however, a risk of infective endocarditis.
- A larger VSD causes a left-to-right shunt and increased volume load on the right ventricle, with symptoms of cardiac failure.

Patent ductus arteriosus (PDA)

- Persistence of the ductus arteriosus after 10 days of life.
- Systemic blood flows from the aorta to the pulmonary artery, causing a left-to-right shunt.
- Blood flow to the lungs is increased 2-fold, as is the volume return to the left side of the heart, causing left ventricular hypertrophy.
- Infective endocarditis is a frequent complication.

Atrial septal defect (ASD)

- An abnormal hole in the atrial septum.
- Most common site is in the middle of the septum away from the atrioventricular valves.
- Blood flows from the left to right atrium, causing an increase in circulation through the lungs.
- May be asymptomatic or cause easy fatiguability in childhood.
- Many present in adulthood due to atrial arrhythmias.

Atrioventricular septal defect (AVSD)

- A defect at the junction of the atrial and ventricular septae.
- In a complete AVSD, there is a combination of a low ASD and high VSD (essentially a hole right in the centre of the heart).
- Most function like a VSD with a volume overload to the right ventricle.
- Most common form of CHD seen in children with Down's syndrome.

Tetralogy of Fallot

- Comprises pulmonary stenosis, VSD, overriding aorta, and right ventricular hypertrophy.
- Pulmonary stenosis causes a right-to-left shunt and reduced blood flow to the lungs, resulting in cyanosis.

Transposition of the great arteries

- Incorrect placement of the aorta to the right ventricle and the pulmonary artery to the left ventricle.
- Always an associated defect to allow mixing of blood from both circulations (e.g. VSD or PDA) or the abnormality is incompatible with life.

Coarctation of the aorta

- A localized narrowing of the lumen of the aortic arch, distal to the origin of the left subclavian artery.
- In the infantile form, a PDA distal to the coarctation allows cardiac output to the lower body, but most of this is deoxygenated blood from the right side of the heart, so there is cyanosis of the lower half of the body.
- In the adult form, there is no PDA. Increased blood flow to the upper half of the body is increased and most patients develop upper extremity hypertension. This form is often not recognized until adult life.

Bicuspid aortic valves

- Tend to function well at birth and go undetected.
- Most bicuspid valves eventually develop calcific aortic stenosis (at an earlier age than typical 'senile' aortic stenosis) or aortic regurgitation.
- Increased risk of aortic dissection in adult life (➔ Aortic dissection, p. 36).

Angina pectoris

Definition

- Recurrent transient episodes of chest pain due to myocardial ischaemia.

Epidemiology

- Very common.

Aetiology

- Virtually always caused by coronary artery atherosclerosis.
- Major risk factors are smoking, hypertension, diabetes, and hyperlipidaemia.
- Hypertension and aortic stenosis may also contribute by causing left ventricular hypertrophy and increased myocardial oxygen demand.

Pathogenesis

- Myocardial ischaemia occurs whenever myocardial oxygen demand outstrips supply.
- A significant fixed stenosis of a coronary artery impairs coronary blood flow when myocardial oxygen demand increases, e.g. during exercise.

Presentation

- Central chest discomfort which is often described as a pressure, heaviness, tightness, or squeezing sensation.
- The pain often radiates up the neck into the jaw and across the shoulders and upper arms.
- May be associated with nausea and sweating.
- Episodes of angina are typically precipitated by exercise or emotional stress, last for a few minutes, and terminate upon resting or taking medication.

Macroscopy

- Significant stenosis of a coronary artery by atherosclerosis.
- No gross changes visible in the myocardium.

Histopathology

- No specific light microscopic features in the myocardium.

Prognosis

- Atherosclerosis is often generalized, so patients are at risk not only from other forms of ischaemic heart disease (acute myocardial infarction, LVF), but also abdominal aortic aneurysm, peripheral vascular disease, and stroke.

Unstable angina

Definition
- Severe acute myocardial ischaemia without myocardial necrosis.

Epidemiology
- Very common.

Aetiology
- Almost always due to coronary artery atherosclerosis.

Pathogenesis
- Erosion of the surface of an unstable atherosclerotic plaque stimulates platelets to aggregate over the plaque.
- Platelet fragments may also break off and embolize down the artery.
- The reduction in coronary blood flow causes acute ischaemia of the affected myocardium, but not myocardial necrosis.

Presentation
- Acute coronary syndrome with sudden onset of prolonged ischaemic cardiac chest pain at rest or on minimal exertion.
- The electrocardiogram (ECG) shows ischaemic changes, but not ST-elevation.

Biochemistry
- Blood troponin levels do not rise.

Macroscopy
- Significant stenosis of the involved coronary artery by a complicated atherosclerotic plaque.
- No gross changes visible in the myocardium.

Histopathology
- No specific light microscopic features in the myocardium.

Prognosis
- Patients are at high risk of future acute coronary events and subsequent development of LVF.

Non-ST-elevation myocardial infarction

Definition

- Partial-thickness necrosis of an area of the myocardium.

Epidemiology

- Very common.

Aetiology

- Almost always due to coronary artery atherosclerosis.

Pathogenesis

- Cracking or fissuring of an unstable atherosclerotic plaque stimulates the formation of a platelet-rich thrombus.
- The thrombus causes significant prolonged narrowing of the artery such that part of the territory of the supplied myocardium undergoes ischaemic necrosis.

Presentation

- Acute coronary syndrome with prolonged ischaemic cardiac chest pain at rest or on minimal exertion.
- ECG shows ischaemic changes, but not ST-elevation.

Biochemistry

- Blood troponin levels are elevated.

Macroscopy

- Significant stenosis of the involved coronary artery by a complicated atherosclerotic plaque.

Histopathology

- The earliest change of myocardial infarction is increased cytoplasmic eosinophilia and loss of nuclei within the affected myocytes after about 8–12h.
- By 24h, neutrophils infiltrate the necrotic area and after a few days, granulation tissue is laid down.
- Over a period of several weeks, the granulation tissue is replaced by scar tissue.

Prognosis

- Patients are at high risk of future acute coronary events and subsequent development of LVF.

ST-elevation myocardial infarction

Definition

- Full-thickness necrosis of an area of the myocardium.

Epidemiology

- Very common.

Aetiology

- Almost always a complication of coronary artery atherosclerosis.

Pathogenesis

- Rupture of an unstable coronary artery atherosclerotic plaque stimulates the formation of an occlusive fibrin-rich thrombus over the plaque.
- Complete occlusion of the coronary artery leads to full-thickness necrosis of the area of myocardium supplied by that artery (Fig. 4.1).

Presentation

- Severe ischaemic cardiac chest pain which does not resolve.
- Patients often describe a feeling as though they are going to die.
- ECG shows ST-elevation or new-onset left bundle branch block.

Biochemistry

- Blood troponin levels are elevated.

Macroscopy

- The affected coronary artery shows complete occlusion by a thrombus overlying an atherosclerotic plaque.
- The infarcted myocardium is not discernible until about 15h after the event where it appears soft and swollen with a darker red colour.
- By 24–48h, the infarct turns yellow.
- Over a period of weeks to months, the infarct is replaced by white scar tissue and the ventricular wall becomes thinned.

Histopathology

- The earliest change of myocardial infarction is cytoplasmic eosinophilia and loss of nuclei within the affected myocytes after ~8–12h.
- By 24h, neutrophils infiltrate the necrotic area and after a few days, granulation tissue is laid down.
- Over a period of weeks to months, the granulation tissue is replaced by fibrous scar tissue.

Prognosis

- Immediate complications include ventricular arrhythmias (which may be fatal) and acute cardiac failure in severe cases. Rupture of the free wall of the infarcted ventricle causes haemopericardium with rapid cardiac tamponade and death. Thrombus forming over the akinetic myocardium can detach and give rise to systemic emboli.
- Later complications include ventricular aneurysm formation and the development of LVF.

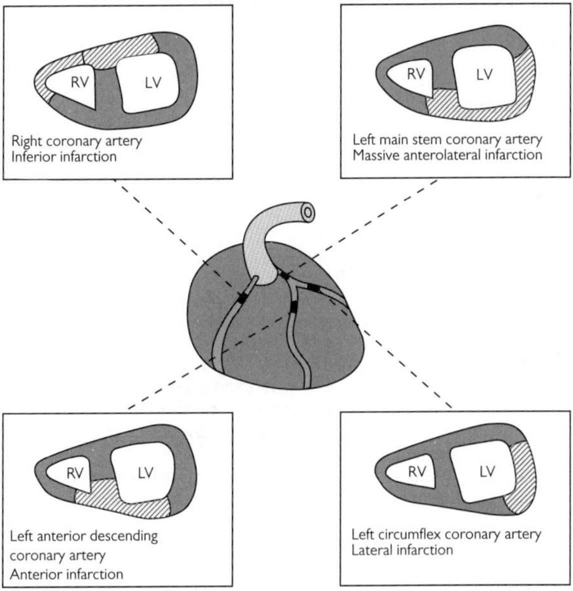

Fig. 4.1 Territories of myocardial infarction according to the coronary artery involved.

Reproduced with permission from *Clinical Pathology* (Oxford Core Texts), Carton, James, Daly, Richard, and Ramani, Pramila, Oxford University Press (2006), p. 90, Figure 6.17.

Left ventricular failure (LVF)

Definition

- A syndrome resulting from insufficient left ventricular output.

Epidemiology

- Very common.
- Occurs in ~1% of people after age 75 and 2% after 80y.

Aetiology

- Ischaemic heart disease.
- Hypertensive heart disease.
- Aortic or mitral valve disease.

► Note that all of these are common and so LVF is often due to a combination of two or more of these conditions.

Pathogenesis

- Falling cardiac output triggers a drop in blood pressure. Low blood pressure stimulates baroreceptors and reduces renal blood flow.
- This leads to sympathetic overdrive and the activation of the renin–angiotensin–aldosterone system.
- Blood pressure is restored at the expense of an increased heart rate, increased peripheral vascular resistance (afterload), and increased blood volume (preload).
- Unfortunately, this short-term solution is deleterious in the long term as the work of the heart is increased even further (Fig. 4.2).
- In response, the left ventricle undergoes hypertrophy, but this reduces the volume of ventricular cavity and lowers the stroke volume.
- Eventually, the heart becomes overloaded with blood and dilates.

Presentation

- Breathlessness, fatigue, palpitations.
- Peripheral oedema and ascites tend to occur in advanced disease.

Macroscopy

- The heart is heavy and the left ventricle is hypertrophic and dilated.
- The underlying cause(s) may also be evident, e.g. coronary artery atherosclerosis or valvular disease.

Histopathology

- Histology is non-specific, usually showing patchy myocyte hypertrophy and interstitial fibrosis as a result of chronic injury to the chamber.

Prognosis

- Poor prognosis, with many patients dying within 3y of diagnosis.
- Associated with a poor quality of life and frequent hospital admissions.
- Fatal ventricular arrhythmias are a common cause of sudden death.

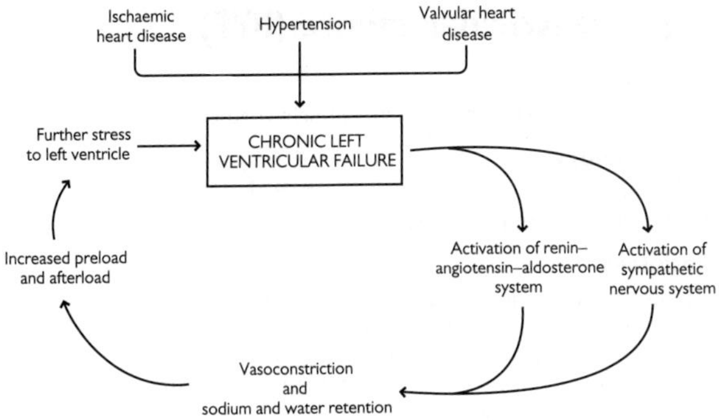

Fig. 4.2 The neurohormonal response in chronic left ventricular failure.

Reproduced with permission from *Clinical Pathology* (Oxford Core Texts), Carton, James, Daly, Richard, and Ramani, Pramila, Oxford University Press (2006), p. 84, Figure 6.13.

Right ventricular failure (RVF)

Definition

- A syndrome resulting from insufficient right ventricular output.

Epidemiology

- Uncommon.
- Seen much less frequently than LVF.

Aetiology

- Most cases are caused by chronic lung diseases such as chronic obstructive pulmonary disease (COPD), pulmonary fibrosis, bronchiectasis, and recurrent pulmonary emboli.
- Rarer causes include ischaemic heart disease affecting the right ventricle and right-sided valvular heart disease.

Pathogenesis

- In most cases, RVF is the result of pulmonary hypertension caused by chronic lung diseases.
- Pulmonary hypertension increases the work of the right ventricle by requiring a higher chamber pressure to maintain adequate output.
- Initially, there is right ventricular hypertrophy, but eventually the chamber dilates and fails.

Presentation

- Worsening of pre-existing breathlessness and development of peripheral oedema.

Macroscopy

- The right ventricle is hypertrophic and dilated.

Histopathology

- Histology is non-specific, usually showing patchy myocyte hypertrophy or atrophy with interstitial fibrosis.

Prognosis

- High chance of death from a combination of cardiac and respiratory failure.
- Many patients die suddenly from a fatal ventricular arrhythmia arising in the diseased right ventricle.

Valvular heart disease

Aortic stenosis

- Most common valve disease.
- Most are caused by calcification of an anatomically normal tricuspid valve in the elderly (senile calcific aortic stenosis). Bicuspid aortic valves calcify at a younger age (Fig. 4.3).
- Chronic rheumatic disease may also cause aortic stenosis.
- Years of turbulent blood flow across the valve is thought to cause damage, followed by calcification.
- Presents with chest pain, syncope, and breathlessness.

Aortic regurgitation

- Caused by diseases which dilate the aortic root, e.g. Marfan's syndrome, ankylosing spondylitis.
- Congenital abnormalities of the valve leaflets may also cause aortic regurgitation.
- Dilation of the aortic root causes pulling on the annulus of the aortic valve and prevents tight closure of the leaflets.
- Presents with breathlessness and palpitations.

Mitral stenosis

- Usually the result of chronic rheumatic valvular heart disease.
- Narrowing of the valve prevents free flow of blood from the left atrium into the left ventricle during ventricular diastole.
- The rise in left atrial pressure is transmitted to the pulmonary venous system, causing pulmonary oedema and breathlessness.
- The left atrium increases in size and becomes prone to developing atrial fibrillation.
- Stenotic mitral valves shows marked thickening of the valve leaflets and attached chordae tendinae. Fusion of the leaflets gives rise to the so-called 'fish mouth' appearance.

Mitral regurgitation

- Usually due to mitral valve prolapse or ischaemic heart disease.
- In mitral valve prolapse, the abnormal valve leaflets balloon into the left atrium during ventricular systole.
- In ischaemic heart disease, the regurgitation is caused by a combination of ischaemic papillary dysfunction and widening of the mitral valve annulus due to left ventricular dilation.
- Patients may remain asymptomatic for some time as the left ventricle and left atrium enlarge to cope with the increased volume, but eventually, there is decompensation and development of LVF.

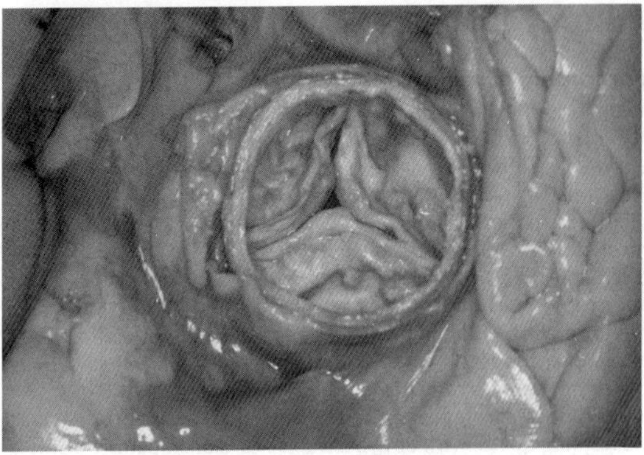

Fig. 4.3 Calcific aortic stenosis. This aortic valve is studded with nodules of calcium causing significant narrowing of the valve orifice (see Plate 1).

Reproduced with permission from *Clinical Pathology* (Oxford Core Texts), Carton, James, Daly, Richard, and Ramani, Pramila, Oxford University Press (2006), p.96, Figure 6.18.

Cardiomyopathies

Hypertrophic cardiomyopathy

- Uncommon with an incidence of 0.5%.
- ~70% of cases have been linked to mutations in genes encoding sarcomeric proteins such as β-myosin heavy chain, troponin T, myosin-binding protein, and α-tropomyosin.
- Wide spectrum of presentation, including breathlessness, angina, syncope, palpitations, and sudden death.
- Macroscopically, most cases show asymmetric left ventricular hypertrophy involving predominantly the septum. Associated systolic anterior motion of the mitral valve often leads to a patch of endocardial fibrosis over the septum known as the sub-aortic mitral impact lesion.
- Some cases cause symmetric left ventricular hypertrophy indistinguishable from that caused by hypertension or aortic stenosis.
- The histological hallmark of hypertrophic cardiomyopathy (HCM) is the presence of myocyte hypertrophy, myocyte disarray, and interstitial fibrosis. Myocyte disarray refers to the loss of the normal parallel arrangement of myocytes which instead adopt haphazard oblique organizations.

Idiopathic dilated cardiomyopathy

- Uncommon with an incidence of 0.2%.
- Mode of inheritance includes autosomal dominant, X-linked, and autosomal recessive forms, as well as mitochondrial inheritance.
- Mutations in a number of genes have been described, including cardiac actin, desmin, sarcoglycan, troponin, and tropomyosin.
- Presents with breathlessness, fatigue, and palpitations. Thrombus formation over the akinetic myocardium can cause systemic emboli.
- Macroscopically, the heart has increased mass with dilation and thinning of the cardiac chambers in the absence of any cause to account for it (e.g. coronary artery disease, valvular disease, hypertension, alcohol abuse).
- Microscopic findings are not specific but may show myocyte attenuation and loss of myofibrils with the enlargement of myocyte nuclei together with interstitial fibrosis.

Arrhythmogenic right ventricular cardiomyopathy

- Exact incidence and prevalence unknown.
- Mutations in genes encoding cell adhesion molecules described.
- Mutations lead to detachment and apoptosis of myocytes under mechanical stress, with subsequent fat replacement and scarring.
- Presents with palpitations or sudden death.
- Macroscopically, there is thinning of the right ventricle, often the right ventricular outflow tract, with a yellow appearance due to fat replacement.
- Microscopically, there is replacement of the normal right ventricular myocardium by fat and fibrosis. The disease process usually starts in the epicardial region and works its way towards the endocardial surface.

Infective endocarditis

Definition

- Infection of the interior surface of the heart, usually a heart valve.

Classification

- Acute endocarditis is caused by pathogenic organisms infecting a structurally normal heart.
- Subacute endocarditis is a more insidious illness caused by weakly pathogenic organisms infecting a structurally abnormal heart.

Epidemiology

- Uncommon, but important to recognize.

Microbiology

- Acute endocarditis is usually due to *Staphylococcus aureus*.
- Subacute endocarditis is most commonly due to *Streptococcus viridans* or enterococci.

Pathogenesis

- *S. aureus* usually gains access to the blood from the skin via indwelling vascular lines or via intravenous drug abuse.
- *S. viridans* gains access to the blood from the oropharynx following tooth brushing or dentistry.
- Enterococci gain access to the bloodstream following instrumentation of the bowel or bladder.

Presentation

- Left-sided acute endocarditis presents acutely with fever and signs of valve damage. Major systemic embolic events are also common; septic emboli can travel to multiple organs and cause abscesses.
- Right-sided acute endocarditis presents with fevers, chills, and prominent pulmonary symptoms due to numerous septic emboli in the lungs.
- Subacute endocarditis causes low-grade fever and constitutional symptoms. The diagnosis may be difficult and easily overlooked.

Macroscopy

See Fig. 4.4.

- The involved endocardial surface is covered with friable vegetations.
- Acute cases may show extensive underlying tissue destruction and abscess formation.

Histopathology

- Vegetations are composed of a mixture of fibrin, inflammatory cells, and bacterial colonies which are usually Gram-positive cocci.

Prognosis

- Acute endocarditis has a high mortality due to rapid valve destruction and the development of acute cardiac failure.
- Subacute endocarditis has a more protracted course but remains a serious disease if undiagnosed and untreated.

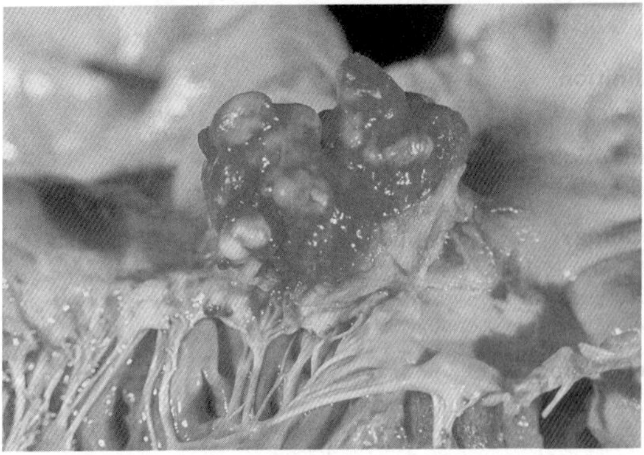

Fig. 4.4 Close-up of a vegetation of infective endocarditis. This is on the mitral valve; you can see the chordae tendinae attached to the valve leaflets (see Plate 2).

Reproduced with permission from *Clinical Pathology* (Oxford Core Texts), Carton, James, Daly, Richard, and Ramani, Pramila, Oxford University Press (2006), p.97, Figure 6.19.

Myocarditis

Definition

- Inflammation of the myocardium unrelated to ischaemia.

Epidemiology

- Rare.

Aetiology

- Most cases are infective in origin.
- Drugs and toxins have also been implicated.
- Some cases are idiopathic.

Microbiology

- Coxsackie virus is the most commonly implicated organism.
- Other organisms include HIV, *Clostridia, Meningococcus, Mycoplasma, Borrelia*, leptospirosis, and Chagas' disease.

Pathogenesis

- Myocyte injury causes a variable degree of necrosis and inflammation.

Presentation

- Depends on the extent of myocardial necrosis.
- Mild cases may cause a flu-like illness without obvious localizing symptoms to the heart and go undiagnosed.
- More severe cases cause breathlessness, chest pain, and palpitations.
- Very severe cases present as a medical emergency with acute cardiac failure and cardiogenic shock, mimicking a massive acute myocardial infarction.

Macroscopy

- Macroscopic changes vary widely, depending on severity.
- Importantly, many cases of myocarditis produce no gross pathology and the heart appears macroscopically normal.
- Very severe cases of myocarditis producing extensive necrosis may give a macroscopic abnormality similar to myocardial infarction.

Histopathology

- All forms of myocarditis show an inflammatory cell infiltrate together with myocardial necrosis or degeneration.
- The infiltrate is usually a mixture of lymphocytes and histiocytes.
- Some cases show an eosinophil-rich infiltrate (hypersensitivity myocarditis) or contain giant cells (giant cell myocarditis).

Prognosis

- In most cases, recovery is complete without complications.
- Giant cell myocarditis runs a fulminant course with an almost inevitable development of cardiac failure and high mortality.

Pericarditis

Definition

- Inflammation of the pericardium.

Epidemiology

- Uncommon.

Aetiology

- Infections are a common cause and these may be viral (Coxsackie, EBV, HIV), bacterial (extension from a pneumonia, acute rheumatic fever, TB), or fungal.
- Full-thickness acute myocardial infarction causes pericarditis overlying the infarct.
- Other miscellaneous causes include severe renal failure ('uraemic' pericarditis), hypothyroidism, multisystem autoimmune diseases (e.g. RA, SLE), cardiac surgery, radiotherapy, malignant infiltration, and some drugs.

Pathogenesis

- Injury to the pericardium causes an inflammatory response.

Presentation

- Central chest pain which is worse on inspiration or lying flat and relieved by sitting forward.
- A superimposed large pericardial effusion may cause breathlessness.

Macroscopy

- The pericardial surface of the heart is roughened due to the presence of an inflammatory exudate.
- Strands of fibrinous material may be present between the two pericardial surfaces.
- The exudate may be purulent if associated with bacterial infection.
- An associated pericardial effusion may be present.

Histopathology

- The pericardium is infiltrated by inflammatory cells, often with fibrin deposition.
- Malignant cells may be seen in cases due to malignant infiltration.

Prognosis

- Infective pericarditis often resolves with appropriate treatment.
- Pericarditis associated with an acute myocardial infarction is governed by the outcome of the infarction.
- Uraemic pericarditis implies severe renal failure with attendant risk of mortality.
- Malignant pericarditis usually implies significant metastatic disease and poor prognosis.
- Any cause of pericarditis may lead to a reactive pericardial effusion which, if large, requires urgent drainage to prevent cardiac tamponade.

Chapter 5

Lung pathology

Respiratory tract malformations

Congenital diaphragmatic hernia

- A defect in the diaphragm caused by failure of the pleuroperitoneal canals to close during 8–10 weeks of gestation.
- Bowel loops and the liver can pass into the thorax and compress the developing lung, causing lung hypoplasia.
- Infants usually present with respiratory failure and 50% die within 24h of birth.

Congenital (cystic) adenomatoid malformation

- A lung mass composed of terminal bronchioles. There are no normal alveoli.
- Usually, a single lobe is involved.
- Many cases diagnosed by antenatal ultrasound at 20 weeks' gestation.
- Most cause a degree of respiratory distress and so are surgically removed.

Pulmonary sequestration

- A discrete mass of lung tissue that has no normal connection with the respiratory tract.
- Sequestrations have a systemic blood supply.
- Most are intrapulmonary and found in the left lower lobe.
- Up to half of extrapulmonary sequestrations may be associated with other anomalies.
- Pulmonary sequestrations may become infected or cause massive haemoptysis.

Respiratory failure

Definition

- Arterial pO_2 <8kPa.

Subtypes

- Type 1 is associated with a normal or low pCO_2.
- Type 2 is associated with a raised pCO_2.

Aetiology

- Type 1: severe pneumonia, pulmonary embolism, acute asthma, pulmonary fibrosis, acute LVF.
- Type 2: COPD, neuromuscular disorders impairing ventilation.

Pathogenesis

- Type 1 respiratory failure is a result of ventilation/perfusion mismatching in areas of the lungs. Increased ventilation removes any excess carbon dioxide but cannot compensate for the low pO_2.
- Type 2 respiratory failure is a result of a generalized alveolar hypoventilation. Transfer of both oxygen and carbon dioxide is impaired, so pCO_2 is raised, in addition to the low pO_2.

Presentation

- Acute respiratory failure typically develops suddenly in a patient with otherwise healthy lungs. There is obvious respiratory distress with hyperventilation.
- Chronic respiratory failure is a more persistent problem in patients with chronic lung diseases. By contrast, the clinical picture may be surprisingly undramatic despite the low pO_2 levels, due to compensatory mechanisms.

Complications

- Prolonged chronic hypoxia causes pulmonary hypertension and ultimately RVF (➲ Right ventricular failure (RVF), p. 52)

Acute respiratory distress syndrome (ARDS)

Definition

- A very severe form of acute lung injury defined as a ratio of PaO_2:FiO_2 <200mmHg in the presence of bilateral alveolar infiltrates on chest X-ray and in the absence of LVF.

Epidemiology

- Incidence rates range from 17 to 34 per 100 000 people years.
- 10–15% of all intensive care patients meet criteria for ARDS.

Aetiology

- Any severe injury to the lung may lead to ARDS.
- Common causes include severe pneumonia, shock, trauma, multiple transfusions, and near drowning.

Pathogenesis

- Severe damage to the lung causes widespread alveolar necrosis with severe impairment of normal gas exchange.

Presentation

- Severe breathlessness, in addition to signs of the underlying cause.

Macroscopy

- Both lungs are typically markedly heavy and fluid-filled, often weighing >1000g each (a normal lung weighs 300–400g).

Histopathology

- The histopathological hallmark is **diffuse alveolar damage**, characterized by the presence of hyaline membranes lining alveolar spaces.
- Hyaline membranes are composed of a mixture of fibrin and necrotic alveolar epithelial cells.

Prognosis

- Severe condition with high mortality rates averaging between 30% and 50%, depending on the cause.
- Survivors usually demonstrate residual pulmonary functional abnormalities.

Bronchiectasis

Definition

- An abnormal permanent dilation of bronchi, accompanied by inflammation in their walls and in adjacent lung parenchyma.

Epidemiology

- Incidence rates between 20 and 35 per 100 000 people years.
- More common in underdeveloped countries due to higher incidence of severe childhood pulmonary infections.

Aetiology

- A structural condition resulting from a number of different causes.
- In developed countries, bronchiectasis is usually related to obstruction to an area of the lung (e.g. tumour or foreign body) or in association with CF. Many cases prove to be idiopathic.
- In less developed countries, severe pulmonary infections are a major cause.

Pathogenesis

- Thought to be the result of weakening in bronchial walls caused by recurrent inflammation.
- Scarring in the adjacent lung parenchyma places traction on the weakened bronchi, causing them to permanently dilate.

Presentation

- Persistent productive cough and haemoptysis (which may be massive).

Macroscopy

- Affected areas of the lung contain visibly dilated airways filled with mucopurulent material which extend right up to the pleural surface.
- In obstructive cases, the cause may be seen proximally, e.g. a tumour.

Histopathology

- Bronchial dilation with marked chronic inflammation in the wall, often with lymphoid aggregates and germinal centres.
- Adjacent alveoli may show an acute and organizing pneumonia.

Complications

- Pulmonary hypertension and RVF.
- Deposition of serum amyloid A protein in β-pleated sheets in multiple organs (AA amyloidosis).

Cystic fibrosis

Definition

- An inherited disorder caused by a mutation in the **cystic fibrosis transmembrane conductance regulator** (CFTR) gene.

Epidemiology

- The most common lethal genetic disease in European populations.
- ~1 in 2500 babies born in the United Kingdom (UK) have CF.

Genetics

- Inherited in an autosomal recessive manner.
- *CFTR* is on chromosome 7q and codes for a chloride ion channel.
- Over 1400 mutations have been described, though the most common is a deletion at position 508 that leads to loss of a phenylalanine amino acid (the ΔF508 mutation).

Pathogenesis

- The ΔF508 mutation causes abnormal folding of the CFTR protein and its subsequent degradation in the cell.
- Other mutations may result in a correctly located protein, but abnormal function.
- Lack of normal CFTR causes a defective electrolyte transfer across epithelial cell membranes, resulting in thick mucus secretions.

Presentation

- Most patients present with pulmonary disease due to recurrent infections. Initially, common bacteria colonize the lungs, but eventually *Pseudomonas aeruginosa* often becomes the dominant organism.
- Pancreatic insufficiency is also common.
- Bowel obstruction may occur in the neonatal period due to thick meconium (meconium ileus) or develop later in childhood.
- Liver disease develops late.
- Some cases may be diagnosed when a raised serum immunoreactive trypsin is picked up on neonatal screening.

Macroscopy

- Lungs from older children usually show widespread bronchiectasis.
- The liver may appear fatty and, in severe cases, may be cirrhotic.

Histopathology

- Lungs show bronchiectatic airways containing thick mucus. Acute inflammation may be seen if there is active infection.
- The liver shows inspissated bile in intrahepatic bile ducts. There may be periportal fibrosis and, in more severe cases, cirrhosis.

Prognosis

- Average lifespan is currently ~35y.
- Most patients die as a result of pulmonary disease.

Pulmonary thromboembolism

Definition

- Occlusion of a pulmonary artery by an embolic thrombus.

Epidemiology

- Common condition with incidence rates of 100 per 100 000 people years.

Aetiology

- As pulmonary emboli originate from deep vein thromboses, the risk factors are the same as for that condition, i.e. immobility, acute medical illness, recent surgery, malignancy, pregnancy, and congenital and acquired thrombotic disorders.

Pathogenesis

- A fragment of a detached thrombus from a deep vein thrombosis embolizes via the right side of the heart into the pulmonary arterial circulation and lodges in a pulmonary artery.

Presentation

- Blockage of a major pulmonary artery usually may cause instant death due to a sudden huge rise in pulmonary arterial pressure, acute RVF, and cardiac arrest.
- Blockage of medium-sized arteries causes an area of ventilation/perfusion mismatch in the lungs with breathlessness.
- Smaller pulmonary emboli may lead to subtle symptoms of breathlessness, chest pain, and dizziness; these can easily go undiagnosed.

Macroscopy

- Emboli are visible as fragments of thrombi within pulmonary arteries.
- Thrombi are firm and brown and the cut surface may show visible bands (lines of Zahn).

Histopathology

- Fresh thromboemboli are composed of a mixture of fibrin and enmeshed blood cells, often arranged in alternating linear bands that correspond to the macroscopic lines of Zahn.
- Thromboemboli organize after 2–3 days with ingrowth of granulation tissue composed of fibroblasts and capillaries from the vessel wall.
- Old thromboemboli may be evident as fibrous nodules projecting from the vessel wall or fibrous bands crossing the lumen of a pulmonary artery.

Prognosis

- Mortality rates range from 3% to 25%.
- Risk of death is higher for larger emboli or if the diagnosis is made late.

Pulmonary hypertension

Definition

- A mean pulmonary artery pressure >25mmHg at rest or >30mmHg during exercise.

Subtypes

- Secondary pulmonary hypertension is a complication of chronic lung or cardiac disease.
- Primary pulmonary hypertension occurs in the absence of chronic lung or heart disease.

Epidemiology

- Secondary pulmonary hypertension is quite common.
- Primary pulmonary hypertension is rare.

Aetiology

- Common causes of secondary hypertension include COPD, interstitial lung disease, LVF, and chronic pulmonary thromboemboli.
- Primary pulmonary hypertension may be idiopathic or associated with certain drugs, HIV infection, collagen vascular disease, and congenital systemic-to-pulmonary shunts.

Pathogenesis

- Chronic hypoxia and obliterative pulmonary fibrosis both lead to the development of raised pressure in the pulmonary arterial circulation.

Presentation

- Secondary pulmonary hypertension causes worsening of the symptoms of the pre-existing condition with increasing breathlessness.
- Primary pulmonary hypertension presents with exertional dyspnoea and fatigue. Dizziness and syncope are also common.

Macroscopy

- The presence of atherosclerosis in large pulmonary arteries is a clue to underlying pulmonary hypertension.
- Right ventricular hypertrophy may also be present.

Histopathology

- Muscular hypertrophy and intimal proliferation of small pulmonary arteries and muscularization of pulmonary arterioles.
- Severe cases show plexiform lesions, characterized by a proliferation of slit-like vascular spaces from the arterial wall.
- Very severe cases may display fibrinoid necrosis of the arterial wall.

Prognosis

- Secondary pulmonary hypertension generally implies significant underlying cardiac or lung disease with poor prognosis.
- Prognosis of primary pulmonary hypertension is also very poor with 5-year survival rates of only 25–50%.

Asthma

Definition

- A chronic inflammatory disorder of large airways characterized by recurrent episodes of reversible airway narrowing.

Epidemiology

- Very common, affecting >10% of children and 5% of adults.

Aetiology

- Most cases are associated with **atopy**, a genetic tendency of the immune system to produce IgE in response to common environmental allergens.
- The aetiology of non-atopic asthma is uncertain, but some have suggested a link with gastro-oesophageal reflux disease.

Pathogenesis

- Atopic individuals respond to common environmental allergens by producing large amounts of allergen-specific IgE which bind to the surface of mast cells.
- Re-exposure to the allergen causes cross-linking of allergen-specific IgE antibodies and degranulation of mast cells.
- Degranulated mast cells stimulate airway inflammation and bronchospasm.
- Ongoing inflammation results in hypersensitive airways which react to a number of stimuli, including exercise, cold air, and cigarette smoke.

Presentation

- Intermittent episodes of breathlessness, wheeze, and chest tightness.
- Cough, particularly at night, is also common.

Macroscopy

- Lungs of most asthmatics may be macroscopically normal.
- Thick mucus plugs in airways may be seen in severe disease.

Histopathology

- Airways show evidence of inflammatory activity with eosinophils which are not usually seen in normal airways.
- There may also be basement membrane thickening, goblet cell hyperplasia, and prominent smooth muscle.

Prognosis

- Generally good with appropriate treatment.
- There is a small mortality rate associated with severe acute asthma.

Chronic obstructive pulmonary disease (COPD)

Definition
- A chronic lung condition characterized by breathlessness due to poorly reversible and progressive airflow obstruction.

Epidemiology
- Very common disease with a prevalence of 1–4% of the population.
- Mostly a disease of middle-aged to elderly adult smokers.

Aetiology
- 85% of cases are caused by smoking.
- Most of the remainder are attributable to previous workplace exposure to dusts and fumes.
- A very small number are related to α1-antitrypsin deficiency.

Pathogenesis
- Inflammation and scarring of small bronchioles are thought to be the main source of airflow obstruction.
- Imbalance of proteases and antiproteases causes destruction of the lung parenchyma with dilation of terminal airspaces (emphysema) and air trapping.
- Mucous gland hyperplasia and irritant effects of smoke causes productive cough (chronic bronchitis).

Presentation
- Sudden onset of exertional breathlessness on a background of prolonged cough and sputum production.
- Spirometry shows ↓ forced expiratory volume in 1s (FEV_1) and ↓ FEV_1/forced vital capacity (FVC) ratio (Fig. 5.1).

Macroscopy
- The lungs are hyperinflated with thick mucus in the airways and dilated terminal airspaces.
- Bullae may be present.

Histopathology
- Chronic inflammation and fibrosis of small bronchioles (chronic obstructive bronchiolitis).
- Finely pigmented macrophages in respiratory bronchioles (respiratory bronchiolitis).
- Dilated terminal airspaces (emphysema).

Prognosis
- Gradual decline in lung function with episodes of acute exacerbation due to infection, pneumothorax, or pulmonary embolism.
- Pulmonary hypertension and RVF then occur.
- LVF often coexists due to ischaemic heart disease.
- Death is often related to both respiratory and cardiac failure.

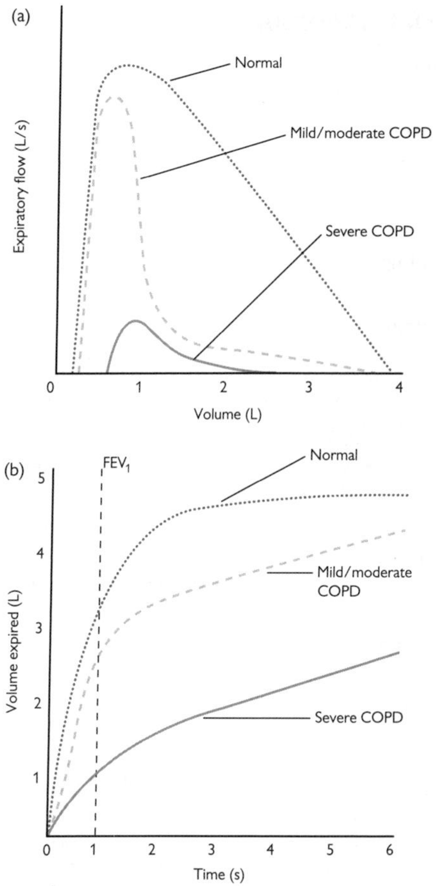

Fig. 5.1 (a) Flow–volume loops in a normal individual, compared with patients with COPD. In mild to moderate COPD, the immediate flow is relatively normal (this is why peak flow can be normal in patients with early COPD), but then the airflow rapidly decreases. In severe COPD, the airflow is very poor with prominent air trapping (note how at the start of expiration, there is already nearly 1L of air in the lungs). (b) Spirometry in a normal individual, compared with patients with COPD. Note how in COPD, the forced expiratory volume in 1s (FEV_1) is reduced, but the final volume expired is relatively normal (they just take longer to get there!), hence the FEV_1-to-FVC ratio is lowered.

Bacterial pneumonia

Definition

- An infection of the lung parenchyma caused by bacterial organisms.

Classification

- Community-acquired.
- Hospital-acquired.
- Aspiration.
- Immunosuppression.

Epidemiology

- Very common.

Microbiology

- Community-acquired: *Streptococcus pneumoniae, Mycoplasma pneumoniae, Haemophilus influenzae, Legionella pneumophila.*
- Hospital-acquired: Gram-negative bacteria, e.g. *Klebsiella, Escherichia coli, Pseudomonas.*
- Aspiration: mixed aerobic and anaerobic bacteria.
- Immunosuppression: all the previously mentioned possible (as well as viral, mycobacterial, and *Pneumocystis*).

► Multiple coexisting infections are common in the immunosuppressed.

Pathogenesis

- Bacterial organisms overcome the defences of the lung and establish infection within alveoli.

Presentation

- Productive cough, breathlessness, chest pain, and fever.

Macroscopy

- The infected lung parenchyma feels firm and appears yellowish.
- Purulent material may be expressed from small airways.
- The overlying pleura may show evidence of pleuritis.

Histopathology

- The alveolar spaces are filled with an inflammatory infiltrate rich in neutrophils. Bacterial colonies are often visible within the exudate.
- In cases of aspiration pneumonia, food material may be present within the lung parenchyma.
- Severe cases complicated by abscess formation show destruction of the lung tissue and replacement by confluent sheets of neutrophils.

Prognosis

- Recovery is usually expected with appropriate antimicrobial therapy in an otherwise healthy individual.
- Complications include respiratory failure, septicaemia, pleural effusion, empyema, and lung abscess. These are more likely with virulent organisms or in patients with coexisting heart and lung disease.

Idiopathic pulmonary fibrosis (IPF)

Definition

- An idiopathic interstitial pneumonia limited to the lung and associated with a histological appearance of usual interstitial pneumonia (UIP).

Epidemiology

- The majority of patients are between 50 and 70y.
- Men are affected about twice as often as women.

Aetiology

- Unknown but thought to be due to an abnormal repair mechanism to alveolar injury in genetically predisposed individuals.

Pathogenesis

- Environmental factors injure alveolar epithelial cells which react by overexpressing profibrotic cytokines, such as transforming growth factor (TGF)-β and interleukin (IL)-10, which stimulate irreversible lung scarring (Fig. 5.2).

Presentation

- Progressive breathlessness and non-productive cough.

Macroscopy

- Marked lung fibrosis with honeycomb change.
- Disease most marked at the peripheries of the lower lobes.

Histopathology

- Heterogeneous, non-uniform fibrotic process, characterized by markedly scarred areas of the lung juxtaposed to islands of relatively normal lung ('spatial variability').
- Evidence of active ongoing fibrosis in the form of numerous fibroblastic foci ('temporal variability').

► This histopathological picture, known as **usual interstitial pneumonia**, is always seen in IPF but is not specific for it.

Prognosis

- Very poor, with average survival of only 2–3 years from diagnosis.
- A common terminal event is an acute exacerbation of IPF, characterized histologically by diffuse alveolar damage on a background of the UIP histological pattern.

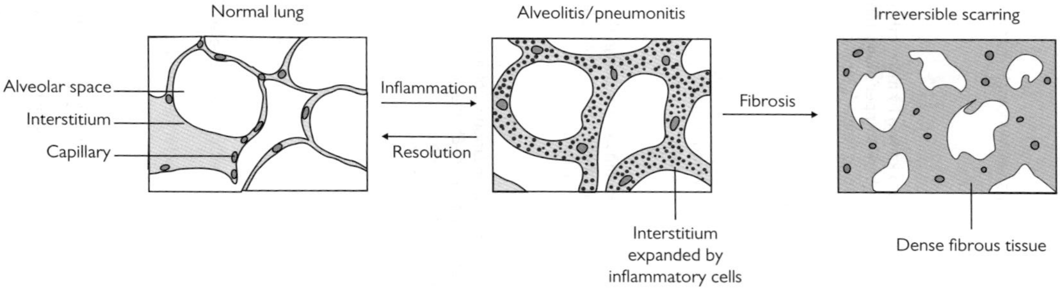

Fig. 5.2 Evolution of diffuse parenchymal lung disease (DPLD). The normal interstitium is thin and contains pulmonary artery capillaries. In DPLD, the interstitium becomes expanded by an inflammatory cell infiltrate ('pneumonitis' or 'alveolitis'), impairing gas exchange. Complete resolution can occur, but the danger is the development of fibrosis which permanently destroys the lung parenchyma.

Reproduced with permission from *Clinical Pathology* (Oxford Core Texts), Carton, James, Daly, Richard, and Ramani, Pramila, Oxford University Press (2006), p. 126, Figure 7.10.

Hypersensitivity pneumonitis

Definition

- An interstitial lung disease caused by an immunologic reaction to inhaled antigens.

Synonyms

- Extrinsic allergic alveolitis.
- Individual forms of the disease are also known by many other names (farmer's lung, humidifier lung, maple bark stripper's lung, mushroom worker's lung, pigeon breeder's lung, bird fancier's lung, etc.).

Epidemiology

- Uncommon.

Aetiology

- Thermophilic bacteria (mouldy hay, compost, air conditioner ducts).
- Fungi (mouldy maple bark, barley, or wood dust).
- Avian proteins (bird droppings and feathers).

Pathogenesis

- Inhaled antigens lead to an abnormal immune reaction in the lungs.
- Involves a combination of antibody (type 2), immune complex (type 3), and cell-mediated (type 4) hypersensitivity reactions (➔ Hypersensitivity reactions, p. 10).

Presentation

- Acute disease follows exposure to large amounts of antigen and causes severe breathlessness, cough, and fever 4–6h after exposure. Resolution occurs within 12–18h after exposure ceases.
- Chronic disease results from prolonged exposure to small amounts of antigen with gradual onset of breathlessness, dry cough, and fatigue.

Radiology

- High-resolution computed tomography (CT) shows middle to upper lobe-predominant linear interstitial opacities and small nodules.
- Often associated with traction bronchiectasis and honeycomb areas.

Histopathology

- Cellular chronic interstitial pneumonia with peribronchiolar accentuation.
- Foci of organizing pneumonia and poorly formed granulomas may also be present.

Prognosis

- Generally good if the causative antigen is identified and exposure is avoided.
- Persistent exposure can lead to irreversible lung fibrosis and respiratory failure.

Lung carcinoma

Definition

- A malignant epithelial tumour arising in the lung.

Epidemiology

- Most common and deadly cancer with >1 million deaths annually.

Aetiology

- Up to 90% of cases are directly attributable to smoking.

Classification

- Adenocarcinoma (40%).
- Squamous cell carcinoma (20%).
- Small cell carcinoma (15%).
- A number of rare subtypes make up the remainder.

Carcinogenesis

- Similar to other carcinomas, lung carcinomas are likely to arise from a precursor phase of epithelial dysplasia, representing neoplastic transformation of lung epithelium without invasion.
- Adenomatous dysplasia/adenocarcinoma *in situ* precedes adenocarcinoma.
- Squamous dysplasia/squamous carcinoma *in situ* precedes squamous cell carcinoma.

Genetic mutations

- *EGFR, ALK, ROS, MET* in adenocarcinomas.
- *TP53* and *CDKN2A* in squamous cell carcinomas.
- *TP53* and *Rb* in small cell carcinomas.

Presentation

- Symptoms related to local growth of the tumour include progressive breathlessness, cough, chest pain, hoarseness or loss of voice, haemoptysis, weight loss, and recurrent pneumonia.
- Abdominal pain, bony pain, and neurological symptoms may occur from metastases.
- A small proportion of small cell carcinomas present with paraneoplastic syndromes or the superior vena cava syndrome.

Macroscopy

- A firm white/grey tumour mass within the lung.
- Yellow consolidation may be seen in the lung parenchyma distal to large proximal tumours due to an obstructive pneumonia (Fig. 5.3)
- Pleural puckering may be seen overlying peripheral tumours that have infiltrated the pleura.
- Metastatic tumour deposits may be seen in hilar lymph nodes.

Histopathology

- Adenocarcinoma is an invasive malignant epithelial tumour showing glandular differentiation and/or mucin production by tumour cells.
- Squamous cell carcinoma is an invasive malignant epithelial tumour showing keratinization and/or intercellular bridges.
- Small cell carcinoma is a poorly differentiated neuroendocrine carcinoma, composed of small cells with scant cytoplasm, ill-defined cell borders, finely granular chromatin, and absent nucleoli. Mitotic activity is high and necrosis is often extensive.

Immunohistochemistry

- The main histological types of lung carcinomas show differing patterns of immunohistochemistry which can aid in diagnosis.
- Adenocarcinomas are usually $CK7^{+}TTF1^{+}p63^{-}CK5^{-}$.
- Squamous cell carcinomas are usually $p63^{+}CK5^{+}CK7^{-}TTF1^{-}$.
- Small cell carcinomas are usually $CD56^{+}CK7^{+}TTF1^{+}p63^{-}CK5^{-}$.

Prognosis

- Poor with 5-year survival rates of ~10% in most countries.

Fig. 5.3 A central lung carcinoma. Note how the lung tissue distal to the tumour shows flecks of yellow consolidation due to an obstructive pneumonia. The tumour was found to be a squamous cell carcinoma when examined microscopically (see Plate 3).

TNM 7 pathological staging of lung carcinomas

Primary tumour (T)

T1a: tumour ≤2cm in size, confined to the lung.

T1b: tumour >2–3cm in size, confined to the lung.

T2: tumour 3–7cm in size; tumour of any size that involves the main bronchus 2cm or more distal to the carina, invades visceral pleura, causes partial atelectasis.

T3: tumour >7cm in size; tumour of any size that invades the chest wall, diaphragm, pericardium, mediastinal pleura, and main bronchus <2cm distal to the carina, causes total atelectasis; multiple tumour nodules in same lobe.

T4: tumour of any size that invades the mediastinum, heart, great vessels, carina, trachea, oesophagus, vertebra; multiple tumour nodules in same lung, but different lobes.

Regional lymph nodes (N)

N0: no regional lymph node metastasis.

N1: metastasis in ipsilateral peribronchial or hilar lymph nodes.

N2: metastasis in ipsilateral mediastinal or subcarinal lymph nodes.

N3: metastasis in contralateral mediastinal or hilar lymph nodes or any scalene or supraclavicular lymph nodes.

Pleural effusion

Definition
- An accumulation of excess fluid within the pleural space.

Epidemiology
- Common.

Aetiology
- LVF.
- Pneumonia.
- Pulmonary embolism.
- Malignancy.
- Multisystem autoimmune diseases (e.g. lupus, RA).

Pathogenesis
- Increased pulmonary venous congestion (LVF), inflammation of the pleura (pneumonia, pulmonary embolism, autoimmune disease), infiltration of the pleura (malignancy).

Presentation
- Small effusions may be asymptomatic (though visible on imaging).
- Large effusions cause breathlessness.

Macroscopy
- Fluid is seen within the pleural space.
- Fluid may be straw-coloured, haemorrhagic, or purulent.

Cytopathology
- Cytological examination of pleural fluid in benign conditions shows mesothelial cells and variable numbers of inflammatory cells, depending on the cause.
- Pleural fluid due to malignancy may contain malignant cells with enlarged pleomorphic nuclei.

Prognosis
- Parapneumonic effusions and those due to pulmonary emboli resolve upon treatment.
- Pleural effusion due to LVF usually implies advanced disease and poor prognosis.
- Pleural effusion due to malignancy is invariably due to metastatic disease and so has a very poor prognosis.

Pneumothorax

Definition

- The presence of air in the pleural space.

Epidemiology

- Common.
- Men are affected more than women.

Aetiology

- Spontaneous pneumothorax typically occurs in thin, tall young men. It is thought to be due to the rupture of small delicate apical blebs of lung tissue which result from stretching of the lungs.
- Underlying lung disease, e.g. COPD, asthma, pneumonia, TB, CF, sarcoidosis, lung carcinoma, IPF. Rare conditions often associated with pneumothorax include pulmonary Langerhans cell histiocytosis, pulmonary lymphangioleiomyomatosis, and thoracic endometriosis.
- Trauma, e.g. penetrating chest wound, rib fractures.
- Iatrogenic, e.g. subclavian vein cannulation, lung biopsy.

Pathogenesis

- Air leaks out of the damaged lung into the pleural space until the pressures equalize.
- The lung collapses to a variable degree, depending on the size of the pneumothorax.
- Rarely, the tissues near the lung defect act as a one-way valve, preventing the equalization of pressure. The continuous build-up of pressure and volume in the pleural space displaces mediastinal structures, causing cardiorespiratory arrest (**tension pneumothorax**).

Presentation

- Sudden onset of unilateral pleuritic chest pain.
- There may be breathlessness, depending on the size of the pneumothorax. Patients with an underlying lung disease will usually notice a worsening in their symptoms.

Radiology

- Air is present within the pleural space, together with varying amounts of lung collapse.

Histopathology

- Apical lung tissue excised from patients with spontaneous pneumothoraces shows one or more bullae associated with subpleural alveolar collapse and fibrosis.
- The overlying visceral pleura shows reactive mesothelial hyperplasia and inflammation which is often rich in eosinophils.

Prognosis

- About one-third of patients with spontaneous pneumothorax suffer from recurrent episodes, usually on the same side.

Malignant mesothelioma

Definition

- A malignant tumour arising in the pleura from mesothelial cells and showing a diffuse pattern of growth over the pleural surfaces.

Epidemiology

- Most cases are seen in males aged over 60 years old.
- Incidence still rising due to the long latency period between asbestos exposure and development of the tumour.
- Incidence is expected to peak between 2015 and 2020.

Aetiology

- >90% of cases are directly attributable to asbestos exposure.
- Amphibole asbestos is the most potent type, followed by chrysotile, and then amosite.
- Other rarer causes include exposure to non-asbestos mineral fibres and therapeutic radiation.

Pathogenesis

- Inhaled asbestos fibres become permanently entrapped in the lung.
- Most do not cause a tissue reaction and these are probably the ones responsible for the carcinogenic effects.
- A minority become coated with iron, forming asbestos bodies.

Genetic mutations

- Deletion of *CDKN2A* is seen in 80% of mesotheliomas.

Presentation

- Breathlessness, often due to a large pleural effusion, and chest pain.
- Weight loss and malaise are often profound.

Macroscopy

- Initially, multiple small nodules stud the parietal pleura.
- As the tumour grows, the nodules become confluent and form a tumour mass that encases the entire lung and fuses to the chest wall (Fig. 5.4)

Cytopathology

- Cytological examination of pleural fluid from a pleural effusion may reveal the presence of malignant cells forming sheets, clusters, and papillae.

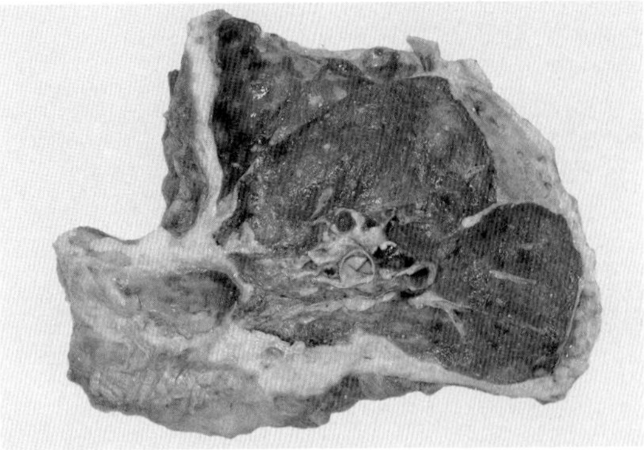

Fig. 5.4 Typical macroscopic appearance of malignant mesothelioma. Note how the tumour encases and compresses the lung (see Plate 4).

Reproduced with permission from *Clinical Pathology* (Oxford Core Texts), Carton, James, Daly, Richard, and Ramani, Pramila, Oxford University Press (2006), p.136, Figure 7.15.

Histopathology

- **Epithelioid mesothelioma** is composed of round malignant cells forming tubules and papillae.
- **Sarcomatoid mesothelioma** is composed of elongated spindled malignant cells.
- **Biphasic mesothelioma** contains a mixture of epithelioid and sarcomatoid types.
- **Desmoplastic mesothelioma** is a variant composed of small numbers of spindled malignant cells set in very dense collagenous tissue.

Immunohistochemistry

- Mesotheliomas are usually positive for cytokeratin 5/6, WT1, D2-40, and calretinin.

Prognosis

- Very poor, with half of patients dying within a year of diagnosis.
- Few survive >2 years from diagnosis.

Chapter 6

Head and neck pathology

Benign oral cavity diseases

Candidiasis

- Fungal infection which is more common in the immunosuppressed.
- Clinically, there is erythema with pseudomembrane formation.

Actinomycosis

- Gram-positive anaerobic bacteria which are part of normal oral flora and colonize tonsillar crypts, dental plaque, and the gums.
- Pathological infection can occur if the organisms enter deeper tissue through trauma (e.g. tooth extraction).

Lichen planus

- Often involves the oral cavity (➔ Lichen planus, p. 388).

Pemphigus vulgaris

- Usually involves the oral cavity (➔ Pemphigus vulgaris, p. 391).

Mucous membrane pemphigoid

- Also known as cicatricial pemphigoid.
- Autoimmune blistering disease predominantly affecting mucosal sites.
- Presents between ages 50–70y with oral blistering.
- The conjunctiva, upper airways, and skin are also often involved.
- Histology shows separation of the squamous epithelium from the underlying connective tissue with a variable inflammatory infiltrate.
- Direct immunofluorescence shows linear deposition of IgG and C3 along the basement membrane zone.

Squamous papilloma

- Benign exophytic proliferation of squamous epithelium.
- Most occur in adults aged 30–50y.
- Predilection for hard and soft palates and the uvula.
- Histology shows papillary fronds lined by squamous epithelium.

Fibroma

- Benign proliferation of fibrous tissue in response to irritation.
- Presents as a painless oral lump in an adult aged 30–50y.
- Histology shows a subepithelial mass of dense collagenous tissue.

Pyogenic granuloma

- Benign vascular lesion, also known as 'lobular capillary haemangioma'.
- Presents as a dark red polypoid mass which often ulcerates.
- Histology shows a lobulated proliferation of small blood vessels.

Mucocele

- Caused by blockage or rupture of a salivary gland duct.
- Presents as a fluctuant lesion, most commonly on the lower lip.
- Histology shows a cystic space filled with mucin and lined by inflammatory tissue.

Oral/oropharyngeal carcinoma

Definition

- Malignant epithelial neoplasm arising in the oral cavity/oropharynx.

Epidemiology

- 5% of all cancers in men and 2% of all cancers in women.

Aetiology

- Smoking and high alcohol intake are the dominant risk factors for oral carcinoma. These two factors are strongly synergistic.
- HPV infection is implicated in a high proportion (~70%) of oropharyngeal carcinomas.

Carcinogenesis

- Smoking-related cancers commonly show *TP53* mutations.
- HPV-related cancers show overexpression of *p16*.

Presentation

- Early oral carcinomas appear as small red/white plaques and may be picked up during routine oral examination, often by dentists.
- Advanced oral carcinomas present with problems with talking and eating due to tumour obstruction. There may be coexisting neck swelling due to cervical lymph node metastasis.
- Sometimes patients present with enlarged cervical lymph nodes in the absence of any symptoms referrable to the primary tumour. This is particularly the case with oropharyngeal carcinomas.

Macroscopy

- Early tumours appear as red/white plaques (Fig. 6.1).
- Advanced tumours appear as ulcerated exophytic masses.

Histopathology

- >90% are squamous cell carcinomas, characterized by invasive growth of epithelial cells showing variable squamous differentiation.
- Tumours are graded into well, moderate, or poorly differentiated.
- Tumour growth at the invasive growth is divided into cohesive or non-cohesive.

Prognosis

- The 5-year survival for smoking-related oral carcinomas is 80% for early disease and 20% for advanced tumours. These patients are also at high risk of developing multiple tumours due to a field change effect throughout the upper aerodigestive tract.
- HPV-associated carcinomas show a much more favourable prognosis, with overall 5-year survival rates of 85%.

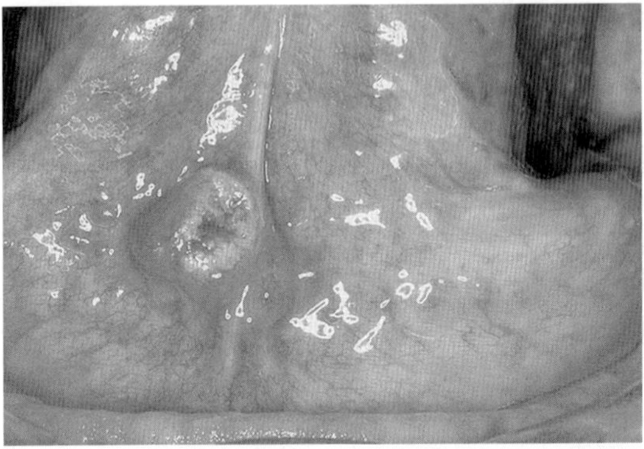

Fig. 6.1 Early squamous cell carcinoma of the oral cavity, presenting as a persistent ulcerated lesion on the undersurface of the tongue (see Plate 5).

Reproduced with permission from *Clinical Pathology* (Oxford Core Texts), Carton, James, Daly, Richard, and Ramani, Pramila, Oxford University Press (2006), p.452, Figure 19.4.

Salivary gland tumours

A diverse array of epithelial tumours have been described in the salivary glands (10 benign and 24 malignant types in the current WHO classification). Only the more common ones will be mentioned here.

Pleomorphic adenoma

- Most common salivary gland neoplasm.
- Majority occur in the parotid gland as a painless, slowly growing lump.
- Cytology is cellular with abundant epithelial and myoepithelial cells and fibrillary stromal fragments.
- Histology shows a circumscribed tumour composed of a mixture of ductal epithelium, myoepithelial cells, and a myxochondroid stroma. (Fig 6.2).
- Benign tumour but may recur following incomplete excision. If left untreated, there is a small risk of malignant transformation ('carcinoma ex pleomorphic adenoma').

Warthin's tumour

- Second most common salivary gland neoplasm.
- Almost all occur in the parotid gland as a painless, slowly growing lump. May be bilateral and multifocal.
- Cytology shows sheets of oncocytic epithelial cells with abundant lymphoid cells in the background.
- Histology shows a circumscribed tumour composed of a double layer of oncocytic epithelium with an underlying dense lymphoid stroma.
- Benign tumour but may recur following incomplete excision.

Mucoepidermoid carcinoma

- Most common malignant salivary gland neoplasm.
- Presents with a tender mass related to a major salivary gland.
- Cytology shows mucus, intermediate cells, and mucus cells.
- Histology shows an infiltrative tumour composed of a mixture of intermediate, squamoid, and mucus cells. Cystic change may be seen.
- Most tumours are low-grade and behave well, with survival >95%.
- High-grade tumours are aggressive, with survival ~45%.

Acinic cell carcinoma

- Malignant salivary gland tumour, mostly arising in the parotid.
- Presents with a mass which may be painful.
- Histology shows a tumour composed of serous acinar cells with granular cytoplasm which may grow in a variety of architectural patterns.
- 5-year survival ~80%.

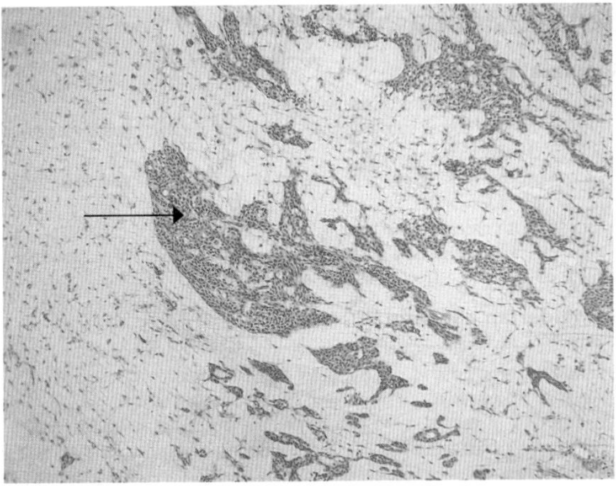

Fig. 6.2 Pleomorphic adenoma. Typical microscopic appearance of a pleomorphic adenoma with an intermingling of epithelial elements (arrow) set within a mesenchymal component (see Plate 6).

Reproduced with permission from *Clinical Pathology* (Oxford Core Texts), Carton, James, Daly, Richard, and Ramani, Pramila, Oxford University Press (2006), p.456, Figure 19.7.

Adenoid cystic carcinoma

- Malignant salivary gland tumour, mostly arising in minor salivary glands.
- Presents with a slowly growing mass which may be painful.
- Histology shows an infiltrative tumour composed of basaloid epithelial and myoepithelial cells, classically forming cribriform sheets. Perineural invasion is very frequently seen.
- The tumour shows a relentless clinical course, with a 5-year survival rate of ~35%. After 10–15 years, up to 90% of patients die of the disease.

Mammary analogue secretory carcinoma

- Recently described low-grade salivary carcinoma, arising predominantly in the parotid gland.
- Histology shows an epithelial tumour with solid, cystic, or papillar growth and eosinophilic secretions.
- Harbours a t(12;15) translocation, leading to an *ETV6-NTRK3* fusion oncogene.

Benign sinonasal diseases

Sinonasal polyps

- Benign polypoid lesions of the sinonasal tract.
- Usually related to repeated episodes of inflammation from infection or allergic rhinitis.
- Occur predominantly in adults. Presence in children should raise the possibility of CF.
- Present with nasal obstruction.
- Histologically, the polyps comprise an oedematous, inflamed stromal core, covered by a sinonasal-type epithelium.

Schneiderian papillomas

- A group of benign papillary lesions arising from the sinonasal epithelium.
- Exophytic type arises from the nasal septum and is composed of papillary fronds covered by a bland squamous epithelium.
- Endophytic (inverted) type arises from the lateral nasal wall and is composed of inverted lobules of transitional/squamous epithelium with many intraepithelial microcysts.
- Oncocytic (cylindrical) type arises from the lateral nasal wall and is composed of exophytic and endophytic proliferation of a columnar oncocytic epithelium with many intraepithelial microcysts.
- All types have a risk of local recurrence if incompletely removed. The recurrence risk is highest with the inverted type.

Allergic fungal sinusitis

- Allergic reaction to ubiquitous fungal antigens.
- Presents with nasal itching and discharge.
- Severe cases can give rise to a large destructive inflammatory mass.
- Histology shows a layered arrangement of mucoid material with abundant eosinophils and eosinophilic cellular debris. Fungal hyphae can be highlighted within the material with special stains.

Sinonasal malignancies

Sinonasal squamous cell carcinoma

- Most common malignant neoplasm of the sinonasal tract.
- Arises in elderly adults with symptoms of a mass lesion.
- Most common sites are the maxillary sinus, lateral nasal wall, and nasal septum.
- Nasal tumours tend to be keratinizing and well differentiated.
- Sinus tumours tend to be non-keratinizing and less well differentiated.
- Prognosis for nasal cavity-confined tumours is good (80% 5-year survival). Prognosis for sinus tumours is less favourable.

Sinonasal adenocarcinomas

- Second most common malignant neoplasm of the sinonasal tract.
- Salivary-type adenocarcinomas have an equal gender incidence and mostly arise in the maxillary sinuses. The most common histological type is adenoid cystic carcinoma.
- Intestinal-type adenocarcinomas show a marked male predilection and usually arise in the ethmoid sinus and nasal cavity. There is a well-recognized association with occupational exposure, particularly in wood workers.
- Non-intestinal-type adenocarcinomas tend to involve the ethmoid sinus and maxillary sinus.

Sinonasal undifferentiated carcinoma

- A rare, but highly aggressive, malignancy arising in the sinonasal tract.
- Presents with a large mass with bone destruction.
- Histology shows sheets of undifferentiated cells with high mitotic activity and necrosis.
- Prognosis is poor (20% 5-year survival).

Olfactory neuroblastoma

- Rare sinonasal malignancy arising from the olfactory epithelium.
- Bimodal age of onset at 10–20y and 50–60y.
- Presents with nasal obstruction, anosmia, and headaches.
- Histology shows lobules of closely packed, small, round, blue cells which may form pseudorosettes or true rosettes.
- A histological grading system from 1 to 4 is used.
- The 5-year survival ranges from 40% to 90%, depending on the stage and grade.

Malignant melanoma

- Very rare sinonasal malignancy which presents with symptoms of nasal obstruction, discharge, and pain.
- Histology shows malignant melanocytes which can grow in a multitude of different patterns.
- Prognosis is generally poor.

Nasopharyngeal diseases

Nasopharyngeal angiofibroma

- Rare benign soft tissue tumour which arises exclusively in the nasopharynx of young males (peak age of onset 15y).
- Histology shows a highly vascular neoplasm, in which variably sized vessels are surrounded by a cellular fibroblastic stroma. The lesion is covered by an intact sinonasal epithelium.
- Local recurrence occurs in about 20% of cases following surgery.

Nasopharyngeal carcinoma

- A malignant epithelial neoplasm arising in the nasopharynx.
- Presents in adults with nasal obstruction, hearing loss, and tinnitus.
- Marked geographical variation in incidence, being particularly common in southern China, Thailand, and the Philippines.
- Strong association with EBV and diet.
- Histology recognizes three subtypes: non-keratinizing, keratinizing, and basaloid.
- Most cases are treated with radical radiotherapy.
- Overall survival rates are 75%, according to WHO data.

Benign laryngeal diseases

Vocal cord nodules

- Benign growths of the laryngeal mucosa.
- Nodules are seen mostly in young women associated with vocal abuse.
- Present with vocal changes.
- Small lesions arising in the middle third of both vocal cords.
- Histology shows a nodule with an oedematous stroma which then becomes fibrotic.

Vocal cord polyp

- Benign growth of the laryngeal mucosa.
- Occurs at any age and with equal gender incidence.
- Presents with vocal changes.
- Involves the ventricular space, or Reinke's space, of one vocal cord.
- Histology shows a polyp with a stroma that may be variably oedematous, myxoid, hyaline, or fibrous.

Laryngeal amyloidosis

- A localized form of amyloidosis.
- Usually arises in the false vocal cord.
- Presents with vocal changes.
- Histology shows deposition of amorphous eosinophilic material beneath the epithelium. Amyloid stains with Congo red and demonstrates chromatic changes under polarized light.
- The amyloid is usually derived from light-chain immunoglobulin.

Squamous papillomas

- Most common benign laryngeal neoplasms.
- Associated with HPV types 6 and 11.
- Bimodal age of incidence <5y and 20–40y.
- Present with vocal changes.
- Histology shows branching exophytic papillary fronds covered by a bland squamous epithelium.
- Children tend to develop a more aggressive disease with early recurrences and a higher change of spread beyond the larynx.
- Adults tend to show a more favourable course with less frequent recurrences.

Laryngeal carcinoma

Definition

- Malignant epithelial neoplasm arising in the larynx.

Epidemiology

- 1% of all cancers.
- Men affected more frequently than women, though the incidence in women is increasing.
- Patients usually present in sixth and seventh decades.

Aetiology

- Strong association with heavy smoking and alcohol consumption.

Carcinogenesis

- *TP53* mutations frequently observed.

Presentation

- Glottic tumours: hoarseness.
- Supraglottic tumours: dysphagia, foreign body sensation in the throat.
- Subglottic tumours: dyspnoea, stridor.

Histopathology

- >90% are squamous cell carcinomas, characterized by invasive growth of epithelial cells showing variable squamous differentiation.
- Tumours are graded into well, moderate, or poorly differentiated.
- Tumour growth at the invasive growth is divided into cohesive or non-cohesive.

Prognosis

- TNM stage correlates well with survival.
- The 5-year survival approaches 90% for T1 lesions, but <50% for T4.

Odontogenic cysts

Radicular (periapical) cyst

- Most common type of odontogenic cyst.
- Inflammatory in origin.
- Arises around the apex of a non-vital tooth, usually due to deep caries or trauma.
- Tends to be asymptomatic, unless it becomes inflamed.
- Radiologically appears as a well-defined, round radiolucency.
- Histologically shows an inflamed fibrous wall lined by a non-keratinizing stratified squamous epithelium.

Dentigerous cyst

- Second most common type of odontogenic cyst.
- Developmental in origin.
- Arises around the crown of an unerupted tooth, most commonly an impacted wisdom tooth.
- Radiologically appears as a radiolucent lesion.
- Histologically lined by a thin layer of stratified epithelium, most likely of dental follicular origin.
- Complete removal is curative.

Odontogenic keratocyst

- Third most common type of odontogenic cyst.
- Developmental in origin.
- Can affect a wide age range, with a peak in the second and third decades.
- Radiologically presents as a well-demarcated radiolucency, often with scalloped margins; 25% are multiloculated.
- 75% occur in the mandible.
- Histology is distinctive with an uninflamed fibrous wall lined by a thin, keratinized stratified squamous epithelium with a corrugated surface. The basal epithelial layer is well defined and palisaded.
- Treatment is by enucleation or surgical resection, though recurrence rates are high, possibly due to the presence of 'daughter cysts' which persist.

► Multiple lesions should prompt consideration of Gorlin's syndrome (naevoid basal cell carcinoma syndrome) caused by mutations in the *PTCH* gene.

Jaw bone neoplasms

Ossifying fibroma

- Benign fibro-osseous neoplasm, arising most commonly in the mandible of patients in the third and fourth decades.
- More common in females.
- Radiologically appears as well-demarcated, radiolucent lesions with varying degrees of radio-opacity.
- Histologically contains cementum-like material or bone in a fibrous connective tissue stroma.

Ameloblastoma

- Rare, slowly growing, locally aggressive odontogenic tumour.
- Most arise in the posterior mandible.
- Occurs mostly from 30 to 60y, with no gender predilection.
- Solid/multicystic type (85%) shows islands of odontogenic epithelium in a mature fibrous stroma.
- Unicystic type (10%) shows a cyst lined by oedematous ameloblastic epithelium with a ragged surface.
- Treated by excision, though recurrences are common.

Central giant cell lesion

- Uncommon lesion of the jaw bones.
- Presents in young adults 20–30y, with a predilection for the mandible.
- Radiologically appears as a radiolucent defect with scalloped borders.
- Histologically composed of osteoclastic giant cells and spindled fibroblasts in a vascular stroma.
- Prognosis good, with recurrence rare if completely removed.

Neck lumps

Thyroglossal cyst

- Derived from persistent remnants of the thyroglossal duct.
- Presents as a 1- to 4-cm diameter lump in the anterior neck.
- Histologically lined by a pseudostratified columnar epithelium with a fibrous wall, often the focus of thyroid tissue.

Branchial cyst

- Most are derived from second branchial arch remnants.
- Presents as a 2- to 5-cm diameter lump in the upper lateral neck.
- Most commonly seen in young adults aged 20–40.
- Histologically, the cysts are lined by stratified squamous or pseudostratified columnar epithelium, with a fibrous wall containing lymphoid tissue with prominent germinal centres.

❗ A cystic lymph node metastasis of squamous cell carcinoma is an important differential diagnosis to exclude.

Carotid body paraganglioma

- Rare tumour derived from the paraganglia of carotid bodies.
- Presents as a slow-growing, painless neck lump.
- Most commonly presents in fifth to sixth decades of life.
- Histologically composed of nests of cells with a surrounding delicate vascular network.
- Immunohistochemistry shows positivity for the neuroendocrine markers chromogranin, synaptophysin, and CD56. S100 stain highlights sustentacular cells around the nests.
- Overall 90% 5-year survival rates if completely resected, but lifelong follow-up is essential as late recurrence/metastasis can occur, leading to death.

Chapter 7

Gastrointestinal pathology

Gastrointestinal malformations

Oesophageal atresia

- Occurs in 1 in 3500 live births.
- Results from faulty division of the foregut into the tracheal and oesophageal channels during the first month of embryonic life.
- In the majority of cases, there is a communication between the distal oesophagus and the trachea known as a tracheo-oesophageal fistula.
- Neonates present with coughing and choking during feeding.
- At least half of affected babies have other congenital abnormalities, and cardiac defects account for the majority of deaths in infants with oesophageal atresia.

Duodenal atresia

- Less common than oesophageal atresia.
- Associated with Down's syndrome in 30% of cases.
- Caused by failure of epithelial apoptosis and incomplete canalization of the duodenal lumen by 8 weeks of gestation.
- The obstruction is usually distal to the ampulla of Vater.
- Prenatal ultrasound shows dilation of the proximal duodenum and stomach with polyhydramnios.

Exomphalos

- An anterior abdominal wall defect at the umbilicus that causes abdominal contents to protrude through the umbilicus.
- The protrusion is covered by a delicate transparent sac composed of the amniotic membrane and peritoneum.
- Arises due to failure of the midgut to return to the abdomen from the umbilical coelom during embryogenesis.

Gastroschisis

- An anterior abdominal wall defect which lies to the side of the umbilicus through which loops of bowel protrude.
- Unlike exomphalos, there is no protective covering sac.

Malrotation

- Malpositioning of the intestine and mesentery due to failure of rotation of the developing gut as it returns from the umbilical coelom to the abdomen during development.
- A malrotated bowel is likely to have a narrow mesenteric base, predisposing to volvulus around the superior mesenteric artery.
- Compromised arterial blood supply leads to ischaemic necrosis of the entire midgut, extending from the duodenum to the transverse colon.
- Necrosis causes bleeding into the bowel and a high risk of perforation.
- Without prompt surgical intervention, the condition can be fatal.

Meckel's diverticulum

- A remnant of the vitellointestinal duct, the structure that connects the primitive gut to the yolk sac.
- Typically said to be '2in (5cm) long, 2ft (60cm) from the ileo-caecal valve in 2% of the population'.
- The mucosa of the diverticulum may contain areas of gastric or pancreatic tissue (heterotopia).
- Most children with a Meckel's diverticulum are asymptomatic.
- The most common symptom is painless rectal bleeding due to ulceration in a diverticulum containing acid-secreting gastric mucosa.
- Small bowel obstruction may also occur, related to intussusception or incarceration.

Imperforate anus

- Umbrella term for any atretic condition of the rectum or anus.
- Lesions range in severity from a stenosed anal canal to anorectal agenesis.
- Surgically, they are considered as either high or low anomalies, depending on the level of termination of the bowel with respect to the pelvic floor.
- Low defects are easier to correct and post-operative function is good.
- Higher defects are more difficult to correct as they are more likely to be associated with fistulae between the rectum and the genitourinary tract, as well as a deficient pelvic floor.

Hirschsprung's disease

- Not strictly a malformation, but a congenital gastrointestinal (GI) condition in which there is absence of ganglion cells from a variable length of the intestinal wall.
- Results from failure of neuroblasts to migrate from the oesophagus to the anal canal during weeks 5–12 of gestation.
- Absence of ganglion cells causes spasm in the aganglionic segment.
- Presents with intestinal obstruction and failure to pass meconium 24h after birth.
- Rectal suction biopsy is the gold standard for the diagnosis of Hirschsprung's disease. The key feature is the absence of ganglion cells in the submucosa and abnormally thick nerve fibres in the mucosal layer. The diagnosis is made at the time of surgery by frozen section with histochemical staining for acetylcholinesterase.

Oesophagitis

Definition

- Inflammation of the oesophagus.

Presentation

- Burning retrosternal pain (heartburn).
- Dysphagia and hiccups may also occur.

Reflux oesophagitis

- Caused by gastric acid refluxing into the lower oesophagus.
- Very common. Most prevalent in adult white males but can occur in men and women of all races and in children.
- Predisposing conditions include alcohol, medications, hypothyroidism, pregnancy, hiatus hernia, diabetes, and obesity.
- Mucosal biopsy shows regenerative changes of the squamous epithelium demonstrated by basal cell hyperplasia and extension of vascular papillae into the upper part of the epithelium. Spongiosis (intercellular oedema) is a characteristic feature. Inflammation is typically mild with scattered neutrophils and eosinophils.
- ~10% of patients develop columnar metaplasia of the lower oesophagus which is visible endoscopically; this is known as **Barrett's oesophagus** or **columnar-lined oesophagus** (Fig. 7.1). There may also be intestinal metaplasia with goblet cells. This is associated with a higher risk of developing oesophageal adenocarcinoma.

▶ Barrett's oesophagus is associated with a 50 times increased risk of oesophageal adenocarcinoma (➲ Oesophageal carcinoma, pp. 112–13). Patients with Barrett's oesophagus should be considered for entry into a surveillance programme of regular endoscopy and biopsy to check for columnar epithelial dysplasia. Dysplasia is divided into high grade and low grade. This is such a subjective assessment that it should always be made by two pathologists.

Drug-induced ('pill') oesophagitis

- Caused by direct toxicity of drugs to the oesophageal mucosa.
- Occurs mostly in the elderly.
- Common culprit drugs are bisphosphonates and iron tablets.
- Mucosal biopsy shows acute inflammation with erosion or ulceration of the surface epithelium. Encrusted golden brown iron pigment may be seen in cases caused by iron tablets.
- Usually resolves after discontinuation of the offending drug.

Eosinophilic oesophagitis

- Uncommon condition which occurs mostly in atopic individuals with a history of allergy, asthma, and drug sensitivities.
- Mucosal biopsy shows heavy infiltration of the mucosa by eosinophils which often form clusters.
- May coexist with reflux oesophagitis.
- Good outlook if diagnosed and treated early. If untreated, it can lead to severe oesophageal strictures.

Infectious oesophagitis

- More commonly seen in debilitated or immunocompromised patients, as the oesophagus is normally highly resistant to infection.
- Common infectious agents include herpes simplex virus (HSV), CMV, and *Candida*.

(a)

(b)

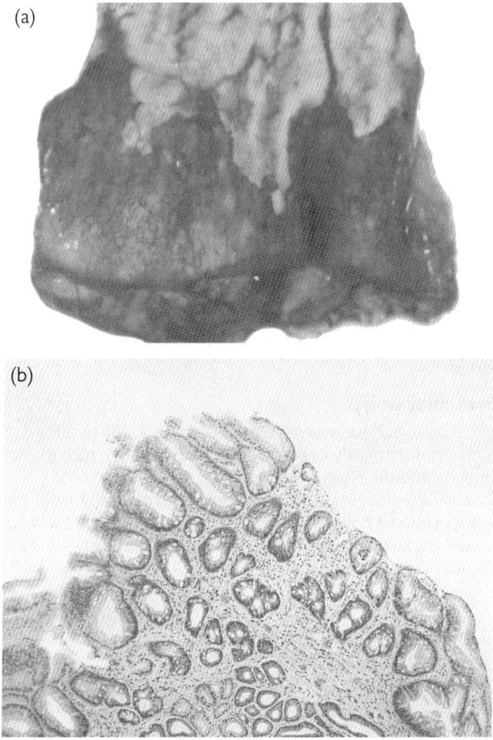

Fig. 7.1 Barrett's oesophagus. (a) This segment from the lower oesophagus shows the white keratinized squamous epithelium at the top. The red area at the bottom represents an area of Barrett's oesophagus. (b) An oesophageal biopsy taken from an area of endoscopic Barrett's oesophagus, confirming the presence of glandular epithelium. (See Plate 7.)

Reproduced with permission from *Clinical Pathology* (Oxford Core Texts), Carton, James, Daly, Richard, and Ramani, Pramila, Oxford University Press (2006), p.139, Figure 8.1.

Oesophageal polyps and nodules

Squamous papilloma

- Uncommon lesion, usually seen as a tiny white polyp in the distal oesophagus at endoscopy.
- Cases have been reported in association with HPV infection.
- Histology shows a bland squamous epithelium forming papillary projections.

Leiomyoma

- Uncommon benign smooth muscle tumour arising from the muscular layers of the oesophagus. More common than GI stromal tumours at this site.
- Usually produces a polypoid mass covered by mucosa that may show surface ulceration.
- Histology shows interlacing fascicles of bland smooth muscle cells.

Granular cell tumour

- Uncommon neural tumour which can occur anywhere in the GI tract, but most frequently in the tongue and oesophagus.
- Forms a small firm, raised mucosal nodule in the lower oesophagus.
- Histologically characterized by aggregates of large polygonal cells with conspicuous granular cytoplasm.
- Almost all are benign, though very rare malignant cases have been reported.

Fibrovascular polyp

- Rare oesophageal lesion which typically presents with dysphagia.
- Can reach an alarmingly large size (up to 25cm long!), such that it can regurgitate into the pharynx or mouth.
- Endoscopically visible as a pedunculated lesion on a long stalk.
- Histology shows a polypoid lesion covered by squamous epithelium with an underlying stromal core composed of loose fibrous tissue, fat, and a prominent vasculature.

Oesophageal carcinoma

Definition

- A malignant epithelial tumour arising in the oesophagus.
- Two major subtypes are distinguished: **squamous cell carcinoma** and **adenocarcinoma**.

Epidemiology

- Both types occur at a median age of 65y.
- Oesophageal adenocarcinoma has attracted much attention in developed countries due to its dramatic and ongoing rise in incidence over recent decades.
- Squamous carcinomas are much more common in Asia and Africa.

Aetiology

- Heavy tobacco and alcohol use for squamous cell carcinoma.
- Chronic gastro-oesophageal reflux disease leading to Barrett's oesophagus is the most common precursor to adenocarcinoma.

Carcinogenesis

- Both types frequently harbour *p53* mutations.

Presentation

- Dysphagia, retrosternal or epigastric pain, and weight loss.
- By the time most patients present, the tumour is already advanced.

Macroscopy

- Tumour mass in the oesophagus which may grow into the lumen in an exophytic manner or infiltrate into the wall in a plaque-like fashion.
- Squamous cell carcinomas tend to occur in the middle oesophagus, whereas adenocarcinomas tend to occur in the lower oesophagus.

Histopathology

- Squamous cell carcinomas show infiltrating malignant epithelial cells, with evidence of squamous differentiation, i.e. intercellular bridges and/or keratinization.
- Adenocarcinomas show infiltrating malignant epithelial cells, with evidence of glandular differentiation, i.e. tubule formation and/or mucin production. The adjacent oesophageal mucosa may show high-grade dysplasia within an area of Barrett's oesophagus.

Prognosis

- Generally poor due to late presentation.
- 5-year survival rates ~10–20%.

TNM 7 pathological staging of oesophageal carcinoma

Primary tumour (T)
pT1a: tumour invades the mucosa.
pT1b: tumour invades the submucosa.
pT2: tumour invades the muscularis propria.
pT3: tumour invades the adventitia.
pT4: tumour invades adjacent structures.

Regional lymph nodes (N)
pN0: no regional lymph node metastasis.
pN1: 1 or 2 regional lymph node metastases.
pN2: 3–6 regional lymph node metastases.
pN3: 7 or more regional lymph node metastases.

In resection specimens, it is important to assess involvement of the circumferential resection margin. In cases which have received neo-adjuvant therapy, the degree of tumour regression can be recorded using the Mandard score.

Gastritis

Acute haemorrhagic gastritis

- Caused by an abrupt insult to the gastric mucosa.
- Often the result of drugs or a severe alcohol binge, but any acute medical illness which reduces gastric blood flow may also cause acute gastritis.
- Endoscopy shows numerous punctate erosions which ooze blood.
- Severe forms can cause significant upper GI haemorrhage.
- Histology shows neutrophilic infiltration of the gastric mucosa with haemorrhage and mucosal necrosis.
- Acute gastritis usually resolves rapidly and uneventfully.

Autoimmune gastritis

- Caused by autoimmune attack directed at parietal cells in fundic glands.
- Histology shows infiltration of the body mucosa by lymphocytes and plasma cells. The infiltrate is directed at fundic glands, with atrophy associated with loss of chief and parietal cells. Pyloric and intestinal-type metaplasia is common.
- Increased risk of gastric neuroendocrine tumours and carcinoma.
- Some patients also develop antibodies to intrinsic factor, leading to depletion of vitamin B12 and megaloblastic anaemia (➔ Megaloblastic anaemias, pp. 330–1).

Bacterial (*Helicobacter*) gastritis

- A very common cause of gastritis which is usually antral-predominant.
- Most are caused by *Helicobacter pylori*, a curved flagellate Gram-negative rod.
- *Helicobacter heilmannii*, which is larger and more tightly coiled, accounts for <1% of cases.
- Histology shows a heavy lymphoid inflammatory infiltrate in the lamina propria, often with lymphoid follicle formation, with neutrophilic infiltration of the superficial mucosa. Infection may be associated with intestinal metaplasia and dysplasia.
- The organisms can be identified on routine stains but are better visualized on special stains that highlight the bacteria.
- In most cases, the gastritis is healed by eradicating the organism.
- In a small proportion of untreated cases, the gastritis can be complicated by peptic ulceration, gastric carcinoma (➔ Gastric carcinoma, pp. 118–19), or gastric marginal zone B-cell lymphoma (➔ Extranodal marginal zone lymphoma, pp. 370–1).

Chemical/reactive gastropathy

- Caused by any low-grade injury to the gastric mucosa.
- Seen mostly in the antrum in relation to bile reflux or non-steroidal anti-inflammatory drugs (NSAIDs).
- Endoscopically, there is erythema of the gastric mucosa.
- Histology shows vascular congestion, foveolar hyperplasia, and smooth muscle proliferation. Inflammation is minimal or absent. It is for this reason the term gastropathy is preferred to gastritis.
- It usually resolves without complication if the offending cause is removed.

Iron pill gastritis

- Caused by the corrosive effects of ingested iron tablets.
- Histology shows it causes acute inflammation with erosion or ulceration of the gastric mucosa. Yellow-brown iron pigment may be seen.

Gastric polyps

Hyperplastic polyp

- Common polyp which occurs mostly in the antrum or body.
- Non-neoplastic reactive lesion thought to represent an exaggerated regenerative response to mucosal injury.
- Often associated with an underlying gastric pathology such as *Helicobacter* or autoimmune gastritis.
- Histology shows a polyp containing a dilated, elongated, tortuous foveolar epithelium in an oedematous, inflamed lamina propria.

Fundic gland polyp

- Common polyp which occurs only in the body or fundus.
- Most frequently seen in patients taking proton pump inhibitors. Can occur sporadically or in association with familial adenomatous polyposis (FAP).
- FAP-associated polyps are more likely to be multiple and occur at a younger age.
- Sporadic polyps are not normally associated with any underlying mucosal pathology.
- Histology shows a polyp containing cystically dilated fundic glands lined by flattened parietal and chief cells.

Gastric adenoma

- Uncommon neoplastic polyp that can occur throughout the stomach.
- Microscopically composed of dysplastic glands with stratified hyperchromatic nuclei.
- Two types are described—an intestinal and a foveolar type.
- Intestinal types are far more likely to show high-grade dysplasia or harbour gastric carcinoma than the foveolar type.

Gastric xanthoma

- Uncommon polyp that occurs anywhere in the stomach.
- Appears as a pale yellow nodule due to its lipid content.
- Histology shows numerous lipid-laden macrophages in the lamina propria.

Inflammatory fibroid polyp

- Rare lesion which occurs mostly in the antrum.
- Histology shows a submucosal lesion composed of bland spindle cells arranged around prominent vessels, all set in a loose myxoid stroma containing conspicuous eosinophils.

Gastric carcinoma

Definition

- A malignant epithelial tumour arising in the stomach.

Epidemiology

- Marked geographical variability in incidence due to differences in diet.
- Changes in nutrition in countries with a traditionally high incidence is leading to a steadily declining global incidence.

Aetiology

- Diet is the most consistent factor. High salt intake is a strong risk factor, whilst fresh fruit and vegetables are protective due to their antioxidant effects.
- *H. pylori* and autoimmune gastritis are the other major risk factors, as they both promote a sequence of chronic gastritis, gastric atrophy, intestinal metaplasia, epithelial dysplasia, and carcinoma. This is referred to as the metaplasia–dysplasia of cancer development and is in contrast with the polyp–carcinoma pathway seen in the large bowel.

Carcinogenesis

- Free radicals, oxidants, and reactive oxygen species produced by *H. pylori* infection and dietary carcinogens cause DNA damage.
- Common gene targets include *p53* and *KRAS*.
- Diffuse-type carcinomas often show E-cadherin loss.

Presentation

- Early gastric cancer may be asymptomatic or cause non-specific symptoms such as dyspepsia.
- Advanced cases cause persistent abdominal pain with weight loss.
- Tumours may also bleed, causing haematemesis, or obstruct the gastric outlet leading to vomiting.

Macroscopy

- A tumour mass in the stomach wall which may be exophytic or diffusely infiltrative ('linitis plastica').

Histopathology

- Almost all are adenocarcinomas. The Lauren classification divides them into intestinal and diffuse.
- Intestinal-type adenocarcinoma shows infiltrating malignant epithelial cells forming recognizable glandular structures.
- Diffuse-type adenocarcinoma shows infiltrating malignant epithelial cells growing as poorly cohesive cells, with little or no gland formation. Individual malignant cells may contain intracytoplasmic vacuoles filled with mucin. Cells distended with mucin, such that the nucleus is displaced to one side, are also known as 'signet ring' cells. Tumours with abundant signet ring cells tend to be widely infiltrative.
- *Her-2* testing is now routinely carried out to predict response to Herceptin® (trastuzumab) therapy.

Prognosis

- Dependent on the stage, but generally presents late with a poor prognosis.

TNM 7 pathological staging of gastric carcinomas

Primary tumour (T)

pT1a: tumour invades the lamina propria.
pT1b: tumour invades the submucosa.
pT2: tumour invades the muscularis propria.
pT3: tumour invades the subserosa.
pT4a: tumour perforates the serosa.
pT4b: tumour invades adjacent structures.

Regional lymph nodes (N)

pN0: no regional lymph node metastasis.
pN1: metastasis in 1 or 2 regional lymph nodes.
pN2: metastasis in 3–6 regional lymph nodes.
pN3: metastasis in 7 or more regional lymph nodes.

In cases which have received neo-adjuvant therapy, the degree of tumour regression can be recorded using the Mandard score.

Gastrointestinal stromal tumours

Definition

- Mesenchymal tumours of variable malignant potential which arise within the wall of the GI tract and recapitulate the phenotype of the interstitial cell of Cajal, the pacemaker cell of the Auerbach plexus.

Epidemiology

- Incidence of about ~15 per million population per year.
- Most arise in adults at a median age of 50–60y.

Aetiology

- Aetiology of sporadic cases unknown.
- A small proportion arise in association with neurofibromatosis type 1 and Carney's triad, and in families with germline *KIT* mutations.

Genetics

- The vast majority show activating mutations of the oncogene *KIT*.
- The remainder show activating mutations in the related gene *PDGFRA*.

Presentation

- Palpable upper abdominal mass, pain, or bleeding.
- Malignant tumours may cause symptoms related to metastasis.

Sites of involvement

- Can occur anywhere in the GI tract, from the oesophagus to the rectum.
- Most arise in the stomach (60–70%) or small intestine (20–30%).
- A small number appear to arise primarily within the omentum.

Macroscopy

- Well-defined tumour mass, centred on the submucosal, muscular, or serosal layer of the bowel.
- Ranges in size from 1 to >20cm.

Histopathology

- Composed of spindle cells, often with paranuclear vacuoles. Plumper epithelioid cells may also be present and some tumours may be entirely epithelioid in nature.
- Small intestinal tumours may also have so-called 'skeinoid' fibres.
- Almost all express the markers CD117 (c-kit) and DOG-1.
- Molecular detection of *KIT* or *PDGFRA* mutations may be necessary in a minority of cases.

Prognosis

- All should be considered potentially malignant.
- Based on location, size, and mitotic activity, they are stratified into very low risk, low risk, intermediate risk, and high risk categories for progressive disease.

Peptic duodenitis

Definition

- Inflammation or ulceration of the duodenal mucosa due to excess gastric acid.

Epidemiology

- Common, affecting up to 10% of the population.
- Mostly seen in male patients aged >40y.

Aetiology

- Chronic *H. pylori* infection is thought to be the key aetiological factor.
- Smoking and NSAIDs are also major risk factors.
- Recurrent multiple duodenal ulcers, particularly if present beyond the first part of the duodenum, should raise suspicion of possible Zollinger–Ellison syndrome (➔ Pancreatic endocrine tumours, pp. 174–5).

Pathogenesis

- Increased gastric acid production causes injury to the duodenal mucosa, varying from mild erosions only through to severe ulceration.

Presentation

- Burning epigastric pain relieved by eating.
- Severe cases cause persistent epigastric pain, nausea, and vomiting.

Macroscopy

- Peptic duodenitis shows mucosal erythema ± superficial erosions.
- Peptic ulcers appear as well-circumscribed, punched-out mucosal defects with granulation tissue at the base.

Histopathology

- Peptic duodenitis shows acute inflammation, oedema, and haemorrhage in the lamina propria. The surface epithelium typically shows areas of gastric metaplasia. *H. pylori* organisms may be identified overlying the metaplastic gastric epithelium.
- Peptic ulcers show complete loss of the whole mucosal layer, with replacement by granulation tissue and underlying scar tissue.

Prognosis

- Eradication of *H. pylori* and acid suppressive therapy improves symptoms and leads to healing.
- Scarring of ulcers can lead to stricture formation and obstruction.
- Breach of a large vessel by a peptic ulcer is a common cause of acute upper GI haemorrhage.
- Free perforation causes acute generalized peritonitis, necessitating urgent surgical intervention.

Coeliac disease

Definition

- An autoimmune disorder caused by an abnormal immune response to dietary gluten.

Epidemiology

- Common, affecting ~1% of the population.

Aetiology

- Dietary gluten and related proteins.

Pathogenesis

- The culprit proteins are poorly digested by intestinal proteases.
- Intact peptides enter the lamina propria and are deamidated by tissue transglutaminase, rendering them negatively charged.
- Negatively charged peptides bind more efficiently to human leucocyte antigen (HLA) receptors on antigen-presenting cells which are recognized by intestinal T-cells.
- Activated T-cells stimulate an immune reaction in the intestinal wall.

Presentation

- Symptoms relating to the GI tract may be present such as weight loss, abdominal pain, and diarrhoea.
- However, many patients are asymptomatic and only diagnosed during investigation of an iron deficiency anaemia.

Serology

- Presence of serum IgA endomysial or transglutaminase antibodies is highly specific and sensitive for coeliac disease. Care must be taken in interpreting these results in patients who are IgA-deficient.

Macroscopy

- Blunting and flattening of villi may be visible under a dissecting microscope.

Histopathology

- Fully developed cases show increased intraepithelial lymphocytes (>20/100 epithelial cells), mainly at the tips of the villi, many lymphocytes and plasma cells in the lamina propria, villous atrophy, and crypt hyperplasia (Fig. 7.2).
- Milder cases may only show increased intraepithelial lymphocytes without villous atrophy.

► Note that none of these changes are specific to coeliac disease; identical changes can be seen in a number of other conditions, e.g. tropical sprue. Biopsy findings must be interpreted in light of the clinical and serological picture.

Prognosis

- Strict adherence to a gluten-free diet leads to resolution of symptoms and normalization of histology, although architectural changes may take some time to normalize. Cases which do not respond to a gluten-free diet need to be carefully assessed for the development of a lymphoma.
- Increased risk of type 1 diabetes, autoimmune thyroid disease, dermatitis herpetiformis, oropharyngeal and oesophageal carcinomas, small bowel adenocarcinoma, and a rare, but highly aggressive, form of T-cell lymphoma known as enteropathy-associated T-cell lymphoma (➔ Mature T-cell non-Hodgkin's lymphomas, pp. 382–3).

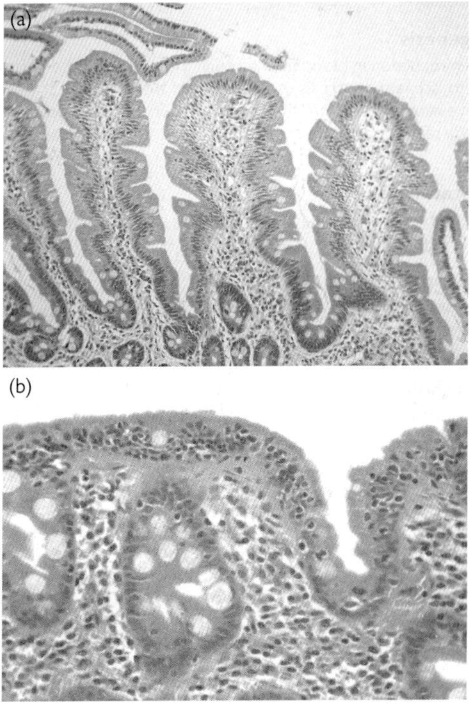

Fig. 7.2 (a) Normal duodenal mucosa. The villi have a normal height and shape, and there is no increase in intraepithelial lymphocytes. (b) Duodenal biopsy from a patient with gluten-sensitive enteropathy. The villi have completely disappeared and the surface epithelium contains many intraepithelial lymphocytes. (See Plate 8.)

Reproduced with permission from *Clinical Pathology* (Oxford Core Texts), Carton, James, Daly, Richard, and Ramani, Pramila, Oxford University Press (2006), p.154, Figure 8.8.

Small bowel infarction

Definition
- Ischaemic necrosis of a segment of the small intestine.

Epidemiology
- Usually seen in patients aged >50y.

Aetiology
- Thrombosis overlying an unstable atherosclerotic plaque in the superior mesenteric artery.
- Thromboemboli from the left ventricle or left atrium.
- Hypovolaemia.

Pathogenesis
- Sudden reduction in blood flow through the superior mesenteric artery leads to ischaemic necrosis of a segment of the small bowel.
- Massive haemorrhage into the infarcted bowel causes hypovolaemia.
- Bacteria rapidly permeate the devitalized intestinal wall, leading to sepsis.

Presentation
- Acute onset of severe abdominal pain with bloody diarrhoea and hypovolaemia.

Macroscopy
- The infarcted small bowel appears dusky purple (Fig. 7.3).
- On opening the segment of bowel, large amounts of blood are present in the lumen and the mucosal surface is friable and necrotic.

Histopathology
- Full-thickness necrosis of the bowel wall. Milder changes include crypt atrophy (withering).

Prognosis
- Early laparotomy is essential to resect the infarcted segment of bowel.
- Survival is generally poor due to the rapid development of hypovolaemia and sepsis, causing multiorgan failure.

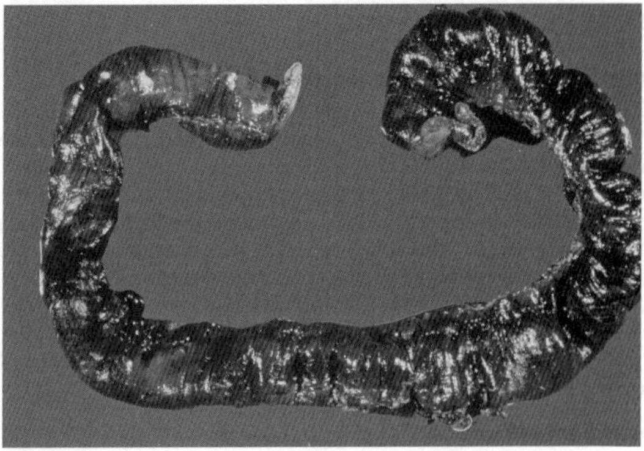

Fig. 7.3 Small bowel infarction. Typical appearance of an infarcted segment of the small bowel. The dark colour is due to the intense congestion and haemorrhage within the intestine as a result of blockage to venous outflow (see Plate 9).

Intestinal infections

Campylobacter, Salmonella, Shigella, Escherichia coli

- Common bacterial causes of GI infection.
- Mucosal biopsies usually show an acute colitis, with neutrophils present in the lamina propria and within crypts.
- Enterotoxigenic *E. coli* (ETEC) is a common cause of diarrhoea in travellers. ETEC possesses fimbriae which allow the bacteria to adhere to small bowel epithelial cells and produce toxins, causing massive fluid loss.
- Enterohaemorrhagic *E. coli* produces a cytotoxin, leading to haemorrhagic necrosis of the colonic mucosa and bloody diarrhoea. Susceptible individuals, particularly children, are at risk of developing thrombotic microangiopathy, leading to haemolysis and ARF (haemolytic uraemic syndrome, HUS).

Clostridium difficile

- An important cause of colitis, often associated with broad-spectrum antibiotic use in hospitalized patients.
- The clinical picture is highly varied, ranging from mild diarrhoea to fulminant colitis with a risk of perforation and death.
- Macroscopically, the colitis leads to the formation of cream-coloured pseudomembranes on the mucosal surface of the colon (Fig. 7.4).
- Microscopically, crypts distended with neutrophils and mucin are covered by pseudomembranes composed of fibrin and neutrophils.

Mycobacterium avium

- Significant opportunistic pathogen in the immunosuppressed.
- Disseminated infection throughout the small and large bowel causes chronic diarrhoea.
- Mucosal biopsy shows extensive infiltration of the lamina propria by macrophages filled with acid-fast bacilli.

Rotavirus

- Most common cause of severe diarrhoea in infants and young children.
- Faecal–oral transmission.
- Immunity develops during childhood, such that adult infection is rare.

Norovirus

- Common cause of epidemic outbreaks of gastroenteritis.
- Highly infectious with transmission through contaminated food or water, person-to-person contact, and contamination of surfaces.
- Often seen in close communities such as institutions, hospitals, and cruise ships.

Cytomegalovirus

- Usually associated with immunocompromise.
- CMV infection is an important cause of a sudden clinical deterioration in immunosuppressed patients with inflammatory bowel disease.
- Microscopically, the changes vary from mild inflammation to deep ulceration. CMV inclusions are found in endothelial and stromal cells.

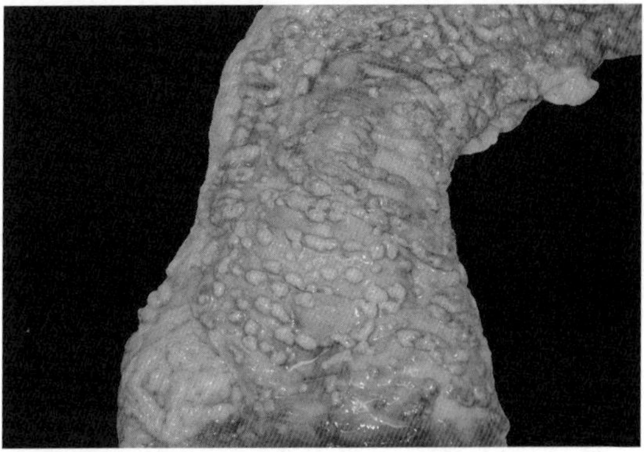

Fig. 7.4 *Clostridium difficile* colitis. This is a freshly opened colon from a patient with profuse diarrhoea, following broad-spectrum antibiotic treatment. Note the large number of cream-coloured plaques studded across the mucosal surface, representing collections of neutrophils, fibrin, and cell debris (see Plate 10).

Reproduced with permission from *Clinical Pathology* (Oxford Core Texts), Carton, James, Daly, Richard, and Ramani, Pramila, Oxford University Press (2006), p. 163, Figure 8.14.

Giardia lamblia

- Protozoan transmitted by drinking water contaminated with cysts of the organism.
- The mature pathogen attaches to the brush border of the epithelial cells of the upper small bowel and may be diagnosed on duodenal biopsy.
- The inflammatory reaction causes a mild diarrhoeal illness which lasts ~1 week and then resolves.
- Immunocompromised individuals may develop chronic infection.

Entamoeba histolytica

- Common protozoal infection, affecting ~10% of people worldwide.
- Symptoms range from mild diarrhoea and abdominal pain to severe fulminant colitis.
- The infection can disseminate to other sites such as the liver, and rarely large inflammatory masses can form (amoebomas).
- Mild cases show neutrophilic infiltration only, but more severe cases are associated with deep ulceration of the bowel.
- The organisms are round structures with a bean-shaped nucleus and foamy cytoplasm containing ingested red blood cells (RBCs).

Enterobius vermicularis

- Nematode pinworm transmitted by hand-to-mouth transfer of eggs.
- Larvae mature into adult organisms, residing mainly in the caecum.
- At night, female organisms migrate to the anus to deposit eggs which cause marked perianal itching.

Necator americanus and *Ancylostoma duodenale*

- Nematode hookworms which attach themselves to the jejunal mucosa.
- A pump mechanism is used to ingest blood and interstitial fluid from the host. High worm loads can lead to significant cumulative blood loss.
- Hookworm infestation is the most common cause of iron deficiency anaemia worldwide.

Intestinal obstruction

Definition

- Mechanical blockage to a segment of the bowel.

Epidemiology

- Common.

Aetiology

- Small bowel obstruction: adhesions, hernias, intussusception, volvulus.
- Large bowel obstruction: tumours, sigmoid volvulus, diverticular strictures.

Pathogenesis

- Mechanical blockage to the bowel prevents normal peristaltic movements.

Presentation

- Small bowel obstruction: acute colicky abdominal pain, abdominal distension, early onset of vomiting, later onset of absolute constipation (neither flatus nor faeces passed).
- Large bowel obstruction: acute colicky abdominal pain, abdominal distension, early onset of absolute constipation, later onset of vomiting.

Macroscopy

- The bowel proximal to the obstruction is usually dilated.
- The underlying cause of the obstruction is usually apparent, e.g. adhesions, tumour, intussusception.

Histopathology

- Ischaemic changes may be present in prolonged cases.
- Features of the underlying cause may also be seen.

Prognosis

- Depends on the underlying cause.
- Benign causes of obstruction generally have a good prognosis, following either spontaneous resolution or surgical intervention.
- Large bowel obstruction due to colorectal carcinoma generally implies advanced disease and poorer prognosis.

Acute appendicitis

Definition

- An acute inflammatory process of the appendix related to obstruction.

Epidemiology

- Peak incidence between ages 5 and 15, but can occur at any age.

Aetiology

- Believed to be the result of obstruction of the appendiceal lumen by a faecolith, undigested food, or enlarged lymphoid tissue.

Pathogenesis

- Obstruction to the appendiceal lumen leads to superimposed infection in the mucosa which then spreads through the whole wall of the appendix.

Presentation

- Right iliac fossa pain accompanied by fever and malaise.
- Many cases do not show typical features, possibly related to the precise positioning of the appendix within the individual.

Macroscopy

- The appendix may appear normal in early cases where the inflammation is confined to the mucosal layer.
- In more advanced cases, the appendix is dilated and a fibrinopurulent exudate may be seen on the serosal surface.

Histopathology

- Acute transmural inflammation is seen involving the mucosa, submucosa, and muscularis propria.
- Extensive necrosis of the muscularis propria can lead to perforation.
- In cases where there is peritonitis, but no underlying crypt inflammation, extra-appendicular causes should be excluded.
- Other types of appendicitis include granulomatous and parasites (e.g. schistosomiasis).

Prognosis

- Prognosis is excellent, provided an appendectomy is performed promptly.
- Delayed treatment risks perforation of the inflamed appendix, with potential complications such as intra-abdominal abscess formation or generalized peritonitis.

Crohn's disease

Definition

- An idiopathic inflammatory bowel disease, characterized by multifocal areas of inflammation which may involve any part of the GI tract.

Epidemiology

- Uncommon.
- Major incidence between 20 and 30y.

Aetiology and pathogenesis

- Thought to be caused by an abnormal mucosal immune response to luminal bacteria in genetically susceptible individuals.
- *NOD2* (nucleotide oligomerization binding domain 2) mutations are relatively common, although only 10% of individuals with risk-associated variants develop the disease.
- Smoking increases the risk.
- A true infectious aetiology remains unproven, although mycobacteria have been long suspected to play a role.

Presentation

- Crampy right iliac fossa pain and diarrhoea which is usually not bloody.
- Fever, malaise, and weight loss are common.

Macroscopy

- Disease usually involves the terminal ileum and colon.
- Affected bowel is thickened with encroachment of mesenteric fat around the anti-mesenteric border of the bowel ('fat wrapping').
- Adhesions and fistulae may be seen between adjacent loops of bowel.
- The mucosal surface shows linear ulceration and 'cobblestoning'.

Histopathology

- Mucosal biopsies: variability of inflammation within a single biopsy and between several biopsies is the key feature. This is typically manifested by discrete areas of inflammation adjacent to histologically normal crypts. Surface erosions and ulceration may be present. Poorly formed granulomas may be seen, but these are generally uncommon.
- There may be evidence of chronicity with architectural changes. If not, the differential diagnosis of focal acute inflammation includes an infectious colitis.
- Resection specimens: deep fissuring ulcers separated by relatively normal mucosa. Lymphoid aggregates are present in the submucosa and muscular layers. Poorly formed granulomas may be seen. Transmural inflammation is the key diagnostic feature, although it may be seen in the toxic megacolon associated with UC.

Prognosis

- Relapsing and remitting course.
- Most patients require surgery at some point to relieve symptoms from obstruction or fistula formation.
- Increased risk of small and large bowel adenocarcinomas.
- Extra-GI manifestations include enteropathic arthropathy (➔ Spondyloarthropathies, p. 429), anterior uveitis, gallstones, erythema nodosum (➔ Erythema nodosum, p. 394), and pyoderma gangrenosum (➔ Pyoderma gangrenosum, p. 395).

Ulcerative colitis

Definition

- An idiopathic inflammatory bowel disease, characterized by inflammation restricted to the large bowel mucosa, which always involves the rectum and extends proximally in a continuous fashion for a variable distance.

Epidemiology

- Uncommon.
- Major incidence between 15 and 25y.

Aetiology and pathogenesis

- Thought to be due to an abnormal mucosal immune response to luminal bacteria.
- The genetic link is weaker than for Crohn's disease (CD).
- Smoking appears to decrease the risk of UC.
- One unusual, but consistently confirmed, observation is the protective effect of appendectomy on the subsequent development of UC.

Presentation

- Recurrent episodes of bloody diarrhoea, often with urgency and tenesmus.

Macroscopy

- Erythematous mucosa with a friable, eroded surface and haemorrhage.
- Inflamed mucosa may form polypoid projections (inflammatory polyps).
- Disease always involves the rectum and extends continuously to involve a variable amount of colon (Fig. 7.5).

Histopathology

- Biopsies show diffuse mucosal inflammation with cryptitis and crypt abscess formation. Inflammation is usually more severe distally.
- Resection specimens show diffuse inflammation limited to the mucosal layer. Inflammatory polyps may be present.
- Extension of inflammation into the submucosa or muscle layers may occur in very severe acute UC, but the inflammation still remains heaviest in the mucosal layer.

Prognosis

- Generally good with treatment.
- Increased risk of colorectal carcinoma, so surveillance colonoscopy is usually recommended several years after diagnosis.
- Extra-GI manifestations include enteropathic arthropathy (➔ Spondyloarthropathies, p. 429), primary sclerosing cholangitis (PSC) (➔ Primary sclerosing cholangitis, p. 156), erythema nodosum (➔ Erythema nodosum, p. 394), pyoderma gangrenosum (➔ Pyoderma gangrenosum, p. 395), uveitis, and AA amyloidosis.

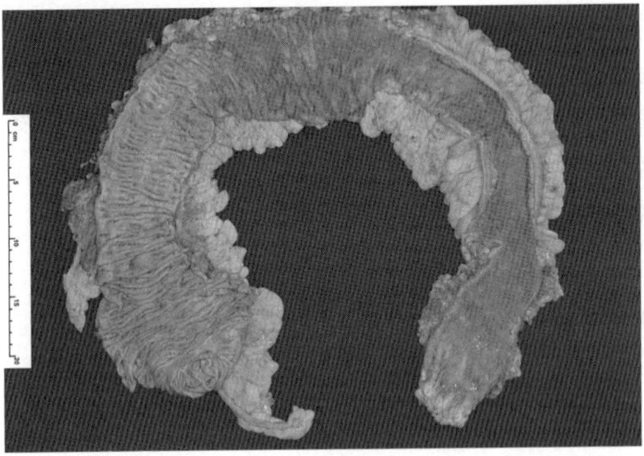

Fig. 7.5 Ulcerative colitis. This is a colectomy specimen from a patient with ulcerative colitis. The right colon is on the left of the picture (note the appendix), and the left colon and rectum are on the right side of the picture. The inflamed mucosa, which looks red, begins at the rectum and continuously affects the left colon until the transverse colon where there is a sharp transition into normal mucosa (see Plate 11).

Reproduced with permission from *Clinical Pathology* (Oxford Core Texts), Carton, James, Daly, Richard, and Ramani, Pramila, Oxford University Press (2006), p. 163, Figure 8.15.

Microscopic colitis

Definition

- A chronic form of colitis, characterized by chronic watery diarrhoea, normal or near normal colonoscopy, and microscopic evidence of colonic inflammation.

Subtypes

- Two types are recognized: lymphocytic and collagenous colitis, although they may coexist.

Lymphocytic colitis

- Incidence of 3 per 100 000 population.
- Equal sex incidence.
- Mean age of onset is 50y.
- Strong association with coeliac disease.
- Mucosal biopsy specimens show increased numbers of plasma cells in the lamina propria and increased intraepithelial lymphocytes (>20/100 epithelial cells).
- Most patients respond to medical therapy.

Collagenous colitis

- Incidence of 1–2 per 100 000 population.
- Significant predilection for women (♀:♂ = 8:1).
- Mean age of onset is 60y.
- Association with NSAIDs and coeliac disease.
- Mucosal biopsy specimens show thickening of the subepithelial collagen plate and increased numbers of plasma cells in the lamina propria, and increased intraepithelial lymphocytes.
- Most patients respond to medical therapy.

Colorectal polyps

Hyperplastic polyps

- Very common polyps, occurring most frequently in the distal colon.
- Usually small lesions, <1cm in size, found on the crest of a mucosal fold.
- Microscopically, they are composed of crypts which are dilated and serrated in the superficial portion and narrow at the base.
- Benign lesions with no risk of progression into carcinoma, unless they show dysplasia which is very uncommon. The hyperplastic polyposis syndrome, in which there are very large numbers of hyperplastic polyps, is also associated with an increased risk.

Sessile serrated lesions (or polyps)

- Relatively recently characterized polyps which tend to be >1cm and more likely to be found in the right colon.
- Genetically, they tend to harbour mutations in mismatch repair genes.
- Microscopically, they show markedly dilated serrated crypts which are widened at their base.
- There may be coexisting dysplasia.

► Associated with an increased risk of subsequent colorectal carcinoma.

Adenomatous polyps

- Very common polyps which may occur anywhere in the large bowel.
- Most occur sporadically, but they are also associated with **familial adenomatous polyposis** (FAP). FAP is an inherited condition in which the colon becomes carpeted with thousands of adenomas at a young age, with the inevitable development of colorectal carcinoma without prophylactic colectomy. There may be polyps in the duodenum as well. Gardener's syndrome, which is a variant of FAP, may be associated with extraintestinal manifestations such as desmoid tumours.
- Neoplastic polyps which harbour frequent mutations of *APC, KRAS*, and *p53*.
- Microscopically, the polyps contain dysplastic glands lined by epithelial cells with stratified hyperchromatic nuclei growing in complex tubules or finger-like villous projections. Depending on the relative proportion of tubules and villi, they are classified as tubular, tubulo-villous, and villous adenomas.
- The dysplasia is graded into low or high grade, according to the degree of cytological and architectural abnormality.
- ~10% of adenomas develop carcinoma.
- The likelihood of malignant transformation is higher with larger polyps, high-grade dysplasia, and a villous architecture. When carcinomas arise in pedunculated polyps, they are staged using the Haggitt system to assess the risk of there being lymph node metastases.

Inflammatory polyps

- Thin, filiform lesions which occur following any mucosal injury, but are often seen in patients with inflammatory bowel disease.
- Microscopically, they are covered by mucosa on all sides, with only a tiny amount of submucosal tissue.

Mucosal prolapse ('solitary rectal ulcer syndrome')

- Prolapsed pieces of mucosa which appear as polypoid projections.
- Can occur at any point in the large bowel, but characteristically seen on the anterior rectal wall or in association with diverticular disease.
- Can ulcerate and mimic colorectal carcinoma.
- Microscopically, they show distorted angulated crypts set in the lamina propria containing bundles of smooth muscle running up from the muscularis mucosae.

Benign fibroblastic polyps

- Almost always incidental polyps picked up in adults undergoing screening colonoscopy.
- Microscopically, they show a bland spindle cell proliferation in the lamina propria. The spindle cells show no specific line of differentiation immunohistochemically.

Leiomyomas

- Benign smooth muscle tumours arising from the muscularis mucosae.
- Usually small polyps, located mostly in the distal large bowel.
- Microscopically, they show bundles of bland smooth muscle cells.

Juvenile (hamartomatous) polyps

- Most common colonic polyp found in children.
- Thought to be hamartomatous in nature.
- Microscopically, they show irregular, markedly dilated, disorganized colonic glands set in an oedematous stroma.
- Presence of multiple juvenile polyps may be a marker for **juvenile polyposis**, an autosomal dominant condition caused by germline mutations in either *SMAD4* or *BMPR1A*.

Colorectal carcinoma

Definition

- A malignant epithelial tumour arising in the colon or rectum.

► Note that only tumours that have penetrated through the muscularis mucosae into the submucosa are considered malignant at this site. This contrasts with carcinomas at other sites where a breach of the basement membrane directly underlying the epithelium is sufficient for the categorization of an epithelial tumour as malignant.

Epidemiology

- Third most common cancer in the UK, with a lifetime risk of 1 in 16 men and 1 in 20 women.
- Second most common cause of cancer-related deaths.

Aetiology

- A diet high in animal fat and low in fibre, together with a sedentary lifestyle, increases the risk.
- Other associations include idiopathic inflammatory bowel disease, FAP, and hereditary non-polyposis colorectal cancer (HNPCC).

Carcinogenesis

- Most develop through a sequence of aberrant crypt focus (dysplasia in a single crypt) → adenomatous polyp → invasive carcinoma.
- Common genetic aberrations include the loss of *APC, TP53,* and *SMAD4.*
- Some tumours are characterized by the inactivation of mismatch repair genes, recognized by the epiphenomenon of microsatellite instability.

Presentation

- Change in bowel habit, tenesmus, abdominal pain, iron deficiency anaemia.
- Asymptomatic tumours may be discovered via screening or surveillance programmes.

Macroscopy

- Most tumours grow as polypoid masses projecting into the bowel lumen, often with areas of surface ulceration (Fig. 7.6). Some tumours, particularly in the distal colon, form circumferential stenosing lesions.
- The cut surface shows a firm, white tumour mass in the bowel wall.
- Large pools of gelatinous material are seen in mucinous carcinomas.

Histopathology

- The vast majority are adenocarcinomas, i.e. infiltrating malignant epithelial tumours showing evidence of glandular differentiation.
- Well-differentiated tumours show plentiful tubular formation, whereas poorly differentiated tumours show minimal gland formation.
- Most tumours are moderately differentiated and often contain abundant necroinflammatory debris within the glandular spaces (so-called 'dirty' necrosis).

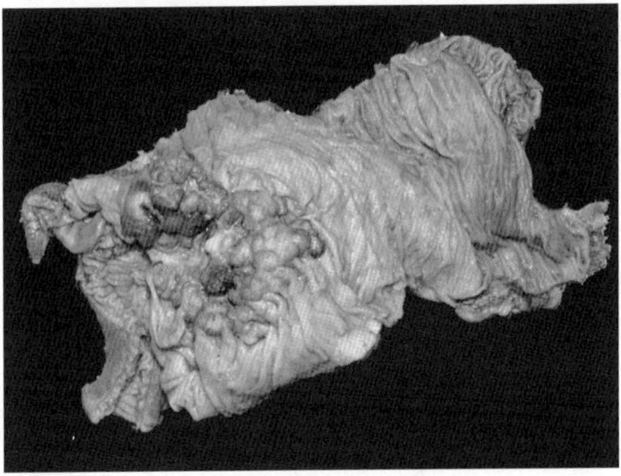

Fig. 7.6 Adenocarcinoma of the caecum. This is a right hemicolectomy specimen, in which a small piece of the terminal ileum, the caecum, the appendix, and the ascending colon have been removed. A large tumour is seen in the caecum, which was confirmed on microscopy to be an adenocarcinoma. This tumour was picked up at colonoscopy performed because the patient was found to have an unexplained iron deficiency anaemia (see Plate 12).

- ~10% of colonic and 30% of rectal tumours show extensive mucin production, such that the malignant cells are seen floating in large pools of extracellular mucin; these are termed **mucinous adenocarcinomas**.
- Patients with tumours which have a pushing margin and/or associated with a marked increase in tumoural lymphocytes have a better prognosis.

Molecular markers

- Current guidelines suggest that all patients with colorectal cancer aged under 50 should be screened for HNPCC by immunohistochemistry for loss of expression of the mismatch repair proteins MLH1, MSH2, MSH6, and PMS2.
- *K-ras* and *BRAF* mutational status is routinely requested in patients with metastatic disease and increasingly in patients with localized disease.

Prognosis

- 5-year survival rate ~50%.
- Important prognostic factors include the stage (particularly the lymph node status), presence of venous invasion, differentiation of the tumour, and completeness of surgical excision.

NHS bowel cancer screening programme

- Two types of screening are offered by the NHS:
  - **Faecal occult blood** (FOB) testing is offered every 2y to men and women aged 60–74. This is a home test kit sent through the post that looks for evidence of blood in the stool.
  - **Bowel scope screening** is currently being introduced in England as a one-off test to men and women at age 55. This involves direct sigmoidoscopy to look for polyps.

TNM 7 pathological staging of colorectal carcinomas

Primary tumour (T)

pT1: tumour invades the submucosa.
pT2: tumour invades the muscularis propria.
pT3: tumour invades through the muscularis propria into the subserosa or into non-peritonealized pericolic or perirectal tissues.
pT4a: tumour perforates the visceral peritoneum.
pT4b: tumour directly invades other organ or structures.

Regional lymph nodes (N)

pN0: no regional lymph node metastasis.
pN1a: metastasis in 1 regional lymph node.
pN1b: metastasis in 2 or 3 regional lymph nodes.
pN2a: metastasis in 4–6 regional lymph nodes.
pN2b: metastasis in 7 or more regional lymph nodes.

Dukes' staging of colorectal carcinomas

A: tumour is confined to the bowel wall.
B: tumour invades through the muscularis propria.
C1: lymph node metastases.
C2: apical lymph node involved.

In rectal cancers, the nature of the perirectal excision must be assessed. It should be smooth and bulky with a mesorectal plain of excision.

In resection specimens, it is important to assess involvement of the circumferential resection margin where there is a bare, non-peritonealized surface, as well as the presence or absence of venous invasion. In cases which have received neo-adjuvant therapy, the degree of tumour regression can be recorded using the Mandard score.

Diverticular disease

Definition

- The presence of outpouchings of the colonic mucosa that have herniated through the circular muscular layer of the large bowel and are therefore only pseudodiverticula.
- The vast majority of cases are seen in the sigmoid colon.

Epidemiology

- Very common. Mostly a disease of patients aged >60y.

Aetiology

- A diet low in fibre and high in meat is the strongest risk factor.

Pathogenesis

- Firm stools require higher intraluminal pressures to propel.
- High intraluminal pressure forces pouches of the colonic mucosa through an anatomical weak point in the muscular layer where blood vessels pass through to supply the mucosal layers.

Presentation

- Intermittent abdominal pain, altered bowel habit, iron deficiency anaemia. ▶ These may closely mimic colorectal carcinoma.
- Acute inflammation in a diverticulum (acute diverticulitis) presents with severe left iliac fossa pain.
- Occasionally, erosion of a large submucosal vessel can cause severe rectal bleeding.

Macroscopy

- Diverticula are seen herniating out between the taenia coli of the sigmoid colon.
- The circular muscle layer is often markedly thickened and numerous redundant mucosal folds are present, projecting into the lumen.
- In acute diverticulitis, an inflammatory mass may be visible surrounding a diverticulum.
- Diverticular strictures cause fibrous narrowing of the bowel lumen which can closely mimic a stenosing carcinoma.

Histopathology

- Diverticula are seen herniating through a thickened circular muscle layer. Only a thin coating of longitudinal muscle separates the diverticulum from the pericolic fat.
- In cases of acute diverticulitis, there is superimposed acute inflammation associated with a diverticulum; severe cases may show pericolic abscess formation.

Prognosis

- Acute diverticulitis can be complicated by pericolic abscess formation, fistula formation, and free perforation.
- Free perforation causes generalized peritonitis which can be fatal in frail elderly patients.

Anal pathology

Haemorrhoids

- Abnormally dilated and prolapsed anal cushions.
- Extremely common.
- Thought to be due to disruption of the normal suspensory mechanisms caused by chronic straining at stool.
- Cause bright red rectal bleeding and discomfort.
- Excised haemorrhoids examined microscopically contain large dilated blood vessels, which may show evidence of thrombosis, with an overlying hyperplastic squamous epithelium.

Anal tags

- Polypoid projections of the anal mucosa and submucosa.
- Unrelated to haemorrhoids, but frequently confused with them.
- Microscopically composed of a fibrovascular core covered by squamous epithelium. The fibrovascular core lacks the typical ectatic vessels of haemorrhoids.

Anal fissure

- A tear in the mucosa of the lower anal canal which is almost always located posteriorly in the midline.
- Cause is unclear, but chronic infection may lead to loss of the normal elasticity of the mucosa, such that passage of hard faeces may precipitate the tear.
- Usually presents with severe pain.
- The presence of granulomas (rather than a foreign body reaction to foreign material) should raise the possibility of CD.

Anorectal abscess

- A collection of pus within deep perianal tissue.
- A complication of infection within a deep anal gland.
- Presents with perianal erythema, swelling, and pain.

Anorectal fistula

- An abnormal epithelial-lined tract connecting the anal canal to the perianal skin.
- Usually the result of infection in an anal gland tracking to the skin surface.
- Multiple perianal fistulae can also be a manifestation of CD.

Anal cancer

- Uncommon and invariably associated with HPV infection.
- Vast majority are squamous cell carcinomas which arise from areas of squamous dysplasia known as anal intraepithelial neoplasia (AIN) which is graded 1–3.

Chapter 8

Hepatobiliary pathology

Acute viral hepatitis

Definition

- Infection of the liver by hepatitis A, B, C, or E, lasting 6 months or less.

Epidemiology

- Hepatitis A virus (HAV) and hepatitis C virus (HCV) are common worldwide.
- Hepatitis B virus (HBV) is common in parts of Asia and China.
- Hepatitis E virus (HEV) is common in South East Asia, India, and Central America. Its importance is being increasingly recognized in the West.
- All ages may be affected.

Virology

- HAV is a positive-sense, single-stranded RNA picornavirus transmitted orally by faecal contamination of food or water.
- HBV is a partially double-stranded DNA hepadnavirus transmitted through contaminated needles, sexual contact, or vertically from an infected mother to her baby.
- HCV is a positive-sense, single-stranded RNA hepacivirus transmitted from contaminated needles, mostly through intravenous drug abuse.
- HEV is positive-sense, single-stranded RNA hepevirus transmitted orally by faecal contamination of food or water.

Immunopathogenesis

- The viruses localize to the liver. After a variable incubation period, a specific T-lymphocyte response to the virus is mounted.
- The necroinflammatory activity in the liver causes an episode of acute hepatitis.

Presentation

- Many cases are clinically silent or cause a non-specific, flu-like illness.
- Clinically apparent cases cause nausea, vomiting, malaise, and jaundice.

Serology

- Presence of serum anti-hepatitis IgM antibodies confirms a recent infection.

Macroscopy

- The liver may be swollen and discoloured with bile.

Histopathology

- Liver lobules are infiltrated by mononuclear inflammatory cells.
- Hepatocyte injury is manifested morphologically by swelling ('ballooning') or shrinkage and pyknosis (acidophil bodies).
- Severe cases show confluent areas of hepatocyte necrosis and parenchymal collapse.

► Note these histological changes are not specific to viral hepatitis and may be seen in acute liver injury from other causes.

Prognosis

- Acute HAV never progresses to chronic infection.
- Acute HBV progresses to chronic infection in ~10% of cases.
- Acute HCV progresses to chronic infection in ~90% of cases.

Chronic viral hepatitis

Definition

- Infection of the liver by hepatitis B, C, or D lasting >6 months.

Epidemiology

- Chronic HCV is common worldwide, with ~3% of the world's population infected.
- Chronic HBV shows more geographical variation, being rarer in western countries, but very common in areas of Asia and China where infection rates are as high as 15%.

Immunopathogenesis

- Chronic viral hepatitis is the result of an immune response that fails to clear the virus following infection.
- 10% of people fail to clear HBV infection.
- 90% of people fail to clear HCV infection.
- Hepatitis D virus (HDV) is an incomplete DNA virus which can only cause infection in patients who already have HBV. If the two infections occur together, this is co-infection; if the HDV follows HBV, this is superinfection. The latter produces more serious diseases.

Presentation

- Often asymptomatic and diagnosed incidentally on abnormal liver function tests (LFTs).
- Many patients do not present till advanced cirrhosis with ascites.

Serology

- Chronic HBV: presence of serum HBsAg (hepatitis B surface antigen) and anti-HBcAg (hepatitis B core antigen) antibodies.
- Chronic HCV: presence of serum anti-HCV antibodies and HCV RNA by PCR.
- HDV: presence of serum IgM anti-HDV antibodies or the detection of the virus in liver biopsies.

Macroscopy

- The liver may feel slightly firm due to fibrosis.

Histopathology

- Portal inflammation is dominant and composed mostly of lymphocytes.
- Interface hepatitis ('piecemeal necrosis') refers to the extension of the portal inflammatory infiltrate into the hepatocytes at the limiting plate, associated with hepatocyte degeneration.
- Lobular inflammation is usually focal and mild in chronic viral hepatitis (compare with acute viral hepatitis where it is the dominant site).
- Fibrosis is a marker of how advanced the disease is. Extensive bridging fibrosis through the liver terminates in cirrhosis.

► Note that all of these changes may be seen in chronic liver injury from a number of causes. Clues to a viral aetiology may be present, however, e.g. 'ground glass' hepatocytes in hepatitis B and portal lymphoid aggregates, inflammatory bile duct damage, and fatty change in hepatitis C. HDV is characterized by lobular damage.

Prognosis

- Prognosis largely depends on the extent of fibrosis present on liver biopsy.
- Viral genotype is also important in hepatitis C.
- High risk of hepatocellular carcinoma (HCC), particularly with chronic HBV. This may occur, especially in endemic areas, in patients without cirrhosis.

Alcoholic liver disease

Definition

- Liver disease due to excessive alcohol consumption.
- Three patterns of disease are recognized: **steatosis**, **alcoholic steatohepatitis** (ASH), and **cirrhosis**.

Epidemiology

- Extremely common.

Pathogenesis

- Alcohol metabolism in the liver generates high levels of nicotinamide adenine dinucleotide dehydrogenase (NADH) which stimulates fatty acid synthesis and production of triglycerides, leading to steatosis.
- In some individuals, oxidative stress from metabolism of alcohol leads to hepatocyte injury and necroinflammatory activity (ASH).
- Ongoing necroinflammatory activity causes liver fibrosis which may progress to cirrhosis.

Presentation

- Steatosis and mild ASH are usually asymptomatic but are a common cause of mildly abnormal LFTs.
- Severe alcoholic hepatitis following binge drinking causes malaise and fever, with marked elevation of LFTs. Jaundice may occur if there is marked loss of liver function.
- Alcoholic cirrhosis presents with complications of cirrhosis, e.g. ascites or ruptured oesophageal varices.

Macroscopy

- Steatosis causes an enlarged soft greasy liver.
- ASH may cause a firm texture due to fibrosis in the liver.
- Cirrhosis causes diffuse nodularity of the liver.

Histopathology

- All the changes are most severe in zone 3 near the central vein.
- Steatosis shows large droplets of fat in hepatocytes which displace the nucleus to one side (macrovesicular steatosis).
- ASH shows ballooned hepatocytes which may contain Mallory–Denk bodies (clumps of dense pink material derived from the cytoskeleton) and an inflammatory infiltrate rich in neutrophils.
- Fibrosis in ASH is typically pericellular but eventually forms fibrous bridges. Cirrhosis shows diffuse replacement of the liver by nodules of regenerating hepatocytes surrounded by fibrous bands. Background steatosis and hepatitis may not be present.

Prognosis

- Simple steatosis is fully reversible if alcohol consumption ceases.
- Alcoholic hepatitis may resolve with cessation of alcohol consumption or may progress to fibrosis and cirrhosis.
- Alcoholic cirrhosis has a poor prognosis, with 5-year survival rates of only 50%.

Non-alcoholic fatty liver disease

Definition

- The hepatic manifestation of the metabolic syndrome (central obesity, abnormal glucose tolerance, hyperlipidaemia). Non-alcoholic fatty liver disease (NAFLD) covers a range of conditions, including simple **steatosis** (fatty liver), **non-alcoholic steatohepatitis** (NASH), and **cirrhosis**.

Epidemiology

- Very common and increasing in incidence due to rising obesity rates.
- Now the most common cause of abnormal LFTs.
- Many cases of cirrhosis once thought to be cryptogenic are now thought to represent end-stage NAFLD.

Aetiology

- Obesity and diabetes are the most common associations.
- Also associated with some drugs and parenteral nutrition.

Pathogenesis

- Insulin resistance seems to be the key factor and is linked to obesity.
- Insulin resistance causes the accumulation of fat and hepatocyte injury.
- Inflammation in response to hepatocyte injury leads to fibrosis, and eventually cirrhosis in some individuals.

Presentation

- Most cases are asymptomatic and discovered because of abnormal LFTs.
- Occasional cases present with complications related to cirrhosis.

Macroscopy

- The liver is enlarged, soft, and greasy.
- Cirrhotic livers are diffusely nodular.

Histopathology

- Steatosis shows accumulation of fat within hepatocytes without significant inflammatory activity.
- NASH shows steatosis, together with the presence of ballooned hepatocytes (which may contain Mallory–Denk bodies) and mixed acute and chronic inflammatory infiltrate. Variable fibrosis may be present, depending on the stage of the disease.

► These histological findings are essentially identical to those seen in alcoholic liver disease. Ruling out alcoholic liver disease can sometimes be difficult, as many patients significantly under-report their alcohol intake.

Prognosis

- Steatosis has a very low risk of progression to chronic liver disease.
- NASH progresses to cirrhosis in ~10–15% of cases over 8y.
- Patients with cirrhosis due to NAFLD generally have a better survival rate than patients with cirrhosis due to alcoholic liver disease.
- Liver cell cancer is being increasingly recognized in patients without cirrhosis.

Autoimmune hepatitis

Definition

- A liver disease due to an autoimmune response targeted against the liver.

Epidemiology

- Uncommon.
- Typically affects middle-aged females.

Aetiology

- Unknown for certain, but thought to be triggered by infection or drugs.

Pathogenesis

- Current thinking suggests that liver damage from an infection or a drug causes genetically susceptible people to become sensitized to their liver and mount an immune response against it.

Presentation

- Most cases are asymptomatic in the early stages but may be diagnosed incidentally due to abnormalities of LFTs.
- Some patients present late with symptoms and signs of chronic liver disease or terminal cirrhosis.
- ~25% of cases present suddenly with an episode of acute hepatitis with jaundice.
- Rarely, massive acute liver damage occurs and the patient presents with acute hepatic failure.

Serology

- Serum IgG is usually raised.
- A variety of autoantibodies may be present, e.g. anti-nuclear antibodies, liver–kidney microsomal antibodies, and smooth muscle antibodies.

Macroscopy

- Few macroscopic changes, except in patients with cirrhosis or in cases of severe acute hepatitis with massive hepatocyte necrosis.

Histopathology

- Chronic hepatitis pattern of injury with portal inflammation, interface hepatitis, lobular inflammation, and variable fibrosis.
- In contrast to chronic viral hepatitis, interface hepatitis and lobular inflammation tend to be more prominent. Plasma cells are often a conspicuous component of the inflammatory cell infiltrate.

Prognosis

- Most cases respond well to immunosuppressive therapy.
- Long-term prognosis is dependent on the extent of fibrosis in the liver at the time of diagnosis.

Primary biliary cholangitis

Definition

- A chronic liver disease characterized by the destruction of small intrahepatic bile ducts and the presence of anti-mitochondrial antibodies.

Terminology

- Previously called primary biliary cirrhosis.
- The name has changed because less than half of patients with this condition have cirrhosis.
- There are cases which have serological features of an autoimmune hepatitis, but pathological features of primary biliary cholangitis (PBC) and these cases are best termed autoimmune cholangitis.

Epidemiology

- Uncommon.
- Occurs most frequently in middle-aged women and is associated with other autoimmune conditions.

Aetiology

- Unknown, but may be triggered by infection with organisms that show molecular mimicry to antigens on the biliary epithelium.

Pathogenesis

- Thought to be an autoimmune disease in which the immune system mounts an abnormal response to the biliary epithelium.

Presentation

- Asymptomatic in its early stages, although may be picked up by elevated alkaline phosphatase levels.
- Patients presenting with symptoms usually do so with fatigue or pruritus due to the accumulation of bile salts.

Serology

- >95% of cases are associated with the presence of anti-mitochondrial antibodies directed at a component of the pyruvate dehydrogenase enzyme complex located in the inner mitochondrial matrix.

Macroscopy

- Early disease shows few macroscopic changes in the liver.
- In advanced disease, the liver is cirrhotic and bile-stained.

Histopathology

- Earliest feature is the infiltration and destruction of interlobular bile ducts by lymphocytes and macrophages ('florid duct lesion'). The macrophages may coalesce into clusters and form granulomas.
- As the disease progresses, there is inflammation and destruction of hepatocytes at the edges of the portal tracts (interface hepatitis) which begins a sequence of periportal fibrosis → portal–portal bridging → cirrhosis.

Prognosis

- Gradual progression towards cirrhosis over 15–20y.
- Ursodeoxycholic acid therapy decreases the rate of progression.

Primary sclerosing cholangitis

Definition

- A chronic liver disease characterized by inflammation and scarring in the biliary tree.
- Usually, the entire biliary tree is affected, but occasionally only small interlobular bile ducts are affected (small duct PSC).

Epidemiology

- Uncommon.
- Seen predominantly in young men with UC.
- ~70% of patients with PSC also have UC.

Aetiology

- Unknown, although there is a genetic link with certain HLA types.

Pathogenesis

- Chronic biliary inflammation is followed by fibrotic scarring which narrows the affected bile ducts. Obstruction within the biliary system leads to progressive fibrosis within the liver which terminates in cirrhosis. Biliary stasis also promotes infection and stone formation.

Presentation

- Asymptomatic in its early stages, but often picked up when elevated alkaline phosphatase levels are found in a patient with UC.

Radiology

- Demonstration of strictures and dilations within the biliary tree on imaging is highly suggestive of PSC.

Macroscopy

- Early PSC usually causes no macroscopic changes. Advanced disease causes a cirrhotic liver with bile staining. Fibrotic biliary strictures may be apparent in the major bile ducts.

Histopathology

- Explanted liver specimens show fibrosis and inflammation in large bile ducts with inspissated bile and stones. There is a biliary pattern of cirrhosis with large, irregular, jigsaw-like nodules of hepatocytes.
- Liver biopsy specimens show variable features, depending on the biopsy site. If the biopsy is taken from an area unaffected by the primary disease, but distal to a large duct stricture, the liver shows features of duct obstruction (i.e. portal oedema with proliferation of bile ductules). If the biopsy comes from an area affected by PSC, then medium-sized bile ducts show periductal oedema and concentric fibrosis, whilst small bile ducts are often completely absent.

Prognosis

- Progressive liver disease eventually terminating in cirrhosis.

►► Patients are at high risk of bile duct carcinoma, which develops in ~20% of patients (➲ Extrahepatic bile duct carcinoma, p. 168) and has a very poor prognosis.

Wilson's disease

Definition

- An inherited disorder of copper metabolism, leading to the accumulation of toxic levels of copper in the liver and brain.

Epidemiology

- Uncommon.
- Most cases present in childhood or young adulthood; however, the diagnosis should be considered as a possible cause of liver disease presenting at any age.
- Males and females are equally affected.

Genetics

- Autosomal recessive disorder due to mutations in the gene *ATP7B* which codes for a copper-transporting ATPase.
- ~100 different mutations have been described and the majority of patients are compound heterozygotes (i.e. they have two differently mutated alleles). This makes genetic screening difficult.

Pathogenesis

- Possession of two mutated *ATP7B* alleles causes disruption of normal copper transport and accumulation of toxic levels of copper in hepatocytes and basal ganglia.

Presentation

- Most patients present in childhood or early adulthood with chronic liver disease or cirrhosis.
- A small proportion of patients present in hepatic failure.
- About half of patients also develop neuropsychiatric symptoms due to copper accumulation in the brain, though this usually occurs after the liver disease presents.

Macroscopy

- By the time of presentation, most patients have advanced disease and the liver is firm due to extensive fibrosis or cirrhotic.

Histopathology

- Liver biopsies show a chronic hepatitis pattern with portal inflammation, scattered lobular inflammation, and variable amounts of fibrosis, depending on the stage of the disease.
- The diagnosis is strongly suggested by the presence of high levels of stainable copper or copper-associated protein in hepatocytes, though this can only be demonstrated in 50% of cases. The diagnosis is best made by measuring tissue copper levels.

Prognosis

- Progressive disease which terminates in cirrhosis, if untreated.
- Lifelong treatment with metal-chelating agents prevents this progression if the diagnosis is made early enough.
- Risk of HCC is low.

Hereditary haemochromatosis

Definition

- An inherited disorder characterized by increased intestinal absorption of iron, leading to iron overload in multiple organs, particularly the liver, and sometimes leading to organ damage.

Epidemiology

- Genetic prevalence of the mutated gene is 0.4% in white races, making it the most common genetic disease in people of Celtic origin, though the clinical penetrance is much lower.
- Males and females are affected equally, though women usually present later in life due to menstrual and pregnancy iron loss.

Genetics

- Autosomal recessive disorder caused by mutations of the *HFE* gene on chromosome 6p.
- *HFE* encodes an iron regulatory hormone called **hepcidin**.
- Most common mutation is a missense mutation at codon 282, causing a cysteine residue to be switched for a tyrosine (C282Y).

Pathogenesis

- Hepcidin controls plasma iron concentrations by inhibiting iron export by ferroportin from duodenal enterocytes and macrophages.
- Deficiency of hepcidin results in raised plasma iron concentrations and accumulation in multiple organs, including the liver, pancreas, heart, joints, and pituitary.

Presentation

- Early symptoms are non-specific, e.g. fatigue and arthropathy.
- Later, there may be skin pigmentation, cirrhosis, hypogonadism, cardiac failure, and diabetes mellitus.
- If transferrin saturation and serum ferritin are raised, then testing for the C282Y mutation should be performed.

Macroscopy

- Advanced cases cause diffuse nodularity due to cirrhosis.

Histopathology

- The earliest histological change is the accumulation of iron within periportal hepatocytes, highlighted by Perl's stain.
- As the disease progresses, iron accumulates within hepatocytes throughout the liver lobules, associated with expansion of portal tracts by fibrosis.
- Eventually, bridging fibrosis occurs which terminates in cirrhosis.

Prognosis

- Overall mortality is not higher in patients with timely diagnosis and adequate iron depletion therapy.
- ~5% of men and 1% of women develop cirrhosis. This has a worse prognosis, even with treatment, and carries a significant risk of HCC (➔ Hepatocellular carcinoma, pp. 164–5).

Cirrhosis

Definition

- Irreversible replacement of the normal liver architecture by bands of fibrous tissue separating nodules of regenerating hepatocytes.

Epidemiology

- Common and increasing in incidence due to alcohol and obesity.

Aetiology

- Alcohol, chronic viral hepatitis, and NAFLD are the most common causes.
- Less commonly, PBC, PSC, autoimmune hepatitis (AIH), Wilson's disease, and haemochromatosis.
- In some cases, the cause remains unclear (cryptogenic cirrhosis) although many of these are thought to be secondary to NAFLD.

Pathogenesis

- Persistent liver injury causes Kupffer cells lining the vascular sinusoids to release cytokines which activate hepatic stellate cells.
- Activated stellate cells proliferate and secrete large quantities of dense collagen, leading to irreversible liver fibrosis and hepatocyte loss.
- Cirrhosis causes a number of functional defects: reduced synthesis of coagulation factors; low glycogen reserves; reduced clearance of organisms by Kupffer cells; portal hypertension with hypersplenism and oesophageal varices; and splanchnic vasodilation → decreased renal blood flow → secondary hyperaldosteronism → ascites.

Presentation

- Non-specific symptoms of tiredness and malaise.
- Signs of chronic liver disease are usually present on clinical examination and LFTs are usually abnormal.
- Patients often present with a complication related to the presence of cirrhosis, e.g. upper GI haemorrhage.

Macroscopy

- The liver may be normal in size, enlarged, or shrunken.
- The cut surface has a firm texture and shows diffuse nodularity (Fig. 8.1).

Histopathology

- The entire liver is replaced by nodules of regenerating hepatocytes surrounded by fibrous bands.
- The size of the nodules is related to the cause: micronodular cirrhosis in alcoholic liver disease and macronodular cirrhosis secondary to viral hepatitis.
- The fibrous bands contain a variable inflammatory infiltrate and reactive bile ductular proliferation.
- In some cases, the features may point to a particular aetiology.

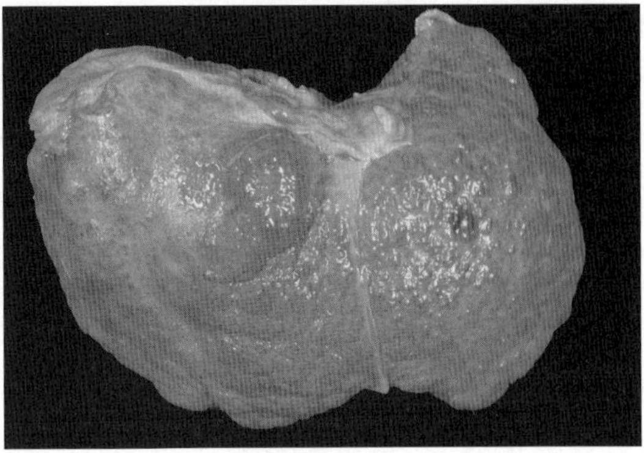

Fig. 8.1 The cirrhotic liver. This liver was removed at post-mortem from a patient known to abuse alcohol. The whole of the liver is studded with nodules. Microscopically, the liver showed nodules of regenerating hepatocytes separated by dense bands of fibrosis, confirming established cirrhosis (see Plate 13).

Reproduced with permission from *Clinical Pathology* (Oxford Core Texts), Carton, James, Daly, Richard, and Ramani, Pramila, Oxford University Press (2006), p. 168, Figure 9.9.

Prognosis

- Generally poor, with a high risk of significant complications such as infections (including bacterial peritonitis), upper GI bleeding, renal failure, and HCC.

▶ Development of complications may tip the patient into terminal hepatic failure, characterized by deep jaundice, severe coagulopathy, hepatic encephalopathy, and high risk of mortality.

Benign liver lesions

Haemangioma

- Most common tumour of the liver.
- Macroscopically, well-circumscribed red tumours with a spongy texture due to the numerous vessels within them.
- Microscopically, composed of numerous dilated blood vessels lined by bland endothelial cells.
- Benign lesions which are usually asymptomatic and require no treatment.

Hepatic adenoma

- Rare tumour seen almost exclusively in young women of reproductive age.
- Thought to be associated with oral contraceptive use.
- Macroscopically, solitary lesions, often >10cm in size, with a softer consistency and a lighter colour than the adjacent liver.
- Microscopically, hepatocytes arranged in plates 1–3 cells thick. Large vessels are often present within the lesion, but portal tracts are absent.
- Surgical resection is often performed to prevent the potentially fatal complication of rupture and haemoperitoneum.

Focal nodular hyperplasia

- Benign, non-neoplastic lesion usually seen in young women of reproductive age.
- Thought to represent a localized area of liver hyperplasia in response to changes in blood flow associated with a pre-existing arterial malformation.
- Macroscopically, a well-defined nodular area with a lighter colour than the adjacent liver. Most lesions have a characteristic central scar.
- Microscopically, nodules of hepatocytes separated by fibrous stroma containing bile ductules. Large, thick-walled vessels are very often present and a helpful diagnostic clue.
- Benign and not associated with a risk of haemorrhage.

Biliary microhamartoma (von Meyenberg's complex)

- Thought to be a ductal plate malformation.
- Macroscopically, it is a small (<5mm), irregular, grey lesion of the liver which may be multifocal.
- Microscopically, it is composed of small, irregular ductules embedded in a dense fibrous stroma. Inspissated bile may be present within the ductules.
- May be associated with other forms of fibro-polycystic liver disease: congenital hepatic fibrosis, polycystic liver diseases, Carol's disease (dilatation of intrahepatic bile ducts), and choledochal cyst (dilatation of extrahepatic bile ducts).

Bile duct adenoma

- May not be a true neoplasm, but rather a reactive proliferation of ductular structures (peribiliary hamartoma).
- Macroscopically, small (but usually larger than biliary microhamartomas), firm, white lesions which are often subcapsular.
- Microscopically, small uniform ductules which are more closely packed than a biliary hamartoma. Bile is not present in the ductules.

Hepatocellular carcinoma (liver cell cancer)

Definition

- A malignant epithelial neoplasm of the liver derived from hepatocytes.

Epidemiology

- Common worldwide, but with a wide geographical variation.
- Incidence figures largely parallel rates of infection with HBV, making HCC particularly common in parts of Africa and Asia.

Aetiology

- HCC usually arises on a background of liver cirrhosis.
- Chronic hepatitis B and haemochromatosis are particularly carcinogenic substrates.
- Dietary ingestion of aflatoxins produced by *Aspergillus* fungi which are also known to be potent liver carcinogens.

Carcinogenesis

- Loss of function of tumour suppressor genes, such as *TP53*, is common.
- Activating mutations of oncogenes appear to be rare.
- Hepatitis B X gene product disrupts p53 function and inhibits nucleotide excision repair.

Presentation

- Presents late with non-specific weight loss and abdominal pain.
- Known cirrhotics may be diagnosed following investigation of a rising serum alpha-fetoprotein (AFP) or on ultrasound surveillance.

Macroscopy

- Expansile tumour mass in the liver, often with satellite deposits (Fig. 8.2).
- Tumour may have a green tinge due to the production of bile.
- Distinguishing tumour deposits from dysplastic nodules in cirrhotic livers can be difficult.

Histopathology

- Classical HCC is composed of epithelial cells resembling hepatocytes, which typically grow in trabeculae that resemble thickened liver cell plates. Bile production may be seen by the tumour. A very typical feature is the loss of reticulin fibres.
- HepPar 1 and CD10 staining to demonstrate canaliculi can be useful to confirm a tumour as being an HCC.
- It is increasingly apparent that many tumours have features of both HCCs and cholangiocarcinomas.
- Fibrolamellar HCC is a rare, but distinctive, variant which typically arises in young patients without background cirrhosis. Histologically, the tumour is composed of nests of very large neoplastic cells with abundant granular pink cytoplasm separated by dense fibrous bands.

Fig. 8.2 Liver cell cancer arising in a cirrhotic liver (see Plate 14).

Prognosis

- Generally very poor, with 5-year survival rates <5%. HCCs of stem cell origin are CK7-positive and carry a worse prognosis.
- Fibrolamellar HCC has a slightly better prognosis, with 5-year survival rates ~60%.

Intrahepatic cholangiocarcinoma

Definition

- A malignant epithelial neoplasm arising in the liver, composed of cells resembling bile ducts.

Epidemiology

- Rare in most populations.

Aetiology

- Liver flukes (*Clonorchis sinensis* and *Opisthorchis viverrini*).
- Hepatolithiasis.
- PSC (➔ Primary sclerosing cholangitis, p. 156).
- Exposure to Thorotrast (a contrast medium used from 1930 to 1955).
- Biliary malformations, e.g. choledochal cyst.

Carcinogenesis

- Mutations of *RAS* and *TP53* are the most common genetic abnormalities.

Presentation

- Most present late, as they can grow to a large size within the liver before causing symptoms of malaise, weight loss, and abdominal pain.
- Tumours infiltrating the hilar region of the liver may present with obstructive jaundice.

Macroscopy

- The liver contains large confluent nodules of a grey-white tumour, often with satellite deposits.
- The background liver is usually non-cirrhotic.

Histopathology

- Adenocarcinomas in which the infiltrating malignant epithelial cells form glandular and papillary structures.
- A typical feature is the presence of abundant fibroblastic stroma.
- It is increasingly apparent that many tumours have features of both HCCs and cholangiocarcinomas.

Prognosis

- Generally poor, with 5-year survival rates of 40–50%, depending on the stage.

Cholecystitis

Definition

- Inflammation of the gall bladder.

Epidemiology

- Very common.

Aetiology

- Most cases are caused by gallstones (calculous cholecystitis).
- Acalculous cholecystitis also occurs, particularly in the elderly.

Pathogenesis

- Thought to be due to chemical injury to the mucosa caused by bile.
- Biliary stasis may be caused by obstruction of the gall bladder outlet by a gallstone or poor gall bladder motility.

Presentation

- Biliary colic, characterized by severe upper abdominal pain which resolves spontaneously after several hours.
- Acute cholecystitis is a more severe illness with prolonged upper abdominal pain, fever, and tachycardia.

Macroscopy

- The gall bladder wall is thickened and the mucosa may be friable.
- Gallstones are usually present.

Histopathology

- Acute cholecystitis shows oedema, acute inflammatory cells, and granulation tissue.
- Chronic cholecystitis shows muscular hypertrophy and fibrosis, mild chronic inflammation, and the presence of mucosal diverticula herniating through the muscular layer (Rokitansky–Aschoff sinuses).
- Xanthogranulomatous cholecystitis is a variant of chronic cholecystitis, in which sheets of macrophages and fibroblasts are present, probably in reaction to a ruptured Rokitansky–Aschoff sinus.

Prognosis

- Most patients with calculous cholecystitis are cured by cholecystectomy.

Extrahepatic bile duct carcinoma

Definition

- A malignant epithelial tumour arising in an extrahepatic bile duct.

Epidemiology

- Rare, with no geographical variations in incidence.

Aetiology

- PSC.
- Liver fluke infestation.
- Choledochal cysts.

► Choledocholithiasis does not seem to be relevant.

Carcinogenesis

- Mutations in *KRAS* and *TP53* are described.

Presentation

- Obstructive jaundice.
- Superimposed cholangitis may cause fevers and rigors.

Macroscopy

- The involved bile duct contains a tumour which may be polypoid, stenosing, or diffusely infiltrative.

Histopathology

- Most are well- or moderately differentiated adenocarcinomas, in which the infiltrating malignant epithelial cells form glandular structures resembling biliary ducts.

Prognosis

- The 5-year survival in patients with resectable tumours and clear surgical margins is in the order of 20–40%.
- Tumours arising on a background of PSC have a particularly poor outlook, with 5-year survival rates of <10%.

Chapter 9

Pancreatic pathology

Pancreatic malformations

Ectopic pancreas

- Common developmental anomaly in which pancreatic tissue is located outside the usual position of the pancreas.
- The duodenum is the most common site, but it can be seen in the jejunum and ileum and within a Meckel's diverticulum (➲ Meckel's diverticulum, p. 107).
- Most cases are incidental findings, but some patients present with symptoms relating to bleeding or obstruction.

Pancreas divisum

- Common developmental anomaly in which the dorsal and ventral pancreatic buds fail to fuse.
- The duct of Santorini becomes the dominant ductal system of the pancreas. As this duct drains into the duodenum via the smaller minor papilla, there is a tendency to stasis of pancreatic secretions and susceptibility to pancreatitis.
- Usually asymptomatic and discovered incidentally on imaging, though some patients may present with pancreatitis in adulthood.

Annular pancreas

- Rare developmental anomaly in which the dorsal and ventral pancreatic buds fuse around the duodenum.
- The ring of the pancreas can cause obstruction to the duodenum.
- Most patients present around 1y of age with vomiting and abdominal distension after meals.

Acute pancreatitis

Definition
- Acute inflammation of the pancreas and peripancreatic tissues.

Epidemiology
- Uncommon.

Aetiology
- Gallstones and alcohol account for the majority of cases.
- Other causes include abdominal trauma, endoscopic retrograde cholangiopancreatography (ERCP), drugs, hypercalcaemia, pancreas divisum, and viral infection.
- Many cases are idiopathic.

Pathogenesis
- Injury to the pancreas leads to release and activation of digestive enzymes, causing necrosis of pancreatic and peripancreatic tissue.
- Exudation of plasma into the retroperitoneal space leads to hypovolaemia and cardiovascular instability.
- Paralytic ileus may also occur as a reaction to extensive inflammation occurring in the vicinity of the bowel.

Presentation
- Sudden onset of severe upper abdominal pain radiating to the back, associated with nausea, vomiting, and fever.
- Hypotension is often present which, in severe cases, causes shock.

Biochemistry
- A significantly raised serum amylase is virtually diagnostic of acute pancreatitis in the correct clinical setting.

Macroscopy
- The pancreas is swollen and soft.
- White flecks of fat necrosis are present in peripancreatic tissues.
- In severe cases, there is haemorrhage into the necrotic pancreas.

Histopathology
- Acute inflammation, oedema, and focal necrosis within the pancreas.
- Surrounding peripancreatic tissue shows fat necrosis.
- Severe cases show widespread necrosis and haemorrhage into the gland.

Prognosis
- Many cases are mild and resolve with supportive treatment.
- Severe cases can be life-threatening and require organ support.
- Superadded infection of the necrotic pancreatic tissue is an ominous complication, often leading to DIC and multiple organ failure.
- Pancreatic pseudocyst (a collection of fluid within the region of the pancreas) is a common late complication.

Chronic pancreatitis

Definition

- A chronic inflammatory process of the pancreas, leading to irreversible loss of pancreatic function.

▶ Chronic pancreatitis can closely mimic pancreatic carcinoma clinically, radiologically, and pathologically.

Epidemiology

- Uncommon.

Aetiology

- Almost all cases are associated with alcohol abuse.
- A small proportion is thought to be autoimmune in origin.

Pathogenesis

- Chronic inflammation in the pancreas leads to the replacement of functional pancreatic tissue by fibrous scar tissue.

Presentation

- Persistent upper abdominal pain and weight loss.
- Steatorrhoea and diabetes mellitus occur late once most of the gland is destroyed.

Macroscopy

- The pancreas is replaced by firm fibrous tissue, within which are dilated ducts and areas of calcification.

▶ The scarred mass is so firm, it can closely mimic carcinoma macroscopically.

Histopathology

- The pancreas shows a chronic inflammatory cell infiltrate with scarring and loss of exocrine tissue. The endocrine tissue is typically spared until late in the disease. Large ducts are dilated and contain inspissated secretions. Calcification is also common. ▶ Small residual atrophic ducts set in a fibrous background can closely mimic an infiltrating pancreatic carcinoma.
- A recently recognized variant of chronic pancreatitis has been described, in which there is a prominent periductal and perivenular chronic inflammatory cell infiltrate rich in $IgG4^+$ plasma cells. Patients often have raised serum IgG4 levels. This variant is thought to be autoimmune in nature.

Prognosis

- Alcoholic chronic pancreatitis tends to be associated with a fairly poor outcome. Treatment is supportive only and most patients will have other alcohol-related pathology.
- The outlook is better for patients with autoimmune pancreatitis, as this responds to steroid therapy.

Pancreatic ductal carcinoma

Definition

- A malignant epithelial tumour arising in the pancreas, composed of infiltrating duct-like structures.

Epidemiology

- Most common type of pancreatic neoplasm.
- Usually seen in people >60y and slightly more commonly in men.
- Incidence in developed countries ranges from 1 to 10 per 100 000.

Aetiology

- Smoking is the main recognized risk factor.

Carcinogenesis

- Activating mutations of *KRAS*.
- Loss of function of *TP53, P16*, and *DPC4*.
- Pancreatic ductal carcinomas may arise from pancreatic intraepithelial neoplasia (PanIN). PanIN is graded 1 to 3, with reference to increasing cytological and architectural atypia.

Presentation

- Persistent upper abdominal pain and profound weight loss.
- Tumours in the head may cause obstructive jaundice.
- Sudden onset of diabetes mellitus is also a suspicious finding.

Macroscopy

- A poorly defined, firm tumour mass is present within the pancreas.
- Most arise within the head, but they can occur anywhere in the pancreas.

Histopathology

- Most pancreatic carcinomas are well to moderately differentiated adenocarcinomas, in which the infiltrating malignant cells form well-developed glandular structures.
- A typical feature is the presence of abundant fibroblastic stroma around the infiltrating glands.
- Perineural invasion is also common and probably accounts for the high rates of peripancreatic tumour extension.

Prognosis

- Extremely poor, with 5-year survival rates of <5%.

Pancreatic neuroendocrine tumours

Definition

- A group of epithelial tumours of the pancreas showing endocrine differentiation. Tumours may be functioning or non-functioning, depending on whether a syndrome of inappropriate hormone secretion is present.

Epidemiology

- Rare tumours, accounting for ~2% of all pancreatic tumours.
- Peak incidence between 30 and 60y.

Aetiology

- Unknown in sporadic cases.
- ~15% associated with multiple endocrine neoplasia (MEN)-1.

Genetics

- Losses at chromosomes 1 and 11q and gains of 9q appear to be early events.
- Accumulation of further alterations is associated with malignant behaviour.

Presentation

- Functioning tumours present with features related to excess hormone production, e.g. hypoglycaemia (insulin-producing tumours), recurrent duodenal ulceration (gastrin-producing tumours), necrolytic migratory erythema (glucagon-producing tumours).
- Non-functioning tumours are either picked up incidentally on imaging or present when they grow large enough to produce symptoms of local disease or metastasis.

Macroscopy

- Most are well-demarcated tumours within the pancreas.

Cytopathology

- Fine-needle aspiration (FNA) smears are cellular and composed of a monotonous population of cells present singly, in loose clusters, or as pseudorosettes.
- The nuclei usually have a distinct granular chromatin pattern ('salt-and-pepper').

Histopathology

- Most tumours are composed of cells with granular cytoplasm, forming solid nests, trabeculae, glands, or rosettes.
- Immunostaining confirms the endocrine nature of the cells with reactivity for the markers CD56, chromogranin, and synaptophysin.
- Tumours are classified according to their Ki-67 labelling index: grade 1 = 2% or less, grade 2 = >2% but <10%, grade 3 = 10% or more.
- Functional tumours can also be stained for the hormones they secrete.

Prognosis

- Often difficult to predict with certainty.
- All tumours should be considered potentially malignant, and long-term follow-up is essential as metastases may develop many years after removal of the primary lesion. The Ki-67 labelling index is not entirely reliable.

Clinicopathological classification of pancreatic endocrine tumours

Well-differentiated endocrine tumour

- Benign behaviour: confined to the pancreas, non-angioinvasive, <2cm in size, ≤2 mitoses/10 high-power field (hpf), ≤2% Ki-67-positive cells/10hpf.
- Uncertain behaviour: confined to the pancreas and one or more of the following features: ≥2cm in size, 2–10 mitoses/10hpf, >2% Ki-67-positive cells/10hpf, angioinvasion, perineural invasion.

Well-differentiated endocrine carcinoma

- Histologically low-grade, but with evidence of gross local invasion and/or metastases.

Poorly differentiated endocrine carcinoma

- Histologically high-grade with >10 mitoses/10hpf.

Pancreatic cystic tumours

Intraductal papillary mucinous neoplasm

- A grossly visible, mucin-producing tumour that grows within the pancreatic ductal system.
- Most arise within the head of the pancreas in men.
- Macroscopically, there are mucin-filled cysts within the pancreas that communicate with the duct system.
- Histologically, the cysts are lined by mucin-secreting columnar epithelial cells which form papillary projections into the cyst. The epithelial cells may show a range of atypia from low to high grade. Invasive carcinoma can arise within this lesion.

Mucinous cystic neoplasms

- A range of lesions, most of which are benign.
- Almost all occur in women and present with symptoms of an abdominal mass.
- Macroscopically, they are well-circumscribed cystic tumours with large locules containing mucoid material. The cysts do not communicate with the pancreatic ductal system.
- Histologically, the cysts are lined by mucus-secreting columnar epithelial cells, beneath which there is a densely cellular, ovarian-like stroma. The epithelial component may show a range of atypia from low to high grade. Invasive carcinomas can arise within these lesions.
- This needs to be distinguished from intraductal papillary neoplasms (IPMNs) which involve the pancreatic ducts and lack the ovarian-type stroma. IPMNs may progress to invasive adenocarcinoma.

Serous cystic neoplasms

- A range of lesions, the majority of which are benign.
- Almost all occur in women and present with symptoms of an abdominal mass.
- The most common type is the **serous microcystic adenoma**, which gives rise to a well-circumscribed pancreatic mass containing numerous small cysts with a central scar. Histologically, the small cysts are lined by cuboidal cells with a round nucleus and clear cytoplasm due to the accumulation of glycogen.

Solid pseudopapillary neoplasm

- A neoplasm of the pancreas which often shows cystic change.
- Occurs in young women with symptoms of an abdominal mass.
- The tumours may occur anywhere in the pancreas as a solid mass with cystic areas and haemorrhage.
- Histologically, the tumour is composed of uniform round cells which form sheets and cords. The cells tend to be poorly cohesive and fall apart, creating pseudopapillary and cystic areas.
- The tumours generally have very low-grade biological behaviour, with most patients remaining tumour-free many years after resection.

Acinar cell carcinoma

Definition

- A malignant epithelial neoplasm of the pancreas, demonstrating evidence of enzyme production by the neoplastic cells.

Epidemiology

- Rare tumour, accounting for ~1% of all pancreatic tumours.
- Most occur in older adults.

Aetiology

- Unknown.

Carcinogenesis

- Abnormalities have been described in the APC/β-catenin pathway.
- Genetic mutations typically found in ductal adenocarcinomas are absent.

Presentation

- Non-specific symptoms of abdominal pain, weight loss, nausea, and diarrhoea.
- ~10% of patients have a syndrome of multifocal fat necrosis and polyarthralgia due to lipase secretion.

Macroscopy

- Large, well-demarcated, soft-tan tumour arising within the pancreas.
- Extension outside the pancreas may be present.

Histopathology

- Cellular tumours composed of neoplastic epithelial cells growing in sheets, trabeculae, and acini.
- Some cells have abundant eosinophilic, finely granular cytoplasm.
- The cells show positive immunoreactivity for lipase, trypsin, and chymotrypsin.

Prognosis

- Aggressive malignant tumours.
- Median survival 18 months from diagnosis, with 5-year survival rates of <10%.

Chapter 10

Renal pathology

Acute kidney injury

Definition

- A significant deterioration in renal function occurring over hours or days. Severity is defined by three stages (1 to 3).

Epidemiology

- Common.
- Often occurs as a complication of a pre-existing illness causing circulatory disturbance.

Aetiology

- **Pre-renal**: hypoperfusion, e.g. hypovolaemia, sepsis.
- **Renal** ('intrinsic'): acute tubular injury, acute interstitial nephritis, glomerulonephritis (GN), renal vasculitis, thrombotic microangiopathy.
- **Post-renal**: bilateral obstruction (or obstruction to a single kidney).

►► The cause of acute kidney injury (AKI) should be determined promptly, with special attention to reversible causes. Several causes may coexist. By far, the most common causes are hypoperfusion and acute tubular injury (e.g. related to contrast, aminoglycosides, or amphotericin B).

Presentation

- Most cases are heralded by the onset of oliguria (passing small volumes of urine), though some cases may produce few symptoms or signs.
- Very severe cases cause marked pulmonary oedema, encephalopathy, and pericarditis.

Biochemistry

- Elevated serum urea and creatinine.
- Hyperkalaemia and metabolic acidosis are also commonly present.

❶ Severe hyperkalaemia is pro-arrhythmic and can lead to a cardiac arrest, so it must be treated promptly.

Prognosis

- Pre-renal and post-renal acute AKI may be reversible if treated promptly by restoring circulating volume or relieving obstruction.
- Treatment is supportive whilst the cause is treated, and dialysis may be needed whilst renal function recovers.
- Prognosis of the intrinsic causes of AKI depends on the underlying disease. A renal biopsy may be required to ascertain the cause of ARF.

Chronic kidney disease

Definition

- Abnormalities of kidney structure or function, present for >3 months, with implications for health. Most cases of chronic kidney disease (CKD) are irreversible, but some cases may be partially or even entirely reversible.
- Abnormalities of kidney function/structure include decreased glomerular filtration rate (GFR), increased albuminuria, urinary sediment abnormalities, electrolyte and other abnormalities due to tubular disorders, abnormalities detected by histology, and structural abnormalities detected by imaging.
- CKD is classified based on the cause, GFR category, and albuminuria category.

Epidemiology

- Common, with a significant impact on health worldwide.

Aetiology

- Diabetic nephropathy and hypertensive nephropathy are the most common causes, particularly in developed countries.
- Other causes include adult polycystic kidney disease (APKD), dysplastic kidneys, reflux nephropathy, obstructive nephropathy, infections, drugs, systemic diseases that affect the kidney (e.g. SLE, amyloidosis, monoclonal gammopathy, or gout), and intrinsic renal diseases (e.g. GN or focal segmental glomerulosclerosis (FSGS)).

Pathogenesis

- Injury may primarily affect glomeruli, vessels, or the tubulo-interstitium, but eventually it leads to reduction in nephron mass with an attendant reduction in renal function.
- The reduction in nephron mass may then cause haemodynamic stress in remaining nephrons, leading to further nephron loss.

Presentation

- Early disease is asymptomatic and can only be picked up if GFR is measured in at-risk patients, e.g. diabetics, hypertensives.
- With progression, patients feel tired and develop bony pain.
- Some patients present in end-stage renal failure, with fluid overload and metabolic derangement requiring immediate renal replacement therapy.

Biochemistry

- ↑ urea and creatinine due to impaired excretion of waste products.
- ↓ calcium due to lack of active calcitriol.
- ↑ phosphate due to impaired excretion of phosphate.
- Secondary hyperparathyroidism due to hypocalcaemia.
- ↓ haemoglobin (Hb) due to reduced erythropoietin secretion.

► Note that loss of acid–base and sodium/potassium balance occurs late in CKD.

Complications

- High incidence of cardiovascular disease due to a combination of hypertension, vascular calcification, and hyperlipidaemia.
- Derangement of calcium and phosphate metabolism leads to renal bone disease, which is a complex mixture of hyperparathyroid bone disease, osteomalacia, and osteoporosis (Fig. 10.1).

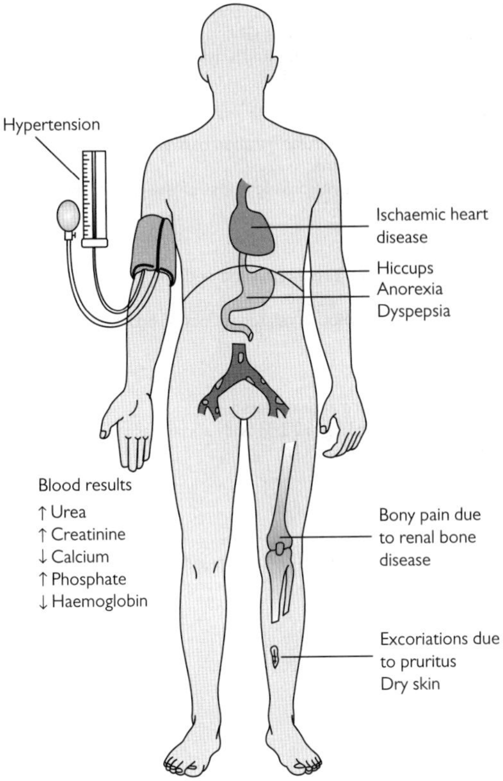

Fig. 10.1 Symptoms and signs of advanced chronic renal failure.

Reproduced with permission from *Clinical Pathology* (Oxford Core Texts), Carton, James, Daly, Richard, and Ramani, Pramila, Oxford University Press (2006), p. 208, Figure 10.4.

Nephrotic syndrome

Definition

- Combination of nephrotic-range proteinuria (>3.5g/1.73m^2 body surface area/24h), hypoalbuminaemia (<30g/L), hyperlipidaemia, and oedema.

Aetiology

- Primary renal diseases, most commonly: minimal change disease (MCD), FSGS, and membranous GN.
- Systemic diseases, e.g. diabetes and amyloidosis (➔ Primary amyloidosis, pp. 380–1)

Pathogenesis

- Dysfunction of the glomerular filtration barrier, which normally prevents loss of protein in the urine.
- Podocyte injury plays a major role in loss of the glomerular filtration barrier function.

Presentation

- Abrupt onset of heavy proteinuria and oedema.
- Hyperlipidaemia.
- Increased risk of thrombosis related to loss of proteins regulating coagulation.

Biochemistry

- Creatinine can be normal or elevated.
- Heavy proteinuria (>3.5g/1.73m^2 body surface area/24h).
- Hypoalbuminaemia (<30g/L).
- Hyperlipidaemia.

Prognosis

- Depends on the cause.
- Procoagulant state due to loss of anticoagulant proteins in the urine may lead to vein thrombosis and life-threatening pulmonary embolism.

Hereditary renal diseases

Definition

- A number of hereditary conditions may affect the kidney primarily or as part of a systemic disease.
- In addition, patients may be predisposed to developing kidney failure because of underlying genetic traits; most importantly, high-risk alleles of *APOL1* confer an increased risk of renal failure to some patients of African descent.

Epidemiology

- Uncommon.
- The prevalence of risk alleles in patients of African origin or descent is variable, between a few % and up to 40% of the population.

Examples

- Cystic kidney diseases such as autosomal dominant polycystic kidney disease.
- Alport's syndrome and thin basement membrane lesion: mutations in the alpha chains of type IV collagen.
- Hereditary FSGS/congenital nephrotic syndrome.
- Sickle cell nephropathy.
- Storage disorders, e.g. Fabry disease.
- Abnormalities of protein folding: uromodulin-associated kidney disease.

Presentation

- Cystic kidney disease may present with renal impairment and/or symptoms related to an increased kidney size.
- Alport's syndrome and thin basement membrane lesion typically present with microhaematuria; some cases progress to chronic renal failure.
- Hereditary FSGS/congenital nephrotic syndrome: nephrotic syndrome *in utero*, in infancy, or later in life.
- Fabry disease: kidney dysfunction is part of a systemic picture with involvement of the skin (angiokeratomas), nerves, heart, brain, and GI tract.
- Uromodulin-associated kidney disease: progressive renal dysfunction with hyperuricaemia and gout, sometimes with renal cysts.

Prognosis

- Depends on the cause; renal transplantation may cure the disease.

Alport's syndrome and thin basement membrane lesion

Definition

- Mutations of the alpha chains of type IV collagen, leading to structural defects in the glomerular basement membrane.

Aetiology

- Most cases of Alport's syndrome are X-linked dominant and due to mutations of the alpha 5 chain of type IV collagen.
- Mutations affecting the alpha 3 and alpha 4 chains of type IV collagen may lead to autosomal dominant or recessive forms of Alport's syndrome or to thin basement membrane lesion.

Presentation

- Typically presents with microhaematuria.
- Patients with Alport's syndrome often have deafness and ocular abnormalities.
- Alport's syndrome is typically a progressive disease, with chronic renal failure in middle age.
- Thin basement membrane lesion may be entirely benign ('benign familial haematuria') or may progress to renal failure, depending on the underlying mutation.

Histopathology

- Light microscopy: normal or progressive scarring in glomeruli (FSGS) and tubules.
- Immunofluorescence: no immunoglobulin or complement deposition; it may be possible, in some cases, to demonstrate an abnormal staining pattern using antibodies directed against the alpha chains of type IV collagen, either within the kidney or within a skin biopsy.
- Electron microscopy: Alport's syndrome shows a typical 'basket-weave' pattern to the glomerular basement membranes; thin basement membrane lesion shows marked and diffuse thinning of glomerular basement membranes.

Prognosis

- Depends on the cause; renal transplantation may cure the disease.

Hypertensive nephropathy

Definition
- CKD thought to be due to hypertension.

Epidemiology
- A common cause of CKD.

Aetiology
- Hypertension.

Pathogenesis
- Two pathophysiological theories have been suggested, which may not be mutually exclusive.
- The first suggests that narrowing of arteries and arterioles causes glomerular ischaemia and global glomerular scarring.
- The second suggests that glomerular hypertension leads to glomerular haemodynamic stress, leading to focal and segmental glomerulosclerosis.

Presentation
- Renal dysfunction and proteinuria in a long-standing hypertensive, in the absence of other causes of renal disease.
- Other signs of hypertension may be present, e.g. left ventricular hypertrophy.

Macroscopy
- Both kidneys are shrunken with finely granular cortical surfaces.

Histopathology
- Hyaline deposits are seen in the walls of afferent arterioles.
- Interlobular and larger arteries show medial hypertrophy and intimal thickening.
- Glomeruli may show wrinkling and shrinkage (due to ischaemia), followed by scarring of the whole tuft (global sclerosis; see first pathogenetic mechanism) and/or enlargement of the tuft with segmental glomerular scarring (see second pathogenetic mechanism).
- This constellation of pathological features is often referred to as **nephrosclerosis**, a term simply meaning hardening of the kidney.

► Note that the presence of nephrosclerosis is not specific for hypertensive nephropathy, as identical changes can be seen with ageing, diabetes, and other causes of chronic renal failure. These features on a renal biopsy support a diagnosis of hypertensive nephropathy, provided other causes of renal failure have been excluded.

Prognosis
- As with all forms of CKD, there is a tendency to progressive disease.
- The decline in renal function can be slowed by aggressive control of blood pressure.

Diabetic nephropathy

Definition

- CKD caused by diabetes mellitus.

Epidemiology

- Common cause of CKD.

Aetiology

- Type 1 or type 2 diabetes mellitus.
- Only 30–40% of diabetics develop nephropathy, so other factors are involved.

Pathogenesis

- Complex.
- High glucose levels are thought to be directly injurious, at least partly through abnormal glycosylation of extracellular proteins, oxidative stress, and enhanced production of TGF-β.

Presentation

- Onset of proteinuria in a patient with diabetes mellitus.
- Typically, this starts as microalbuminuria but progresses to overt proteinuria, which may be heavy enough to cause the nephrotic syndrome.
- Hypertension is invariably present.

Histopathology

- Glomerular changes develop progressively and are classed by severity, from early to late lesions:
  - class I: thickening of the glomerular basement membranes on electron microscopy only (light microscopy normal or near normal);
  - class II: increase in the mesangial matrix, without nodules (IIa, mild; IIb, severe);
  - class III: nodular glomerulosclerosis/Kimmelstiel–Wilson lesion (Fig. 10.2);
  - class IV: advanced diabetic glomerulosclerosis.
- Hyalinization of arterioles, typically affecting both afferent and efferent arterioles.
- Tubulo-interstitial fibrosis proportional to the degree of glomerular damage.

► Note that renal biopsy is not necessary to confirm a diagnosis of diabetic nephropathy, provided the clinical picture is typical. Biopsy is usually reserved for atypical cases where an alternative or additional diagnosis is suspected.

Immunofluorescence

- Linear enhancement of glomerular and tubular basement membranes with IgG may be seen.

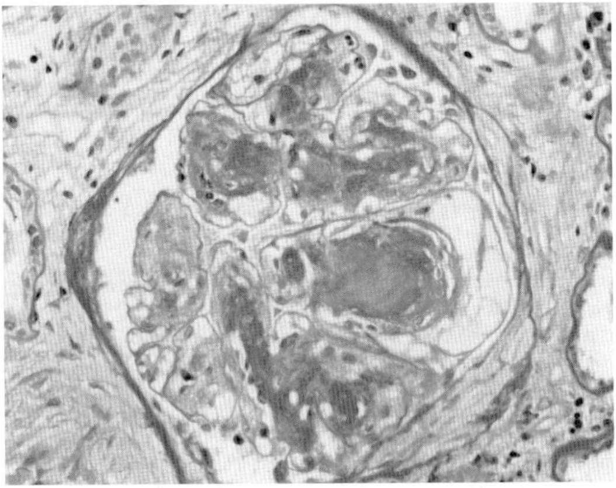

Fig. 10.2 Nodular diabetic glomerulosclerosis (periodic acid–Schiff stain) (see Plate 15).

Electron microscopy

- Diffuse glomerular basement membrane thickening and expansion of the mesangial matrix are seen.
- No immune complexes are present.

Prognosis

- Gradual deterioration in renal function.
- Patients with severe hypertension and marked proteinuria fare worse.
- Control of blood pressure and glycaemic control are cornerstones of slowing the disease process.

Minimal change disease

Definition

- A glomerulopathy characterized clinically by the nephrotic syndrome and histologically by glomeruli that appear normal on light microscopy.

Epidemiology

- Main cause of nephrotic syndrome in children, but also occurs in adults.

Aetiology

- As a primary disease: aetiology uncertain, but current evidence points towards an immune dysfunction.
- As a secondary disease, minimal change disease (MCD) can occur following drug administration (NSAIDs), bee stings, venom exposure, and lymphoma.

Pathogenesis

- The podocyte is thought to be the key cell affected in MCD.
- Normal podocyte function is lost, such that the glomerular filtration barrier becomes abnormally permeable to proteins.

Presentation

- Nephrotic syndrome.

Light microscopy

- By definition, the glomeruli appear normal on light microscopy.

Immunofluorescence

- Negative for immunoglobulins (IgG, IgA, and IgM) and complement components (C3 and C1q), as well as for light chains (kappa and lambda).

Electron microscopy

- Extensive effacement of podocyte foot processes.
- No electron-dense deposits are present.

Prognosis

- Complete recovery usually occurs in MCD, particularly in children.

► Adults with steroid-resistant disease should be carefully monitored, as they may turn out to have FSGS (➔ Focal segmental glomerulosclerosis, pp. 192–3) which was not apparent on biopsy due to the focal nature of that condition.

Focal segmental glomerulosclerosis

Definition

- Primary glomerulopathy, characterized histologically by sclerosis involving some, but not all, glomeruli (focal) and affecting only a portion of the glomerular tuft (segmental).
- FSGS can also occur as a pattern of injury secondary to glomerular injury of any type and cause; therefore, segmental glomerular scarring can be seen in many contexts and does not always indicate primary FSGS.

► Careful exclusion of other underlying diseases through histological examination and clinical correlation is therefore essential before making a diagnosis of primary FSGS.

Epidemiology

- Common cause of nephrotic syndrome in adults.
- Patients of African origin or descent are at increased risk of FSGS, if they carry risk alleles of *APO-L1*.

Aetiology

- Idiopathic primary FSGS: unknown, although recurrence of the disease in transplanted kidneys suggests a circulating factor.
- Rare cases are due to genetic mutations, particularly in podocyte proteins and in children (e.g. congenital nephrotic syndrome of Finnish type due to mutations of *NPHS1*, or diffuse mesangial sclerosis/Dennis Drash syndrome/Frasier syndrome related to mutations of *WT-1*).
- Other cases develop following viral infections (e.g. HIV), drugs (e.g. pamidronate), and in relation to haemodynamic stress to the glomerulus (e.g. obesity, anabolic steroids, sickle-cell anaemia, and reduced nephron mass of any cause).

Pathogenesis

- Podocyte injury and loss cause heavy proteinuria and segmental glomerular scarring.

Presentation

- Primary FSGS: nephrotic syndrome.
- Secondary FSGS: heavy proteinuria

Light microscopy

- Involved glomeruli show replacement of a segment of the glomerular tuft by sclerosis (Fig. 10.3).
- The sclerotic segment often shows adhesion to the overlying epithelial cells of the Bowman's space.
- Glomerulosclerosis is usually accompanied by tubulo-interstitial fibrosis around the involved glomerulus.
- Primary FSGS can be classified into five different morphological patterns: not otherwise specified (NOS), tip variant, cellular variant, collapsing variant, perihilar variant.

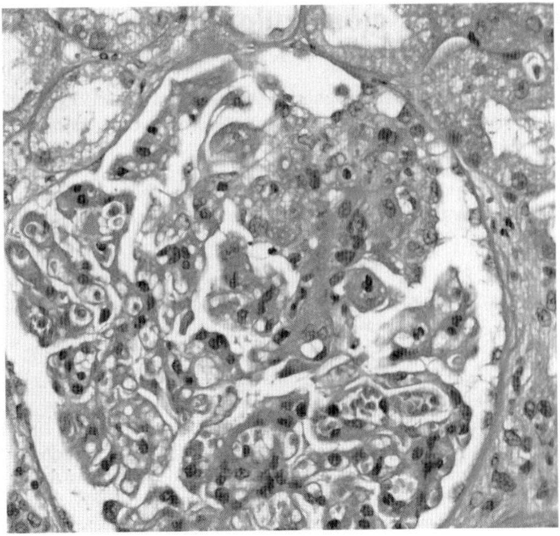

Fig. 10.3 Focal and segmental glomerulosclerosis (see Plate 16).

Immunofluorescence

- Non-specific entrapment of IgM and C3 may be seen in areas of sclerosis.

Electron microscopy

- Primary FSGS: extensive podocyte foot process effacement. There are no electron-dense deposits.
- Secondary FSGS: segmental podocyte foot process effacement; there may also be evidence of an underlying disease causing the scarring, such as immune complex GN, with electron-dense deposits.

Prognosis

- Depends on whether primary or secondary and on the histological variant.
- Commonly leads to progressive renal insufficiency.
- Tip variant has a better outcome, and collapsing variant has a worse outcome.

Membranous glomerulopathy

Definition

- Glomerulopathy caused by subepithelial (between the podocyte and glomerular basement membrane) immune complex deposition.

Epidemiology

- Most common primary renal cause of nephrotic syndrome in adults, except in patients of African origin or descent where FSGS is more common.

Aetiology

- Primary/idiopathic membranous is an autoimmune disease; antibodies against phospholipase A2 type M receptor (a protein expressed in podocytes) have been identified in about 75% of cases of idiopathic membranous glomerulopathy. In rare cases, other autoantibodies have been identified. In some, the antigen remains unidentified.
- Secondary membranous: malignancies (in particular, epithelial malignancies), drugs (e.g. captopril, gold, penicillamine), infections (e.g. hepatitis B, syphilis, and malaria), and SLE. In these cases, the immune complexes probably form elsewhere and circulate to the kidneys where they are deposited within the glomeruli.

Pathogenesis

- Immune complexes within the subepithelial space injure podocytes and disrupt the normal filtration barrier, causing heavy proteinuria.

Presentation

- Nephrotic syndrome.

Light microscopy

- All of the glomeruli have thickened, rigid capillary loops.
- Silver staining shows 'holes' in the glomerular basement membrane which represent the immune deposits, and 'spikes' which represent the glomerular basement membrane reaction to the deposits.
- More advanced cases may also show glomerular sclerosis and tubulo-interstitial fibrosis.

Immunofluorescence

- Granular deposits of IgG and C3 along the capillary walls.
- If deposits of IgA, IgM, and C1q are also present, then membranous nephropathy secondary to SLE should be considered.

Electron microscopy

- Subepithelial electron-dense immune complex deposits are present with a variable reaction of the adjacent basement membrane, which may surround them.
- Podocytes show diffuse foot process effacement.

Prognosis

- About one-third of patients develop progressive disease.

Glomerulonephritis

Definition

- GN is characterized by increased glomerular cellularity, caused by proliferation of indigenous cells and/or leucocyte infiltration

Aetiology

- On the basis of aetiology, there are five classes of GN:
  - immune complex GN (including IgA nephropathy (IgAN), post-infectious GN, lupus nephritis, and cryoglobinaemic GN) (for lupus nephritis and cryoglobulinaemia;
  - pauci-immune GN;
  - anti-glomerular basement membrane antibody (anti-GBM) GN;
  - monoclonal immunoglobulin GN;
  - C3 glomerulopathy.
- These are primarily autoimmune diseases, although some may have a hereditary component. Monoclonal immunoglobulin GN is due to monoclonal immunoglobulins produced by clonal B-cell populations.

Pathogenesis

- Damage to the glomerulus with leakage of protein and blood into the urine. There may be rupture of the glomerular basement membrane, with a cellular reaction in the Bowman's space (crescent formation). The cause of the damage to the glomerulus depends on the cause:
  - immune complex GN and monoclonal immunoglobulin GN: deposition of polyclonal or monoclonal immune complexes, respectively, within the glomerulus; these deposits lead to local cellular proliferation and inflammation;
  - pauci-immune GN: 80–90% of patients have serologic evidence of anti-neutrophil cytoplasmic antibodies (ANCA). There is glomerular necrosis; the pathogenetic link with ANCA is not fully characterized;
  - anti-GBM GN: circulating antibodies against the GBM cause glomerular damage;
  - C3 glomerulopathy: abnormalities in regulation of the alternative pathway of complement activation, with deposition of C3 in the glomerulus, leading to glomerular injury.

Presentation

- Haematuria (microscopic or macroscopic), proteinuria, and a variable degree of renal dysfunction.

Light microscopy

- Cases with immune complex or C3 deposition often show diffuse glomerular hypercellularity, which varies from mild mesangial hypercellularity to marked hypercellularity with capillary loop occlusion by cells.
- Pauci-immune and anti-GBM GN show necrosis of the glomerular tuft, most often without hypercellularity in the unaffected glomerular portions.
- Crescents (Fig. 10.4) may be seen in all types of GN but are particularly large and common in pauci-immune and anti-GBM GN.

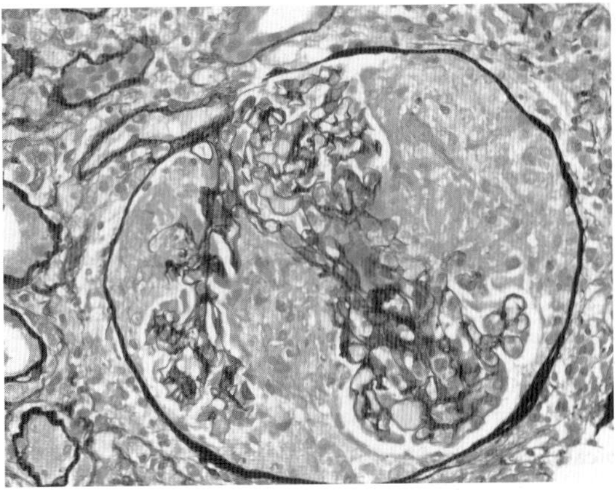

Fig. 10.4 Segmental glomerular necrosis with cellular crescent (Jones silver stain) (see Plate 17).

Immunofluorescence

- Immune complex GN: deposition of immunoglobulins, often with complement, in glomeruli. The type and location of the immune deposits often point to the underlying aetiology—IgAN shows dominant or co-dominant staining with IgA; lupus nephritis shows a 'full-house' pattern with IgG, IgM, IgA, C3, and C1q positivity. In the case of monoclonal immunoglobulin GN, there is restriction of light chains to one type (kappa or lambda).
- C3 GN: dominant C3 deposits in the glomeruli with minimal or no Ig deposits.
- ANCA: negative for immunoglobulins and complement.
- Anti-GBM GN: linear deposition of IgG and C3 along glomerular basement membranes.

Electron microscopy

- Immune complex and C3 GN: electron-dense immune deposits are present; variable distribution (mesangial, subendothelial, subepithelial).
- Immune complex GN: rarely the deposits are fibrillary (polyclonal in fibrillary GN, and monoclonal in cryoglobulinaemic GN and immunotactoid GN).
- ANCA and anti-GBM GN: no electron-dense deposits.

Prognosis

- Variable, depending on the underlying cause.
- Cases presenting with crescents and rapidly progressive renal failure require urgent treatment.

IgA nephropathy

Definition

- Immune complex GN related to glomerular deposition of immune complexes containing IgA.

Epidemiology

- The most common GN worldwide.

Aetiology

- Primary: incompletely understood; an abnormal mucosal immune system and the production of abnormally glycosylated IgA molecules play a role.
- Secondary: IgA can be deposited in glomeruli, in association with liver disease, bowel disease, and dermatitis herpetiformis.
- Systemic form with small-vessel vasculitis (Henoch–Schönlein purpura).

Typical pathological features

- IgAN can cause a number of changes in the glomeruli, ranging from mild mesangial hypercellularity only to global glomerular hypercellularity.
- Crescents may be seen in the most severe cases.
- Immunofluorescence: by definition, there is dominant or co-dominant staining with IgA in the mesangial region of the glomeruli.
- Electron microscopy: electron-dense immune deposits are present, mainly in the mesangium.

Prognosis

- About one-third of patients develop progressive renal disease.
- A number of clinical features can help predict the risk of progression (proteinuria, hypertension, renal function).
- The Oxford Classification of IgA Nephropathy (MEST score) documents four features known to provide independent prognostic values in predicting the outcome: mesangial hypercellularity (M), endocapillary hypercellularity (E), segmental glomerulosclerosis (S), and tubular atrophy/interstitial fibrosis (T).

Post-infectious glomerulonephritis

Definition

- Immune complex GN related to infection.

Aetiology

- Acute post-streptococcal GN: mainly caused by group A streptococci—classical association of upper respiratory tract infection (e.g. pharyngitis), followed a few weeks later by ARF.
- Other microorganisms can also cause post-infectious GN, with acute or chronic renal failure, most notably staphylococcal infections (including meticillin-resistant *Staphylococcus aureus*, MRSA) of the viscera, skin, bones and teeth, shunts, and heart valves (endocarditis). These infections may be occult at the time of the renal presentation.

Typical pathological features

- Acute post-streptococcal GN: global glomerular hypercellularity with neutrophils; predominant C3 on immunofluorescence; typical subepithelial 'humps' (dome-shaped electron-dense deposits) on electron microscopy.
- Non-streptococcal post-infectious GN: less typical findings, with variable glomerular proliferation; immunoglobulins and complement on immunofluorescence, and electron-dense deposits on electron microscopy, but often no 'humps'.

Prognosis

- Mostly self-limiting; disappears after treatment of infection.
- Rare cases are progressive.

C3 glomerulopathy

Definition

- C3 glomerulopathy comprises C3 GN and dense deposit disease (DDD); both are characterized by C3-predominant deposits within glomeruli, and sometimes tubules, with little or no immune complexes.

Aetiology

- These diseases are related to dysregulation of the alternative pathway of complement activation (inherited or acquired) and can be due to mutation or autoimmune dysregulation of various components of the alternative pathway, e.g. DDD is often due to a C3 nephritic factor which is an autoantibody against C3; C3 GN can be due to mutations in factor H.

Typical pathological features

- Variable glomerular hypercellularity.
- Immunofluorescence: C3 predominance, with or without immunoglobulins.
- Electron microscopy: electron-dense deposits in variable locations within the glomeruli; DDD is characterized by electron-dense transformation of the glomerular and tubular basement membranes.

Prognosis

- Depends on the underlying pathogenetic mechanism; cases with autoantibodies may respond well to immunosuppression or removal of the antibody by plasmapheresis, whereas cases due to defective proteins may respond well to replacement of the defective proteins by fresh plasma.

Anti-glomerular basement membrane disease

Definition

- Severe GN caused by the development of autoantibodies to the glomerular basement membrane.

Epidemiology

- Rare.

Aetiology

- Autoantibodies to the C-terminal domain of type IV collagen, a component of the glomerular basement membrane.

Pathogenesis

- Autoantibodies bind to the glomerular basement membrane and initiate an autoimmune attack on the glomeruli.

Presentation

- ARF due to severe acute glomerular injury.
- Usually presents as rapidly progressive renal failure.
- Some patients also present with pulmonary haemorrhage if the autoantibody also cross-reacts with the alveolar basement membrane.

Light microscopy

- Glomeruli show a segmental, necrotizing GN with breaches in the glomerular basement membrane and the formation of crescents in the Bowman's space.
- Unaffected segments of the glomeruli appear normal.

Immunofluorescence

- Strong linear staining of IgG and C3 is seen in the glomerular basement membrane.

Electron microscopy

- No immune deposits are present.

Prognosis

- Although prompt immunosuppressive therapies can halt ongoing disease activity, damage already suffered in the kidneys may be irreversible.

Monoclonal gammopathy-associated kidney disease

Definition

- The production of monoclonal immunoglobulins or free light chains by clonal proliferations of plasma cells or B-cells can cause a range of renal lesions, referred to collectively as monoclonal gammopathy-associated kidney disease.

Epidemiology

- Monoclonal gammopathy-associated kidney disease can be seen in association with myeloma, monoclonal gammopathy of unknown significance, and lymphomas, and rarely in the absence of any of these.

Aetiology

- Abnormal light and/or heavy chains accumulate in the glomeruli, the tubules, the interstitium, and/or vessels.

Pathogenesis

- Free light chains can lead to light chain cast nephropathy, light chain tubulopathy, or AL amyloidosis (Congo red-positive fibrils).
- Abnormal complete immunoglobulins can deposit in glomeruli, leading to an immune complex GN, either with structured deposits in the form of microtubules or crystals (immunotactoid GN, cryoglobulinaemic GN) or with linear granular deposits (monoclonal immunoglobulin deposition disease) or with circumscribed granular deposits (proliferative GN with monoclonal immunoglobulins).
- The different patterns that develop are mostly determined by the physicochemical properties of the pathogenic monoclonal proteins produced. Rate of production of the monoclonal proteins is also important, e.g. light chain cast nephropathy is often related to high monoclonal light chain production.

Presentation

- Variable, from tubular dysfunction in light chain tubulopathy, to ARF in light chain cast nephropathy, nephrotic syndrome in AL amyloidosis, and nephritic syndrome in immune complex GN.

Light microscopy

- Light chain cast nephropathy: casts in tubules with 'cracks' and a cellular reaction at the periphery, staining weakly with periodic acid–Schiff (PAS) (Fig. 10.5).
- Light chain tubulopathy: vacuolation of tubular epithelial cells.
- AL amyloidosis: amorphous deposits in glomeruli, the interstitium, and vessels; Congo Red stain-positive.
- Immune complex GN: variable glomerular hypercellularity.

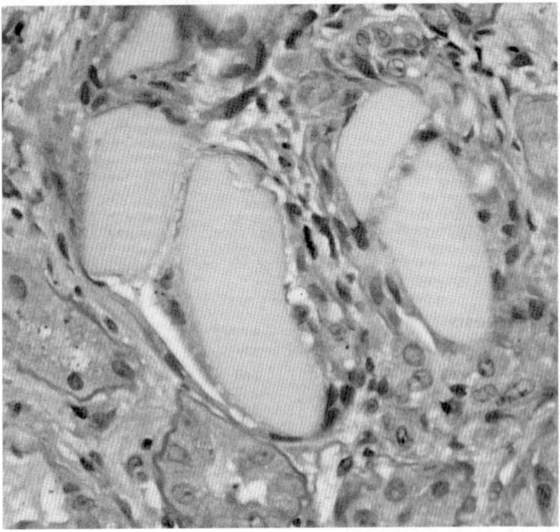

Fig. 10.5 Light chain cast nephropathy (PAS stain) (see Plate 18).

Immunofluorescence

- Monoclonal immunoglobulin and/or light chains can be identified by light chain restriction (i.e. staining for only kappa or only lambda light chain).
- Distribution will depend on the type of lesion (i.e. tubular, glomerular, etc.).

Electron microscopy

- In immune complex GN, microtubular, amorphous granular, and/or crystalline electron densities are seen, with a variable distribution.

Prognosis

- Successful treatment of the underlying clonal population is necessary for renal recovery.

Acute tubular injury

Definition

- Acute renal impairment caused by injury to renal tubules.

Epidemiology

- One of the most common causes of AKI.

Aetiology

- Ischaemia due to prolonged hypoperfusion.
- Nephrotoxins such as drugs, radiological contrast, uric acid, Hb, myoglobin, and ethylene glycol.

Pathogenesis

- Tubular epithelial cells are metabolically active and very sensitive to damage from ischaemia or toxins.

Presentation

- ARF.

Histopathology

- The injured tubules are dilated, with flattening of tubular epithelial cells and loss of the brush border.
- Casts of sloughed necrotic epithelial cells may be seen in the lumen of distal tubules.
- The interstitial compartment is expanded by oedema, but there is no significant inflammatory cell infiltrate.
- Clues to the underlying cause may be present, e.g. birefringent oxalate crystals in ethylene glycol poisoning or pigmented casts in rhabdomyolysis.

Prognosis

- Often associated with a severe circulatory disturbance and significant mortality rate.

Acute tubulo-interstitial nephritis

Definition

- Renal impairment caused by an immune injury to the tubules and interstitium.

Aetiology

- The main causes are drugs, autoimmune diseases, and infections.
- Drug-related tubulo-interstitial nephritis (TIN) is due to a hypersensitivity reaction to a drug.
- Any drugs can cause acute TIN, but the most common culprits are:
  - NSAIDs;
  - antibiotics;
  - diuretics;
  - allopurinol;
  - proton pump inhibitors.

Pathogenesis

- Tubulo-interstitial inflammation and tubular damage can be due to a hypersensitivity reaction to a drug, to a local infection or an idiosyncratic reaction to an infection, or to autoimmunity.

Presentation

- The typical presentation is ARF.
- In drug-related TIN, presentation occurs within days of starting the drug, though occasionally it only occurs after several months of exposure. Patients often have fever, rash, eosinophilia, eosinophiluria, and raised serum IgE levels.
- Patients with NSAID-induced disease may also show heavy proteinuria.

Histopathology

- The interstitium is expanded by oedema and a predominantly monocytic inflammatory cell infiltrate.
- Lymphocytes are also seen infiltrating into the tubules ('tubulitis').
- In drug-related TIN, there are often eosinophils.
- In granulomatous TIN, there are, in addition, well-formed granulomas in the interstitium. This is seen in drug-related TIN, sarcoidosis, and mycobacterial infections.

Prognosis

- Treatment of the underlying autoimmune disease or infection, or cessation of the offending drug may result in complete recovery. A short course of steroids is given to clear the local inflammatory injury to the tubules.

Reflux nephropathy

Definition

- Renal scarring associated with vesicoureteric reflux (VUR), a congenital disorder in which urine regurgitates from the bladder into the upper urinary tract.

Epidemiology

- An important cause of CKD, responsible for up to 30% of cases in children and 10% of cases in adults.

Aetiology

- VUR.

► Note not all VUR cases are complicated by reflux nephropathy.

Pathogenesis

- Thought to be the result of reflux of infected urine into the kidney.
- Intra-renal reflux tends to occur at the poles of the kidneys where compound papillae are found.
- Compound papillae are more susceptible to reflux, as the papillary ducts open at less oblique angles onto a flat or concave surface.
- The inflammatory response to the infection causes renal scarring.
- Once sufficient nephron mass is lost, progressive renal disease occurs.

Presentation

- Patients typically present with hypertension and/or proteinuria.
- Once renal scarring is extensive, biochemical evidence of renal dysfunction becomes evident.

Macroscopy

- The poles of the kidneys show areas of coarse renal cortical scarring.

Histopathology

- The scarred areas show features of chronic pyelonephritis with tubular atrophy and interstitial fibrosis, associated with a mononuclear inflammatory cell infiltrate.
- Some tubules are collapsed, whereas others may be dilated and filled with proteinaceous material ('thyroidization').
- Residual glomeruli show hypertrophy and secondary glomerulosclerosis.

► This constellation of features is not specific to reflux nephropathy and may be seen in other contexts, most notably obstructive nephropathy. Distinction between the two is usually possible, based on the clinical picture and the pattern of scarring.

Complications

- Recurrent urinary tract infection (UTI).
- Renal stones.
- CKD.

Obstructive nephropathy

Definition

- Renal damage caused by obstruction in the urinary tract.

Epidemiology

- Predominantly seen in children (due to congenital anomalies of the urinary tract) and elderly men (due to prostatic hyperplasia).

Aetiology

- Obstruction may occur anywhere in the urinary tract (➔ Urinary tract obstruction, p. 214–15).
- Common causes include urinary calculi, pelviureteric junction obstruction, prostatic hyperplasia, urothelial tumours, and compression of the ureters by abdominal/pelvic masses.

Pathogenesis

- Renal damage is thought to be predominantly a pressure-related phenomenon, though superimposed infection may also be contributory.

Presentation

- The clinical features are diverse, depending on the extent of disease and laterality.
- Patients may be asymptomatic or present with hypertension, polyuria, or renal failure.

Macroscopy

- The kidney is small and shrunken, with hydronephrosis, diffuse calyceal dilation, blunting of papillae, and cortical thinning.

Histopathology

- The renal parenchyma shows features of chronic pyelonephritis with extensive tubulo-interstitial fibrosis and tubular atrophy.
- Atrophic tubules are often dilated and filled with proteinaceous material ('thyroidization').
- The collecting system shows marked chronic inflammation with lymphoid aggregates and follicles.
- Residual glomeruli may show hypertrophy and secondary glomerulosclerosis.

► Note that the term 'chronic pyelonephritis' refers to a constellation of pathological features which are not specific to obstructive nephropathy and may be seen in other contexts such as reflux nephropathy. Distinction is usually possible, based on the clinical picture and pattern of scarring.

Prognosis

- Patients with significant bilateral disease are at risk of developing progressive renal impairment.

Further reading

Fogo AB, Kashgarian M (2012). *Diagnostic Atlas of Renal Pathology*, second edition. Philadelphia: Elsevier Saunders.

Jennette JC, Olson JL, Silva FG, D'Agati VD (2015). *Heptinstall's Pathology of the Kidney*, seventh edition. Philadelphia: Wolters Kluwer.

Kidney Disease: Improving Global Outcomes (KDIGO) Acute Kidney Injury Work Group. KDIGO Clinical Practice Guideline for Acute Kidney Injury. *Kidney Int Suppl* 2012;**2**:1–138.

Kidney Disease: Improving Global Outcomes (KDIGO) CKD Work Group. KDIGO 2012 Clinical Practice Guideline for the Evaluation and Management of Chronic Kidney Disease. *Kidney Int Suppl* 2013;**3**:1–15.

Sethi S, Haas M, Markowitz GS, *et al*. Mayo Clinic/Renal Pathology Society Consensus Report on Pathologic Classification, Diagnosis and Reporting of GN. *J Am Soc Nephrol* 2016;**27**:1278–87.

Tervaert TW, Mooyaart AL, Amann K, *et al*.; Renal Pathology Society. Pathologic classification of diabetic nephropathy. *J Am Soc Nephrol* 2010;**21**:556–63.

Chapter 11

Urological pathology

Genitourinary malformations

Renal agenesis

- Absence of one or both kidneys.
- Bilateral renal agenesis is uniformly fatal *in utero* or shortly after birth.
- Unilateral renal agenesis is usually asymptomatic, though it is often associated with other anomalies of the genital tract.

Renal fusion

- May involve some or all portions of each kidney.
- The most common form of renal fusion is the **horseshoe kidney**, in which the lower poles of each kidney are fused into a single renal mass in the midline.
- Patients are prone to developing obstruction.

Rotational anomalies

- Occur due to failure of the renal pelvis to rotate from an anterior position to a medial position.
- May occur in an otherwise normal kidney or accompany renal fusion or ectopia.

Renal dysplasia

- Refers to a kidney with abnormal development.
- Unilateral disease causes renal enlargement and a flank mass in infancy.
- Bilateral disease is usually fatal.
- Grossly, the kidney may be enlarged and cystic or small and solid.
- Histologically, the kidney contains abnormally formed nephron structures, often with cystic change. The presence of fetal cartilage is a characteristic feature.

Pelviureteric junction obstruction

- A common cause of congenital obstructive uropathy.
- Due to an intrinsic malformation of the smooth muscle of the wall of the outflow tract at that site.
- More common in boys.
- Usually unilateral, more common on the left.
- May present in childhood with abdominal pain.

Ureteral duplication

- Common anomaly in which the kidney has two separate renal pelves, accompanied by partial to complete reduplication of the ureter.
- When there is complete reduplication, the upper ureter typically enters the bladder posteriorly at the normal site of the ureteric orifice on the trigone of the bladder. The lower ureter usually enters the bladder laterally with a short intramural course, predisposing it to VUR.

Vesicoureteric reflux

- Failure of the vesicoureteric valve causes abnormal reflux of urine into the ureter when the bladder contracts.
- Predisposes to UTI in children. In severe cases, may be complicated by intra-renal reflux and renal scarring, a condition known as **reflux nephropathy** (➔ Reflux nephropathy, p. 206).

Posterior urethral valves

- Abnormal mucosal folds in the posterior prostatic urethra that cause obstructive uropathy.
- Their presence is usually indicated when bilateral hydronephrosis is detected on antenatal ultrasound.

Cryptorchidism

- Occurs when the testis fails to descend into its normal position in the scrotum.
- Mobilization of the testis and fixation in the scrotum (orchidopexy) should be performed by the age of 2y to preserve fertility.
- Cryptorchidism is important due to its association with a higher risk of testicular germ cell tumours (➔ Testicular germ cell tumours, pp. 234–7).

Hypospadias

- The most common anomaly of the penis.
- Refers to the abnormal opening of the urethral meatus on the undersurface of the penis.
- Usually an isolated defect, though the incidence of cryptorchidism appears to be higher in boys with hypospadias.

Urinary tract infection

Pathogens

- *Escherichia coli* is the main organism.
- *Staphylococcus saprophyticus* and *Proteus mirabilis* are other causes.

Epidemiology

- Extremely common.
- ~60% of women will have a UTI at some point in their life.

Transmission

- Ascending spread of endogenous gut bacteria into the urethra.
- The shorter urethra of women and its closer proximity to the anus are thought to be the main reason why females are more susceptible.

Risk factors

- Female gender, sexual intercourse, pregnancy, diabetes, catheterization, urinary tract obstruction or malformation.

Pathogenesis

- Pathogenic strains of *E. coli* have pili which allow them to bind to galactose-containing receptors on the surface of urothelial cells.
- Other important virulence factors include haemolysin which allows invasion of tissues and the K antigen which protects the organism from neutrophil phagocytosis.

Presentation

- Bladder infection (**cystitis**) causes frequency, urgency, dysuria, haematuria, and suprapubic pain.
- Ascending spread into the kidneys (**acute pyelonephritis**) causes a more severe illness with fever, rigors, vomiting, and loin pain.

► May present with acute confusion in the elderly.

Diagnosis

- Urinalysis showing leucocytes or nitrites is a useful quick screening test.
- The gold standard is microbiological culture of a correctly collected midstream urine specimen. A pure growth of $>10^5$ organisms/mL of urine is considered diagnostic.

Urinary tract obstruction

Definition

- Urinary tract obstruction (**obstructive uropathy**) is a blockage to the flow of urine at some point in the urinary tract (Fig. 11.1).

Epidemiology

- Seen mostly in older men (due to BPH) and children (due to congenital anomalies of the urinary tract).

Aetiology

- Urinary stones.
- Urothelial tumours.
- Extrinsic compression by abdominal/pelvic masses.
- Prostatic hyperplasia.
- Urinary tract malformations.
- Strictures.

Presentation

- Symptoms directly suggestive of obstruction (e.g. ureteric colic).
- Impaired renal function.
- Recurrent UTIs.

The precise clinical picture will depend on whether the obstruction is acute or chronic, whether it involves the upper or lower urinary tract, and whether it is unilateral or bilateral.

Macroscopy

- There is dilation of the urinary tract above the level of the obstruction, causing hydroureter and hydronephrosis.
- Renal damage is associated with loss of renal tissue and scarring.

Complications

- Obstruction increases the risk of infection, stone formation, and renal damage (**obstructive nephropathy**) (➔ Obstructive nephropathy, p. 207).

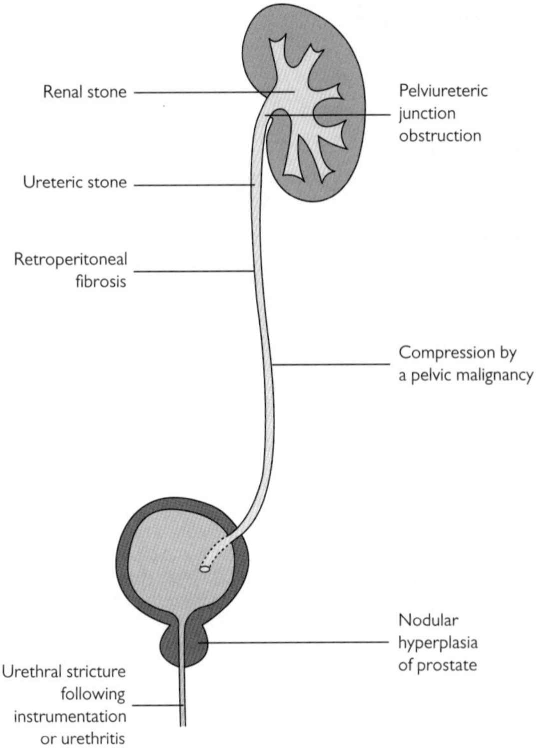

Fig. 11.1 Common causes of obstruction in the urinary tract.

Reproduced with permission from *Clinical Pathology* (Oxford Core Texts), Carton, James, Daly, Richard, and Ramani, Pramila, Oxford University Press (2006), p. 226, Figure 11.2.

Urinary calculi

Definition

- Crystal aggregates which form in the renal collecting ducts but may become deposited anywhere in the urinary tract.

Epidemiology

- Common, with a lifetime incidence of up to 15%.
- Males are at higher risk than females (3:1).

Stone types

- Calcium oxalate (75%).
- Magnesium ammonium phosphate (15%).
- Uric acid stones (5%).

Pathogenesis

- Calcium stones are associated with hypercalciuria. Most patients have absorptive hypercalciuria, in which too much calcium is absorbed from the gut. Others have renal hypercalciuria, in which calcium absorption from the proximal tubule is impaired. Only a minority have hypercalciuria due to hypercalcaemia which is usually due to primary hyperparathyroidism.
- Triple stones are formed largely as a result of infections with organisms such as *Proteus* that produce the enzyme urease which splits urea to ammonia. The ammonia alkalinizes the urine and promotes precipitation of magnesium ammonium phosphate salts. Triple stones can become very large and may form branching masses filling the entire renal pelvis and calyces (**staghorn calculus**).
- Uric acid stones may form in patients with hyperuricaemia, e.g. patients with gout and conditions of rapid cell turnover, e.g. leukaemias. However, most patients do not have hyperuricaemia nor increased urinary excretion of uric acid. It is thought that these patients have a tendency to make slightly acidic urine which is prone to forming uric acid stones.

Presentation

- Large stones tend to remain confined to the kidney. They may be asymptomatic or picked up following investigation of haematuria or recurrent UTIs.
- Smaller stones may pass into the ureter and become impacted, causing ureteric colic. Common points of impaction are the pelviureteric junction, the pelvic brim, and the vesicoureteric junction.

Complications

► Complete obstruction of the urinary tract requires urgent intervention to remove the stone.

►► Superadded infection in an obstructed urinary tract or any obstruction within the tract of a solitary kidney is a urological emergency requiring immediate intervention.

Cystic renal diseases

Adult (dominant) polycystic kidney disease

- The most common cystic renal disease, with a frequency of up to 1 in 500 and a leading cause of end-stage renal failure.
- 90% of cases are caused by an inherited mutation in the *PKD1* gene on chromosome 16.
- Defects in the function of the PKD1 protein lead to cystic change in renal tubules and loss of normal renal tissue.
- Most patients present in adulthood, usually aged 30–40, with hypertension, flank pain, and haematuria.
- Grossly, the kidneys are massively enlarged (weighing >2kg) and completely replaced with cysts.
- Histologically, both kidneys contain numerous cysts lined by flattened cuboidal epithelium with little intervening normal renal parenchyma.
- Extra-renal manifestations include liver cysts and berry aneurysms.

► Subarachnoid haemorrhage from a ruptured berry aneurysm can cause sudden death.

Infantile (recessive) polycystic kidney disease

- A rare, inherited condition causing bilateral polycystic kidneys and congenital hepatic fibrosis.
- Caused by mutations in the gene *PKHD1* on chromosome 6p which encodes a component of the cilia on collecting duct epithelial cells.
- Grossly, the kidneys are enlarged and contain numerous cysts.
- Histologically, the cysts are lined by flattened cuboidal epithelium.
- Severe cases cause neonatal death from pulmonary hypoplasia.
- Children with less severe renal disease who survive suffer from congenital hepatic fibrosis and complications of portal hypertension.

Medullary cystic disease

- Congenital presence of numerous cysts at the corticomedullary junction which vary in size from <1mm to 2cm.
- The childhood disease (juvenile nephronophthisis) is autosomal recessive and associated with mutations in the genes *NPH1, 2*, or *3*.
- The adult disease (uraemic medullary cystic disease) is autosomal dominant and associated with mutations in the genes *MCDK1* or *2*.

Medullary sponge kidney

- Associated with an irregular enlargement of the collecting ducts, leading to microcystic change of the renal medullae and papillae with calcification.
- The condition usually presents in adult life with recurrent infections.

Acquired renal cystic disease

- Development of multiple bilateral cortical and medullary cysts in patients with end-stage kidneys on dialysis.
- An important additional feature is the increased occurrence of renal tumours which are often papillary in type and may be multiple.

Benign renal tumours

Papillary adenoma

- Benign unencapsulated renal epithelial tumour with a papillary or tubulopapillary architecture and size <15mm.
- Frequently found incidentally in nephrectomy specimens or at autopsy.
- Macroscopically, they are well-circumscribed, unencapsulated cortical nodules which measure <15mm.
- Histologically, they are composed of bland epithelial cells growing in papillary or tubulopapillary patterns.

Oncocytoma

- Benign oncocytic renal epithelial tumour which is usually discovered incidentally in adults.
- Most cases are sporadic, but some are associated with genetic syndromes (e.g. Birt–Hogg–Dubé syndrome).
- Macroscopically, they are well-circumscribed tumours with a mahogany brown colour, often with central scarring.
- Histologically, they are characterized by cells with abundant granular eosinophilic cytoplasm, growing in nests within an oedematous stroma.
- Oncocytomas are benign tumours with no capacity for metastatic spread. Large tumours are nevertheless often excised.
- Infiltration of tumour cells into perinephric fat may be seen and this has no adverse consequence.

Angiomyolipoma

- Benign mesenchymal tumour of the kidney composed of variable amounts of fat, smooth muscle, and thick-walled blood vessels.
- Most occur sporadically in adults, but a small proportion is associated with tuberous sclerosis. These are more likely to be multiple and bilateral.
- Although most are picked up incidentally, occasionally they present with flank pain due to haemorrhage into the tumour.
- Macroscopically, they are lobulated renal masses which may appear rather yellow if their fat content is high.
- Histologically, they are composed of a mixture of adipose tissue, smooth muscle bundles, and thick-walled blood vessels in variable amounts.

Cystic nephroma

- Benign cystic renal tumour which shows a marked predilection for women.
- Macroscopically, they are encapsulated multicystic lesions without a solid component.
- Microscopically, the cysts are lined by a single layer of attenuated cuboidal epithelial cells.
- The septa may show cellular areas resembling ovarian stroma, and interestingly the nuclei of the cells within the septa often react with antibodies to oestrogen and progesterone receptors.

Leiomyoma

- Benign smooth muscle tumours which usually arise from the renal capsule.
- Most occur in adults as incidental small, well-circumscribed, capsular tumours.
- Histologically, they show bundles of bland smooth muscle cells.

Renomedullary interstitial cell tumour

- Common benign renal tumours which are often encountered incidentally in kidneys at autopsy.
- Macroscopically, they are small (1–5mm) white nodules centred on a medullary pyramid.
- Histologically, they are composed of small stellate or polygonal cells set in a loose stroma. Entrapped tubules may be found at the edge of the lesion.

Renal cell carcinoma

Definition

- A malignant epithelial tumour arising in the kidney.

Epidemiology

- Accounts for ~2% of all cancers worldwide.
- More common in developed countries, with an average incidence of ~10 per 100 000 in men and 3 per 100 000 in women.

Aetiology

- Recognized risk factors include smoking, hypertension, obesity, environmental chemicals, and long-term dialysis.
- Some genetic syndromes are associated with renal cell carcinoma (RCC), e.g. von Hippel–Lindau and tuberous sclerosis.

Presentation

- About half of all cases present with painless haematuria.
- Most of the remainder is picked up incidentally on imaging.
- A small proportion presents with metastatic disease.

Subtypes

- 70% clear cell RCC.
- 15% papillary RCC.
- 5% chromophobe RCC.
- A number of rare subtypes make up the remainder of cases.

Clear cell renal cell carcinoma

- Macroscopically, heterogenous tumours with golden yellow and haemorrhagic areas (Fig. 11.2).
- Histologically composed of epithelial cells with clear or eosinophilic cytoplasm, set within a delicate vascular network.
- Immunohistochemically positive for AE1/AE3, EMA, CD10, vimentin, Pax8, RCC, and CAIX, and negative for CK7 and CD117.
- Genetically demonstrates losses at chromosome 3p.

Papillary renal cell carcinoma

- Macroscopically, well-circumscribed, friable tumours with a surrounding fibrous pseudocapsule.
- Histologically composed of epithelial cells arranged in a papillary or tubulopapillary growth pattern with a size of >5mm.
- Immunohistochemically positive for AE1/AE3, CK7, Pax8, and racemase.
- Genetically shows trisomy of chromosomes 7 and 17 and loss of chromosome Y in men.

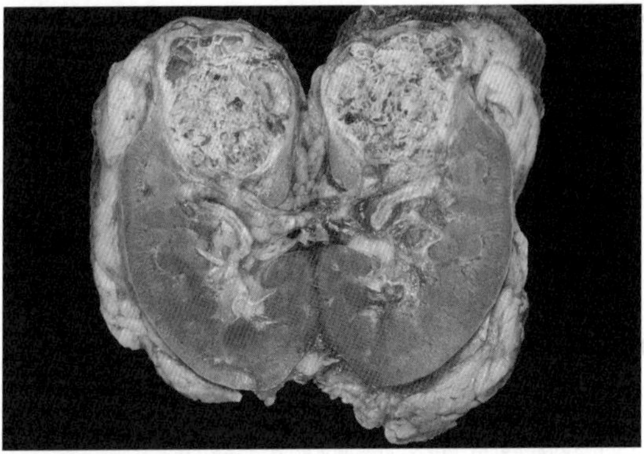

Fig. 11.2 This patient presented with macroscopic haematuria and was found to have a solid renal mass on CT imaging. A nephrectomy was performed and sent to pathology. The kidney has been sliced open by the pathologist to reveal a large tumour in the upper pole of the kidney. Subsequent microscopic examination of samples of the tumour revealed this to be a clear cell renal cell carcinoma (see Plate 19).

Reproduced with permission from *Clinical Pathology* (Oxford Core Texts), Carton, James, Daly, Richard, and Ramani, Pramila, Oxford University Press (2006), p.233, Figure 11.6.

Chromophobe renal cell carcinoma

- Macroscopically, well-circumscribed, solid light brown tumours.
- Histologically composed of sheets of large, round epithelial cells with distinct cell borders and finely reticulated cytoplasm. The vasculature within the tumour is thick-walled.
- Immunohistochemically positive for CK7, Pax8, E-cadherin, and CD117, and negative for CAIX.
- Genetically shows extensive chromosomal losses.

Prognosis

- Overall 5-year survival rate is ~60%.
- Stage and grade are the most important prognostic factors.
- The recommended grading system for clear cell RCC and papillary RCC is the ISUP (International Society of Urologic Pathologists) nucleolar grade. Grade 1 has the best prognosis, and grade 4 the worst. Chromophobe RCC is not graded.
- The Leibovich risk model may also be used for clear cell RCC to predict the likelihood of progression. Tumour stage, size, grade, and necrosis are each scored to give a maximum possible total of 11: 0–2 = low risk, 3–5 = intermediate risk, 6 or more = high risk.

ISUP nucleolar grading system for clear cell and papillary RCC

Grade 1: nucleoli are inconspicuous or absent at high-power magnification.

Grade 2: nucleoli are clearly visible at high-power magnification but are not prominent.

Grade 3: nucleoli are prominent and are easily visualized at low-power magnification.

Grade 4: presence of tumour giant cells and/or marked pleomorphism.

TNM 7 pathological staging of renal cell carcinomas

Primary tumour (T)

pT1a: tumour ≤4cm, limited to the kidney.
pT1b: tumour >4cm, but ≤7cm, limited to the kidney.
pT2a: tumour >7cm, but ≤10cm, limited to the kidney.
pT2b: tumour >10cm, limited to the kidney.
pT3a: tumour extends into perinephric fat or renal veins.
pT3b: tumour extends into the vena cava below the diaphragm.
pT3c: tumour extends into the vena cava above the diaphragm.
pT4: tumour directly invades the adrenal gland or beyond the Gerota fascia.

Regional lymph nodes (N)

pN0: no regional lymph node metastasis.
pN1: metastasis in regional lymph nodes.

Childhood renal tumours

Nephroblastoma (Wilms' tumour)

- A malignant childhood renal neoplasm.
- Second most common childhood malignancy, with an incidence of ~1 in 8000.
- Most children present aged 2–5 years old with an abdominal mass.
- Macroscopically, they are well-demarcated tumours with a grey or tan colour.
- Histologically, most nephroblastomas contain a mixture of undifferentiated small, round, blue cells (blastema), with areas of more differentiated epithelial and stromal components (so-called 'triphasic' tumours).
- Most nephroblastomas are of low stage with a favourable histology and have an excellent prognosis with treatment.
- ~5% of cases show unfavourable histology, characterized by nuclear anaplasia or the presence of multipolar mitotic figures; these cases are associated with an adverse outcome.

Clear cell sarcoma

- A rare childhood renal sarcoma with a marked propensity to metastasize to bone.
- Most children present between 1 and 2y of age.
- Macroscopically, they are typically large tumours centred on the renal medulla.
- Histologically, the classical pattern is of nests or cords of cells separated by fibrovascular septae.

Rhabdoid tumour

- A rare, highly malignant renal tumour of young children.
- Most present around 1y of age with either haematuria or symptoms of disseminated disease.
- Macroscopically, tumours are large and infiltrative with necrosis.
- Histologically, the malignant cells have vesicular chromatin, prominent cherry red nucleoli, and hyaline pink intracytoplasmic inclusions. Extensive vascular invasion is usually evident.
- Prognosis is extremely poor, with mortality rates in excess of 80% within 2y of diagnosis.

Congenital mesoblastic nephroma

- A low-grade fibroblastic renal sarcoma arising in young children.
- May be diagnosed on antenatal ultrasound or present within the first year of life with an abdominal mass.
- Macroscopically, the tumour is centred on the renal sinus and has either a firm, whorled appearance or a softer cystic cut surface.
- Histologically, two types are recognized: a 'classic' type composed of fascicles of bland spindled cells and a 'cellular' type composed of sheets of densely packed rounder cells.
- Prognosis is generally excellent when the tumour is completely excised by nephrectomy.

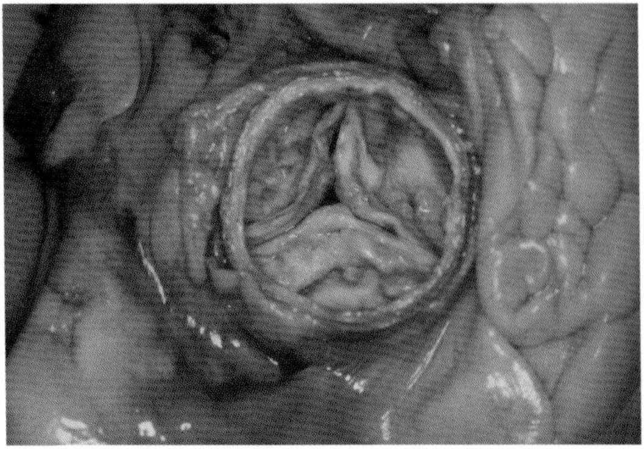

Plate 1 Calcific aortic stenosis. This aortic valve is studded with nodules of calcium causing significant narrowing of the valve orifice.

Reproduced with permission from *Clinical Pathology* (Oxford Core Texts), Carton, James, Daly, Richard, and Ramani, Pramila, Oxford University Press (2006), p.96, Figure 6.18.

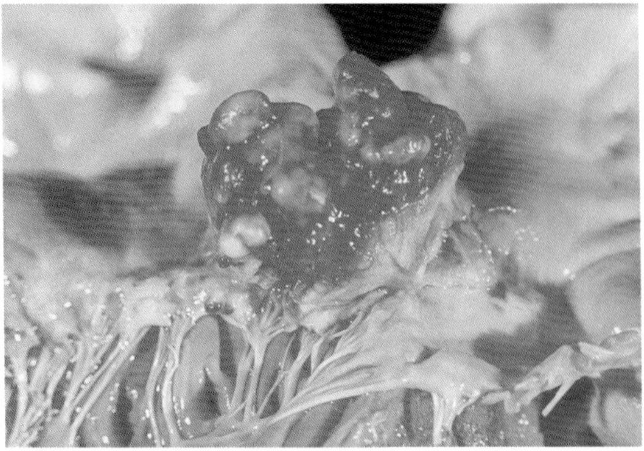

Plate 2 Close-up of a vegetation of infective endocarditis. This is on the mitral valve; you can see the chordae tendinae attached to the valve leaflets.

Reproduced with permission from *Clinical Pathology* (Oxford Core Texts), Carton, James, Daly, Richard, and Ramani, Pramila, Oxford University Press (2006), p.97, Figure 6.19.

Plate 3 A central lung carcinoma. Note how the lung tissue distal to the tumour shows flecks of yellow consolidation due to an obstructive pneumonia. The tumour was found to be a squamous cell carcinoma when examined microscopically.

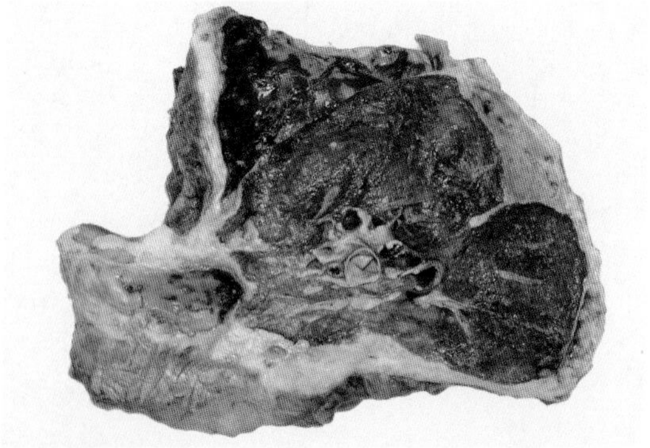

Plate 4 Typical macroscopic appearance of malignant mesothelioma. Note how the tumour encases and compresses the lung.

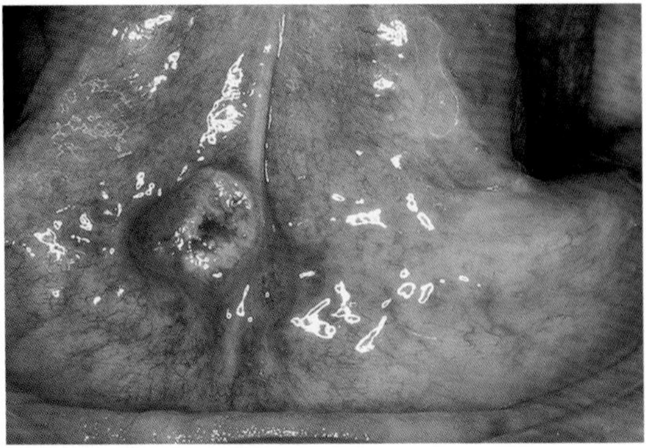

Plate 5 Early squamous cell carcinoma of the oral cavity, presenting as a persistent ulcerated lesion on the undersurface of the tongue.

Reproduced with permission from *Clinical Pathology* (Oxford Core Texts), Carton, James, Daly, Richard, and Ramani, Pramila, Oxford University Press (2006), p.452, Figure 19.4.

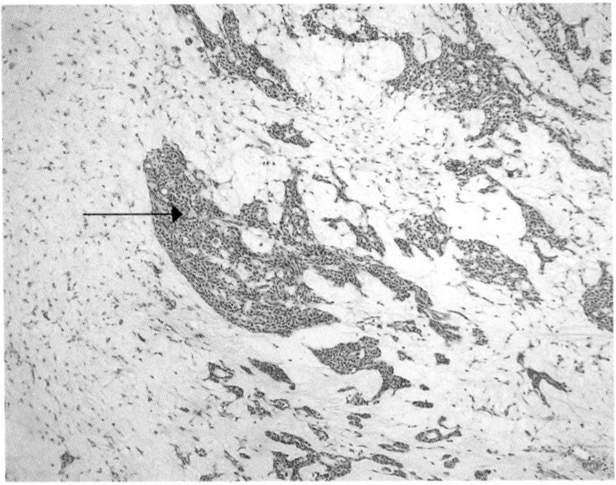

Plate 6 Pleomorphic adenoma. Typical microscopic appearance of a pleomorphic adenoma with an intermingling of epithelial elements (arrow) set within a mesenchymal component.

Reproduced with permission from *Clinical Pathology* (Oxford Core Texts), Carton, James, Daly, Richard, and Ramani, Pramila, Oxford University Press (2006), p.456, Figure 19.7.

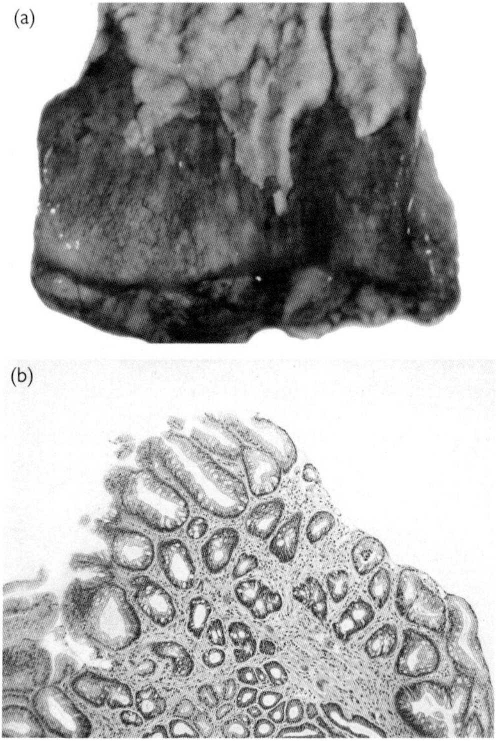

Plate 7 Barrett's oesophagus. (a) This segment from the lower oesophagus shows the white keratinized squamous epithelium at the top. The red area at the bottom represents an area of Barrett's oesophagus. (b) An oesophageal biopsy taken from an area of endoscopic Barrett's oesophagus, confirming the presence of glandular epithelium.

Reproduced with permission from *Clinical Pathology* (Oxford Core Texts), Carton, James, Daly, Richard, and Ramani, Pramila, Oxford University Press (2006), p.139, Figure 8.1.

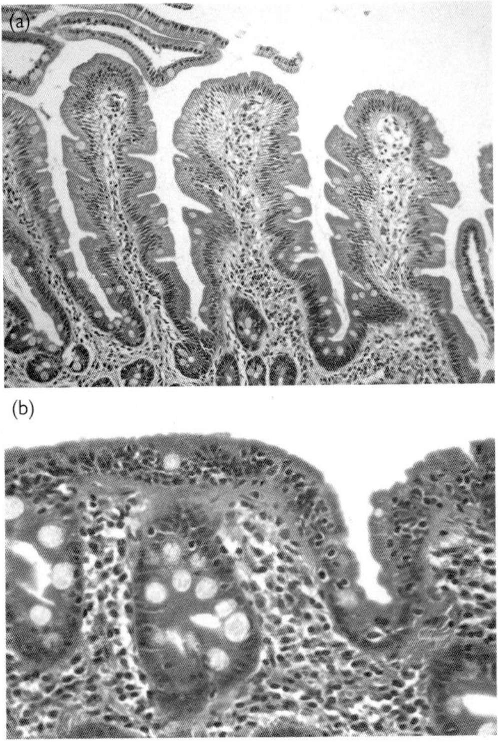

Plate 8 (a) Normal duodenal mucosa. The villi have a normal height and shape, and there is no increase in intraepithelial lymphocytes. (b) Duodenal biopsy from a patient with gluten-sensitive enteropathy. The villi have completely disappeared and the surface epithelium contains many intraepithelial lymphocytes.

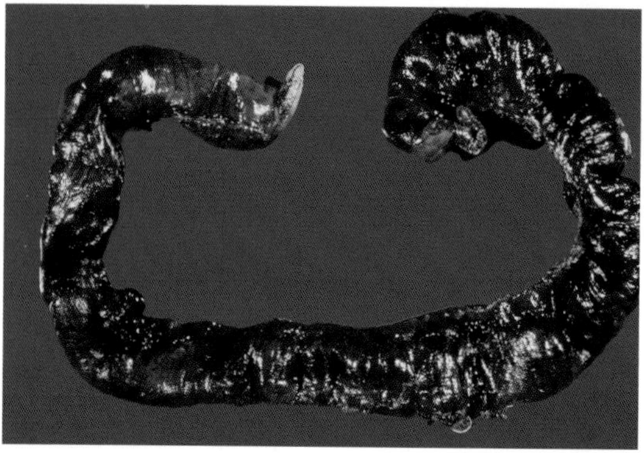

Plate 9 Small bowel infarction. Typical appearance of an infarcted segment of the small bowel. The dark colour is due to the intense congestion and haemorrhage within the intestine as a result of blockage to venous outflow.

Reproduced with permission from *Clinical Pathology* (Oxford Core Texts), Carton, James, Daly, Richard, and Ramani, Pramila, Oxford University Press (2006)), p.159, Figure 8.11.

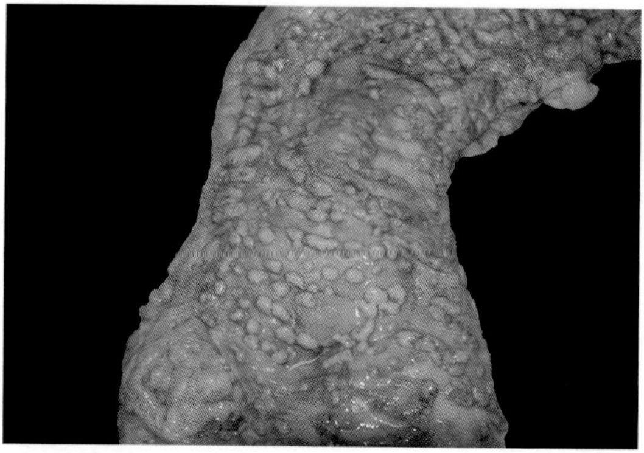

Plate 10 *Clostridium difficile* colitis. This is a freshly opened colon from a patient with profuse diarrhoea, following broad-spectrum antibiotic treatment. Note the large number of cream-coloured plaques studded across the mucosal surface, representing collections of neutrophils, fibrin, and cell debris.

Reproduced with permission from *Clinical Pathology* (Oxford Core Texts), Carton, James, Daly, Richard, and Ramani, Pramila, Oxford University Press (2006), p. 163, Figure 8.14.

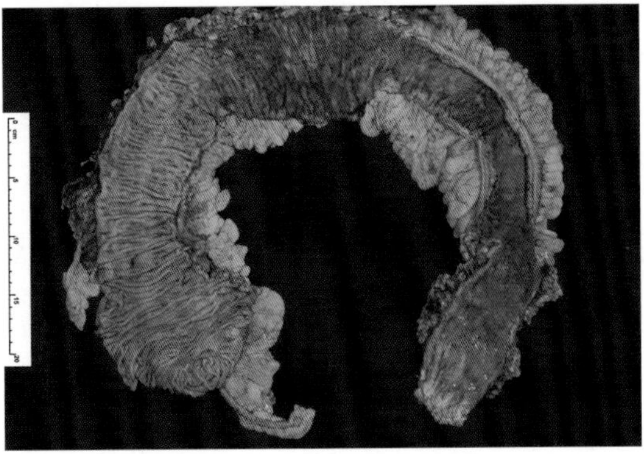

Plate 11 Ulcerative colitis. This is a colectomy specimen from a patient with ulcerative colitis. The right colon is on the left of the picture (note the appendix), and the left colon and rectum are on the right side of the picture. The inflamed mucosa, which looks red, begins at the rectum and continuously affects the left colon until the transverse colon where there is a sharp transition into normal mucosa.

Reproduced with permission from *Clinical Pathology* (Oxford Core Texts), Carton, James, Daly, Richard, and Ramani, Pramila, Oxford University Press (2006), p. 163, Figure 8.15.

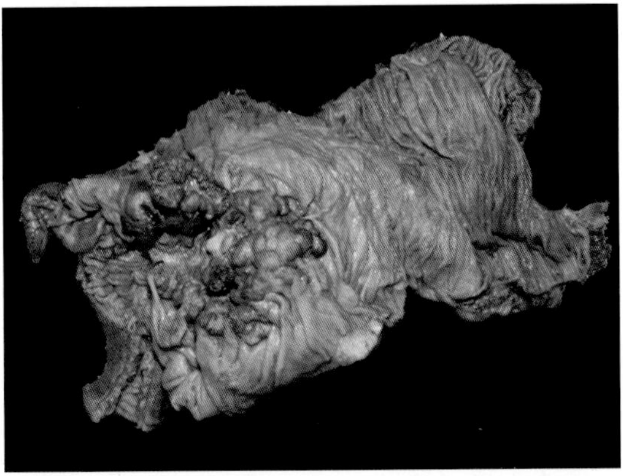

Plate 12 Adenocarcinoma of the caecum. This is a right hemicolectomy specimen, in which a small piece of the terminal ileum, the caecum, the appendix, and the ascending colon have been removed. A large tumour is seen in the caecum, which was confirmed on microscopy to be an adenocarcinoma. This tumour was picked up at colonoscopy performed because the patient was found to have an unexplained iron deficiency anaemia.

Reproduced with permission from *Clinical Pathology* (Oxford Core Texts), Carton, James, Daly, Richard, and Ramani, Pramila, Oxford University Press (2006), p.168, figure 8.20.

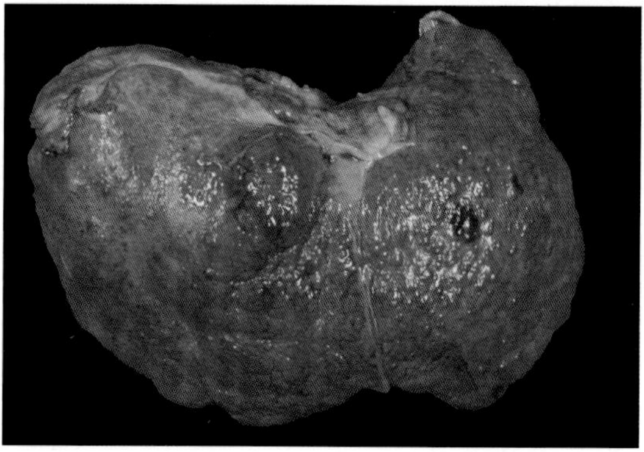

Plate 13 The cirrhotic liver. This liver was removed at post-mortem from a patient known to abuse alcohol. The whole of the liver is studded with nodules. Microscopically, the liver showed nodules of regenerating hepatocytes separated by dense bands of fibrosis, confirming established cirrhosis.

Reproduced with permission from *Clinical Pathology* (Oxford Core Texts), Carton, James, Daly, Richard, and Ramani, Pramila, Oxford University Press (2006), p. 168, Figure 9.9.

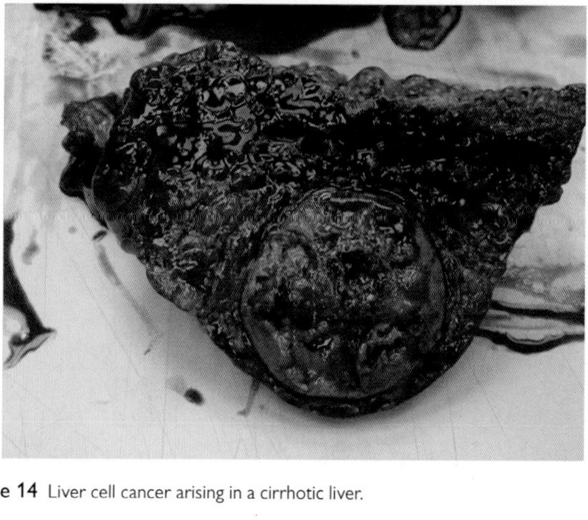

Plate 14 Liver cell cancer arising in a cirrhotic liver.

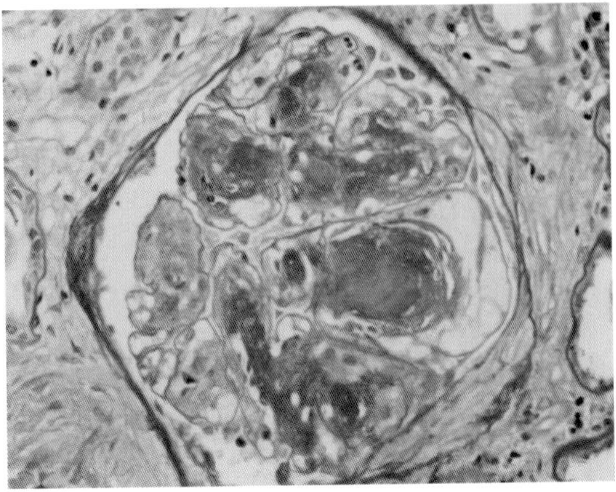

Plate 15 Nodular diabetic glomerulosclerosis (periodic acid–Schiff stain).

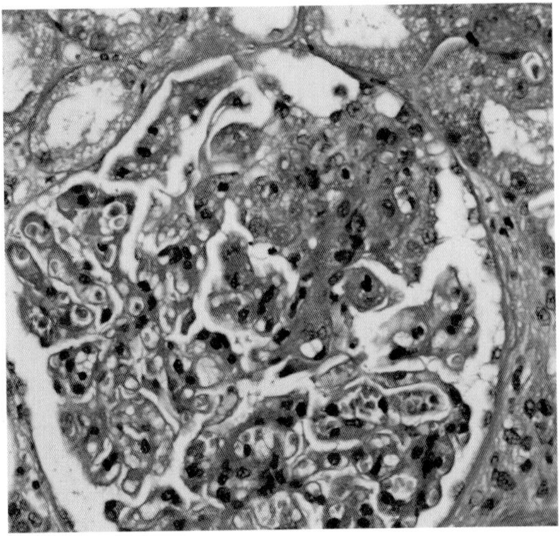

Plate 16 Focal and segmental glomerulosclerosis.

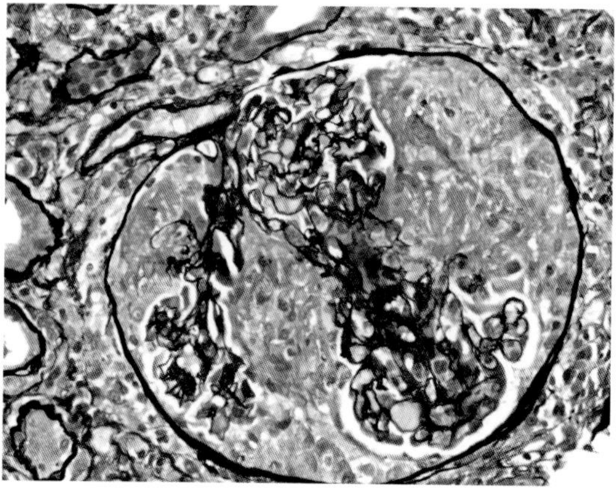

Plate 17 Segmental glomerular necrosis with cellular crescent (Jones silver stain).

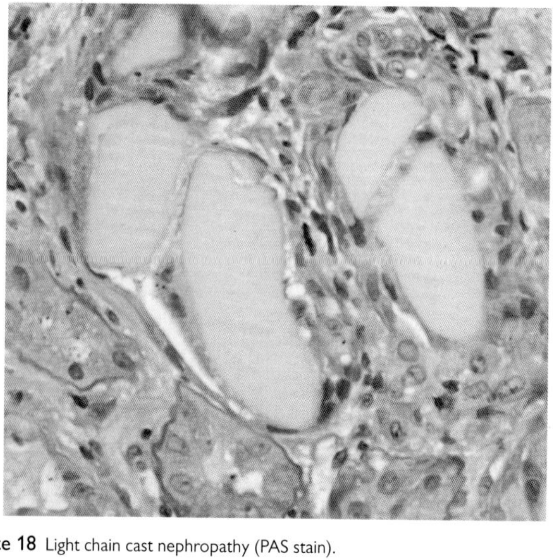

Plate 18 Light chain cast nephropathy (PAS stain).

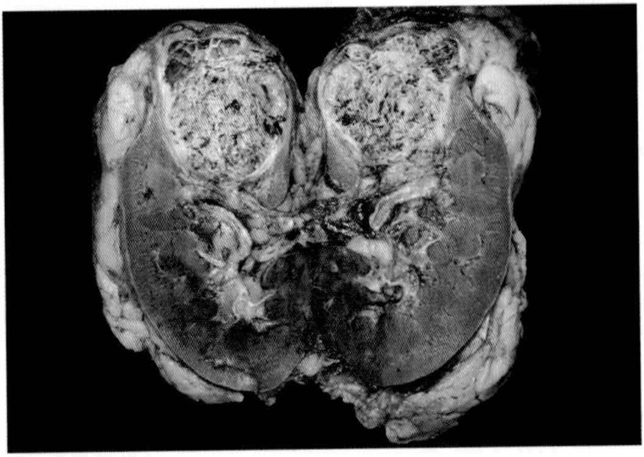

Plate 19 This patient presented with macroscopic haematuria and was found to have a solid renal mass on CT imaging. Anephrectomy was performed and sent to pathology. The kidney has been sliced open by the pathologist to reveal a large tumour in the upper pole of the kidney. Subsequent microscopic examination of samples of the tumour revealed this to be a clear cell renal cell carcinoma.

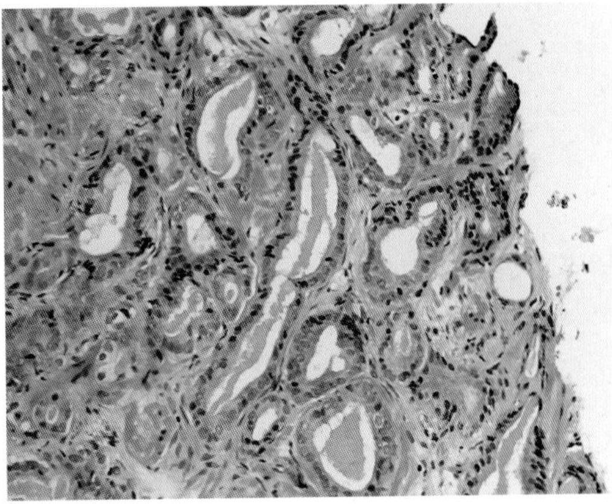

Plate 20 Gleason pattern 3 prostate adenocarcinoma composed of individual well-formed glandular acini.

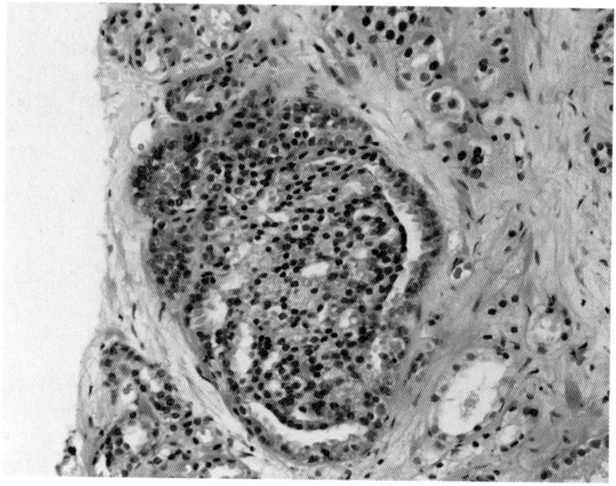

Plate 21 Gleason pattern 4 prostate adenocarcinoma showing a fused cribriform unit.

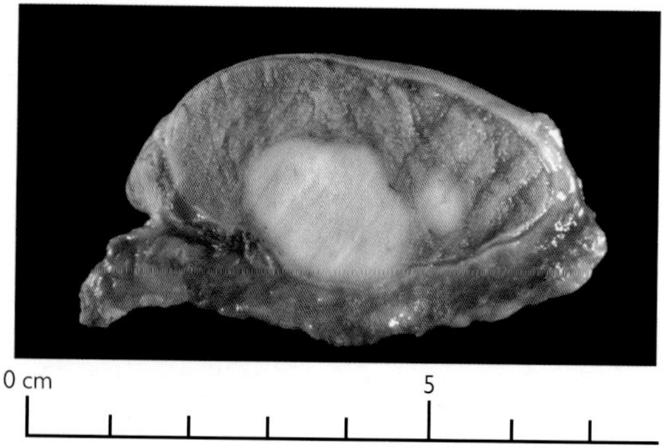

Plate 22 This is a testis from a young man who presented with an enlarging testicular lump. Following an ultrasound scan which was suspicious for a neoplasm, he underwent orchidectomy. The testis has been sliced in the pathology department, revealing this white solid mass in the testis. This appearance is typical of a seminoma, and microscopic examination confirmed this.

Reproduced with permission from *Clinical Pathology* (Oxford Core Texts), Carton, James, Daly, Richard, and Ramani, Pramila, Oxford University Press (2006), p. 244, Figure 11.14.

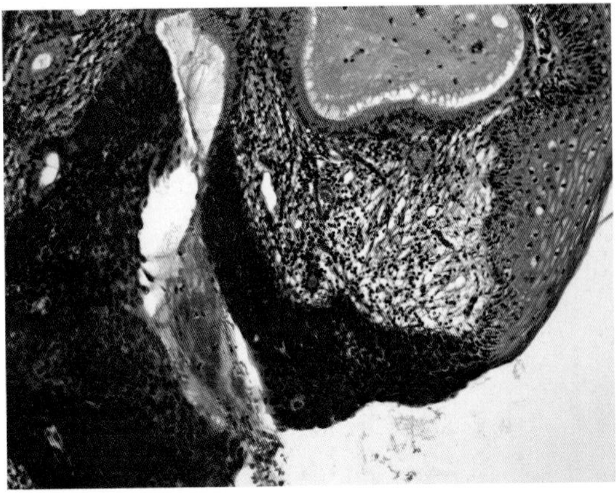

Plate 23 CIN 3 extending into an endocervical crypt.

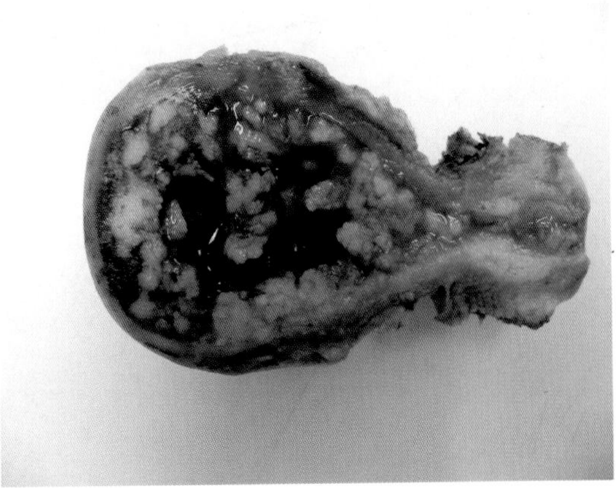

Plate 24 Endometrial carcinoma filling the uterine cavity.

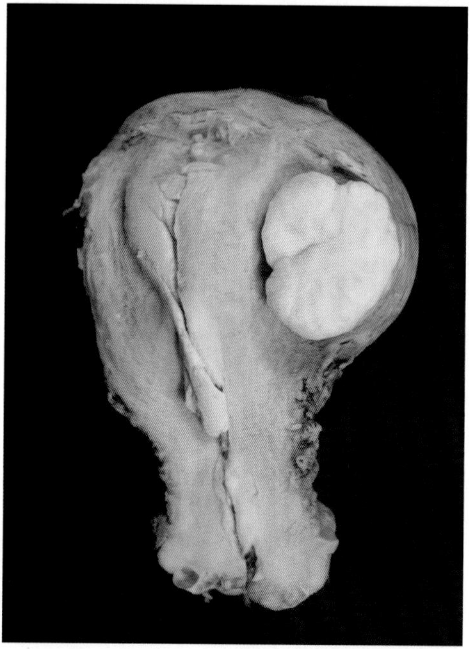

Plate 25 Leiomyoma. This uterus was removed due to severe menorrhagia. On bisecting the uterus, a well-circumscribed white mass is seen in the myometrium which bulges from the cut surface. This is the typical macroscopic appearance of a leiomyoma (fibroid) and this was confirmed on microscopic examination.

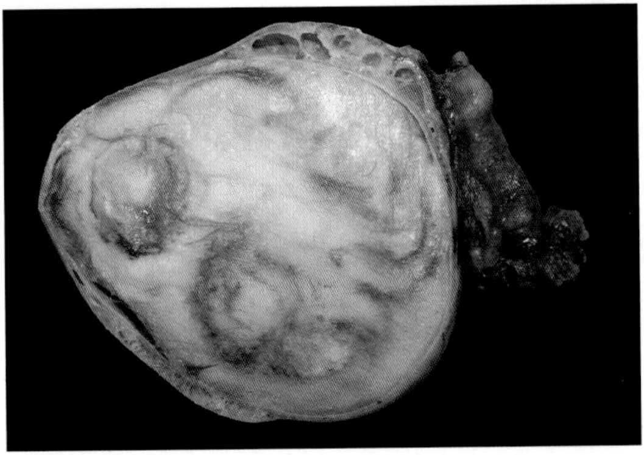

Plate 26 Mature cystic teratoma. Typical appearance of a mature cystic teratoma (dermoid cyst) filled with greasy yellow material and hair.

Reproduced with permission from *Clinical Pathology* (Oxford Core Texts), Carton, James, Daly, Richard, and Ramani, Pramila, Oxford University Press (2006), p. 278, Figure 12.17.

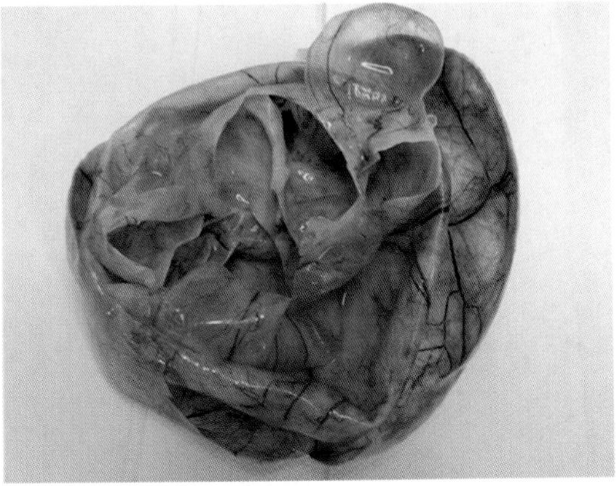

Plate 27 Benign mucinous cystadenoma of the ovary.

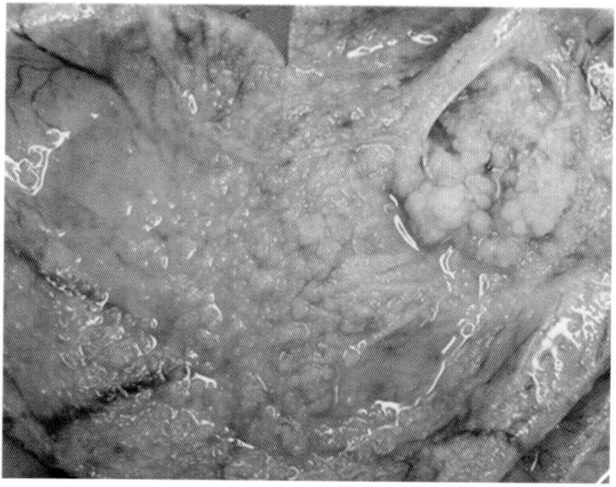

Plate 28 Borderline serous tumour of the ovary.

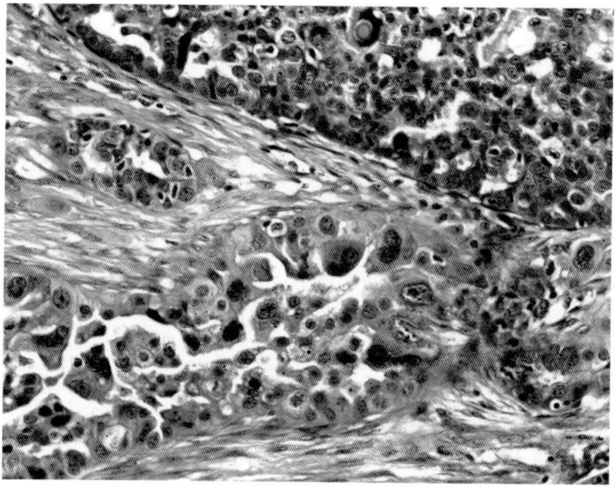

Plate 29 High-grade serous carcinoma of the ovary.

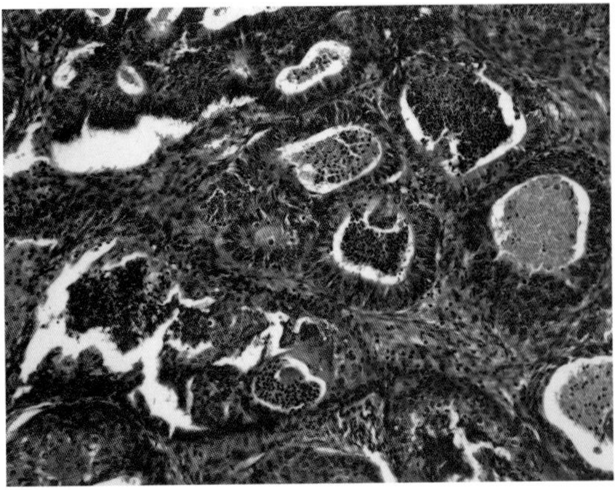

Plate 30 Endometrioid carcinoma of the ovary.

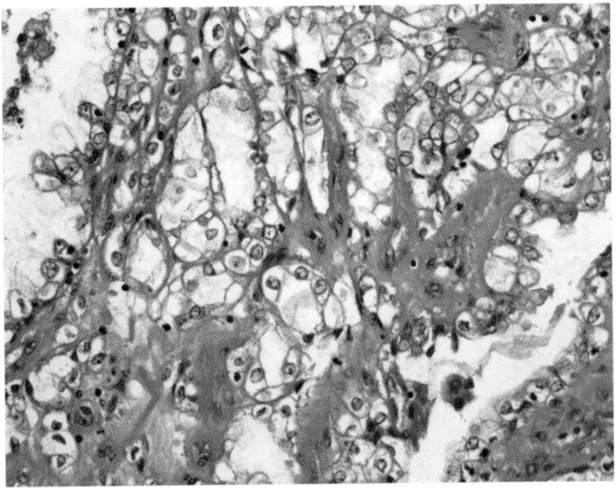

Plate 31 Clear cell carcinoma of the ovary.

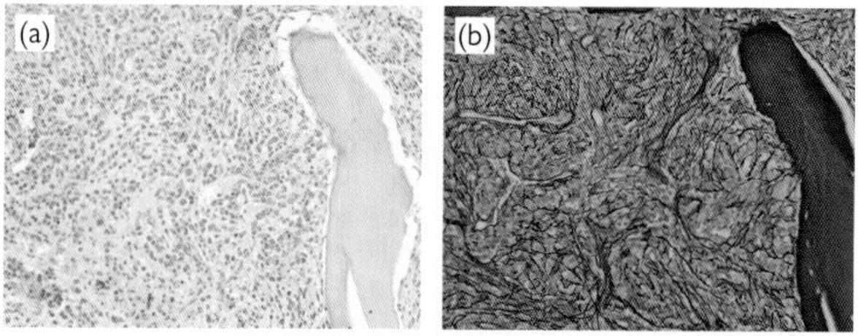

Plate 32 Acute myeloid leukaemia with myelofibrosis. (a) Bone marrow trephine showing sheets of myeloid blasts (haematoxylin and eosin stain). (b) Diffuse and dense increase in reticulin fibres (reticulin stain).

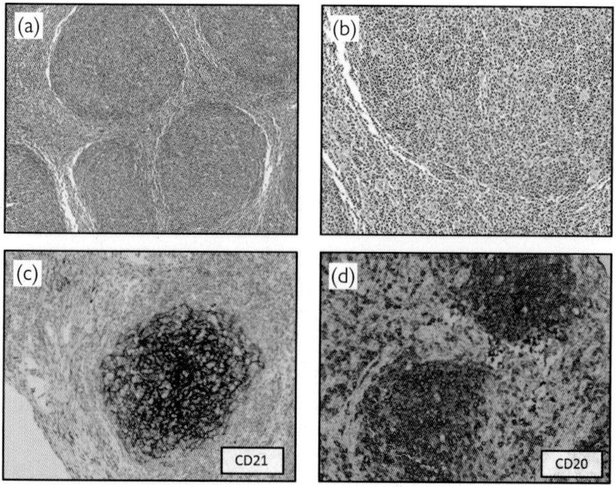

Plate 33 Follicular lymphoma. (a, b) Lymphoma characterized by a nodular pattern. The nodules are well defined and lack mantle areas (haematoxylin and eosin). (c) Follicular pattern highlighted with CD21 (staining follicular dendritic cells). (d) The cells in the follicle centres are CD20-positive (B-cell marker).

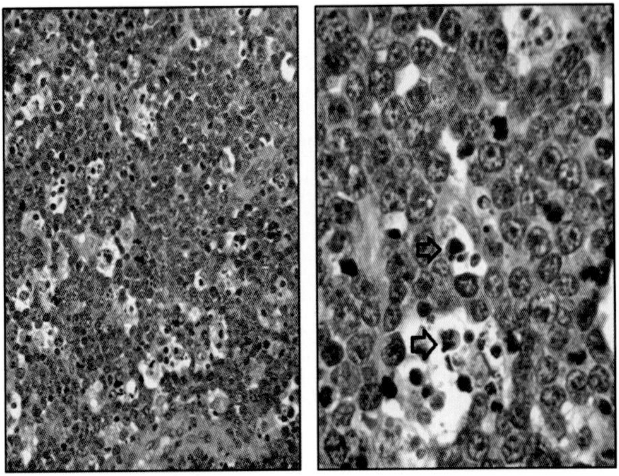

Plate 34 Burkitt's lymphoma. Lymphoma characterized by monomorphic medium-sized lymphoid cells with a 'starry sky' pattern. Detail of tingible body macrophages containing apoptotic tumour cells (arrows).

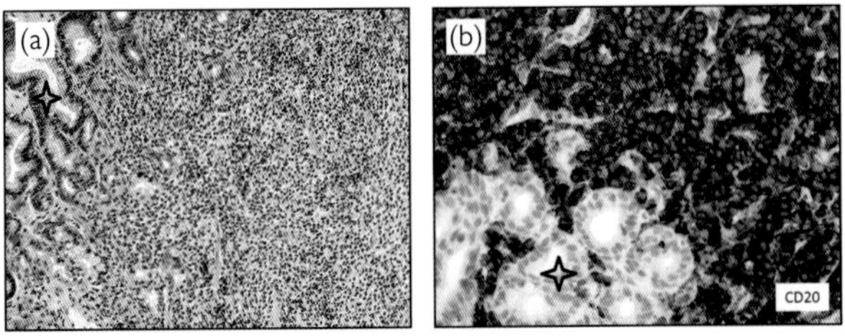

Plate 35 Extranodal marginal zone lymphoma involving the stomach. (a) Gastric mucosa (asterisk indicates gastric glands) infiltrated by a lymphoma composed of small centrocyte-like lymphocytes (haematoxylin and eosin). (b) The lymphoma cells are CD20 diffuse-positive.

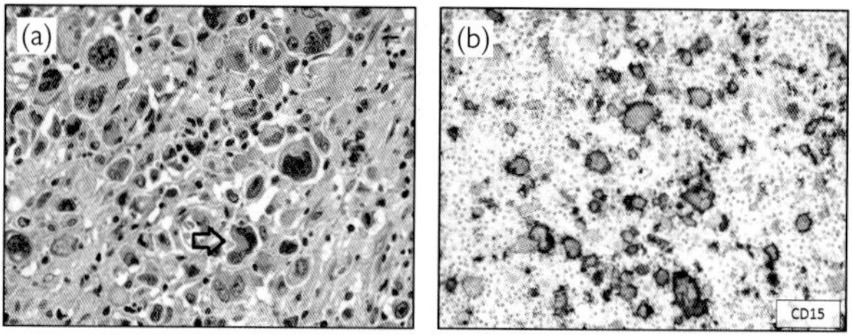

Plate 36 Classical Hodgkin's lymphoma. (a) Mononuclear Hodgkin cells and large atypical Reed–Sternberg cells (arrow), multinucleated with prominent nucleoli. (b) The cells are positive with CD15 (membrane staining).

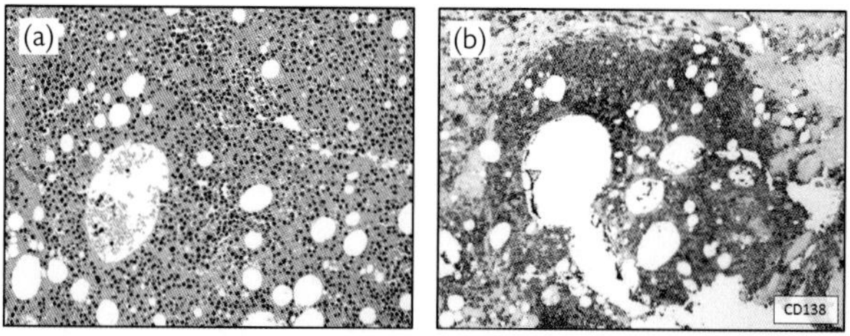

Plate 37 Multiple myeloma. (a) Bone marrow trephine biopsy infiltrated by sheets of plasma cells. The plasma cells have a round eccentric nucleus and abundant basophilic cytoplasm (haematoxylin and eosin staining). (b) The plasma cells are diffusely and strongly positive with CD138 (plasma cell marker).

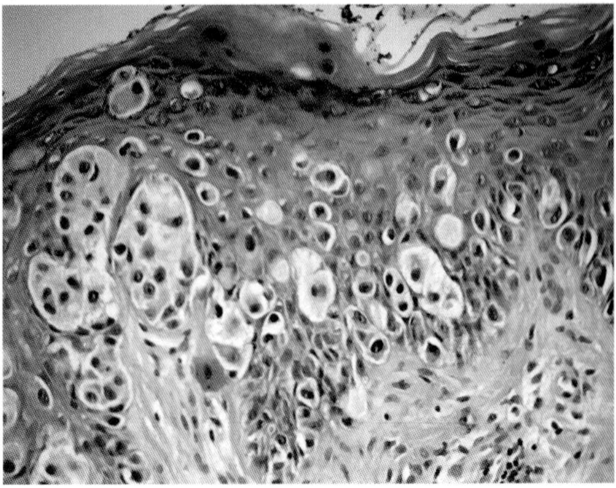

Plate 38 Superficial spreading malignant melanoma *in situ* showing severely atypical melanocytes proliferating in the epidermis with cells present at all levels of the epidermis (pagetoid spread).

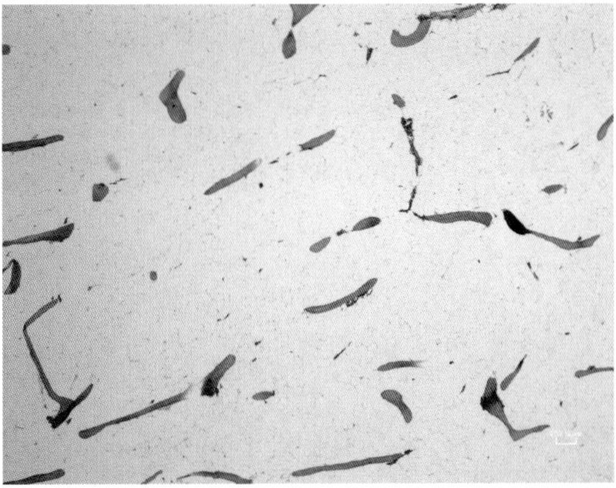

Plate 39 Osteoporosis characterized by thin, disconnected trabeculae of lamellar bone within fatty marrow.

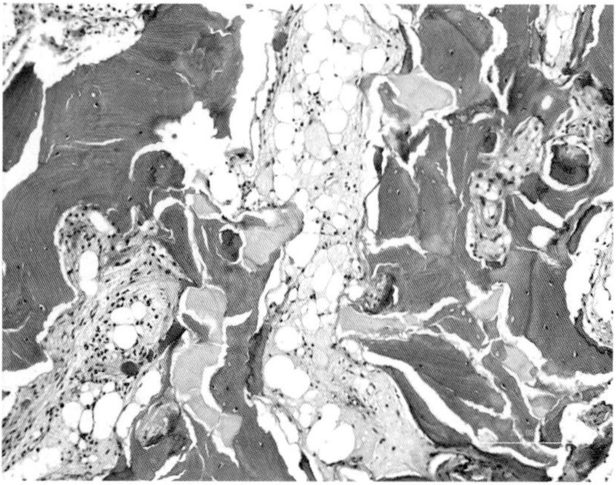

Plate 40 Osteopetrosis is characterized by a distorted bony architecture, with thick trabecular and compact bone largely obliterating the bone marrow space.

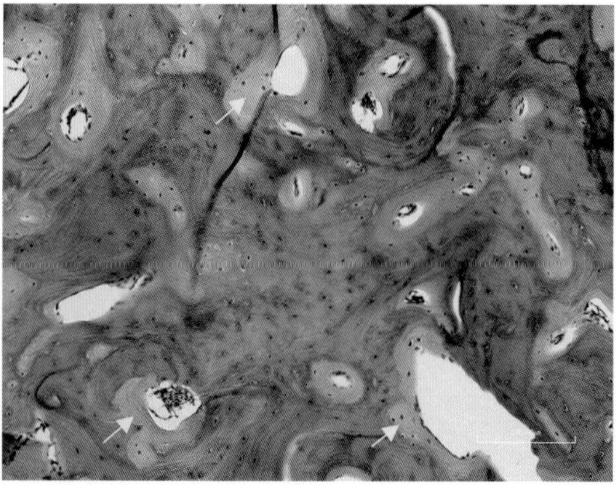

Plate 41 Osteomalacia, as seen in compact bone, showing mature viable bone covered by a thick layer of unmineralized matrix (osteoid)—pale pink (arrows). Similar features are seen in rickets. Haematoxylin and eosin section.

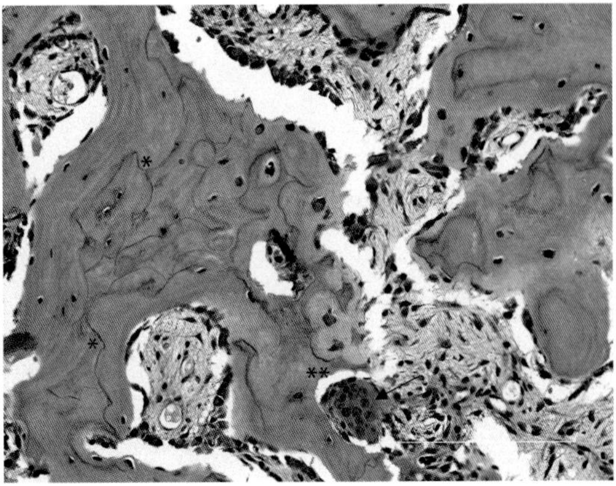

Plate 42 Paget's disease. Diffuse remodelled cancellous bone with prominent cement lines* and deep Howship's lacunae** which, in areas, are associated with osteoclasts, containing very large numbers of nuclei (arrow).

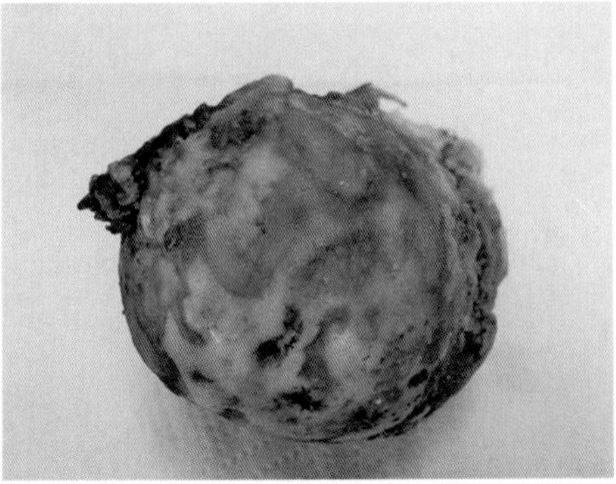

Plate 43 Osteoarthritis. Femoral head shows an eroded and irregular articular surface.

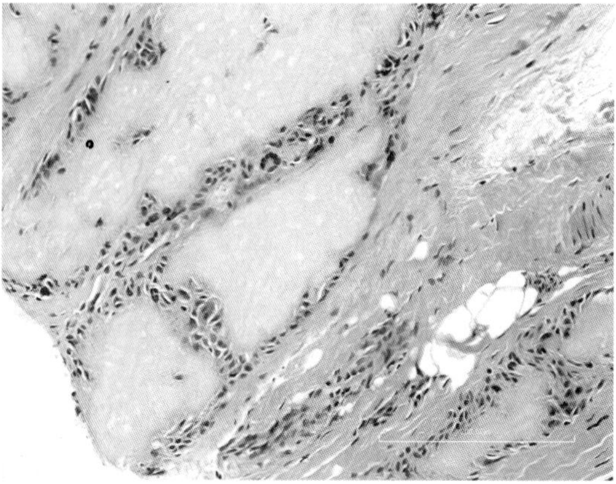

Plate 44 Microscopic features of gout showing amorphous eosinophilic deposits surrounded by epithelioid macrophages and multinucleated giant cells. Haematoxylin and eosin section.

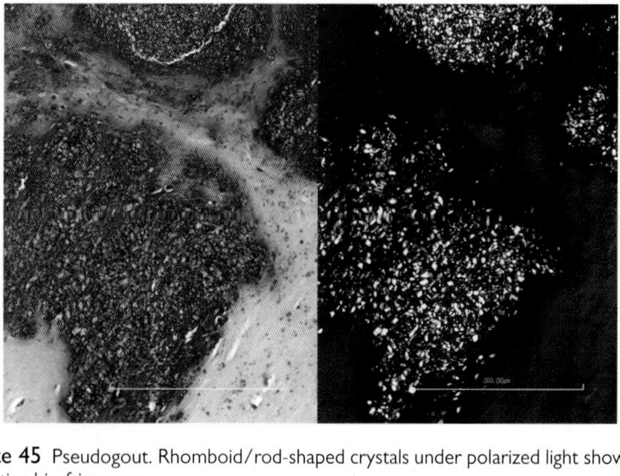

Plate 45 Pseudogout. Rhomboid/rod-shaped crystals under polarized light showing positive birefringence.

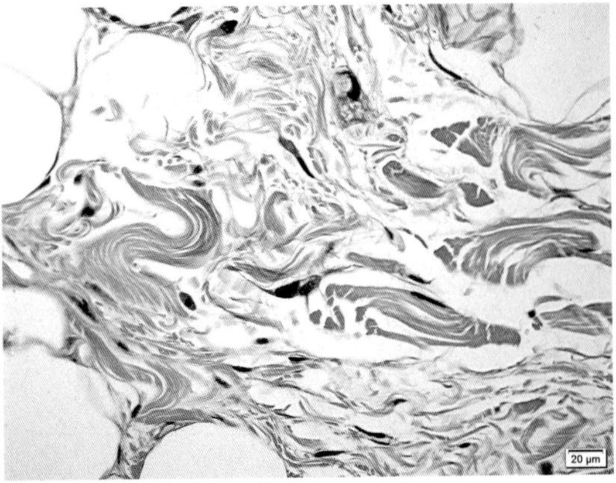

Plate 46 Atypical lipomatous tumour. Mature adipocytes with scattered spindle hyperchromatic stromal cells.

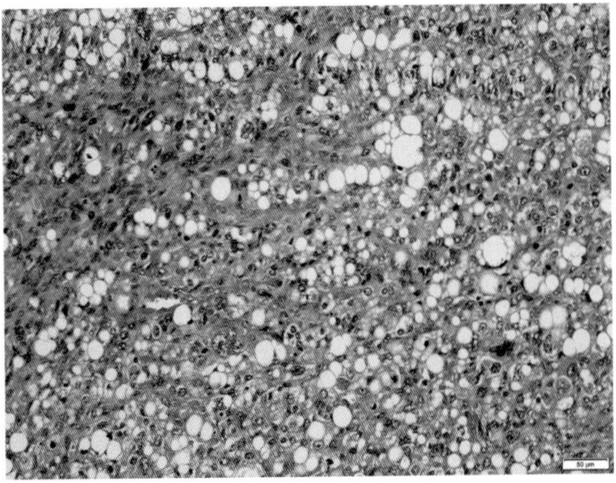

Plate 47 Pleomorphic liposarcoma. Sheets of severely pleomorphic lipoblasts admixed with spindle cells.

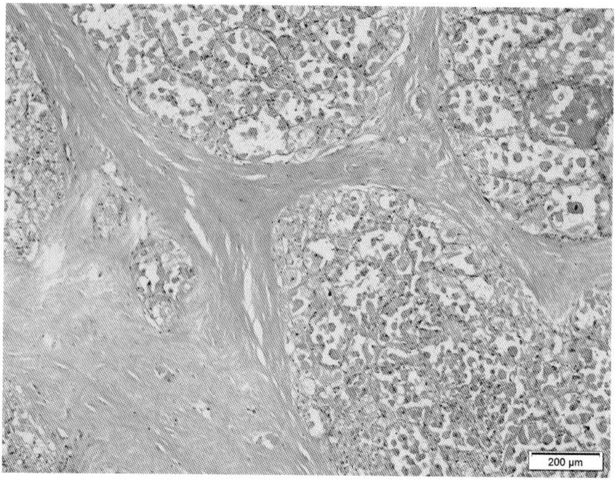

Plate 48 Clear cell sarcoma. Closely packed nests of polygonal to spindle cells with clear/pink cytoplasm and central nuclei.

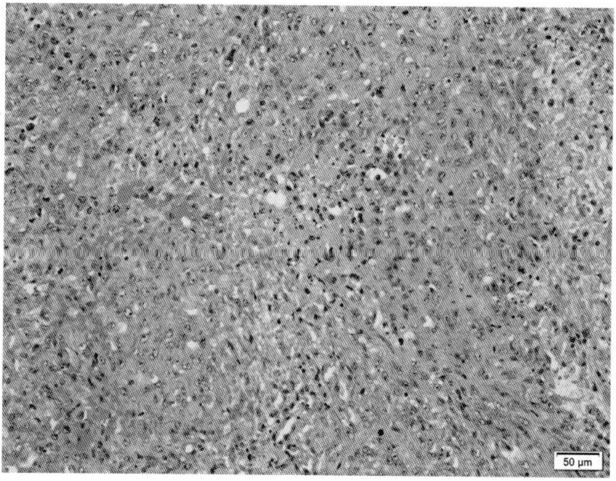

Plate 49 Epithelioid sarcoma. Atypical epithelioid cells forming aggregates and surrounding necrotic areas in a granuloma-like pattern. This could be mistaken for a carcinoma.

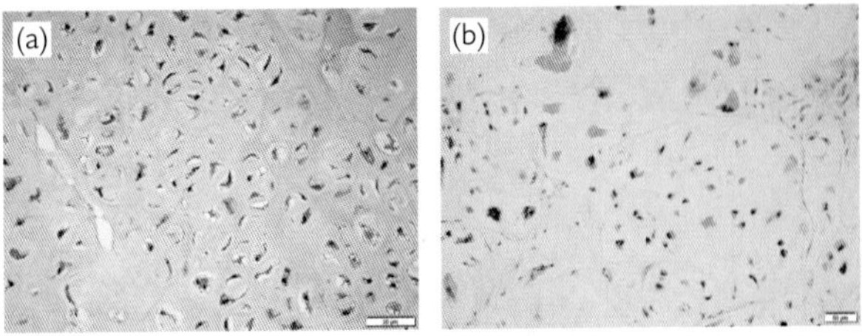

Plate 50 Chondrosarcoma. Histology shows an increase in cellularity and atypia between grades I (a) and III (b) in chondrosarcoma (haematoxylin and eosin sections).

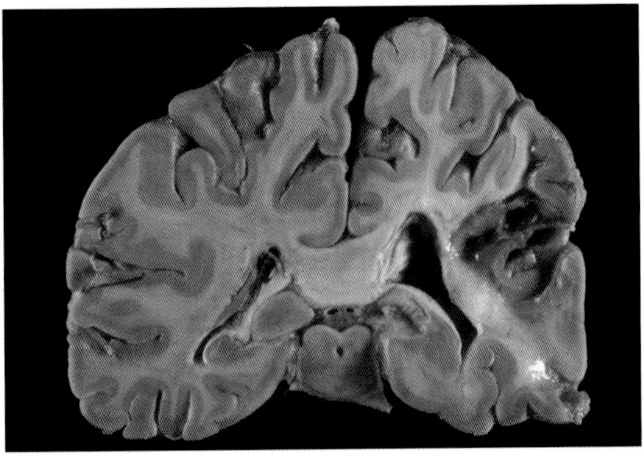

Plate 51 Cerebral infarction.

Reproduced with permission from Clinical Pathology (Oxford Core Texts), Carton, James, Daly, Richard, and Ramani, Pramila, Oxford University Press (2006).

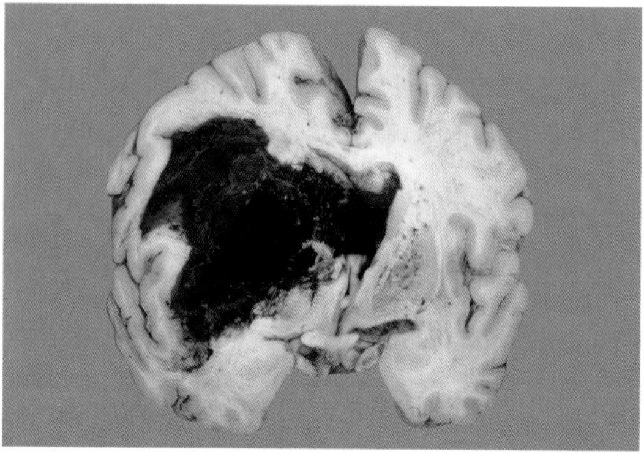

Plate 52 Intracerebral haemorrhage. This is a slice of brain taken at post-mortem from a patient who suddenly collapsed and died. There is a massive intracerebral haematoma which led to a huge rise in intracranial pressure and herniation. The cause in this case was hypertension, and other changes of hypertension at post-mortem included left ventricular hypertrophy and nephrosclerosis of both kidneys.

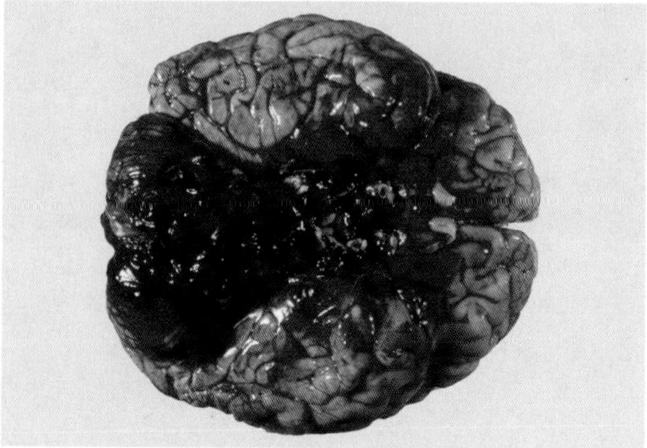

Plate 53 Subarachnoid haemorrhage. This is the undersurface of the brain removed at post-mortem from a patient who suddenly cried out, collapsed, and died. Blood is seen filling the subarachnoid space. When the blood clot was cleared away, a ruptured berry aneurysm was found in the circle of Willis.

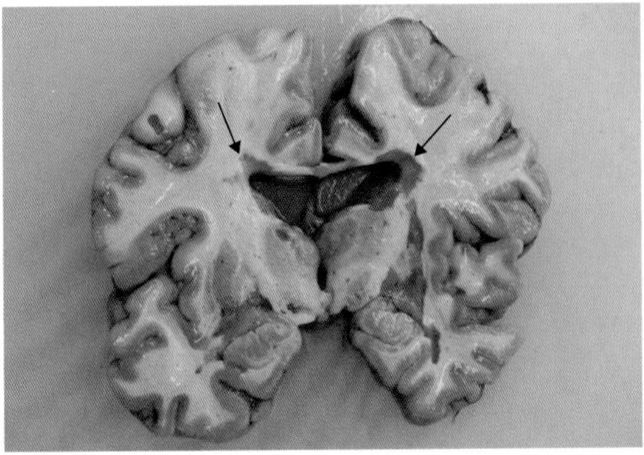

Plate 54 Multiple sclerosis plaques. Brown appearance of multiple sclerosis plaques, seen here in a characteristic location around the lateral ventricles (arrows).

Reproduced with permission from *Clinical Pathology* (Oxford Core Texts), Carton, James, Daly, Richard, and Ramani, Pramila, Oxford University Press (2006).

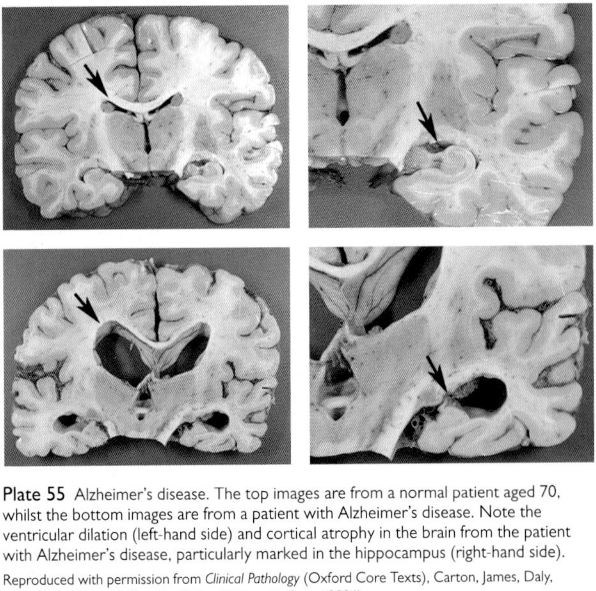

Plate 55 Alzheimer's disease. The top images are from a normal patient aged 70, whilst the bottom images are from a patient with Alzheimer's disease. Note the ventricular dilation (left-hand side) and cortical atrophy in the brain from the patient with Alzheimer's disease, particularly marked in the hippocampus (right-hand side).

Reproduced with permission from *Clinical Pathology* (Oxford Core Texts), Carton, James, Daly, Richard, and Ramani, Pramila, Oxford University Press (2006).

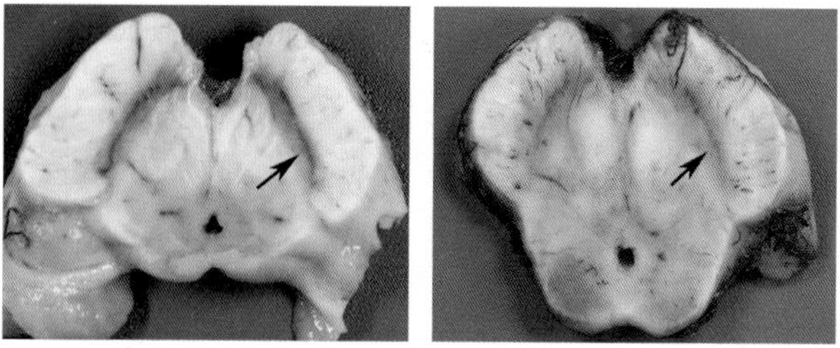

Plate 56 Substantia nigra in Parkinson's disease. Slices through the midbrain of a normal person (left) and a patient with Parkinson's disease (right) showing loss of pigmentation in the substantia nigra in Parkinson's disease (arrows).

Reproduced with permission from *Clinical Pathology* (Oxford Core Texts), Carton, James, Daly, Richard, and Ramani, Pramila, Oxford University Press (2006).

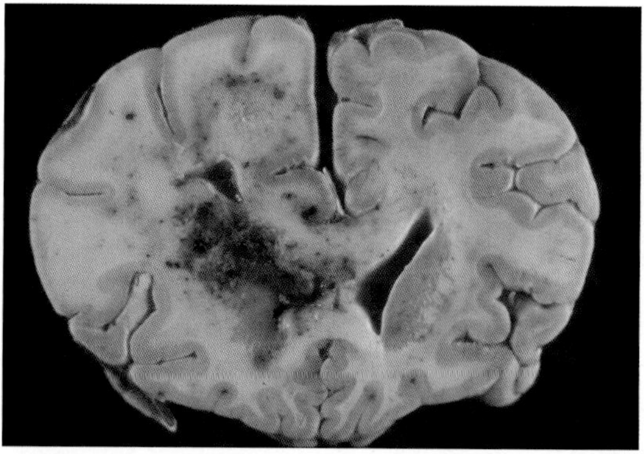

Plate 57 Glioblastoma. This is a section of the brain from a patient who presented with signs of raised intracranial pressure, rapidly deteriorated, and died. There is an ill-defined tumour with areas of haemorrhage. Microscopy revealed this to be a glioblastoma which was much more extensive than was apparent macroscopically.

Reproduced with permission from *Clinical Pathology* (Oxford Core Texts), Carton, James, Daly, Richard, and Ramani, Pramila, Oxford University Press (2006).

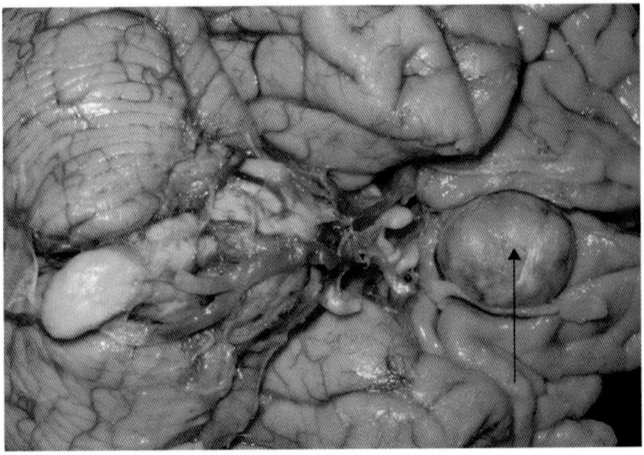

Plate 58 Meningioma. This very well-circumscribed tumour (arrow) has the typical macroscopic appearance of a meningioma, a suspicion that was confirmed microscopically.

Reproduced with permission from *Clinical Pathology* (Oxford Core Texts), Carton, James, Daly, Richard, and Ramani, Pramila, Oxford University Press (2006).

Urothelial carcinoma

Definition
- A group of urothelial neoplasms arising in the urothelial tract.

Epidemiology
- Common with over 250 000 new cases worldwide.
- Can occur anywhere in the urothelial tract, but the vast majority arises in the bladder, then the renal pelvis, then the ureters (50:3:1, respectively).

Aetiology
- Cigarette smoking.
- Occupational exposure to aromatic amines.

Presentation
- Most present with haematuria.

Subtypes
- Non-invasive urothelial carcinoma (low-grade and high-grade).
- Invasive urothelial carcinoma.
- Urothelial carcinoma *in situ* (CIS).

Genetics
- Low-grade, non-invasive urothelial carcinomas show relatively few genetic alterations, the most common being losses of chromosome 9.
- High-grade, non-invasive urothelial carcinomas, invasive urothelial carcinomas, and urothelial CIS are genetically unstable lesions with many chromosomal aberrations, including *TP53* and *RB* mutations.

Non-invasive papillary urothelial carcinoma
- Macroscopically appear as exophytic frond-like masses.
- Histologically composed of atypical urothelium growing in papillary fronds. Low-grade tumours show mild disorganization and low-grade nuclear atypia. High grade tumours show marked disorganization and high-grade nuclear atypia.

Invasive urothelial carcinoma
- Macroscopically appear as solid masses which infiltrate into underlying tissues.
- Histologically composed of an atypical urothelium growing as tumour nests infiltrating into the bladder wall.
- Tumours showing divergent differentiation (usually squamous or glandular) show more aggressive biology.
- Immunohistochemically show a $CK7^{+}p63^{+}GATA3^{+}$ phenotype.

Urothelial carcinoma *in situ*
- Macroscopically may be invisible or manifest as an erythematous area of mucosa.
- Histologically, a flat lesion in which the urothelium displays unequivocally high-grade nuclear atypia.

Urine cytology

- Poorly sensitive at picking up low-grade urothelial carcinomas.
- Good at detecting high-grade lesions where shed severely atypical urothelial cells can be visualized due to their large pleomorphic nuclei with dark coarsely granular chromatin.

Prognosis

- All show a tendency to multifocality and recurrence.
- Non-invasive, low-grade papillary urothelial carcinomas carry a very low risk of progression to invasion and death (<5%).
- Non-invasive, high-grade papillary urothelial carcinomas and urothelial CIS carry a much higher risk of progression.
- The prognosis of infiltrating urothelial carcinoma is mostly dependent on disease stage.

TNM 7 pathological staging of renal pelvis and ureter carcinomas

Primary tumour (T)

pTa: non-invasive tumour.
pT1: tumour invades the lamina propria.
pT2: tumour invades the muscularis propria.
pT3: tumour invades beyond the muscularis into peripelvic fat or renal parenchyma (renal pelvis) or into periureteric fat (ureter).
pT4: tumour invades adjacent organs or through the kidney into perinephric fat.

Regional lymph nodes (N)

pN0: no regional lymph node metastases.
pN1: metastasis in a single lymph node, 2cm or less in dimension.
pN2: metastasis in a single lymph node, >2cm, but not >5cm, or multiple lymph nodes, none >5cm.
pN3: metastasis in a lymph node, >5cm in dimension.

TNM 7 pathological staging of bladder carcinomas

Primary tumour (T)

pTa: non-invasive tumour.
pT1: tumour invades the lamina propria.
pT2: tumour invades the muscularis propria.
pT3: tumour invades perivesical tissue.
pT4: tumour invades adjacent organs (prostate, uterus, vagina, pelvic wall).

Regional lymph nodes (N)

pN1: single positive node in the primary drainage region.
pN2: multiple positive nodes in the primary drainage region.
pN3: common iliac node involvement.

Benign prostatic hyperplasia

Definition

- Enlargement of the prostate gland due to an increase in cell number.

Epidemiology

- Very common.
- Symptomatic disease affects ~3% of men aged 45–49, rising to nearly 25% of men by age 80.
- Histological evidence is present in 90% of men by age 80.

Aetiology

- Unclear.

Pathogenesis

- Androgens are critical in the development of BPH, more specifically increased levels of dihydrotestosterone locally in the prostate.
- Current evidence suggests that increased oestrogen levels in blood (which rise with age) induce androgen receptors in prostate tissue and stimulate hyperplasia.

Presentation

- Frequency, urgency, nocturia, hesitancy, poor flow, and terminal dribbling (collectively known as lower urinary tract symptoms or 'LUTS').
- Some patients present with UTI, acute urinary retention, or renal failure.

Macroscopy

- The prostate shows nodular enlargement which usually involves the transition zone.
- There is a poor correlation between the size of the prostate and the severity of symptoms.

Histopathology

- There is proliferation of both epithelial and stromal elements of the prostate, which form nodules.
- The proportion of epithelial and stromal elements varies considerably between cases, with some being predominantly epithelial and some being predominantly stromal.

Complications

- Urinary retention.
- Recurrent UTIs.
- Bladder stones.
- Obstructive nephropathy (➔ Obstructive nephropathy, p. 207).

Prostate carcinoma

Definition

- A malignant epithelial tumour arising in the prostate.

Epidemiology

- The most common malignant tumour in men, accounting for about 25% of all male cancers.
- About 1 in 8 men will develop prostate cancer in their lifetime.
- Prevalence rising due to longer life expectancy and increased detection rates.
- A less prominent cause of cancer-related deaths, as many cases behave in a relatively indolent fashion.

Aetiology

- Racial background and genetic factors are important, with a 5- to 10-fold increased risk in men with two or more affected first-degree relatives.
- Dietary association with animal products, particularly red meat.

Carcinogenesis

- Arises from a precursor lesion known as **prostatic intraepithelial neoplasia** (PIN), characterized by neoplastic transformation of the epithelium lining of the prostatic ducts and acini.
- Harbour mutations in a number of genes, including *GST-pi, PTEN, AMACR, p27*, and *E-cadherin* (note these are not classical tumour suppressor genes or oncogenes).

Presentation

- The vast majority of prostate cancers are asymptomatic and diagnosed when needle biopsy is performed to investigate a raised serum prostate-specific antigen (PSA) level or a suspicious-feeling prostate on digital rectal examination.
- LUTS may be present.
- Rarely, patients present with symptoms of metastatic disease.

Prostate biopsy

- Prostate needle core biopsies are required to make the diagnosis.
- As prostate cancer rarely forms a discrete mass, random biopsies have to be taken from the prostate in an attempt to locate the tumour.
- The standard approach is a 12-core biopsy specimen (six biopsies from each lobe) taken transrectally.
- Some patients may be suitable candidates for extended biopsy regimes taken transperineally using a mapped template. This approach is better at sampling areas of the prostate which may be missed by the transrectal approach (especially the anterior prostate).
- As imaging techniques improve, there is a move towards focused targeted biopsies from radiologically suspicious areas.

Histopathology

- The most common type of prostate cancer is acinar adenocarcinoma, in which the malignant epithelial cells are from acinar structures.
- One of the key diagnostic features of prostate cancer is the abnormal architecture of the malignant glands which are crowded and show infiltration between benign glands and ducts.
- Malignant epithelial cells have enlarged nuclei with prominent nucleoli and denser amphophilic cytoplasm.
- Malignant glands often have intraluminal crystalloids (dense crystal-like structures), amorphous pink secretions, or blue-tinged mucin.

Gleason scoring

- Prostate cancers are graded using the Gleason scoring system.
- Gleason **scores** are expressed in the format $x + y = z$ and are based on the two most common Gleason **patterns** present in the tumour.
- Gleason patterns range from 1 to 5 and are based on the architectural growth of the tumour.
- In practice, patterns 1 and 2 are never diagnosed, and so all prostate cancers have a Gleason score of between 6 and 10.
- Gleason pattern 3 tumours are composed of well-formed discrete glandular units (Fig. 11.3).
- Gleason pattern 4 tumours are composed of poorly formed, fused, or cribriform glands (Fig. 11.4).
- Gleason pattern 5 tumours are composed of solid sheets, cords, or single cells showing no glandular differentiation.

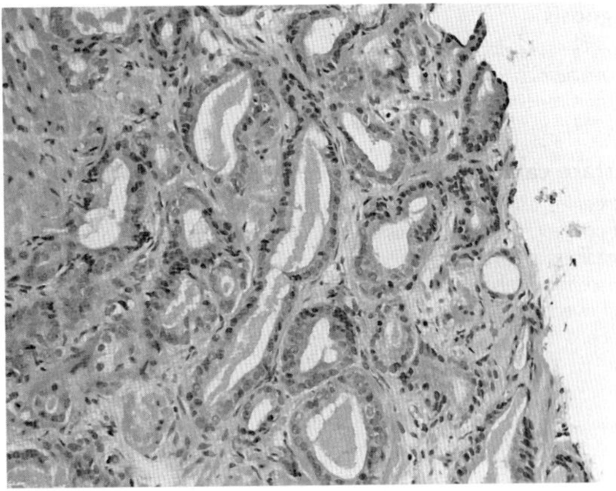

Fig. 11.3 Gleason pattern 3 prostate adenocarcinoma composed of individual well-formed glandular acini (see Plate 20).

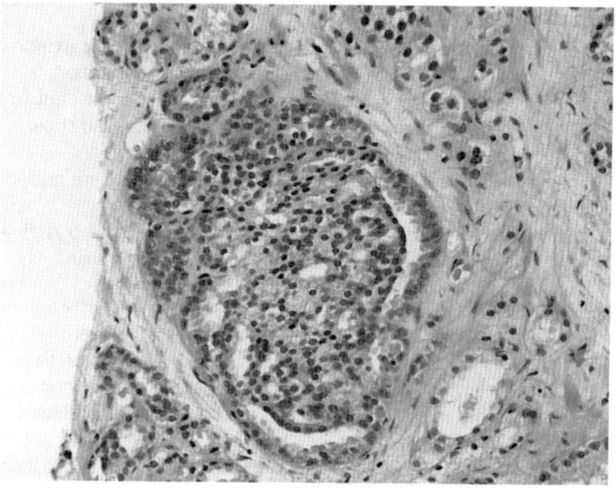

Fig. 11.4 Gleason pattern 4 prostate adenocarcinoma showing a fused cribriform unit (see Plate 21).

Immunohistochemistry

- Prostate cancer shows a $CK7^{-}CK20^{-}PSA^{+}$ phenotype.
- Basal cell markers, e.g. p63 or cytokeratin 5, can be used to confirm a morphological diagnosis of prostate cancer by demonstrating the absence of basal cells around the prostate cancer glands.

Prognosis

- The Gleason score is a powerful prognostic indicator, with a higher score associated with a worse outcome.
- Other important factors include the serum PSA level and the stage of the disease.

Prostate cancer screening

- Screening using serum PSA is a controversial subject.
- At present, most countries do not operate an organized prostate screening programme.
- Current evidence suggests that screening would result in overdiagnosis and overtreatment of many men with prostate cancers that are unlikely to behave in an aggressive manner.

Prostate cancer grade groups

The WHO have adopted a new grading system for prostate cancer that simplifies the existing Gleason scoring system into a 5-point system:

Gleason score	Grade group
3 + 3 = 6	1
3 + 4 = 7	2
4 + 3 = 7	3
4 + 4 = 8	4
9 or 10	5

TNM 7 pathological staging of prostatic carcinomas

Primary tumour (T)

pT1a: tumour as incidental histological finding in 5% or less of TURP tissue.
pT1b: tumour as incidental histological finding in >5% of TURP tissue.
pT1c: tumour identified by needle biopsy (e.g. because of elevated PSA).
pT2a: tumour involves one-half of one lobe or less.
pT2b: tumour involves more than half of one lobe, but not both lobes.
pT2c: tumour involves both lobes.
pT3a: extracapsular extension or microscopic bladder neck invasion.
pT3b: tumour invades seminal vesicle(s).
pT4: tumour invades adjacent structures other than seminal vesicles.

Regional lymph nodes (N)

pN0: no regional lymph node metastasis.
pN1: regional lymph node metastasis.

TURP, transurethral resection of the prostate.

Testicular germ cell tumours

Definition

- A group of malignant tumours of the testis arising from germ cells.

Epidemiology

- >90% of all testicular tumours are germ cell tumours.
- Most arise in young men aged from 20 to 45.

Aetiology

- The most consistent risk factor is the presence of cryptorchidism (➲ Cryptorchidism, p. 211), which increases the risk by 3- to 5-fold.
- Other prenatal risk factors include low birthweight and small-for-gestational age.
- No consistent adulthood risk factors have been identified.

Carcinogenesis

- Most germ cell tumours arise from a precursor lesion known as **germ cell neoplasia *in situ*** (GCNIS), characterized by the presence of neoplastic germ cells confined to the seminiferous tubules.
- It is likely that the malignant process begins in fetal life and that GCNIS is present during childhood and young adulthood, during which time further genetic aberrations lead to malignant transformation.
- One consistently observed structural chromosomal aberration is gain of 12p sequences.

Presentation

- Most patients present with a painless testicular lump.
- ~10% present with symptoms related to metastatic disease, most commonly back pain from retroperitoneal lymph node metastases or cough/dyspnoea from pulmonary metastases.

Serum tumour markers

- AFP is typically associated with the presence of yolk sac elements.
- β-human chorionic gonadotrophin (HCG) is associated with the presence of syncytiotrophoblastic cells; these may be present individually within a pure seminoma or as an integral component of a choriocarcinoma.

Macroscopy

- Pure seminomas tend to produce lobulated tan lesions (Fig. 11.5).
- Teratomas often show cystic and solid areas.
- Mixed tumours tend to have a variegated appearance.

Histopathology

- **Seminoma** is composed of sheets or nests of polygonal cells with clear or eosinophilic cytoplasm and round nuclei containing one or two nucleoli. A lymphocytic infiltrate is commonly present within the tumour.
- **Teratoma** is composed of tissues resembling immature fetal-type tissues and/or mature adult-type tissues.

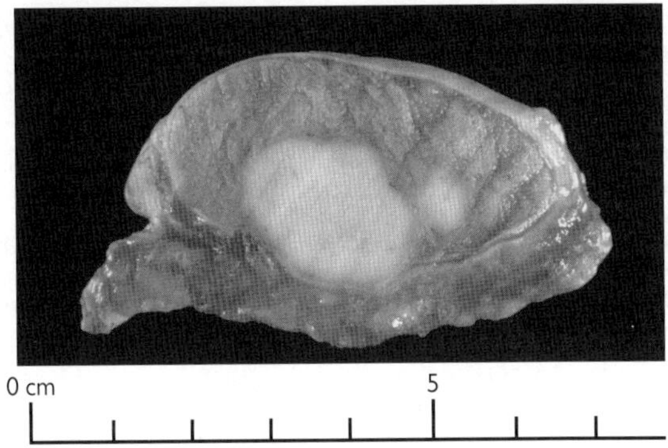

Fig. 11.5 This is a testis from a young man who presented with an enlarging testicular lump. Following an ultrasound scan which was suspicious for a neoplasm, he underwent orchidectomy. The testis has been sliced in the pathology department, revealing this white solid mass in the testis. This appearance is typical of a seminoma, and microscopic examination confirmed this (see Plate 22).

Reproduced with permission from *Clinical Pathology* (Oxford Core Texts), Carton, James, Daly, Richard, and Ramani, Pramila, Oxford University Press (2006), p. 244, Figure 11.14.

- **Embryonal carcinoma** is composed of anaplastic cells with large vesicular nuclei containing large nucleoli. The tumours may grow in solid sheets or form glandular structures.
- **Yolk sac tumour** is composed of small mildly pleomorphic cells which form a wide variety of architectural patterns, of which the most common are reticular and microcystic.
- **Choriocarcinoma** is composed of a mixture of syncytiotrophoblastic and cytotrophoblastic cells. There is often extensive haemorrhage and necrosis.

► Germ cell tumours may be composed entirely of one subtype or a mixture of different subtypes.

Immunohistochemistry

- Seminoma: Oct3/4$^+$CD117$^+$CD30$^-$AEI/AE3$^-$.
- Embryonal carcinoma: Oct3/4$^+$CD117$^-$CD30$^+$AEI/AE3$^+$.
- Yolk sac tumour: Oct3/4$^-$Glypican 3$^+$AFP$^+$HCG$^-$.
- Choriocarcinoma: Oct3/4$^-$Gypican 3$^{+/-}$AFP$^-$HCG$^+$.

Prognosis

- Excellent 5-year survival rates of ~98% in most countries.
- This reflects the high sensitivity of germ cell tumours to modern platinum-based chemotherapeutic regimes.

TNM 7 pathological staging of testicular germ cell tumours

Primary tumour (T)

pT1: tumour limited to the testis without lymphovascular invasion.

pT2: tumour limited to the testis with lymphovascular invasion or tumour extending through the tunica albuginea with involvement of the tunica vaginalis.

pT3: tumour invades the spermatic cord with or without lymphovascular invasion.

pT4: tumour invades the scrotum with or without lymphovascular invasion.

Testicular non-germ cell tumours

Testicular lymphomas

- ~5% of all testicular tumours.
- Mostly seen in elderly men.
- The testis is usually replaced by a large grey/tan mass which may extend into the cord.
- Histologically, the most common type is **diffuse large B-cell lymphoma** (➲ Diffuse large B-cell lymphoma, pp. 366–7).
- Survival is generally poor.

Leydig cell tumour

- A sex cord stromal tumour which accounts for ~3% of all testicular tumours.
- May occur at any age.
- Prepubertally, they tend to present with signs of precocious puberty due to androgen production.
- Post-pubertally, they present with a testicular mass.
- Macroscopically, they are well-circumscribed tumours, often with a brown cut surface.
- Histologically, they are composed of sheets or nests of polygonal cells with eosinophilic cytoplasm and round nuclei with a single nucleolus. Reinke's crystals (rhomboid-shaped, intracytoplasmic crystals) may be seen.
- The majority of Leydig cell tumours behave in a benign fashion; however, ~10% show malignant behaviour.
- Histology is not always entirely reliable at predicting which tumours will behave aggressively; however, worrying findings include tumour size >5cm, necrosis, vascular invasion, cellular pleomorphism, and raised mitotic activity.

Sertoli cell tumour

- A sex cord stromal tumour which accounts for ~1% of all testicular tumours.
- Most present as a testicular mass in young and middle-aged men.
- Macroscopically, they are usually solid yellow or white tumours.
- Histologically, they are composed of oval cells forming hollow or solid tubular structures.
- ~10% of tumours are malignant; similar histological criteria are used to predict malignant behaviour as for Leydig cell tumours.

Paratesticular diseases

Epididymal cyst

- Benign cystic lesion of the epididymis.
- Usually presents as a small paratesticular swelling which may be tender.
- Grossly appears as a thin-walled, translucent cystic lesion.
- Histologically, the cyst is lined by a thin attenuated layer of bland epithelial cells.

Epididymitis

- Usually results from an ascending infection from the lower urinary tract.
- In young men <35y, it is usually due to a sexually transmitted infection such as *Chlamydia trachomatis* or *Neisseria gonorrhoeae*.
- In men >35y, it is usually due to *E. coli*.

Varicocele

- A persistent abnormal dilation of the pampiniform venous plexus in the spermatic cord.
- More common on the left side where the testicular vein drains into the renal vein.
- Usually presents with nodularity on the lateral side of the scrotum.
- Some cause a dull ache, especially after prolonged standing or towards the end of the day.
- May contribute to male subfertility, as the increased blood flow raises the scrotal temperature and impairs spermatogenesis.

Hydrocele

- An abnormal accumulation of fluid in the space between the two layers of the tunica vaginalis.
- A common cause of scrotal swelling.
- Usually caused by trauma or a reaction to an underlying pathology such as epididymitis, orchitis, or a tumour.

Adenomatoid tumour

- The most common benign paratesticular neoplasm.
- Can occur in the epididymis, spermatic cord, and tunica albuginea.
- Most present in young adults.
- Grossly, they are small solid, firm, grey/white tumours which are usually <3cm.
- Histologically, they are composed of dilated tubular structures lined by attenuated mesothelial cells.

Paratesticular sarcomas

- Rare, but well-recognized, paratesticular tumours.
- The two most common types are **well-differentiated liposarcoma** in adults and **embryonal rhabdomyosarcoma** in children/adolescents.

Urethral diseases

Urethritis

- Usually caused by sexually transmitted infections.
- Divided into gonococcal and non-gonococcal urethritis.
- Non-gonococcal urethritis is more common and most are caused by *C. trachomatis*. Patients typically describe a sensation of urethral 'itching'.
- Gonococcal urethritis is due to infection with *N. gonorrhoeae*. Patients tend to present with a more purulent discharge and dysuria.
- Gram staining of urethral discharge can detect *N. gonorrhoeae* as intracellular Gram-negative diplococci. If these organisms are not detected, but numerous neutrophils confirm a urethritis, then non-gonococcal urethritis is presumed.
- Detection of *C. trachomatis* is usually by molecular methods, as culture is slow and unreliable.

Prostatic urethral polyp

- Lesion of the prostatic urethra containing prostatic epithelium.
- Typically presents with haematuria.
- Grossly appears as a papillary lesion projecting into the prostatic urethra.
- Histologically composed of crowded collections of prostatic-type glands covered by urothelium.

Urethral caruncle

- Relatively common polypoid lesion of the distal urethra in women.
- Presents with dysuria and spotty bleeding.
- The caruncle is visible as a polypoid mass at the urethral meatus.
- Histologically, it contains a dense inflammatory cell infiltrate rich in blood vessels and is covered by hyperplastic epithelium.

Urethral carcinomas

- These are rare, but more common in women.
- Often present at a high stage with poor prognosis.
- Most are squamous cell carcinomas (70%) and arise in the distal urethra near the meatus.
- The others are either urothelial carcinomas (20%) or adenocarcinomas (10%) and tend to arise in the proximal urethra.

Malignant melanoma

- Rare, but recognized, tumour in the urethra.
- Grossly, they appear as polypoid or ulcerated urethral masses.
- Histologically, they are composed of atypical epithelioid or spindled cells. Frequently amelanotic, which can lead to diagnostic difficulty.
- Immunohistochemical reactivity of the malignant cells for melanocytic markers (S100, HMB-45, Melan-A) helps to clinch the diagnosis.

Penile diseases

Lichen sclerosus

- Penile lichen sclerosus (balanitis xerotica obliterans) is an inflammatory disease that usually affects the foreskin or glans penis.
- Most cases present in adulthood with phimosis.
- Macroscopically, the affected areas appear white and atrophic.
- Histologically, there is epidermal atrophy and hyperkeratosis with underlying bands of hyalinized collagen and a chronic inflammatory cell infiltrate.

Lichen planus

- Penile involvement is commonly seen in patients with generalized lichen planus (➔ Lichen planus, p. 388).
- The lesions often involve the glans penis.
- Histology shows a band-like inflammatory infiltrate hugging the epithelium.

Zoon's balanitis

- Usually presents as a solitary red area in uncircumcised elderly men.
- Clinically mimics penile Bowen's disease.
- Histology shows thinning of the epidermis with spongiosis and an underlying band-like inflammatory infiltrate rich in plasma cells.

Condylomas

- Caused by HPV infection, usually types 6 and 11. Seen mostly in sexually active young men.
- Macroscopically, condylomas appear as either flat or frond-like papillary growths.
- Histologically, they show a papillomatous squamous proliferation with koilocytes (keratinocytes showing viral cytopathic changes).

Peyronie's disease

- Also known as penile fibromatosis, but probably unrelated to the other forms of fibromatosis (➔ Benign superficial fibromatoses, p. 436).
- Presents between ages 40 and 60 with thickening of the corpus cavernosa, leading to penile pain and curvature on erection.
- Histological examination of excised tissue shows hypocellular collagenous scar tissue with aggregates of chronic inflammatory cells.

Penile carcinoma

- Rare malignancy, usually arising on the glans penis of elderly men.
- Risk factors include HPV infection, smoking, phimosis, and long-standing lichen sclerosus. Circumcision is associated with a reduction in risk.
- Macroscopically, they are exophytic masses which may ulcerate.
- Histologically, the majority are squamous cell carcinomas which arise from areas of squamous dysplasia (sometimes termed penile intraepithelial neoplasia).

Scrotal diseases

Epidermoid cysts

- Common cause of a scrotal skin lump.
- Macroscopically, they contain yellow keratinous debris.
- Histologically, they are lined by squamous epithelium showing epidermoid-type keratinization.

Scrotal calcinosis

- An uncommon disorder in which multiple calcified nodules develop in the scrotal skin.
- The calcification is thought to be dystrophic in type and probably represents calcification of old epidermoid cysts.

Angiokeratomas

- Benign vascular lesions which usually present as multiple small blue/red lesions of the scrotal skin.
- Histologically, they are composed of dilated vascular channels in the papillary dermis, associated with hyperplasia and hyperkeratosis of the overlying epidermis.

Fournier's gangrene

- A clinical variant of necrotizing fasciitis (➔ Necrotizing fasciitis, p. 398) which involves the penis, scrotum, perineum, and abdominal wall in men.
- Main risk factors are diabetes and immunosuppression.
- Usually, a polymicrobial infection caused by a mixture of aerobic and anaerobic bacteria.
- Histology shows a severe necrotizing inflammatory process involving the skin and deep subcutaneous tissue.
- Mortality is in the order of 15–20%.

Scrotal squamous cell carcinoma

- A very rare malignancy.
- Mostly of historical interest due to its association with occupational exposure to carcinogens in chimney workers.

Chapter 12

Gynaecological pathology

Vulval skin diseases

Eczemas

- Commonly arise on vulval skin.
- Seborrhoeic dermatitis and irritant contact dermatitis are the two most frequent types.
- These have similar appearances to elsewhere on the skin (➲ Eczema, p. 386).

Lichen simplex chronicus

- Thickened patches of skin which probably represent a non-specific reaction to chronic itching.
- The labium majus is the predominant site on the vulva.
- Histologically, there is marked epidermal thickening with overlying hyperkeratosis and hypergranulosis.

Psoriasis

- Vulval psoriasis is typically of flexural type with marked erythema and absence of scaling.
- Typical histology shows regular psoriasiform epidermal hyperplasia with plaques of parakeratosis and loss of the granular layer. Neutrophils are present within parakeratosis.
- Vulval psoriasis may, however, show atypical histology, making the diagnosis more difficult to make.

Lichen planus

- May be found in patients with generalized disease (➲ Lichen planus, p. 388) or restricted to the genital region.
- The lesions are purple, flat-topped, shiny papules. Erosive disease may occur which can lead to scarring.
- Histologically, there is a band-like inflammatory cell infiltrate containing lymphocytes, histiocytes, and plasma cells. The overlying epidermis shows basal cell damage and may be thickened or atrophic.
- Lichen planus carries a small increased risk of development of vulval intraepithelial neoplasia (VIN) and squamous cell carcinoma.

Lichen sclerosus

- An inflammatory dermatosis of unknown cause, with a predilection for the anogenital skin of women.
- Clinically, there are white papules and plaques with a wrinkled surface. There may be areas of atrophy and haemorrhage. Itching, burning, and dyspareunia are common symptoms.
- Histologically, the epidermis is thinned and there is interface change. There is a band of hyalinization beneath the epidermis and an underlying chronic inflammatory cell infiltrate.
- Lichen sclerosus carries a small increase of development of VIN and squamous cell carcinoma.

Benign vulval tumours

Bartholin's duct cyst

- Arise due to obstruction of the vestibular orifice of the Bartholin's gland duct and accumulation of secretions.
- Usually present as painless lumps in the lateral wall of the vaginal opening (introitus) in young women.
- Histologically, they are lined by a transitional-type epithelium with areas of squamous metaplasia.

Papillary hidradenoma

- Benign sweat gland tumour which usually presents in middle-aged women as a small, painless lump on the labia majora or minora.
- Histologically, they are well-circumscribed papillary tumours of the dermis. The epithelium covering the papillae is double-layered, with inner tall columnar cells and outer small myoepithelial cells.

Condylomas

- Warty lesions related to low-risk HPV infection (types 6 or 11).
- Histologically, they show papillary squamous proliferations with koilocytes.
- Widespread condylomas may be seen in the immunosuppressed.

Granular cell tumour

- Tumour of neural Schwann cell origin that may occur in the vulva.
- Histologically composed of nests of large polygonal cells with abundant granular cytoplasm.
- The vast majority behave in a benign fashion.

Angiomyofibroblastoma

- Benign mesenchymal neoplasm that occurs almost exclusively in the vulvovaginal region of young women.
- Presents as a small subcutaneous lump, often mistaken for a cyst.
- Histologically, they are well-circumscribed lesions composed of dilated capillary-sized vessels set in an oedematous stroma containing many plump epithelioid stromal cells.

Cellular angiofibroma

- Benign mesenchymal neoplasm presenting as a small, painless subcutaneous mass in the vulvovaginal area.
- Occur in reproductive and post-menopausal age groups.
- Histologically, they are well-circumscribed cellular lesions composed of bland spindle cells and small, thick-walled blood vessels.

Deep (aggressive) angiomyxoma

- Locally infiltrative, but non-metastasizing, mesenchymal neoplasm that presents as a large, deep-seated mass in the pelvis and perineum of reproductive age women.
- Histologically, they are infiltrative, paucicellular tumours composed of small numbers of bland spindle cells set in a myxoid stroma containing thick-walled blood vessels.

Vulval carcinoma

Definition

- A malignant epithelial tumour arising in the vulva.
- Most are squamous carcinomas.

Epidemiology

- Rare with an age-standardized annual incidence of 4 per 100 000.
- 1300 cases per year; 20th most common cancer in UK females.
- Most arise in women >65y, but it can occur in younger women.

Aetiology

- Some are linked to chronic vulval inflammatory disorders such as lichen sclerosus or lichen planus.
- Most cases arising in younger women are linked to high-risk HPV infection of the vulva and cigarette smoking.

Carcinogenesis

- Most cases arise from a precursor lesion known as **vulval intraepithelial neoplasia (VIN)**.
- VIN is a dysplastic lesion of the squamous epithelium of the vulva and is divided into two types: **classical** and **differentiated**.
- The classical type is seen in young women and is related to HPV infection and smoking.
- The differentiated type is seen in older women and is related to chronic vulval inflammation.
- Both differentiated VIN and vulval carcinomas arising from it display genetic aberrations, which include mutations of the tumour suppressor genes *p53* and *PTEN*.

Presentation

- Most present with a mass or ulcer which, with time, may bleed or become painful.

Macroscopy

- Firm nodule, warty mass, or ulcerated with raised firm edges.

Histopathology

- Almost all cases are **squamous cell carcinomas**, composed of infiltrating malignant epithelial cells showing squamous differentiation.
- The squamous epithelium adjacent to the tumour often shows VIN.

Prognosis

- The most important prognostic indicators are tumour size, depth of invasion, involvement of adjacent structures, and extent of lymph node metastasis.
- Tumours with depth of invasion ≤1mm have a very low risk of lymph node metastasis and a good chance of cure following local excision.
- The 5-year survival rates in patients with unilateral lymph node disease is 65%, whereas with bilateral disease it falls to 25%.

FIGO 2009 staging of vulval carcinomas

IA: tumour confined to the vulva or perineum, ≤2cm in size with stromal invasion ≤1mm, negative nodes.

IB: tumour confined to the vulva or perineum, >2cm in size or with stromal invasion >1mm, negative nodes.

II: tumour of any size with adjacent spread (1/3 lower urethra, 1/3 lower vagina, anus), negative nodes.

IIIA: tumour of any size with positive inguino-femoral lymph nodes:

(i) 1 lymph node metastasis ≥5mm

(ii) 1–2 lymph node metastasis(es) of <5mm.

IIIB:

(i) 2 or more lymph nodes metastases ≥5mm

(ii) 3 or more lymph nodes metastases <5mm.

IIIC: positive node(s) with extracapsular spread.

IVA:

(i) tumour invades other regional structures (2/3 upper urethra, 2/3 upper vagina), bladder mucosa, rectal mucosa, or fixed to pelvic bone

(ii) fixed or ulcerated inguino-femoral lymph nodes.

IVB: any distant metastasis including pelvic lymph nodes.

Vaginal infections

Bacterial vaginosis

- Most common cause of an abnormal vaginal discharge.
- Occurs when the normal balance of vaginal bacteria is disrupted.
- Caused by overgrowth of anaerobic bacteria such as *Gardnerella vaginalis* and *Bacteroides* species.
- The metabolic products of these bacteria include volatile amines which give the discharge a distinctive fishy odour.
- There is no actual inflammation in the vaginal wall, hence why the term vaginosis is applied, rather than vaginitis.

Vulvovaginal candidosis

- Also known as 'thrush' or 'yeast infection'.
- Very common infection in young women caused by *Candida albicans*.
- Increased risk of occurrence if pregnant, diabetic, immunosuppressed, or taking contraceptive pill or antibiotics.
- The typical presentation is vulvovaginal itching and burning, dyspareunia, and dysuria. A thick, white ('cheesy') discharge is common.
- Diagnosed by a history of typical symptoms and discharge.
- The organism can also be cultured in the microbiology laboratory but is not usually necessary.

Trichomoniasis

- Sexually transmitted infection caused by the flagellate protozoan *Trichomonas vaginalis*.
- The male partner is usually asymptomatic and half of all affected women are also asymptomatic.
- Women with symptoms usually complain of vaginal itching and a thin, thick, or frothy yellow-green offensive discharge. Dyspareunia and dysuria may also occur.
- Wet mount microscopy of the discharge shows motile trichomonads.

Vaginal tumours

Vaginal carcinoma

- Uncommon in comparison to cervical and vulval carcinomas.
- Most are squamous cell carcinomas which arise from a precursor dysplastic lesion known as **vaginal intraepithelial neoplasia** (VAIN).
- Most arise in women over 50 years of age.
- Risk factors include HPV infection, smoking, and immunosuppression.
- Prognosis is generally poor, with 5-year survival rates of ~60%.

Fibroepithelial stromal polyp

- Benign lesion of the distal female genital tract which most commonly involves the vagina but may also arise in the vulva.
- Hormonally responsive lesions which occur in reproductive age women as a small polypoid mass.
- Histologically, they are composed of a central fibrovascular core covered by hyperplastic squamous epithelium. Stellate and multinucleate stromal cells are typically seen within the core near the epithelial surface.

Vaginal leiomyoma

- Most common mesenchymal tumour of the vagina, but relatively rare.
- Derived from smooth muscle.
- Histologically composed of bundles of bland smooth muscle.
- Treated by local excision.

Genital rhabdomyoma

- Rare benign tumour showing skeletal muscle differentiation.
- Presents in middle-aged women as a nodule and may cause dyspareunia or bleeding.
- Histologically, it is composed of a haphazard proliferation of spindle cells with abundant brightly eosinophilic cytoplasm containing cross-striations.

Embryonal rhabdomyosarcoma

- Rare malignant tumour showing skeletal muscle differentiation which can arise in the vagina of children.
- Most cases present in children <5 years old with vaginal bleeding. The tumour may be seen projecting through the vaginal opening.
- Macroscopically, the tumour is composed of oedematous 'grape-like' polypoid nodules projecting from the vaginal wall.
- Histologically, the tumour is composed of small, round, and spindled tumour cells condensed beneath the squamous epithelium of the vaginal wall. Some tumour cells have brightly eosinophilic cytoplasm; cytoplasmic cross-striations may be visible.
- Prognosis following treatment is generally excellent, with 10-year survival rates of >90%.

Cervical carcinoma

Definition

- A malignant epithelial tumour arising in the cervix.

Epidemiology

- Worldwide, cervical carcinoma is the most common malignancy of the female genital tract and the second most common non-cutaneous malignancy in women following breast cancer.
- In developed countries, cervical carcinoma is the third most common malignancy of the female genital tract after endometrial and ovarian carcinomas. The lower incidence is largely attributable to the success of cervical screening programmes.

Aetiology

- Virtually all are caused by high-risk HPV infection (mostly types 16 and 18).
- Other risk factors include smoking and oral contraceptive use, which probably act by enhancing HPV persistence in the cervix.

► HPV vaccines are highly effective in preventing infection.

Carcinogenesis

- 80% are squamous cell carcinomas which arise from a precursor lesion known as **cervical intraepithelial neoplasia** (CIN).
- 20% are adenocarcinomas which arise from a precursor lesion known as **cervical glandular intraepithelial neoplasia** (CGIN).
- HPV-mediated cervical carcinogenesis is linked to the presence of two viral genes *E6* and *E7*.
- The E6 and E7 proteins interact with the tumour suppressor proteins p53 and Rb, targeting them for degradation. Loss of function of these proteins results in uncontrolled proliferation of the infected cells.

Presentation

- Non-menstrual vaginal bleeding and discharge.

Macroscopy

- Solid tumour mass or ulcer.

Histopathology

- **Squamous cell carcinomas** are characterized by infiltrating irregular nests of malignant epithelial cells showing squamous differentiation. Residual CIN may be seen adjacent to small tumours.
- **Adenocarcinomas** are characterized by infiltrating malignant epithelial cells forming glandular structures. Residual CGIN may be seen adjacent to small tumours.

Prognosis

- Depends on a number of factors, including age, stage, and presence or absence of lymphovascular invasion.

FIGO 2009 staging of cervical carcinomas

IA1: confined to the cervix, diagnosed only by microscopy with invasion of <3mm in depth and lateral spread <7mm.

IA2: confined to the cervix, diagnosed with microscopy with invasion of >3mm and <5mm with lateral spread <7mm.

IB1: clinically visible lesion or >A2, <4cm in greatest dimension.

IB2: clinically visible lesion, >4 cm in greatest dimension.

II: involvement beyond uterus, but not lower third of vagina or pelvic wall:

- IIA: without parametrial invasion
- IIA1: <4cm in greatest dimension
- IIA2: >4cm in greatest dimension
- IIB: with parametrial involvement.

IIIA: extends to lower third of vagina.

IIIB: extends to pelvic side wall, causes hydronephrosis or non-functioning kidney.

IVA: tumour invades the mucosa of bladder or rectum and/or extends beyond true pelvis.

IVB: distant metastasis.

Cervical screening

► The main aim of cervical screening is the detection of CIN.

NHS cervical screening programme

- Women aged between 25 and 64 are eligible for cervical screening.
- Routine screening is performed every 3y from 25 to 49 and every 5y from 50 to 64.
- The test is a cervical brush sample for **liquid-based cytology**.
- A special device is used to brush cells from the cervix. The head of the brush is then broken off into a small glass vial containing a fixative or rinsed directly in the fixative.
- The sample is then sent to the local laboratory where a processing machine creates a thin monolayer of cells on a glass slide for cytological examination.

Cytopathology

- The principal aim of cytological examination of cervical samples is detection of **dyskaryotic squamous epithelial cells**.
- Dyskaryosis is graded into borderline, mild, moderate, or severe, depending on how abnormal the cell appears.
- A test showing moderate or severe dyskaryosis will result in the woman being referred for colposcopy.
- If the test shows borderline or mild dyskaryosis, it will undergo further testing for HPV. If HPV is detected, the woman will be referred for colposcopy. A negative HPV result allows the woman to carry on being routinely screened as normal.
- In some areas, an HPV test is done first and then the sample submitted for cytological examination only if HPV positive.

Colposcopy

- Colposcopy is a detailed examination of the cervix using a binocular microscopy called a colposcope and an intense light source.
- Application of acetic acid and iodine to the cervix helps identify areas of possible CIN for directed biopsy.

Histopathology

- Directed cervical biopsies are sent for histopathological examination to confirm the presence of CIN and provide a grade from 1 to 3.
- CIN 1 shows squamous dysplasia, in which the abnormalities are concentrated in the basal third of the epidermis.
- CIN 2 shows squamous dysplasia, in which the abnormalities are concentrated in the basal two-thirds of the epithelium.
- CIN 3 shows squamous dysplasia, in which the abnormalities extend into the upper one-third of the epithelium (Fig. 12.1).

Management

- CIN 2 and 3 are high-grade lesions which are removed by excision of the transformation zone (large loop excision of the transformation zone (LLETZ)).
- CIN 1 is a low-grade lesion and may be managed conservatively or excised, depending on the clinical situation.

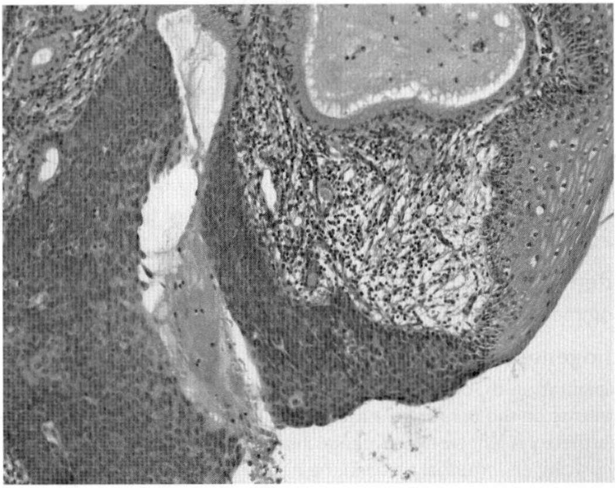

Fig. 12.1 CIN 3 extending into an endocervical crypt (see Plate 23).

Endometriosis

Definition

- The presence of endometrial tissue outside the uterine body.
- Almost all cases occur in the pelvis, most commonly the ovaries, uterosacral ligaments, peritoneum, pouch of Douglas, and sigmoid colon.
- Endometriosis is also recognized at sites outside of the pelvis, such as surgical scars and the lungs, but this is rarer.

Epidemiology

- Common, affecting up to 10% of women.

Pathogenesis

- **Implantation theory** proposes that endometrial tissue enters and implants on the peritoneal surface during menstruation. Credence to this theory is lent by experimental induction of endometriosis in animals by placing endometrial tissue in the peritoneal cavity. Changes in the immune response may prevent elimination of the endometrial tissue and promote the implantation and growth of endometrial cells.
- **Metaplastic theory** proposes that endometriosis arises due to metaplasia of the peritoneal surface epithelium into endometrial-type epithelium. Given that the peritoneum and female genital tract arise from the same embryological cells (coelomic epithelium), this seems plausible and would account for endometriotic deposits in areas in which implantation is unlikely.
- **Metastatic theory** proposes that endometriosis arises due to haematogenous spread of endometrial tissue that enters the circulation during menstruation. This would account for cases arising in locations where implantation or metaplasia are improbable, e.g. the lung.

Presentation

- Dysmenorrhoea, caused by swelling of endometriotic deposits.
- Subfertility, through unclear mechanisms, though implantation failure and/or endocrine dysfunction have been proposed. There is little evidence to support tubal distortion as a cause in most women.

Macroscopy

- Ovarian involvement typically gives rise to cysts filled with dark brown altered blood ('chocolate cysts'). Peritoneal involvement causes small nodules which often appear brown/black.

Histopathology

- Microscopy is diagnostic, demonstrating endometrial glands and endometrial stromal cells in tissues other than the uterine body.

Prognosis

- Endometriosis is chronic and progressive in 50% of cases.
- Ovarian endometriosis is thought to be a precursor to ovarian endometrioid and clear cell carcinomas (➔ Ovarian carcinomas, pp. 268–71).

Endometrial carcinoma

Definition

- A malignant epithelial tumour arising in the endometrium.

Epidemiology

- The most frequent malignant tumour of the female genital tract in developed countries.
- 80% are oestrogen-dependent, low-grade (type 1) carcinomas, occurring in women in their 50s and 60s.
- 10% are oestrogen-independent, high-grade (type 2) carcinomas, occurring in older women in their 70s and 80s

Aetiology

- Oestrogen-dependent tumours are associated with diabetes, obesity, nulliparity, early menarche, late menopause, polycystic ovarian syndrome, oestrogen-secreting ovarian tumours, and exogenous oestrogens or tamoxifen therapy. Lynch syndrome and Cowden syndrome also increase the risk of developing endometrial carcinoma.
- The aetiology of oestrogen-independent tumours is less clear, but they are associated with multiparity and a history of breast carcinoma/ tamoxifen use. *BRCA1/2* mutation carriers are more susceptible to the development of these tumours.

Genetic alterations

- Type 1 carcinomas:
  - *PTEN* (sporadic and Cowden syndrome-associated)
  - *PIK3CA*
  - *PIK3R1*
  - *ARID1A*
  - *KRAS*
  - microsatellite instability (sporadic and Lynch syndrome-associated).
- Type 2 carcinomas:
  - *TP53*
  - *PIK3CA*
  - *FBXW7*
  - *PPP2R1A*.

Carcinogenesis

- Oestrogen-dependent tumours develop from a precursor lesion called **atypical endometrial hyperplasia**. This often results from continuous unopposed oestrogenic stimulation of the endometrium and progression from endometrial hyperplasia without atypia. Loss of function of PTEN is typical.
- Most oestrogen-independent carcinomas develop from a precursor lesion called **serous endometrial intraepithelial carcinoma** on a background of endometrial atrophy. Loss of function of TP53 is typical.

Presentation

- Post-menopausal bleeding is the key symptom.

Macroscopy

- An exophytic friable mass fills the endometrial cavity and infiltrates to a varying extent into the underlying myometrium (Fig. 12.2).
- In advanced cases, the tumour may breach the serosal surface or invade the cervix.

Histopathology

- Oestrogen-dependent tumours are usually well-differentiated **endometrioid adenocarcinomas**, in which the malignant epithelial cells form complex glandular structures.
- Oestrogen-independent tumours are usually **serous carcinomas** or the uncommon **clear cell carcinomas** which look identical to their ovarian counterparts. Both are high-grade malignancies and usually have extensive spread at presentation.

Prognosis

- Oestrogen-dependent tumours generally have a better outcome.
- Oestrogen-independent tumours are highly aggressive and usually fatal.

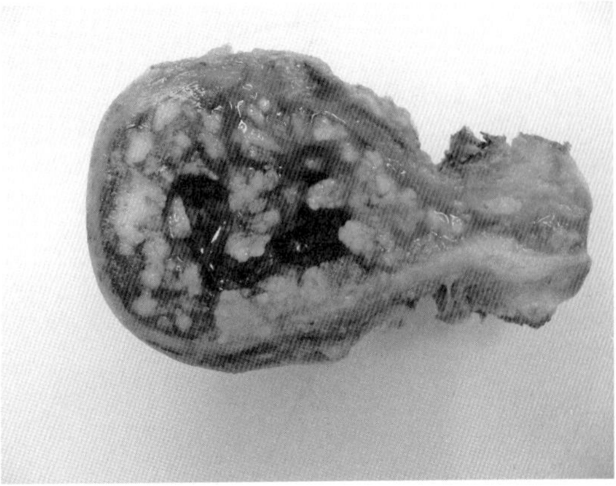

Fig. 12.2 Endometrial carcinoma filling the uterine cavity (see Plate 24).

FIGO 2009 staging of endometrial carcinomas

IA: tumour confined to the endometrium or invades less than half of the myometrium.

IB: tumour invades one half or more of the myometrium.

II: tumour invades the cervical stroma but does not extend beyond the uterus.

IIIA: tumour invades the uterine serosa and/or adnexa.

IIIB: tumour invades the vagina and/or parametrium.

IIIC1: metastases to pelvic lymph nodes.

IIIC2: metastasis to para-aortic lymph nodes.

IVA: tumour invades the bladder and/or bowel mucosa.

IVB: distant metastases.

Uterine leiomyomas (fibroids)

Definition

- Benign smooth muscle tumours arising in the myometrium.

Epidemiology

- Extremely common tumours, found in up to 75% of all women.
- Symptomatic fibroids affect about 20% of women.

Aetiology

- The precise cause is unclear, but Afro-Caribbean origin, heredity, nulliparity, and obesity are risk factors.
- No single causative genetic mutation has been identified. However, the mitochondrial enzyme fumarate hydratase has been linked to rare uterine fibroid syndromes.

Pathogenesis

- Growth is driven by oestrogen, progesterone, growth factors, and angiogenesis.
- They occur almost exclusively in reproductive age women, rapidly grow in pregnancy, and regress after the menopause.
- Genetic studies show that they are clonal neoplasms with chromosomal aberrations.

Presentation

- Menorrhagia.
- Pelvic pain. This may be related to tumour infarction or twisting of a pedunculated fibroid.
- Palpable mass. Fibroids may be large enough to be felt abdominally.
- Pressure symptoms. Large fibroids may affect adjacent organs, such as the bowel or bladder, or complicate pregnancy and delivery.

Macroscopy

- Well-circumscribed, white, whorled tumours which characteristically bulge from the surrounding myometrium when cut (Fig. 12.3).
- Often multiple and may be intramural or project from the serosal surface (subserosal) or into the endometrial cavity (submucosal).
- Calcification is very common.
- Infarcted tumours appear red, rather than white ('red degeneration').

Histopathology

- Classical fibroids are composed of intersecting fascicles of bland smooth muscle cells with blunt-ended nuclei and eosinophilic cytoplasm. Areas of hyalinization and calcification are common.
- A number of histological variants are recognized: cellular leiomyoma, mitotically active leiomyoma, symplastic leiomyoma, hydropic leiomyoma, epithelioid leiomyoma.

Prognosis

- Benign tumours with no capacity for malignant behaviour.

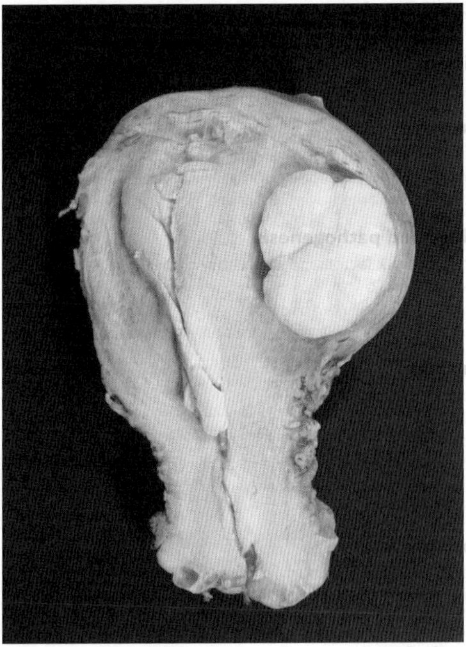

Fig. 12.3 Leiomyoma. This uterus was removed due to severe menorrhagia. On bisecting the uterus, a well-circumscribed white mass is seen in the myometrium which bulges from the cut surface. This is the typical macroscopic appearance of a leiomyoma (fibroid) and this was confirmed on microscopic examination (see Plate 25).

Reproduced with permission from *Clinical Pathology* (Oxford Core Texts), Carton, James, Daly, Richard, and Ramani, Pramila, Oxford University Press (2006), p. 269, Figure 12.9.

Uterine leiomyosarcoma

Definition

- A malignant smooth muscle tumour arising in the myometrium.

Epidemiology

- Although uncommon, representing 1–2% of uterine malignancies, it is the most common uterine sarcoma.
- Most occur in women over 50y of age.

Aetiology and pathogenesis

- Unclear, but risk factors include history of pelvic radiation and Afro-Caribbean origin.
- Thought to arise *de novo* and not usually from leiomyomas.
- Abnormalities of the *Rb* gene commonly seen in these tumours.

Presentation

- Abnormal vaginal bleeding.
- Palpable mass.
- Pelvic pain.
- Rapid enlargement of a uterine mass may prompt suspicion for leiomyosarcoma; however, many are unsuspected preoperatively and assumed to be large fibroids.

Macroscopy

- Leiomyosarcomas are poorly circumscribed and tend not to bulge from the surrounding myometrium due to their infiltrative nature.
- They are softer than fibroids and may show evidence of necrosis.

Histopathology

- Histologically, leiomyosarcomas are composed of spindle cells and/or pleomorphic cells which demonstrate a number of atypical features such as cytological atypia, tumour cell necrosis, and high mitotic activity.

Prognosis

- Leiomyosarcomas are aggressive malignancies with a tendency to local recurrence and metastasis, particularly to the liver and lungs.

Functional ovarian cysts

Definition

- Ovarian follicles showing pathological cystic change.
- A proposed cut-off between normal cystic follicles and follicular cysts is 2.5cm.

Terminology

- Cysts derived from preovulatory follicles are known as **follicular cysts** and those derived from the corpus luteum are known as **corpus luteum cysts**.

Epidemiology

- Very common.

Aetiology

- Follicular cysts: disordered function of the pituitary–ovarian axis.
- Corpus luteum cysts: excessive haemorrhage in a corpus luteum.

Presentation

- Almost all are discovered incidentally, either on imaging or by a surgeon exploring the pelvis.
- Occasionally, large cysts may present as a pelvic mass.

Macroscopy

- Follicular cysts are usually single and measure from 2.5 to 10cm in size. They are smooth-lined and contain clear fluid.
- Corpus luteum cysts usually measure from 2.5 to 5cm in size. The cyst contains bloody fluid and the wall often is yellow.

Cytopathology

- Aspirated fluid from a follicular cyst contains many granulosa cells with round nuclei, coarse chromatin, and a small rim of cytoplasm. Nuclear grooves may be seen. Luteinized cells may also be seen.
- Aspirated fluid from a corpus luteum cyst contains blood, haemosiderin-laden macrophages, and many fully luteinized granulosa cells. These are large polyhedral cells with abundant finely granular cytoplasm. The nuclei are round to oval with finely granular chromatin and prominent nucleoli. Nuclear grooves are not present.

Histopathology

- Follicular cysts are lined by granulosa cells and theca cells which may show some luteinization.
- Corpus luteum cysts contain abundant central haemorrhage. The lining is composed of fully luteinized granulosa and theca cells.

Prognosis

- Functional ovarian cysts are entirely benign. They are predominantly of clinical importance, as large cysts may raise concern for a cystic neoplasm.

Benign non-epithelial ovarian tumours

Mature cystic teratoma

- Benign germ cell ovarian tumour, also known as a 'dermoid cyst'.
- Occurs in young women, with peak incidence between 20 and 29 years old.
- Many are asymptomatic and discovered incidentally, but larger tumours may cause pelvic pain. The most serious complication is torsion or rupture, leading to an acute abdomen.
- Macroscopically, the tumour is cystic and contains greasy, soft, yellow material. Hair, cartilage, bone, and teeth may be visible (Fig. 12.4).
- Histologically, the tumour comprises mature adult-type tissues of virtually any type, including skin, brain, fat, smooth muscle, cartilage, respiratory, and GI tissue.

► Note that although other ovarian germ cell tumours (e.g. dysgerminoma, immature teratoma) are much rarer, they behave in a malignant fashion.

Ovarian fibroma

- Benign sex cord stromal ovarian tumour, composed of fibroblasts and collagen.
- Occur over a wide age range, though most are found in women over 50 years old. They are often small and discovered incidentally. Large tumours may cause abdominal pain and ascites.
- Macroscopically, the tumour is firm with a solid white cut surface.
- Histologically, the tumour is composed of bland spindled cells growing in a collagenous stroma.

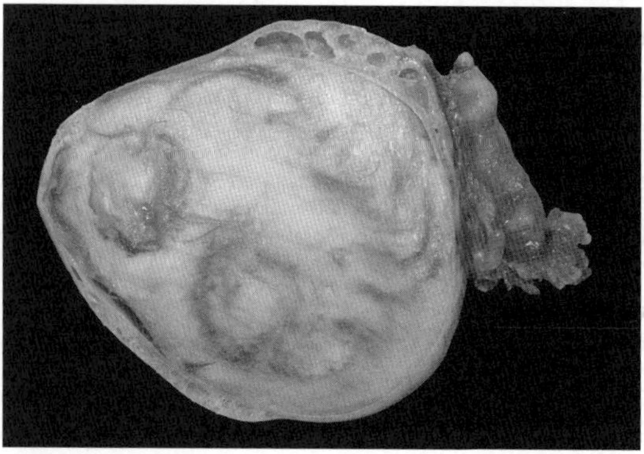

Fig. 12.4 Mature cystic teratoma. Typical appearance of a mature cystic teratoma (dermoid cyst) filled with greasy yellow material and hair (see Plate 26).

Benign epithelial ovarian tumours

Serous cystadenoma

- Benign epithelial ovarian tumour which usually occurs in premenopausal women.
- May be picked up incidentally, with symptoms of a pelvic mass, or with an acute abdomen due to torsion.
- Macroscopically, it is cystic and may be unilocular or multilocular. The cysts contain clear, straw-coloured or water-like fluid and have a thin wall with a smooth lining.
- Histologically, the cysts are lined by a single layer of bland columnar cells which may be ciliated or non-ciliated, similar to Fallopian tube epithelium.

Mucinous cystadenoma

- Benign epithelial ovarian tumour which usually occurs in premenopausal women.
- May be picked up incidentally, with symptoms of a pelvic mass, or with an acute abdomen due to torsion.
- Macroscopically, the tumour is usually unilateral, with a mean size of 10cm, but massive tumours have been reported. They may be unilocular or multilocular with either a thin or thick fibrous wall. They often contain a watery mucinous fluid (Fig. 12.5).
- Histologically, the tumours are composed of glands and cysts separated by varying amounts of fibrous stroma. The lining cells comprising a single layer of columnar epithelium with basal nuclei and apical mucinous cytoplasm.

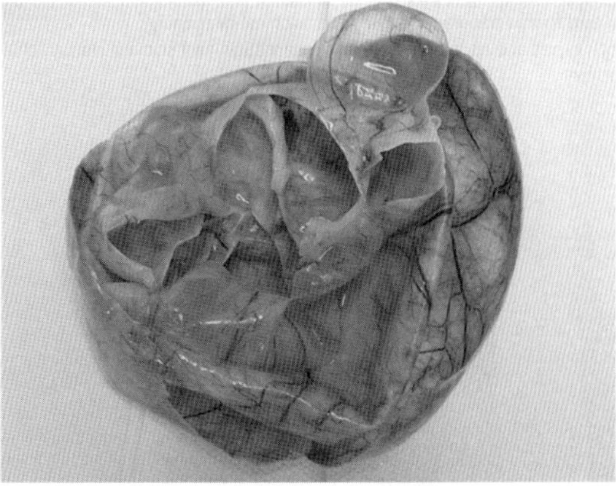

Fig. 12.5 Benign mucinous cystadenoma of the ovary (see Plate 27).

Borderline epithelial ovarian tumours

Borderline serous tumours

- Usually confined to the ovary at presentation but may be bilateral.
- Present with similar pressure symptoms as benign tumours but may present with ascites if extra-ovarian involvement.
- Macroscopically, these tumours show exuberant papillary growths within the cyst wall of the tumour or on the ovarian surface (Fig. 12.6).
- Histologically, the tumours show structural complexity, with complex cyst walls containing branching papillary structures. They are lined by stratified or non-stratified columnar cells, many of which are ciliated. The cells show mild to moderate cytological atypia with characteristic budding.
- There is no evidence of stromal invasion.
- Around 10% may have implants of similarly appearing tumours on the surface of pelvic structures that do not invade underlying tissue.
- Most are benign clinically, but a minority recur.
- Rarely may progress to low-grade serous carcinoma.

Borderline mucinous tumours

- Divided into intestinal-type and endocervical-type.
- Intestinal-type:
  - large (mean 19cm) multiloculated tumours containing mucin
  - usually unilateral (90%)
  - epithelial lining is enteric in type with goblet cells and forms tufts and papillae.
- Endocervical-type:
  - smaller than the intestinal type (mean 8cm)
  - more often bilateral (40%)
  - epithelial lining is endocervical in type with mucinous columnar cells and forms papillae showing hierarchical branching.
- Both types are usually stage I at presentation and show a benign clinical course.

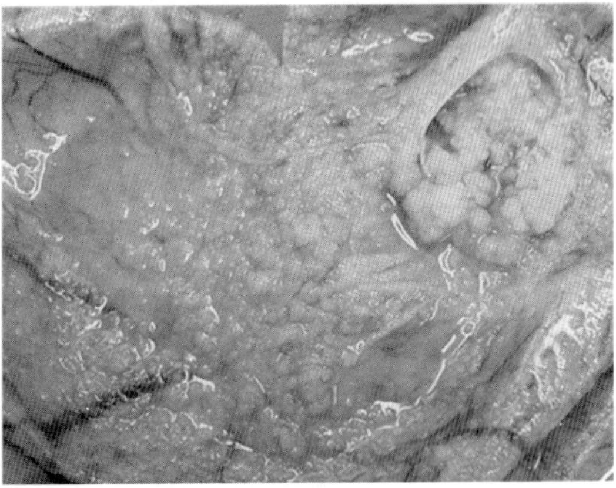

Fig. 12.6 Borderline serous tumour of the ovary (see Plate 28).

Ovarian carcinomas

Definition
- A group of malignant epithelial tumours arising in the ovary.

Epidemiology
- Fifth most common cause of cancer death and a leading cause of gynaecological cancer mortality due to late presentation.

Aetiology
- Multiparity, oral contraceptive use, hysterectomy, and tubal ligation are associated with a reduced risk of ovarian carcinoma.
- Family history, oestrogen replacement therapy, and obesity are associated with an increased risk.
- Hereditary factors account for up to 20% of ovarian cancers.

BRCA1 and 2 mutations
- Women with these mutations are at higher risk of developing high-grade serous carcinoma.
- The lifetime risk of developing ovarian cancer is around 50% for *BRCA1* carriers at an average age of between 49 and 53y. For *BRCA2* mutation carriers, the lifetime risk is between 11 and 37% and tends to develop later (average age 55–58y).
- Prophylactic bilateral salpingo-oophorectomy reduces risk.

Lynch syndrome (HNPCC)
- Most cancers associated with this syndrome are endometrioid or clear cell carcinomas.
- Nine to 12% lifetime risk of developing ovarian cancer and 40–60% of developing endometrial cancer.
- Related to mutations in DNA mismatch repair genes, especially *MLH1*, *MSH2*, and *MSH6*.

Presentation
- Abdominal pain, fatigue, abdominal distension, and diarrhoea.
- The vague and non-specific nature of the symptoms often cause women to dismiss the symptoms as stress or menopause-related.
- Women who do seek medical attention are easily misdiagnosed with benign GI or urinary conditions.
- Raised serum Ca125.

High-grade serous carcinoma
- Most common ovarian cancer.
- Associated with inactivation of *BRCA1/2* and *TP53* mutations.
- Arises from a precursor lesion known as **serous tubal intraepithelial carcinoma** (STIC).
- STIC is now thought to originate in most cases within the Fallopian tube fimbrial epithelium, with subsequent spread to the ovary.
- Histologically comprises high-grade malignant epithelial cells showing papillary and micropapillary growth with slit-like glandular spaces (Fig. 12.7).
- Immunohistochemistry shows CK7, WT-1, and Pax-8 positivity.

► Usually advanced stage at presentation, rapidly growing, and aggressive with poor survival.

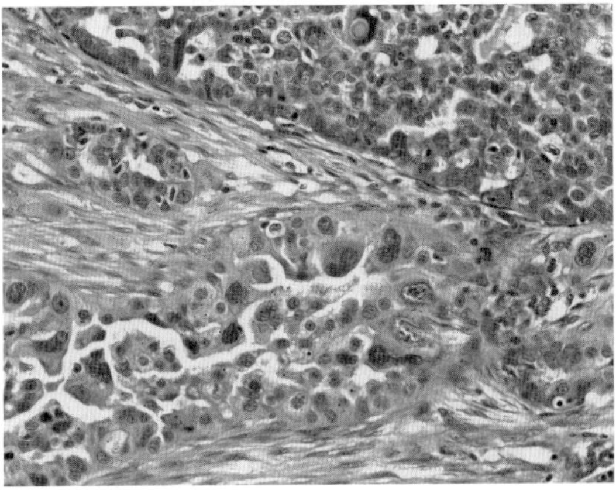

Fig. 12.7 High-grade serous carcinoma of the ovary (see Plate 29).

Low-grade serous carcinoma

- *KRAS* and *BRAF* mutations, but no *TP53* mutations and few chromosomal abnormalities.
- Arises through progression from serous cystadenoma → borderline tumour → low-grade serous carcinoma.
- Histologically comprise low-grade malignant epithelial cells growing in papillae. Psammoma bodies may be seen. Necrosis is not usually a feature.
- Prognosis excellent if confined to the ovary.

Endometrioid carcinoma

- Many are associated with endometriosis.
- Show *PTEN, PIK3CA*, and *ARID1A* mutations, as well as microsatellite instability in some.
- Soft solid or partly cystic mass with haemorrhage and necrosis.
- May appear as polypoid mass projecting into the endometriotic cyst.
- Usually unilateral.
- Histologically comprise malignant epithelial cells forming round or oval glands resembling endometrial carcinomas. Areas of squamous differentiation are common (Fig. 12.8).
- Survival dependent on stage, with 5-year survival rates of 78% for stage 1 cancers and 6% for stage 4.

Mucinous carcinoma

- Large, solid, and cystic tumour.
- Histologically comprise adenocarcinomas of intestinal type, growing in complex, crowded, fused glands.
- Immunohistochemistry shows CK7, CK20, and CDX2 positivity.
- 50% are stage I, with 83% 5-year survival.
- The 5-year survival for stages II, III, and IV are 55, 21, and 9%, respectively.

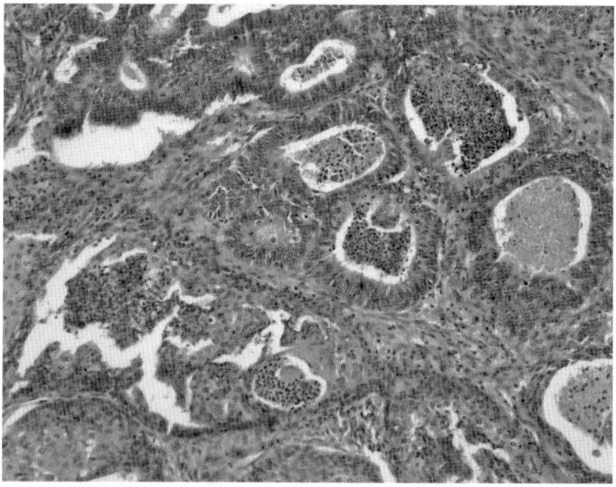

Fig. 12.8 Endometrioid carcinoma of the ovary (see Plate 30).

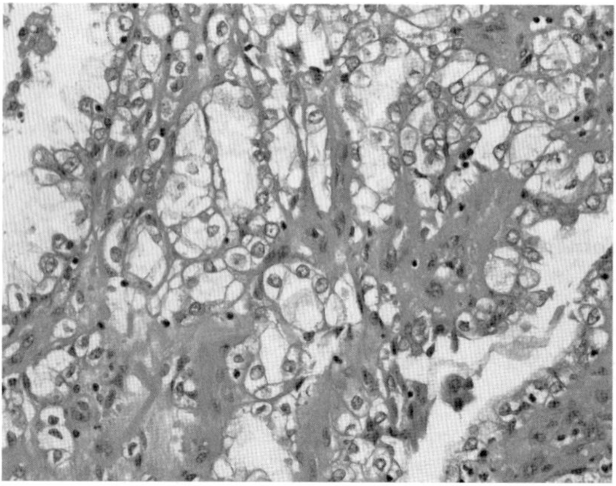

Fig. 12.9 Clear cell carcinoma of the ovary (see Plate 31).

Clear cell carcinoma

- Arise in most cases within endometriosis.
- They are composed of malignant epithelial cells with clear cytoplasm and hobnailing which grow in small tubules and papillae (Fig. 12.9).
- Survival for early stage 1a tumours is excellent, but high-stage disease survival is poor due to resistance to platinum-based chemotherapy.

FIGO staging of ovarian and Fallopian tube carcinomas (2014)

IA: tumour limited to one ovary (capsule intact) or Fallopian tube; no tumour on ovarian or Fallopian tube surface; no malignant cells in ascites or peritoneal washings.

IB: tumour limited to both ovaries (capsule intact) or Fallopian tubes; no tumour on ovarian or Fallopian tube surface; no malignant cells in ascites or peritoneal washings.

IC: tumour limited to one or both ovaries or Fallopian tubes, with any of the following:

- IC1: surgical spill
- IC2: capsule ruptured before surgery or tumour on ovarian or Fallopian tube surface
- IC3: malignant cells in ascites or peritoneal washings.

IIA: extension and/or implants on uterus and/or tubes and/or ovaries.

IIB: extension to other pelvic intraperitoneal tissues.

III: tumour involves one or both ovaries or Fallopian tubes, or primary peritoneal cancer, with cytologically or histologically confirmed spread to the peritoneum outside the pelvis and/or metastasis to the retroperitoneal lymph nodes:

- IIIA1: positive retroperitoneal lymph nodes only:
  - IIIA1(i): metastasis up to 10mm in greatest dimension
  - IIIA1(ii): metastasis >10mm in greatest dimension
- IIIA2: microscopic extrapelvic (above pelvic brim) peritoneal involvement with or without positive retroperitoneal lymph nodes
- IIIB: macroscopic peritoneal metastasis beyond the pelvis 2cm or less in size, with or without metastasis to the retroperitoneal lymph nodes
- IIIC: peritoneal metastasis beyond the pelvis >2cm in size and/or regional lymph node metastasis (includes extension of tumour to capsule of the liver and spleen without parenchymal involvement of either organ.

IV: distant metastasis, excluding peritoneal metastases.

IVA: pleural effusion with positive cytology.

IVB: parenchymal metastases and metastases to extra-abdominal organs (including inguinal lymph nodes and lymph nodes outside of the abdominal cavity).

Pelvic inflammatory disease

Definition

- An infection of the upper female genital tract.

Epidemiology

- Most cases are seen in young sexually active women aged 15–25.
- True incidence is difficult to estimate, as many cases go undiagnosed.

Aetiology

- Most cases are caused by ascending infection by either *Chlamydia trachomatis* or *Neisseria gonorrhoeae*. Both organisms are sexually transmitted bacteria.
- Cases unrelated to a sexually transmitted infection are often associated with intrauterine devices or retained products of conception postpartum or post-miscarriage.

Presentation

- Usually there are persistent symptoms of pelvic pain, dyspareunia, and post-coital or intermenstrual bleeding.
- Severe cases may cause an acute illness with fever, abdominal pain, and peritonism.

► Note that many women are asymptomatic and go undiagnosed.

Complications

- Infertility. The risk of infertility increases with each episode of infection. Women with three or more episodes of pelvic inflammatory disease (PID) have a 40% chance of being infertile.
- Ectopic pregnancy. There is a 6-fold increased risk, presumably due to tubal distortion and scarring.
- Chronic pelvic pain and dyspareunia.

Ectopic pregnancy

Definition

- Abnormal implantation of a fertilized ovum outside the uterine cavity. Nearly all occur in the Fallopian tubes, usually in the ampullary region. Other sites include the ovaries and abdominal cavity, but these are rare.

Epidemiology

- Annual incidence is 12 per 1000 pregnancies and rising.

Aetiology

- Tubal scarring from previous episodes of PID is the most common predisposing factor.
- Other risk factors include previous tubal surgery and endometriosis.
- About half occur for no apparent underlying reason.

Pathogenesis

- Trophoblast implanting within the Fallopian tube causes intense haemorrhage into the tube.
- The embryo may be dislodged and shed, or absorbed into the tubal wall.
- Rupture of the tubal wall may be sudden or gradual.

Presentation

- The typical presentation is gradually increasing abdominal pain and vaginal bleeding.
- Sudden rupture causes an acute abdomen with peritonism and shock.

► Consider the diagnosis in any woman of reproductive age with abdominal pain.

Macroscopy

- The involved Fallopian tube is markedly dilated and congested.
- The tubal lumen is filled with blood and friable material.

Histopathology

- Chorionic villi and infiltrating extravillous trophoblast are seen within the Fallopian tube.

Prognosis

- Prognosis is good, provided the diagnosis is made and appropriate management follows.
- Having one ectopic pregnancy is associated with a higher risk of future ectopics.

Polycystic ovarian syndrome

Definition

- A metabolic syndrome characterized by androgen excess, ovulatory failure, and, in some women, polycystic ovaries.

Epidemiology

- Common, affecting about 5% of women.

Aetiology

- Insulin resistance appears to be the key underlying cause (Fig. 12.10).

Pathogenesis

- Insulin resistance → obesity and ↑ androgen production by the ovaries.
- ↑ androgens → hirsutism, acne, and abnormal follicle maturation.
- Abnormal follicle maturation → polycystic ovaries in some women.
- Chronic anovulation → subfertility and ↑ oestrogen production.
- Prolonged oestrogen exposure → endometrial hyperplasia and risk of development of endometrial hyperplasia and endometrial carcinoma (➔ Endometrial carcinoma, pp. 256–9).

Presentation

- Subfertility is a common presentation.
- Irregular periods or no periods.
- Weight gain.
- Some women present with hirsutism and acne.

Radiology

- Polycystic ovaries may be seen in some, but not all, women.

Biochemistry

- Elevated blood androgens.
- Impaired glucose tolerance or frank diabetes.

Prognosis

- The main issues are the complications associated with obesity and the risk of endometrial carcinoma.
- Weight reduction, insulin-lowering agents, and progesterone administration all act to reduce these complications.

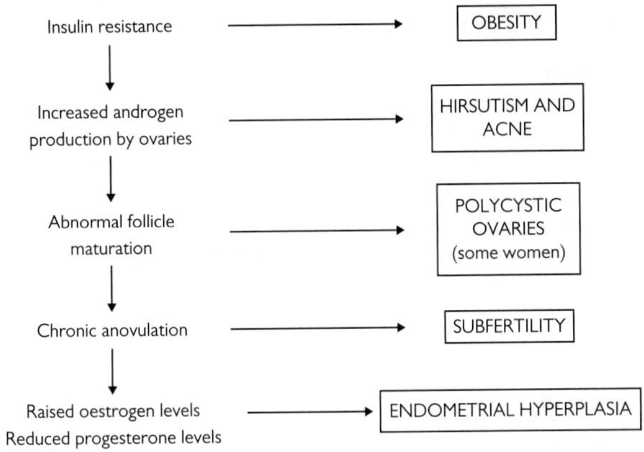

Fig. 12.10 Pathophysiology and clinical features of polycystic ovarian syndrome.
Reproduced with permission from *Clinical Pathology* (Oxford Core Texts), Carton, James, Daly, Richard, and Ramani, Pramila, Oxford University Press (2006), p. 272, Figure 12.11.

Hydatidiform moles

Definition

- A type of gestational trophoblastic disease characterized by abnormal trophoblastic proliferation.
- Two types are recognized: **complete moles** and **partial moles**.

Epidemiology

- About 1 in 1000 pregnancies in the western world are molar.
- For unknown reasons, they are much more common in areas of the Far East where incidence rates are as high as 1 in 80.

Genetics

- Complete moles are usually diploid (46 XX or 46 XY), with all chromosomes being paternally derived. They arise from fertilization of an anucleate ovum by a haploid sperm which then duplicates its genetic material.
- Partial moles are triploid (69 XXY, 69 XXX, or 69 XYY), with one set of maternal chromosomes and two sets of paternal chromosomes. They arise from fertilization of an ovum by two sperm.

Presentation

- Most present with early miscarriage. Usually there is no clinical suspicion of molar pregnancy, the diagnosis being made following histopathological examination of the evacuated products of conception.

Macroscopy

- Most molar products of conception are grossly unremarkable.
- Cases presenting late may contain visibly hydropic villi.

Histopathology

- Complete moles show villi with a characteristic lobulated 'budding' architecture. The villi have a myxoid stroma containing collapsed empty blood vessels and karyorrhectic debris. There is abnormal non-polar trophoblastic hyperplasia and sheets of pleomorphic extravillous trophoblast may be present. A prominent implantation site reaction is often seen, but with absence of the normal trophoblast plugging of decidual blood vessels.
- Partial moles show villi with irregular, 'dentate', or 'geographic' outlines. The villi are often fibrotic and contain prominent villous pseudoinclusions and villous blood vessels with nucleated fetal red cells. Abnormal non-polar trophoblastic hyperplasia is present, though this is usually focal and less marked than in complete moles. The implantation site is usually unremarkable with normal trophoblast plugging of decidual blood vessels.

Prognosis

- In most cases, evacuation of molar tissue is curative and β-HCG levels rapidly fall to normal.
- Persistence of β-HCG levels is indicative of persistent gestational trophoblastic disease; this complicates ~15% of complete moles and ~1% of partial moles, and requires chemotherapy to cure.

Gestational choriocarcinoma

One other type of gestational trophoblastic disease is **choriocarcinoma**, a rare, but highly malignant, trophoblastic tumour. About half develop from a preceding hydatidiform mole, with the remainder following a normal pregnancy or non-molar miscarriage.

Histologically, choriocarcinomas are composed of a mixture of cytotrophoblast and syncytiotrophoblast, typically forming bilaminar structures. By definition, chorionic villi are absent.

Choriocarcinomas have a great propensity for vascular invasion, leading to early dissemination to multiple distant sites. Fortunately, gestational choriocarcinomas respond extremely well to chemotherapy, and the prognosis for most women is very good.

Pre-eclampsia

Definition
- Pregnancy-induced hypertension with proteinuria.

Epidemiology
- Complicates about 6% of pregnancies.
- More frequent in women carrying their first child.

Aetiology
- Exact cause unknown, but abnormal placentation is key (Fig. 12.11).

Pathogenesis
- Abnormally shallow invasion of the trophoblast, with failure of physiological conversion of intradecidual spiral arteries and basal arteries into large low-resistance vessels.
- Maternal blood pressure rises in an attempt to compensate, but the net result is placental ischaemia.
- Toxic substances released from the ischaemic placenta enter the maternal circulation and cause endothelial damage.
- Progression to eclampsia is heralded by widespread formation of fibrin thrombi within the microcirculation and risk of renal failure, hepatic failure, cardiac failure, and cerebral haemorrhage.

Presentation
- Usually routine antenatal surveillance picks up hypertension after 20 weeks' gestation, together with proteinuria.

Macroscopy
- Placentas tend to be smaller than those from normal pregnancies.
- The incidence of placental infarcts is much higher.

Histopathology
- Placental villi show increased number and prominence of villous cytotrophoblast with irregular thickening of the basement membrane. Villous blood vessels are often small and inconspicuous. Maternal decidual arteries show failure of physiological conversion by the trophoblast. A minority also show fibrinoid necrosis of the arterial wall, together with intramural accumulation of lipid-laden macrophages ('atherosis').
- The kidneys show enlarged 'bloodless' glomeruli containing swollen endothelial cells. Fibrin microthrombi may be seen within glomerular capillary loops in more severe cases.
- The liver may show fibrin thrombi in hepatic sinusoids, with hepatic necrosis and haemorrhage in severe cases.

Prognosis
►► Delivery is the only cure. The danger to the fetus from premature delivery must be weighed against the risks to the mother. The disease behaves very unpredictably and can progress very rapidly, so patients must be closely monitored for signs of deterioration.

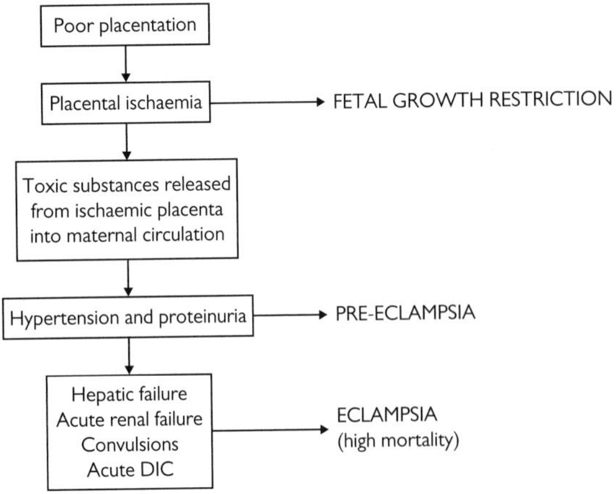

Fig. 12.11 Postulated pathogenesis of pre-eclampsia.

Reproduced with permission from *Clinical Pathology* (Oxford Core Texts), Carton, James, Daly, Richard, and Ramani, Pramila, Oxford University Press (2006), p. 282, Figure 12.18.

Chapter 13

Breast pathology

Duct ectasia

Definition

- Inflammation and dilation of large breast ducts.

Epidemiology

- Common in adult women of all ages.

Aetiology

- Unclear.
- Whilst infection may complicate duct ectasia, it does not seem to be the underlying cause.

Presentation

- Nipple discharge is the most common presenting symptom. The discharge may be clear, creamy, or bloodstained.
- More florid cases may cause pain, a breast mass, and nipple retraction.

Macroscopy

- Subareolar ducts are visibly dilated and contain thick secretions.

Cytopathology

- Smears prepared from a sample of nipple discharge contain proteinaceous debris and macrophages.
- Ductal epithelial cells are usually not seen.

Histopathology

- Subareolar ducts are dilated and filled with proteinaceous material and macrophages.
- Periductal chronic inflammation and fibrosis are also seen.

Prognosis

- Duct ectasia is a benign condition with no increased risk of malignancy.

Granulomatous mastitis

Definition

- Granulomatous inflammation in and around the breast lobules (granulomatous lobulitis).
- Appears after pregnancy.

Clinical features

- Linked to pregnancy, hormone therapy, or infection (*Corynebacterium*-linked).
- Presents as a hard mass; may mimic carcinoma.
- May present as an abscess; can grow to large sizes.

Microbiology

- *Corynebacterium* has been recently implicated.
- Staphylococci and streptococci in lactating women.

Pathogenesis

- *Corynebacterium* is a resident of normal skin. Likely bacterial access to the breast and lowered immunity promotes infection.

Presentation

- A painful breast is the most common presentation.
- Abscess formation may produce a breast mass.

Macroscopy

- A firm to hard breast mass with a nodular pattern.
- Purulent material may be present with abscess formation.

Histopathology

- Granulomatous inflammation in the perilobular region.
- Inflammatory reaction comprises granulomas, multinucleate giant cells, and eosinophils; small lipogranuloma with a central degenerate vacuole.
- Fat necrosis and abscess formation.
- Special stains (Gram) show *Corynebacterium* bacteria, thought to be the source of abscess.

Histologic mimics

- Plasma cell mastitis.
- Tuberculous mastitis.
- Breast abscess.
- Sarcoidosis.
- Drainage and appropriate antibiotic treatment usually result in resolution.

Prognosis

- No relationship to carcinoma.

Fat necrosis

Definition
- An inflammatory reaction to damaged adipose tissue.

Epidemiology
- Common.

Aetiology
- Related to trauma, breast surgery, radiation, infection; idiopathic.

Pathogenesis
- Damaged adipocytes spill their lipid contents, resulting in an inflammatory reaction which gives rise to a palpable mass.

Presentation
- Palpable breast.
- Clinically mimics carcinoma.

Macroscopy
- The breast tissue shows yellow-white flecks of discoloration.

Cytopathology
- FNA cytology shows foamy macrophages, multinucleated giant cells, and background debris.

Histopathology
- Degenerating adipocytes are present, surrounded by foamy macrophages, multinucleated giant cells, lymphocytes, and plasma cells.
- Scar and calcifications are common in late lesions.
- Later changes include fibrosis and calcification.

Differential diagnosis
- Ductal carcinoma.

Prognosis
- Benign with no increased risk of breast cancer.

Fibrocystic change

Definition

- A number of alterations within the breast, which reflect normal, albeit exaggerated, responses to hormonal influences.

Epidemiology

- Very common.
- Found in more than one-third of premenopausal adult women.

Aetiology

- A hormonally driven condition in response to oestrogens.

Pathogenesis

- Somewhat unclear, though some workers speculate that the initial event is apocrine metaplasia of breast ducts.
- Secretions produced by these cells lead to duct dilation and formation of cysts.

Presentation

- Breast nodularity and lumpiness are the main features.
- There may also be cyclical tenderness.

Macroscopy

- The breast tissue has a firm, rubbery texture.
- Visible cysts are usually evident with a brown or bluish hue.

Cytopathology

- Aspirates of cysts show debris, foamy macrophages, and apocrine cells.
- Aspirates of non-cystic areas contain cohesive fragments of bland ductal epithelial cells and many background bare bipolar nuclei.

Histopathology

- Associated with a number of histological changes, including cystic change, apocrine metaplasia, adenosis, mild epithelial hyperplasia, and stromal hyperplasia.

Prognosis

- Benign with no increased risk for subsequent invasive breast carcinoma.

Fibroadenoma

Definition

- A benign fibroepithelial tumour of the breast.

Epidemiology

- Common.
- Occurs mostly in young women aged 20–30y.

Aetiology

- Most authorities believe them to be neoplastic growths of fibroblasts within the specialized connective tissue of the intralobular stroma.

Pathogenesis

- As the neoplastic fibroblasts multiply within the intralobular stroma, they entrap and compress the terminal duct lobular units and interlobular stroma to form a well-circumscribed nodular mass.

Macroscopy

- Well-circumscribed mobile breast masses which usually measure 3cm or less.
- The cut surface is usually solid, whorled, and grey-white in colour.

Cytopathology

- Aspirates are cellular, containing many branching sheets of cohesive bland ductal epithelial cells and abundant bare bipolar nuclei in the background.
- Fragments of stromal material may also be seen.

Histopathology

- Histology shows a multinodular mass which is well demarcated from the surrounding breast tissue.
- Each nodule contains an expanded myxoid intralobular stromal compartment containing bland spindled fibroblastic cells. The terminal duct lobular unit is compressed into slit-like channels.
- Narrow strands of interlobular stroma are present between each nodule of the fibroadenoma.
- Older lesions often show fibrosis and calcification.

Prognosis

- Benign lesions with no capacity for malignant behaviour.
- Surgical excision with simple 'shelling out' is virtually always curative, with little chance of recurrence.

Phyllodes tumour

Definition

- Rare fibroepithelial tumour.
- Hypercellular mesenchymal component in a leaf-like pattern.

Epidemiology

- 1% of breast tumour.
- Usually affects adults (fifth/sixth decades). Rare in children.
- Rapidly growing, discrete, palpable breast mass.

Aetio-pathogenesis

- A biphasic fibroepithelial tumour.
- Considered as a stromal tumour with the capacity to induce glandular formation.

Macroscopy

- Well-circumscribed, bulging masses.
- Cut surface is fleshy.
- Whorled pattern with curved clefts resembling a 'leaf' (nomenclature derived from the leaf-shaped clefts).
- May show myxoid areas, haemorrhage, or necrosis.

Histopathology

- Circumscribed pushing border, stromal hypercellularity and overgrowth.
- Stroma typically overgrows the glandular component.
- Stromal nodules project into the lumen, producing characteristic 'leaf-like' fronds.
- Mitotic counts important (0–4/hpf for benign, 4–10 for borderline, and >10/hpf for malignant lesions).
- May show haemorrhage, fat, cartilage, or skeletal muscle.
- May show variable atypia.

Treatment

- Previously benign tumours were excised with a margin of normal breast tissue. More recent studies suggest that simple excision usually suffices, particularly in young women.
- In borderline lesions, wide local excision is suggested, with follow-up.
- Malignant lesions should be treated as sarcoma and followed up at specialized sarcoma units.

Prognosis

- Traditional classification includes benign, borderline, and malignant lesions.
- New classification; low and high grade, due to difficulty in predicting behaviour on histology alone.
- Positive margin status increases the recurrence rate.
- Overall good prognosis; rare chance of metastases.

Intraductal papilloma

Definition

- A benign papillary tumour arising within the duct system of the breast.
- Papillomas can develop anywhere in the ductal system but show a predilection for either small terminal ductules (peripheral papillomas) or large lactiferous ducts (central papillomas).

Epidemiology

- Common.
- Seen mostly in women in their 40s and 50s.

Aetiology

- Believed to be neoplastic growths of glandular and stromal breast tissue.

Presentation

- Most women with central papillomas present with nipple discharge.
- Small peripheral papillomas usually present with a breast mass.

Macroscopy

- Large papillomas are visible as friable masses within a dilated duct.

Cytopathology

- Smears prepared from nipple discharge may contain branching papillaroid groups of epithelial cells, which suggests the diagnosis.

Histopathology

- A papillary mass is present with a duct space.
- The papillae are broad and rounded, such that the fronds fit neatly around each other.
- Each frond contains abundant stroma composed of blood vessels and fibrous tissue.
- The epithelium covering the fronds is double-layered, composed of inner columnar epithelial cells and outer myoepithelial cells.

Prognosis

- Benign papillomas, particularly those involving a single duct, have little risk of carcinoma. When multiple papillomas are present, there is a 2-fold increased risk of subsequent invasive breast carcinoma.

Radial scar

Definition

- A benign sclerosing breast lesion, characterized by a central zone of scarring surrounded by a radiating rim of proliferating glandular tissue.
- Radial scars range in size from tiny microscopic lesions to larger clinically apparent masses. Large lesions >1cm in size are sometimes called 'complex sclerosing lesions'.

Epidemiology

- Radial scars are reasonably common lesions.
- Incidence rates vary widely, depending on how they are defined.

Aetiology

- Little is known about the aetiology or pathogenesis of radial scars.
- One hypothesis is that they represent a reparative phenomenon in response to areas of tissue damage in the breast.

Presentation

- Large foci of sclerosing adenosis and radial scars are usually detected on mammography as stellate or spiculated masses.

► They can closely mimic the appearance of a carcinoma.

Macroscopy

- Grossly, radial scars are stellate, firm masses which appear to infiltrate the surrounding parenchyma.
- They may be easily confused for invasive carcinomas macroscopically.

Histopathology

- Symmetrical stellate breast lesion with a characteristic zonal architecture.
- The centre of the lesion (nidus) comprises fibroelastotic collagen tissue, within which are entrapped haphazardly arranged tubules.
- Surrounding the nidus are radially arranged clusters of ducts and lobules, each of which points towards the centre of the lesion. The ducts and lobules within this zone typically exhibit florid benign changes, including fibrocystic change, sclerosing adenosis, and marked usual epithelial hyperplasia.

Prognosis

- Radial scars, also known as complex sclerosing lesions, are benign lesions and thought to have a 2-fold increased cancer risk.
- Recent reports, however, suggest an increased risk when atypia is present.

Proliferative breast diseases with/without atypia

Definition

- A diverse group of intraductal proliferative lesions of the breast, associated with a variably increased risk for subsequent development of invasive breast carcinoma.

Epidemiology

- Commonly seen in the breast.
- Increasingly identified since the introduction of breast screening programmes.

Aetiology

- Similar to invasive breast carcinoma (➲ Invasive breast carcinomas, pp. 294–6).

Genetics

- Most cases of flat epithelial atypia and *in situ* lobular neoplasia show genetic abnormalities, most notably the loss of heterozygosity of chromosome 16p.
- Only a minority of cases of usual epithelial hyperplasia show genetic abnormalities.

Macroscopy

- The vast majority are picked up either on screening mammography or incidentally in breast tissue removed for other reasons.

Histopathology

- **Usual epithelial hyperplasia** is a haphazard proliferation of ductal epithelial cells which form fenestrations and irregular slit-like spaces.
- **Flat epithelial atypia** represents cyto-architectural atypia seen within the acini, comprising flattened epithelial cells, usually single but occasionally more than one layer of cells thick. The cells are mildly atypical with nucleoli. This pattern is thought to be the precursor of flat-type low-grade ductal carcinoma *in situ* (DCIS).
- **Atypical ductal hyperplasia (ADH)** or atypical intraductal proliferation (AIDP) is a high-risk lesion comprising atypical ductal cells showing cytological and architectural atypia falling short of DCIS. Lesions are usually <2 duct spaces or <2mm in size.
- ***In situ* lobular neoplasia** is a proliferation of small, poorly cohesive epithelial cells arising in the terminal duct lobular system and characterized by a monomorphic population of small cells showing loss of E-cadherin expression immunohistochemically. Morphologically, lesion of atypical lobular hyperplasia (ALH) and lobular carcinoma *in situ* (LCIS) are included in this category.

Prognosis

- Usual epithelial hyperplasia is not considered a direct precursor lesion to invasive breast carcinoma but is a marker for a slightly increased risk (relative risk of 1.5–2.0) for subsequent invasive carcinoma.
- Large series on relative risk and flat epithelial atypia are lacking, but it appears to have a risk similar to ADH (four times), albeit a little less.
- A third up to a half of ADH lesions may show genetic changes similar to DCIS, i.e. loss of 16q and 17p. ADH has an increased risk of invasive breast carcinoma (4–5 times that of the general population). This risk is further increased if the patient has a first-degree relative with breast cancer.
- ALH and LCIS are bilateral and multifocal in a high proportion of cases. Current evidence suggests that *in situ* lobular neoplasia is a risk factor for subsequent invasive breast carcinoma in either breast and it is now widely realized that these lesions are more closely related to ADH than to DCIS. The relative risk appears to be similar (4–5 times) to that expected in women without lobular neoplasia.

Ductal carcinoma *in situ*

Definition

- Neoplastic heterogeneous intraductal epithelial proliferations arising from the terminal duct lobular unit, with an increased risk of progression to invasive breast carcinoma.

Epidemiology

- Common.
- Incidence has markedly increased since the introduction of breast screening programmes.

Aetiology

- Risks similar to invasive breast carcinoma (➔ Invasive breast carcinomas, pp. 294–6).

Genetics

- Low-grade DCIS often is associated with loss of 16q.
- High-grade DCIS is genetically distinct with a more complex karyotype with gains of 17q and 8q, and 5p with losses of 11q, 13q, and 14q.

Presentation

- 85% are detected on mammography as areas of microcalcification.
- 10% produce clinical findings such as a lump, nipple discharge, or eczematous change of the nipple (**Paget's disease of the nipple**).
- 5% are diagnosed incidentally in breast specimens removed for other reasons.

Macroscopy

- DCIS is often macroscopically invisible, even to an experienced pathologist.
- Extensive high-grade DCIS may be visible as gritty, yellow flecks due to calcified necrotic debris in the involved ducts.

Histopathology

- DCIS is subclassified into low, intermediate, and high nuclear grade.
- **Low-grade DCIS** has small monotonous cells growing in cribriform, solid, or micropapillary patterns with good cellular polarization (cells have basally positioned nuclei and apical cytoplasm directed towards the duct lumen). Necrosis in the centre of the duct is unusual.
- **Intermediate-grade DCIS** has cells with moderately sized nuclei and coarse chromatin growing in solid, cribriform, or micropapillary patterns with a moderate degree of cellular polarization. Central necrosis may be present.
- **High-grade DCIS** has cells with large, markedly pleomorphic nuclei with clumped chromatin, prominent nucleoli, and poor cellular polarization. Central necrosis is common.

Biology

- Microarray and laser capture microdissection have shown that gene expression signatures of DCIS may be similar to invasive carcinoma.
- Low-grade DCIS frequently shows loss of 16q, whilst high-grade DCIS shows more complex mutational changes.

Prognosis

- Complete surgical excision with clear margins is curative. Prognosis depends on the persistence of any neoplastic cells after treatment. Recurrence is more likely with extensive disease, high nuclear grade, and the presence of comedo necrosis.
- Van Nuy's prognostic index uses tumour size, margin width, and grade of DCIS to prognosticate pure DCIS lesions, dividing this into low-, intermediate-, and high-risk categories for local recurrence that may benefit from radiation therapy.

Invasive breast carcinomas

Definition

- A group of malignant invasive epithelial tumours of the breast derived from a terminal duct lobular unit with the capacity to spread to distant sites.

Epidemiology

- The most common cancer in women, with a lifetime risk of 1 in 8.
- Incidence rates rise rapidly with increasing age, such that most cases occur in older women.
- Rarely in 20s and 30s with a family history of breast carcinoma.
- The most common site is the upper outer quadrant, although it can occur anywhere in the breast.

Aetiology

- Early menarche, late menopause, increased weight, high alcohol consumption, oral contraceptive use, and a positive family history are all associated with increased risk.
- ~5% show clear evidence of inheritance. *BRCA* mutations cause a lifetime risk of invasive breast carcinoma of up to 85%.

Carcinogenesis

- Recent genetic studies have led to the hypothesis that breast cancer evolution is broadly classified into two groups: luminal and basal/abluminal phenotypes. These are also defined by differential expression of hormone receptors.
- The luminal subtype (e.g. low-grade invasive ductal carcinoma, classical lobular carcinoma, tubule-lobular, cribriform, mucinous carcinoma, tubular carcinoma) classically expresses oestrogen (ER) and progesterone (PR) receptors with lack of HER2 overexpression. These are thought to arise within luminal ductal cells and do not express basal markers. Genetically, they have simple diploid or near diploid karyotypes and, as a hallmark, show deletion of 16q and gains of 1q.
- The basal subtype (e.g. high-grade invasive ductal carcinoma, including medullary and atypical medullary, metaplastic carcinoma, apocrine carcinoma, secretory carcinoma, adenoid cystic carcinoma, and acinic carcinoma) frequently lacks hormone receptors and may show overexpression of HER2 (or lack all three ER/PR/HER2). These often express basal markers. Genetically, they have complex karyotypes with many unbalanced chromosomal aberrations showing frequent gains of 1q, 2q, and 1p and losses of 1p, 12q, 17q, 8p, and 17p.

Presentation

- Most cases present symptomatically with a breast lump, usually an ill-defined mass, sometimes adherent to the skin or the underlying pectoralis muscle.
- An increasing proportion of asymptomatic cases and small tumours are detected on screening mammography.

Macroscopy

- Most breast carcinomas produce a firm, stellate mass in the breast.

Cytopathology

- FNA from breast carcinomas are typically highly cellular, containing a poorly cohesive population of malignant epithelial cells. Background bare bipolar nuclei are absent.

Histopathology

- **Invasive ductal carcinomas** (80%) are infiltrating carcinomas which do not exhibit sufficient characteristics to achieve classification as a specific histological type such as lobular or tubular carcinoma (hence, they are also sometimes referred to as 'no special type'). They therefore represent a heterogeneous group of tumours, rather than a distinct type. It is likely in the future that this group will become divided up into more meaningful entities on the basis of their genetic profiles.
- **Invasive lobular carcinomas** (15%) are composed of small, poorly cohesive cells with scant cytoplasm, which characteristically grow in linear cords and encircle pre-existing normal ducts.
- **Tubular carcinomas** (5%) are composed of well-formed tubular structures lined by a single layer of epithelial cells with low-grade atypia.
- **Mucinous carcinomas** (5%) are characterized by the production of abundant quantities of mucin within which the tumour cells float.
- **Basal-like carcinomas** are a recently described group of tumours discovered by the genetic profiling of large numbers of breast carcinomas. They often occur in young women and are linked to *BRCA* mutations. Morphologically, they typically show sheets of highly atypical epithelial cells with a prominent lymphocytic inflammatory infiltrate and central necrosis. Immunohistochemically, they are characterized by the expression of basal-type keratins, e.g. cytokeratins 5 and 14. Basal-like tumours are frequently ER- and PR-negative and HER2-non-amplified (so-called 'triple-negative' tumours). About 15% of tumours tend to be ER/PR-negative and HER2 overexpressors. These tumours appear to have a propensity to visceral metastasis, notably to the lungs and brain. These, however, also show good response with chemotherapeutic agents.

Grading

- All invasive breast cancers are graded histologically by assessing nuclear pleomorphism, tubule formation, and mitotic activity.
- Each parameter is scored from 1 to 3, and the three values are added together to produce total scores from 3 to 9.
- 3–5 points = grade 1 (well differentiated).
- 6–7 points = grade 2 (moderately differentiated).
- 8–9 points = grade 3 (poorly differentiated).

Prognosis

- The single most important prognostic factor is the status of the axillary lymph nodes.
- Other important factors include tumour size, histological type, and histological grade.

Simplified TNM 7 pathological staging of breast carcinomas

Primary tumour (T)
pT1: tumour 2cm or less in size.
pT2: tumour >2cm, but not >5cm in size.
pT3: tumour >5cm in size.
pT4: tumour of any size with extension to the chest wall and/or skin.

Regional lymph nodes (N)
pN0: no regional lymph node metastasis.
pN1: metastasis in 1–3 ipsilateral axillary lymph nodes.
pN2: metastasis in 4–9 ipsilateral axillary lymph nodes.
pN3: metastasis in 10 or more ipsilateral axillary lymph nodes.

Treatment

- Based on prognostic factors that include tumour size, histological grade, nodal stage, and hormone receptor status, invasive cancers are treated with a combination regimen that includes surgery (localized or radical), chemotherapy, hormone manipulation, and local radiotherapy.

Genomic tests

- These are NHS-funded and are predictive tests that analyze a group of genes that can affect how a cancer is likely to behave and respond to treatment. The test include Oncotype DX® and EndoPredict®.
- **EndoPredict®** testing is a multi-gene test used to predict the risk of distant recurrence of early-stage, ER-positive, HER2-negative invasive breast cancer that is either node-negative (pN0) or has up to three positive nodes (pN1). The EndoPredict® clinical score (EP clinscore) categorizes patients into low- and high-risk groups. The low-risk group is less likely to develop recurrences, compared with high-risk groups, and hence can be spared the side effects of chemotherapy.
- **Oncotype DX®** testing is done for low-stage (1 and 2), ER-positive, and lymph-node negative (pN0) invasive breast cancers. A recurrence score (RI) is generated by testing for the activity of 21 genes.
- Invasive cancer with a low score (<18) is deemed to have a low chance of recurrence and less likely to derive benefit from chemotherapy.
- Invasive cancer with a high score (≥31) have a higher risk of recurrence and likely to derive benefit from chemotherapy
- Invasive cancer with intermediate score (18–30): risk is unclear.

Breast screening

► The aim of screening is to pick up DCIS or early invasive carcinoma.

NHS breast screening programme

- Women aged 50–70 are invited for screening every 3y.
- The NHS is in the process of extending this to women aged 47–73.
- The screening test is a mammogram which looks for abnormal areas of calcification or a mass within the breast.

Assessment clinic

- ~5% of women have an abnormal mammogram and are recalled to an assessment clinic for further investigation.
- This may include more mammograms or an ultrasound, followed by sampling of the abnormal area, usually by core biopsy.

Histopathology

- Core biopsies taken from breast screening patients are given a B code from 1 to 5.
- B1 is normal breast tissue. This usually implies the biopsy missed the area of interest.
- B2 is a core containing a benign abnormality. This is appropriate for a range of lesions, including fibroadenomas, fibrocystic change, sclerosing adenosis, and fat necrosis.
- B3 is a lesion of uncertain malignant potential. This category mainly consists of lesions which may be benign in the core but are known to show heterogeneity or to have an increased risk (albeit low) of an adjacent malignancy. This is appropriate for cores showing flat epithelial atypia, *in situ* lobular neoplasia, ADH, partly sampled papillomas, phyllodes tumours, and radial scars.
- B4 is a core showing features suspicious of malignancy, but in which unequivocal diagnosis is not possible due to reasons such as insufficient abnormal tissue or crushing of the biopsy.
- B5 is a core biopsy showing unequivocal features of malignancy. This is subdivided into B5a for DCIS or B5b for invasive carcinoma.

Management

- B1: rebiopsy.
- B2: reassure and return to normal recall.
- B3: excision of the abnormal area.
- B4: rebiopsy or excision of the abnormal area.
- B5: surgical excision with wide local excision or mastectomy.

Effectiveness

- Published figures state that the NHS breast screening programme saves about 1250 lives each year.

Male breast diseases

Gynaecomastia

- Refers to the enlargement of the male breast.
- Usually seen in boys around puberty and older men aged >50.
- Most cases are either idiopathic or associated with drugs (both therapeutic and recreational).
- Histologically, the breast ducts show epithelial hyperplasia with typical finger-like projections extending into the duct lumen. The periductal stroma is often cellular and oedematous.
- The condition is benign, with no increased risk of malignancy.

Male breast cancer

- Carcinoma of the male breast is rare (0.2% of all cancers).
- The median age at diagnosis is 65y.
- Most patients present with a palpable lump.
- Grossly, the tumours are firm, irregular masses.
- Histologically, the tumours show similar features to female breast cancers.

Chapter 14

Endocrine pathology

Diabetes mellitus

Definition

- A metabolic disorder characterized by chronic hyperglycaemia due to lack of insulin.

Epidemiology

- Very common, affecting ~2% of the population.
- Rising in incidence.

Aetiology

- Type 1 diabetes is due to the autoimmune destruction of insulin-producing beta cells by CD4+ and CD8+ T-lymphocytes. Autoantibodies against beta cells and insulin may also be relevant.
- Type 2 diabetes is strongly related to obesity and insulin resistance. Initially, the pancreas compensates for insulin resistance by increasing insulin secretion, but eventually beta cells suffer from 'secretory exhaustion' and insulin levels then become inappropriately low.

Pathogenesis

- Lack of insulin drives the mobilization of energy stores from muscle, fat, and the liver (Fig. 14.1).
- Glucose accumulates in the blood, causing hyperglycaemia.
- In the kidneys, the glucose reabsorption mechanism becomes saturated and glucose appears in the urine.
- Glucose within renal tubules draws water in by osmosis, leading to osmotic diuresis.
- The raised plasma osmolality stimulates the thirst centre.
- Over time, diabetes damages capillaries and markedly accelerates atherosclerosis.

Presentation

- Polyuria and polydipsia are the classic symptoms of diabetes mellitus.
- Hyperglycaemia also predisposes to recurrent skin and urinary tract infections.
- Type 1 diabetics may present acutely in diabetic ketoacidosis.

Biochemistry

- Fasting plasma glucose >7.0mmol/L or a random plasma glucose >11.1mmol/L.
- Patients with borderline values should have an oral glucose tolerance test.

Complications

- A number of organ systems are at risk in diabetes (Fig. 14.2).
- Ischaemic heart disease due to coronary artery atherosclerosis.
- CKD due to diabetic nephropathy (➔ Diabetic nephropathy, pp. 188–9).
- Visual impairment due to cataract and diabetic retinopathy.
- Peripheral vascular disease due to atherosclerosis.
- Foot ulceration due to peripheral neuropathy and ischaemia.

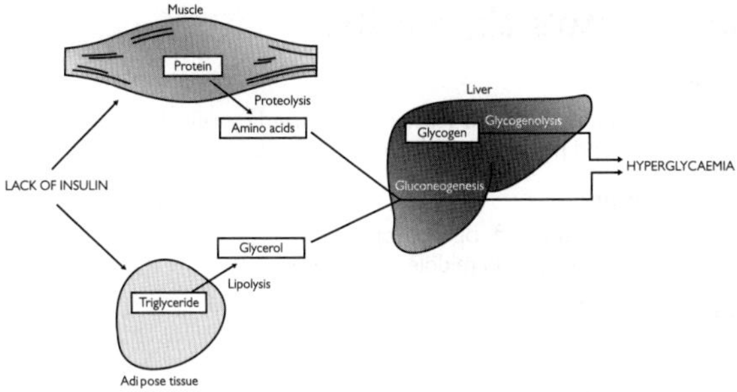

Fig. 14.1 Mechanism of hyperglycaemia in diabetes mellitus. Lack of insulin causes the breakdown of protein in muscle and of triglyceride in fat, providing substrates for gluconeogenesis in the liver. This, together with glucose formed from glycogen in the liver, causes hyperglycaemia.

Reproduced with permission from *Clinical Pathology* (Oxford Core Texts), Carton, James, Daly, Richard, and Ramani, Pramila, Oxford University Press (2006), p. 324, Figure 14.13.

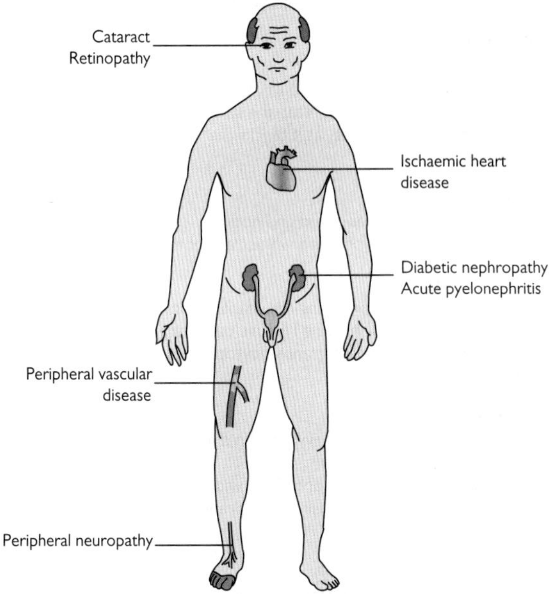

Fig. 14.2 Long-term complications of diabetes mellitus.

Reproduced with permission from *Clinical Pathology* (Oxford Core Texts), Carton, James, Daly, Richard, and Ramani, Pramila, Oxford University Press (2006), p. 326, Figure 14.14.

Hashimoto's thyroiditis

Definition

- An autoimmune thyroid disease characterized by diffuse enlargement of the thyroid and high titres of thyroid autoantibodies.

Epidemiology

- Common, affecting ~1% of the population.
- Predominantly occurs in middle-aged women.

Aetiology

- Unknown.

Pathogenesis

- Activated CD4+ helper T-cells recruit CD8+ cytotoxic T-cells which destroy thyroid follicular epithelial cells.
- Anti-thyroid autoantibodies produced by activated B-cells may also contribute.

Presentation

- Diffuse firm goitre and features of hypothyroidism.

Biochemistry

- ↑ TSH and ↓ T4.
- Autoantibodies against thyroglobulin, thyroid peroxidase, and TSH receptor are usually present. Note the latter antibody is different from that seen in Graves' disease, as it blocks the TSH receptor rather than activates it.

Macroscopy

- The thyroid is diffusely enlarged and nodular.
- The cut surface is often soft and white, resembling lymphoid tissue.

Cytopathology

- Aspirates are cellular, containing abundant lymphoid cells and scanty follicular epithelial cells showing Hurthle cell change.
- Hurthle cells have abundant granular cytoplasm and enlarged nuclei with vesicular chromatin.

Histopathology

- The thyroid shows diffuse heavy lymphoid infiltration with the formation of germinal centres.
- Thyroid follicles are atrophic and show widespread Hurthle cell change characterized by abundant eosinophilic granular cytoplasm and nuclear enlargement.

Prognosis

- Good with thyroxine replacement therapy.

► There is an increased incidence of thyroid lymphoma, usually extranodal marginal zone B-cell lymphoma (➔ Extranodal marginal zone lymphoma, pp. 370–1).

Graves' disease

Definition

- An autoimmune thyroid disease characterized by thyrotoxicosis and diffuse hyperplasia of the thyroid.

Epidemiology

- Common, affecting up to 1% of the population.
- Peak incidence is in young adults in their 30s and 40s.
- Women are affected much more frequently than men.

Aetiology

- Production of TSH receptor-stimulating antibodies.

Pathogenesis

- TSH receptor-stimulating antibodies bind to the TSH receptor and activate it, stimulating hyperplasia of the thyroid follicular epithelium and unregulated secretion of thyroid hormones.

Presentation

- Patients present with thyrotoxicosis and a diffuse goitre.
- Some patients also develop a form of orbital disease known as Graves' ophthalmopathy.

Macroscopy

- The thyroid is diffusely enlarged with a firm, red cut surface.
- If treatment has been administered, the thyroid may show a nodular appearance.

Cytopathology

- Aspirates are highly cellular with little colloid and many follicular epithelial cells showing hyperplastic changes.

► In practice, aspiration is rarely performed in cases of active Graves' disease, as the diagnosis is usually straightforward clinically. This is fortunate as the highly cellular aspirates can easily be mistaken for a neoplastic process by the unwary.

Histopathology

- The thyroid shows diffuse hyperplasia with loss of colloid and marked hyperplastic changes of the follicular epithelium.
- A variable lymphoid infiltrate, with or without germinal centres, is usually present.

Prognosis

- Excellent with appropriate thyroid ablative therapy.

Nodular goitre

Definition
- Nodular enlargement of the thyroid gland.

Epidemiology
- Very common.
- Clinically apparent nodular goitre affects up to 5% of the population.

Aetiology
- Endemic goitre occurs due to dietary iodine deficiency in geographic areas of the world with low levels of iodine in soil and water.
- Sporadic goitre may be due to ingestion of substances that interfere with thyroid hormone synthesis or due to genetic variations in components of the thyroid hormone synthetic apparatus.

Pathogenesis
- Reduced levels of thyroid hormones stimulate the release of TSH from the anterior pituitary, causing growth of the thyroid.

Presentation
- A palpably enlarged, nodular goitre.
- Most patients are euthyroid.

Macroscopy
See Fig. 14.3.
- The thyroid gland is enlarged and multinodular.
- Slicing reveals numerous unencapsulated nodules of varying size, usually containing abundant colloid.
- Areas of cystic change, haemorrhage, and calcification are common.

Cytopathology
- Aspirates contain abundant colloid with scanty thyroid follicular epithelium.
- Haemosiderin-laden macrophages may be present due to previous haemorrhage.
- Foamy macrophages often indicate cystic change within a nodule.

Histopathology
- The thyroid contains numerous nodules of varying sizes with areas of cystic change and haemorrhage.
- The follicles within the nodules are heterogeneous in appearance. Some are markedly distended with colloid; some appear hyperplastic, whilst others are small and tightly packed, forming cellular 'adenomatoid' nodules.

Prognosis
- Nodular goitre is a benign condition, with no reported increased risk of development of thyroid carcinoma.
- The main potential complication is compression of nearby structures, such as the trachea, by a markedly enlarged nodular goitre.

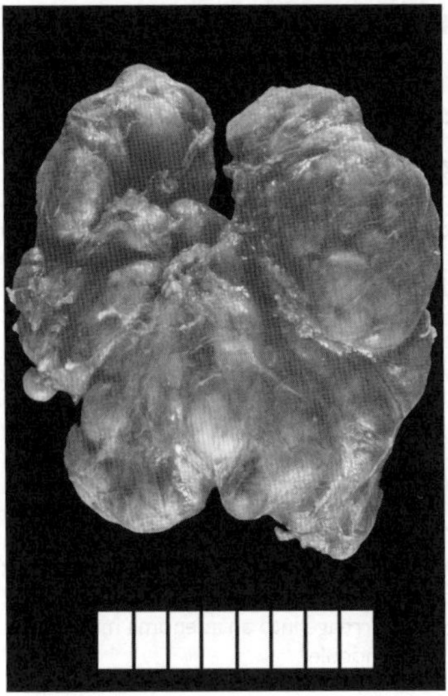

Fig. 14.3 Multinodular goitre. This massive multinodular goitre was removed from an elderly lady because it was compressing her trachea.

Reproduced with permission from *Clinical Pathology* (Oxford Core Texts), Carton, James, Daly, Richard, and Ramani, Pramila, Oxford University Press (2006), p. 269, Figure 12.9.

Follicular adenoma

Definition
- A benign encapsulated thyroid tumour showing follicular differentiation.

Epidemiology
- Most common thyroid neoplasm.
- True incidence is difficult to ascertain due to a lack of consistent diagnostic criteria in distinguishing follicular adenomas from cellular adenomatoid nodules in nodular goitres.

Aetiology
- Associated with radiation exposure and iodine deficiency.

Genetics
- Chromosomal trisomies (particularly trisomy 7) are the most frequent type of genetic aberration.

Presentation
- Most present with a solitary thyroid nodule, either palpated by the patient or picked up incidentally on imaging.
- Spontaneous haemorrhage into an adenoma may cause acute pain and enlargement of the nodule.

Macroscopy
- The thyroid contains a well-demarcated, thinly encapsulated solid nodule with a grey, tan, or brown cut surface.

Cytopathology
- Aspirates are cellular, containing numerous follicular cells and little colloid.
- The follicular cells are both dissociated and present in small microfollicular arrangements.

▶ Note that it is not possible to distinguish between follicular adenoma and follicular carcinoma on cytology. This can only be done histologically.

Histopathology
- Follicular adenomas are encapsulated epithelial tumours showing follicular differentiation.
- By definition, there is no capsular or vascular invasion.

Prognosis
- Follicular adenomas are benign lesions which are cured by excision.

Thyroid carcinomas

Definition

- A group of malignant epithelial tumours arising in the thyroid.

Subtypes

- Papillary carcinoma.
- Follicular carcinoma (subdivided into minimally or widely invasive).
- Medullary carcinoma.
- Anaplastic carcinoma.

Epidemiology

- Uncommon, accounting for ~1% of all malignancies.
- Mean age at diagnosis: mid 40s to early 50s for papillary, 50s for follicular and medullary, and 60s for anaplastic carcinoma.

Aetiology

- Radiation exposure is a well-documented risk factor for thyroid carcinoma, most notably papillary carcinoma.
- Iodine deficiency, particularly for follicular carcinomas.
- ~25% of medullary carcinomas are linked to the inherited syndromes MEN-2A, MEN-2B, and familial medullary thyroid cancer (FMTC).

Presentation

- Most well-differentiated thyroid carcinomas present with a solitary thyroid nodule. Thyroid function is usually normal.
- Anaplastic carcinoma usually presents with a rapidly enlarging neck mass; involvement of nearby structures causes hoarseness, dysphagia, and dyspnoea.

Papillary carcinoma

- Cytology aspirates contain papillaroid fragments of follicular epithelial cells with the characteristic nuclear features of papillary carcinoma, i.e. powdery chromatin, thick nuclear membranes, nuclear grooves, and nuclear pseudoinclusions. Multinucleated giant cells, psammoma bodies, and thick colloid may be present.
- Histology shows an epithelial tumour, usually with a papillary architecture, showing characteristic nuclear features: oval shape, overlapping, clearing of the nuclear chromatin, nuclear grooves, and pseudoinclusions (Fig. 14.4).
- Demonstrates gain-of-function mutations in *RET/TRK* or *BRAF*.

Follicular carcinoma

- Cytology aspirates are cellular, containing follicular epithelial cells present singly and in microfollicular arrangements. ► Note these appearances are identical to follicular adenomas; cytology cannot distinguish between these entities (➔ Follicular adenoma, p. 308).
- Histology shows an invasive follicular neoplasm that lacks the nuclear features of papillary thyroid carcinoma. **Minimally invasive** tumours

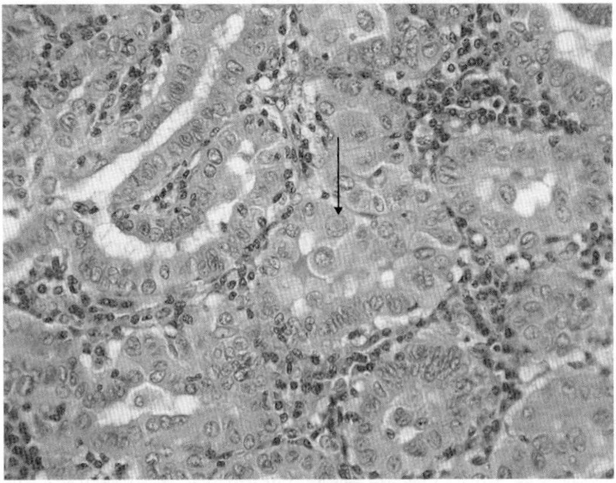

Fig. 14.4 Papillary carcinoma. This histological image from a papillary carcinoma of the thyroid shows the diagnostic nuclear features of nuclear clearing, nuclear grooving, and intranuclear inclusions (arrow).

Reproduced with permission from *Clinical Pathology* (Oxford Core Texts), Carton, James, Daly, Richard, and Ramani, Pramila, Oxford University Press (2006), p. 269, Figure 12.9.

show limited capsular invasion and/or vascular invasion. **Widely invasive** tumours show widespread infiltration of the thyroid and/or blood vessels.
- Demonstrates gain-of-function mutations in *RAS* or *PI-3K*.

Medullary carcinoma
- Cytology aspirates are cellular, containing loosely cohesive epithelial cells which may be round or spindled. Some cells may have eccentric nuclei with a plasmacytoid appearance. The nuclei contain coarsely granular chromatin. Fragments of amyloid may be seen.
- Histology shows sheets, nests, or trabeculae of round or spindled neoplastic epithelial cells with granular cytoplasm and nuclei with coarse chromatin. Amyloid deposits may be seen. The diagnosis can be confirmed by immunoreactivity for calcitonin.

Anaplastic carcinoma
- Cytology aspirates are highly cellular, containing markedly atypical malignant cells.
- Histology shows highly pleomorphic epithelioid and spindled cells with extensive necrosis and vascular invasion.
- Demonstrates inactivating mutations in *TP53*, in addition to mutations seen in follicular or papillary carcinomas.

Prognosis

- Papillary carcinomas and minimally invasive follicular carcinomas are low-grade malignancies with excellent prognosis.
- Widely invasive follicular carcinomas and medullary carcinomas are intermediate-grade malignancies with a higher risk of metastasis.
- Anaplastic carcinomas are highly malignant and almost always fatal.

TNM 7 pathological staging of thyroid carcinomas

Primary tumour (T)

pT1a: tumour ≤10mm in size, limited to the thyroid.
pT1b: tumour ≤20mm, but >10mm in size, limited to the thyroid.
pT2: tumour >20mm, but ≤40mm in size, limited to the thyroid.
pT3: tumour >40mm in size, limited to the thyroid, or any tumour with minimal extrathyroid extension.
pT4a: tumour of any size extending beyond the thyroid capsule to invade subcutaneous soft tissues and the larynx, trachea, oesophagus, or recurrent laryngeal nerve.
pT4b: tumour invades the prevertebral fascia and mediastinal vessels, or encases the carotid artery.

► Note that all anaplastic tumours are considered T4.

Regional lymph nodes (N)

pN0: no regional lymph node metastasis.
pN1a: metastases in level VI cervical lymph nodes.
pN1b: metastases in levels I–V cervical, retropharyngeal, or superior mediastinal lymph nodes.

Non-invasive follicular thyroid neoplasm with papillary-like nuclear features (NIFTP)

Definition

- Recently described indolent thyroid neoplasm, formally known as 'encapsulated follicular variant of papillary thyroid carcinoma without invasion'.

Genetics

- Strong association with *RAS* mutations.

Presentation

- Most present with a solitary thyroid nodule, either palpated by the patient or picked up incidentally on imaging.

Macroscopy

- Well-circumscribed, encapsulated solid nodule.

Histopathology

- Well-circumscribed tumour surrounded by a well-formed fibrous capsule.
- Dominant follicular pattern growth.
- Characteristic nuclear features of papillary thyroid carcinoma must be seen, although this may be focal and patchy in the tumour.

Prognosis

- Indolent tumour with excellent long-term survival following simple thyroid lobectomy.

Parathyroid hyperplasia

Definition

- An increase in parathyroid cell mass without an apparent stimulus.

Epidemiology

- Uncommon, accounting for ~20% of primary hyperparathyroidism.
- Women are affected more than men (3:1).

Aetiology

- Most patients have sporadic hyperplasia with no clear underlying cause.
- ~20% of cases have familial disease, most commonly one of the MEN syndromes (➲ Multiple endocrine neoplasia syndromes, p. 326).

Pathogenesis

- Parathyroid hyperplasia leads to overproduction of parathyroid hormone (PTH).
- Raised PTH levels cause hypercalcaemia by stimulating an increased absorption of calcium from the gut and kidneys and increasing osteoclastic activity in bone.

Presentation

- Patients present with primary hyperparathyroidism, a biochemical syndrome defined by the presence of hypercalcaemia and an inappropriately normal or raised PTH level.
- Many patients are asymptomatic when this is discovered.
- Some may present with vague symptoms of fatigue, nausea, constipation, polyuria, and arthralgias.

Macroscopy

- All of the parathyroid glands are increased in weight (>60mg) and size (>6mm), though this may be to varying degrees between the glands.

Histopathology

- The key feature is an increase in cell mass within the gland, associated with a decrease in fat content.
- Generally, both chief and oncocytic cell types are increased.
- Secondary fibrosis and haemorrhage are common findings.

Prognosis

- Excellent following subtotal parathyroidectomy.

Parathyroid adenoma

Definition

- A benign epithelial neoplasm of the parathyroid.

Epidemiology

- Common, accounting for ~80% of primary hyperparathyroidism.
- Peak incidence 50–60 years old.
- Women are affected more than men (3:1).

Aetiology

- Poorly understood, although prior irradiation of the neck appears to increase the risk.

Pathogenesis

- Autonomous production of PTH from the adenoma causes hypercalcaemia due to an unregulated mobilization of calcium from the bone and enhanced absorption of calcium from the kidneys and gut.

Presentation

- Patients present with primary hyperparathyroidism, i.e. hypercalcaemia together with an inappropriately normal or raised PTH level.
- Many patients are asymptomatic when this is discovered incidentally.
- Some may present with vague symptoms of fatigue, nausea, constipation, polyuria, and arthralgias.

Macroscopy

- A single parathyroid gland is enlarged in size (>6mm) and weight (>60mg).
- The adenoma is usually smooth, solid, soft, and light brown in colour.

Histopathology

- The parathyroid gland contains a well-circumscribed, usually encapsulated, mass composed of parathyroid epithelial cells without fat. A compressed rim of normal parathyroid tissue is often present at one edge.
- Chief cells tend to predominate, though an intermingling of oncocytic cells is also commonly present. The cells may be arranged in solid sheets, trabeculae, or follicles.
- Stromal oedema, fibrosis, and haemorrhage are often present.

Prognosis

- Parathyroid adenomas are benign lesions which are cured by excision.

Parathyroid carcinoma

Definition

- A malignant epithelial neoplasm of the parathyroid.

Epidemiology

- Rare, accounting for ~1% of cases of primary hyperparathyroidism.
- Peak incidence 40–50 years old, with no gender predilection.

Aetiology

- Unknown, though anecdotal reports have linked it with secondary hyperparathyroidism and prior neck irradiation.
- Parathyroid carcinoma has not been linked with MEN-1.

Carcinogenesis

- Loss of genetic material at chromosome 13q is the most frequently reported aberration.

Presentation

- Unlike patients with parathyroid hyperplasia or adenoma, patients usually present with symptomatic primary hyperparathyroidism and a palpable neck mass.
- Calcium levels are usually very high (3.5–4mmol/L) with symptoms of polyuria, polydipsia, weakness, renal colic, and bone pain.

Macroscopy

- Parathyroid carcinomas are generally much larger than adenomas, weighing on average 12g.
- They may be well circumscribed or have clearly infiltrative borders.

Histopathology

- Parathyroid carcinomas are composed of sheets of epithelial cells which are often deceptively bland. Follicle formation is unusual.
- They often have a thick capsule and are traversed by thick bands of fibrous tissue which divide the tumour into multiple expansile nodules.
- Capsular invasion, vascular invasion, tumour necrosis, and a high mitotic index are all very suggestive of malignancy.

Prognosis

- The 10-year survival rates are ~50%.
- Most patients succumb to the uncontrollable metabolic effects of severe hyperparathyroidism secreted by a recurrent tumour.

Addison's disease

Definition

- Primary adrenocortical insufficiency.

Epidemiology

- Rare with an estimated annual incidence of 1 in 100 000 people.
- Most cases present in young to middle-aged adults.
- Women are affected more than men.

Aetiology

- Autoimmune destruction in developed countries.
- Disseminated TB in developing countries.
- Other causes such as adrenal metastases are rare.

Pathogenesis

- Addison's disease leads to a marked lack of glucocorticoid and mineralocorticoid production from the adrenal cortex. Clinical features do not become manifest until ~90% of the gland has been destroyed.

Presentation

- Tiredness, lethargy, and weakness.
- Anorexia, nausea, vomiting, and diarrhoea.
- Loss of weight may be prominent.

► The clinical presentation is often insidious and non-specific, making the diagnosis challenging.

Biochemistry

- ↓ sodium and ↑ potassium.
- ↑ urea due to dehydration.
- Up to half of patients have hypoglycaemia.
- Circulating anti-adrenal autoantibodies are often present.

Diagnosis

- Patients suspected of having Addison's disease should have dynamic testing of the adrenal cortex with a **Synacthen® test**. This involves an intramuscular injection of synthetic adrenocorticotropic hormone (ACTH). The normal response is a rise in plasma cortisol. In Addison's disease, there is either no cortisol rise or only a minimal rise.

Prognosis

- Good, provided the diagnosis is made and lifelong replacement therapy is started with a synthetic glucocorticoid (hydrocortisone) and mineralocorticoid (fludrocortisone).

► It is vital that patients understand they must increase their dose of hydrocortisone during any intercurrent illness.

►► Untreated or undertreated, Addison's disease can cause acute adrenal failure ('Addisonian crisis') with a deadly combination of hypovolaemic shock, marked hypoglycaemia, and hyponatraemia.

Adrenal cortical adenoma

Definition

- A benign epithelial neoplasm of the adrenal cortex.

Epidemiology

- Most cases occur in adults, with no gender predilection.
- True incidence figures are unknown, largely due to the inability to distinguish nodular adrenal hyperplasia from true neoplastic adenomas.

Aetiology

- Unknown in most cases.

Genetics

- No consistent genetic aberrations have been described.

Presentation

- Most non-functional tumours are diagnosed incidentally when the abdomen is imaged for unrelated reasons.
- Aldosterone-producing adenomas present with primary hyperaldosteronism (Conn's syndrome) characterized by hypertension and, in some patients, hypokalaemia.
- Cortisol-producing adenomas present with Cushing's syndrome.

Macroscopy

- The adrenal gland contains a well-circumscribed tumour which may be encapsulated.
- The median tumour weight is 40g.
- Aldosterone-producing adenomas may be bright yellow, whilst those associated with Cushing's syndrome may be yellow to tan.
- A small number of adenomas have a black colour ('black adenoma').

Histopathology

- The tumours are composed of large polygonal cells arranged in nests and trabeculae separated by a fine vascular network.
- The cells have cytoplasm which is either clear and microvesicular or compact and eosinophilic. Nuclei are round to oval and usually bland.
- Occasionally, striking nuclear pleomorphism may be seen, though this does not equate with malignant behaviour.
- A compressed rim of normal adrenal cortex may be seen at the edge.

Prognosis

- Adrenal cortical adenomas are benign tumours with no capacity for malignant behaviour.
- Prognosis is largely determined by the severity of the endocrine effects of functional tumours.

Adrenal cortical carcinoma

Definition

- A malignant epithelial neoplasm arising in the adrenal cortex.

Epidemiology

- Rare tumours, with an annual incidence of 1 per million population.
- Most occur in adults aged >60 years old.

Aetiology

- Unknown in most cases.

Carcinogenesis

- The most frequent genetic aberrations are overexpression of *IGF2* and *EGFR* and loss of function of p21 and p16.

Presentation

- Most are functioning tumours which present with endocrine manifestations related to hormone overproduction.
- Flank pain may be present if the adrenal mass is large.
- 45% overproduce glucocorticoids alone, causing Cushing's syndrome.
- 45% overproduce glucocorticoids and androgens which induce virilization in women.
- 10% overproduce androgens alone.
- Overproduction of mineralocorticoids is extremely rare.

Macroscopy

- A large bulky tumour mass replaces the adrenal gland.
- Most tumours weigh >100g. The mean size is 12cm.
- The cut surface of the tumour appears lobulated and heterogeneous with areas of necrosis and haemorrhage.
- Invasion into adjacent structures may be seen in some cases.

Histopathology

- Most tumours show obvious invasive growth, with extension beyond the capsule and vascular invasion.
- Broad fibrous bands are often present which divide the tumour into expansile nodules.
- The tumour cells are highly pleomorphic and arranged in sheets, nests, and trabeculae.
- Areas of necrosis may be seen.

Prognosis

- The 5-year survival rate is 50–70%.
- The most important prognostic factors are age and stage.

Phaeochromocytoma

Definition

- A neoplasm of the chromaffin cells of the adrenal medulla.

Epidemiology

- Rare with an annual incidence of 8 per million.

Aetiology

- Most are sporadic.
- ~10% are associated with inherited syndromes such as MEN-2, neurofibromatosis 1, and von Hippel–Lindau disease.
- Inherited tumours are more likely to occur at a younger age and be bilateral.

Genetics

- Sporadic tumours show a high frequency of 1p loss of heterozygosity.

Presentation

- Patients suffer from abrupt episodes of throbbing headaches, sweating, palpitations, chest pain, and abdominal pain due to excess circulating catecholamines produced by the tumour.
- Hypertension is often present (➔ Hypertension, p. 33).

Biochemistry

- Raised urinary catecholamines and their metabolites is an important diagnostic aid.

Macroscopy

- A well-circumscribed tumour with a firm, grey cut surface.
- Mean size of 6cm and weight of 200g.

Histopathology

- The tumour cells form characteristic balls of cells ('zellballen') separated by a delicate vascular network.
- The cells are polygonal with granular basophilic cytoplasm.
- Nuclei have a typical stippled chromatin pattern.
- Scattered pleomorphic nuclei may be seen.

Prognosis

- 90% behave in a benign manner.
- Unfortunately, histology is not reliable at predicting the 10% which will be malignant, although worrying factors include invasive growth, necrosis, and high mitotic activity.

Neuroblastoma

Definition

- A malignant childhood tumour arising from neural crest-derived cells of the sympathetic nervous system.
- Most arise in the adrenal medulla or paraspinal sympathetic ganglia.

Epidemiology

- Third most common malignant childhood tumour.
- Incidence of 1 in 10 000 live births per year.
- Most arise in the first 4y of life.

Aetiology

- Unknown.

Genetics

- Tumour genetics have important prognostic implications.
- Amplification of MYCN, diploidy, and deletions at chromosome 1p are all associated with poorer prognosis.

Presentation

- Most children present unwell with weight loss, fever, watery diarrhoea, and a palpable abdominal mass.

Biochemistry

- High urinary concentrations of catecholamines and their metabolites vanillylmandelic acid (VMA) and homovanillic acid (HMA) are an important diagnostic aid.

Macroscopy

- A lobulated, soft, grey tumour mass averaging 6–8cm in size, which is intimately related to the adrenal gland or sympathetic chain.

Histopathology

- **Undifferentiated neuroblastoma** is composed of undifferentiated neuroblasts with no evidence of ganglionic differentiation. They appear identical to a number of other 'small, round, blue cell tumours' of childhood and so require ancillary techniques to confirm the diagnosis (e.g. immunoreactivity for CD56 and synaptophysin).
- **Poorly differentiated neuroblastoma** shows limited evidence of ganglionic differentiation (<5% cells) with neurofibrillary stroma.
- **Differentiating neuroblastoma** contains many ganglionic cells (>5%, but <50% cells) and plentiful neurofibrillary stroma.
- **Ganglioneuroblastoma** is composed almost entirely of ganglionic cells (>50% cells) and neurofibrillary stroma.

Prognosis

- Depends on several factors, including stage, age, histology, and genetics.
- Cure rates are >90% for low-risk disease and 70–90% for intermediate-risk disease, but only 10–40% for high-risk disease.

Pituitary adenoma

Definition

- A benign epithelial neoplasm of the anterior pituitary.
- Most are functioning tumours which overproduce prolactin, growth hormone (GH), or ACTH, in descending order of frequency.
- Functional adenomas producing TSH, follicle-stimulating hormone (FSH), or luteinizing hormone (LH) are very rare.

Epidemiology

- Uncommon with an incidence of 1 in 100 000 per year.
- Most arise in middle-aged adults.
- Women are affected more than men.

Aetiology

- Unknown in the majority of cases.
- A small proportion is seen in association with inherited tumour syndromes, e.g. MEN-1.

Genetics

- The two best characterized gene aberrations are *MEN 1* and *gsp*, a mutation in the G-protein alpha subunit.

Presentation

- Features of endocrine hyperfunction, depending on the hormone produced, e.g. galactorrhoea and sexual dysfunction (prolactin-secreting), acromegaly (Fig. 14.5) if GH-secreting, or Cushing's syndrome (Fig. 14.6) if ACTH-secreting.
- Large adenomas may also produce symptoms of mass effect, such as headache, nausea, and visual field disturbance, due to compression of the overlying optic chiasm.
- Many patients will also have symptoms and signs of hypopituitarism, though they rarely present with these.

Macroscopy

- Soft tumours which may be very small microadenomas (<10mm in size) or larger macroadenomas (>10mm in size).

Histopathology

- Composed of solid nests or trabeculae of neoplastic cells with uniform round nuclei, stippled chromatin, and inconspicuous nucleoli.
- Immunohistochemistry using antibodies against prolactin, GH, and ACTH can be used to identify the hormone produced by the tumour.

Prognosis

- Generally good, following appropriate medical or surgical treatment, though some patients may suffer from recurrences.

► The endocrine effects of these tumours may, however, have significant consequences, e.g. cardiovascular disease in acromegaly.

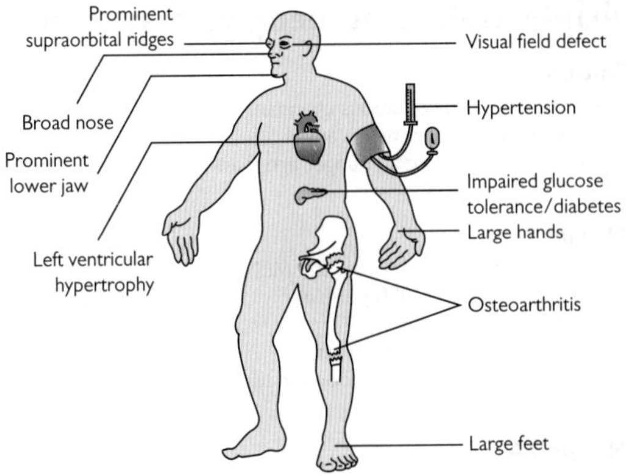

Fig. 14.5 Clinical features of acromegaly.

Reproduced with permission from *Clinical Pathology* (Oxford Core Texts), Carton, James, Daly, Richard, and Ramani, Pramila, Oxford University Press (2006), p. 303, Figure 14.5.

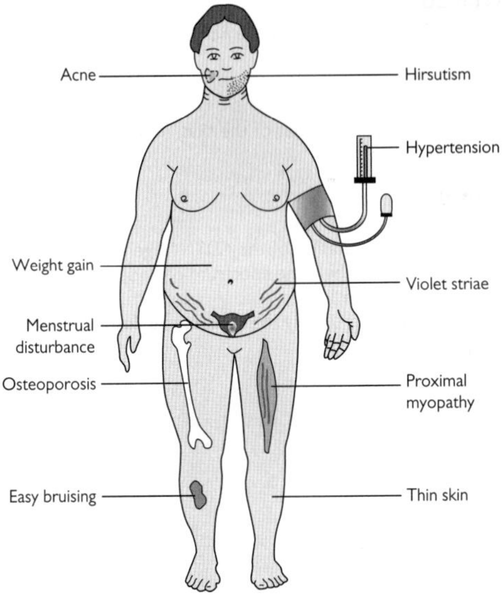

Fig. 14.6 Clinical features of Cushing's syndrome.

Reproduced with permission from *Clinical Pathology* (Oxford Core Texts), Carton, James, Daly, Richard, and Ramani, Pramila, Oxford University Press (2006), p. 303, Figure 14.5.

Multiple endocrine neoplasia syndromes

Definition

- A group of inherited conditions characterized by proliferative lesions arising in multiple endocrine organs.
- Lesions typically occur at a younger age than sporadic lesions and may be multifocal.

MEN type 1

- Caused by germline mutation of the *MEN 1* gene.
- Prevalence of 2 per 100 000 people.
- Common lesions include:
  - multiple parathyroid adenomas
  - pancreatic and duodenal endocrine tumours
  - pituitary tumours.

MEN type 2A

- Caused by activating germline mutation of the *RET* gene.
- Characterized by:
  - medullary thyroid carcinoma (virtually 100%)
  - multiple parathyroid adenomas in 10–20%.

MEN type 2B

- Caused by germline mutation of the *RET* gene.
- Characterized by:
  - medullary thyroid carcinoma
  - phaeochromocytomas
  - neuromas/ganglioneuromas of the skin, mouth, and gut
  - Marfanoid habitus.

MEN type 4

- Relatively new subset of MEN.
- Caused by germline mutation of the *CDKN1B* gene.
- Propensity to develop the same spectrum of endocrine tumours as patients with MEN type 1.
- Hyperparathyroidism is usually the earliest manifestation of the syndrome.

Chapter 15
Haematopathology

Iron deficiency anaemia

Definition

- A reduction in Hb concentration due to inadequate iron supply.

Epidemiology

- The most common cause of anaemia.

Aetiology

- Chronic blood loss from the gut is the most common cause.
- Worldwide, this is usually related to hookworm infection.
- Common causes in developed countries include peptic ulcers (NSAID intake), gastric carcinoma, sigmoid diverticular disease, and colorectal carcinoma.
- Heavy menstrual loss in women (menorrhagia) can also lead to iron deficiency.
- GI diseases causing malabsorption of iron can also cause iron deficiency, e.g. coeliac disease, atrophic gastritis, and history of partial gastrectomy.

► Ruling out a GI tract malignancy is mandatory in any adult patient with unexplained iron deficiency anaemia.

Pathogenesis

- Iron is an essential constituent of the haem group of Hb.
- Chronic iron deficiency interrupts the final step in haem synthesis.

Presentation

- May be asymptomatic and diagnosed on routine full blood count.
- Pallor of the mucous membranes, palm, and nail beds is common (usually when Hb is <9g/dL).
- Symptoms include tiredness and breathlessness on exertion.
- Some cases may cause additional features such as koilonychia, angular cheilitis, and glossitis.

Full blood count

- ↓ Hb.
- ↓ mean corpuscular volume (MCV).
- ↓ serum ferritin, ↓ serum iron, ↓ transferrin saturation, ↑ total iron binding capacity (TIBC).
- Platelet count might be raised, particularly if haemorrhagic episodes.

Peripheral blood film

- Small red cells (microcytic).
- Pale red cells (hypochromic).
- Variability in red cell size (anisocytosis) and shape (poikilocytosis).
- Long elliptical red cells are often seen ('pencil cells').

Bone marrow

- Mild to moderate erythyroid hyperplasia (normoblastic).
- Absence of stainable iron (Perl's staining).

Anaemia of chronic disease

Definition

- A reduction in Hb concentration related to chronic inflammatory disorders, chronic infections, and malignancy.

Epidemiology

- Second most common cause of anaemia.

Aetiology

- Any chronic inflammatory disease, chronic infection, or malignancy.
- Most frequent causes include: autoimmune disorders (e.g. inflammatory bowel disease, RA, lupus, vasculitis, sarcoidosis), long-term infections (e.g. hepatitis, HIV), cancer, and CKD.

Pathogenesis

- The underlying mechanisms are complex and multifactorial.
- Microorganisms, malignant cells, or autoimmune dysregulation lead to activation of CD3+ T-cells and monocytes, with subsequent production of cytokines (IFN-gamma; TNF-α; IL-1, 6, and 10).
- IL-6 stimulates the hepatic expression of the acute phase protein hepcidin, which inhibits the duodenal absorption of iron. TNF-α, IL-1, IL-6, and IL-10 induce ferritin expression and stimulate the storage and retention of iron within macrophages, leading to a decreased iron concentration in the circulation.
- TNF-α and IFN-gamma inhibit the production of erythropoietin in the kidney.
- The end result is a reduction in erythropoiesis which is often ineffective.

Presentation

- Tiredness and breathlessness.

Full blood count

- ↓ Hb which is usually mild to moderate (8–9.5g/dL).
- MCV is usually normal but may be low.
- ↓ iron; normal/low transferrin; ↓ transferrin saturation; normal/increased ferritin; ↓ ratio of soluble transferrin receptor to log ferritin; ↑ cytokine levels.

Peripheral blood film

- Red cells usually normochromic and normocytic, but can be small.
- There is no noticeable variation in size or shape.

Bone marrow

- The marrow is usually of normal cellularity.
- Decreased bone marrow sideroblasts, but stainable iron is present.

Megaloblastic anaemias

Definition

- A reduction in Hb concentration due to impaired erythroid DNA synthesis. Most cases are related to either vitamin B12 or folate deficiency.

Aetiology

- Autoimmune gastritis (➔ Autoimmune gastritis, p. 114) is the most common cause of vitamin B12 deficiency. Megaloblastic anaemia due to autoimmune gastritis is also known as **pernicious anaemia**. This affects about 1 in 1000 people, with a female predilection.
- Poor diet is the most common cause of folate deficiency. The main dietary sources of folate are leafy green vegetables. Deficiency is typically seen in the elderly and alcoholics.
- Some cases might be secondary to medication: antifolate drugs (methotrexate) or drugs interfering with DNA synthesis (e.g. mercaptopurine, hydroxyurea).

Pathogenesis

- Vitamin B12 and folate are both required to convert deoxyuridine monophosphate into deoxythymidine monophosphate, a molecule required for DNA synthesis.
- Developing red cells are unable to divide because they cannot make enough DNA to form two nuclei.
- Therefore, RBCs become arrested in their development as large immature cells (megaloblasts), many of which die in the bone marrow.
- Some megaloblasts survive and develop into abnormally large red cells (macrocytes) which are released into the circulation.

Presentation

- Usually insidious onset and symptoms do not appear until anaemia is severe.
- Mild jaundice may be present due to haemolysis and ineffective erythropoiesis. Lactate dehydrogenase (LDH) might be also increased.
- Vitamin B12 deficiency may also cause neurological symptoms, including cognitive impairment, peripheral neuropathy, and subacute combined degeneration of the spinal cord.
- Glossitis and angular cheilosis are also present.

Full blood count

- Hb concentration is typically very low (approaching only 2g/dL).
- MCV is typically very high.

Peripheral blood film

- Prominent anisocytosis and poikilocytosis with large oval macrocytes.
- Nucleated RBCs may be seen.
- Hypersegmented neutrophils (>5 lobes).

Bone marrow

- The marrow is hypercellular, containing many immature large erythroid blasts (megaloblasts) and large metamyelocytes.
- The myeloid:erythroid ratio is reversed due to an increase in erythroid precursors.
- Megakaryocytes might be hypersegmented and show open chromatin.

Hereditary spherocytosis

Definition

- An inherited (dominant pattern) haemolytic condition caused by mutations in genes encoding proteins involved in maintaining the integrity of the red cell membrane.

Epidemiology

- Common with an incidence of up to 1 in 2000.

Aetiology

- Mutations in genes encoding red cell membrane proteins (ankyrin, band 3, and β-spectrin), leading to protein deficiency.

Pathogenesis

- Mutations cause destabilization of the red cell membrane, with loss of lipid from the membrane.
- Reduction in the surface area of the membrane forces red cells to assume a spherical shape (spherocyte).
- Spherocytes are less deformable than normal red cells and are susceptible to becoming trapped in the spleen and destroyed by splenic macrophages.

Presentation

- Clinically, findings vary from asymptomatic patients to severe haemolysis. Diagnosis is usually made in childhood or young adult life.
- Most patients have mild to moderate anaemia (Hb 8–12g/dL).
- Jaundice and splenomegaly are common. However, some patients have normal bilirubin values.

Full blood count

- Mild to moderate anaemia (Hb 8–12g/dL).
- Raised reticulocyte count.
- Raised mean corpuscular haemoglobin concentration (MCHC).

Peripheral blood film

- Spherocytes are readily identifiable.
- Reticulocytes are also present.

Ancillary tests

- The **direct antiglobulin test** is negative, distinguishing spherocytosis from immune haemolytic anaemia, which has similar blood film findings but is rare in children.
- The recommended laboratory tests are the eosin-5-maleimide (EMA) binding test or the cryohaemolysis test.

Prognosis

- Most patients have well-compensated disease and only require folate supplements to avoid megaloblastic anaemia.
- Splenectomy might be beneficial in children with severe disease, but not to be performed in those with mild disease as splenectomy is associated with an increased risk of infection.
- Recognized complications include gallstone disease (from pigment gallstones) and aplastic crisis due to parvovirus B19 infection. The latter is potentially fatal.

Glucose-6-phosphate dehydrogenase deficiency

Definition

- An inherited haemolytic condition caused by a mutation in the glucose-6-phosphate dehydrogenase (G6PD) gene.
- Several variants have been proposed, based on the extent of enzyme deficiency and on the severity of haemolysis: (a) class I: severe, associated with non-spherocytic haemolytic anemia; (b) class II: <10% activity; (c) class III: 10–60% activity; (d) class IV: normal activity; and (e) class V: increased activity.

Epidemiology

- Common, affecting up to 10% of the population worldwide.
- There is much geographical variability, with the highest rates in Africans (prevalence 28% in Nigeria), Asians, Italians, and Greeks.

Genetics

- The G6PD gene is located on the long arm of the X chromosome (Xq28).
- A single mutated copy therefore causes G6PD deficiency in men.
- Homozygous women are also affected, but such individuals are not often seen.
- Heterozygous women do not have clinical manifestations, as the other normal copy produces enough enzyme activity.
- Polymorphisms of the G6PD gene are common and ~200 variant alleles are described.

Pathogenesis

- G6PD is one of the enzymes of the hexose monophosphate pathway, a metabolic process necessary for generating reduced glutathione.
- Reduced glutathione protects the red cell membrane from oxidative damage.
- Individuals with G6PD deficiency suffer from episodes of haemolysis following oxidant stress.

Presentation

- Most individuals are asymptomatic with normal Hb levels.
- If exposed to oxidants, however, they suffer from an acute haemolytic episode with fever, jaundice, and dark urine, due to haemoglobinuria.
- Common precipitants include drugs (especially antimalarials), fava beans (a common food in Mediterranean countries), severe infection, and diabetic ketoacidosis.
- Haemoglobinuria and neonatal jaundice can also occur.

Full blood count

- ↓ Hb during an acute haemolytic episode.

Peripheral blood film

- Variation in red cell shape (poikilocytosis).
- Red cells with punched-out defects in their contours ('bite cells') are characteristic.
- Spherocytes may also be seen.

Ancillary tests

- Screening tests for G6PD deficiency are available which indirectly assess G6PD activity by testing the ability of red cells to reduce dyes.
- The NADPH fluorescence test is a qualitative test and is the gold standard for G6PD deficiency screening.
- Definitive diagnosis requires direct assay of the enzyme.

Thalassaemias

Definition

- A group of inherited red cell disorders caused by the underproduction of α- or β-globin chains.

Pathogenesis and genetics

- Underproduction of either α- or β-globin chains causes accumulation of excess unpaired chains.
- This leads to the destruction of developing red cells and premature removal of circulating red cells in the spleen.
- The anaemia in thalassaemia is therefore a combination of ineffective erythropoiesis and haemolysis in the spleen.
- Point mutations in or near the globin gene are responsible for the majority of the β-thalassaemias. More than 400 genetic alterations have been documented in β-thalassaemias.

Beta-thalassaemia major

- Caused by mutations in both β-globin genes.
- Problems begin in the first few months of life (usually <6 months of age), as HbF levels decline and excess α-chains begin to accumulate in red cells.
- Worsening anaemia leads to intense erythropoietic drive, with expansion of the bone marrow compartment and resumption of extramedullary haematopoiesis. Osteoporosis is frequent, even in well-transfused patients, and spontaneous fractures might occur.
- Presents in infancy with pallor, poor feeding, and failure to thrive.
- Full blood count shows a hypochromic, microcytic anaemia.
- Bone marrow shows red cell hyperplasia with precipitated α-chains in the cytoplasm of erythroblasts.
- Diagnosis is confirmed by the near absence of HbA on Hb electrophoresis.
- Regular transfusions from the age of onset is the standard treatment, but this results in iron overload, and splenectomy might be needed to reduce transfusion requirements.

Beta-thalassaemia minor

- Caused by mutations in only one β-globin gene.
- Silent carriers who have an asymptomatic mild microcytic anaemia with a high red cell count.
- A raised HbA2 level on Hb electrophoresis is a key diagnostic feature.

Alpha-thalassaemia

- Alpha-chains are required for both adult and fetal Hb.
- In the fetus, excess γ-chains form tetramers known as Hb Bart's.
- In adults, excess β-chains form tetramers known as HbH.
- Alpha-thalassaemias are classified according to the number of genes affected.

- Deletion of all four α-globin genes (the more severe form) causes severe fetal anaemia, generalized oedema, massive hepatosplenomegaly, and fetal demise between 28 and 40 weeks' gestation.
- Deletion of three α-globin genes causes HbH disease with variable levels of chronic haemolysis. Most patients have a moderate chronic haemolytic anaemia throughout life (Hb 7–10g/dL) and splenomegaly.
- Deletion of one or two α-globin genes leads to α-thalassaemia minor or α-thalassaemia trait which is usually asymptomatic. There may be a very mild microcytic anaemia.

Sickle-cell disorders

Definition

- A group of inherited red cell disorders caused by HbS (sickle Hb)

Epidemiology

- Seen most frequently in people of African descent and other areas of current or previous malaria endemicity.
- The mutant gene has survived because heterozygote carriers are protected against the effects of severe *Plasmodium falciparum* malaria.

Genetics

- HbS is caused by a point mutation in the β-globin gene on chromosome 11, which causes a replacement of valine for glutamic acid in the sixth position of the β-chain.
- Heterozygotes are said to have the **sickle-cell trait**.
- Homozygotes suffer from **sickle-cell disease** or **sickle-cell anaemia**.

Pathogenesis

- HbS is 50 times less soluble than HbA.
- Under conditions of low oxygen tension, HbS polymerizes into rod-like aggregates which cause the red cell to adopt a sickled shape.

Presentation

- Individuals with the sickle-cell trait do not suffer from sickling because the normal HbA protein reduces the formation of HbS aggregates. Patients are usually asymptomatic and have normal Hb levels. They are nevertheless genetically important as carriers of the sickle-cell gene.
- Typically, patients present with asthenia, jaundice, and ulcers around the ankles. Bone deformities and infections can also occur.
- Individuals with sickle-cell disease present at around 2y of age once they have lost most of their HbF, and virtually all their Hb is HbS. Their red cells sickle in venous blood, causing persistent haemolysis and episodes of vascular crises.

Full blood count

- ↓ Hb, typically between 7 and 9g/dL.

Peripheral blood film

- Sickled red cells and their variants are present.
- In adults, there is also evidence of hyposplenism/splenic atrophy (target cells, Howell–Jolly bodies, Pappenheimer bodies).
- In the marrow, the myeloid:erythroid ratio is preserved.

Diagnosis

- The **sickle-cell solubility test** is a useful screening test in which a reducing agent is added to Hb extracted from red cells. HbS readily precipitates and the solution goes cloudy.
- Definitive diagnosis requires **Hb electrophoresis** which shows a single major HbS band and no normal HbA.

Prognosis

- Patients with sickle-cell disease have a significantly decreased lifespan.
- The median age of death is ~42y in men and 48y in women.

Complications of sickle-cell disease

Childhood

- Hand and foot syndrome (unequal growth of small bones of the hands and feet).
- Splenic sequestration crisis.
- Stroke (usually as a result of embolism from fractured bones and stenosis of vessels in the circle of Willis).

Later life

- Bacterial infections, including osteomyelitis from *Salmonella* species.
- CKD.
- Priapism.
- Lower limb ulceration.
- Pigment gallstones.
- Avascular necrosis of the femoral head.
- Pulmonary syndrome.

Idiopathic thrombocytopenic purpura

Definition

- A reduction in platelet number due to platelet autoantibodies, which contributes to accelerate platelet destruction and inhibit their production.

Epidemiology

- Uncommon with an incidence of 1.6–3.9 per 100 000 persons per year.
- Occurs in adults and children.
- The female-to-male ratio ranges from 1.2 to 1.9.
- Adult idiopathic thrombocytopenic purpura (ITP) is more common in women (3:1).
- Childhood ITP has a peak incidence between ages 5 and 6, with no gender predilection.
- 20% of cases are secondary.

Aetiology

- Platelet autoantibodies are formed for unknown reasons.
- The majority are idiopathic, but some forms are secondary (e.g. lupus, antiphospholipid syndrome, common variable immunodeficiency (CVID), chronic lymphocytic leukaemia (CLL), infection, drugs).

Pathogenesis

- Platelets become coated with autoantibodies and are destroyed in the spleen. However, platelet antibodies are only detected in ~60% of patients.

Presentation

- Sudden onset of cutaneous petechiae, nosebleeds (epistaxis), and gum bleeding.
- A preceding viral infection is often noted in childhood cases.
- Annual risk of fatal haemorrhage is 1.6–3.9 cases per 100 patient years.

Full blood count

- Severe thrombocytopenia (platelet count $<100 \times 10^9$/L).
- Normal Hb and white cell count (WCC).
- Anaemia may exist if there is concomitant immune haemolytic anaemia (Evan syndrome).

Peripheral blood film

- A mixture of normal and large platelets is present.
- Platelet counts are reduced.

Bone marrow findings

- Normal or increased numbers of megakaryocytes.
- Normal megakaryocyte morphology.
- Normal haematopoiesis.

► Note that ITP is a diagnosis of exclusion once other causes of thrombocytopenia have been ruled out.

Prognosis

- Childhood cases usually resolve within 1–2 months.
- Adult cases are more likely to persist with a chronic mild to moderate bleeding tendency.
- Risk of thrombosis.
- B-lymphocyte depletion with anti-CD20 (rituximab) has proved to be useful in some patients with chronic ITP.

Thrombotic thrombocytopenic purpura

Definition

- A thrombotic microangiopathy associated with haemolytic anaemia due to lack of ADAMTS13.

Epidemiology

- Rare; annual incidence of 6–11.3 per 10^6 population.

Aetiology

- Inherited cases are due to genetic mutations of ADAMTS13 (von Willebrand factor (vWF) cleaving protein).
- Sporadic cases are due to autoantibodies against ADAMTS13 (incidence of 6 per 10^6 population per year).

Pathogenesis

- ADAMTS13 is a metalloproteinase which cleaves vWF into small fragments.
- Deficiency of ADAMTS13 leads to the accumulation of ultra-high molecular-weight forms of vWF which attach to endothelial cells and stimulate microthrombus formation in small vessels.
- Microthrombi cause organ impairment, most notably affecting the brain and kidneys.
- Platelets are rapidly consumed in the microthrombi, causing thrombocytopenia.
- RBCs passing through the microthrombi are sheared apart, causing anaemia.

Presentation

- Fever, petechiae, jaundice, and bleeding (epistaxis, gingival bleeding, GI bleeding).
- Neurological symptoms are typically prominent, including confusion, headache, aphasia, and visual problems.
- Acute renal failure may also occur (proteinuria and microhaematuria).

Haematology

- ↓ Hb with normal MCV.
- ↑ reticulocyte count.
- ↓ platelets.
- Normal clotting (prothrombin time (PT), fibrinogen).
- Troponin T levels are raised (50% cases).
- LDH raised due to haemolysis.

Blood film

- Red cell anisocytosis.
- Prominent schistocytes (fragmented red cells).

Prognosis

- If untreated, the mortality is 90%, but survival rates are 80–90% with early diagnosis and plasma exchange.
- Around one-third of patients suffer from relapses within 2y.
- Patients with refractory or relapsing immune-mediated thrombotic thrombocytopenic purpura (TTP) might benefit from rituximab therapy.

von Willebrand disease

Definition

- An inherited bleeding tendency caused by a quantitative or qualitative deficiency of vWF.

Epidemiology

- The most common inherited bleeding disorder.
- Incidence varies from 23 to 100 per 10^6 population.
- Type 1 (75%) is a quantitative defect.
- Type 2 (20%) is a qualitative defect and includes four subtypes (2A, 2B, 2M, and 2N) on the basis of the phenotype.
- Type 3, although rarer, is the most severe form of the disease (virtually complete deficiency of vWF).
- Acquired forms of von Willebrand disease also exist probably due related to autoimmune disorders or medications.

Genetics

- The vWF gene is located on the short arm of chromosome 12 (12p13.3).
- Type 1 is autosomal dominant, and type 2 can be autosomal dominant or recessive depending on the type (2A: dominant or recessive, 2B dominant, 2M dominant or recessive, and 2N recessive).
- Type 3 is an autosomal recessive trait.

Pathogenesis

- vWF acts as an adhesion molecule which allows platelets to bind to subendothelial tissues and it also acts as a carrier for factor VIII.
- Lack of vWF activity leads to a bleeding tendency due to a combination of failure of platelet adhesion and factor VIII deficiency.

Presentation

- Mucosal bleeding, particularly nosebleeds, and bleeding after injury or surgery are the main manifestations.
- Joint and muscle bleeds are rare and only occur in type 3 disease.

Clotting studies

- Prolonged activated partial thromboplastin time (APTT).
- Prolonged bleeding time.
- Normal PT.
- Formal diagnosis requires the measurement of plasma vWF (VWF:Ag) and testing of vWF functionality (e.g. ristocetin-induced platelet agglutination assay or VWF:RCo which measures the ability of vWF to bind to platelets).

Prognosis

- Most patients require no regular treatment.
- Prophylactic treatment is given before surgery.

Haemophilia

Definition

- An inherited disorder of haemostasis characterized by bleeding tendency due to a deficiency of either factor VIII (haemophilia A) or factor IX (haemophilia B).

Epidemiology

- Prevalence of 10 in 100 000 people.
- Haemophilia A occurs in about 1 in 5–10 000 male births.
- Haemophilia B, also called Christmas disease, is less common with an incidence of about 1 in 20–30 000 male births.

Genetics

- The factor VIII and factor IX genes are both located on the X chromosome, so haemophilia demonstrates sex-linked inheritance, with males being predominantly affected. Both disorders are X-linked recessive disorders.
- Numerous mutations have been described, leading to a wide variation in the severity of haemophilia. Other alterations (deletions, insertions, inversions) are also associated with haemophilia in some patients.

Pathogenesis

- Factors VIII and IX together form the factor VIII–factor IX complex which activates factor X in the clotting cascade.
- Lack of these factors impairs clotting.

Presentation

- Easy bruising and massive bleeding after trauma or surgery.
- Spontaneous haemorrhages into large weight-bearing joints, such as the knee, elbow, and ankles (haemarthroses), are common.
- Median age for the diagnosis is 1y if the disease is severe, but in >9% of cases, the mean age for diagnosis is 15y.
- Despite the inherited nature of the disease, a positive family history is not recorded in 30% of cases.

Clotting studies

- Both forms of haemophilia cause a prolonged APTT and a normal PT.
- The two can only be distinguished by measuring levels of each factor.

Prognosis

- Long-term complications include haemarthropathy (repeated bleeding episodes in the joints).
- Replacement of the missing factor is the key therapeutic intervention.
- Factor concentrates are pooled from multiple donors and carry a much higher risk of transmission of infection.
- Although stringent donor screening and viral inactivation of concentrates reduce this risk, there is a move towards the use of synthetic factors.
- Trials with gene therapy are under way using adenovirus vectors containing the genes for factors VIII and IX.

Thrombophilia

Definition

- An inherited predisposition to venous thrombosis.
- Thrombophilia is a multigenetic and heterogeneous disease.

Presentation

- Deep vein thrombosis or pulmonary embolus, which may be recurrent.
- Venous thrombosis at unusual sites, e.g. axillary or cerebral veins, may also occur.
- It is associated with pregnancy complications and recurrent miscarriage.

Activated protein C resistance

- The most common form of thrombophilia, affecting 5–10% of people, most commonly Caucasian individuals.
- Due to a single point mutation in the factor V gene (known as factor V Leiden mutation), due to replacement of Arg506 with a Gln.
- Factor V Leiden protein has normal procoagulant activity but is not inhibited in the normal way by activated protein C, resulting in a hypercoagulative state and a tendency to thrombosis.

Prothrombin G20210A mutation

- Affects ~1–5% of people.
- Caused by a single nucleotide change of guanine for adenine at position 20210 of the PT gene (called F2).
- Associated with elevated PT levels and an increased risk of venous thrombosis, possibly due to increased rates of thrombin generation, excess growth of fibrin clots, and possibly increased activation of platelets.
- May increase the risk of pregnancy loss.
- Heterozygous and homozygous women with a history of venous thrombosis should avoid use of contraceptive treatment containing oestrogens and HRT.

Protein C and S deficiency

- Protein C deficiency can be found in 1 in 200–500 persons in the general population, but the majority of cases are asymptomatic. Severe homozygous protein C deficiency affects 1 in 500 000 to 1 in 750 000 live births
- Heterozygous protein C deficiency is an inherited (autosomal dominant) disease. The gene is located in the long arm of chromosome 2.
- More than 200 mutations have been described. The deficiency in protein can be classified as: type I (quantitative) and type II (less frequent and characterized by decreased functional activity of the protein).
- Protein C and S are natural anticoagulants which inactivate clotting factors and regulated normal coagulation.
- Defects in these proteins therefore predispose to thrombosis.

Acute B-lymphoblastic leukaemia

Definition

- A haematological neoplasm composed of malignant B-lymphoid blasts with bone marrow and blood involvement.
- The WHO classification (2008) includes: acute B-lymphoblastic leukaemia (B-ALL) not otherwise specific and B-ALL with recurrent genetic abnormalities.

Epidemiology

- Incidence 1–4.75/100 000 persons per year.
- Primarily a disease of children (75% of cases occur aged <6y).

Aetiology

- Largely unknown, though there is a suggestion of an inherited component in some cases.

Genetics

- Clonal DJ rearrangement of the *IGH* gene. T-cell receptor gene rearrangement also frequent (up to 70% of cases).
- B-ALL with recurrent genetic abnormalities include: t(9,22) *BCR–ABL1* fusion gene; t(v;11q23) MLL rearranged; B-ALL with hyperploidy, B-ALL with hypoploidy; t(1;19) E2A-PBX1; t(12;21) TEL-AML1.

Pathogenesis

- Mutations in a haematopoietic stem cell lead to the clonal expansion of immature B-lymphoid blasts.
- Rapidly proliferating lymphoid blasts overwhelm the normal bone marrow, spill into the peripheral blood, and infiltrate other organs.

Presentation

- Sudden onset of bone marrow failure with profound anaemia and thrombocytopenia. The leucocyte count may be decreased, normal, or increased.
- Infiltration of other organs is common, causing lymphadenopathy, hepatosplenomegaly, bone pain, headache, vomiting, and cranial nerve palsies.

Microscopy

- By definition, >20% of cells in the peripheral blood or bone marrow are lymphoid blasts, relatively monomorphic medium to large cells with a high nuclear-to-cytoplasmic ratio and finely dispersed chromatin.

Immunophenotype

- B-lymphoid blasts usually express CD19, CD79a, CD22, CD10, Pax5, and TdT.
- PAX5 is probably the most sensitive and specific marker for B-cell lineage in bone marrow trephines.
- MPO is usually negative.
- Myeloid-associated antigens (CD13 and CD33) are positive in t(9;22) acute lymphoblastic leukaemia (ALL) and CD34+ blasts are common in t(12;21) ALL.

Prognosis

- Modern treatment regimens have excellent success rates, with complete remission achieved in >95% of children. The prognosis in adults is less favourable.
- Central nervous system (CNS) involvement at presentation is associated with aggressive disease and requires specific treatment.
- t(9;22) ALL has the worst prognosis among patients with ALL.

T-lymphoblastic leukaemia/lymphoma

Approximately 15% of childhood ALL and 25% of adult ALL are of T-cell lineage (T-lymphoblastic leukaemia/lymphoma).

T-ALL presents with a high leucocyte count and frequently with a mediastinal mass and pleural effusions. Morphologically, blasts are difficult to distinguish from B-lineage blasts and require flow cytometry, immunophenotyping (TdT, CD1a, CD2, CD3, CD4, CD5, CD7, and CD8), and T-cell receptor clonal rearrangement.

T-ALL in childhood is more aggressive than B-ALL, with early relapses and CNS involvement.

Acute myeloid leukaemias

Definition

- A group of haematological neoplasms composed of malignant myeloid blasts found in the bone marrow and blood.

Classification

- Different classifications have been proposed to classify acute myeloid leukaemia (AML).
- The French–American–British (FAB) scheme is based on morphological findings (M0 to M7).
- The WHO classification relies primarily on cytogenetic findings and includes: AML with recurrent genetic abnormalities; AML with myelodysplasia-related changes; therapy-related myeloid neoplasms; AML NOS; myeloid sarcoma; myeloid proliferations related to Down's syndrome; and blastic plasmacytoid dendritic cell neoplasm.

Epidemiology

- Worldwide incidence is 3.7–4 per 100 000 population per year.
- It shows two peaks in occurrence—in early childhood and later adulthood (mean age at diagnosis is 65y).
- AML represent <2% of all new cancer cases.

Aetiology

- AML may be sporadic or occur as a complication of previous chemotherapy or as a terminal event in a pre-existing myeloproliferative or myelodysplastic disease.

Genetics

- Favourable cytogenetic abnormalities include: t(8;21); Inv(16); and t(15;17) promyelocytic subtype.
- Chromosomal rearrangements involving the *MLL* gene on chromosome 11 are common in myelomonocytic leukaemias.
- Unfavourable cytogenetics include: t(6;9); −7; inv(3); and complex karyotypes.
- 50% of adult AMLs have normal cytogenetics, and gene mutations are frequent in this group; mainly in the *FTL3, NPM1* (nucleophosmin member 1), and tumour suppressor *TET2* genes.

Pathogenesis

- Mutations in a haematopoietic stem cell lead to the clonal expansion of immature myeloid blasts.
- Rapidly proliferative myeloid blasts overwhelm the bone marrow and spill into the peripheral blood.
- Infiltration of organs by myeloid blasts can occur in AML, but this is less common than in acute B-lymphoblastic leukaemia.

Presentation

- Most cases present with bone marrow failure, leading to anaemia, thrombocytopenia, and neutropenia. There may be leucocytosis.
- Infections, bruising, and haemorrhage are also frequent.
- Organs involved include: lymph nodes, CNS, testes (although this is more frequent in ALL), and skin.

Microscopy

See Fig. 15.1.

- By definition, >20% of the cells in the peripheral blood or bone marrow are myeloid blasts.
- The blasts are medium- to large-sized cells with a high nuclear-to-cytoplasmic ratio. Some myeloid blasts contain cytoplasmic granules or Auer rods.

Immunophenotype

- Myeloid blasts usually express CD13, CD117, CD33, and CD34.
- They do not express B-lymphoid markers such as CD79a or PAX5, except t(8;21) AML.
- AMLs with *NPM1* mutation express markers of monocytic differentiation such as CD11c, CD68, and CD163.

Prognosis

- Outcome is dependent on the precise type of AML; however, most are aggressive diseases requiring intensive ablative regimes to achieve remission.
- AML associated with previous chemotherapy or a pre-existing myeloid disorder generally has a poor outcome.
- The overall survival as a group is 26% (SEER 2005–2011).

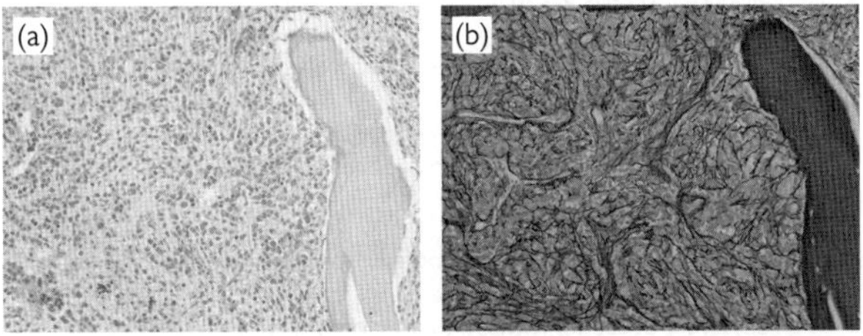

Fig. 15.1 Acute myeloid leukaemia with myelofibrosis. (a) Bone marrow trephine showing sheets of myeloid blasts (haematoxylin and eosin stain). (b) Diffuse and dense increase in reticulin fibres (reticulin stain) (see Plate 32).

Chronic lymphocytic leukaemia

Definition

- A malignant neoplasm composed of monomorphic small B-cells, involving peripheral blood, bone marrow, spleen, and lymph nodes.
- Small lymphocytic lymphoma (B-CLL/SLL) represent different manifestations of the same disease entity, but with a different anatomical distribution (non-leukaemic).

Epidemiology

- The most common leukaemia in Western countries; incidence of 2–6 cases per 100 000 person per year.
- A disease of older adults, with a peak incidence between 60 and 80y, although younger individuals might also be affected.
- Men are affected twice as often as women; ratio 1.5–2:1.
- Very rare disease in Eastern countries.

Aetiology

- Unknown.
- Familial predisposition is high; first-degree relatives of CLL patients have a 2–7 times increased risk of developing leukaemia.

Genetics

- Rearrangement of immunoglobulin genes and somatic hypermutation are the most common alterations.
- Expression of the *ZAP-70* gene (tyrosine kinase) is associated with IG unmutated cases.
- 80% cases have cytogenetic abnormalities, del 13q14.3 and trisomy 12 being the most frequent alterations.

Pathogenesis

- The neoplastic B-cells gradually fill the bone marrow and then spill into the peripheral blood.
- With progression, lymph nodes become involved, and then the liver and spleen.
- In the final stages of the disease, the neoplastic cells overwhelm the bone marrow and cause bone marrow failure.

Presentation

- Many patients are asymptomatic and diagnosed incidentally when a full blood count reveals a leucocytosis.
- The remainder presents with lymphadenopathy or autoimmune phenomena such as autoimmune haemolytic anaemia or autoimmune thrombocytopenia.
- Splenomegaly, hepatomegaly, and lymphadenopathy are also common.
- The diagnosis requires the presence of lymphadenopathy and/or splenomegaly and lymphocytosis ($>5 \times 10^9$/L monoclonal lymphocytes in the absence of extramedullary disease).

Peripheral blood film

- Excess of mature lymphocytes with clumped chromatin and scanty cytoplasm.
- Proportion of prolymphocytes varies but usually <2%.
- So-called 'smear cells' are characteristic of CLL; these represent neoplastic cells which are smudged during preparation of the film.
- Atypical variants exist and are usually associated with trisomy of chromosome 12.

Histopathology

- Lymph nodes are replaced by small, slightly irregular B-cells with variable numbers of 'lighter areas', the so-called proliferation centres containing larger lymphoid cells (prolymphocytes and paraimmunoblasts).
- Some cases show large cells resembling Reed–Sternberg cells (seen in Hodgkin's disease).
- Involved bone marrow contains collections of monomorphic neoplastic lymphoid cells with round nuclei and coarse chromatin.

Immunophenotype

- Positive for PAX5, CD20, CD79a, CD5, and CD23.
- CD23 expression is better detected by flow cytometry than immunohistochemistry.
- Negative for cyclin D1.
- LEF1 (lymphoid-enhancer-binding factor 1) is a highly sensitive and specific marker.

Prognosis

- Generally behaves indolently, with many patients surviving for several years after diagnosis, often without treatment.
- However, different risk factors are associated with a worse prognosis: unmutated CLL, expression of ZAP-70, deletions of 11q22-23 and 17p13.
- A small proportion of cases are complicated by the development of diffuse large B-cell lymphoma (DLBCL) (Richter's syndrome) which has a poor prognosis.
- Rare cases (<1%) might develop Hodgkin's disease.

Chronic myelogenous leukaemia

Definition

- A myeloproliferative neoplasm that predominantly involves the granulocytic lineage and is consistently associated with the *BCR–ABL1* fusion gene located on the Philadelphia chromosome.

Epidemiology

- Incidence of 1–2 per 100 000 population per year.
- The peak age of onset is between 50 and 70y.
- Slight male predominance.

Aetiology

- Unknown.
- An inherited predisposition has not been documented.

Genetics

- By definition, typical cases of chronic myelogenous leukaemia (CML) have the characteristic t(9;22) translocation that results in the Philadelphia chromosome.
- The translocation results in fusion of the *BCR* gene on chromosome 22 to the *ABL1* gene on chromosome 9.
- The *BCR–ABL1* protein (210-kDa protein) has enhanced tyrosine kinase activity, leading to the constitutive activation of signal transduction pathways and deregulated proliferation of myeloid cells.
- Breakpoints on chromosome 2 can be seen outside the major *BCR* region, resulting in different transcripts/shorter fusion proteins (p190), but carrying also an enhanced tyrosine kinase activity.

Presentation

- Most patients are diagnosed during the chronic phase of the disease when a WCC is abnormally raised.
- Symptomatic patients complain of fatigue and night sweats.
- Anaemia and hepatosplenomegaly are often present at diagnosis.
- Several phases are described: chronic phase, accelerated phase, and blastic phase.

Peripheral blood

- Leucocytosis (~100×10^9/L) due to the presence of increased numbers of neutrophils in various stages of maturation.
- Basophilia and eosinophilia are common in the chronic phase.
- No dysplasia is present in the chronic phase.

Bone marrow

- Bone marrow trephines are hypercellular due to increased numbers of neutrophils and their precursors.
- Eosinophils might be prominent.
- Megakaryocytes are typically small and hypolobated ('dwarf megakaryocytes').

- Blasts account for <5% of marrow cells in the chronic phase. Immunostaining with CD34 and TdT highlights clusters of blasts (>20%) in the accelerated phase.
- Transformation may be myeloblastic, lymphoblastic, or mixed.
- Reticulin fibrosis in 30% of cases.

Prognosis

- Outcome is much improved since the development of the tyrosine kinase inhibitor imatinib, with 5-year survival rates of 80–90%.
- Disease progression is usually heralded by an increase in circulating blasts to >10% (accelerated phase) and terminates in acute leukaemia when blasts account for >20% of circulating cells.

Rare types of CML

- **Atypical chronic myeloid leukaemia, *BCR–ABL1* negative,** now included in the myelodysplastic/myeloproliferative neoplasms (WHO classification 2008), usually with worse prognosis than *BCR–ABL*-positive cases.
- **Chronic neutrophilic leukaemia,** characterized by peripheral blood neutrophilia and no evidence of myelodysplastic/myeloproliferative neoplasm. In 20% of cases, another neoplasm is present (most frequently multiple myeloma).
- **Chronic eosinophilic leukaemia not otherwise specified,** a multisystemic disease characterized by persistent blood eosinophilia and organ damage by eosinophilic infiltrate (heart, CNS, skin, GI tract, and lungs).
- **Chronic myelomonocytic leukaemia** (myelodysplastic/ myeloproliferative neoplasms in the WHO classification 2008), defined by persistent monocytosis, <20% of blasts in the marrow, dysplasia in one or more myeloid lineages and absence of the *BCR–ABL* fusion gene.
- **Juvenile myelomonocytic leukaemia,** 75% of cases presenting in children <3 years of age. Young infants with Noonan's syndrome and neurofibromatosis type 1 (NF1) are at risk of developing juvenile myelomonocytic leukaemia. Transformation to AML is rare, but if untreated, it is a fatal disorder with children dying from organ failure due to leukaemic infiltration.

Polycythaemia vera

Definition

- A chronic myeloproliferative neoplasm that predominantly involves the erythroid lineage and is almost always associated with a somatic gain-of-function mutation of the *JAK2* gene.

Epidemiology

- Incidence of 1–2.5 cases per 100 000 population per year.
- Affects middle-aged and elderly patients; median age at diagnosis is 60.
- There is a slight male predominance (male:female ratio 1–2:1).

Aetiology

- Unknown in the majority of cases.
- Familial clustering has been reported.
- There are rare cases of primary congenital polycythaemia associated with mutation in genes in the hypoxia pathway (von Hippel–Lindau gene (VHL); hypoxia inducible factor (HIF) gene).

Genetics

- More than 95% of cases have the JAK2 V617F mutation, leading to a deregulated proliferation of all myeloid cells through cytokines and grown factors, including erythropoietin. The erythroid lineage is the most notably increased.
- Philadelphia chromosome or *BCR–ABL1* gene fusion are absent.
- Progression of the disease is associated with the acquisition of cytogenetic abnormalities.

Presentation

- May present incidentally on full blood count or with symptoms related to hyperviscosity (headache, dizziness, visual disturbance, venous or arterial thrombosis).
- Suffusion of the conjunctiva and engorgement of retinal vessels are also present.
- Most patients are plethoric and have hepatosplenomegaly.
- Three phases described: (1) prodromal (mid-erythrocytosis); (2) overt polycythaemic phase; and (3) 'spent' with myelofibrosis, anaemia, and ineffective haematopoiesis.

Full blood count

- ↑ Hb, ↑ red cell count, ↑ haematocrit (HCT), ↑ packed cell volume (PCV).
- Often ↑ WCC and ↑ platelets.
- Subnormal erythropoietin levels.

Bone marrow

- The marrow is hypercellular due to an increase in all myeloid lineages ('panmyelosis'). Haematopoietic tissue makes up to 90% of the intertrabecular space.
- Erythroid precursors and megakaryocytes are most prominent.
- Megakaryocytes form loose clusters and often show significant variation in size and shape.
- There is an increase in reticulin fibre density.

Prognosis

- Median survival is >10y with treatment. Most patients die from thrombosis or haemorrhage.
- Progression to myelofibrosis occurs in ~30% of patients
- Development of myelodysplasia or AML occurs in 20% of patients, and death from AML occurs in <10% of patients.

Essential thrombocythaemia

Definition

- A chronic myeloproliferative neoplasm that predominantly involves the megakaryocytic lineage.

Epidemiology

- Estimated at 0.6–2.5 per 100 000 people per year.
- Most cases present in adults aged 50–60. A second peak at ~30y of age is also described in women.
- There is no gender predilection.

Aetiology

- Unknown.

Genetics

- No recurring molecular genetic or cytogenetic abnormality is known.
- The presence of a *BCR–ABL1* fusion gene excludes the diagnosis of essential thrombocythaemia (ET).
- A JAK2 V617F mutation is found in 50–60% of patients.
- Mutations in the thrombopoietin receptor gene *MPL* detected in 5% of patients.
- Abnormal karyotype in 5–10% of cases.

Presentation

- About half of patients present incidentally when a markedly raised platelet count is found on full blood count.
- The remainder presents with symptoms related to vascular occlusion or haemorrhage (transient ischaemic attacks (TIAs), digital ischaemia and gangrene, major arterial and venous thrombosis).
- Bleeding from the GI tract and less frequently from upper airway or genitourinary tracts.
- Splenomegaly is present in only a minority of patients.

Full blood count

- Sustained elevated platelet count ($>450 \times 10^9$/L).
- The WCC and red cell count are usually normal, but low Hb levels can be seen with progression to fibrosis.
- Ferritin is usually normal (>20 micrograms/L).

Bone marrow

- The marrow is of normal cellularity but contains increased numbers of large and giant megakaryocytes with abundant cytoplasm and deeply lobated 'stag-horn' nuclei.
- Increase in reticulin fibres is not significant.
- There is no significant erythroid or granulocytic proliferation.
- Absence of increase in myeloblasts.

Prognosis

- Relatively indolent disease with median survival of 10–15y.
- Only a very small proportion of patients progress to bone marrow fibrosis.
- Transformation to AML occurs in <5% of patients and it is usually associated with previous cytotoxic treatment.

Primary myelofibrosis

Definition

- A clonal myeloproliferative neoplasm characterized by predominant proliferation of megakaryocytes and granulocytes in the bone marrow, associated with reactive deposition of fibrous connective tissue and with extramedullary haematopoiesis.

Epidemiology

- Estimated annual incidence of 0.5–1.5 per 100 000 population.
- Occurs mostly in adults aged 60–70, with no gender predilection.

Aetiology

- Unknown in most cases.
- Cases associated with exposure to toxins or ionizing radiation.
- Familial cases are rare, and in a subset of these patients, an autosomal recessive inherited condition might be the cause.
- A previous history of polycythaemia vera (PV) is recorded in 30% of patients.

Genetics

- No specific genetic defect has been identified.
- JAK2 V617F mutation detected in 50% of patients.
- Gain-of-function mutation of MPL in 5% of cases.
- Abnormal karyotype in 30% of cases, del(20q) and partial trisomy 1q being the most common alterations.
- Absence of Philadelphia chromosome or *BCR–ABL1* fusion gene.

Presentation

- Abdominal discomfort due to massive splenomegaly.
- Symptoms related to hypermetabolism such as night sweats, fever, anorexia, and weight loss.
- Two stages described: prefibrotic/early stage and fibrotic.

Peripheral blood

- ↑ platelets and/or WCC.
- ↓ Hb. Normochromic anaemia.
- Gouty arthritis and renal stones if hyperuricaemia.
- Blood film shows leuckoerythroblastosis with teardrop-shaped RBCs.
- Serum LDH might be increased.

Bone marrow

- Megakaryocytes are markedly abnormal with extensive clustering and marked cytological atypia.
- With progression, there is increasing marrow fibrosis (reticulin grade 2 or 3, on a scale of 0–3) and in 10% of osteosclerosis.
- Increase of myeloblasts not a feature.
- Lymphoid nodules seen in bone marrow trephine biopsies in 20–30% of cases.

- Marked vascular proliferation (tortuous vessels) as fibrosis progresses.
- Extramedullary haematopoiesis can be confirmed in liver biopsies or in splenectomy specimens.

Prognosis

- Survival depends on the extent of marrow fibrosis at diagnosis.
- Patients with marked fibrosis have median survival times of 3–7y.
- The major causes of death are bone marrow failure, thromboemboli, and the development of AML.
- Incidence of AML in primary myelofibrosis (PMF) is 5–30%, some of which might be associated with previous cytotoxic treatment.

Myelodysplastic syndromes

Definition

- A group of clonal haematopoietic neoplasms characterized by dysplasia in one or more of the myeloid cell lineages and associated with ineffective myelopoiesis, cytopenias, and an increased risk of development of AML.

Classification

- The 2008 WHO classification includes: refractory cytopenia with unilineage dysplasia (RCU); refractory anaemia with ring sideroblasts (RARS); refractory cytopenia with multilineage dysplasia (RCMD), 30% of all MDS patients; refractory anaemia with excess of blasts (RAEB), 40% of all patients with MDS; myelodysplastic syndrome with isolated del(5q); myelodysplastic syndrome, unclassified (MDS-U).

Epidemiology

- Estimated annual incidence of 3–5 per 100 000 population.
- Occur mostly in older adults at a median age of 70.
- No significant sex predilection, except del5q (or 5q− syndrome) which is more often seen in women.

Aetiology

- Unknown in most cases.
- Exposure to toxins has been documented.
- Inherited haematological disorders might predispose to MDS (e.g. Fanconi anaemia, Diamond–Blackfan syndrome, dyskeratosis congenita).
- Therapy-related myelodysplastic syndrome (t-MDS) occurs as a late complication of chemo- or radiotherapy treatment and might account for up to 20% of all MDS.

Genetics

- A number of recurring chromosomal aberrations have been described in MDS, in 50% of primary MDS and 90% of secondary MDS:
  - chromosomal deletion or loss, e.g. del5q, 17p loss
  - chromosomal gains: trisomy 8, trisomy 11
  - chromosome rearrangement: t3q26, t11q23
  - complex karytotypes (>3 abnormalities).
- Cytogenetic and molecular studies are important in proving clonality and determining the prognosis.

Presentation

- Refractory anaemia is the most common presentation.
- Neutropenia and thrombocytopenia are less frequent.
- Symptoms related to bone marrow failure: infective episodes, bleeding abnormalities.

► Note that hepatosplenomegaly is uncommon in MDS.

Peripheral blood

- Blood film abnormalities vary, depending on each entity, but cytopenias in one or more myeloid lineages are common.
- Blood films may show macrocytes, abnormal neutrophils with poorly developed nuclear segmentation and hypogranular cytoplasm, and giant platelets.
- Leukoerythroblastic changes are present in patients with RAEB, and thrombocytosis is seen in patients with 5q−.

Bone marrow

- Morphological evidence of myelodysplasia may be seen in one or more myeloid lineages in the bone marrow.
- Dyserythropoiesis is characterized by nuclear budding, internuclear bridging, karyorrhexis, multinuclearity, nuclear hypolobation, megaloblastic changes, ring sideroblasts, and cytoplasmic vacuolization.
- Dysgranulopoiesis is characterized by small size, nuclear hypolobation, irregular hypersegmentation, and cytoplasmic hypogranularity.
- Dysmegakaryocytopoiesis is characterized by small size, nuclear hypolobation, or multinucleation.
- Bone marrow is usually hypercellular and an increase in reticulin fibres is noted (myelofibrosis might be prominent in 10% of cases). Some MDS are hypoplastic (~10%), although per se this group has no independent prognostic significance.
- CD34 immunohistochemistry can help to highlight clusters of blasts away from the bone trabeculae and vascular structures, particularly in cases of RAEB.

Prognosis

- Survival depends on a number of factors, including morphological subtype, karyotype, severity of cytopenia, and age.
- A scoring system to predict survival and evolution to AML has been proposed by the International Myelodysplastic Syndrome Working group based on: blasts count in the marrow, number of cytopenias, and karyotype abnormalities.
- Low-risk forms of MDS (RCUD and RARS) tend to have a more prolonged natural history, with a very low incidence of progression into AML.
- High-risk forms (RAEB-2) are more aggressive, with many patients succumbing rapidly to bone marrow failure or AML.

Follicular lymphoma

Definition

- A mature B-cell neoplasm composed of germinal centre cells (centrocytes and centroblasts).

Epidemiology

- Accounts for ~20% of all non-Hodgkin's lymphomas.
- Predominantly affects adults aged 50–60; slight female predominance.
- More common in Western countries.

Aetiology

- Unknown.

Genetics

- 90% of cases have a characteristic t(14;18) translocation which results in fusion of the *BCL2* gene to the *IGH* locus.
- Deregulated production of the anti-apoptotic Bcl-2 protein results in clonal proliferation. However, overexpression of BCL2 is insufficient to induce lymphomagenesis.
- Other chromosomal alterations: random losses of 1p36 and 6q; gains in chromosomes 7 and 18.
- Recurrent mutations in some genes (*MLL2, EZH2*) are detected.
- The microenvironment is essential through expression of CXCR4 and CXCR5 by lymphoma cells, the role of T-regulatory cells and M2 polarized macrophages.

Presentation

- Widespread lymphadenopathy and splenomegaly.
- Patients are otherwise relatively asymptomatic.
- The bone marrow is frequently involved.
- Some variants are recognized: paediatric follicular lymphoma; primary intestinal follicular lymphoma; testicular follicular lymphoma.

Histopathology

See Fig. 15.2.

- Nodal architecture is replaced by back-to-back neoplastic follicles, but areas of diffuse proliferation of neoplastic cells are also observed.
- Neoplastic follicles lack mantle zones and are composed of randomly distributed neoplastic centroblasts and/or centrocytes.
- Tingible body macrophages are usually absent.
- Interfollicular spread of neoplastic cells is usually present.
- Bone marrow involvement is characterized by paratrabecular aggregates of neoplastic centrocytes and centroblasts.

Immunophenotype

- B-cell markers PAX5, CD20, and CD79a are positive.
- Bcl-2, Bcl-6, and CD10 are also positive in the follicle centres, and CD20/CD10 cells are also detected in the interfollicular areas.
- CD5, CD23, and cyclin D1 are negative.

- CD21/CD23 stain follicular dendritic cells and highlight the follicular growth pattern.
- The proliferation index (assessed with Ki67/MIB1) is usually 20–30%.

Prognosis

- Related to the extent of disease and tumour grade.
- 25–35% progress into a high-grade lymphoma, usually DLBCL, associated with a rapid clinical decline and death.
- Transformation usually associated with acquisition of additional chromosomal abnormalities (e.g. MYC translocations).

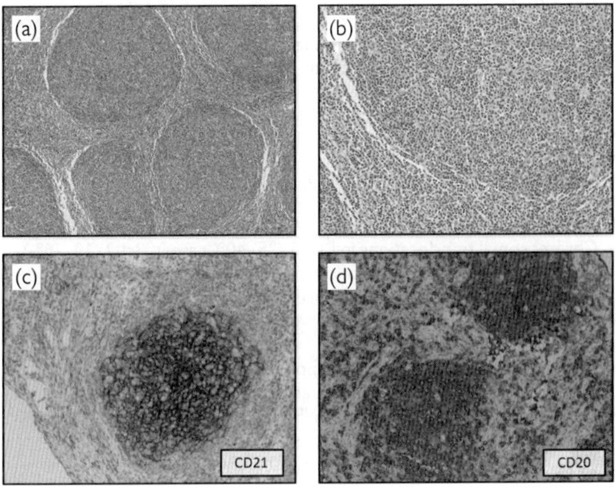

Fig. 15.2 Follicular lymphoma. (a, b) Lymphoma characterized by a nodular pattern. The nodules are well defined and lack mantle areas (haematoxylin and eosin). (c) Follicular pattern highlighted with CD21 (staining follicular dendritic cells). (d) The cells in the follicle centres are CD20-positive (B-cell marker) (see Plate 33).

Diffuse large B-cell lymphoma

Definition

- A mature B-cell neoplasm composed of large B-lymphoid cells with a diffuse growth pattern.
- Clinically and biologically heterogeneous disease, including a wide range of subtypes and related entities.

Epidemiology

- Accounts for 30–40% of all non-Hodgkin's lymphomas.
- Predominantly affects elderly adults aged >60.
- Slight predominance in males.
- The majority are *de novo*, but some cases represent transformation from pre-existing low-grade lymphomas (e.g. follicular lymphoma, Richter's transformation of small lymphocytic lymphoma/leukaemia).

Aetiology

- Remains unknown in many cases.
- Immunodeficiency/immunosuppression is a risk factor where the lymphoma is driven by EBV, HHV-8, or both.

Genetics

- Chromosomal translocations in BCL6 (35–40% cases), Bcl-2 (10–15%), and c-MYC (5–10%) and somatic hypermutations in germinal centre genes (e.g. BCL6, c-MYC, PAX5) are well known.
- Alterations in genes and proteins involved in cell cycle control, cell survival, and apoptosis.
- Activation of the nuclear factor kappa B (NF-κB) pathway, including mutations in CD79A/B, CARD11, and MYD88.
- Different micro-RNA signatures (miR221, miR22, mir93, miR331, and miR491) have been linked with more aggressive disease.
- MYC rearrangements occur in 5–10% of DLBCL.

Presentation

- Rapidly growing mass which may be nodal (60%) or extranodal (40%).
- The most common extranodal site is the GI tract, but virtually any site may be affected.
- Up to one-third of the cases have extranodal involvement at the time of presentation.
- Bone marrow involvement occurs in ~20–33% of patients.

Histopathology

- Involved tissues are replaced by diffuse sheets of large atypical lymphoid cells which are usually more than twice the size of a normal lymphocyte.
- The involved lymph nodes show effacement of the normal architecture, partial or total, with frequent extension of the neoplastic cells into the surrounded perinodal tissue.
- Three variants (immunoblastic, centroblastic, anaplastic), based on the predominant type of the neoplastic cells.
- Apoptotic debris are usually seen and there may be confluent areas of tumour necrosis.

Immunophenotype

- Positive with at least one pan B-cell marker (CD20, CD19, CD22, CD79a, Pax5).
- Cyclin D1 usually negative but can be positive in 2% cases.
- Other frequent expressed markers are CD10, Bcl6, MUM1/IRFA4, GCTE1, and FOXP1.
- High proliferation index (usually 40–90% of cells).
- MYC protein expression (>40% cells) is associated with inferior overall survival, particularly when BCL2 protein is co-expressed.

Prognosis

- DLBCL as a group is an aggressive disease but potentially curable with chemotherapy.
- Survival is much improved since the introduction of the anti-CD20 inhibitor rituximab, with long-term survival rates of around 60–75%.
- Bone marrow involvement is generally associated with poor prognosis.
- Non-anti-CD20 antibodies targeting tumour cells and stroma have shown promising results (e.g. proteasome inhibitors, immunomodulatory drugs, anti-CD22).

Burkitt's lymphoma

Definition

- An aggressive B-cell tumour of germinal centre cell origin.

Variants

- Three variants have been described: **endemic** (equatorial Africa); **sporadic** (children and young adults); and **immunodeficiency associated**-Burkitt's lymphoma (BL) in association with HIV infection.

Epidemiology

- BL accounts for 0.3–1.3% of all non-Hodgkin's lymphomas.
- BL is the most frequent childhood malignancy in equatorial Africa in patients between 3 and 7y.

Aetiology

- EBV might a play a role in the aetiology of the disease.
- In endemic areas, there is an epidemiological link with malaria.
- Immunosuppression (HIV, post-transplant) appears to increase the risk.

Genetics

- Translocation and deregulation of the c-*myc* gene (on chromosome 8) is present in the majority of cases.
- The translocation partner is usually *IGH* (14q21) and less commonly *IGK* and *IGL*. The molecular consequence of the different types of translocations is deregulated expression of the *MYC* oncogene, which plays an essential role in cell cycle control.
- Gains in 12q, 20q, 22q, and Xq and losses of 13q have also been described.
- Amplifications in 1q and gains in 7q are associated with a poor clinical outcome.

Presentation

- Bulky disease, rapid and aggressive clinical course with frequent bone marrow and CNS involvement.
- Extranodal involvement is common, jaws/facial bones (endemic variant) and ileocaecal junction (sporadic) being the most frequent sites.
- Nodal involvement is more frequent in adults.

Histopathology

See Fig. 15.3.

- Diffuse monomorphic infiltrate of small to medium lymphoid cells with rounded nuclei, small nucleoli, and small to moderate amount of basophilic cytoplasm.
- Mitotic figures are frequent, and almost all cases show apoptotic debris.
- Classical 'starry sky pattern', secondary to debris concentrated in the cytoplasm of macrophages admixed with sheets of neoplastic cells.

Immunophenotype

- Prototype CD20+, CD10+, Bcl6+, Bcl2−, IgM+, and TdT− with a proliferation ratio with Ki-67 of nearly 100%.
- VpreB3, a protein in the pre-B-cell receptor, is highly expressed in all cases of BL.
- EBER (EBV-encoded small RNAs detected by *in situ* hybridization) is present in 90% of African BL, but only in 30% of cases in Western areas.

Prognosis

- Overall cure rate for sporadic BL in Western countries is ~90% in the absence of adverse prognostic factors.
- If CNS involvement is present at presentation, the reported 5-year event-free survival is 84%. Older patients have poorer outcomes than young patients on most therapies.
- Treatment consists of initial cytoreduction with cyclophosphamide, prednisolone, and vincristine, followed by intensive chemotherapy in varying combinations.

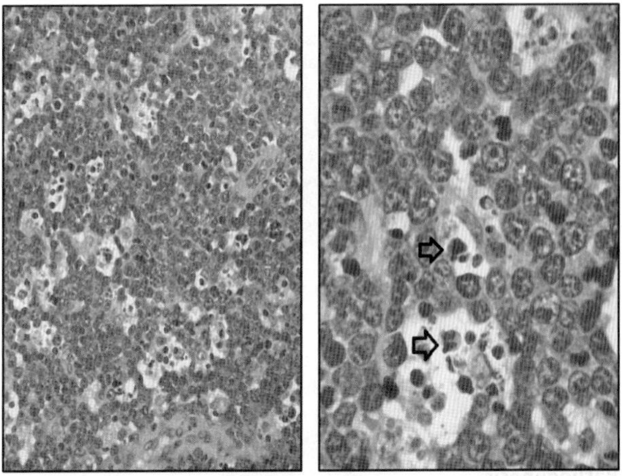

Fig. 15.3 Burkitt's lymphoma. Lymphoma characterized by monomorphic medium-sized lymphoid cells with a 'starry sky' pattern. Detail of tingible body macrophages containing apoptotic tumour cells (arrows) (see Plate 34).

Extranodal marginal zone lymphoma of mucosa-associated lymphoid tissue (MALT lymphoma)

Definition

- An extranodal mature B-cell neoplasm composed predominantly of small neoplastic marginal zone (centrocyte-like) cells.

Epidemiology

- Accounts for 7–8% of all non-Hodgkin's B-cell lymphomas.
- Gastric MALT lymphomas account for 50% of all gastric lymphomas.
- Predominantly arises in adults at a mean age of 60.
- Variation in different geographic areas.

Sites of involvement

- The GI tract accounts for 50% of all cases, with the stomach being the most common location.
- Other sites include the lung, salivary gland, skin, thyroid, and breast.
- Involvement of the small intestine is usually in the form of 'immunoproliferative small intestinal disease' (IPSID).

Aetiology

- Gastric cases are typically associated with *Helicobacter pylori*.
- Other implicated organisms include *Campylobacter jejuni* (jejunum) and *Borrelia burgdorferi* (skin).
- Autoimmune diseases are also associated, e.g. Hashimoto's thyroiditis (thyroid) and Sjögren's syndrome (salivary gland).

Genetics

- t(11;18) involving the *AP12–MALT12* fusion gene is present in the majority of MALT lymphomas not responsive to *H. pylori* eradication therapy.
- Other well-known chromosomal abnormalities include t(1;14) (p22;q32)/*BCL10–IGH* and t(14;18) (q32;q21)/*IGH–MALT1*.
- These translocations involve genes which play an important role in the activation of the NF-κB pathway.

Pathogenesis

- Most cases are preceded by a chronic inflammatory disorder that causes the accumulation of extranodal lymphoid tissue.
- Prolonged stimulation of lymphoid proliferation eventually leads to transformation into a neoplastic process.
- In the stomach, growth of neoplastic B-cells is stimulated by tumour-infiltrating *H. pylori*-specific T-cells through the interaction between B- and T-cells involving CD40 and CD40L co-stimulatory molecules.
- *A20* mutation and deletion are commonly seen in MALT lymphoma of the ocular adnexa, salivary glands, and thyroid.

Presentation

- Symptoms relating to a mass at the involved site.
- Patients usually present with low-stage disease.
- Multiple extranodal sites might be affected in the same patient.
- Bone marrow involvement is seen more frequently in extra-gastric MALT lymphomas.
- Advanced disease at diagnosis appears to be more common in MALT lymphomas that arise outside of the GI tract.

Histopathology

See Fig. 15.4.

- Involved tissues contain a heterogeneous population of small neoplastic B-cells which surround and may overrun background reactive lymphoid follicles.
- The cells include marginal zone cells, cells resembling monocytoid cells, small lymphocytes, and scattered immunoblasts and centroblast-like cells.
- In epithelial-lined tissues, the neoplastic lymphoid cells typically infiltrate and destroy the epithelium, creating so-called lymphoepithelial lesions.

Immunophenotype

- B-cell markers, including CD20, CD79a, and Pax5, are positive.
- CD5, CD10, CD23, and cyclin D1 are all negative.
- Marginal zone markers (CD21 and CD35) are usually positive.
- Neoplastic cells express IgM but lack IgD expression.
- IRTA-1 and MNDA, recently added markers, are positive.

Prognosis

- Tends to show indolent behaviour with prolonged disease-free remissions following treatment.
- Usually favourable outcome; overall survival at 5y >85%.
- Histologic transformation to large-cell lymphoma in ~10% of cases.
- *H. pylori* eradication therapy is recommended to all localized (stages I–II) gastric lymphomas, independently of histological grade.

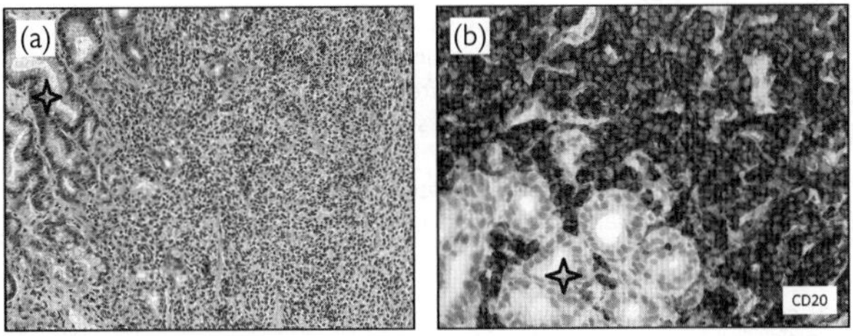

Fig. 15.4 Extranodal marginal zone lymphoma involving the stomach. (a) Gastric mucosa (asterisk indicates gastric glands) infiltrated by a lymphoma composed of small centrocyte-like lymphocytes (haematoxylin and eosin). (b) The lymphoma cells are CD20 diffuse-positive (see Plate 35).

Mantle cell lymphoma

Definition

- A mature B-cell neoplasm composed of monomorphic, small to medium-sized lymphoid cells with irregular nuclear contours and a CCND1 translocation.

Epidemiology

- Accounts for 3–10% of all non-Hodgkin's B-cell lymphomas.
- Predominantly arises in adults at a mean age of 60.
- Slight male predominance.

Aetiology

- Unknown in the majority of cases.
- Familial aggregation is recognized, and candidate genes in these familial cases include germline mutations in the ataxia-telangiectasia mutated (ATM) and CHK2 genes.

Genetics

- Virtually all cases show a t(11;14) translocation involving the *CCND1* (cyclin D1) and *IGH* genes.
- Deregulated expression of cyclin D1 results in uncontrolled proliferation of the lymphoid cells.
- Cases with lack of t(11;14) and lack of cyclin D1 expression do exist.
- Many other chromosomal alterations are described.
- Oncogenic mutations in genes targeting the DNA damage response pathway are described.
- *TP53* mutations are present in cases with a high proliferation index.

Presentation

- Most patients present with lymph node involvement and stage III or IV disease.
- The liver, spleen, marrow, or peripheral blood may also be involved.
- Extranodal sites may also be affected, particularly the GI tract.

Histopathology

- Involved tissues are replaced by sheets of monomorphic, small to medium-sized lymphoid cells with irregular nuclear contours.
- Vaguely nodular growth pattern often seen.
- Hyalinized small blood vessels and scattered epithelioid histiocytes are often present.
- Some morphological variants are recognized, some associated with a more aggressive behaviour (e.g. blastoid and pleomorphic variants).

Immunophenotype

- B-cell markers are positive as well as surface IgM/IgD.
- CD5 and cyclin D1 are positive.
- CD23 and CD10 are usually negative.
- SOX11, a neural transcription factor, is expressed in the majority of mantle cell lymphomas, including cyclin 1-negative cases.

Prognosis

- Despite its relatively bland appearance, prognosis is generally poor, with a median survival of only 3–5y.
- High-proliferation index (assessed with Ki67) correlates with poor prognosis.
- Other adverse prognostic factors include: morphological variants, presence of trisomy 12, *TP53* mutation, and complex karyotype.

Classical Hodgkin's lymphoma

Definition

- A lymphoid neoplasm composed of crippled neoplastic B-cells, known as Hodgkin/Reed Sternberg (HRS) cells, within a rich, non-neoplastic inflammatory background.

Epidemiology

- Bimodal age distribution, with a peak at 15–35y and a smaller peak in adults (>55 years old).
- Classical Hodgkin's lymphoma (cHL) accounts for 20% of all malignant lymphomas.
- Men are more commonly affected than women (ratio 1.5:1), with the exception of the nodular sclerosis variant which has an equal gender incidence.
- Lower incidence in developing countries, with the exception of EBV+ cHL in younger patients.

Aetiology

- Unknown, though EBV infection has been implicated in some types.
- Immunosuppression (e.g. HIV infection) might contribute to the development of EBV+ cHL.
- Familial clustering has been described.

Genetics

- HRS cells are of B-cell lineage and derive from germinal centre B-cells.
- NF-κB pathway is frequently activated, contributing to evasion of apoptosis, survival, and proliferation of neoplastic cells.

Presentation

- Most patients present with localized lymphadenopathy, most frequently cervical, axillary, and inguinal nodes.
- Fever, night sweats, weight loss are common (so-called 'B symptoms') in 40% of cases.
- Nodular sclerosis subtype typically presents with mediastinal involvement (bulky mass in >50% of cases).
- Bone marrow involvement is infrequent (3–5%) in immunocompetent patients.

Histopathology

- Lymph nodes are replaced by small numbers of neoplastic HRS cells (usually 0.1–2%) within a rich inflammatory background.
- The textbook diagnostic Reed Sternberg cell is a very large cell with two or more large nuclei, a thick nuclear membrane, and prominent eosinophilic nucleoli (Fig. 15.5).
- Four histological subtypes are recognized, depending on the number and nature of the HRS cells and the reactive background: nodular sclerosis (50–80% cases), mixed cellularity (20–30%), lymphocyte-rich (5%), and lymphocyte-depleted (very rare).

Immunophenotype

- HRS cells are CD30+ and CD15+ with a typical membranous and Golgi staining pattern.
- MUM-1 is strongly positive and there is reduced/weak expression of PAX5. CD45 (pan-leucocyte marker) is negative and a subset of cases express CD20.
- EBV (either latent membrane protein-1 or EBER *in situ*) positive, depending on age, geographic factors, and subtype (frequently positive in mixed cellularity type and less frequent in nodular sclerosis).

Prognosis

- Modern treatment regimes cure cHL in >85% of cases.
- Histological subtype has limited value to predict prognosis.

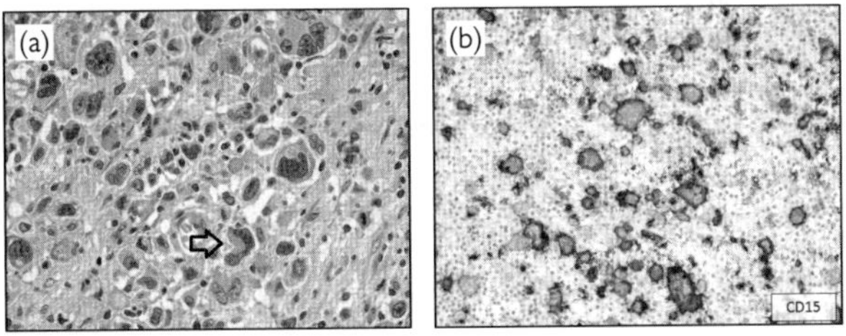

Fig. 15.5 Classical Hodgkin's lymphoma. (a) Mononuclear Hodgkin cells and large atypical Reed–Sternberg cells (arrow), multinucleated with prominent nucleoli. (b) The cells are positive with CD15 (membrane staining) (see Plate 36).

Nodular lymphocyte-predominant Hodgkin's lymphoma

A distinct subtype of Hodgkin's lymphoma, known as **nodular lymphocyte-predominant Hodgkin's lymphoma (NLPHL)**, is also recognized.

NLPHL accounts for 5% of all Hodgkin's lymphomas and typically arises in young to middle-aged adults aged 30–50. Localized peripheral lymphadenopathy is the most frequent clinical presentation.

The abnormal B-cells, known as lymphocyte-predominant (LP) or 'popcorn' cells, are immunophenotypically distinct from classical HRS cells; they usually lack CD30 and CD15 and strongly express B-cell markers (CD20, CD79a, Oct2, BOB1) and EMA. Large numbers of follicular T-helper cells (CD57+, PD1+) are noted, forming rosettes around the LP cells.

The disease behaves indolently; it is rarely fatal, but frequent relapses are common. In early stages, radiotherapy is the standard treatment, and in other stages the therapeutic regime is similar to cHL.

Lymphoplasmacytic lymphoma

Definition

- A neoplasm of small B-lymphocytes, plasma cells, and plasmacytoid lymphocytes involving the bone marrow and sometimes the spleen and lymph nodes.
- Cases with lymphoplasmacytic lymphoma (LPL) in the bone marrow and IgM monoclonal gammopathy are referred to as Waldenström macroglobulinaemia.

Epidemiology

- Median age 63–68y, male predominance.
- Incidence of 3 per 10^6 people per year.
- More frequent in Caucasians, compared with other ethnic groups.

Aetiology

- Family predisposition.
- Chronic hepatitis C, in addition to type II cryoglobulinaemia, drives proliferation of LPL.
- Some patients with Sjögren's syndrome might be at higher risk for LPL.

Genetics

- The most common alteration is a mutation in the *MYD88* gene (90% patients).
- Mutations in *DXCR4* are also frequent.
- Trisomy of chromosomes 4, 3, and 18.

Presentation

- Symptoms related to 'hyperviscosity' such as mucosal bleeding, visual disturbances due to retinopathy, and neurological disorders.
- Precipitation of cryoglobulins results in purpura, arthralgia, and cutaneous vasculitis.

Histopathology

- Nodular, interstitial, and/or diffuse infiltrate of small lymphocytes, plasma cells, and lymphoplasmacytoid cells in the bone marrow.
- Paratrabecular aggregates are also frequent.
- In the lymph nodes, the architecture might be partially preserved or replaced by nodules of neoplastic cells.
- Intranuclear inclusions (Dutcher bodies) are often seen.
- Mast cell hyperplasia is common.

Immunophenotype

- Positive with pan-B-cell markers CD20, CD19, CD20, CD22, and CD79a.
- Usually CD5-negative.
- Negative also with CD10, CD23.
- Plasma cells are highlighted with CD138 and are monotypic with light chains.
- Expression of surface immunoglobulins, mainly IgM and sometimes IgG.

Prognosis

- Indolent disease; median survival 5–10y.
- Main causes of death are transformation to high-grade lymphoma and infection.
- Standard treatment in symptomatic patients include rituximab (anti-CD20 antibody), cyclophosphamide, and dexamethasone.

Plasma cell myeloma

Definition

- A disseminated bone marrow-based plasma cell neoplasm associated with a serum and/or urine paraprotein (usually M-protein).

Epidemiology

- Incidence 3–5 per 100 000 population.
- Occurs in older adults, with a mean age at diagnosis of 70y.
- There is a male predominance (1.5:1) and it is more frequent in Afro-Caribbean ethnic groups.
- Cases can occur *de novo*, but the majority are preceded by monoclonal gammopathy of undetermined significance (MGUS).

Aetiology

- Unknown in most cases.
- Chronic antigenic stimulation (chronic bacterial diseases and inflammatory conditions) might play a role in some cases of multiple myeloma.

Genetics

- Frequent translocations involving the heavy chain locus on chromosome 14q32. The most frequent partner is cyclin D1 (11q13).
- Trisomies of odd-numbered chromosomes (3, 5, 7, 9, 11, 15, 19, and 2).
- Activating mutations of *RAS* (*K-* and *NRAS*).
- Activation of the NF-κB pathway by mutations in upstream genes.
- Epigenetic changes are also important, mainly DNA methylation, histone modifications, and non-coding RNAs.

Pathogenesis

- The neoplastic plasma cells secrete cytokines which activate osteoclasts, causing lytic bone lesions.
- Circulating paraprotein depresses normal immunoglobulin production, increasing the risk of infections.
- Free light chains passing through the kidney contribute to renal failure.
- The interaction between myeloma cells and bone marrow stromal cells increases myeloma cell growth and it is a target for new treatments.

Presentation

- Bone pain, pathological fractures, and recurrent infections.
- Anaemia, increased erythrocyte sedimentation rate (ESR), hypercalcaemia, and renal impairment are common.
- Clinical variants include: asymptomatic (smouldering) plasma cell myeloma; non-secretory myeloma and plasma cell leukaemia ($>2 \times 10^9$/L clonal plasma cells in the peripheral blood).

Histopathology

- Definite diagnosis requires bone marrow biopsy.
- The bone marrow contains an excess of monoclonal plasma cells present in clusters, nodules, or sheets (Fig. 15.6).
- Plasma cells might contain globular inclusions: Russell bodies (cytoplasmic) and less frequently Dutcher bodies (nuclear inclusions).
- Prominent osteoclastic activity can also be seen in bone marrow biopsies.
- Clonality can be proven immunohistochemically by demonstrating kappa or lambda light chain restriction, and tumour burden can be assessed by CD138 immunostaining.

Immunophenotype

- Positive with CD138, CD38, VS38c, and CD79a.
- CD56 is aberrantly expressed.
- Some cases are cyclin D1-positive and this correlates with the presence of t(11;14).
- Less frequently, plasma cells can express CD117, CD20, and rarely CD10.

Prognosis

- Myeloma remains an incurable disease.
- Typical survival is 3–4y from diagnosis.
- Prognostic factors include: renal function, β_2 microglobulin levels, cytogenetics abnormalities, and high degree of bone marrow involvement.

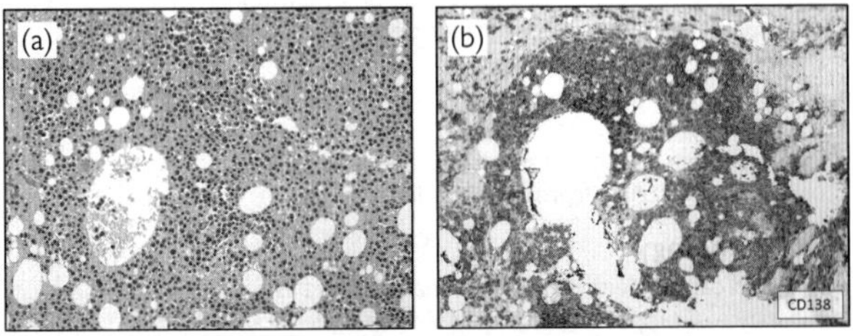

Fig. 15.6 Multiple myeloma. (a) Bone marrow trephine biopsy infiltrated by sheets of plasma cells. The plasma cells have a round eccentric nucleus and abundant basophilic cytoplasm (haematoxylin and eosin staining). (b) The plasma cells are diffusely and strongly positive with CD138 (plasma cell marker) (see Plate 37).

Primary amyloidosis

Definition

- A plasma cell neoplasm, or rarely a lymphoplasmacytic disorder, associated with secretion of abnormal immunoglobulin light chains and the deposition of AL amyloid in multiple tissues.

Epidemiology

- Rare disease.
- Median age at diagnosis 65y, with clear male predominance.

Aetiology

- Up to 20% of patients have an underlying plasma cell myeloma and even a higher proportion will have criteria for MGUS.

Genetics

- Genetic abnormalities similar to those described in MGUS and plasma cell myeloma.
- t(11;14) present in >40% of cases of primary amyloidosis.

Pathogenesis

- AL amyloid is composed of immunoglobulin light chains (intact or fragments) secreted by monoclonal plasma cells which deposit in various tissues in a β-pleated sheet structure.
- Accumulated amyloid includes intact light chain and fragments of the variable NH2-terminus region.
- Rarely, immunoglobulin heavy chains are involved in the pathogenesis.

Presentation

- Clinical features related to the deposition of amyloid in multiple organs.
- Common sites of involvement include the skin, kidney, heart, liver, bowel, and peripheral nerves.
- Typical features include purpura, peripheral neuropathy, cardiac failure, nephrotic syndrome, bone pain, and malabsorption.
- Haemorrhage is a common complication, usually as consequence of blood vessel fragility from amyloid deposition.

Histopathology

- Amyloid can be demonstrated in many tissues as a pink amorphous substance. Congo red stains amyloid red under standard light microscopy and 'apple green' under polarized light.
- Amyloid is usually present in thickened blood vessel walls, and in the bone marrow it is seen in the interstitium.
- Bone marrow biopsies typically show a mild increase in plasma cells which may appear normal or atypical. The plasma cells are monotypic for either kappa or lambda light chains.

Immunophenotype

- Staining for amyloid P component.
- Anti-amyloid fibril antibodies against AL kappa and lambda and amyloid AA component might be useful.

Prognosis

- Poor prognosis with a median survival of only 2y from diagnosis or shorter for patient with coexisting plasma cell myeloma.
- Treatment options include reduction in the production of the amyloid-forming protein and supporting the function of damaged organs.
- Most frequent cause of death is amyloid-associated cardiac failure.

Mature T-cell non-Hodgkin's lymphomas

Definition

- A group of lymphoid neoplasms derived from natural killer (NK) or T-cells.

Classification

- The WHO classification includes >20 entities, accounting for 12–15% of all the malignant lymphomas.
- Peripheral T-cell lymphoma not otherwise specified (PTCL-NOS) and angioimmunoblastic T-cell lymphoma (AITL) are the most common types.
- Other types include enteropathy-associated T-cell lymphoma (EATL), adult T-cell lymphoma (ATLL), AITL, anaplastic large cell lymphoma (ALCL), and extranodal NK nasal-type lymphoma.

Epidemiology

- Some geographic variation, depending on the type (EATL in the UK, ATLL in Japan, extranodal NK nasal-type in the Far East).
- The mature T-cell and NK-cell neoplasms usually affect adults, and most of the entities described are more commonly reported in males than in females. However, some types (e.g. ALCL) are commonly seen in children/young adults.

Aetiology

- EBV might play a role particularly in some entities (e.g. EBV+ T-cell lymphoproliferative diseases of childhood).
- Chronic immunosuppression (e.g. post-transplant) contributes to the development of some types (e.g. hepatosplenic T-cell lymphoma).

Genetics

- Monoclonal or oligoclonal rearrangement of the T-cell receptor.
- RHO-A mutations are common in AITL.
- ALK gene translocation, most commonly t(2;5)(p23;q35)(NPM-ALK), in ALCL–ALK+.
- Complex karyotype with recurrent chromosomal gains (7q, 9q, 17q) and losses (4q, 5q, 6q, 9p) in PTCL-NOS.

Presentation

- Might be nodal (PTCL-NOS, AITL, ALCL), extranodal (nasal type, EATL, hepatosplenic), cutaneous only, or disseminated (AITL, aggressive NK-cell leukaemia).
- The majority are clinically aggressive.
- Compared to aggressive B-cell lymphomas, patients tend to present with more advanced disease, a poorer performance status, and an increased incidence of B-symptoms.

Histopathology

- Varies, depending on the entity, but effacement of the nodal architecture is common in cases with nodal involvement.
- AITL shows prominent vascularization by arborizing venules and expansion of CD21+ follicular dendritic cell networks. An oligoclonal or monoclonal B-cell population due to the expansion of B-cells infected with EBV can be seen in some cases.
- ALCL are characterized by 'hallmark cells' with a horseshoe-shaped nucleus, infiltrating sinusoids, and diffuse sheets surrounding residual follicles.
- PTCL-NOS is defined by medium-sized or large pleomorphic cells with irregular nuclei, in a diffuse pattern most frequently. Reed Sternberg-like cells can be seen.

Immunophenotype

- Lack of at least one T-cell marker (CD5 and CD7 the most frequently lost). CD4 and CD8 might be positive or negative.
- CD30 is frequently expressed in ALCL and in a proportion of cutaneous T-cell lymphomas and PTCL-NOS.
- Cytotoxic markers (TIA-1, granzyme B, perforin) are positive in ALCL.
- Follicular T-helper cell markers (CD10, PD1, CXCL13, and ICOS) are expressed in AITL and in some cases of PTCL-NOS.
- ALK (subcellular localization) varies according to the type of translocation in ALCL. EMA is usually positive.
- NK cell markers: CD56, CD57, CD16.
- AITL and some entities (e.g. EBV+ lymphoproliferative chronic disease of childhood) are EBV-positive (especially by EBER *in situ* hybridization).

Prognosis

- The 5-year overall survival with standard chemotherapy varies between 25 and 45%.
- A clinical score (peripheral T-cell index PIT) has been proposed to allow prognostic stratification.
- Morphology usually does not correlate with outcome.
- Monoclonal antibodies (e.g. anti-CD30) might improve prognosis in some cases (e.g. ALCL).

Chapter 16

Skin pathology

Eczema/dermatitis

Definition

- A group of inflammatory skin diseases characterized clinically by an erythematous papulovesicular rash and histologically by the presence of intraepidermal oedema (spongiosis).

Atopic dermatitis

- Chronic dermatitis occurring in people with atopy.
- Very common disorder with incidences as high as 15%.
- Typically occurs in infants and children.
- Clinically causes an itchy, erythematous papulovesicular rash involving the face and extensor surfaces of the arms and legs.
- Biopsies from acute lesions show epidermal spongiosis and dermal inflammation.
- Biopsies from later lesions show epidermal thickening and hyperkeratosis with mild spongiosis.

Irritant contact dermatitis

- Inflammatory skin disease caused by direct toxic effect of an irritant.
- A common cause of occupational skin disease.
- Clinically causes erythema with vesiculation.
- Biopsies show epidermal spongiosis and dermal inflammation.

Allergic contact dermatitis

- Inflammatory skin disease caused by a delayed-type hypersensitivity reaction to an allergen to which the patient has been sensitized.
- Common occupational skin disease (well-described in hairdressers).
- Clinically causes itchy papules and vesicles 12–48h after exposure.
- Common culprits include nickel, cosmetics, and foodstuffs.
- Biopsies show epidermal spongiosis with vesicle formation and an inflammatory infiltrate which usually includes eosinophils.

Nummular dermatitis

- Inflammatory skin disease of unknown cause.
- Clinically shows tiny papules and vesicles that coalesce into coin-shaped patches.
- Biopsies show epidermal spongiosis and inflammation in early lesions. Older lesions show epidermal hyperplasia.

Seborrhoeic dermatitis

- Common inflammatory skin disease affecting 1–3% of people.
- Some evidence suggests it may be the result of an abnormal immune response to *Malassezia* organisms, but this is controversial.
- Clinically causes erythematous, scaly papules and plaques, sometimes with a greasy appearance, on the scalp, ears, eyebrows, and nasolabial area.
- Biopsies show variable epidermal spongiosis and hyperplasia with parakeratosis centred on hair follicles.

Psoriasis

Definition

- A chronic relapsing skin disorder associated with abnormal hyperproliferation of the epidermis.

Epidemiology

- Common, affecting ~2% of people.
- Mean age of onset 25y.

Aetiology

- Current evidence suggests that psoriasis is the result of an abnormal immune reaction to an external trigger in a genetically susceptible individual.
- Factors known to trigger or exacerbate the condition include stress, infections, climate, alcohol, smoking, and trauma.
- Genome-wide linkage analysis studies have identified at least nine chromosomal loci associated with psoriasis; most of these appear to be genes encoding HLA proteins, cytokines, or cytokine receptors.

Pathogenesis

- Activated plasmacytoid dendritic cells in the skin migrate to draining lymph nodes where they induce the differentiation of naïve T-cells into type 1 and type 17 helper and cytotoxic T-cells.
- Effector T-cells circulate to the skin where they elaborate cytokines, including IL-17, IL-22, IFN-γ, and TNF-α, which stimulate the hyperproliferation of epidermal keratinocytes.

Presentation

- Well-demarcated erythematous plaques with adherent silvery scale.
- Sites of predilection are the elbows, knees, and scalp.
- Nail involvement is common with pitting and onycholysis.
- Guttate psoriasis is a clinical variant, characterized by small, 1–5mm in size, erythematous papules. Many of these cases are preceded by streptococcal infection.
- Severe psoriasis may cause erythroderma (erythrodermic psoriasis).

Histopathology

- Typical lesions show psoriasiform epidermal hyperplasia with thinning of the suprapapillary plates. Plaques of parakeratosis are present, with a diminution of the granular layer beneath the parakeratosis.
- Collections of neutrophils are seen in the stratum corneum (Munro microabscesses) and may also be found within the stratum spinosum.
- The dermis contains dilated capillaries and an inflammatory infiltrate.

Prognosis

- Usually runs a chronic course.
- May have a significant impact on quality of life.

Lichen planus

Definition

- An inflammatory skin disease associated with itchy purple papules clinically and a lichenoid reaction pattern histologically.

Epidemiology

- Affects ~1% of the population.
- Usually arises in middle-aged adults, with a slight female predominance.

Aetiology

- Unknown.

Pathogenesis

- Thought to represent a delayed-type hypersensitivity reaction to an unidentified epidermal antigen.

Presentation

- The skin lesions are small, flat-topped, violaceous papules which are usually intensely itchy.
- Fine white lines (Wickham's striae) usually cross the surface.
- The lesions usually occur on the flexor aspect of the wrists, the extensor aspects of the hands, and the forearms.
- Oral involvement is common (➔ Oral cavity diseases, p. 90) as are genital lesions (➔ Penile diseases, p. 241 and ➔ Vulval skin diseases, p. 244), particularly in men.

Histopathology

- A heavy, band-like inflammatory infiltrate containing lymphocytes and macrophages is present beneath the epidermis.
- The basal layer of the epidermis shows vacuolar damage with cytoid body formation and melanin spillage.
- The epidermis shows irregular acanthosis, hyperkeratosis, and wedge-shaped hypergranulosis.

Prognosis

- In most cases, the disease resolves spontaneously over a variable period of time from weeks to a year.

Erythema multiforme

Definition

- An inflammatory skin disorder associated with distinctive targetoid lesions clinically and an interface reaction pattern histologically.

Epidemiology

- Relatively common.
- Mainly affects young people, including children.

Aetiology

- Most cases are linked to current or previous infections with HSV (which may not always be clinically apparent).
- Other infective agents have also been implicated, e.g. *Mycoplasma*.
- Drugs are also a recognized cause.

Pathogenesis

- Thought to represent a delayed-type hypersensitivity reaction to HSV antigens transported to the skin in circulating lymphocytes.

Presentation

- Discrete, round erythematous patches, 1–2cm in size, with central discoloration which may blister ('target' lesions).
- Most cases involve the extremities.
- Mild oral involvement is common.

Histopathology

- Biopsies show an interface dermatitis characterized by a superficial lymphohistiocytic inflammatory infiltrate with prominent basal cell vacuolar degeneration and keratinocyte apoptosis.
- Cases with marked basal cell damage may result in subepidermal clefting and blistering.

Prognosis

- Most cases are self-limiting, but recurrent episodes are common.

Granuloma annulare

Definition

- An inflammatory skin disease classically associated with annular lesions clinically and necrobiotic granulomatous inflammation histologically.

Epidemiology

- Common.

Aetiology

- Unknown in the majority of cases.
- *Borrelia* infection has been linked in a small number of cases.

Pathogenesis

- Current evidence suggests it represents a cutaneous reaction pattern to as yet undefined antigens.

Presentation

- Localized lesions of granuloma annulare consist of flesh-coloured or red papules which line up to form an annular lesion of 1–5cm.
- Acral sites are usually affected, especially the knuckles and fingers.

Histopathology

- The dermis contains a palisading granuloma, characterized by a central area of degenerate (necrobiotic) collagen surrounded by radially arranged histiocytes, lymphocytes, and fibroblasts.
- Mucin is often present within the necrobiotic focus.
- Occasionally, the process forms a more subtle ill-defined lesion in the dermis, rather than a typical well-formed palisaded granuloma (interstitial granuloma annulare).

Prognosis

- About half of cases resolve within 2y of onset, though recurrences are quite common.

Pemphigus vulgaris

Definition

- An immunobullous skin disease due to autoantibodies against epidermal desmosomal proteins.

Epidemiology

- Rare with an incidence of 0.1–1 per 100 000 people per year.
- Usually affects middle-aged adults of 40–60y.

Aetiology

- Production of autoantibodies directed against the epidermal desmosomal cadherin desmoglein-3.

Pathogenesis

- The autoantibody binds to the extracellular domain of desmoglein-3, leading to desmosomal damage and acantholysis.
- The traditional view was that complement fixation led to acantholysis; however, some workers have suggested that the acantholysis may be due to cytoskeletal collapse, independent of the action of complement.

Presentation

- Most cases start with oral erosions and blisters, followed weeks or months later by the development of skin lesions.
- The skin lesions are fragile blisters developing on normal or erythematous skin. The blisters easily rupture, leaving a painful area of erosion.
- The skin lesions typically occur on the face, scalp, axillae, and groins.

Histopathology

- Biopsies show a blister cavity within the epidermis containing acantholytic keratinocytes.
- Typically, the level of the split is suprabasal, such that the floor of the blister is lined by a single layer of intact basal keratinocytes.
- The acantholysis may also involve the epidermis of adnexal structures.
- There is usually an underlying dermal inflammatory infiltrate which includes many eosinophils.

Immunofluorescence

- Direct immunofluorescence on perilesional skin reveals a deposition of IgG and C3 in the intercellular region of the epidermis.

Prognosis

- Mortality rates are low with appropriate immunosuppressive regimes.
- Most complications are therapy-related.

Bullous pemphigoid

Definition

- An immunobullous skin disease due to autoantibodies against epidermal hemidesmosomal proteins.

Epidemiology

- Most common immunobullous skin disorder, but still a rare disease with an annual incidence of 7 per million population.
- Most cases arise in elderly adults aged >70.

Aetiology

- Production of autoantibodies directed against epidermal hemidesmosomal proteins.
- The two key antigens are known as BPAg1 and BPAg2.

Pathogenesis

- Binding of the antibody leads to fixation of complement and an influx of inflammatory cells, including eosinophils.
- Direct cytotoxic action leads to the disruption of the hemidesmosomes anchoring the epidermis to the dermis and the resultant separation of the entire epidermis from the dermis.

Presentation

- The typical skin lesions are large, tense, intact blisters which develop on normal or erythematous skin.
- Sites of predilection include the lower trunk, inner thighs, forearms, axillae, and groins.

Histopathology

- Biopsies show a subepidermal blister containing numerous eosinophils.
- The underlying dermis is oedematous and also contains an inflammatory infiltrate rich in eosinophils.

Immunofluorescence

- Direct immunofluorescence on perilesional skin reveals linear deposition of IgG and C3 along the basement membrane zone.

Prognosis

- Mortality rates are low with appropriate immunosuppressive regimes.
- Most complications are therapy-related.

Dermatitis herpetiformis

Definition

- An immunobullous skin disorder characterized by intensely itchy papules and vesicles, granular deposition of IgA in the papillary dermis, and a strong association with coeliac disease.

Epidemiology

- Rare.
- Any age may be affected, but the peak incidence is young adults aged 20–40y.
- Males are affected twice as often as females.
- The condition is particularly common in Northern Europe and Ireland.
- Up to 90% of people have evidence of coeliac disease, though this may be subclinical.

Aetiology

- IgA transglutaminase antibodies formed in the gut appear to be the key mediator.

Pathogenesis

- IgA transglutaminase antibodies react with transglutaminase enzymes in the skin.
- Fixation of complement stimulates chemotaxis of neutrophils into the papillary dermis.
- Enzymes released from neutrophils lead to blister formation.

Presentation

- The rash is composed of groups of papules and vesicles which are intensely itchy.
- Sites of predilection are the shoulders, back, buttocks, elbows, and knees.

Histopathology

- Biopsies from early lesions show collections of neutrophils within the papillary dermis (papillary dermal microabscesses).
- Biopsies from established lesions show a subepidermal blister rich in neutrophils.

Immunofluorescence

- Direct immunofluorescence of perilesional skin reveals granular deposition of IgA in the papillary dermis.

Prognosis

- The disease is usually chronic and lifelong but shows a dramatic response to the drug dapsone.

Erythema nodosum

Definition

- A syndrome characterized clinically by an acute painful erythematous nodular skin eruption and histologically by a septal panniculitis.

Epidemiology

- Typically affects young adults, with a marked predilection for women.

Aetiology

- Numerous aetiologies have been described.
- Most common associations are sarcoidosis (➲ Sarcoidosis, p. 495), infections, inflammatory bowel disease (➲ Crohn's disease, pp. 132–3 and ➲ Ulcerative colitis, pp. 134–5), and drugs.

Pathogenesis

- Unknown, but probably represents a form of hypersensitivity reaction to infection, drug, or an underlying systemic disease.

Presentation

- Sudden onset of red, warm, tender skin nodules.
- Classically involves the shins, but other sites may be affected.
- Systemic symptoms, such as fever and malaise, may also be present.

Histopathology

- Biopsies show a septal panniculitis characterized by an inflammatory infiltrate centred on the septa of subcutaneous fat.
- The inflammatory infiltrate is composed predominantly of lymphocytes and macrophages.
- Collections of histiocytes surrounded by cleft-like spaces are well described (Mieschner's radial granuloma).

Prognosis

- The condition is usually self-limiting over a period of weeks, with the skin nodules eventually fading and discolouring rather like a bruise.

Pyoderma gangrenosum

Definition

- An inflammatory skin disease characterized by the development of one or more large necrotic ulcers with ragged undermined violaceous borders.

Epidemiology

- Uncommon.
- Typically affects middle-aged adults.

Aetiology

- Unknown, though more than half of all cases are associated with a systemic disease (particularly inflammatory bowel disease and arthritis).

Pathogenesis

- Unknown, though many immune abnormalities have been described.
- Whether it represents a form of vasculitis is controversial.

Presentation

- The lesion begins as an erythematous pustule or nodule, typically on the lower extremity.
- Often there is a history of preceding minor trauma (pathergy).
- There is then rapid evolution into a necrotic ulcer with undermined red-purple edges.

Histopathology

- Histology is variable and non-specific.
- There is epidermal ulceration with extensive underlying dermal inflammation and abscess formation.

Prognosis

- Recurrence is common and more than half of patients require long-term therapy to control the disease.

Acne vulgaris

Definition

- A cutaneous disorder of pilosebaceous units leading to comedones ± inflammatory papules and pustules.

Epidemiology

- Extremely common disorder affecting ~85% of adolescents and ~15% of the general population.
- Worldwide distribution with equal sex incidence, though males tend to have more severe disease.

Aetiology

- Most cases are related to increased androgen production during adolescence.
- Endocrine conditions resulting in increased androgen production (e.g. polycystic ovarian syndrome, ➲ Polycystic ovarian syndrome, pp. 274–5) can also cause acne.
- Drugs, e.g. contraceptives, steroids, can exacerbate acne.

Pathogenesis

- Increased sebum production and hyperkeratosis cause blockage to hair follicles and formations of comedones.
- Overgrowth of the bacterium *Propionibacterium acnes* causes secondary inflammation with eventual rupture of the follicle with scarring.

Presentation

- Non-inflammatory acne is characterized by the presence of comedones only, which may be open or closed.
- Inflammatory acne causes superimposed papules and pustules which may be complicated by scarring in more severe cases.

Histopathology

- Comedones show a dilated hair follicle plugged with keratin.
- Inflammatory acne shows an acute inflammatory reaction around the involved hair follicle. More severe cases may shows abscess formation and scarring.

Prognosis

- Most cases can be controlled with treatment and the condition generally improves as the patient passes through adolescence.
- Severe cases can lead to permanent scarring.

Rosacea

Definition

- A chronic skin condition characterized by facial flushing ± persistent erythema, papules, and pustules.

Epidemiology

- Common disease affecting ~3% of the population.
- 2–3 times more common in women.

Aetiology

- Exact cause unknown, but possibilities include vascular abnormalities or a reaction to Demodex mites.
- Numerous triggering factors may exacerbate the condition, including sunlight, stress, exercise, hot/cold weather, alcohol, caffeine, and certain foods.

Pathogenesis

- Triggering factors lead to a vascular reaction with dilation and flushing.
- Some patients develop also an inflammatory reaction leading to papules and pustules.

Presentation

- Erythematous subtype: flushing and persistent facial erythema.
- Papulopustular subtype: persistent facial erythema with papules ± pustules.
- Phymatous subtype: thickened nodular skin on the nose, chin, forehead, cheeks, or ears.
- Granulomatous subtype: hard, brown yellow or red papules or nodules.

Histopathology

- Erythematous subtype: dermal oedema, telangiectasia, and mild inflammation.
- Papulopustular subtype: acute inflammation around hair follicles. Demodex mites are often present.
- Phymatous subtype: marked follicular dilation and plugging.
- Granulomatous subtype: perifollicular non-caseating granulomas.

Prognosis

- Usually persistent with a relapsing and remitting course.
- Can have significant psychological effects.

Skin infections

Acute folliculitis

- Infection of hair follicles, usually due to *Staphylococcus aureus*.
- Presents with small, red, tender pustules.
- Deep extension of the acute inflammation may lead to a furuncle with more surrounding erythema and pain.

Impetigo

- Highly infectious superficial bacterial skin infection.
- Very common, particularly in children.
- Caused by either *S. aureus* or *Staphylococcus pyogenes*.
- Presents with vesicles covered by a golden yellow crust, typically around the mouth and nose.

Staphylococcal scalded skin syndrome

- A superficial blistering skin disease caused by strains of *S. aureus* producing an epidermolytic toxin.
- Seen almost exclusively in neonates and young children.
- The skin rash is initially erythematous and then extensively blisters with an appearance likened to a scald.
- Healing occurs within 2–3 weeks without scarring.

Cellulitis

- Deep skin infection caused by *S. pyogenes*.
- Mostly occurs on the legs as an erythematous rash with oedema.

► Clinically may closely mimic deep venous thrombosis (➔ Deep vein thrombosis, p. 39).

Necrotizing fasciitis

- Rapidly progressive necrotizing infection of subcutaneous tissues.
- *S. aureus* and group A β-haemolytic streptococci (dubbed 'flesh-eating bacteria') are the most commonly cultured organisms, but infection is often polymicrobial.
- Fournier's gangrene is a variant on the scrotum (➔ Fournier's gangrene, p. 242).
- Rapid surgical debridement is essential to avoid systemic sepsis.

Cutaneous tuberculosis

- Most cases are caused by haematogenous spread from a tuberculous infection elsewhere in the body.
- Lesions occur mostly on the face (particularly around the nose) as red papules and plaques with a gelatinous consistency.
- Biopsies show granulomatous inflammation ± necrosis.

Non-tuberculous mycobacterial infections

- Non-tuberculous environmental mycobacteria may cause infection if inoculated into the skin, e.g. *Mycobacterium marinum* (associated with underwater injuries), *Mycobacterium fortuitum/chelonae*, and *Mycobacterium kansasii*.

- Biopsies typically show areas of suppurative granulomatous inflammation within which small numbers of acid-fast bacilli may be found.

Viral warts

- Very common skin lesions caused by HPV infection.
- May occur anywhere on the skin in people of any age.
- Clinically appear as keratotic papules.
- Immunosuppressed individuals may have them in large numbers.
- Biopsies show marked papillomatosis with hyperkeratosis and tiers of parakeratosis. The keratinocytes show typical viral cytopathic effects with vacuolation and large keratohyaline granules.

Herpes simplex

- Caused by HSV types 1 and 2.
- Infections involve the oral and/or genital areas.
- Infection is lifelong due to viral latency within sensory ganglia.
- Recurrent episodes may be precipitated by many factors and is characterized by the onset of groups of vesicles on an erythematous base.
- Biopsies show ballooning degeneration of keratinocytes with acantholysis. Keratinocyte nuclei contain characteristic pale intranuclear inclusions.

Varicella-zoster

- Varicella-zoster virus (VZV) is highly contagious and most individuals are infected in childhood, leading to chickenpox.
- Infection is lifelong due to viral latency within sensory ganglia.
- Reactivation of the virus in adulthood leads to herpes zoster (shingles), presenting as a band-like vesicular eruption along the distribution of a sensory nerve.

Molluscum contagiosum

- Caused by molluscipoxvirus infection.
- Results in the eruption of groups of small umbilicated papules on the face, limbs, and trunk of young children or the genital region of young adults.
- Biopsies show a highly distinctive lobular epidermal proliferation in which the keratinocytes contain large basophilic cytoplasmic inclusions.

Dermatophytoses

- Common superficial fungal infections caused by 'ringworm' fungi.
- Cause slowly enlarging scaly erythematous annular lesions on the body (tinea corporis), head (tinea capitis), or foot (tinea pedis).

Tinea (pityriasis) versicolor

- Superficial fungal infection caused by the yeast *Malassezia globosa*.
- Presents with multiple areas of hypo- or hyperpigmentation with fine scale in young adults.
- Biopsies show budding yeasts and hyphae within the stratum corneum ('spaghetti and meatballs').

Benign epidermal tumours

Fibroepithelial polyps

- Very common lesions which typically occur as multiple small pedunculated papules around the neck, axillae, and groin.
- Most are removed for cosmetic reasons or because they catch on clothing.
- Histologically, they are composed of a core of fibrovascular tissue covered by normal or hyperplastic epidermis.

Epidermoid cysts

- Common cutaneous cysts typically arising on the face, neck, upper trunk, vulva, or scrotum.
- Histologically, the cyst is filled with laminated keratin and lined by squamous epithelium with a granular layer.

Pilar (tricholemmal) cysts

- Common cutaneous cysts which almost always occur on the scalp.
- Histologically, the cyst is lined by pale squamous epithelial cells showing abrupt keratinization without formation of a granular layer.

Seborrhoeic keratoses

- Very common lesions seen in middle-aged and elderly adults.
- Appear as brown-black greasy warty nodules which are often multiple.
- May occur anywhere on the body, apart from the palms and soles.
- Histologically composed of a proliferation of basaloid keratinocytes showing variable squamous differentiation, often with hyperkeratosis and horn cyst formation.

Benign melanocytic tumours

Lentigo simplex

- Very common melanocytic lesion presenting as brown to black well-circumscribed macules which may occur anywhere on the body.
- Histology shows elongation of epidermal rete ridges associated with an increased number of basal melanocytes. Pigmentation is increased within the epidermis and in the papillary dermis.

Melanocytic naevi

- Extremely common melanocytic lesions which are virtually universal in white individuals and may be found anywhere on the body.
- Typically show temporal evolution from junctional naevus → compound naevus → intradermal naevus.
- Histologically, junctional naevi show nests of melanocytes located at the tips of the rete ridges. Compound naevi contain a dermal population of melanocytes, in addition to junctional nests. Intradermal naevi contain only dermal melanocytes.
- Most melanocytic naevi have activating mutations in *BRAF*.
- Malignant transformation is rare.

Common blue naevus

- A relatively common dermal melanocytic naevus which appears as a dark blue papule across a wide age range.
- May occur anywhere on the body, but more commonly on the hands, feet, buttocks, scalp, and face.
- Histologically composed of heavily pigmented spindled and dendritic dermal melanocytes.

Spitz naevus

- Benign melanocytic lesion typically presenting in children or young adults as a pink or red/brown papule or nodule.
- Usually seen on the head, neck, and extremities.
- Histologically, Spitz naevi are usually compound melanocytic lesions composed of large epithelioid and/or spindled cells containing abundant eosinophilic cytoplasm and a conspicuous nucleolus.
- Spitz naevi are of particular importance histologically because the large size of the melanocytes can lead to misdiagnosis as melanoma.

Atypical/dysplastic naevus

- Dysplastic melanocytic lesion typically presenting as larger (>6mm) pigmented lesion with irregular margins and variable pigmentation.
- Histologically, the junctional component shows architectural disarray with bridging of nests, together with evidence of cytological atypia.
- Lesions may be graded as mild, moderate, or severe, depending on the degree of atypia.
- Some melanomas arise within pre-existing dysplastic naevi.

Benign cutaneous soft tissue tumours

Dermatofibroma

- Common benign fibrous tumour of the skin.
- Presents as a reddish brown papule on the trunk or lower legs.
- Histologically composed of an ill-defined dermal lesion composed of short interlacing spindle cells within variable amounts of collagen, foamy macrophages, blood vessels, and inflammatory cells.

Lobular capillary haemangioma

- Benign vascular tumour, also widely known as pyogenic granuloma.
- Present as red papules or nodules which often ulcerate and bleed.
- Occurs mostly on the head and neck or extremities.
- Histologically composed of a polypoid dermal lesion composed of lobules of small capillaries.

Neurofibroma

- Common benign cutaneous nerve sheath tumour.
- Most cases are sporadic, but note that multiple neurofibromas and café-au-lait spots are associated with neurofibromatosis type 1.
- Presents as a soft, flesh-coloured papule or nodule at any skin site.
- Histologically characterized by a dermal tumour containing Schwann cells and fibroblasts in a fibrillar background.

Benign skin adnexal tumours

Pilomatrixoma

- Common benign skin tumour showing hair matrix differentiation.
- Presents as a firm papule or nodule in a child or young adult.
- Often occur on the cheek.
- Histologically composed of nodules of basaloid cells showing transformation into anucleate eosinophilic cells ('ghost cells') in the centre of the nodules. Calcification is very common.

Trichoepithelioma

- Benign skin adnexal tumour showing hair germ differentiation.
- Presents as a flesh-coloured papule, usually on the face.
- Histologically composed of organoid nests of basaloid epithelium showing primitive hair follicle formation.

Sebaceous adenoma

- Histologically composed of lobules of cells with peripheral basaloid cells with mature sebocytes centrally.
- Multiple sebaceous tumours may be associated with the Muir–Torre syndrome, an inherited syndrome caused by germline mutations in mismatch repair genes.

Cylindroma

- Benign skin adnexal tumour showing sweat gland differentiation.
- Presents as a solitary pink or red lesion, usually on the head or neck.
- Histologically composed of islands of basaloid cells showing ductal differentiation. The tumour islands characteristically fit together like pieces of a jigsaw puzzle.

Poroma

- Benign skin adnexal tumour showing sweat gland differentiation.
- Presents as a solitary lesion with a wide distribution.
- Histologically composed of broad trabeculae of small epithelial cells growing down from the epidermis.

Syringoma

- Benign skin adnexal tumour showing sweat gland differentiation.
- Present as multiple small papules around the eyelids.
- Histologically composed of clusters of small ducts in the dermis with 'tadpole' shapes.

Basal cell carcinoma

Definition

- A group of malignant epidermal tumours composed of basaloid cells.

Epidemiology

- Very common tumours, accounting for 70% of all skin malignancies.
- Seen predominantly in fair-skinned adults with sun damage.

Aetiology

- Cumulative ultraviolet (UV) radiation exposure is the key risk factor.

Carcinogenesis

- Almost all show mutations in genes encoding proteins involved in the sonic hedgehog pathway, most commonly PTCH1.
- A smaller proportion display mutations in SMOOTHENED which encodes the protein normally inhibited by the PATCHED1 protein.

Presentation

- Most appear as pearly papules or nodules on sun-exposed skin. Ulceration may occur.
- Superficial variants present as persistent scaly/erythematous lesions.

Histopathology

- The tumour is composed of groups of small basaloid cells with scanty cytoplasm which grow in a variety of patterns. The cells at the edge of the groups typically line up in a palisade (peripheral palisading).
- The tumour stroma is typically loose and mucinous.
- Artefactual retraction spaces between the tumour cells and stroma are often seen and can be a useful diagnostic feature.
- A number of morphological subtypes are recognized, including nodular, superficial, infiltrative, morphoeic, and micronodular.

Prognosis

- Show locally invasive behaviour, but metastasis is extremely rare.
- Complete excision is usually curative.
- Recurrences are more common at high-risk sites (head and neck) and with certain morphological subtypes (infiltrative, morphoeic, micronodular).

Pathological staging of skin carcinomas

Primary tumour (T)

pT1: tumour measures 2cm or less in size.
pT2: tumour measures >2cm in size.
pT3: tumour invades muscle, bone, cartilage, jaws, and orbit.
pT4: tumour invades skull base and axial skeleton.

Regional lymph nodes (N)

pN1: single nodal metastasis measuring <3cm in size.
pN2: single nodal metastasis measuring 3–6cm in size or multiple nodal metastases, none measuring >6cm.
pN3: any nodal metastasis measuring >6cm.

Squamous cell carcinoma

Definition

- A malignant epidermal tumour showing squamous differentiation.

Epidemiology

- Common tumours accounting for ~15% of all skin malignancies.
- Most arise on sun-exposed skin of elderly fair-skinned adults.

Aetiology

- Most are related to cumulative UV radiation exposure.
- Immunosuppression increases the risk. Transplant recipients are particularly prone to developing multiple tumours.

Carcinogenesis

- Most arise from **actinic keratoses** which are dysplastic epidermal lesions arising on sun-damaged skin.
- UV radiation, particularly UVB, induces DNA damage in growth-controlling genes such as *KRAS* and *CDK4*.

Presentation

- Skin plaques or nodules, often with a keratinous surface crust.
- Ulceration may be present.

Histopathology

- Nests, sheets, and cords of atypical squamous epithelial cells are seen arising from the epidermis and infiltrating into the underlying dermis.
- Tumours are graded into well, moderately, or poorly differentiated, depending on the extent of keratinization.

Prognosis

- Most are only locally infiltrative at the time of diagnosis and cured by surgical excision.
- Risk factors for recurrence or metastasis include depth of invasion, poor differentiation, perineural invasion, narrow excision, and immunosuppression.

Pathological staging of skin carcinomas

Primary tumour (T)

pT1: tumour measures 2cm or less in size.
pT2: tumour measures >2cm in size.
pT3: tumour invades muscle, bone, cartilage, jaws, and orbit.
pT4: tumour invades skull base and axial skeleton.

Regional lymph nodes (N)

pN1: single nodal metastasis measuring <3cm in size.
pN2: single nodal metastasis measuring 3–6cm in size or multiple nodal metastases, none measuring >6cm.
pN3: any nodal metastasis measuring >6cm.

Malignant melanoma

Definition

- A malignant melanocytic tumour.

Epidemiology

- Less common than basal or squamous cell carcinomas of the skin, but much more frequently fatal.
- Seen predominantly in fair-skinned individuals with sun exposure.

Aetiology

- UV radiation exposure is the major risk factor.
- An element of genetic susceptibility may also be relevant.

Genetics

- *BRAF* mutations are very common (70%) in melanomas arising in non-chronically sun-damaged skin.
- *KIT* mutations are seen in about 30% of melanomas arising in chronically sun-damaged skin.

Presentation

- Most melanomas present as pigmented skin lesions demonstrating **A**symmetry, irregular **B**orders, uneven **C**olour, and **D**iameter >6mm (the 'ABCD' acronym).

Histopathology

- Common to all forms of malignant melanoma is the presence of a neoplastic proliferation of severely atypical melanocytes.
- If the process is confined to the epidermis, the term **melanoma *in situ*** may be employed (Fig. 16.1).
- Once invasion into the dermis has occurred, the term **invasive melanoma** may be employed.

Evolution

- Most melanomas initially grow as a flat lesion in a radial fashion, known as the **radial growth phase**. During this phase, either there is no dermal invasion or cells within the dermis are not able to survive and proliferate.
- With progression, the growth switches such that cells within the dermis are able to proliferate. This is known as the **vertical growth phase** and is associated with the emergence of metastatic potential (Fig. 16.2).

Prognosis

- Survival is related to the stage of the disease at diagnosis.
- Key determinants of stage are the thickness of the melanoma (known as the **Breslow thickness**) and the presence of ulceration.
- Mitotic rate is also now recognized as a strong prognostic indicator in vertical growth phase melanomas.

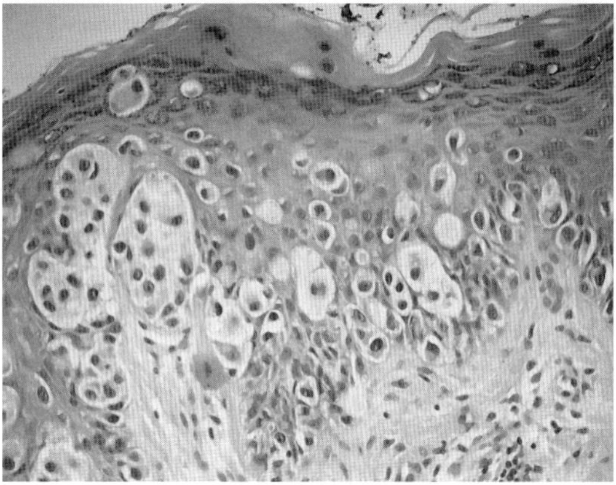

Fig. 16.1 Superficial spreading malignant melanoma *in situ* showing severely atypical melanocytes proliferating in the epidermis with cells present at all levels of the epidermis (pagetoid spread) (see Plate 38).

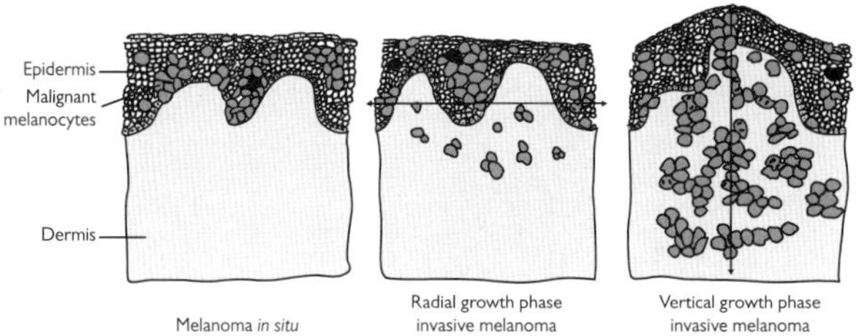

Fig. 16.2 Diagrammatic representation of different stages of melanoma. Melanoma *in situ* comprises malignant melanocytes confined to the epidermis. In radial growth phase invasive melanoma, malignant melanocytes invade the dermis, but growth of the tumour is still confined to the epidermis. In vertical growth phase invasive melanoma, growth of the tumour switches from the epidermis to the dermis.

Reproduced with permission from *Clinical Pathology* (Oxford Core Texts), Carton, James, Daly, Richard, and Ramani, Pramila, Oxford University Press (2006), p. 381, Figure 16.14.

TNM 7 pathological staging of malignant melanoma

Primary tumour (T)

pT1a: tumour ≤1.0mm thick, without ulceration, mitoses <1/mm^2.
pT1b: tumour ≤1.0mm thick, with ulceration or mitoses ≥1/mm^2.
pT2a: tumour 1.01–2.0mm thick, without ulceration.
pT2b: tumour 1.01–2.0mm thick, with ulceration.
pT3a: tumour 2.01–4.0mm thick, without ulceration.
pT3b: tumour 2.01–4.0mm thick, with ulceration.
pT4a: tumour >4.0mm thick, without ulceration.
pT4b: tumour >4.0mm thick, with ulceration.

Mycosis fungoides

Definition

- A low-grade T-cell lymphoma of variably epidermotropic skin-homing T-lymphocytes.

Epidemiology

- Most common form of primary cutaneous lymphoma, but overall an uncommon disease, affecting 0.3 per 100 000 people annually.
- Usually a disease of adulthood but occasionally affects children.

Aetiology

- Unknown.

Genetics

- Disease progression is associated with chromosomal aberrations, particularly involving chromosomes 8 and 17.

Presentation

- Sequential appearance of patches, plaques, and tumours on non-sun-exposed skin (particularly around the buttocks and trunk).
- Patches are multiple large (>10mm), flat, erythematous, scaly lesions.
- Plaques are elevated lesions arising either within patches or *de novo*.
- Nodules are large exophytic tumour masses.
- Sometimes the disease presents with erythroderma.
- Bone marrow, lymph nodes, and visceral organs may be involved in advanced disease.

Histopathology

- Patch stage shows a mild upper dermal T-cell infiltrate associated with variable epidermotropism. Early disease is often difficult to diagnose as the features overlap with a number of inflammatory conditions.
- Plaque stage shows a more prominent and band-like infiltrate of T-cells with more epidermotropism. Collections of neoplastic lymphocytes within the epidermis may be seen (Pautrier microabscesses). Nuclear atypia of the lymphocytes is more appreciable.
- Tumour stage shows a more diffuse dermal infiltrate which may extend into subcutaneous fat. Epidermotropism may be lost.

Immunophenotype

- Most cases show a T-helper cell phenotype, i.e. CD3+CD4+CD8−.

Prognosis

- Risk of progression and death correlates with the stage of disease at presentation.
- The 10-year survival rates are high (85–95%) in patch and plaque stage disease, dropping to 40% in tumour stage, and to 20% if there is nodal involvement.

Dermatofibrosarcoma protuberans

Definition

- A superficially located low-grade fibroblastic sarcoma.

Acronym

- DFSP.

Epidemiology

- Rare tumour.
- Most commonly arises in young adults.

Aetiology

- Unknown.

Genetics

- Translocation t(17;22) juxtaposes the *COLA1* and *PDGFB* genes, resulting in overexpression of PDGFB and autocrine stimulation of tumour cell growth.

Presentation

- Slowly growing plaque with nodules.
- Trunk and proximal extremities most common sites.

Histopathology

- Tumour filling the dermis and extending into subcutaneous fat with a characteristic 'honeycomb pattern'.
- Storiform grown pattern.
- Tumour cells are uniform and spindled with only mild cytological atypia and low mitotic activity.

Immunohistochemistry

- CD34 diffusely positive.
- S100, cytokeratin, desmin negative.

Prognosis

- Locally aggressive growth, often with repeated local recurrences.
- Metastatic behaviour is extremely rare (<0.5%).

Fibrosarcomatous DFSP (FS-DFSP)

A small proportion of DFSPs progress to FS-DFSP, in which there is transition into areas where the cells become arranged in cellular 'herringbone' fascicles with more atypia and higher mitotic activity. CD34 expression may be lost in the fibrosarcomatous areas and there is increased p53 expression. FS-DFSP shows a high risk (10–15%) of metastatic spread.

Chapter 17

Osteoarticular pathology

Osteoporosis

Definition

- A metabolic bone disease characterized by a generalized reduction in bone mass, increased bone fragility, and predisposition to fracture.

Epidemiology

- Very common.
- Typically presents in elderly women, though people of all ages may have clinically silent disease.

Aetiology

- Primary: post-menopausal and age-related (>70y).
- Secondary: a wide variety of causes, including therapeutic agents, notably glucocorticoid therapy, anti-androgens and anti-oestrogens, Cushing's syndrome, hyperparathyroidism, hyperthyroidism, hypogonadism (low levels of testosterone), coeliac disease, inflammatory bowel disease, alcohol, poor nutrition, immobilization.

Pathogenesis

- Bone mass in later life is determined by the peak bone mass attained in early adulthood and the subsequent rate of bone loss.
- Peak bone mass is largely genetically determined but is modified by factors such as nutrition, physical activity, and health early in life.
- Bone loss occurs in both women and men with increasing age due to decreasing bone turnover, decreasing physical activity, reduced sex hormones, and reduced calcium absorption from the gut.
- In women, oestrogen deficiency after the menopause markedly accelerates bone loss.
- Glucocorticoids decrease osteoblastic activity and lifespan, reduce calcium absorption from the gut, and increase renal calcium loss. Sex hormone production is also suppressed which increases bone turnover and loss.

Presentation

- Most cases are clinically silent until fragility fractures occur.
- Classic sites of involvement: vertebrae, distal radius (Colles'), neck of femur following a fall.
- Vertebral fractures lead to loss of height and kyphosis. May occur spontaneously and after lifting, coughing, and bending down.

Histopathology

See Fig. 17.1.

- Cancellous bone is thinned with disconnectivity of bony trabeculae.
- Cortical bone is thinned with enlargement of Haversian canals.

Prognosis

- Neck of femur fractures are the most problematic, as these require hospital admission and surgical fixation.
- Elderly patients with significant coexisting medical problems may have a significant risk of post-operative mortality.

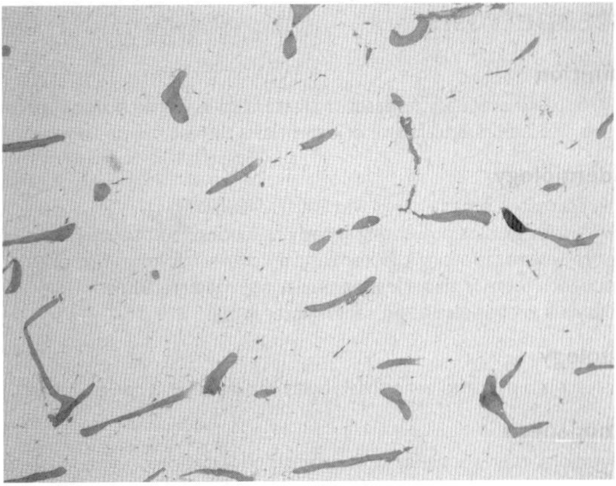

Fig. 17.1 Osteoporosis characterized by thin, disconnected trabeculae of lamellar bone within fatty marrow (see Plate 39).

Osteopetrosis

Definition

- A group of hereditary diseases characterized by dense bones ('marble bone disease') due to failure of osteoclasts to resorb bone adequately.

Epidemiology

- The estimated prevalence is 1 in 100 000–500 000.
- Two major groups presenting in early childhood: autosomal recessive (more severe, affecting children) and autosomal dominant (more frequent); there is also a less common intermediate autosomal dominant osteopetrosis presenting later in life.

Aetiology

- At least ten mutated genes have been implicated in its development.

Pathogenesis

- Mutations interfere either with osteoclast formation or osteoclast function, resulting in dense, brittle bone.

Presentation

- Individuals may be asymptomatic or experience severe symptoms, including visual impairment, stunted growth, and bone marrow failure.
- The most common clinical manifestation is increased fragility of bone, leading to fractures.
- Radiographs show an abnormally high bone density.

Histopathology

See Fig. 17.2.

- If the genetic alteration results in osteoclast formation, very few osteoclasts are present.
- If the genetic alteration results in osteoclast function, abundant and very large osteoclasts are present, but there is little evidence of osteoclast resorption (Howship's lacunae).
- Foci of intra-trabecular hyaline cartilage representing persistent primary spongiosa.

Prognosis

- If severe, there is a high postnatal mortality.
- The only known cure for the infantile malignant form is allogeneic haematopoietic stem cell transplant.

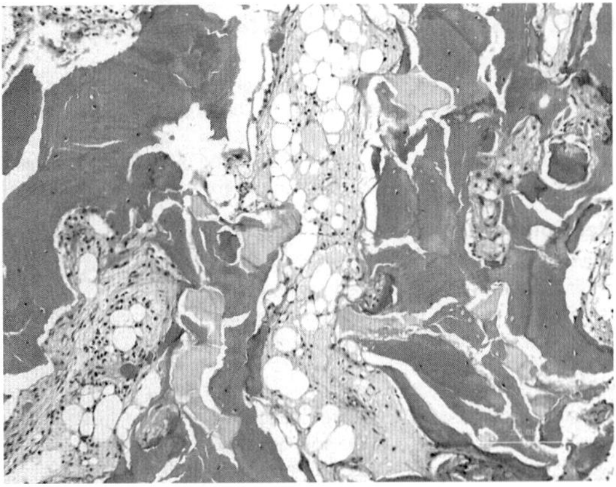

Fig. 17.2 Osteopetrosis is characterized by a distorted bony architecture, with thick trabecular and compact bone largely obliterating the bone marrow space (see Plate 40).

Rickets and osteomalacia

Definition

- Osteomalacia: a metabolic bone disease characterized by inadequate mineralization of bone in the mature skeleton.
- Rickets: a metabolic bone disease characterized by inadequate mineralization of bone and epiphyseal cartilage in the growing skeleton of children.

Epidemiology

- Osteomalacia is common in elderly people resident in institutions (care homes) and anyone with limited exposure to sunlight.
- Osteomalacia is becoming more common in sunny countries because of higher awareness of risk of skin cancer to sun exposure.

Aetiology

- Almost all cases are due to calcium deficiency which, in most cases, is due to vitamin D deficiency, the source of which is sunlight.
- Calcium deficiency is also caused by nutritional deficiency: diet, malabsorption of calcium due to chronic liver disease, CKD, GI bypass surgery, nutritional.
- Vitamin D resistance can result in hypophosphataemic rickets, characterized by low serum phosphate levels and resistance to treatment with UV radiation and vitamin D, mainly caused by genetic defects involving renal absorption of phosphate.
- Tumour-induced osteomalacia: mesenchymal tumours secreting fibroblast growth factor (FGF)-23.

Pathogenesis

- Inadequate mineralization of bone matrix (osteoid) due to lack of calcium and, much less commonly, phosphate.
- Bones become abnormally soft and prone to deformity and fracture.
- In children, the soft bone formed at the epiphyseal plate results in skeletal deformity (bowing of the legs) and short stature.

Presentation

- Diffuse bone pain and tenderness.
- Weakness of proximal muscles.
- Imaging: osteopenia; multiple stress fractures are common.
- Many cases go undiagnosed due to the insidious, non-specific nature of the presenting symptoms.

Histopathology

See Fig. 17.3.

- Bony trabeculae are covered by an excessively thick layer of unmineralized osteoid.
- Bone biopsies must not be decalcified if mineralization is to be assessed.

Prognosis

- Vitamin D supplementation usually results in rapid mineralization of bone and resolution of symptoms, though some deformity may remain.
- Failure to respond requires exclusion of vitamin D-resistant rickets.

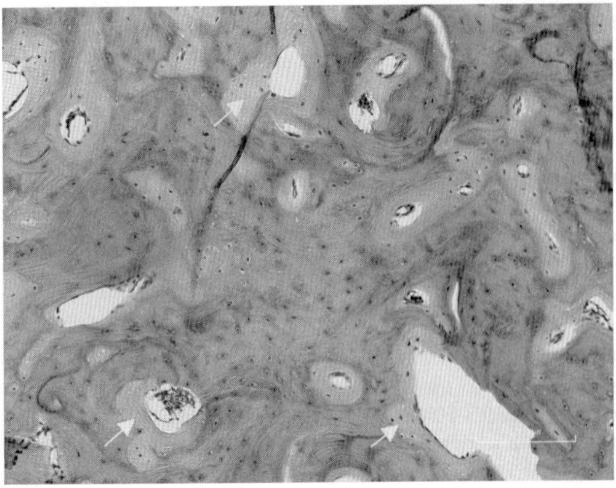

Fig. 17.3 Osteomalacia, as seen in compact bone, showing mature viable bone covered by a thick layer of unmineralized matrix (osteoid)—pale pink (arrows). Similar features are seen in rickets. Haematoxylin and eosin section (see Plate 41).

Paget's disease

Definition

- A metabolic bone disease characterized by excessive chaotic bone turnover in localized parts of the skeleton.

Epidemiology

- Marked geographic variation, being particularly common in the UK—appears that the incidence is reducing.
- Seen mostly in older adults (>50).
- Presentation in the young is usually associated with a genetic (germline) alteration.

Aetiology

- Mutations account for ~70% of all cases, with *SQSTM* alterations accounting for 25–50% of familial Paget's disease.
- Familial Paget's disease also associated with mutations in *RANK*, a gene which plays a pivotal role in osteoclast formation.
- Inclusion identified on electron microscopy in Pagetic osteoclasts has implicated, although not proven, a paramyxoviral aetiology.

Pathogenesis

- The disease passes through a number of stages, all of which may be seen simultaneously within the same bone or in different bones.
- Initially, there is intense osteoclastic bone resorption.
- Osteoblastic activity then becomes exaggerated with laying down of grossly thickened, poorly organized weak bone which is prone to deformity and pathological fracture.

Presentation

- The vast majority of patients are asymptomatic, the diagnosis being made incidentally on radiology.
- Symptomatic disease usually presents with bony pain and deformity.

Biochemistry

- ↑↑ serum alkaline phosphatase associated with osteoblastic activity.
- Serum calcium is usually normal.

Histopathology

See Fig. 17.4.

- Bony trabeculae are thickened with a 'mosaic' pattern of cement lines indicating repetitive phases of bone resorption and formation.
- Striking numbers of osteoclasts with more nucleic than normal.
- Cortical Haversian canals are replaced by irregular trabeculae.
- The bone marrow becomes densely fibrotic.

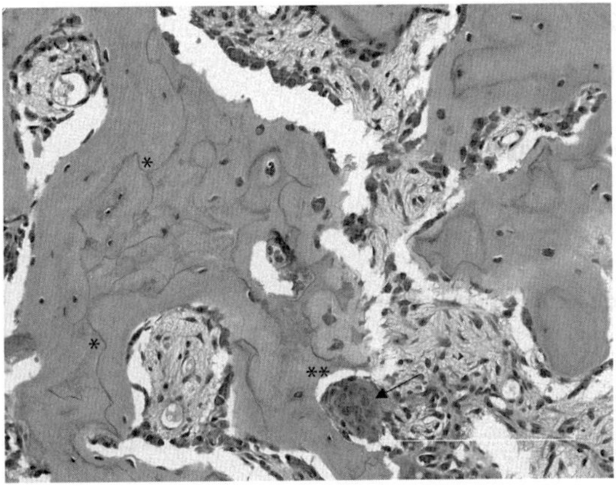

Fig. 17.4 Paget's disease. Diffuse remodelled cancellous bone with prominent cement lines* and deep Howship's lacunae** which, in areas, are associated with osteoclasts, containing very large numbers of nuclei (arrow) (see Plate 42).

Prognosis

- Most patients do not suffer from any significant problems.
- Potential complications include pathological fractures and deafness due to compression of cranial nerve VIII by enlarging skull bones.
- Treated with bisphosphonates which block osteoclasts from resorbing bone.

► Osteosarcoma (➔ Conventional osteosarcoma, p. 448) is the most significant complication of Paget's disease. Although it only occurs in <1% of cases, it has a very poor prognosis. Osteosarcoma should be considered in any patient known to have Paget's disease if their bony pain rapidly worsens.

Osteomyelitis

Definition

- Infection of a bone.

Epidemiology

- May develop at any age.
- Acute haematogenous osteomyelitis is typically a disease of children.
- The vast majority of chronic infections result from unresolved acute osteomyelitis.

Acquisition of infection

- Haematogenous spread—this is typically the case in acute osteomyelitis in children.
- Penetrating trauma, e.g. open fracture.
- Iatrogenic, e.g. following joint replacement or root canal treatment.
- Direct spread from an adjacent infection, e.g. as a complication of a foot ulcer in a diabetic.

Microbiology

- Most infections are caused by *Staphylococcus aureus*.
- Sickle-cell disease increases susceptibility to *Salmonella* osteomyelitis.
- Because of the low levels of causative organisms in chronic infections, cultures may be negative.

Pathogenesis

- Infection leads to an influx of acute inflammatory cells into the bone and suppurative inflammation.
- Destruction of bone leads to necrotic bone known as sequestrum.
- Failure to eradicate infection may lead to chronic osteomyelitis with areas of infected necrotic bone surrounded by areas of new bone formation (involucrum).

Presentation

- Fever and pain in the affected bone.
- Children may present with failure to weight-bear.

Prognosis

- Aggressive treatment is needed with intravenous antibiotics and surgical debridement of any necrotic bone if cure is to be achieved.
- Development of osteomyelitis following joint replacement may lead to failure of the prosthesis (periprosthetic reactions; ➔ Periprosthetic reactions, p. 433).
- Chronic sinus formation and an associated squamous carcinoma (Marjolin's ulcer) may occur.
- AA amyloidosis may occur as with other chronic infections (TB, bronchiectasis).

Osteoarthritis

Definition

- A group of diseases characterized by joint degeneration.

Epidemiology

- The most common joint disease.
- About 2 million people in the UK have symptomatic disease.
- Predominantly a disease of the elderly.

Aetiology

- Primary osteoarthritis: most common, with no clear cause.
- Secondary osteoarthritis: brought about by conditions causing damage to joints, e.g. rheumatoid arthritis (RA), gout, trauma.

Pathogenesis

- Insult to joint tissue (not always understood) initiating a cycle of cellular events, including low-grade chronic inflammation of the synovium, release of metalloproteinases, and degradation of articular cartilage matrix (fibrillation, erosion and cracking, and exposure eventually of bone (eburnation)).

Presentation

- Joint pain, tenderness, swelling (seen in small joints), stiffness.
- Symptoms typically worsen during the day with activity.
- Principally affects the hip, knee, spine, and small joints of the hands.

Histopathology

See Fig. 17.5.

- Articular cartilage is thinned and lost.
- Subchondral bone is exposed and thickened.
- Subchondral cysts may be present.
- Osteophytes can occur at the periphery of the joint.

Prognosis

- The condition tends to progress with time and requires analgesics.
- Severe disease usually requires joint replacement.

Fig. 17.5 Osteoarthritis. Femoral head shows an eroded and irregular articular surface (see Plate 43).

Rheumatoid arthritis

Definition

- A multisystem autoimmune disease in which the brunt of disease activity falls upon synovial joints.

Epidemiology

- Common, affecting about 1% of people.
- Particularly affects young and middle-aged women.

Aetiology

- The initial trigger remains unknown.
- Once inflammation begins, it appears to become self-perpetuating.

Pathogenesis

- Infiltration of synovium by CD4+ T-cells, B-cells, plasma cells, and macrophages.

Presentation

- Symmetrical, swollen, painful, stiff, small joints of hands and feet.
- Symptoms are typically worse in the morning.

Serology

- ~70% of patients are positive for rheumatoid factor (RhF), an autoantibody which binds the Fc portion of IgG. RhF is often positive in other autoimmune diseases and some apparently healthy individuals.
- Newer antibodies, known as anti-citrullinated protein antibodies, have a much greater specificity, though they are not widely available.

Extra-articular manifestations

- Cardiac disease: ischaemic heart disease, pericarditis.
- Vascular disease: accelerated atherosclerosis, vasculitis.
- Haematological disease: anaemia, splenomegaly.
- Pulmonary disease: pulmonary fibrosis, pleuritis.
- Skin: rheumatoid nodules, erythema nodosum, pyoderma gangrenosum.
- Neurological: peripheral neuropathy, stroke.
- Deposition of serum amyloid A as β-pleated sheets in multiple organs (AA amyloidosis).

Histopathology

- Marked synovial hyperplasia with a heavy inflammatory infiltrate of lymphocytes, with germinal centre formation, and plasma cells, along with pannus formation over the articular cartilage (fibroblastic granulation tissue).

Prognosis

- The disease shows variable behaviour, but there are considerable recent advances in the successful treatment of this disease (anti-TNF-α).

Spondyloarthropathies

Definition

- A group of inflammatory joint diseases characterized by arthritis affecting the spinal column and peripheral joints, and enthesitis (inflammation at the insertion site of tendons and ligaments to bone).

Epidemiology

- Common diseases, affecting nearly 1% of people.
- Usually in young adults aged 20–40; slight male predominance.

Genetics

- Strong genetic association with possession of HLA-B27 allele.

Pathogenesis

- Traditional theories proposed that an unidentified 'arthritogenic peptide' is presented by HLA-B27 to CD8+ cytotoxic T-cells, leading to joint inflammation.
- Studies show that misfolded HLA-B27 causes endoplasmic reticulum stress and production of IL-23 via the T-helper 17 axis.

Ankylosing spondylitis

- Affects 0.5% of people, usually in young adults aged 20–40.
- Lower back pain due to sacroiliitis is the typical presentation.
- Extra-articular manifestations include iritis, pulmonary fibrosis, and aortitis.

Reactive arthritis

- Occurs within 1 month of an infection elsewhere in the body.
- Usually related to a genitourinary infection with *Chlamydia* or a GI infection with *Shigella, Salmonella*, or *Campylobacter*.
- May be due to deposition of bacterial antigens and DNA in joints, but this has not been conclusively proven.
- Typically presents with pain and stiffness in the lower back, knees, ankles, and feet. Enthesitis is also common.

Psoriatic arthropathy

- Seen in about 5% of patients with psoriasis (➔ Psoriasis, p. 387).
- Mostly affects the distal interphalangeal joints and may lead to severe deformation.

Enteropathic arthropathy

- Seen in about 10% of patients with inflammatory bowel disease.
- Typically affects sacroiliac and lower limb joints asymmetrically.
- Cause unknown.

Crystal arthropathies

Definition

- A group of joint diseases caused by deposition of crystals in joints.

Pathogenesis

- Crystals are deposited in joints.
- Neutrophils ingest the crystals and degranulate, releasing enzymes that damage the joint.

Gout

- Caused by deposition of monosodium urate crystals in a joint.
- Most cases are related to hyperuricaemia due to impaired excretion of urate by the kidneys.
- Acute gout causes an acute, painful, swollen, red joint. Any joint may be involved, but the first metatarsophalangeal joint is typical.
- Individuals with high urate levels may develop chronic tophaceous gout, in which large deposits of urate (tophi—chalky white material) occur in the skin and around joints (Fig. 17.6).

Calcium pyrophosphate crystal deposition (CPPD) (pseudogout)

- Caused by deposition of calcium pyrophosphate crystals in a joint.
- Also referred to as chondrocalcinosis.
- Pyrophosphate is a by-product of the hydrolysis of nucleotide triphosphates within chondrocytes of cartilage.
- Shedding of crystals into a joint precipitates an acute arthritis which mimics gout.
- Typically elderly women; usually affects the knee, wrist, and vertebral joints.

Calcific tendinitis

- Caused by deposition of hydroxyapatite crystals in a tendon.
- The most common deposits appear as small granular aggregates within capsular and tendinous tissues without a cellular reaction.
- Macroscopically, deposits have a chalky white appearance; may be bulky or punctate.
- The largest deposits are seen in tumoral calcinosis.

Microscopy

- Joint fluid contains neutrophils and crystals.
- Urate crystals (gout): needle-shaped with negative birefringence.
- CPPD (pseudogout): rhomboid/rod-shaped with positive birefringence (Fig. 17.7).

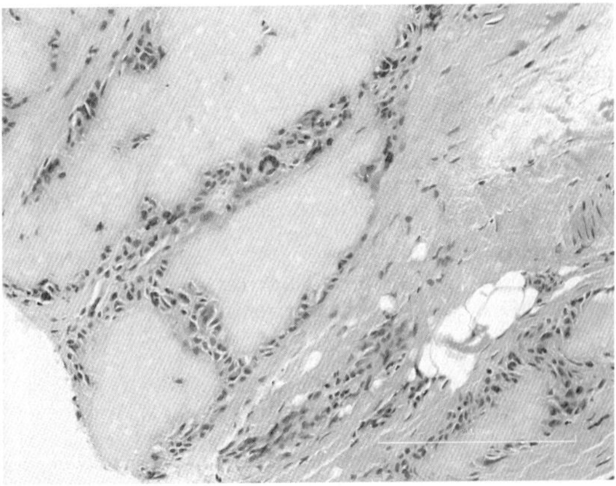

Fig. 17.6 Microscopic features of gout showing amorphous eosinophilic deposits surrounded by epithelioid macrophages and multinucleated giant cells. Haematoxylin and eosin section (see Plate 44).

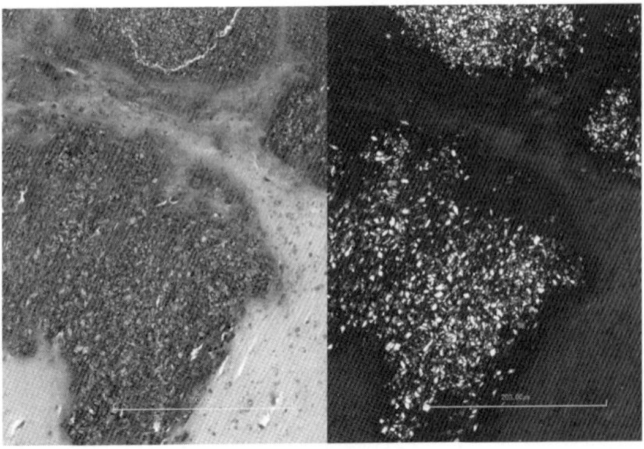

Fig. 17.7 Pseudogout. Rhomboid/rod-shaped crystals under polarized light showing positive birefringence (see Plate 45).

Septic arthritis

Definition

- Infection within a joint.

Epidemiology

- May occur at any age.
- Patients with pre-existing joint disease are at higher risk.

Acquisition of infection

- Infection is usually via haematogenous spread.
- Occasionally may follow penetrating trauma.

Microbiology

- Almost all cases are caused by *Staphylococcus aureus*.

Pathogenesis

- Establishment of infection is favoured by the relative inability of phagocytes to enter the joint space.
- Infection spreads quickly, leading to rapid and irreversible joint destruction if antibiotic treatment is not started early.

Presentation

► An extremely painful, hot, red, swollen joint.

Microscopy

- Joint fluid contains neutrophils but no crystals.

Culture

- Microbiological culture of joint fluid and blood is essential to identify the causative organism and provide antibiotic sensitivities.

Prognosis

- Irreversible joint destruction occurs without treatment.

Periprosthetic reactions

Definition

- Adverse biological reactions (local and systemic) caused by wear debris from prosthetic implants.

Epidemiology

- Mostly seen in total hip arthroplasties or hip resurfacing procedures but can be seen in knee or vertebral disc arthroplasties.
- Affects mainly metal-on-metal (MoM) prosthesis, but also in prosthesis manufactured from other materials (polyethylene, ceramic).

Pathogenesis

- Initiated as a foreign body-type response to wear debris (inflammatory mediators), and the presence of a lymphocytic infiltrate suggests a T-lymphocyte-mediated immune reaction.

Presentation

- Adverse tissue reactions may be systemic or local.
- Local: painful inflammatory synovitis, large joint effusions, osteomyelitis, pseudotumours, and periprosthetic osteolysis with prosthesis loosening.
- Systemic: toxicity due to elevated levels of metal particles and ions.

Histopathology

- Metallosis: stromal deposition or phagocytosed black particulate material, and amorphous intracytoplasmic brown debris (the latter are found in association with MoM prosthesis).
- Necrosis and pseudotumours (granulomatous or destructive cystic lesion, neither infective nor neoplastic).
- Variability in the number, type, and arrangement of inflammatory cells. May show massive synovial surface ulceration and fibrin, synovial hyperplasia, and the presence of thick areas of fibrosis.
- The presence of neutrophil polymorphs suggests an active infection.
- ALVAL score (aseptic lymphocytic vasculitis-associated lesion seen in MoM prosthesis) used for assessment and circulating metal ions.

Prognosis

- Irreversible joint destruction occurs without treatment.

Soft tissue and bone tumours

There are ~200 different types of soft tissue and bone tumours, including benign and malignant (sarcoma) lesions. Although some show a clear line of cellular differentiation (fat, smooth muscle, skeletal muscle, endothelial/vascular, nerve sheath, bone, cartilage), there are many where the line of cellular differentiation/cell of origin is not known (synovial sarcoma, Ewing sarcoma, and many others).

Malignant soft tissue and bone tumours (sarcomas) represent <2% of all cancers, with carcinoma representing ~85% and lymphohaematological malignancies representing ~15%.

In some cases, the benign connective tissue tumour represents the precursor of the malignant variant, e.g. a proportion of neurofibroma transforms to become a malignant peripheral nerve sheath tumour, and an enchondroma can progress to a chondrosarcoma. However, in many cases, the benign lesions do not transform into malignant disease (chondroblastoma, chondromyxoid fibroma). Furthermore, in many cases of sarcoma, a benign precursor is not recognized, in which case the malignant tumours appear to present '*de novo*', e.g. there is no benign precursor of Ewing sarcoma, synovial sarcoma, and osteosarcoma.

Sarcomas generally metastasize to the lungs.

High-grade sarcomas metastasize in about one-third of cases.

TNM 7 pathological staging of soft tissue tumours

Primary tumour (T)

pT1a: superficial tumour ≤5cm in size.
pT1b: deep tumour ≤5cm in size.
pT2a: superficial tumour >5cm in size.
pT2b: deep tumour >5cm in size.

Regional lymph nodes (N)

N0: no regional lymph node metastasis.
N1: regional lymph node metastasis.

TNM 7 pathological staging of bone tumours

Primary tumour (T)

pT1: tumour 8cm or less in greatest dimension.
pT2: tumour >8cm in greatest dimension.
pT3: discontinuous tumour in the primary bone site.

Regional lymph nodes (N)

N0: no regional lymph node metastasis.
N1: regional lymph node metastasis.

Benign soft tissue tumours

Fibroblastic tumours

Fibroma of tendon sheath
- Presents as a firm nodule attached to a tendon, usually in a finger.
- Seen in young and middle-aged adults, with a male preponderance.
- Histologically shows a well-circumscribed tumour composed of bland fibroblasts and thin, slit-like blood vessels in a fibrous stroma.

Superficial fibromatoses
- Presents as nodule and contracture: palms (Dupuytren's contracture)—trigger finger, plantar fascial fibromatosis (Ledderhose's disease), penile fibromatosis (Peyronie's disease).
- Not larger than 2cm.
- Histologically, all show bland spindled fibroblasts arranged in broad, long fascicles infiltrating into surrounding structures. May be mitotically active.
- No predilection for large growth or malignant transformation.

Deep fibromatosis (desmoid-type)
- Occurs deep to subcutaneous tissue.
- Larger than 2cm and as large as 20cm.
- May cause pain and problems if encroach on vital structures.
- Fibroblastic tumour, poorly circumscribed: little mitotic activity, no necrosis.
- Sporadic deep fibromatosis harbour a *CTNNB1* mutation in >90% of tumours.
- Patients with FAP caused by an *APC* germline mutation may also present with extracolonic tumours, including deep fibromatosis. In this setting, the fibromatosis most frequently arises in the aponeurosis of the rectus abdominis muscle of women.
- Sensitive to oestrogen and has a tendency to grow at pregnancy.
- High recurrence rate post-surgery.
- No predilection for malignant transformation.

Nodular fasciitis
- A self-limiting tumour as a result of trauma, usually presenting in young adults.
- Subcutaneous, rapidly growing lump in the upper body.
- Histologically shows fascicles of fibroblasts/myofibroblasts in a whorled growth pattern ('tissue culture' appearance) in a myxoid to collagenous stroma, with extravasated erythrocytes.
- Rearrangements of the USP6 locus (17p13) have been detected in 90% of cases of nodular fasciitis (characteristic *MYH9–USP6* fusion gene). Similar *USP6* rearrangements are seen in aneurysmal bone cyst.
- No predilection to becoming malignant.

Solitary fibrous tumour

- Presents as a slowly enlarging mass in deep and superficial soft tissues of adults at any site in the body.
- Histologically composed of haphazardly arranged bland fibroblastic cells ('patternless pattern'), with variation in cellularity and collagenization. Dilated branching blood vessels (haemangipericytoma-like) are characteristically seen.
- In most cases, an inversion at 12q13 leads to a pathogenic fusion transcript involving *NAB2–STAT6*.
- The vast majority are benign, though a small proportion metastasize.

Fibrohistiocytic tumours

Tenosynovial giant cell tumour

- Presents as a painless, slowly growing nodule arising from tendon sheath, joint, bursae, or adjacent soft tissue (usually on a finger, toe, wrist, or knee).
- Peak age at presentation 20–40y, with a female preponderance.
- Histologically shows a lobulated tumour composed of round mononuclear cells, osteoclast-like multinucleated cells, foamy macrophages, and haemosiderin-laden macrophages.
- Most common cytogenetic aberration results in the *COL6A3–CSF1* fusion gene, resulting in overproduction of CSF1, a critical growth factor in osteoclast formation.

Lipomatous tumours

Lipoma

- A tumour of mature white fat.
- The most common soft tissue tumour.
- Presents as a painless subcutaneous and less frequently in deep mass in the limbs or trunk of adults.
- Histologically composed of lobules of mature adipocytes without a predilection to becoming malignant.

Spindle cell/pleomorphic lipoma

- Presents as a painless subcutaneous mass in the upper back, shoulders, or neck of adults. Marked predilection for men.
- A well-circumscribed lesion composed of a mixture of mature adipocytes, short spindle, and/or pleomorphic cells in a fibromyxoid stroma containing thick 'ropy' collagen bundles.
- Pleomorphic lipoma represents a spectrum of this entity with the presence of pleomorphic and multinucleated cells.
- Spindle and pleomorphic cells are immunoreactive for CD34.

Nerve sheath tumours

Neurofibroma

- A benign peripheral nerve sheath tumour composed of a mixed population of Schwann cells, fibroblasts, and perineural-like cells with scattered intermingled axons.
- Lesions may be localized, diffuse, or plexiform, the latter two having a strong association with neurofibromatosis type 1.

- Usually occurs in the dermal or subcutaneous tissues of young adults.
- Histologically shows bland spindle cells arranged haphazardly, set in a fibromyxoid stroma admixed with dense collagen bundles. Mild nuclear atypia is common and does not mean malignant transformation.
- Malignant transformation occurs in about 3% of neurofibromas associated with neurofibromatosis type 1.

Schwannoma

- A benign nerve sheath tumour showing Schwann cell differentiation.
- Can present at any age as solitary, slow-growing, painless nodules.
- Multiple schwannomas are associated with neurofibromatosis type 2 germline genetic alterations.
- Histologically shows a nodular encapsulated tumour composed of spindle cells, alternating hypocellular myxoid areas (Antoni B), and compact cellular areas (Antoni A) with focal nuclear palisading (Verocay bodies).
- No predilection for malignant transformation.

Smooth muscle tumours

Angioleiomyoma

- Presents as a small, painful subcutaneous mass, typically on the lower limbs.
- More common in women.
- Histologically shows a well-circumscribed lesion composed of mature smooth muscle cells arranged around thick-walled blood vessels. There is no predilection for malignant transformation.

Vascular tumours

Haemangiomas

- Benign neoplasms that usually have well-formed vessels; there is a wide variety of patterns and clinical manifestations.
- Many arise in the dermis, but they also occur in superficial and deep soft tissue, bone, and viscera.
- Vascular malformations are frequently clinically and histologically indistinguishable from haemangiomas.

Uncertain histogenesis

Intramuscular myxoma

- Usually presents as a painless mass in the lower extremities, <10cm.
- Affects middle-aged adults, with a female predominance.
- Mazabraud syndrome: intramuscular myxoma and fibrous dysplasia.
- A circumscribed sparsely cellular tumour composed of bland stellate to spindle cells embedded in an abundant myxoid stroma.
- The majority harbour activating mutations in *GNAS*.

Malignant soft tissue tumours

- Sarcoma representing <2% of all cancers.
- At least 100 subtypes.
- Generally metastasize to the lungs.
- High-grade tumours metastasize in about one-third of cases.

Tumours of specific lineage

Liposarcomas

- The most common soft tissue sarcoma showing fatty/lipomatous differentiation. There are various subtypes.
- Present in adulthood with a deep-seated mass in an extremity, the limb girdle, or the retroperitoneum.
- **Well-differentiated liposarcoma/atypical lipomatous tumour (ALT)** is the most frequent subtype. Histologically composed of relatively mature adipocytes with scattered bizarre hyperchromatic stromal cells (Fig. 17.8). Local recurrence is common following incomplete excision, but metastasis does not occur.
- Characteristic genetic alteration: amplification of the *MDM2* gene.
- Outcome is excellent other than when the tumour is sited in body cavities (retroperitoneum, chest, spermatic cord) when recurrence is almost inevitable and can result in dedifferentiation and death.
- **Dedifferentiated liposarcoma**: a high-grade sarcoma which occurs as a result of transformation of ALT. Histologically, there is an abrupt transition from the mature fatty tumour to the non-lipomatous sarcoma—tumour cells harbour *MDM2* amplification.
- **Myxoid/round cell liposarcoma**: a high-grade sarcoma composed of round to spindle cells showing lipoblasts. Characterized genetically by t(12;16)(q13;p11), producing an *FUS–DDIT3* fusion gene.
- **Pleomorphic liposarcoma**: the least common form. High-grade disease. Histologically composed of markedly pleomorphic cells (Fig. 17.9). No characteristic genetic alteration.

Leiomyosarcoma (smooth muscle differentiation)

- Malignant tumour showing smooth muscle differentiation; immunoreactive for the smooth muscle markers desmin and/or caldesmon.
- Presents with an enlarging mass in the retroperitoneum (including the uterus) and limbs of adults. Represents 10–15% of limb sarcomas.
- Histologically composed of intersecting fascicles of atypical smooth muscle cells with 'cigar-shaped' nuclei.
- Half of all cases metastasize and cause death.

Rhabdomyosarcoma (skeletal muscle differentiation)

- Sarcoma showing skeletal muscle differentiation: immunoreactive for the skeletal muscle markers MyoD1 and/or myogenin.
- Represents <2% of all muscular tumours.
- **Embryonal rhabdomyosarcoma**: young children, most commonly in the head and neck region or the genitourinary tract. Histologically, primitive spindle cells and a subset of cells with dense eosinophilic cytoplasm embedded in a myxoid stroma.

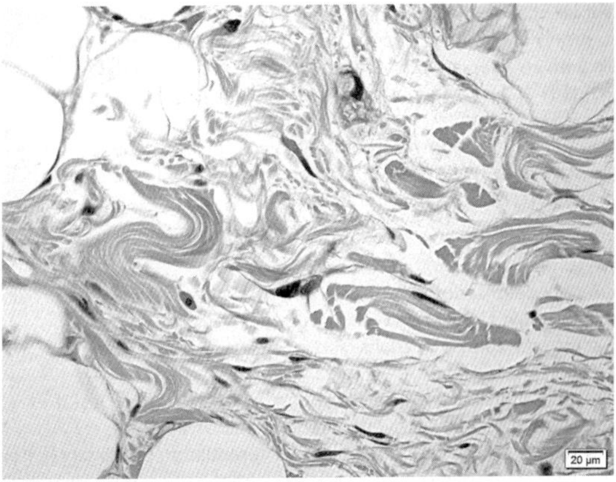

Fig. 17.8 Atypical lipomatous tumour. Mature adipocytes with scattered spindle hyperchromatic stromal cells (see Plate 46).

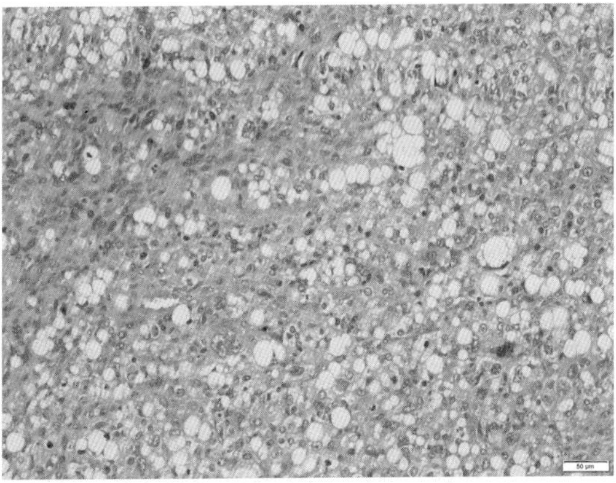

Fig. 17.9 Pleomorphic liposarcoma. Sheets of severely pleomorphic lipoblasts admixed with spindle cells (see Plate 47).

- **Alveolar rhabdomyosarcoma**: older children and adolescents, most commonly in the limbs. Histologically round hyperchromatic tumour cells with an alveolar architecture. Mostly associated with t(2;13)(q35;q14) or, less frequently, t(1;13)(p36;q14) producing a *PAX3* or *PAX7–FKHR* fusion.
- **Pleomorphic rhabdomyosarcoma**: limbs of adults and behaves very aggressively. Composed of bizarre polygonal, round, and spindle cells. No characteristic genetic alteration.

Malignant peripheral nerve sheath tumour (MPNST)
- Rare tumour (up to 5% of soft tissue sarcomas).
- Generally deep-seated tumours arising most commonly in the proximal extremities, in association with a major nerve trunk.
- Presents sporadically in adults, and in younger patients with neurofibromatosis type 1.
- Histology: alternating hypercellular and hypocellular fascicles of monotonous spindle cells with extensive necrosis.
- MPNST may show rhabdomyoblastic differentiation (malignant Triton tumour) or osteosarcomatous differentiation.

Tumours of uncertain lineage (in alphabetical order)

Clear cell sarcoma of soft tissue
- Also known as malignant melanoma of soft parts.
- Rare tumour (<1% of all soft tissue tumours).
- Deep-seated tumours frequently associated with tendons or aponeuroses.
- Histology: round to spindle cells with clear/eosinophilic cytoplasm, arranged in lobules, separated by fibrous septa. Intracellular melanin pigment occasionally seen (Fig. 17.10).
- The tumour cells express melanocytic markers (S100, HMB45, Melan-A), but genetically not similar to melanoma.
- Characterized by t(12;22)(q13;q12 that results in *EWSR1–ATF1* fusion—which is not specific for this neoplasm.

Desmoplastic small round cell tumour
- Rare tumour (<200 cases have been reported).
- Sarcoma of the abdominal cavity, primarily affecting children and young adults, with a male predominance.
- Presents with abdominal pain with extensive peritoneal spread.
- Histology: nests of small, round cells with uniform hyperchromatic nuclei, separated by desmoplastic stroma.
- Polyphenotypic differentiation, expressing epithelial, muscle, and neural markers.
- Characterized by t(11;22)(p13;q12) producing an *EWSR1–WT1* fusion.
- Overall survival poor.

Epithelioid sarcoma
- Rare tumour (0.6–1% of all sarcomas).
- Typically seen in male adolescents and young adults.
- Presents as a slowly growing, painless nodule, usually on the flexor surfaces of the extremities.

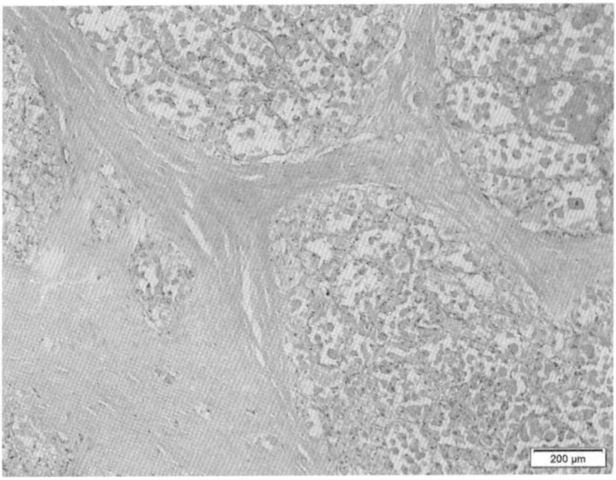

Fig. 17.10 Clear cell sarcoma. Closely packed nests of polygonal to spindle cells with clear/pink cytoplasm and central nuclei (see Plate 48).

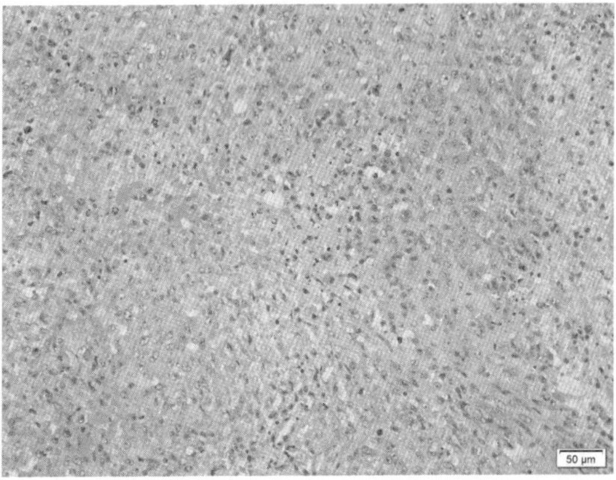

Fig. 17.11 Epithelioid sarcoma. Atypical epithelioid cells forming aggregates and surrounding necrotic areas in a granuloma-like pattern. This could be mistaken for a carcinoma (see Plate 49).

- Most common sarcoma of distal extremities.
- Histology: multinodular arrangement of epithelioid and spindle cells, with extensive central necrosis, round vesicular nuclei, prominent nucleoli, and ample eosinophilic cytoplasm (Fig. 17.11).
- Immunohistochemistry: cytokeratin positive and loss of *INI1* expression in 50% of cases.

Ewing sarcoma

- Round cell sarcoma of soft tissue with neuroectodermal differentiation; morphologically, immunophenotypically, and genetically similar to Ewing sarcoma of bone (➔ Ewing sarcoma, p. 449–50) but affects older patients (adolescents and young adults).

Low-grade fibromyxoid sarcoma

- First described by Evans in 1987. Rare tumour with about 350 reported cases.
- Presents as slow-growing, deep, soft tissue mass, most often in proximal extremities or trunk, deep to fascia, of young to middle-aged patients.
- Histology: a well-circumscribed tumour with bland spindle cells set in a biphasic collagenized and myxoid stroma with elongated thin-walled vessels.
- Immunohistochemistry: MUC4 positivity.
- A subset is associated with t(7;16) or, less frequently, t(11;16), producing a *FUS–CREB3L2* or *CREB3L1* fusion, respectively.
- Good prognosis if widely excised.

Myxofibrosarcoma

- One of the most common sarcoma in elderly patients.
- Presents as a slow-growing, painless mass in extremities, usually superficial to fascia.
- Histology: alternating hypocellular myxoid areas and hypercellular areas with atypical spindle cells and variable amount of pleomorphic cells. Characteristic curvilinear blood vessels.
- No characteristic immunohistochemistry or genetic profile.
- High local recurrence rate.

Pleomorphic undifferentiated sarcoma

- Previously known as malignant fibrous histiocytoma (MFH).
- Account for 5–10% of sarcomas in adults older than 40y.
- High-grade sarcoma in which exhaustive investigation reveals no specific line of differentiation or characteristic genetic alteration—a diagnosis of exclusion.
- Tend to be large, deep-seated tumours which behave aggressively.

Synovial sarcoma

- High-grade sarcoma of uncertain differentiation, representing 10–15% of adult soft tissue sarcomas.
- Presents in young adults with long-standing pain and a palpable mass in deep soft tissue.
- Histology: highly cellular spindle cells, often with epithelioid differentiation. Includes biphasic, monophasic, or poorly differentiated variants.
- Genetics: chromosomal translocation t(X;18), producing fusion genes between *SS18* (*SYT*) and *SSX1*, *SSX2*, or *SSX4*.
- Behave aggressively with poor long-term survival.

FNCLCC grading system: definition of parameters

Tumour differentiation

1: sarcomas closely resembling normal adult mesenchymal tissue.
2: sarcomas for which histologic typing is certain.
3: embryonal and undifferentiated sarcomas, sarcomas of doubtful type, synovial sarcomas, osteosarcomas, primitive neuroectodermal tumour.

Mitotic count

1: 0–9 mitoses per 10 hpf.
2: 10–19 mitoses per 10 hpf.
3: 20 mitoses per 10 hpf.

Tumour necrosis

0: no necrosis.
1: 50% tumour necrosis.
2: 50% tumour necrosis.

Histologic grade

Grade 1: total score 2, 3
Grade 2: total score 4, 5.
Grade 3: total score 6, 7, 8.

Modified from Trojani *et al* [Trojani M, Contesso G, Coindre JM, *et al*. Soft tissue sarcomas of adults: study of pathological prognostic variables and definition of histopathological grading system. *Int J Cancer*. 1984;33:37–42]

FNCLCC: Fédération Nationale des Centres de Lutte de Cancer; hpf: high-power field; PNET: primitive neuroectodermal tumour.

Benign bone tumours

Cartilage-forming bone tumours

Osteochondroma (exostosis)

- A benign conventional cartilaginous-forming tumour of bone.
- Typically grows as a solitary metaphyseal exophytic tumour.
- Multiple osteochondromas: inherited in an autosomal dominant manner (*EXT1, EXT2* germline alterations), Langer–Giedion syndrome and DEFECT-11 syndrome, and generally present in young children with reduction in skeletal growth, bony deformity, restricted joint motion, and shortened stature.
- Histology: a cartilage cap, connected to the underlying bone marrow by a bony stalk.
- A minority progress to become a peripheral chondrosarcoma.

Chondroma

- A benign conventional cartilage-forming tumour of bone. Usually discovered incidentally.
- **Enchondroma** arise in the medulla of the bone, most commonly in the hands and feet.
- **Periosteal chondroma** arises on the bone surface, the proximal humerus being a characteristic site.
- Histologically, the lesions are composed of lobules of mature hyaline cartilage.
- *IDH1/IDH2* somatic point mutation is detected in ~50% of cases.
- Ollier's disease: a mosaic disorder describing the presence of multiple enchondromas caused by mutations in *IDH1* and *IDH2*; small risk of other tumours (brain tumours).

Chondroblastoma

- A rare benign, non-conventional cartilage-forming tumour of bone.
- Typically involves the epiphyses of the long bones in skeletally immature patients but may present later in life.
- Histology: immature chondroblasts set in a cartilaginous matrix, classically with pericellular 'chicken wire' calcification. Numerous multinucleated osteoclast-like giant cells can be seen.
- Somatic driver mutations in the *H3F3A* and *H3F3B* genes (K36M) in >90% of cases.
- Does not progress to a malignant tumour.

Chondromyxoid fibroma

- Extremely rare non-conventional benign cartilaginous bone tumour.
- Most cases occur before the age of 40, in the metaphyses of long bones in the lower extremity.
- Histologically composed of lobules of stellate and chondrocyte-like cells set in a fibromyxoid matrix, with greater cellularity at the periphery.
- Rarely reported to transform to malignant disease.

Bone-forming tumours

Osteoid osteoma

- A benign bone-forming tumour of bone.
- Most commonly arises in the cortex of a long bone of a child or young adult, especially the proximal femur.
- Characteristically painful, especially at night; relieved with NSAIDs.
- Readily identified on plain radiographs as a small lucent nidus <1 cm in size.
- Histology: a central nidus of anastomosing trabeculae of woven bone with a peripheral zone of dense osteosclerosis.
- No risk of malignant transformation.

Osteoblastoma

- A benign bone-forming tumour of bone.
- Most commonly arises in the medulla in the axial skeleton of a child or young adult but can present later in life.
- Radiographs: focal cortical expansion or destruction that can be misdiagnosed as a malignancy.
- Histology: features similar to osteoid osteoma; however, these tumours are larger (>1.5cm) and occur in the medullary cavity.
- No risk of malignant transformation, but they can recur.
- Can be difficult to diagnose under the microscope and can be mistaken for osteosarcoma.

Fibrous dysplasia

- A benign intramedullary fibro-osseous lesion.
- Presents in a wide age range, with a peak of incidence before 30y of age.
- Syndromic associations: McCune–Albright and Mazabraud disease.
- Not inherited—a mosaic disorder (early post-zygotic mutation).
- Histology: bland spindle cell proliferation with thin and irregularly curved immature woven bone ('Chinese letters') lacking a rim of osteoblasts. Foci of cartilaginous differentiation may occur.
- *GNAS1* mutation detected in >90% of cases.
- Malignant transformation very rarely occurs.

Osteoclast-rich bone tumours

Giant cell tumour of bone

- A benign, locally aggressive neoplasm of bone (intramedullary) that arises in the ends of long bones.
- Only seen in the mature skeleton.
- Typically presents between 20 and 45y with pain and swelling over the site of the tumour.
- Histology: sheets of neoplastic ovoid mononuclear cells of osteoblastic lineage interspersed with non-neoplastic, uniformly distributed large, osteoclast-like giant cells.
- Local recurrence following excision occurs in about 25% of cases. Distant 'benign' metastases are very rare but have been reported.
- Somatic driver mutations in the *H3F3A* gene (G34W/L) in >90% of cases.
- Calcium and phosphate serum levels should be evaluated to exclude hyperparathyroidism (brown tumour) and Paget's disease of the bone.
- Rarely reported to transform to malignant disease.

Malignant bone tumours

Metastases

- The vast majority of malignant bone tumours are metastases, with most originating from carcinomas of the lung, breast, kidney, thyroid, and prostate.
- Most metastatic deposits are osteolytic, i.e. they destroy bone, but some metastases induce bone formation (osteoblastic), e.g. prostate.
- Bony metastases are one of the common causes of hypercalcaemia.

Myeloma

- The most common malignant tumour arising in bone (➲ Plasma cell myeloma, pp. 378–9).

Conventional osteosarcoma

- A malignant bone-forming tumour.
- The most common malignant primary bone tumour.
- Most present between the ages of 5 and 25 with persistent deep pain within a long bone. A palpable mass may be present.
- The most common malignant bone tumour in the paediatric age group.
- Cases arising in the elderly are usually secondary to Paget's disease, radiation, and bone infarcts.
- Histology: atypical spindle cells associated with osteoid production that may exhibit osteoblastic, chondroblastic, or fibroblastic differentiation.
- The histological subtypes of high-grade disease do not inform on prognosis or predict response to chemotherapy.
- High-grade osteosarcoma is a highly malignant tumour which shows early and rapid haematogenous dissemination, particularly to the lungs.
- Prognosis is largely related to response to preoperative chemotherapy. The 5-year survival for 'good responders' is 60%, whereas non-responders have poor survival rates of <15%.
- Other rare variants exist.

Conventional chondrosarcoma

- A malignant cartilage-forming tumour.
- The second most common malignant primary bone tumour.
- Most occur in adults aged over 50y.
- The most common site is the pelvic bones.
- Histology: atypical chondrocytes distributed in a cartilage matrix. They are graded (grades I–III) according to cellularity, cytological atypia, and mitotic activity (Fig. 17.12).
- Histological grade is the most important prognostic factor. The 5-year survival for low-grade chondrosarcoma (grade I) is 90%, whereas for grade II and II disease it is closer to 50%.
- *IDH1* and *IDH2* mutations are found in 60% of central (intramedullary), not peripheral, chondrosarcoma. Tumours with and without the mutation have the same prognosis.
- Other very rare non-conventional histological variants exist.

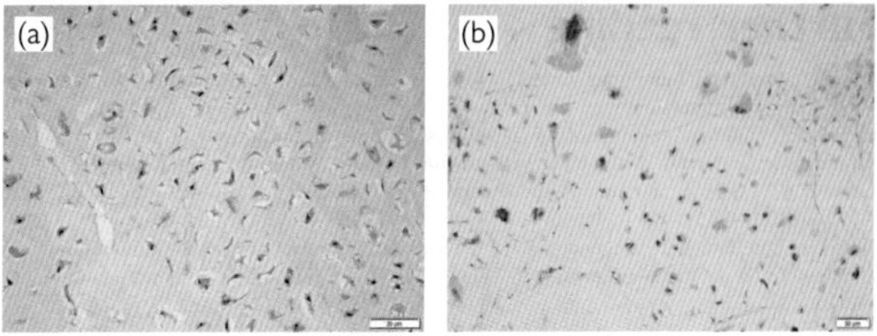

Fig. 17.12 Chondrosarcoma. Histology shows an increase in cellularity and atypia between grades I (a) and III (b) in chondrosarcoma (haematoxylin and eosin sections) (see Plate 50).

Chordoma

- A malignant midline bone tumour showing notochordal differentiation.
- Most occur in Caucasian patients older than 30.
- The vast majority occur sporadically. Familial (autosomal dominant) chordomas occur exceptionally; most are associated with tandem duplication in *brachyury*, a gene involved in notochordal development.
- Midline tumours found from the base of the skull to the coccyx.
- Slow-growing mass, often clinically silent until late stage. Symptoms depend on the site of the lesion, but generally pain is present.
- Histology: lobulated epithelioid cells with bubbly, vacuolated cytoplasm (physaliphorous cells), in a myxoid stroma.
- The tumour cells are immunoreactive for brachyury and cytokeratin.
- Complete surgical resection is the treatment of choice and the most important predictor of survival. Local recurrence is common. Metastatic disease occurs late in the disease process.
- Median survival 7y.

Ewing sarcoma

- A malignant round cell tumour of bone of neuroectodermal origin.
- 6–8% of primary malignant bone tumours.
- Most occur in children or adolescents aged <20y. It is the second most common bone sarcoma in the paediatric age group (the first is osteosarcoma).
- Rarely occurs in black African populations.
- Tends to present with pain and a mass in a long bone, pelvis, or rib.
- Radiology shows an ill-defined lytic or sclerotic diaphyseal mass with discontinuous periosteal reaction (sunburst or onion skin pattern).
- Histology shows a uniform small, round tumour cells with hyperchromatic nuclei and scant cytoplasm. In some cases, the tumour cells form rosette-like structures. Necrosis is commonly seen.
- Most cases show a *EWSR1–FLI* translocation (t[11;22][q24;q12]) and a minor subset show a *EWSR1–ERG* translocation (t[21;22][q22;q12]); <1% have non-*EWSR1* translocations.
- Survival rates are <50%. Prognosis depends on stage, anatomic location, size of the tumour, and tumour necrosis.

Further reading

BoSTT App. Available at: https://www.rnoh.nhs.uk/our-services/cellular-and-molecular-pathology/bostt-app.

Campbell P, Ebramzadeh E, Nelson S, Takamura K, De Smet K, Amstutz HC. Histological features of pseudotumour-like tissues from metal-on-metal hips. *Clin Orthop Relat Res* 2010;**468**:2321–7

Coindre JM. Grading of Soft Tissue Sarcomas: review and update. *Arch Pathol Lab Med* 2006;**130**:1448–53.

Fletcher CDM, Bridge JA, Hogendoom P, Mertens F (2013). *WHO classification of tumours of soft tissue and bone*. Lyon: IARC Press.

Chapter 18

Neuropathology

Nervous system malformations

Neural tube defects

- Due to defective closure of the neural tube during embryogenesis.
- Both genetic and environmental factors are involved.
- Maternal folate deficiency in early gestation is a risk factor.
- **Anencephaly** is a uniformly fatal malformation of the anterior neural tube, leading to absence of the brain and cranial vault.
- **Encephalocele** is a protrusion of malformed brain tissue through a midline skull defect, usually in the occipital region. Large encephaloceles are usually fatal.
- **Spina bifida** is a group of malformations of the spinal cord due to defective closure of the caudal end of the neural tube and lack of fusion of the vertebral arches and skin coverings. There may be associated outpouchings of meninges (**meningocele**) or meninges and spinal cord (**myelomeningocele**). The latter may cause problems such as urinary incontinence, constipation, and variable degrees of motor and sensory impairment of the legs.

Agenesis of the corpus callosum

- Occurs if the glial bridge fails to form between the two cerebral hemispheres or if axons fail to cross it. May be complete or partial.
- Often associated with other malformations (e.g. holoprosencephaly).
- May cause varying degrees of psychomotor retardation.

Aqueductal stenosis

- Developmental anomaly causing narrowing of the cerebral aqueduct.
- A component of complex malformations and may be inherited in an autosomal recessive or X-linked manner.
- Presents with congenital hydrocephalus.

Chiari malformations

- Type II (Arnold–Chiari) causes a small posterior fossa with downward displacement of the cerebellar vermis and deformity of the medulla. There is usually also a lumbar myelomeningocele.
- Type I is a milder version in which the cerebellar tonsils extend into the spinal canal. Some patients may be asymptomatic.

Dandy–Walker malformation

- Absent or rudimentary cerebellar vermis leading to filling of the posterior fossa by a large cyst representing a dilated fourth ventricle.
- May be associated with other malformations.

Syringomyelia

- Fluid-filled cavity within the central grey matter of the spinal cord.
- Usually affects the cervical and upper thoracic segments. Extension of the syrinx into the medulla is known as syringobulbia.
- Expansion of the syrinx causes atrophy of the adjacent spinal cord.
- Presents in early adulthood with isolated loss of pain and temperature in the upper limbs due to damage to spinothalamic tracts.

Epilepsy

Definition

- A recurrent tendency to spontaneous episodes of abnormal electrical activity within the brain which manifest as seizures.

Epidemiology

- Common (1–2% of population worldwide affected), second most common neurological disorder after stroke.

Aetiology

- Very often idiopathic with no clear cause found.
- May be associated with underlying structural lesions (trauma, neoplasms, malformations), metabolic conditions (alcohol, electrolyte disorders), infections, and rare genetic diseases (e.g. ion channel mutations).

Partial seizures

- Features attributable to a localized part of one hemisphere.
- In simple partial seizures, consciousness is unimpaired (e.g. a focal motor seizure).
- In complex partial seizures, consciousness is impaired (e.g. motionless staring).

Generalized seizures

- No features referrable to one hemisphere (no focality); consciousness is always impaired.
- Absence seizures ('petit mal') cause brief (<10s) pauses, e.g. stopping talking in mid-sentence and then carrying on where left off.
- Tonic–clonic seizures ('grand mal') cause sudden loss of consciousness with stiffening (tonic) of limbs and then jerking (clonic).
- Myoclonic jerks cause sudden violent movements of the limbs.

Temporal lobe epilepsy

- Typical onset in late childhood and adolescence.
- Usually presents with complex partial seizures, e.g. strange feeling in the gut or sense of déjà vu or strange smell followed by automatism.
- Secondary generalized tonic–clonic seizures may also occur.
- In most cases, an epileptogenic focus is present in midline temporal structures.

Childhood absence epilepsy

- Idiopathic generalized epilepsy syndrome affecting children aged 4–12.
- Characterized by recurrent absence seizures.
- Some children also develop tonic–clonic-type seizures.

Juvenile myoclonic epilepsy

- Idiopathic generalized epilepsy syndrome affecting children and adolescents aged 8–20.
- Most common seizure type is a myoclonic jerk, but tonic–clonic and absence seizures may also occur.

Head injury

Epidemiology

- About 50 000 severe head injuries occur each year in the UK.
- Responsible for some 20% of deaths in young people aged 5–45.
- May cause severe disability in those who survive.

Skull fracture

- Severe head injury may cause skull fracture at the site of impact.
- A marker of serious head injury with increased risk of an underlying intracranial injury such as contusions and haematomas.
- Base of skull fractures may cause lower cranial nerve palsies or CSF discharge from the nose or ear.

Cerebral contusions

- Bruises on the surface of the brain.
- Occur when the brain suddenly moves within the cranial cavity and is crushed against the skull.
- Typically, there is injury at the site of impact (the 'coup' lesion) and at the site diagonally opposite this point (the 'contrecoup' lesion).
- Oozing of blood into the brain parenchyma and associated cerebral oedema are important contributors to raised intracranial pressure.

Extradural haematoma

- Due to haemorrhage between the dura and the skull.
- The bleeding vessel is often the middle meningeal artery which is torn following fracture of the squamous temporal bone.
- Accumulation of extradural blood is slow, as the firmly adherent dura is slowly peeled away from the inner surface of the skull.
- Patients may appear well for several hours following a head injury ('lucid' interval') but then quickly deteriorate as the haematoma enlarges and compresses the brain.

Subdural haematoma

- Due to haemorrhage between the dura and the arachnoid.
- Results from tearing of delicate bridging veins that traverse the subdural space to drain into the cerebral venous sinuses.
- Blood from these veins spreads freely through the subdural space, enveloping the entire cerebral hemisphere on the side of the injury.
- Often seen in elderly people following relatively minor trauma where it takes a more chronic course and may present with confusion.

Traumatic axonal injury

- Typically follows sudden acceleration–deceleration injuries.
- The most severe form is known as **diffuse axonal injury**, which causes immediate unconsciousness and almost inevitable death.
- Histologically, there is widespread axonal swelling with increased numbers of microglia and eventually degeneration of the involved fibre tracts.

Cerebral infarction

Definition

- Ischaemic necrosis of an area of the brain.

Epidemiology

- Common, accounting for about 80% of strokes.
- Mostly seen in the elderly.

Aetiology

- Most are caused by thromboemboli from either the internal carotid artery or the left side of the heart lodging in a cerebral artery.
- A small proportion are due to *in situ* thrombosis of an atherosclerotic plaque within a cerebral artery.

Pathogenesis

- Sustained occlusion of a cerebral artery leads to ischaemic necrosis of the territory of the brain supplied by the affected artery.

Presentation

- Rapid onset of focal CNS signs and symptoms related to the distribution of the affected artery (stroke, cerebrovascular accident).
- The majority involve the territory of the middle cerebral artery of a cerebral hemisphere, resulting in varying degrees of contralateral hemiplegia and hemiparesis, homonymous hemianopia, and dysphasia.

► TIAs (sudden episodes of focal CNS signs which resolve within 24h or less) are important warning signs to the risk of future cerebral infarction.

Macroscopy

See Fig. 18.1.

- After 24h, the infarcted area softens and there is loss of the normal sharp definition between the grey and white matter. Cerebral oedema within and around the infarct often causes midline shift.
- From 48h to 10 days, the infarct becomes gelatinous and the distinction between the infarct and normal brain becomes clearer.
- From 10 days to 3 weeks, the infarct liquefies and undergoes cystic change.
- In some cases, reperfusion leads to bleeding into the infarct, visible as punctate haemorrhages ('haemorrhagic infarct').

Histopathology

- Within the first 48h, there are ischaemic neuronal changes (shrunken eosinophilic neurones) with influx of neutrophils.
- Mononuclear cells then phagocytose myelin breakdown products and astrocytes proliferate as the infarct organizes over 2–3 weeks.

Prognosis

- Mortality is 20% at 1 month, then about 10% per year.
- Common complications include pneumonia, depression, contractures, constipation, and bed sores. Emotional effects may be significant.

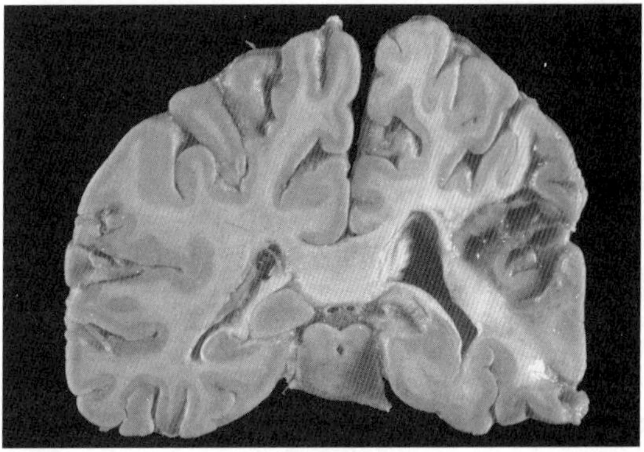

Fig. 18.1 Cerebral infarction (see Plate 51).

Reproduced with permission from Clinical Pathology (Oxford Core Texts), Carton, James, Daly, Richard, and Ramani, Pramila, Oxford University Press (2006).

Intracerebral haemorrhage

Definition

- Primary intracerebral haemorrhage is a spontaneous (non-traumatic) bleed into the substance of the brain.

Epidemiology

- Accounts for about 20% of strokes.
- Mostly occurs in late middle age.

Aetiology

- Hypertension is the most common cause.
- Rarer causes include cerebral amyloid angiopathy, rupture of an arteriovenous malformation, and coagulation disorders.

Pathogenesis

- Most cases related to hypertension are due to ruptured Charcot–Bouchard microaneurysms.
- A haematoma forms which destroys the brain structure and causes a sudden rise in intracranial pressure.

Presentation

- Sudden onset of focal CNS signs related to the area of the haemorrhage, together with symptoms and signs of raised intracranial pressure.
- Large haemorrhages are a common cause of sudden death due to a rapid rise in intracranial pressure and tonsillar herniation.
- Even small haemorrhages within the brainstem may cause sudden death if they disrupt areas vital for cardiorespiratory function.

Macroscopy

See Fig. 18.2.

- A haematoma is seen replacing the underlying brain structure with associated mass effect (midline shift, herniation).
- Hypertensive bleeds typically involve deep brain structures (basal ganglia/internal capsule), but also the pons or cerebellum.
- Bleeds related to other causes are more likely to be lobar (out in the lobes and less deep).

Histopathology

- Early lesions show blood clot surrounded by brain tissue characterized by hypoxic neural changes and oedema.
- Reactive astrocytes, then proliferative, and the damaged area organizes much like an area of infarction.

► Histological examination of the surrounding tissue may give important clues to the underlying cause of the haemorrhage (e.g. hypertensive small-vessel disease or cerebral amyloid angiopathy).

Prognosis

- Mortality is high (over 40%) due to effects of raised intracranial pressure.

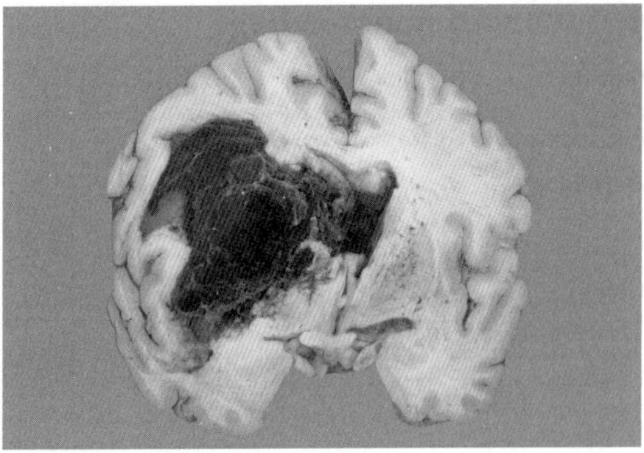

Fig. 18.2 Intracerebral haemorrhage. This is a slice of brain taken at post-mortem from a patient who suddenly collapsed and died. There is a massive intracerebral haematoma which led to a huge rise in intracranial pressure and herniation. The cause in this case was hypertension, and other changes of hypertension at post-mortem included left ventricular hypertrophy and nephrosclerosis of both kidneys (see Plate 52).

Subarachnoid haemorrhage

Definition

- Primary subarachnoid haemorrhage is a spontaneous (non-traumatic) bleed into the subarachnoid space.

Epidemiology

- Incidence of 8 per 100 000 per year.
- Most occur in adults aged 35–65.

Aetiology

- Most commonly due to rupture of a **berry aneurysm**.
- It has been hypothesized that a congenital defect in the tunica media of the cerebral vessels leads to aneurysm formation later in life due to atherosclerosis and hypertension.
- Most do not rupture.

Pathogenesis

- Most berry aneurysms arise at sites of arterial bifurcation at the base of the brain.
- Rupture of the aneurysm usually results in extensive bleeding through the subarachnoid space. The haemorrhage may extend into the brain tissue, as well as the ventricular system.

Presentation

- Sudden severe headache often described as 'like being struck on the back of the head'.
- May be precipitated by exertion or straining.
- There may be loss of consciousness or instant death in severe cases.

► Complications, such as rebleeding from the aneurysm, CSF malabsorption problems, and arterial vasospasm, may cause further deterioration.

Macroscopy

See Fig. 18.3.

- Blood is present within the subarachnoid space, often with abundant clots around the circle of Willis at the base of the brain.
- After clearing the blood clot, the ruptured berry aneurysm may be found in the circle of Willis.

Histopathology

- The aneurysm sac itself is composed of a thick fibrous intimal layer and an outer adventitial layer. No muscular media is present.

Prognosis

- One-third die instantly from tonsillar herniation caused by a massive rise in intracranial pressure.
- One-third become unconscious with a high risk of mortality or permanent neurological deficit.
- One-third have a good outcome, provided there is no rebleeding.

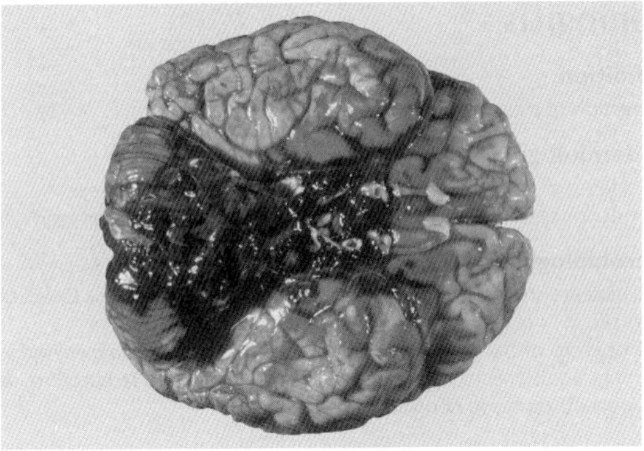

Fig. 18.3 Subarachnoid haemorrhage. This is the undersurface of the brain removed at post-mortem from a patient who suddenly cried out, collapsed, and died. Blood is seen filling the subarachnoid space. When the blood clot was cleared away, a ruptured berry aneurysm was found in the circle of Willis (see Plate 53).

Meningitis

Definition

- Infection of the subarachnoid space.

Epidemiology

- Incidence of viral meningitis of about 11 per 100 000 per year.
- Incidence of bacterial meningitis of about 3 per 100 000 per year.

Microbiology

- Viruses are the most common cause, usually echoviruses or Coxsackie viruses.
- Most cases of bacterial meningitis are caused by *Neisseria meningitidis* or *Streptococcus pneumoniae*. *Escherichia coli* and group B streptococci are important causes in neonates.

Pathogenesis

- Bacteria usually reach the meninges via the bloodstream from the nasal cavity, often following a viral upper respiratory tract infection.
- Both *Meningococcus* and *Pneumococcus* have capsules which render them resistant to phagocytosis and complement.
- The bacteria enter the subarachnoid space where the blood–brain barrier is weak, e.g. the choroid plexus.
- Once in the CSF, the bacteria multiply rapidly and stimulate an acute inflammatory response within the meninges.

Presentation

- Headache, fever, neck stiffness, photophobia.
- The symptoms are usually more severe in bacterial meningitis.

Microbiology

- Examination of CSF fluid obtained through lumbar puncture shows a predominance of lymphocytes in viral meningitis and many neutrophils in bacterial meningitis.
- Gram staining helps narrow down the likely cause in cases of bacterial meningitis.
- Culture of CSF and/or blood cultures should grow the causative organisms in cases of bacterial meningitis.
- No organism will be cultured in cases of viral meningitis.

Prognosis

- Viral meningitis usually runs a mild course with complete recovery.
- Bacterial meningitis is a much more serious, potentially life-threatening, infection if not treated early with appropriate antibiotics. Survivors of severe cases may be left with permanent neurological sequelae, including hearing loss, learning difficulties, paralysis, and epilepsy.

Cerebral infections

Encephalitis

- Infection of the brain parenchyma.
- Viruses are the most common cause, usually HSV.
- HSV encephalitis occurs following reactivation of the virus in the trigeminal ganglion, from which the virus can pass into the temporal lobe.
- Simultaneous perioral involvement may be a clue to the diagnosis.
- Presents with confusion, behavioural changes, and altered consciousness. Seizures may occur in severe cases.
- Brain imaging may highlight abnormalities in the temporal lobe.
- PCR on a CSF sample can identify the virus.
- Histologically, there is a necrotizing inflammation with typical herpetic intranuclear inclusions within neurones and glial cells.

►► Urgent antiviral treatment is essential.

Cerebral abscess

- Foci of infection associated with destruction of brain tissue.
- Usually bacterial infections, often with a mixture of organisms.
- Most arise by direct spread from an infection in a paranasal sinus, the middle ear, or a tooth.
- Can also arise from haematogenous spread, usually from septic emboli originating from infective endocarditis.
- Presents with symptoms of an infected intracranial mass, i.e. headache, nausea, vomiting, fever, seizures, and localizing neurological signs.
- CT scanning is usually diagnostic.
- Treatment requires surgical drainage and prolonged antibiotics.
- Considerable risk of mortality (20%) and morbidity (50% of survivors are left with persistent neurological deficits or epilepsy).

Progressive multifocal leukoencephalopathy

- Caused by the JC virus of the polyoma group of papovaviruses.
- Seen almost exclusively in the immunocompromised.
- Infection causes multiple small foci of demyelination within white matter which may coalesce into larger cystic areas. Histologically, viral inclusions are found within the enlarged nuclei of oligodendrocytes towards the periphery of demyelinated areas. The inclusions stain with SV40 antibody (which also labels JC virus). A striking feature (particularly in older lesions) is the presence of very large astrocytes with bizarre pleomorphic hyperchromatic nuclei.
- Diagnosis relies on presenting neurological features, characteristic brain magnetic resonance imaging (MRI) findings, and the presence of JC virus DNA in the CSF.
- Progression is usually relentless and mortality may be up to 50% within the first 3 months. Treatment of the cause for the underlying immunosuppression can lead to remission of progressive multifocal leukoencephalopathy. However, reconstitution of the immune system (e.g. in AIDS therapy) can occasionally result in an increased inflammatory response to the virus with exacerbation of disease.

Multiple sclerosis

Definition

- A relapsing and remitting demyelinating disease of the CNS, in which episodes of neurological disturbance affect different parts of the CNS at different times.

Epidemiology

- Most common demyelinating disease of the CNS.
- Peak age of onset age 20–30y.
- Females slightly more commonly affected.
- Increased risk in family members, highest in monozygotic twins (30%).
- Striking geographical variation, with annual incidence rates of up to 1 in 500 at highest latitudes and near absence near the equator.

Aetiology

- Precise cause remains unknown but thought to involve a complex interaction of both environmental and genetic factors.
- It has been hypothesized that immune-mediated demyelination is triggered by an unknown pathogen (e.g. infective organism?) acquired during childhood or adolescence in genetically susceptible individuals.
- Candidate genes are involved with regulation of immune responses.
- More recently, sun exposure has been implicated as a factor for the geographical variation with vitamin D deficiency due to low UV light exposure. Vitamin D, a secosteroid, is known to influence the immune system and the expression of genes relevant to the disease.

Pathogenesis

- Episodes of demyelination lead to attacks of acute neurological deficit, which develop over a period of a few days and remain for a few weeks before symptom recovery.
- In the early stages of the disease, complete or almost complete recovery from an episode of demyelination is typical.
- As the disease progresses, recovery is slower and residual deficit remains as a critical threshold of axonal death. Eventually, extensive axonal death results in permanent neurological disability, characteristic of progressive disease.

Presentation

- Symptoms may be highly variable, depending on the lesion site in the CNS.
- Blurred vision/loss of colour vision due to optic nerve demyelination.
- Vertigo and incoordination due to cerebellar demyelination.
- Eye movement disorders due to brainstem demyelination.
- Patchy numbness and tingling in a limb, with progression to paraplegia, incontinence, and sexual dysfunction due to spinal cord demyelination.

► CSF examination typically shows oligoclonal bands (raised intrathecal immunoglobulin synthesis).

Macroscopy

See Fig. 18.4.

- Well-circumscribed grey plaques are present, most clearly seen within the CNS white matter (grey matter demyelination, such as in the cortex, does occur but is not readily seen macroscopically).
- Chronic plaques feel hardened/'sclerosed' on palpation, hence the name 'multiple sclerosis'.
- Sites of predilection include the optic nerves, periventricular white matter, brainstem, and cervical spinal cord.

Histopathology

- Active plaques contain a prominent inflammatory infiltrate with destruction of myelin sheaths. There are sheets of macrophages containing myelin debris and there is perivascular lymphocytic inflammation.
- Established plaques show complete loss of myelin, with a reduction in oligodendrocytes. There is relative preservation of axons. However, axonal loss does occur and may vary in extent. There is astrocytosis (reactive astrocytes), which is responsible for the firmness of the plaques. Astrocytosis or glial scarring is the equivalent of fibrous scarring elsewhere in the body.

Prognosis

- Most patients eventually suffer from progressive disease where irreversible accumulation of disability is a key feature and complications related to this are common (pneumonia, UTIs, pressure sores, etc.). An overall reduction of life expectancy is recognized.
- A small proportion of patients can present with an aggressive form of multiple sclerosis ('Marburg's disease') where life expectancy can be weeks to months in the most severe cases.

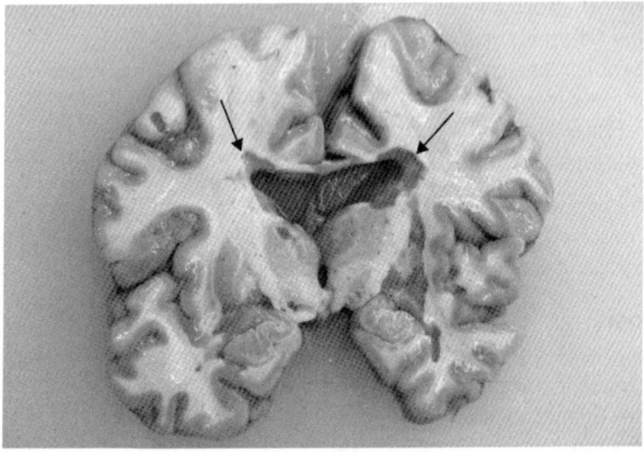

Fig. 18.4 Multiple sclerosis plaques. Brown appearance of multiple sclerosis plaques, seen here in a characteristic location around the lateral ventricles (arrows) (see Plate 54).

Guillain–Barré syndrome

Definition

- Classical Guillain–Barré syndrome (GBS) is an acute demyelinating polyneuropathy which usually follows 1–2 weeks after an upper respiratory tract or GI infection.

Epidemiology

- Rare disease.
- Annual incidence of 1–2 per 100 000.

Aetiology

- Common triggers are *Clostridium jejuni, Mycoplasma*, CMV, HIV, VZV, and EBV.
- Other associations include vaccination, surgery, and malignancy.
- In many cases, no clear cause can be identified.

Pathogenesis

- Theories suggest that the immune response mounted to an antigen on a pathogen cross-reacts with components of the peripheral nerve, particularly myelin.
- Demyelination leads to an acute polyneuropathy.

Presentation

- Sudden onset of tingling and numbness of fingers and toes.
- Over a period of weeks, the weakness spreads proximally.
- Classical form is acute inflammatory demyelinating polyneuropathy (AIDP). Antibodies to gangliosides, basal lamina components, and several myelin proteins.
- 'Axonal' form increasingly recognized (acute motor axonal neuropathy or AMAN), more aggressive, more common in Japan and China. Immune target is the axon.
- Acute motor sensory axonal neuropathy (AMSAN) has more extensive sensory involvement.
- Miller–Fisher syndrome has a triad of ataxia, areflexia, and ophthalmoplegia). Anti-GQ1b ganglioside autoantibodies are common.

► Progressive ventilatory failure is the main danger and ventilatory support may be required. Lumbar puncture typically shows increased CSF protein with a normal cell count (albuminocytological dissociation).

Prognosis

- Plasmapheresis and intravenous immunoglobulins reduce morbidity.
- ~85% make a complete or near complete recovery.
- 10% are unable to walk unaided at 1y.
- Modern mortality rates of 1–2.5%.

Myasthenia gravis

Definition

- An autoimmune disease caused by production of autoantibodies directed against various antigens of the neuromuscular junction, typically the nicotinic acetylcholine receptor (nAChR), rarely MuSK (a tyrosine kinase receptor), and very rarely LRPP4 (low-density lipoprotein receptor-related protein 4).

Epidemiology

- Uncommon disease with an annual incidence of 20 per 100 000.
- Mostly seen in women under 50 and men over 50 years old.

Aetiology

- Precisely what leads to the production of the autoantibodies is unclear.
- Interestingly, up to 75% of patients with nAChR autoantibodies have an abnormality of the thymus, either a neoplasm (thymoma) or hyperplasia. Thymectomy may help in these patients. The autoantibodies may be generated in the abnormal thymus.

Pathogenesis

- The nAChR is the receptor at the motor endplate, through which the neurotransmitter acetylcholine acts to stimulate muscular contraction.
- Autoantibodies binding to the nAChR limit depolarization at the endplate and thus impair muscular contraction.
- MuSK is involved with clustering of nAChR, which is important for its normal function.

Presentation

- The key feature is muscular fatiguability.
- Muscle groups affected, in order, are: extraocular, bulbar, face, neck, limb girdle, and trunk.
- Symptoms can be very subtle and the diagnosis is easily missed or mistaken for other conditions. Lambert–Eaton syndrome is typically a paraneoplastic syndrome (most commonly associated with small cell carcinoma of the lung) and patients develop autoantibodies against voltage-gated calcium channel on the presynaptic nerve terminal. There are also a rising number of very rare genetic mutations described as the cause of congenital myasthenic syndromes which may present later in life and may mimic myasthenia gravis.

Prognosis

- Most patients respond to medical treatment, which typically involves a combination of acetylcholinesterase inhibitors (such as pyridostigmine) and immunomodulatory therapies. Patients tend to have relapsing, but not progressive, symptoms.
- Patients with an aggressive form of thymoma may have a lower life expectancy.

Alzheimer's disease

Definition

- A neurodegenerative disease characterized clinically by dementia and histopathologically by neuronal loss in the cerebral cortex, in association with numerous amyloid plaques and neurofibrillary tangles.

Epidemiology

- Most common cause of dementia.
- Increasing incidence with age (5% of people >65, 20% of people >80).
- Represents an enormous social and financial burden to health care.

Aetiology

- Unknown in the vast majority of cases.
- The allele ε4 of the apolipoprotein E gene (APOE) is a major risk factor for the disease. A single allele increases the risk of developing the disease 3-fold; two alleles increase it more than 10-fold.
- A very small proportion of cases are familial, typically occurring in younger individuals and linked to autosomal dominant genetic mutations in genes such as amyloid precursor protein (APP) on chromosome 21, presenilin 1 (PSEN1) on chromosome 14, and presenilin 2 (PSEN2) on chromosome 1.
- Patients with Down's syndrome (trisomy 21) invariably develop Alzheimer's disease in later life. This is attributed to the presence of three copies of the APP gene on chromosome 21, resulting in increased production of Aβ.

Pathogenesis

- Current evidence suggests Alzheimer's disease is a 'proteinopathy' related to abnormal accumulation of Aβ amyloid and the protein *tau*.
- Aβ peptides are derived from APP by the action of secretase enzymes (presenilin forms part of the γ secretase complex).
- Precisely how Aβ amyloid interacts with tau and how the accumulation leads to neuronal loss is unclear.
- Progression of tau pathology is more tightly linked to anatomical connections than progression of Aβ pathology. This is probably responsible for the hierarchical distribution of the lesions ('march of the tangles') which forms the basis of the Braak neurofibrillary tangle staging.

Presentation

- Typically, it begins with memory loss, particularly day-to-day memory and new learning, which correlates with the early involvement of the medial temporal lobe and the hippocampus. Over time, there is increasing disability in managing daily activities such as finances and shopping.
- Loss of motor skills then causes difficulty dressing, cooking, and cleaning.
- Late in the disease, there is agitation, restlessness, wandering, and disinhibition. This may cause considerable upset to the family and carers.

- Terminal stages cause reduced speech, immobility, and incontinence.
- It is recognized that the disease has a long preclinical phase and there is an active search for biomarkers which might help with early diagnosis. Positron emission tomography (PET) scanning for amyloid in living persons is now possible and is one of the tests which might help in the appropriate clinical context. A variety of CSF biomarkers are also under evaluation.

Macroscopy

See Fig. 18.5.
- Brain weight reduced, often to <1000 g.
- Cortical atrophy involving narrowing of gyri and widening of sulci, particularly in the medial temporal lobe and hippocampus.
- Compensatory enlargement of the temporal horns of the lateral ventricles is often seen with significant medial temporal lobe atrophy.

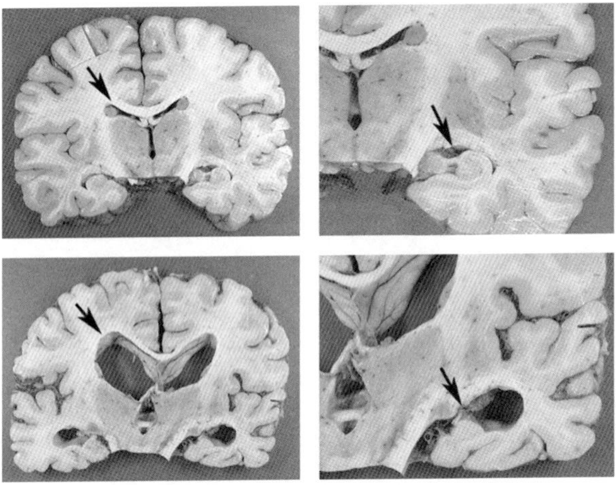

Fig. 18.5 Alzheimer's disease. The top images are from a normal patient aged 70, whilst the bottom images are from a patient with Alzheimer's disease. Note the ventricular dilation (left-hand side) and cortical atrophy in the brain from the patient with Alzheimer's disease, particularly marked in the hippocampus (right-hand side) (see Plate 55).

Histopathology

- There are positive and negative signs.
- The key microscopic features are the presence of abundant **neuritic plaques** and **neurofibrillary tangles** in the cerebral cortex (positive signs). The positive signs form the basis of the diagnostic criteria.
- There is associated loss of neurones and synapses, which is more difficult to measure on microscopy (negative signs).
- Neuritic plaques are spherical collections of tortuous neuritic processes surrounding a central amyloid core. The key component of the amyloid core is the Aβ protein.
- Neurofibrillary tangles are neuronal cytoplasmic inclusions composed of paired helical filaments, the main constituent of which is the tau protein.
- Aβ deposits may also be found in the vessels (referred to as cerebral amyloid angiopathy). Varying amounts of vascular amyloid are present in Alzheimer's disease.

Prognosis

- Death occurs ~10y from diagnosis, often from terminal pneumonia.

Vascular dementia

Definition

- A disease characterized clinically by dementia and histopathologically by injury to the brain parenchyma, associated with a wide range of cerebrovascular lesions (e.g. diffuse white matter chronic ischaemic damage, multiple infarcts, strategic infarcts).

Epidemiology

- Common cause of dementia (estimated 4.2% of people >85).
- Cerebrovascular disease often not the sole cause of dementia. It frequently coexists with other pathologies, particularly Alzheimer's.

Aetiology

- Risk factors similar to those for cerebrovascular disease or stroke.
- Hypertension and age linked to small-vessel disease (arteriolosclerosis), the most common pathological substrate for vascular dementia.
- CADASIL (cerebral autosomal dominant arteriopathy with subcortical infarcts and leukoencephalopathy) is a rare genetic cause of small-vessel disease due to mutations in the *NOTCH3* gene.

Pathogenesis

- Small-vessel disease (arteriolosclerosis) may cause chronic ischaemia and diffuse white matter injury (was known as Binswanger's disease).
- Multiple infarcts caused by vascular occlusion due to thrombosis or thromboemboli commonly due to atherosclerosis. Hypoperfusion may contribute.

Presentation

- Impairment of executive function and slowing of mental processing may be prominent, particularly with diffuse subcortical involvement. May be difficult to capture on standard cognitive testing (Mini-Mental State Examination, MMSE).
- May present with stepwise progression (multi-infarct dementia) and focal neurology (depending on infarct location).

Macroscopy

- Atherosclerosis affecting the circle of Willis at the base of the brain.
- Small infarcts (lacunar infarcts) in the basal ganglia.
- Subtle findings such as loss of white matter bulk.
- Multiple large infarcts are relatively rare.
- Small strategic infarcts (e.g. thalamus) are also rare.

Histopathology

- Atherosclerosis (large vessels), arteriosclerosis (small vessels).
- Parenchymal damage: myelin pallor (diffuse ischaemic damage) with perivascular accentuation and microinfarcts.

Prognosis

- Highly variable, given the heterogeneous nature of the disease.

Dementia with Lewy bodies

Definition

- A neurodegenerative disease characterized clinically by dementia and histopathologically by the presence of Lewy bodies in cortical and subcortical neurones.

Epidemiology

- Common cause of dementia (10–25% in hospital-based series).
- About 5% of people over 85 are affected.
- Slightly more common in men.

Aetiology

- Unknown.

Pathogenesis

- Presumably accumulation of Lewy bodies within neurones leads to damage and cellular loss.

Presentation

- Progressively worsening dementia very similar to Alzheimer's disease.
- Useful distinguishing features from Alzheimer's disease include fluctuating levels of cognition, recurrent visual hallucinations, features of parkinsonism, and hypersensitivity to neuroleptics (antipsychotics, major tranquillizers). Autonomic nervous system problems (dysautonomia) and sleep disorders are also described.

Macroscopy

- Cerebral atrophy, particularly in the temporal and parietal lobes. May be similar to Alzheimer's disease, but atrophy tends to be milder.
- Loss of pigment from the substantia nigra.

Histopathology

- Intracytoplasmic inclusions known as Lewy bodies are present within neurones of cortical grey matter and subcortical nuclei. Cortical Lewy bodies are best demonstrated by immunohistochemistry for α-synuclein or p62. Immunohistochemistry also labels Lewy neurites (neurites involved by synuclein pathology).
- Lewy bodies are composed of α-synuclein and other proteins such as ubiquitin, p62, and parkin.
- Changes typical of Alzheimer's (amyloid plaques and neurofibrillary tangles) are also often present, though areas severely involved in Alzheimer's disease (e.g. the hippocampus) are usually spared.

Prognosis

- Highly variable, but survival following diagnosis is usually 5–7y.

Parkinson's disease

Definition

- A neurodegenerative hypokinetic movement disorder characterized clinically by parkinsonism and histologically by neuronal loss and Lewy bodies concentrated in the substantia nigra.

Epidemiology

- Most common hypokinetic movement disorder.
- Occurs mostly in the elderly.
- Higher incidence in men.
- Prevalence of 1% in people aged over 60.

Aetiology

- Unknown in the majority of cases.
- Rare cases are due to inherited mutations in *SNCA* on chromosome 4 which encodes α-synuclein, a component of Lewy bodies. Inherited mutations also found in a number of other genes, including *LRRK2*, *PARK2* (encoding parkin), and *PINK1*.
- Around 10% of cases thought to be familial.

Pathogenesis

- Neurones from the substantia nigra connect to the putamen and globus pallidus where they release dopamine and control movement.
- Lack of dopamine release results in movement disorder.
- It is recognized that other parts of the nervous system are involved, resulting in additional symptoms (see further text).
- One hypothesis advocates the caudorostral progression of pathology from the enteric nervous system and olfactory bulb to the lower brainstem and then up to the neocortex along a network of interconnecting neurons (possible even with 'prion-like' propagation).

Presentation

- Onset is typically unilateral (e.g. 'pill rolling' tremor at rest).
- Classic triad of tremor, rigidity, and bradykinesia (parkinsonism).
- Autonomic dysfunction, cognitive neurobehavioural disturbances, and sleep dysfunction are also common. Rapid eye movement (REM) sleep behaviour disorder may precede parkinsonism.
- Dysphagia may be seen with disease progression.
- Patients may develop dementia (overlap with dementia with Lewy bodies; if clinical onset 1y after parkinsonism, it is called Parkinson's disease with dementia).

► Note that parkinsonism is not specific to Parkinson's disease; it merely reflects dysfunction of the substantia nigra system. Other causes of parkinsonism include drugs, toxins, infections, and trauma.

Macroscopy

See Fig. 18.6.

- Pallor of the substantia nigra and locus coeruleus.
- Brain weight within normal limits for age.

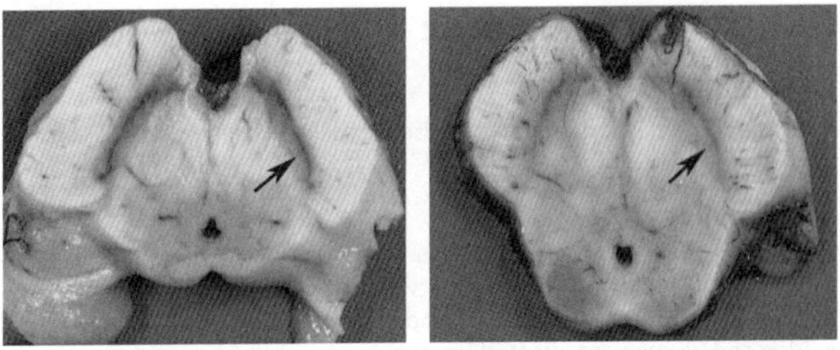

Fig. 18.6 Substantia nigra in Parkinson's disease. Slices through the midbrain of a normal person (left) and a patient with Parkinson's disease (right) showing loss of pigmentation in the substantia nigra in Parkinson's disease (arrows) (see Plate 56).

Reproduced with permission from *Clinical Pathology* (Oxford Core Texts), Carton, James, Daly, Richard, and Ramani, Pramila, Oxford University Press (2006).

Histopathology

- Loss of pigmented neurones from the substantia nigra in the midbrain and locus coeruleus in the pons; the dorsal motor nucleus of the vagus nerve in the medulla may also be affected (clinical correlate: parasympathetic nervous system effects).
- Residual neurones contain intracytoplasmic inclusions known as Lewy bodies. Immunohistochemistry for α-synuclein labels Lewy bodies. It also labels Lewy neurites, which show abnormal α-synuclein deposition.
- Other regions may be involved, e.g. cerebral cortex, autonomic nervous system. Alpha-synuclein pathology has been demonstrated in the gut (enteric nervous system) of Parkinson's disease patients.

► Note that the possibility of diagnosing Parkinson's disease or its early stages based on gut biopsies is an active area of research.

Prognosis

- Treatment with dopaminergic drugs eases symptoms of parkinsonism but does not slow the progression of the disease. Patients on long-term treatment with levodopa (most common medication used for the disease) develop severe dyskinesias (involuntary flailing or jerking body movements) as a side effect.
- Deep brain stimulation of the subthalamic nucleus works by rebalancing aspects of the basal ganglia circuit and is helpful in a small number of selected patients with severe tremor.
- Loss of balance may cause falls, and difficulty swallowing may cause aspiration pneumonia.
- The speed of progression varies considerably between individuals.

Huntington's disease

Definition

- An inherited neurodegenerative disorder caused by mutation of the *HTT* gene.

Epidemiology

- Worldwide prevalence of 5–10 per 100 000 population, but there is considerable geographical variability.
- Most cases present between 35 and 45y but can occur at any age.
- Men and women are affected equally.
- Inherited in an autosomal dominant fashion.

Genetics

- *HTT* contains a sequence of CAG trinucleotide repeats which usually number <36.
- Mutant *HTT* has >36 trinucleotide repeats. The higher the number of trinucleotide repeats, the fuller the penetrance and the younger the age of onset.
- Instability of the repeat sequences tends to result in their expansion in each successive generation, a phenomenon known as **anticipation**.

Pathogenesis

- Huntingtin, the protein coded by *HTT*, interacts with many other proteins and has many biological functions. It is expressed in all cells but is present in highest concentration in the brain and testis.
- Mutated huntingtin is thought to be cytotoxic to certain cell types, most notably neurones in the caudate nucleus and putamen.

Presentation

- Uncontrolled, random, jerky movements (chorea).
- Over time, there is motor, neuropsychiatric, and cognitive decline, ultimately terminating in dementia.

Macroscopy

- Striking atrophy of the caudate nucleus and putamen.
- Cortical atrophy may also be present.

Histopathology

- Marked neuronal loss from the caudate nucleus.
- Surviving neurones contain intranuclear dot-like inclusions composed of huntingtin protein aggregates.

Prognosis

- Survival is on average 20y from onset of symptoms, but this is dependent on the length of the triplet repeat.
- Death is usually due to pneumonia or cardiac failure (abnormal huntingtin is expressed in cardiac muscle). Suicides are a recognized feature in this patient group.

Motor neurone disease

Definition

- A group of neurodegenerative diseases characterized by selective loss of motor neurones.

Epidemiology

- Annual incidence of 1–5 people per 100 000.
- Men slightly more commonly involved than women.
- Most present between ages 50 and 70y.

Aetiology

- Large proportion of cases are idiopathic with no clear cause.
- ~10% are inherited with a Mendelian pattern.
- Largest group of genetically determined amyotrophic lateral sclerosis (ALS) in both sporadic and familial ALS settings is due to an intronic hexanucleotide repeat expansion in C9ORF72 (European founder mutation).
- A number of other genes have been linked to familial motor neurone disease, including *SOD1*, *TDP-43*, and *FUS*.

Pathogenesis

- Little is still known, though research into familial cases has provided interesting insights into the disease.
- *TDP-43* and *FUS* are both RNA/DNA-binding proteins with very similar molecular structures.
- Theories suggest that defects in RNA metabolism may be a key event leading to motor neurone degeneration.

Presentation

- Asymmetric weakness, wasting, fasciculation, and spasticity of limb muscles.
- Difficulty swallowing, chewing, speaking, coughing, and breathing.
- Cognitive changes may also occur (overlap with frontotemporal dementia).

Macroscopy

- Anterior roots of the spinal cord appear grey and thinned.

Histopathology

- Selective loss of motor neurones is seen within the motor cortex and anterior horns of the spinal cord.
- The hypoglossal nucleus in the medulla may be selectively affected.
- In sporadic cases, residual motor neurones contain inclusions containing TDP-43. Inclusions are also labelled with p62 and ubiquitin.
- Cases linked to *C9ORF72* mutations show TDP-43 pathology. Additional p62-positive inclusions are present, particularly in the hippocampus and the cerebellar granule cell layer.

Prognosis

- The disease is usually progressive and fatal within a few years.
- Death is usually from aspiration pneumonia.

Creutzfeldt–Jacob disease

Definition

- A spongiform encephalopathy caused by accumulation of an abnormal form of prion protein (PrP) which is resistant to proteinase breakdown.

Epidemiology

- Rare, but the most common human prion disease.
- Annual incidence of about 1 per 1 000 000.

Aetiology

- Sporadic cases are thought to be due to chance spontaneous conversion of PrP into the abnormal form.
- Familial cases are due to inherited mutations in the *PRP* gene which predispose the protein to converting into the abnormal form.
- Variant Creutzfeldt–Jacob disease (CJD) is thought to be transmitted through consumption of beef contaminated with abnormal PrP derived from cows with bovine spongiform encephalopathy (BSE).

Pathogenesis

- Presence of abnormal PrP promotes refolding of normal native PrP proteins into the abnormal form.
- An exponential increase in abnormal PrP results in cell death.

Presentation

- Sporadic CJD typically presents in the middle-aged and elderly with an obvious neurological illness that follows a rapidly progressive course.
- Variant CJD is clinically distinct. It affects younger people aged under 30 and initially presents with psychiatric symptoms followed by cerebellar ataxia and dementia.

Histopathology

- Sporadic CJD is associated with vacuolation of grey matter (spongiform change) with neuronal loss and gliosis.
- Variant CJD also shows spongiform change, neuronal loss, and gliosis, together with numerous so-called 'florid plaques' composed of deposits of amyloid forms of PrP.

► Florid plaques are the neuropathological hallmark of variant CJD and do not occur in other forms of CJD.

❗ Given the transmissible nature of prion disease, special precautions are taken for patients with suspected CJD if they undergo surgery, particularly brain surgery. Special precautions also apply to suspected CJD autopsy cases.

Prognosis

- No specific treatment currently exists and the disease is usually fatal.

Astrocytomas (including glioblastoma)

Definition

- CNS tumours formed by glial cells showing astrocytic differentiation.
- Include the common diffusely infiltrative astrocytomas (e.g. glioblastoma) as well as the less common low-grade circumscribed variants (e.g. pilocytic astrocytoma). Biologically, these two groups are distinct. The diffusely infiltrative astrocytomas are subdivided by the degree of malignancy into diffuse astrocytoma (WHO grade II), anaplastic astrocytoma (WHO grade III), and glioblastoma (WHO grade IV).

Epidemiology

- Diffusely infiltrating astrocytomas are the most frequent primary CNS tumours (60% of primary CNS tumours), and glioblastoma (GBM) is the most common tumour in this subgroup (incidence of 3–4/100 000).
- On average, grade correlates directly with age of presentation (pilocytic astrocytoma (WHO grade I) in childhood and adolescence, diffuse astrocytoma (WHO grade II) in young adults, and GBM (WHO grade IV) in the sixth decade).

Aetiology

- The majority of tumours are sporadic (previous irradiation plays a role in an insignificant fraction of tumours).
- Increased risk of astrocytomas in neurofibromatosis type 1 (mostly pilocytic astrocytomas of the optic pathways).
- Very rare glioblastomas due to inherited tumour syndromes (e.g. *TP53* mutations in Li Fraumeni syndrome).

Pathogenesis

- It is suggested that malignant gliomas arise from neural stem or progenitor cells. It is thought that the tumours maintain a primitive population of cells responsible for repopulating tumours as they grow.
- Isocitrate dehydrogenase (IDH) mutations are common in grade II and III diffusely infiltrative gliomas (astrocytomas and oligodendrogliomas) and are present in 70–80% of them. Ninety per cent of *IDH*-mutated tumours harbour a hotspot mutation within codon 132, leading to an amino acid substitution from arginine to histidine (R132H). *IDH* mutations result in the production of an oncometabolite (2-hydroxyglutarate) which leads to a hypermethylator phenotype.
- It is believed that *IDH* mutations occur early on in the development of diffuse gliomas and that further genetic alterations determine whether the tumour shows astrocytic (*TP53* and *ATRX* mutations) or oligodendroglial differentiation (1p19q losses).
- *IDH* mutations are seen in secondary GBMs, which arise from lower-grade diffuse astrocytomas. They are typically absent from primary (*de novo*) GBMs, which commonly show EGFR amplifications.
- Evolution from grade II astrocytomas into higher-grade tumours is characterized by mutations in *CDKN2A* and *RB*.

- Methylation of the promoter of the *MGMT* gene is associated with increased progression-free survival of adult GBMs and a better response to temozolamide (standard alkylating chemotherapy agent).
- A tandem duplication or fusion event between the *KIAA1549* and *BRAF* genes is the most common genetic alteration in pilocytic astrocytomas. It results in constitutive activation of the MAPK/ERK signalling pathway.

Presentation

- Focal neurology is related to tumour location (e.g. weakness, sensory and visual symptoms). GBM typically occurs in the cerebral hemispheres.
- Seizures may be the main or only symptom in low-grade tumours.
- As tumours progress, increased intracranial pressure symptoms (headaches, vomiting) develop due to mass effect.
- Primary GBMs present with a short history (months, even weeks) and increased intracranial pressure symptoms early on.

Macroscopy

- GBMs are poorly delineated grey-pink tumours with central areas of yellowish necrosis (Fig 18.7).
- Lower-grade diffusely infiltrative astrocytomas typically enlarge and distort involved brain structures. They may be firm to the touch.
- Pilocytic astrocytomas are relatively well-circumscribed, often cystic, tumours.

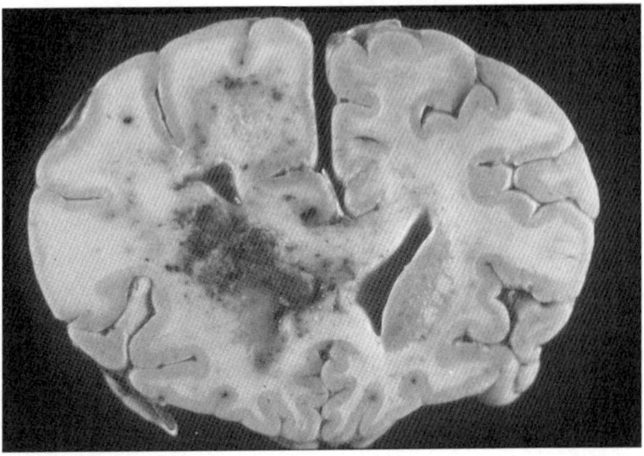

Fig. 18.7 Glioblastoma. This is a section of the brain from a patient who presented with signs of raised intracranial pressure, rapidly deteriorated, and died. There is an ill-defined tumour with areas of haemorrhage. Microscopy revealed this to be a glioblastoma which was much more extensive than was apparent macroscopically (see Plate 57).

Reproduced with permission from *Clinical Pathology* (Oxford Core Texts), Carton, James, Daly, Richard, and Ramani, Pramila, Oxford University Press (2006).

Histopathology

- Diffuse astrocytoma (WHO grade II) shows a mild to moderate increase in glial cellularity, compared to normal brain, and mild nuclear atypia. There may be microcystic change.
- Anaplastic astrocytoma (WHO grade III) is more cellular with greater nuclear atypia and presence of significant mitotic activity.
- Glioblastoma (WHO grade IV) is a highly aggressive neoplasm composed of atypical astrocytes similar to those seen in anaplastic astrocytoma but with superadded areas of necrosis and/or microvascular proliferation.
- Pilocytic astrocytoma shows a biphasic pattern of compact areas with bipolar astrocytes and loose areas with multipolar astrocytes. Rosenthal fibres are typically seen in the compact areas. Mitoses are rare.

Prognosis

- Average survival for diffuse astrocytoma (WHO grade II) is about 5y. For anaplastic astrocytomas (WHO grade III), it is reduced to about 3y, and for GBMs it is <1y. Long survival is the rule for pilocytic astrocytoma (95% 5-year survival).

Oligodendroglioma

Definition

- Diffusely infiltrative CNS tumours formed by glial cells showing oligodendroglial differentiation. They are subdivided by the degree of malignancy into 'classical' oligodendrogliomas (WHO grade II) and anaplastic oligodendrogliomas (WHO grade III).

Epidemiology

- The majority of oligodendrogliomas occur in adults (peak incidence: 30–60 years of age).
- They account for ~2.5% of all primary brain tumours and 5–6% of all gliomas.

Aetiology

- The tumours are generally sporadic (previous irradiation plays a role in an insignificant fraction of tumours).

Pathogenesis

- Oligodendrogliomas are thought to derive from neural stem or progenitor cells similar to diffuse astroglial tumours. *IDH* mutations are believed to be an early event in tumourigenesis and are shared with low-grade diffuse astrocytomas.
- Most show co-deletions of chromosomal arms 1p and 19q, and *CIC* and *FUBP1* mutations, in addition to *IDH* mutations.
- Progression to anaplastic histology is associated with the loss of 9p and 10q and mutations in *CDKN2A*.

Presentation

- Most oligodendrogliomas occur in the cerebral hemisphere. They frequently involve the cortex and hence seizures are the most common presenting symptom (two-thirds of patients). Focal neurological deficits, headaches, and other signs of increased intracranial pressure may also occur.

Macroscopy

- Tumours are well circumscribed and greyish pink with areas of mucoid change, cystic degeneration, focal haemorrhage, and calcification.

Histopathology

- Oligodendroglioma (WHO grade II) is composed of cells resembling normal oligodendrocytes with round nuclei and fine chromatin surrounded by clear cytoplasm. There is a fine network of branching (chicken-wire) capillaries. Calcification is very commonly seen.
- Anaplastic oligodendroglioma (WHO grade III) is an oligodendroglial neoplasm in which there are areas of higher cellularity, atypia, and increased mitotic activity.

Prognosis

- Average survival for grade II tumours is 10y and for grade III tumours 2–3y.

Ependymoma

Definition

- CNS tumour composed of neoplastic ependymal cells arising from the ependymal-lined ventricular system or the spinal canal.
- Subdivided by the degree of malignancy into 'classical' ependymomas (WHO grade II) and anaplastic ependymomas (WHO grade III).

Epidemiology

- Account for ~6% of intracranial gliomas.
- Occur at any age, more frequently in childhood and adolescence.
- In adults, most arise in the spinal cord.
- • In children, most arise around the fourth ventricle.

Aetiology

- The majority of tumours are sporadic.
- Neurofibromatosis type 2 (NF2) is associated with the occurrence of spinal ependymomas.

Pathogenesis

- Current data favour an origin from neural stem or progenitor cells, particularly region-specific radial glia.
- The most common genetic alterations involve chromosome 22.
- Genomic studies have shown a complex landscape of mutations, the clinical significance of which is still being evaluated.

Presentation

- Symptoms depend on tumour location.
- Posterior fossa ependymomas often present with nausea, vomiting, and headache related to hydrocephalus due to obstruction of the fourth ventricle. Cerebellar symptoms may also be present. Spinal ependymomas present with motor and sensory disturbances, depending on which tracts are involved.

Macroscopy

- Grey-red, lobulated, and usually well-demarcated tumours.
- There is often a relationship to a ventricular cavity.
- Some ependymomas may spread widely throughout the CSF.

Histopathology

- Ependymomas are composed of cells with regular plump oval nuclei and fibrillary processes. The cells may form glandular structures (rosettes) and perivascular pseudorosettes, in which the cells are radially arranged around blood vessels.
- Anaplastic ependymomas (WHO grade III) show increased cellularity and significant mitotic activity. Necrosis and microvascular proliferation may also be present.

Prognosis

- Children with posterior fossa tumours have 5-year survival of about 50%. Outcome for adult patients with spinal tumours is better.

Meningioma

Definition

- Tumours from meningothelial (arachnoid cap) cells and attached to the inner surface of the dura mater.
- Majority are benign and correspond to WHO grade I.
- Certain histological subtypes are associated with a less favourable outcome and correspond to WHO grade II (atypical) and very rarely grade III (anaplastic).

Epidemiology

- 13–25% of primary intracranial tumours and 25% of intraspinal tumours.
- Most occur in adults between the ages of 20–60.
- More common in females.

Aetiology

- The majority are sporadic tumours.
- Irradiation is a risk factor. There were a number of patients previously irradiated for tinea capitis (fungal scalp infection) who developed meningiomas. This treatment is no longer used.
- Radiation-induced meningiomas are more commonly multiple and show atypical or anaplastic morphology.
- Multiple meningiomas may occur in patients with neurofibromatosis type 2.

Pathogenesis

- The most common molecular alterations in meningiomas are loss of chromosome 22q and mutations in the NF2 gene.
- As meningiomas increase in histological grade, they may acquire loss of the short arm of chromosome 1, the long arms of chromosomes 10 and 14, and 9p21 deletions.

Presentation

- Meningiomas are typically slow-growing tumours and produce symptoms and signs by compression of adjacent structures. Deficits depend on the location of the tumour. Headaches and seizures are common symptoms more generally.

Macroscopy

See Fig. 18.8.

- Most are smooth, lobulated, well-circumscribed tumours with a homogeneous cream beige cut surface. They are adherent to the dura mater and compress, rather than invade, the underlying brain.
- They may infiltrate the overlying skull or induce hyperostosis (thickening of the bone).

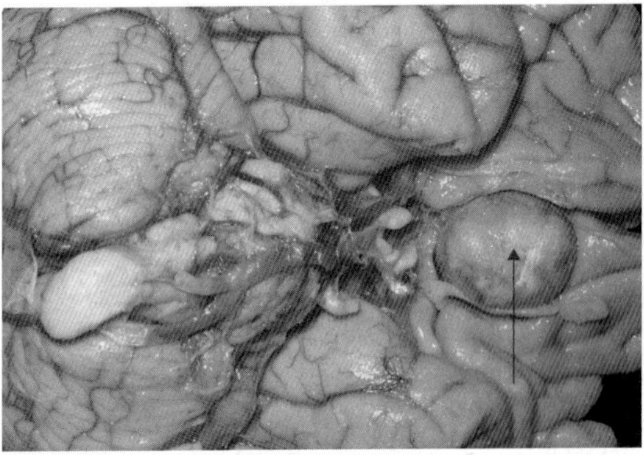

Fig. 18.8 Meningioma. This very well-circumscribed tumour (arrow) has the typical macroscopic appearance of a meningioma, a suspicion that was confirmed microscopically (Plate 58).

Histopathology

- Classical meningiomas are syncytial tumours composed of lobules and whorls of meningothelial cells. Calcified round concretions (psammoma bodies) may be present. However, the histology may vary considerably.
- Atypical meningiomas (WHO grade II) typically show increased mitotic activity and a specific combination of other features (e.g. tumour cell necrosis, hypercellularity).
- Anaplastic meningiomas (WHO grade III) show significantly increased mitotic activity and severe pleomorphism. They may be barely recognizable as meningiomas.

Prognosis

- Benign meningiomas (the majority) have a low risk of recurrence following surgical resection.
- Atypical meningiomas have a higher rate of local recurrence and so may require radiotherapy following surgical excision.
- Anaplastic meningiomas are aggressive malignant tumours.

Medulloblastoma

Definition

- A primitive embryonal tumour of the cerebellum (WHO grade IV).

Epidemiology

- Most common malignant primary brain tumour in children, rare in adults (10–20% of primary paediatric brain tumours, <2% of brain tumours overall).

Aetiology

- Most are sporadic, but rare examples are inherited (e.g. in patients with Gorlin's syndrome (*PTCH* mutations), Turcot's syndrome (*APC* mutations), and Li Fraumeni syndrome (*TP53* mutations).

Pathogenesis

- There are four molecular subgroups of medulloblastomas, each with significant clinical and pathological associations. Group 1 (WNT activation) with the best clinical outcome, group 2 (SHH activation) with a good/intermediate outcome, group 3 with a poor outcome, and group 4 with an intermediate/poor outcome.
- Abnormalities affecting chromosome 17 are most common and are concentrated in medulloblastoma subgroups 3 and 4.
- MYCC and MYCN amplifications are linked with poor prognosis.
- Histogenesis is complex and may vary for the different subgroups. For group 2, the cerebellar external granule cell layer has been postulated as the source of progenitor cells and for group 1 the dorsal brainstem progenitor cells.

Presentation

- Hydrocephalus (increased intracranial pressure, headache, vomiting). Cerebellar signs may be present.

Macroscopy

- Childhood medulloblastomas are typically located in the midline (vermis), rare adult tumours in the cerebellar hemispheres.
- Many are circumscribed, pink or grey, with areas of haemorrhage or necrosis. Texture may vary from soft to firm.
- There may be evidence of CSF dissemination.

Histopathology

- Highly cellular tumour composed of mitotically active small cells with hyperchromatic nuclei and scant cytoplasm ('small round blue cell tumour').

Prognosis

- Like all embryonal tumours, the tumour grows rapidly and is fatal without treatment. The overall prognosis with modern therapy is favourable, depending on tumour stage, subtype, and extent of surgical resection (overall 5-year survival about 75%).

Primary CNS lymphomas

Definition

- Primary extranodal lymphomas arising in the CNS.

Epidemiology

- Incidence has increased from around 1% to around 6% of primary intracranial neoplasms, mainly due to the AIDS epidemic.
- CNS involvement also occurs in 22% of post-transplant lymphomas whereby about 55% are confined to the CNS.
- Typically occurs in two distinct groups: in **immunocompetent** individuals, the peak incidence is from 50 to 70; in **immunocompromised** individuals, it is typically seen at a younger age.

Aetiology

- Inherited or acquired immune deficiency increases the risk of primary CNS lymphoma.
- EBV plays a role in immunocompromised patients.

Pathogenesis

- Histogenetic origin in immunocompetent patients is a late germinal centre exit B-cells (as evidenced by transcriptional profile).
- EBV is expressed in virtually all AIDS- and transplant-associated CNS lymphomas.

Presentation

- Symptoms may vary considerably and tumours may present with focal neurological deficits, neuropsychiatric symptoms, increased intracranial pressure, and seizures.

Macroscopy

- Single or multiple masses in the cerebral hemispheres, often deep-seated and close to the ventricles. Lesions are typically ill-circumscribed, grey to yellow, and fleshy. There may be haemorrhages and necrosis. There may be CSF involvement.

Histopathology

- More than 95% of primary CNS lymphomas are DLBCLs composed of large atypical B-lymphocytes. Tumour cells typically show an angiocentric pattern of arrangement.

► Lymphocytes are highly susceptible to steroid-induced apoptosis. Steroids are commonly given to patients with brain tumours to help reduce oedema. Tissue diagnosis may be difficult in this situation, as the tumour may have temporarily 'vanished'. Steroids are avoided pre-biopsy.

Prognosis

- Median survival of primary CNS lymphoma (DLBCL) of 2.5–5y with radiotherapy and chemotherapy (especially methotrexate).

Cerebral metastases

Definition

- Tumours with origin outside the CNS which spread secondarily to the CNS via the haematogenous route. Rarely, there may be direct invasion from adjacent tissues, as opposed to metastatic disease.

Epidemiology

- Metastatic tumours are the most common CNS neoplasms.
- In autopsy studies, CNS metastases are found in about 25% of patients who die of cancer.

Origin of CNS metastases

- Most common brain metastases in adults in descending order are from lung cancer (particularly small cell and adenocarcinoma), breast cancer, melanoma, renal cancer, and colon cancer.
- In children, they arise from leukaemia, lymphoma, osteogenic sarcoma, rhabdomyosarcoma, and Ewing sarcoma.

Pathogenesis

- Tumours typically spread to the CNS via the haematogenous route. Metastases tend to arise at the grey–white matter junction.
- Leptomeningeal, dural, and spinal epidural metastases may also occur.
- There may be isolated CSF involvement (malignant meningitis).

► Primary tumours may involve the CNS via 'remote' effects and there are a variety of paraneoplastic syndromes involving antibodies to tumour antigens which cross-react with normal CNS autoantigens.

Presentation

- Raised intracranial pressure or local effect of the tumour on the adjacent brain tissue.
- Patients may also present with seizures, infarcts, or intra-tumoural haemorrhage.

Macroscopy

- Typically well-circumscribed, round, grey-white or tan masses with variable necrosis and significant peritumoural oedema.
- Haemorrhage is often seen with choriocarcinoma, melanoma, and renal cell carcinoma.
- Melanoma may appear dark brown/black due to pigment content.

Histopathology

- Histology resembles the primary tumours from which they arise.
- Immunohistochemistry is used for metastases of unknown primary origin to aid with identification of the site of origin.

Prognosis

- Best outcome with surgical resection and/or radiotherapy is achieved in young patients with good performance status, single brain metastasis, and no extracranial metastases.

Chapter 19
Multisystem diseases

Systemic lupus erythematosus

Definition

- A multisystem autoimmune disease characterized by autoantibody production against a number of nuclear and cytoplasmic autoantigens.

Epidemiology

- Incidence of 4 per 100 000 people per year.
- Most cases occur in women of childbearing age.
- More common in Africans and Asians.

Aetiology

- Unknown for certain.
- One theory is that defective phagocytosis of apoptotic bodies leads to priming of the immune system to intracellular self-antigens.

Pathogenesis

- Activation of autoreactive B- and T-cells leads to formation of immune complexes between autoantibodies and self-antigens.
- Circulating immune complexes become deposited in tissues such as the skin, joints, and kidneys where they stimulate inflammation and tissue damage (Fig. 19.1).

Presentation

- Protean manifestations, depending on sites of involvement.
- Fatigue, weight loss, and low-grade fever are common.
- Joint involvement causes arthralgia.
- Skin involvement causes scaly red lesions on sun-exposed sites.
- Pulmonary involvement causes pleuritis and pleural effusion. Pneumonitis may also occur, leading to pulmonary fibrosis.
- Renal involvement causes glomerulonephritis (lupus nephritis), leading to CKD.
- Haematological involvement causes anaemia, lymphopenia, and thrombocytopenia.

Immunology

- >95% have anti-nuclear antibodies.
- 60% have anti-double-stranded DNA antibodies.
- 20–30% have anti-Smith antigen antibodies.
- 20–30% have antiphospholipid antibodies which cause a hypercoagulable state.

Histopathology

- Skin biopsies from involved skin show an interface dermatitis with vacuolar degeneration and apoptosis of basal keratinocytes.

Prognosis

- 15-year survival from diagnosis is 80%.
- Deaths are usually related to severe renal and lung involvement.

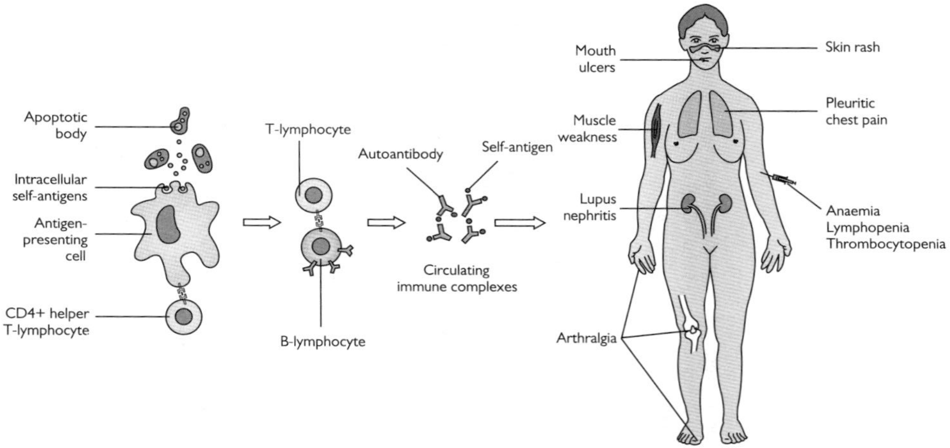

Fig. 19.1 Postulated pathogenesis of systemic lupus erythematosus. Defective phagocytosis of apoptotic bodies leads to the priming of the immune system to intracellular antigens and activation of autoreactive B- and T-lymphocytes. Circulating immune complexes formed between autoantibodies and self-antigens then become deposited in various tissues around the body (skin, joints, kidneys), stimulating inflammation and tissue damage.

Reproduced with permission from *Clinical Pathology* (Oxford Core Texts), Carton, James, Daly, Richard, and Ramani, Pramila, Oxford University Press (2006) p. 478, Figure 21.1.

Systemic sclerosis

Definition

- A multisystem autoimmune disease in which fibrous tissue accumulates in multiple organs.

Epidemiology

- Rare disease with an annual incidence of 2–10 per million.
- Most cases arise in women aged 30–40y.

Aetiology

- Unknown.

Pathogenesis

- An abnormal immune response to an unidentified trigger results in production of cytokines such as IL-4 and TGF-β that stimulate collagen deposition by fibroblasts.

Presentation

- **Limited systemic sclerosis** (SS) usually starts with long-standing Raynaud's phenomenon. Then there is gradual tightening and thickening of the skin of the fingers, face, and neck. Calcium deposition is common, particularly in the finger pads. Small bowel involvement and pulmonary hypertension may occur as late complications after 10–15y.
- **Diffuse systemic sclerosis** presents more abruptly with widespread skin thickening, contractures, and skin ulcers. Visceral involvement occurs early with pulmonary fibrosis. An important complication is severe hypertension, leading to acute renal failure ('scleroderma renal crisis').

Immunology

- Anti-nuclear antibodies present in 65%.
- Anti-centromere antibodies present in 70–80% of limited SS.
- Anti-topoisomerase (Scl70) antibodies present in 40% of diffuse SS.

Prognosis

- No cure at present.
- Immunosuppressive regimes are used for organ involvement or progressive skin disease.
- Deaths are usually related to renal and lung disease.

Sarcoidosis

Definition

- A multisystem disease of unknown cause in which tissues are infiltrated by granulomas.

Epidemiology

- Prevalence of 10–20 per 100 000 population in the UK.
- Peak age of onset 20–40y.
- Those of African descent tend to show more severe disease.

Aetiology

- Unknown.

Pathogenesis

- Presumably the granulomatous inflammation is a reaction to an as yet unidentified antigen.

Presentation

- Virtually any organ may be involved, but the most common sites are lymph nodes, lungs, and skin.
- Acute sarcoidosis tends to present suddenly with manifestations such as erythema nodosum (➲ Erythema nodosum, p. 394), anterior uveitis, and cranial nerve VII palsy. Bilateral hilar lymphadenopathy is frequently present on chest radiography.
- Chronic sarcoidosis is more insidious and is characterized by lupus pernio (cutaneous sarcoidosis of the nose), pulmonary fibrosis, and posterior uveitis.

Histopathology

- Involved tissues contain non-necrotizing granulomas.
- The typical sarcoidal granuloma is well circumscribed with little surrounding lymphoid inflammation (so-called 'naked' granulomas).
- Variable degrees of fibrosis may accompany the granulomas.
- No other explanation for the presence of granulomas can be found (e.g. pathogens, foreign material, tumour).

Prognosis

- Acute sarcoidosis tends to behave favourably, with spontaneous resolution within 1–2y of diagnosis.
- Chronic sarcoidosis is associated with a higher risk of complications, such as progressive lung fibrosis, leading to respiratory failure and RVF (➲ Right ventricular failure, p. 52).

Vasculitis

Definition

- A group of conditions in which inflammation and damage to blood vessels is the primary underlying pathology.

Giant cell (cranial or temporal) arteritis

- A vasculitis of medium and large vessels which preferentially affects head and neck arteries. Most patients are adults aged >50y.
- Presents over weeks or months with fever, anorexia, and weight loss.
- Involvement of the temporal artery causes headache, scalp tenderness, and jaw claudication.
- ❶ Involvement of ocular vessels can cause blindness.
- Aortic involvement occurs in ~25% of cases and may lead to thoracic or abdominal aortic aneurysm formation.
- Positive temporal artery biopsies show a lymphohistiocytic infiltrate with disruption of the media. A giant cell reaction is often present.
- Only 60% of patients with clinical evidence of disease show biopsy evidence of arteritis, as the pattern of involvement may be focal.

Polyarteritis nodosa (PAN)

- A systemic medium-vessel vasculitis, leading to areas of aneurysm formation and narrowing in involved vessels.
- A rare disease if diagnostic criteria are strictly applied.
- Main organs involved are the GI tract (abdominal pain), nervous system (peripheral nerve palsies), and muscles (muscle aches).
- Imaging showing areas of vessel narrowing and aneurysm formation is highly suggestive. Biopsy proof of a necrotizing vasculitis is also helpful.

Granulomatosis with polyangiitis (GPA)

- A systemic ANCA-associated vasculitis characterized by dominant upper respiratory tract, lung, and renal involvement and cANCA positivity.
- Formally known as Wegener's granulomatosis.
- Presents with nasal symptoms, acute renal failure, and pulmonary symptoms.
- Renal biopsies show a focal segmental necrotizing glomerulonephritis with crescent formation (identical to microscopic polyangiitis).
- Lung biopsies show large 'geographical' areas of necrotizing granulomatous inflammation and a necrotizing vasculitis.
- Aggressive immunosuppression is needed to prevent mortality.

Microscopic polyangiitis (MPA)

- A systemic ANCA-associated vasculitis characterized by dominant renal and lung involvement and pANCA positivity.
- Most patients are adults with a median age of 55.
- Presents with acute renal failure and pulmonary symptoms.
- Renal biopsies show a focal segmental necrotizing glomerulonephritis with crescents (identical to Wegener's granulomatosis).

- Lung biopsies show marked alveolar haemorrhage and a necrotizing capillaritis within alveolar septae.
- Aggressive immunosuppression is needed to prevent mortality.

Eosinophilic granulomatosis with polyangiitis (EPA)

- A systemic vasculitis characterized by dominant lung and skin involvement, blood eosinophilia, and a history of asthma.
- Formally known as Churg–Strauss syndrome.
- Most patients are adults with a mean age of 40 at presentation.

Index

A

D

E

M

R

T

U